I1043809

Estonia, Latvia & Lithuania

Helsinki
(FINLAND)
p180

Estonia
p46

Latvia
p192

Lithuania
p285

Kaliningrad
(RUSSIA)
p398

The Urbana Free Library

To renew: call 217-367-4057
or go to **urbanafreelibrary.org**
and select "My Account"

THIS EDITION WRITTEN AND RESEARCHED BY
Peter Dragicevich, Hugh McNaughtan and Leonid Ragozin

Contents

LAHEMAA NATIONAL PARK,
ESTONIA P86

NICO TONDINI/ROBERTHARDING/GETTY IMAGES ©

HILL OF CROSSES,
LITHUANIA P347

PAUL BIRIS/GETTY IMAGES ©

KAVALENKAVA/VOLHA/GETTY IMAGES ©

Contents

OLD TOWN, RĪGA, LATVIA P196

Welcome to Estonia, Latvia & Lithuania

A land of crumbling castles, soaring dunes, enchanting forests and magical lakes – a trip to the Baltic proves that fairy tales do come true.

Teensy but Diverse

Estonia, Latvia and Lithuania are tiny. Yet in this wonderfully compact space there are three completely distinct cultures to discover – with different languages, different traditions and markedly different temperaments. By way of example, you need only look at the three unique yet equally compelling capitals: majestically medieval Tallinn, chic art-nouveau Rīga and flamboyantly baroque Vilnius. When it comes to cultural mileage, the Baltic is as fuel-efficient a destination as you could ever hope for.

Cold War Comrades

For all their differences, the Baltic States suffered the slings and arrows of 20th-century misfortune together. And when the time came, they answered the 'to be or not to be' question hand-in-hand, singing loudly in the affirmative. Visitors will find myriad opportunities to engage with the heart-breaking and horrifying stories of the Nazi and Soviet occupations of these lands: numerous war relics, mass-grave memorials and excellent social-history museums ensure that they're never forgotten. Meantime, distinctive Stalinist architecture and striking Socialist Realist art continue to fascinate. And doesn't everyone love a happy ending?

Super Nature

Endless sandy beaches, a multitude of lakes, large tracts of forest and wildlife-rich wetlands: the Baltic States may be flat but they're not lacking in natural appeal. Best of all, the relatively low population density means there's plenty to go around. Many of Europe's large mammals have found quiet corners to linger in here, although the wolves, bears, elk and lynx know better than to mug for tourist snapshots. You're more likely to see white storks in their bathtub-sized nests balanced on lamp posts, or woodpeckers tap-tapping away, or the odd startled deer scampering along the side of the road.

Magic in the Air

From Tallinn's storybook turrets to the ghostly ruins of Ludza Castle, romantic adults and spellbound children will find plenty of intrigue in this ancient and alluring landscape. Folk tales abound of holy lakes, magic springs and the witches and goblins that inhabit the darkest forests and most treacherous bogs. This was the last corner of Europe to be Christianised and, even now, in out-of-the-way places, you'll occasionally stumble across ribbons tied to trees in sacred groves and coins deposited on mysterious offertory stones. Suspend your disbelief just a little and let your imagination take flight.

Why I Love Estonia, Latvia & Lithuania

By Peter Dragicevich, Writer

Growing up in New Zealand, where you simply won't find a building that's even 200 years old, probably makes me more susceptible than most to the charms of a place such as Tallinn. From the moment I first set eyes on its cobbled lanes, crooked walls and soaring steeples, I was smitten. The collision of history with the modern world has rendered all three Baltic States places of ardent fascination for me. And each time I visit, there's something new to love.

For more about our writers, see page 448

Above: A 13th-century castle in Cēsis (p264), Latvia

Estonia, Latvia & Lithuania

Tallinn
Magical, fairy-tale Old Town (p47)

Lahemaa National Park
One-stop shop for all of Estonia's ecosystems (p86)

Tartu
Engage in the clichés of undergraduate life (p103)

Gauja National Park
Crumbling castle ruins and pine-peppered terrain (p256)

Pärnu
Estonia's most popular beachside resort (p132)

Saaremaa
Forested coastlines and languid lifestyle (p142)

Kurzeme Coast
Constellation of villages and haunting sea stacks (p233)

Jūrmala
The former Russian empire's ultimate spa centre (p228)

Riga
Ethereal—almost eerie— art-nouveau facades (p193)

ELEVATION

250m
200m
150m
100m
50m
0

Vilnius
A funky capital clad
in cobblestone (p288)

Curonian Spit
Enjoy the redemptive powers
of the elements (p363)

Hill of Crosses
Myriad crucifixes in all
shapes and sizes (p347)

Baltic Sea

56°N
55°N
21°E

BELARUS

★ MINSK

LATGALE

LITHUANIA

RUSSIA

POLAND

★ VILNIUS

Liepāja
Saldus
Dobele
Jelgava
Bauska
Jēkabpils
Daugavpils
Rēzekne
Ludza

Klaipėda
Neringa
Nida
Šilutė
Tauragė
Plungė
Kretinga
Telšiai
Mažeikiai
Skuodas
Kuršėnai
Šiauliai
Joniškis
Kėdainiai
Panevėžys
Biržai
Kupiškis
Rokiškis
Anykščiai
Utena
Molėtai
Ukmergė
Jonava
Kaunas
Jurbakas
Marijampolė
Alytus
Trakai
Vievis
Druskininkai

Kaliningrad
Zelenogradsk
Sovetsk
Nesterov

Daugava (Zapadnaya Dvina)

Neman (Nemunas)

Nemunas (Neman)

Estonia, Latvia & Lithuania's
Top 17

Tallinn's Fairy-Tale Old Town

1 There was a time when sturdy walls and turreted towers enclosed most of Europe's cities, but wartime bombing and the advent of the car put paid to most of them. Tallinn's Old Town (p51) is a magical window into that bygone world, inducing visions of knights and ladies, merchants and peasants – not least due to the locals' proclivity for period dress. Rambling lanes lined with medieval dwellings open onto squares once covered in the filth of everyday commerce – now lined with cafes and altogether less gory markets selling souvenirs and handicrafts.

Midsummer's Eve

2 Although church affiliations are widespread, ancient pagan rituals are still deeply woven into the fabric of all three countries. Storks are revered, even-numbered bouquets of flowers are superstitiously rebuffed and the summer solstice is held in the highest regard. Though the spiritual element of Midsummer's Eve has largely disappeared, family and friends continue to gather in the countryside for a bright night of beer and bonfires. While every town and village has a celebration, one great place to see in the solstice is Lithuania's Lake Plateliai (p381).

Right: Midsummer celebrations in Klaipėda, Lithuania

KAVALENKAVAVOLHA/GETTY IMAGES ©

YEVGEN BELICH/SHUTTERSTOCK ©

Castles & Manor Houses

3 A quick glance at a map reveals the Baltics' key position along the ancient trade routes between Western Europe and Russia. Crumbling castle ruins abound in the pine-peppered terrain, each a testament to a forgotten kingdom. For centuries, the region was divided into feudal puzzle pieces, and thus you'll find dozens of manor houses dotting the landscape. Spending the night at one of these elegantly restored mansions, such as those in Latvia's Gauja Valley (p262), is an unforgettable experience.

Top: Turaida Castle in Sigulda, Gauja National Park

Curonian Spit

4 There's something elemental – even slightly old-fashioned – about Lithuania's loveliest seaside retreat: a long thin strip of rare and majestic sand dunes that lines the southeastern corner of the Baltic Sea. Maybe it's the pine scent or the sea breezes, or the relative isolation that so vividly recalls German writer Thomas Mann's sojourns here in the early 1930s. Come to Curonian Spit (p363) to recharge your batteries and renew your faith in the redemptive powers of wind, water, earth and sky.

A. ALEKSANDRAVICIUS/SHUTTERSTOCK ©

HOLGER LEUE/GETTY IMAGES ©

Vilnius' Baroque Old Town

5 Tempting hideaways, inviting courtyards, baroque churches and terrace bars serving beer – the Lithuanian capital's Old Town (p291) one of the best places to get lost in throughout the Baltics. Old and new seem to coexist seamlessly here: whether you're looking for that thrift-shop boutique, an organic bakery, a cosy little bookshop or just a quiet spot to have a coffee, they're all likely to be standing side-by-side down some as-yet-unexplored cobblestone leyway.

Saaremaa

6 There's something about heading out to an island that lifts a trip out of the ordinary, and while Saaremaa (p142) in Estonia is no tropical paradise, the languid pace of this forested place weaves a magic all its own. The highlight is Kuressaare Castle, the Baltics' best-preserved medieval fortress, looming proudly behind its moat by the harbour. Yet it's the island's windmills, particularly the photogenic quintet at Angla, that provide the iconic Saaremaa image that you'll see on bottles of beer, vodka and water throughout Estonia.

Top right: Angla Windmill Hill, Saaremaa

Rīga's Art Nouveau Architecture

7 If you ask any Rīgan where to find the city's world-famous art nouveau architecture, you will always get the same answer: 'Look up!' Over 750 buildings in Latvia's capital – more than any other city in Europe – boast this flamboyant and haunting style of decor. Spend a breezy afternoon snapping your camera at the imaginative facades in the city's Quiet Centre (p203) district to find an ethereal (and almost eerie) melange of screaming demons, enraptured deities, overgrown flora and bizarre geometric patterns.

BOKSTAZ/SHUTTERSTOCK ©

Foraged Food

8 Cast away your preconceived notions about potatoes and pork tongue – the Baltic table no longer feels like a Soviet cafeteria. The locavore movement isn't just up-and-coming: it has arrived with much ado, and its mascot is the mushroom. Mushrooming isn't simply a pastime in these parts, it's a regional obsession. The damp climate makes places Dzūkija National Park (p332) a wonderful spot for finding all sorts of scrumptious fungi. But if you want to indulge in some foraging of your own, it's safer to wait until berry season.

Hill of Crosses

9 Your first thought as you traverse the flat Lithuanian landscape in search of this landmark is likely to be something along the lines of, 'Where did they ever find a hill?' And then you glimpse it in the distance – more a mound than a mountain – covered in crosses by the tens of thousands. The hill (p347) takes on even more significance when you realise that the crosses planted here represent not just religious faith but an affirmation of the country's very identity.

Saunas & Spas

10 Although the Finns, Turks and Russians may be more famous for their saunas, the Baltic folk love to hop into their birthday suits for a good soak and steam as well. There are plenty of spa centres around the Baltics – such as the wonderful Aqva (p93) in Rakvere – where you can purr like a kitten while being pummelled by experts, but most here prefer to go native (so to speak) and indulge in a traditional sauna experience: getting whipped by dried birch branches while sweating it out in temperatures beyond 60°C. Sound relaxing...

Bottom right: Wooden smoke sauna, Estonia

Gauja National Park

11 Dotted with sweet little towns and dramatic fortifications, Latvia's Gauja National Park (p256) entrances all who visit. The tower of Turaida Castle rises majestically over the huddling pines, a glorious reminder of the fairy-tale kingdoms that once ruled the land. And after you've had your history lesson, it's time to spice things up with a bevy of adrenaline-inducing sports, such as bungee jumping from a cable car or careering down a frozen bobsled track.

Tartu

12 Tartu (p103) is to Estonia what Oxford and Cambridge are to England. Like those towns, it's the presence of an esteemed ancient university and its attendant student population that gives it its special character. There's a museum on nearly every corner and, it seems, a grungy bar in every other cellar. When the sun shines, the hill in the centre of town is the place to best observe those eternal clichés of undergraduate life: earnest prattling, hopeless romancing and enthusiastic drinking.

Bottom: University of Tartu building

Lahemaa National Park

13 Providing a one-stop shop of all of Estonia's major habitats – coast, forests, plains, peat bogs, lakes and rivers – within a very convenient 80km of the capital, Lahemaa (p86) is the slice of rural Estonia that travellers on a tight schedule really shouldn't miss. On top of the natural attractions, there are graceful baroque manors to peruse, pocket-sized villages to visit and country taverns to take refuge in whenever the weather turns and the stomach growls.

Jūrmala

14 Jūrmala (p229) was once the most fashionable spa centre and beach resort in all of the former Russian Empire. And while the sanatorium craze has come and gone, it's still an uberpopular place to pamper oneself silly, with unending menus of bizarre services (chocolate massages?). Even if you're not particularly keen to swim at the shallow beach, it's well worth the day trip from the Latvian capital to check out the wonderful old wooden mansions and witness the ostentatious presentations of the nouveau riche.

Pärnu

15 Chances are you're not visiting the Baltic with images of endless sandy beaches hovering before your eyes, but Pärnu (p132) offers exactly that. When the quirky notion of sea-bathing became fashionable at the dawn of the 20th century, Pärnu became Estonia's most popular seaside resort – and it's hardly less so today. Architectural gems of that period combine with relics of the Hanseatic past to create very pleasant streets to explore, with interesting eateries and bars lurking within them.

Above left: St Catherine's Orthodox Church, Pärnu

Kurzeme Coast

16 While Lithuanians relish dune-riddled Curonian Spit and Estonians embrace island life on Saaremaa and Hiiumaa, Latvia's Kurzeme (p233) coastline in between is a rather desolate place, with but a small constellation of towns betwixt haunting sea stacks and crumbling Soviet watchtowers. There's punky Liepāja in the south and the cream-coloured beaches of Ventspils further along, but things come to a crashing climax in the north at Kolka, where the Baltic Sea meets the Gulf of Rīga in a most dramatic fashion.

Soviet Relics

17 It's been just over 20 years since the Baltic States ripped the iron curtain to shreds – and while these newborn nations soar towards globalisation with alacrity, there are still plenty of dour tenements and crumbling coastal watchtowers that remind us of harder times. Many of the other Soviet relics, however, allow visitors to explore the past à la James Bond. One-time secret facilities, such as the Pension bunker (p264) in Latvia's Gauja National Park, offer mirth, melancholy and wonderment for even the slightest of history buffs.

Above right: Camouflaged entrance to the Pension bunker

Need to Know

For more information, see Directory A–Z (p408)

Currency
Euro (€)

Languages
Estonia: Estonian
Latvia: Latvian
Lithuania: Lithuanian

Russian is also commonly spoken.

Visas
Citizens from the EU, Australia, Canada, Japan, New Zealand and the US do not require visas for entry into Estonia, Latvia or Lithuania.

Money
ATMs are widely available. Credit cards are commonly accepted at most restaurants and hotels.

Mobile Phones
Prepaid local SIM cards are available and compatible with most foreign phones.

Time
Eastern European Time (GMT/UTC plus two hours)

When to Go

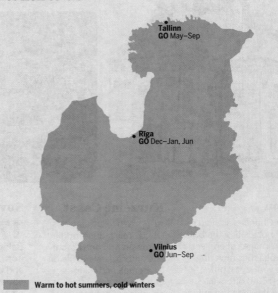

Tallinn
GO May–Sep

Rīga
GO Dec–Jan, Jun

Vilnius
GO Jun–Sep

Warm to hot summers, cold winters

High Season
(Jun–Aug)

➡ Beds in the capitals get booked out – plan ahead!

➡ Endless daylight and warm weather encourage alfresco dining.

➡ Midsummer festivities during the summer solstice are not to be missed.

Shoulder Season
(May & Sep)

➡ Airfare drops significantly outside of the summer rush.

➡ Weather is relatively mild.

➡ Many attractions reduce their hours of operation.

Low Season
(Oct–Apr)

➡ Expect frigid temperatures and limited daylight.

➡ Coastal towns are almost completely shut down.

➡ Crowds converge on the capitals and cross-country ski areas during the holiday season.

Useful Websites

Baltic Times (www.baltictimes.com) English-language newspaper covering all three Baltic countries.

Visit Estonia (www.visitestonia.com) Estonia's official tourism site.

Latvia (www.latvia.travel) Latvia's official tourism website.

Lithuanian Travel (www.lithuania.travel) Lithuania's leading tourism portal.

Baltic Country Holidays (www.traveller.lv) Extensive booking network for rural accommodation throughout all three countries.

Lonely Planet (www.lonelyplanet.com) Destination information, traveller forum and more.

Important Numbers

Estonia country code	☏372
Latvia country code	☏371
Lithuania country code	☏370
International access code	☏00
Emergency	☏112

Exchange Rates

Australia	A$1	€0.65
Canada	C$1	€0.67
Japan	¥100	€0.74
New Zealand	NZ$1	€0.61
Russia	R100	€1.31
UK	£1	€1.38
US	US$1	€0.90

For current exchange rates see www.xe.com.

Daily Costs

Budget: Under €60

➡ Hostel or guesthouse: €10 to €35

➡ Two meals: €15

➡ Walking around town: free

➡ Museum entry: €3

➡ Drinks at a beer garden: €7

Midrange: €60 to €120

➡ Hotel room: €50

➡ Two meals: €28

➡ Public transport: €2

➡ Average entry to two top museums: €10

➡ Drinks at a posh lounge: €15

Top End: Over €120

➡ Luxury hotel room: €75

➡ Two meals: €55

➡ Taxis: €8

➡ A day spent at museums: €15

➡ Pub crawl: €20

Opening Hours

Hours can vary widely depending on the season and the size of the town, but the following are fairly standard:

Banks 9am–4pm or 5pm Monday to Friday

Bars noon–midnight Sunday to Thursday, until 2am or 3am Friday and Saturday

Cafes 9am–10pm

Post offices 8am–6pm Monday to Friday, 9am–2pm Saturday

Restaurants Noon–11pm or midnight daily

Shops 10am–6pm Monday to Friday, 10am–3pm Saturday

Supermarkets 8am–10pm daily

Arriving in the Region

Rīga Airport (p416)

Bus 22 (€2, 25 minutes) runs to the city centre, 13km away, at least every 30 minutes. A taxi to the city typically costs €12.

Tallinn Airport (p416)

Bus 2 will take you to the city centre (€1.60) in about 20 minutes. A taxi should cost less than €10.

Vilnius Airport (p416)

Bus 1 runs between the airport and the train station; trains run to the central station every 30 minutes between 6am and 11.30pm. On-board tickets cost €0.72 and the trip is only 10 minutes. A taxi to the centre, 5km away, will cost €10 to €15.

Getting Around

Public transport in the Baltic States is reasonably priced, quick and efficient.

Car Useful for travelling at your own pace, or for visiting regions with minimal public transport. Cars can be hired in every town or city. Drive on the right.

Bus Estonia, Latvia and Lithuania have extensive domestic networks, covering all the major towns and linking smaller destinations to them.

Train Train services are more limited; you'll need to change trains to travel between the three countries.

Air Each of the three capitals is linked through regular flights.

For much more on **getting around**, see p421

What's New

Estonia's Culinary Contagion

Foodies in the know may already be aware of Tallinn's excellent New Nordic-influenced dining scene. Now the culinary revolution is spreading, taking on the tyrannical rule of pork and potatoes in the Estonian heartland. Of the nation's 50 top-rated restaurants, nearly half are now outside the capital – up from only a handful a couple of years ago.

Kalamaja goes overground

Long the favoured neighbourhood of Tallinn's bohemians, Kalamaja has seen a flurry of restaurant, cafe and bar openings in recent years, abetted by the success of the neighbouring Telliskivi Creative City. (p60)

Lennusadam Seaplane Harbour

The transformation of this architecturally important hanger into a cutting-edge maritime museum has done the improbable: it's succeeded in luring package tourists out of Tallinn's Old Town. (p60)

Tallinn TV Tower

After five years of renovation Tallinn's iconic teletorn has reopened, with new interactive displays, an open-air 'edge walk' and the same brilliant views from its 175m viewing floor. (p67)

Daugavpils Mark Rothko Art Centre

The birthplace of Latvian Mark Rothko, a giant of the 20th-century art world, has just become a whole lot more interesting with the opening of this gallery in his honour. (p269)

Corner House

The grandeur of this building in Rīga stands in contrast to the grimness of its history, but this former Soviet secret police (KGB) headquarters once again has a purpose – telling the stories of its victims. (p207)

Vilnius Takes Off

The Lithuanian capital is in a state of creative flux, with the restaurant and bar scene exploding and a growing awareness of its place within Europe, artistically and culturally. (p288)

Lithuania Gets Crafty

Lithuania's craft scene keeps getting bigger and better. Vilnius, in particular, has thriving 'producer' subcultures: people weaving on traditional looms and making their own paper, jewellery, clothes and puppets. (p315)

Baltic Beer Gets Craftier

The global craft-beer wave has broken over the Baltic, big time. The hipster districts of Estonia and Latvia, in particular, are full of beardy boutique brewers producing quality drops. (p176)

For more recommendations and reviews, see lonelyplanet.com

If You Like...

Castles

The Baltic was once a jigsaw puzzle of feudal territories. Its surviving castles, both ruined and restored, are a testament to the region's strategic importance on the edge of civilisations.

Trakai Castle This fairy-tale-worthy red-brick castle atop a tiny island provides a scenic backdrop for lake paddles. (p319)

Kuressaare Castle The Baltic's best preserved medieval castle, moat and all. (p146)

Narva Hermann Castle A chess match writ large, facing off with its Russian counterpart across the river. (p96)

Rakvere Castle Pint-sized princesses and knights don costumes, pet farm animals and have a rollicking good time. (p93)

Bauska Castle A Latvian two-for-one: a ruined 15th-century castle with an intact 16th-century one grafted on. (p251)

Livonian Order Castle This blocky fortress in the Latvian seaside town of Ventspils houses a fascinating museum of local history. (p253)

Museums

There's a lot of history to document here, but many of the region's museums pay tribute to a bevy of quirkier interests in addition to the region's war-torn past.

Museum of the Occupation of Latvia Five decades of occupation are brought to life through the personal stories of the survivors. (p215)

Pedvāle Open-Air Art Museum Large-scale sculptures embellish a farm secluded deep in the heart of Latvia's Abava Valley. (p243)

Museum of Devils Lucifer in all of his (or her) various guises lurks in Kaunas' New Town. (p339)

City Museum The tale of Tallinn is told across 10 different sites, including this 14th-century merchant's house. (p55)

Lithuanian Art Museum Occupies multiple locations across the country, including this branch in Vilnius' Radvilos Palace. (p300)

Estonian Open-Air Museum Venerable buildings from all around the country, relocated to the forest on Tallinn's fringes. (p67)

Wartime Relics

From Soviet strife and Nazi rule to ancient tribal battles and invading medieval forces, the Baltic has seen more than its share of bloodshed.

Pension Concealed for decades, this high-security bunker is now a tribute to the Soviet spy game. (p264)

Paneriai A sombre memorial to the 100,000 people murdered here by the Nazis in WWII. (p318)

Karosta Prison This Russian military prison offers visitors the unique opportunity to experience life as a detainee. (p240)

Cold War Museum Žemaitija National Park hides one of the great Soviet secrets: an underground nuclear missile base. (p381)

Kiek in de Kök The museum contained within this imposing tower is devoted to Tallinn's fortifications and military history. (p60)

Sõrve Peninsula Saaremaa island's lonely extremity contains battle sites, war graves, bunkers and a military museum. (p150)

Beaches

The Baltic summers may be short but beach bums are handsomely rewarded with endless stretches of flaxen shoreline during the warmer months.

Nida Peace, quiet and unrivalled natural beauty amid sand dunes and pine trees. (p367)

Jūrmala The Baltic's original posh beachside spa resort still teems with Russian tycoons and their families. (p229)

Pärnu Synonymous in Estonia with summertime fun, Pärnu has golden sand aplenty. (p132)

Tuhkana Accessed by a forest path on the Estonian island of Saaremaa, Tuhkana offers comparative serenity. (p144)

Palanga Get your party on at Lithuania's premier summertime fun-in-the-sun destination. (p375)

Saulkrasti A beautiful sandy Latvian beach with surprisingly few bods on it. (p254)

Architecture

The architecture in all three of the Baltic's capitals is as wonderful as it is varied, be it baroque flourishes, medieval gables, dazzling art nouveau, Stalinist confections or modern masterpieces.

Rīga's Art Nouveau Architecture Overly adorned facades cloak the hundreds of imposing structures that radiate beyond the city's core. (p208)

Vilnius' Old Town All steeples, domes and pillars, the capital's wonderfully preserved Old Town revels in the baroque. (p291)

Tallinn's Old Town A treasure trove of medieval battlements,

Top: Latvian National Library by architect Gunnar Birkerts
Bottom: Peat bog in Soomaa National Park

dwellings and public buildings. (p51)

Kumu Seven stories of lime-stone, glass and copper, Tallinn's art museum has set a new standard. (p65)

Latvian National Library A new 'castle of light' on the Daugava river bank. (p209)

St Anne's Church Not Vilnius' most imposing church, but widely regarded to be its most beautiful. (p292)

Quaint Villages

You want charming farm-steads and whisper-quiet villages? The Baltic's got them in spades, especially as locals trade in their bu-colic lifestyles for life in the big city.

Koguva Trapped in a pictur-esque time rift, this fishing village offers a window to the past. (p139)

Labanoras An achingly pretty wooded village smack-dab in the middle of a protected region. (p326)

Kuldīga The place 'where salmon fly' is frequently used as the backdrop for Latvian period films. (p245)

Rõuge Set in a valley puncti-ated by seven small lakes, Rõuge is the Estonian rural idyll personified. (p119)

Plateliai A pretty spot right by the lake and the gateway to Žemaitija National Park. (p381)

Pāvilosta The sleepy, beachy setting for a particularly active water sports scene. (p239)

National Parks

Estonia, Latvia and Lithu-ania stole a lead on their fellow Soviet Republics, establishing the first na-tional parks in the USSR in the early 1970s. They've been entrancing visitors ever since.

Lahemaa National Park Estonia's 'Land of Bays' is a wonderland of beaches, forests, bogs and rivers. (p86)

Gauja National Park This heavily forested Latvian river valley is liberally sprinkled with enchanting castles. (p256)

Rāzna National Park A quiet reserve protecting a large chunk of Latvia's Latgale lakeland. (p274)

Žemaitija National Park A mys-terious landscape of forest and lake, great for camping, walking and water sports. (p381)

Soomaa National Park Wander through Estonia's 'Bogland' on well-maintained boardwalks in search of witches, goblins, bears and wolves. (p130)

Palaces & Manor Houses

When they weren't at war, the Baltic aristoc-racy traded fortresses for comfortable country piles. Some have been carefully restored, while others lie in ruins.

Rundāle Palace Latvia's primo palatial gem is a tribute to the opulence of the Baltic-German elite. (p252)

Kadriorg Palace Built by Russian Tsar Peter the Great, Tallinn's pretty palace now houses a branch of the Estonian Art Museum. (p65)

Palace of the Grand Dukes of Lithuania A painstaking reproduction of the 17th-century seat of power, right in the heart of Vilnius. (p289)

Muižas of the Gauja Spend the night at one of the striking muižas (manor houses) dot-ting the Latvian countryside. (p262)

Palmse Manor The centrepiece of Estonia's Lahemaa National Park has been fully restored, along with its many outbuildings. (p89)

Kau Manor In the heart of the Estonian countryside, this recently derelict mansion now houses a kooky hotel and an ac-claimed restaurant. (p87)

Month by Month

January

New Year's celebrations and continued festive cheer warm the hearts of locals as they weather the limited daylight of what already feels like an endless winter.

✿ New Year's Day

Festivities from the night before continue during this public holiday as locals incorporate pagan practices at family gatherings to ensure a happy and healthy year.

February

The cold, dark and icy winter continues, but locals make the most of it as they flock to the countryside for some cross-country skiing.

🎿 Tartu Ski Marathon

This 63km cross-country race draws about 10,000 competitors to the Estonian countryside; winners complete the course in less than three hours. Participants slide off in sportsmad Otepää.

🍴 Palanga Seals Festival

Held in the Lithuanian seaside resort of Palanga over three days in mid-February, this festival lures hungry fish lovers to try the city's beloved smelts. There's also the annual 'polar bear' event, at which hardy swimmers frolic in the freezing Baltic waters.

March

Locals pull aside the curtains to check the weather outside...and yup, it's still winter out there. The main causes for celebration are the Easter holidays, although they sometimes fall during April.

✿ Lithuanian Folk Art

The annual St Casimir's Fair (Kaziuko *mugė*), a festival of folk arts and crafts, is held at the beginning of March in both Vilnius and Kaunas.

April

Frosty nights officially come to an end as the mean temperature stabilises well above zero. Hope of spring has arrived; locals burst forth from their shuttered houses to inhale the fickle spring air.

☆ Haapsalu Horror & Fantasy Film Festival

Zombies take over the streets and screens of Haapsalu, on Estonia's west coast. This showcase of creepy and kooky films is timed to coincide with the April full moon.

☆ Jazz in Tallinn

Jazz greats from around the world converge on Tallinn, Estonia, in mid-April during the two-week Jazzkaar Festival. Musicians play not just at concert halls but on the streets, in squares and parks, and even at the airport.

✨ Tartu Student Days

Tartu's students let their hair down in this wild pagan celebration marking the end of term and the dawn of spring in Estonia. A second, smaller version occurs in mid-October.

☆ Jazz in Kaunas

The annual Kaunas Jazz Festival, held in late April, is arguably Lithuania's most prestigious and popular jazz event.

May

The days are noticeably longer now as weather conditions dramatically improve. Tourist-focused businesses start revving their engines; excitement fills the air in anticipation of a fruitful summer.

✨ Old Town Days

Held in Tallinn's cinematic 14th-century streets, this is a week of themed days involving dancing, concerts, costumed performers, sports and plenty of medieval merrymaking.

☆ New Baltic Dance Festival

This annual festival in early May features contemporary and modern dance, drawing companies from around Lithuania and the world to Vilnius for a week of performances.

☆ Baltic Ballet

The International Baltic Ballet Festival in Rīga features stirring performances by Latvian and international companies over three weeks.

June

After several fits and bursts of spring sun, the warm weather is finally here to stay. The region-wide Midsummer's Eve festivities herald the peak of the summer season.

✨ Baltica International Folklore Festival

Alternating between Tallinn (2016, 2019), Vilnius (2017, 2020) and Rīga (2018, 2021) annually, this large festival celebrates Baltic folk traditions, with thousands of performers.

☆ Rīga Opera Festival

The Latvian National Opera's showcase event takes place over 10 days and includes performances by world-renowned talent.

🍴 Grillfest Good Food Festival

Join tens of thousands of holidaymakers tucking into barbecued food in the Estonian beach resort of Pärnu.

☆ Culture Night

Visual artists and musicians fill the Lithuanian capital of Vilnius with all manner of installations and performances over the course of a single June night. (www.kulturosnaktis.lt)

✨ Baltic Pride

The Baltic's annual gay and lesbian pride festival alternates between each of the three capitals, with Vilnius taking the reins in 2016 (and 2019), Tallinn in 2017 (and 2020), and Rīga in 2018 (and 2019).

✨ Midsummer's Eve

The region's biggest annual night out is best experienced in the countryside, where huge bonfires flare for all-night revellers.

✨ International Folk Festival

Held in the town of Nida on Curonian Spit, this annual festival draws folk musicians and dance troupes from various Lithuanian regions and from around Europe. It's held over a weekend in late June.

✨ Hanseatic Days

The Estonian towns of Viljandi and Pärnu celebrate their past as part of the Hanseatic League of northern trading cities with much medieval merrymaking.

July

Summer is in full swing as locals gather on terraces and verandahs during the week to sip mugs of beer alfresco. On the weekends everyone flees the cities for their countryside abodes.

☆ Rīga's Rhythms

Held in early July, Rīgas Ritmi is the Latvian capital's international festival of jazz, world and improvised music. Additional concerts are held in winter and spring.

☆ Classical Concerts

The Christopher Summer Festival offers two months of classical, jazz and world music concerts held around the Lithuanian capital Vilnius in July and August.

☆ Pärnu
Film Festival

Coordinated by the city's Museum of New Art, this festival showcases documentary films from all over the world. It's held early in the month in the museum and at other venues around Estonia's premier beach resort.

☆ Beer & Bands

An extremely popular ale-guzzling and rock-music extravaganza, Õllesummer (Beer Summer) is held over three days at the historic Song Festival Grounds in Estonia's capital, Tallinn, in early July.

🎭 Klaipėda
Sea Festival

This five-day annual festival is held over the third weekend in July and celebrates the Lithuanian seaport's rich nautical heritage.

☆ Devilstone
Music Festival

This rock and metal music festival is held in the central Lithuanian town of Anykščiai in mid-July. Acts perform hard rock, heavy metal, goth, electronica and speed metal. If you've got the hair, you know where to be. (www.devil stone.net)

🎭 Võru Folklore
Festival

Mid-July in Võru sees a whir of dancers, singers and musicians decked out in the colourful folk costumes of Estonia and a dozen other nations, celebrating their respective ethnic traditions and cultures.

Top: A performer at the Positivus festival
Bottom: A Christmas market in Old Rīga

🎭 Tartu Hanseatic Days

Tartu goes medieval in mid-July with three days of costumed peasants, ladies, jesters, knights, crafts demonstrations, markets, family-friendly performances and more.

🍷 Wine Festival

The village of Sabile, Latvia, is famed for its vineyard – the world's most northern open-air grape grower. Your only chance to taste local wine is at this festival.

☆ Song & Dance Festival

Held separately in each Baltic country every five years, these massive festivals attract people with Baltic roots from all over the world to perform in mammoth choirs or large-scale dance routines that give North Koreans a run for their money.

☆ Positivus

Taking place amid the quiet pines of northern Vidzeme, Positivus has become an annual pilgrimage for many Latvians, who flock here for several days of rock, electronic and indie music-fueled revelry.

☆ Summer Sound

Liepāja holds the title as Latvia's haven for punk and garage bands, so any of its local music festivals are well worth checking out – especially Summer Sound, which draws up to 40,000 people each year. (www.summersound.lv)

☆ Viljandi Folk Music Festival

The Estonian town of Viljandi is overrun with folk-music aficionados during this hugely popular four-day festival, featuring musicians from Estonia and abroad. Over 100 concerts are held, attended by more than 20,000 people.

☆ Sigulda Opera Festival

An open-air opera festival attracts internationally acclaimed singers to the castle ruins of Sigulda, Latvia, for three days at the end of the month. (www.opersvetki.lv)

☆ Nida Jazz Marathon

Jazz comes to the sand dunes of a Lithuanian Baltic Sea resort during this annual festival. You can expect several days of concerts – with jam sessions afterwards – held at various venues around Curonian Spit in late July and early August.

August

Long cloudless afternoons are perfect for the beach and extended holidays from work, as locals savour every drop of golden sun – despite the occasional rainstorm.

🎭 Maritime Merriment

Early in the month, Kuressaare (on the Estonian island of Saaremaa) celebrates its marine credentials with its Maritime Festival, a weekend of sea-related activities including a regatta, fair, herring-cooking demonstrations, bands and a strong naval presence.

☆ Film Alfresco

The week-long tARTuFF open-air film festival has free screenings of art-house features and documentaries in the atmospheric Town Hall Square in the heart of Tartu, Estonia. Poetry readings and concerts round out the program.

🎭 Ghost Stories

Held in the grounds of Haapsalu's castle in western Estonia, the White Lady Festival culminates in the appearance of a ghostly apparition in the cathedral window, caused by the reflection of the full moon in the glass.

☆ Pagan Music

The popular MJR Alternative Music Festival (Mėnuo Juodaragis) celebrates – nominally – Lithuania's pagan roots; it's really just a chance to hear music rarely heard anywhere else. Held over the last weekend in August on an island near the eastern Lithuanian city of Zarasai. (www.mjr.lt)

☆ Birgitta Festival

The atmospheric ruins of Pirita Convent in Tallinn's most popular beach suburb offer an excellent backdrop to classical concerts, ballet, opera, choral works and modern dance.

🎭 Art by Night

Baltā Nakts (White Night), sponsored by the Contemporary Art Forum, mirrors Paris' night-long showcase of artists and culture around Rīga, Latvia's capital.

🎭 Piens Fest

A hipster's dream festival, Piens Fest feels like an

almost-accidental gathering of local artists (musical and otherwise) in the Miera iela area of Rīga. Devour fried food, peruse vintage attire and listen to indie beats while sitting on the grass. (www.piens.nu/fest/)

☆ Ezera Skaņas Festival

Surely Latvia's most esoteric musical event: people take to boats on Kāla Lake at 5am to hear otherworldly music wafting over the water. (www.ezeraskanas.lv)

☆ Future Shorts

This film festival celebrates short films from all over the world. (www.facebook.com/pages/Future-Shorts-Latvia/137370992955145)

September

The last days of summer quickly turn into the mild beginning of autumn. Rain is more frequent by the end of the month, while leaves turn brilliant colours and tumble off the trees.

☆ World Theatre

Sirenos (Sirens) International Theatre Festival is a popular annual drama festival held in Vilnius, Lithuania, from mid-September to mid-October, drawing people from around the world for a robust roster of live theatre.

October

Days are noticeably shorter and afternoons on the beach are but a memory now; tourist-focused businesses start shuttering their windows as everyone prepares to hibernate.

☆ Gaida Music Festival

One of the highlights of Lithuania's musical calendar is this annual celebration of classical and new music from Central and Eastern Europe. Held in Vilnius.

November

Autumn turns to winter as rainy days blend into snowy ones. This is perhaps one of the quietest months of the year – summer is long gone, yet winter holiday festivities have yet to begin.

☆ Scanorama

Held in Lithuania's four biggest cities (Vilnius, Kaunas, Klaipėda and Šiauliai), this festival showcases European films in various formats and genres. (www.scanorama.lt)

☆ Mama Jazz

Vilnius's biggest jazz event is held every November, usually drawing a banner list of top performers from around Europe and the world.

☆ Black Nights Film Festival

Estonia's biggest film festival showcases films from all over the world in the nation's capital over two weeks from mid-November. Subfestivals focus on animated films, children's films and student-made films.

☆ Latvian National Day

A whole week of festivities surrounds the anniversary of Latvia's 1918 proclamation of independence on 18 November, including the Rīga Festival of Light.

☆ Arēna New Music Festival

Showcases contemporary composers and artists working in what might be loosely dubbed the classical tradition; held at venues throughout Rīga, Latvia.

December

Yuletide festivities provide the perfect distraction from freezing temperatures as decorations cheer the streets and families gather from all over to celebrate.

☆ Christmas in Tartu

Watch the Advent candles being lit while the choirs sing on a fairy-lit Town Hall Square on the four Sundays leading up to Christmas (Estonia).

☆ Christmas Markets

Festive decorations, arts and crafts, traditional foods and entertainment brighten the dark days in the lead-up to Christmas, in each capital's Old Town (and in many other towns around the region).

☆ New Year's Eve

Enjoy fireworks and revelry on the main squares of Tallinn, Rīga and Vilnius in the countdown to midnight.

Itineraries

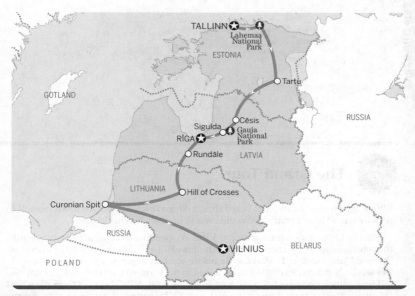

 Best of the Baltic

If you've only got limited time but you're keen on seeing the very best of what each of the Baltic states has to offer, this short itinerary ticks off many of the big-ticket destinations.

Inaugurate your tour in **Tallinn** and roam the magnificent medieval streets of the Estonian capital's **Old Town**. Delve into the city's treasure trove of gastronomic delights before trekking out to **Lahemaa National Park**. The electric university town of **Tartu** awaits; then skip south into Latvia to take in the crumbling castles of **Cēsis** and **Sigulda** in **Gauja National Park**. Spend the night at one of the posh *muižas* (manor houses) nearby, then plough through to reach **Rīga**, home to a dizzying array of decorated facades. Next, head south to **Rundāle** to visit the opulent palace – the Baltic's version of Versailles – built by the architect responsible for St Petersburg's Winter Palace. From Rundāle, hop the border into Lithuania and stop for a quick look at the **Hill of Crosses** in Šiauliai before shooting west to **Curonian Spit**. Spend some time amid the quaint cottages, shifting sand dunes and roving boar before ending your trip in flamboyant, baroque **Vilnius**.

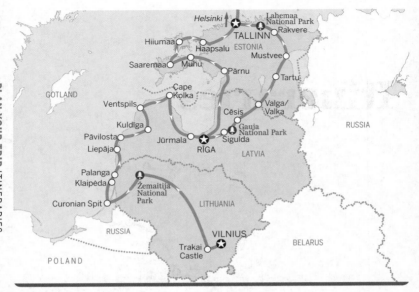

The Grand Tour

4 WEEKS

With a month you can roster in beach time, hiking excursions and see much more of the region's quaint little towns – you could even fit in a side trip to Helsinki.

Start in Lithuania's beautiful capital **Vilnius**, spending a couple of days wandering the cobblestone streets, checking out Gediminas Hill and taking in the city's historical charms. Make a stop at **Trakai Castle** before heading west towards the sea. Stop at **Žemaitija National Park** for a quick lesson in Soviet missile tactics, then reward yourself with some uninterrupted relaxation along the dune-filled shores of **Curonian Spit**. Follow the Baltic Sea up through the port city of **Klaipėda** and family-friendly **Palanga** to reach the Latvian border.

Over the border the first stop is **Liepāja**, famous for its gilded cathedral and hulking Soviet tenements. If the weather's behaving, head north to surfside **Pāvilosta** before detouring inland to the picturesque village of **Kuldīga**. Continue on to the lovely long sands of **Ventspils**, staying overnight before hitting windy and wild **Cape Kolka**. Follow the coast as it traces a snaking line past forests and quiet villages to the spa retreat of **Jūrmala** – a hot spot for Russian tycoons and an excellent pit stop. From here **Rīga** is only a short hop away.

After a couple of days in the Latvian capital, jump the border into Estonia for some beach bliss in **Pärnu**. Move west to play hopscotch between the forested islands of **Muhu**, **Saaremaa** and **Hiiumaa**. Stop for lunch and a castle visit in **Haapsalu** before continuing on to **Tallinn**. Allow at least three days to take in the Estonian capital's treasures before ferrying over to **Helsinki** for a night. Back in Estonia, stop overnight in **Lahemaa National Park** before heading through **Rakvere** and **Mustvee**, on the shores of Lake Peipsi, to **Tartu** for a night or two.

Stop to check out the oddball border town of **Valga/Valka** before continuing on to Latvia's **Gauja National Park**. Stop in charming **Cēsis** to wander among the fortress ruins, and in **Sigulda** for a side of bobsledding and bungee jumping. End your Baltic odyssey back in Rīga or motor on to Vilnius to return your hire car.

 ## 1 WEEK — Absolute Latvia

A full week in Latvia offers time to explore a good number of the nation's treasures beyond the attention-stealing capital.

After exploring **Rīga**, visit the castle-clad forests near **Sigulda** before moving on to the secret Soviet bunker at **Līgatne** and the stone fortress of **Cēsis**. Swing through to the peaceful Latgale Lakelands, where you can stay overnight in a guesthouse or a camp site on the shores of **Lake Rāzna** and visit the basilica at **Aglona**.

Loop back to **Rundāle** to take in the opulence of the palace before blasting on to the coast at **Liepāja**, home to Latvia's garage-band scene and the strikingly dour Karosta district. Detour inland to **Kuldīga**, one of the country's quaintest towns, then stop overnight in beachy **Ventspils**. Then it's on to **Cape Kolka**, where the Gulf of Rīga meets the Baltic Sea in dramatic fashion.

Follow the coastline through the constellation of lonely seaside villages to **Jūrmala**, the Baltic's most famous resort town, then finish up back in Rīga.

 ## 10 DAYS — Capital Drop-in

Ten days in the Baltic is just the right amount of time to get a feel for each of the region's capitals.

Start your journey in **Vilnius** (Lithuania) to appreciate the sumptuous baroque architecture amid the curving cobbled streets. Two days will give you plenty of time to snap photos of Gediminas Hill and take in the city's rich Jewish history.

A side trip to the castle at **Trakai** is a must before visiting Latvia's capital, **Rīga**: the Baltic's largest city. Haggle for huckleberries at the Central Market and crane your neck to take in the glorious art nouveau architecture soaring above. You'll be spoilt for choice with day-tripping detours – cavort with the Russian elite in **Jūrmala**, Latvia's spa centre; or crank up the adrenalin in **Sigulda**, with its clutch of adventure sports.

Next it's on to Estonia and **Tallinn**, where you'll be treated to a fairy-tale kingdom of quaint medieval houses. Indulge in the city's world-class culinary scene and finish off the journey with a day at quiet **Lahemaa National Park**.

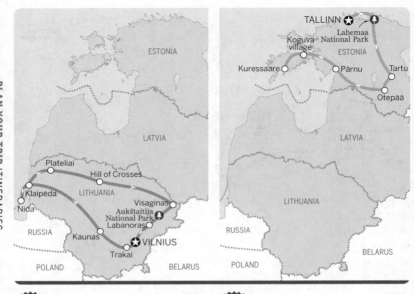

Lithuanian Solo
1 WEEK

You can jam a lot into a week in compact Lithuania, but if you've got the time, you could easily stretch this intinerary out to a more relaxed 10 days.

After taking in the cathedral and museums of **Vilnius**, drop by **Trakai** to see the island castle and then continue on to vibrant, rough-edged **Kaunas**. Beach bums should then head to the Baltic coast, dropping in to the port city of **Klaipėda** before continuing on to Curonian Spit. The best place to base yourself here is the enchanting town of **Nida**.

Leaving the coast, stop at **Plateliai** in Žemaitija National Park to see the abandoned Soviet missile base, which now houses the Cold War Museum. Break up your journey east with a visit to the **Hill of Crosses** before continuing on your way to **Visaginas**, built in the '70s to house workers at the now-shuttered Ignalina Nuclear Power Station. Continue on to **Aukštaitija National Park**, with its lakes and hiking paths, and stop overnight in **Labanoras**, the centrepiece of Labanoras Regional Park, before heading back to Vilnius.

Essential Estonia
1 WEEK

If you can drag yourself away from the wonderland that is Tallinn, this itinerary covers a little of everything Estonia has to offer: beaches, countryside, castles, historic towns and quaint villages.

On a week's journey through Estonia, it's best to give **Tallinn** at least two days – so you can fully explore each crooked nook in the charming medieval core while sampling the spoils of the nation's foodie scene. **Lahemaa National Park** makes for a lovely day trip, while the university town of **Tartu** awaits those looking for cultured city life away from the capital. Swing through **Otepää**, Estonia's self-proclaimed 'winter capital', then switch seasons in **Pärnu**, where sun worshippers come in droves for a bit of beach-lazing.

Round off the week on Estonia's western islands. Stop by time-warped **Koguva village** on Muhu, then base yourself at **Kuressaare** on Saaremaa – Estonia's prettiest spa town, set around an ancient moated castle. From here explore the island's forested expanse of whooshing windmills, lonely churches and soaring sea cliffs. At the end of the week, there are direct flights back to Tallinn.

Plan Your Trip
Road Trips

Whether you plan your itinerary extensively or simply follow the smell of salt and smoked fish up the coastline, you'll find driving in the Baltics a breeze. Roads are pretty good, traffic is light and drivers reasonably sane. Driving is not only an easy way to explore this region – it's a pleasure.

Planning Essentials
Driving vs Public Transport

To be honest, it's quite possible to explore the Baltics using public transport. Hire a car here purely for pleasure, convenience and freedom (plus it makes a great travelling suitcase). A car gives you the flexibility to explore the countries' quiet hinterlands, from the towering dunes of Lithuania's Curonian Spit to Estonia's windswept western islands to Latvia's pine-studded inner forests. Take your car off the main roads and stumble upon tiny villages locked away in time, or curious relics from the Soviet era, when the Russians used space-station technology to spy on the West.

Private vehicles far outshine public transport when it comes to convenience. If you're simply travelling between large towns and capitals, we recommend using the bus and train system, which is geared towards commuting professionals and is thus very comfortable. If you plan on exploring the national parks, rural backwaters or the Estonian islands, the limited bus services just aren't up to the job.

If you're travelling with your family or a small group of friends you'll find the freedom of a car versus the rather high petrol prices a much more amenable equation. However, parking a car can be a hassle in the capital cities, so allow yourself several days to explore them on

Best Day Trips by Car
From Tallinn

Enjoy Estonia's natural beauty and head east early in the morning to watch the forest come to life at Lahemaa National Park. If time permits, swing down to Rakvere to check out the castle before looping back to the capital.

From Rīga

If you've got your own wheels you won't be limited to the most obvious day trips (Gauja National Park, Rundāle, Jūrmala). Go west instead. Consider a stop at Pedvāle to peruse the sculptures at the open-air art museum, then venture on to quaint Kuldīga, a charming village frozen in time.

From Vilnius

Most visitors head west to the castle at Trakai, so buck the trend and venture northeast to check out the quiet lakes and hiking paths of Aukštaitija National Park, stopping at Labanoras along the way.

foot before collecting your hire car and hitting the road.

When to Go

For fairly obvious reasons, the best time of year to travel with a vehicle is during the summer months (June to August), which are blissfully free from snow, sleet and any other weather that could have a negative impact on your driving. The summer months are not, however, completely free of rain – and you'll have to consider booking ahead for ferries to the Estonian islands at busy times (on weekends especially, and around Midsummer). The summer days are long, which means that driving is relatively safe even in the late evening.

Where to Start & End

You'll be pleased to know that almost all car-hire companies allow mobility throughout all three Baltic countries (although some will charge a fee for the privilege). However, you'll be hard-pressed to find a service that will allow you to take a vehicle to any countries beyond.

If you hire a car from a smaller local agency, you'll be expected to return the vehicle to the location from which you picked it up. Larger franchise operators will allow you to drop the car off in a different town or even a different Baltic country for an additional fee – making a flight into Tallinn and out of Vilnius entirely possible. If you want to save on the relocation fee and start and end at the same point, leave from Rīga, complete a figure-eight circuit up into Estonia and down through Lithuania (or vice versa), then return.

Petrol & Servicing

Although the Baltic countryside can feel desolate and underpopulated, there is a healthy number of service stations in all three countries – it would take some seriously bad judgement to run out of petrol. Before taking your vehicle off the lot, make sure to arm yourself with a service phone number for each of the Baltic countries, just in case your car should require any attention while on the road. Tyres have been known to get punctures – especially in Latvia, where the road-maintenance infrastructure isn't as solid as it is in Lithuania or Estonia.

Road Rules

Traffic drives on the right-hand side of the road. Older towns and villages have a proliferation of one-way streets and roundabouts. Blood-alcohol limits are low in all three countries (0.2 in Estonia, 0.4 in Lithuania, 0.5 in Latvia).

Although the Baltic nations have a fairly poor reputation when it comes to road etiquette and collisions, this stereotype is mostly unfounded. Drivers in the big cities can be aggressive but you'll find that most are forgiving of wrong turns and lane-changing. You should, however, avoid inner-city driving during the workday rush hour – especially on Friday afternoons in the warmer months, when locals tend to make a beeline to their countryside cottages. Driving in the region's rural parts is rarely a laborious task as populations are sparse. Do, however, be careful of passing vehicles, which tend to speed by unannounced and at surprisingly inopportune moments.

Take extra care on the Tallinn–Tartu highway, known by locals as 'the road of death'. Numerous speed cameras are in effect here, as well as on the Tallinn–Narva highway and throughout Latvia.

Plan Your Trip
Outdoor Activities

The Baltic countries offer visitors plenty of up-close-and-personal encounters with Mother Nature at her gentlest: paddling on sparkling lakes, rambling or cycling through pretty forests, lazing on beaches. Instead of craning your neck at sky-reaching peaks, here you can marvel over accessible nature and superb rural scenery.

The Great Outdoors

While the flat Baltic countries lack the drama of more mountainous regions, there are places where you're left in no doubt that it's tempestuous nature that's calling the shots – witness the awesome shifting sands of Curonian Spit, or the windswept, desolate Cape Kolka.

There's plenty of breathing space in these countries, too, offering some of the continent's best opportunities to ditch the crowds and simply frolic in the wilderness. Check the population figures and you'll be in no doubt that open space abounds here.

A smorgasbord of active endeavours awaits anyone wanting to delve into the outdoors. You can whet your appetite with berry-picking before feeding on an alfresco meal of brisk, salty air, pristine white-sand beaches and icy-blue Baltic Sea vistas. Want seconds? Try cycling through dense, pine-scented forests; canoeing down a lazy river; or checking out the flora and fauna in a quiet nature reserve. Those craving an adrenalin fix can find some surprising options, too, from bobsledding to bungee jumping. If you still have room for dessert, try baby-gentle downhill or cross-country skiing, or just get hot and sweaty in a traditional rural sauna.

Best of the Outdoors

Ultimate Cycling Route
Follow the Baltic coastline from Curonian Spit, up through the Kurzeme Coast, around the Gulf of Rīga and onto the quiet western islands of Estonia.

Best Authentic Sauna Experience
Try a *pirts,* a traditional Latvian cleanse involving extreme temperatures, a birch-branch beating and jumping into a pond.

Top Forest Hikes
Lahemaa National Park (Estonia), Gauja National Park (Latvia), Žemaitija National Park (Lithuania)

Excellent Canoeing Spots
Haanja Nature Park (Estonia), Latgale Lakelands (Latvia), Aukštaitija National Park (Lithuania)

Must-See Wildlife
Blue cows in Latvia's Kurzeme Region, wild boar on Lithuania's Curonian Spit, storks nesting on power poles throughout the Estonian countryside.

Outdoor Activities Web Resource
Country Holidays (www.traveller.lv) Pan-Baltic website offering details on cycling routes, hiking trails and landmarks.

Cycling

The Baltic offers superb cycling territory. The region's flatness makes tooling around the countryside on a bicycle an option for anyone: casual cyclists can get the hang of things on gentle paved paths, while hardcore fanatics can rack up the kilometres on more challenging multiday treks. Although there's not much along the lines of steep single-track trails, dirt tracks through forests abound, and the varied but always peaceful scenery ensures you'll never tire of the view.

The capital cities of the Baltic are also doing their share to increase the usability of bicycles. Urban cycling paths are multiplying each year as bike-share and easy-access rental programs proliferate.

Among the most popular places to cycle in Lithuania are spectacular Curonian Spit, lake-studded Dzūkija National Park, around Lake Plateliai and on the forest paths in Labanoras Regional Park.

In Estonia, try the quiet back roads of the islands of Muhu, Saaremaa and Hiiumaa, as well as the bay-fringed, forested confines of Lahemaa National Park.

In Latvia, bicycle is the best way to explore Liepaja, Ventspils, Sigulda and Jūrmala. For a longer adventure, the Latgale Lakelands are ideal, with plenty of paved and unpaved roads leading through beautiful wilderness. The Cape Kolka area is also very popular.

WORKING UP A SWEAT

Given that it's cold and snowy for many months of the year, it's little surprise that the sauna is an integral part of local culture. Most hotels have one, and some cities have public bathhouses with saunas. But it's those that smoulder silently next to a lake or river, by the sea or deep in the forest that provide the most authentic experience.

There are three main types of sauna in the Baltic:

➡ In Finnish-style saunas an electric stove keeps the air temperature high (between 70°C and 95°C) and humidity low. These are found in plenty of private homes, most hotels and all spas and water parks etc. Public sauna complexes charge an hourly fee and there are plenty of small private saunas that can be rented by the hour. Some hotels will charge but others have free facilities for guests, or a free morning or evening sauna included as part of the rate; some hotel suites have a private sauna attached to the bathroom.

➡ The smoke sauna is the most archaic type, where a fire is lit directly under rocks in the chimney-less building (generally a one-room wooden hut) – heating can take up to five hours. After the fire is put out in the hearth, the heat comes from the warmed rocks. The smoke is let out just before participants enter; the soot-blackened walls are part of the experience. Smoke saunas are rare but have become more popular in recent times.

➡ The 'Russian sauna', or steam sauna/steam bath, is not as popular in the Baltic region as the Finnish style of sauna, but is found mainly in spas or water parks. In these, the air temperature is medium (about 50°C) and air humidity is high.

Locals use a bunch of birch twigs to lightly slap or flick the body, stimulating circulation, irrespective of which sauna type they're sweating in. Some also lather their bodies in various oils and unguents (honey products are popular).

Cooling down is an equally integral part of the experience: most Finnish-style saunas have showers or pools attached, while the more authentic smoke saunas are usually next to a lake or river. In the depths of winter, rolling in snow or cutting out a square metre of ice from a frozen lake in order to take a quick dip is not unheard of.

In public saunas, such as those in spa hotels, a set of rules is usually posted outlining sauna etiquette and what to wear. Swimming costumes are generally required in mixed-gender areas (for men, Speedo-style briefs are the strong preference – some places forbid board shorts), while people tend to go nude in single-sex facilities. Some places provide towels or paper sheets to sit on.

Plan Your Trip

If you want someone to help with planning, a band of dedicated cycling operators offer everything from itinerary-planning services to fully guided treks. For DIY planning, check out info-laden www.eurovelo.org.

BaltiCCycle (www.bicycle.lt; Lithuania)

City Bike (www.citybike.ee; Estonia)

Spas & Saunas
Estonia

Spa-going is extremely popular among Estonians, who share their sauna habits with the Finns next door. You can try a traditional smoke sauna at the Mihkli Farm Museum on Hiiumaa island. Many Estonians refer to Saaremaa island as 'Sparemaa' for its proliferation of spa resorts, particularly in Kuressaare. You'll find excellent spa spots in Pärnu, Rakvere, Võru and Tallinn as well.

Latvia

Latvia's seaside town of Jūrmala is undoubtedly the spa capital of the Baltic. In its heyday it was the holiday centre of the entire Russian Empire – thousands of aristocrats travelled here in droves to slather themselves in curative mud, rinse in sulphur water and enjoy the glorious views of the bay. Today, much of Jūrmala's allure remains, and it's still a popular spot for Russian tycoons to build a holiday home and get massage treatments. For an authentic cleansing experience, however, you'll have to venture far away from the crowds of Rīga or Jūrmala and head to the countryside, where locals have constructed their own private *pirts* close to the water's edge (pond, river, lake or sea). Several private *pirts* can be booked by travellers, such as the one shared by several hotels in Sigulda; otherwise you'll have to befriend some locals to gain access.

Lithuania

Lithuania has a less-developed spa and sauna scene than its Baltic brothers, but there are nonetheless a few places to indulge. The two most popular spa destinations are Birštonas and the fabled 19th-century spa town of Druskininkai, on the Nemunas River; of the two, Druskininkai is the destination of choice for serious spaseekers. The town, which has been in the healing business for more than 200 years, boasts mineral spas for sipping (with a reputedly recuperative effect on everything from the stomach to the heart), mud baths, a relatively mild climate and miles and miles of surrounding forest that keep the air fresh and clean. Added to that are modern diversions, such as a huge water park, that make the town a perfect respite for the healthy as well as the ailing.

Hiking

While the Baltic countries lack the craggy grandeur or wild expanses of some of their neighbours, a day or two hiking in one of the forested national parks is rewarding all the same. All that forest (it covers 51% of Estonia, 45% of Latvia and 33% of Lithuania) just begs to be explored, especially if there are beaver dams to spot, berries to pick or tales of resident witches and fairies to hear along the way.

Grab your hiking boots, breathe deeply of the pine-fresh air and hit the trails in the likes of Žemaitija National Park in Lithuania, Gauja National Park in Latvia, and Lahemaa National Park in Estonia. Pretty villages that make good bases for exploration include Estonia's Otepää and Rõuge; Valmiera and Cēsis in Latvia; and Nida in Lithuania. If ordinary walking doesn't float your boat, make a beeline for Estonia's Soomaa National Park, where you can go on a guided walk through the park's wetlands using special 'bog shoes' that give you access to otherwise hard-to-reach areas.

Water Sports

Having been cooped up for most of the winter, the region comes alive in summer, with locals and visitors taking any opportunity to soak up some vitamin D during the gloriously long days. You're never far from the sea or a lake offering fishing, sailing, windsurfing and swimming. And when the weather doesn't favour outdoor frolicking, there's no shortage of wet and wild water parks (with indoor pools, slides, saunas etc) in big cities and holiday areas – these operators know from experience that a Baltic summer is no guarantee for beach-going weather.

Great Baltic beachy spots are Pärnu, Narva-Jõesuu and Saaremaa in Estonia; Jūrmala, Ventspils, Pāvilosta and Liepāja in Latvia; and Palanga, Klaipėda and Nida in Lithuania. More heart-pounding water sports, such as kiteboarding, can be attempted at Pāvilosta in Latvia.

Canoeing & Rafting

Watching the landscape slide slowly by while paddling down a lazy river is a fabulous way to experience the natural world from a different angle. As the region's rivers are not known for their wild rapids, this is a great place for beginners to hone their skills or for families to entertain the kids. Even if you're usually more into wild than mild, the region's scenic beauty and tranquillity create such a Zen experience you'll quickly forget you haven't hit a single rapid.

In Latvia, the Gauja and Abava Rivers offer uninterrupted routes stretching for several days, and you can join an organised tour or rent gear and run the routes on your own – the best places to start are Sigulda (for the Gauja) and Kandava (for the Abava). The Latgale Lakelands are also excellent. In Lithuania, Aukštaitija National Park, Labanoras Regional Park, Dzūkija National Park, Trakai and Nemunas Loops Regional Park all offer the opportunity for great canoeing. Canoes or traditional *haabjas* (Finno-Ugric boats carved from a single log) are a good way to explore Soomaa National Park in southwest Estonia – you can even learn to build your own *haabjas*. Otepää is another good Estonian spot to organise and access canoe trips, as is Haanja Nature Park.

Fishing

Abundant lakes and miles of rivers and streams provide ample fishing opportunities in all three countries. Visit a regional tourist office for the scoop on the best angling spots and information pertaining to permits.

In the dark depths of the Baltic winter there is no finer experience than dabbling in a touch of ice-fishing with vodka-warmed local fishing folk on the frozen Curonian Lagoon, off the west coast of Lithuania, or at Trakai. The Nemunas Delta Regional Park is another good western Lithuanian fishing spot. In Latvia, the Latgale Lakelands are packed with hundreds of deep-blue lakes offering fishing opportunities galore. In northern Kurzeme, Lake Engure is another favourite angling spot. Huge Lake Peipsi is popular in Estonia.

Berrying & Mushrooming

The Balts' deep-rooted attachment to the land is reflected in their obsession with berrying and mushrooming – national pastimes in all three countries. Accompanying a local friend into the forest on a summer berrying trip or autumn mushrooming expedition is an enchanting way to appreciate this traditional rural pastime.

If you're keen on picking but lack a local invitation, join an organised tour (locals closely guard the location of their favourite spots, so just asking around probably won't reap any useful information). For info on berrying and mushrooming tours, check out www.atostogoskaime.lt (Lithuania), www.maaturism.ee (Estonia) and www.traveller.lv (Latvia), and ask at local tourist offices.

Of the more than a thousand types of mushroom found in the region, around 400 are edible and about 100 are poisonous – never eat anything you're not 100% sure about. Unless you're accompanied by a local expert, you're better off heading to a market and checking out the freshly picked produce. The crinkle-topped, yellow chanterelle and stubby boletus are among the best. You can also peruse menus for in-season treasures from local forests.

For fungi fanatics, there's Varėna's mushroom festival, held in September every year.

Birdwatching

Thanks to a key position on north–south migration routes, the Baltic countries are a birder's paradise. Each year hundreds of

Top: A young cormorant in Curonian Spit National Park (p363)

Bottom: Kayaking on the Gaja River, Sigulda (p256)

MARTINS VANAGS/SHUTTERSTOCK ©

MIDSUMMER MADNESS

In pagan times it was a night of magic and sorcery, when witches ran naked and wild, bewitching flowers and ferns, people and animals. In the agricultural calendar, it marked the end of the spring sowing and the start of the summer harvest. In Soviet times it became a political celebration: a torch of independence was lit in each capital and its flame used to light bonfires throughout the country.

Today Midsummer Day, aka summer solstice or St John's Day, falling on 24 June, is the Balts' biggest party of the year. On this night darkness barely falls – reason alone to celebrate in a part of the world with such short summers and such long, dark winters. In Estonia it is known as Jaanipäev; in Latvia it's Jāņi, Jānu Diena or Līgo; and in Lithuania, Joninés or Rasos (the old pagan name).

Celebrations start on 23 June, particularly in Latvia, where the festival is generally met with the most gusto. Traditionally, people flock to the countryside to celebrate this special night amid lakes and pine forests. Special beers, cheeses and pies are prepared and wreaths are strung together from grasses, while flowers and herbs are hung around the home to bring good luck and keep families safe from evil spirits. Men adorn themselves with crowns made from oak leaves; women wear crowns of flowers.

Come Midsummer's Eve bonfires are lit and the music and drinking begins. No one is allowed to sleep until the sun has sunk and risen again – anyone who does will be cursed with bad luck for the coming year. Traditional folk songs are sung, dances danced and those special beers, cheeses and pies eaten! To ensure good luck, you have to leap back and forth over the bonfire. In Lithuania, clearing a burning wheel of fire as it is rolled down the nearest hill brings you even better fortune. In Estonia, revellers swing on special double-sided Jaanipäev swings, strung from trees in forest clearings or in village squares.

Midsummer's night is a night for lovers. In Estonia the mythical Koit (dawn) and Hämarik (dusk) meet but once a year for an embrace lasting as long as the shortest night of the year. Throughout the Baltic region, lovers seek the mythical fern flower, which blooms only on this night. The dew coating flowers and ferns on Midsummer's night is held to be a purifying force, a magical healer and a much sought-after cure for wrinkles – bathe your face in it and you will instantly become more beautiful and more youthful. However, beware the witches of Jaanipäev/Jāni/Joninés, who are known to use it for less enchanting means.

bird species descend upon the region, attracted by fish-packed wetlands and wide-open spaces relatively devoid of people. White storks arrive by the thousands each spring, nesting on rooftops and telegraph poles throughout the region. Other annual visitors include corncrakes, bitterns, cranes, mute swans, black storks and all types of geese.

Estonia

In Estonia, some of the best birdwatching in the Baltic is found in Matsalu National Park, where 280 different species (many migratory) can be spotted, and where regular tours are run. Spring migration peaks in April/May, but some species arrive as early as March. Autumn migration begins in July and can last until November. Vilsandi National Park, off Saaremaa, is another prime spot for feathery friends; the park's headquarters can help arrange birdwatching tours.

Lithuania

Some of 270 of the 330 bird species found in Lithuania frequent the Nemunas Delta Regional Park, making it a must-visit for serious birders. Park authorities can help organise birdwatching expeditions during the peak migratory seasons. The nearby Curonian Spit National Park offers opportunities for spotting up to 200 different species of birds amid dramatic coastal scenery.

Latvia

In Latvia, keep an eye out for some of Europe's rarest birds in splendid Gauja National Park. With thick forests and numerous wetlands, Ķemeri National Park in northern Kurzeme is another great birdwatching spot. Lake Engure, in northern Kurzeme, is a major bird reservation with 186 species (44 endangered) nesting around the lake and its seven islets.

Skiing

They might not have anything closely resembling a mountain, but Estonia and Latvia haven't let this geographic hurdle hinder their ski-resort efforts. Instead, these countries have become masters at working with what they've got – and that means constructing lifts and runs on the tiniest of hills, and using rooftops and dirt mounds to create vertical drops. At least they've got the climate working for them, with cold temperatures ensuring snow cover for at least four months of the year. Don't expect much in the way of technical terrain or long powder runs – but you've got to admit that saying you've skied the Baltics is pretty damn cool.

Otepää in southeast Estonia is probably the best of the Baltic winter resorts. It offers limited downhill skiing, myriad cross-country trails, a ski jump and plenty of outlets from which to hire gear. Lively nightlife and a ski-town vibe heighten the appeal. Kicksledding, cross-country skiing and snowshoe excursions are available at Soomaa National Park.

The Gauja Valley is the centre of Latvia's winter-sports scene. Cēsis offers short-but-sweet downhill runs and loads of cross-country trails. Adrenalin junkies disappointed by Sigulda's gentle slopes can get their fix swishing down the town's 1200m-long artificial bobsled run – the five-person contraptions reach speeds of 80km/h!

Lithuania offers downhill skiing at Anykščiai, as well as cross-country skiing amid deep, whispering forests and frozen blue lakes in beautiful Aukštaitija National Park. There's also a huge indoor slope at Druskininkai.

Horse Riding

The gentle pace of horseback exploration is definitely in keeping with the yester-year feel of parts of the Baltic countries. Some of the best and most bucolic places to get saddle-sore include Lahemaa National Park and the islands of Hiiumaa and Saaremaa in Estonia – operators here will usually combine rural and coastal rides, and can arrange multiday treks. In Latvia, head to Plosti, between Kandava and Sabile in the picturesque Abava Valley; **Untumi country ranch** (✆6463 1255; www.untumi.lv), 7km northwest of Rēzekne; or the well-established Klajumi stables, outside Krāslava in the Latgale Lakelands. For some four-legged fun in Lithuania, head to Trakai or to the horse museum in the village of Niūronys, outside Anykščiai.

Plan Your Trip
Travel with Children

Relax. The Baltic states present no particular challenges for parents with kids in tow – whether they're beaming babies or tempestuous teens – and there's oodles of opportunity for family fun. Even when the weather puts a dampener on things, there's plenty to see and do.

Best Regions for Kids

Estonia

Estonia will delight splash-loving kids with its endless shallow, sandy, toddler-friendly beaches and excellent water parks. Other fun includes good child-focused museums, fairy-tale castles and medieval town centres.

Latvia

Gauja National Park is an enchanted forest of towering pines, fairy-tale castles, hidden ogres, secreted Soviet bunkers and myriad adventure activities, such as ropes courses, Tarzan swings and canoeing. Latvia's western coastline is a delightful jumble of water parks and sandy strips of beach.

Lithuania

Lithuania's entire coastline is a veritable playground for kids, be it the funfair amusements and in-house restaurant entertainers in Palanga and Šventoji or the bikes and boats to rent on Curonian Spit. Further inland there are plenty of forested landscapes to be explored by foot or canoe. In Vilnius kids will enjoy a climb up the TV Tower, a ride on the funicular up Gediminas Hill and a dip at the local water park.

Estonia, Latvia & Lithuania for Kids

While it may have been a little daunting travelling with kids in Estonia, Latvia and Lithuania back when they were Soviet Socialist Republics, nowadays it's a breeze. All three are part of the EU, so you can expect the same high standards of regulation as you would in London or Vienna for everything from baby food to car seats.

The Baltic countries have a fascinating history; this might be of keen interest to most adult visitors, but a visit to a social-history museum can be lost on toddlers and teens alike. Fortunately, there are tons of opportunities for younger travellers to engage with their surroundings in a fun and meaningful manner at various castles, farm complexes, interactive museums and the like. Almost all attractions offer half-price tickets for school-age children and free entry for toddlers.

Throughout the region you'll find tours – particularly day trips from the capital cities – that shuttle visitors to the various attractions of note around the region's major centres. These trips are, in general, not well suited to youngsters. If you have little ones in tow, it's best to tailor-make your own adventure.

Feeding Time

Well-behaved children are welcome at almost all eateries throughout the region, although the more relaxed, family-style restaurants will probably be more enjoyable for parents and children alike. In Latvia, look out for the LIDO chain of self-service bistros: the massive Atpūtas Centrs (p220) branch on the outskirts of Rīga is particularly good, with a giant windmill and a fun park next door. In Estonia, anything labelled *kõrts* (tavern) is a good bet.

The stodgy, somewhat bland nature of traditional Baltic food will suit the palates of most children. While they might baulk at the pickled herrings and sauerkraut, the myriad versions of pork, chicken and potatoes should pose no particular challenges.

Favourite standbys such as pizza and pasta are ubiquitous, and usually of sufficient quality to please an adult palate as well. In any event, many places have children's menus serving smaller portions. For something a little different but equally as cheap, filling and crowd-pleasing, try a plate of Russian-style *pelmeņi* dumplings.

On the downside, you won't find many high chairs in restaurants, and nappy-changing rooms are virtually unheard of.

Other Practicalities

Nappies (diapers) and known-brand baby foods, including some organic ones, are widely available in supermarkets in the main towns.

All of the big-name car-rental brands should be able to supply appropriate car seats, but it's best to check what's available and to book in advance. If you've got a good-quality, comfortable, capsule-style baby seat of your own that you're familiar with, you might want to consider bringing it with you, as they can be very handy as portable cots.

Children's Highlights

History Comes Alive

➡ **Tallinn's Old Town, Estonia** Fairy-tale turrets, medieval streetscapes and waitstaff dressed as peasant wenches and farmboys. (p71)

➡ **Turaida Museum Reserve, Latvia** Explore the castle, watch blacksmiths at work and seek out the kooky sculptures in the song garden. (p257)

➡ **Grūtas Park, Lithuania** A step back into the Soviet era, with the added bonus of vintage play equipment and a mini zoo for the little ones. (p329)

➡ **Rakvere Castle, Estonia** Smaller kids can dress up as princesses and knights and pet farm animals; older kids can can scream their heads off in the torture chamber and watch alchemists blow things up. (p93)

➡ **The Pension, Līgatne, Latvia** A hidden bunker stocked with heaps of relics from the Soviet era – truly interesting for all ages. (p264)

➡ **Narva Hermann Castle, Estonia** In summer there's a mock-up of a 17th-century town in the castle yard. (p96)

➡ **Ludza Craftsmen Centre, Latvia** Put your kids to work spinning wool, making pottery and sewing. (p275)

➡ **House of Crafts, Ventspils, Latvia** An old-school classroom features craft demonstrations. (p236)

Fun Museums & Galleries

➡ **Science Centre AHHAA, Tartu, Estonia** Experiential, science-based displays designed to turn your progeny into mad scientists. (p108)

➡ **Tartu Toy Museum, Estonia** Toys to covet, toys to play with, toys to make grown-ups feel nostalgic. (p107)

➡ **Lennusadam Seaplane Harbour, Tallinn, Estonia** Loads of interactive displays, with a real submarine, ice-breaker and mine-hunter to explore. (p60)

➡ **Narrow-Gauge Railway Museum, Anykščiai, Lithuania** Take a ride on a manual rail car and a historic train. (p353)

➡ **Tallinn Zoo, Estonia** Lots of big beasts and cute critters to see and learn about. (p68)

➡ **Horse Museum, Niūronys, Lithuania** Check out the historic carts and carriages, take a ride and bake your own black bread. (p353)

➡ **O. Luts Parish School Museum, Palamuse, Estonia** Where else will adults encourage kids to grab a slingshot and shoot a stone through a real glass window? (p103)

➡ **Nuku, Tallinn, Estonia** The national puppet museum offers dress-ups, puppets to play with and look at, and regular shows. (p69)

➡ **Ilon's Wonderland, Haapsalu, Estonia** Child-focused gallery showcasing the work of noted kids' book illustrator Ilon Wikland. (p153)

Activities

➡ **Sigulda, Latvia** Long established as the go-to spot for adrenalin lovers. Heart-pounding bungee jumps and bobsled tracks are the main attraction, but there are plenty of more subdued options for younger children. (p256)

➡ **Curonian Spit, Lithuania** Shifting sand dunes and miles of windswept beaches make it the best place in the Baltic to build the ultimate sandcastle. (p363)

➡ **Ventspils, Latvia** A huge playground (Children's Town), a narrow-gauge railway and loads of fun things to do on the beach. (p235)

➡ **Palanga, Lithuania** A seaside resort lined with kid-friendly amusements: inflatable slides, merry-go-rounds, electric cars etc. (p375)

➡ **Pärnu, Estonia** This historic town is a veritable magnet for families, with its leafy parks, large indoor water park and lovely shallow, sandy beach. (p132)

➡ **Otepää, Estonia** Estonia's self-proclaimed 'winter capital' actually offers a bevy of nature-related activities throughout the year, including an excellent high-ropes course. (p122)

➡ **Jūrmala, Latvia** A particularly family-friendly beach resort. (p229)

➡ **Aqua Park, Druskininkai, Lithuania** There's a fabulous water park for the kids – and spa treatments for parents! (p329)

Planning

When to Go

The long days and mild weather make summer the perfect time to travel around the Baltic with children – although the virtual lack of darkness during midsummer can play havoc with children's sleeping schedules. In summertime, outdoor tourist amenities are in full swing: beach towns come alive and myriad rental cottages dot the interior. It is, however, very popular with all types of holidaymakers, so it's crucial that you book accommodation and car rental in advance (remembering to request cots and car seats if you require them).

What to Pack

Don't stress too much about the packing, as whatever you forget should easily be found for purchase in any of the capital cities. Whatever the season, a bathing suit is a must, as there are many heated indoor pools to enjoy when it's too miserable to hit the beaches.

Make sure you've got insect repellent handy before you head onto the islands or into the national parks – the mosquitoes are enormous and voracious.

Accommodation

Most hotels will do their best to help make kids feel at home. Many have family rooms with a double bed for parents and a single or bunks for the kids. Cots are often available, especially in the larger establishments, although it's best to enquire and request one in advance. There might be a small charge for the cot, but in most instances infants can stay in a double room for free.

Regions at a Glance

At a glance, the Baltic states look like three easily interchangeable slices, neatly stacked on Europe's northeastern frontier. Although the region's shared history and topography may be the ties that bind, each country is quite different in other respects – language, religion and temperament being the most obvious examples.

The three capitals are a case in point. Estonia's presents itself as a Gothic fairy tale and Lithuania's is full of the thrilling frills of the baroque, while Latvia's is properly kooky, its famous art nouveau buildings embellished with gods, monsters, crazed cats and nature motifs.

Less variations on a theme than separate movements of a symphony, each of the Baltic states can be savoured individually or combined into a magnum opus. And you can play them in any order you like.

Estonia

Historic Towns
Castles
Nature

Hanseatic Heritage

From Tallinn's magnificent medieval Old Town to the genteel lanes and parks of Pärnu and the university precinct of Tartu, Estonia has a wealth of streets that time seemingly forgot.

Brooding Battlements

There has to be a bright side to being precariously positioned on the edge of civilisations – in Estonia's case, the legacy of a millennium of warfare is a spectacular crop of fortresses scattered throughout the country.

Forests & Wetlands

Estonia's countryside may be flat and unassuming compared with craggier parts of Europe, but its low population density and extensive forests, bogs and wetlands make it an important habitat for a multitude of mammals large and small, as well as a biannual seasonal influx of feathered visitors.

p46

Latvia

Architecture
Castles
Nature

Art Nouveau Rīga

No one mastered art nouveau like Rīga's coterie of architects at the turn of the 20th century, who covered the city's myriad facades with screaming goblins, praying goddesses, creeping vines and geometric emblems.

Noble Remains

Once the feudal playground for dozens of German nobles, Latvia is riddled with crumbling reminders of a sumptuous bygone era. Many of these castles and manor houses have been lovingly restored and transformed into memorable inns – the perfect place to live out your fairy-tale fantasies.

Scenery & Serenity

Beyond Rīga's clutch of twisting spires and towering housing blocks you'll find miles and miles of quiet forests, intimate lakelands and flaxen shores that beckon the crashing Baltic tides.

p192

Lithuania

Nature
Architecture
Nightlife

Untouched Landscapes

The Baltic coast, the dunes of Curonian Spit and the large forests broken up by meadows and lakes: Lithuania's landscape is blissfully unspoiled. Good tourist infrastructure allows you to hike it, bike it or boat it at your own pace.

Colour & Grandeur

Vilnius' attractive Old Town is filled with Renaissance, baroque and neoclassical architecture. Outside the city, the simple wooden structures of the countryside will wow you with vivid colours and intricate carvings.

Vilnius after Dark

Vilnius and Kaunas are home to thousands of students, who provide a critical mass for hundreds of cafes, bars, restaurants and clubs. The centre of Vilnius' action is Old Town, but there are plenty of places all around the city.

p285

On the Road

Helsinki (FINLAND)
p180

Estonia
p46

Latvia
p192

Lithuania
p285

Kaliningrad (RUSSIA)
p398

Estonia

📞 372 / POP 1.3 MILLION

Best Places to Stay

➡ Pädaste Manor (p140)

➡ Antonius Hotel (p110)

➡ Georg Ots Spa Hotel (p147)

➡ Villa Theresa (p94)

➡ Tabinoya (p71)

Best Places to Eat

➡ Mr Jakob (p126)

➡ Kuur (p159)

➡ Ö (p77)

➡ Rataskaevu 16 (p75)

➡ Retro (p149)

Why Go?

Estonia doesn't have to struggle to find a point of difference: it's completely unique. It shares a similar geography and history with Latvia and Lithuania, but culturally it's distinct. Its closest ethnic and linguistic buddy is Finland, and although they may love to get naked together in the sauna, 50 years of Soviet rule in Estonia have separated the two. For the last 300 years Estonia's been linked to Russia, but the two states have as much in common as a barn swallow and a bear (their respective national symbols).

With a newfound confidence, singular Estonia has crept from under the Soviet blanket and leapt into the arms of Europe. The love affair is mutual. Europe has fallen head-over-heels for the charms of Tallinn and its Unesco-protected Old Town. Put simply, Tallinn is now one of the continent's most captivating cities. And in overcrowded Europe, Estonia's sparsely populated countryside and extensive swaths of forest provide spiritual sustenance for nature lovers.

When to Go

➡ The most clement weather is from May to September, and while it can get a little crazy in Tallinn and Pärnu (especially in July and August), it's still the best time to visit.

➡ Almost all festivals are scheduled for summer, with the biggest celebrations saved for Midsummer's Eve.

➡ Fans of cross-country skiing should make for Otepää, the unofficial winter capital from December to March.

➡ Yuletide in Tallinn is unforgettable, with Christmas markets and a nearly 600-year-old tradition of raising a Christmas tree on the main square.

TALLINN

POP 414,000

If you're labouring under the misconception that 'former Soviet' means dull and grey and that all tourist traps are soulless, Tallinn will delight in proving you wrong. This city has charm by the bucketload, fusing the modern and medieval to come up with a vibrant vibe all of its own. It's an intoxicating mix of ancient church spires, glass skyscrapers, baroque palaces, appealing eateries, brooding battlements, shiny shopping malls, run-down wooden houses and cafes set on sunny squares – with a few Soviet throwbacks in the mix, for added spice.

Despite the boom of 21st-century development, Tallinn remains loyal to the fairytale charms of its two-tiered Old Town – one of Europe's most beguiling walled cities. That wasn't always the case. For a while it appeared to be willing to sell its soul to become the Bangkok of the Baltic: attracting groups of young men with the lure of cheap booze and rampant prostitution. That's calmed down somewhat and although sleazy elements remain, the city seems to have realised that there's more money to be made from being classy than brassy. Hence an ever-expanding roster of first-rate restaurants, atmospheric hotels and a well-oiled tourist machine that makes visiting a breeze, no matter which language you speak.

Increasingly sophisticated without being overly sanitised, forward-focused while embracing the past, Tallinn is a truly fascinating city.

History

The site of Tallinn is thought to have been settled by Finno-Ugric people around 2500 BC. There was probably an Estonian trading settlement here from around the 9th century AD and a wooden stronghold was built on Toompea (*tawm*-pe-ah; the hill dominating Tallinn) in the 11th century. The Danes under King Waldemar II (who conquered northern Estonia in 1219) met tough resistance at Tallinn and were on the verge of retreat when it's said that a red flag with a white cross fell from the sky into their bishop's hands. Taking this as a sign of God's support, they went on to win the battle and gain a national flag. The Danes built their own castle on Toompea. The origin of the name Tallinn is thought to be from *Taani linn*, Estonian for 'Danish town'.

The Knights of the Sword took Tallinn from the Danes in 1227 and built the first stone fort on Toompea. German traders arrived from Visby on the Baltic island of Gotland and founded a colony of about 200 people beneath the fortress. In 1238 Tallinn returned to Danish control but in 1285 it joined the German-dominated Hanseatic League as a channel for trade between Novgorod, Pihkva (Russian: Pskov) and the West. Furs, honey, leather and seal fat moved west; salt, cloth, herring and wine went east.

By the mid-14th century, when the Danes sold northern Estonia to the Teutonic Order, Tallinn was a major Hanseatic town with about 4000 people. Conflict with the knights and bishop on the hill led the mainly German artisans and merchants in the Lower Town to build a fortified wall to separate themselves from Toompea. Tallinn prospered regardless and became one of northern Europe's biggest towns. Tallinn's German name, Reval, coexisted with the local name until 1918.

Prosperity faded in the 16th century. The Hanseatic League had weakened, and Russians, Swedes, Danes, Poles and Lithuanians fought over the Baltic region. Tallinn survived a 29-week siege by Russia's Ivan the Terrible between 1570 and 1571. It was held by Sweden from 1561 to 1710, when, decimated by plague, Tallinn surrendered to Russia's Peter the Great.

In 1870 a railway was completed from St Petersburg, and Tallinn became a chief port of the Russian Empire. Freed peasants converged on the city from the countryside, increasing the percentage of Estonians in its population from 52% in 1867 to 89% in 1897. By WWI Tallinn had big shipyards and a working class of over 100,000.

Tallinn suffered badly in WWII, with thousands of buildings destroyed during Soviet bombing in 1944. After the war, under Soviet

ESTONIA AT A GLANCE

Currency
Euro (€)

Language
Estonian

Capital
Tallinn

Area
45,339 sq km

Estonia Highlights

1 Embark on a medieval quest for atmospheric restaurants and hidden bars in the history-saturated lanes of **Tallinn** (p47).

2 Wander the forest paths, bog boardwalks, abandoned beaches and manor-house halls of **Lahemaa National Park** (p86).

3 Further your education among the museums and student bars of **Tartu** (p103), Estonia's second city.

4 Unwind among the windmills on **Saaremaa**

(p142) and explore the island's castles, churches, cliffs, coast and crater.

5 Hop over to **Muhu** (p139) for frozen-in-island-time Koguva village and the gastronomic delights of Pädaste Manor.

6 Stroll the golden sands and genteel streets of Estonia's 'summer capital', **Pärnu** (p132).

7 Get back to nature, even if the snow's a no-show, at the 'winter capital' **Otepää** (p122).

Tallinn

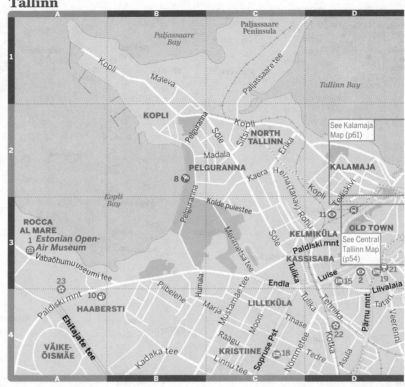

Tallinn

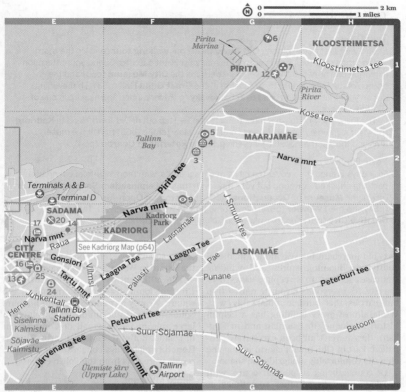

control, large-scale industry was developed – including the USSR's biggest grain-handling port – and the city expanded, its population growing to nearly 500,000 from a 1937 level of 175,000. Much of the new population came from Russia and new high-rise suburbs were built on the outskirts to house the workers.

The explosion of Soviet-style settlements in the suburbs meant a loss of cultural life in the centre. By the 1980s Old Town was run down, with most people preferring to live in the new housing developments. It began to be renovated late in the decade, with the fight for independence largely playing out on the streets of Tallinn.

The 1990s saw the city transformed into a contemporary midsized city, with a restored Old Town and a modern business district. Tallinn shows a taste for all things new, extending to IT-driven business at the fore of the new economy and an e-savvy, wi-fi-connected populace hoping for a brighter future. Mean-while, the outskirts of the city have yet to get the facelift that the centre has received. In those parts that few tourists see, poverty and unemployment is more evident.

◉ Sights

While most of the city's sights are conveniently located within the medieval Old Town's walls, it's worth venturing out to the further-flung attractions – and given Tallinn's relatively compact size, there's really no excuse not to. Kadriorg, in particular, should not be missed.

◉ Old Town

The medieval jewel of Estonia, Tallinn's Old Town (Vanalinn) is without a doubt the country's most fascinating locality. Picking your way along the narrow, cobbled streets is like strolling into the 15th century – not least due to the tendency of local businesses to dress their staff up in peasant garb. You'll

TALLINN IN...

Two Days

Spend your first day exploring **Old Town**. Tackle our **walking tour** (p58) in the morning and then stop for lunch in one of the many excellent eateries. Spend your afternoon exploring one or two of the museums – perhaps the **City Museum** (p55) and the branch of the Estonian History Museum at the **Great Guild Hall** (p53). That evening, put on your glad rags and head to **Tchaikovsky** (p75) for dinner, finishing up in one of Old Town's bars.

The following day, do what most tourists don't – step out of Old Town. Head to **Kadriorg** (p64) for a greenery and art fix and continue to **Maarjamäe** (p65) to visit the museums and the war memorial. That evening, hit the **Rotermann Quarter** (p64).

Four Days

Four days is enough to cover the city's main highlights, with more nights of eating and partying chucked in. Round out your days with trips to **Lennusadam Seaplane Harbour** (p60), the **Museum of Occupations** (p60), the **Estonian Open-Air Museum** (p67) and the **TV Tower** (p67). Allow some time to wander around the **Telliskivi Creative City** (p61) and to explore the Kalamaja neighbourhood.

pass old merchant houses, hidden medieval courtyards, looming spires and winding staircases leading to sweeping views over the city. It's everyone's favourite tourist trap but carries this burden remarkably well. While almost every building has a helpful historical plaque (in Estonian and in English), they haven't all been excessively gentrified. Part of Old Town's charm is that the chic sits comfortably alongside the shabby.

Of course, being so popular comes with its downsides. In summer sometimes as many as six giant cruise ships descend at a time, disgorging their human cargo in slow-moving, flag-following phalanxes. If you're travelling on such a ship, it's worth noting that Old Town is within walking distance of the harbour; you'll have a much better time if you dodge the organised tours and follow your own path. For everyone else, rest assured that most of the boats steam off again in the afternoon, leaving the streets relatively clear by 5pm.

Lower Town

Freedom Square SQUARE
(Vabaduse väljak; Map p54) This large paved plaza is used for summer concerts, skateboarding, impromptu ball games and watching heats of *Estonian Idol (Eesti Otsib Superstaari)* on the big screen at the southern end. The square sits just outside one of the former town gates, the remains of which are preserved under glass near the northwestern corner. A gigantic glass cross at the square's western end commemorates the Estonian War of Independence.

The 19th-century **St John's Lutheran Church** dominates the eastern end of the square. Nearby a **memorial stone** honours Solidarity, the trade union which played a large role in the downfall of Communism in Poland. Both this and the nearby **Chopin Bench** (which plays concertos by the composer) were gifts from the Polish embassy.

Photo Museum MUSEUM
(Fotomuuseum; Map p54; www.linnamuuseum. ee; Raekoja 6; adult/child €2/1; ⊙10.30am-5.30pm Thu-Tue) Only enthusiasts are likely to find much of interest in this little museum housed in the former town prison. Exhibits include old cameras and prints from photography's earliest days in Estonia.

★ **Town Hall Square** SQUARE
(Raekoja plats; Map p54) Raekoja plats has been the pulsing heart of Tallinn since markets began here in the 11th century. One side is taken is taken up by the Gothic town hall, while the rest is ringed by pretty pastel-coloured buildings dating from the 15th to 17th centuries. Whether bathed in sunlight or sprinkled with snow, it's always a photogenic spot.

All through summer, outdoor cafes implore you to sit and people watch. Come Christmas, a huge pine tree stands in the middle of the square just as it did in 1441 when local guild the Brotherhood of the Blackheads erected the world's first publicly displayed Christmas tree (a claim hotly contested by Rīga).

Tallinn Town Hall
HISTORIC BUILDING

(Tallinna Raekoda; Map p54; ☑ 645 7900; www.raekoda.tallinn.ee; Raekoja plats; adult/student €5/2; ☉ 10am-4pm Mon-Sat Jul-Aug, by appointment Sep-Jun) Completed in 1404, this is the only surviving Gothic town hall in northern Europe. Inside, you can visit the Trade Hall (housing a visitor book dripping in royal signatures), the Council Chamber (featuring Estonia's oldest woodcarvings, dating from 1374), the vaulted Citizens' Hall, a yellow-and-black-tiled councillor's office and a small kitchen. The steeply sloped attic has displays on the building and its restoration.

Occasionally the building is used to host prominent visiting art exhibitions, in which case the entry fee may be considerably higher.

If the kids are getting restive, draw their attention to the iron shackles still hanging on the exterior wall facing the square.

Town Hall Tower
VIEWPOINT

(Map p54; adult/child €3/1; ☉ 11am-6pm Jun-Aug) Old Thomas (Vana Toomas), Tallinn's symbol and guardian, has been keeping watch from his perch on the Town Hall's weathervane since 1530 (although his previous incarnation now resides in the City Museum). You can enjoy much the same views as Thomas by climbing the 115 steps to the top of the tower. According to legend, this elegant 64m minaret-like structure was modelled on a sketch made by an explorer following his visit to the Orient.

Town Council Pharmacy
HISTORIC BUILDING

(Raeapteek; Map p54; www.raeapteek.ee; Raekoja plats 11; ☉ 10am-6pm Tue-Sat) Nobody's too sure on the exact date it opened but by 1422 this pharmacy was already on to its third owner, making it the oldest continually operating pharmacy in Europe. In 1583 Johann Burchardt took the helm, and a descendant with the same name ran the shop right up until 1913 – 10 generations in all! Inside there are painted beams and a small historical display, or you can just drop in to stock up on painkillers and prophylactics.

Holy Spirit Lutheran Church
CHURCH

(Pühavaimu kirik; Map p54; www.eelk.ee/tallinna.puhavaimu/; Pühavaimu 2; adult/child €1/0.50; ☉ noon-2pm Mon-Fri, 10am-4pm Sat Jan–mid-Mar, 10am-3pm Mon-Sat mid-Mar–Apr & Oct-Dec, 10am-5pm Mon-Sat May-Sep) The blue-and-gold clock on the facade of this striking 13th-century Gothic church is the oldest in Tallinn, dating from 1684. Inside there are exquisite woodcarvings and painted panels, including an altarpiece dating to 1483 and a 17th-century baroque pulpit.

Johann Koell, a former pastor here, is considered the author of the first Estonian book, a catechism published in 1535. The church hosts regular classical music concerts.

Great Guild Hall
MUSEUM

(Suurgildi hoone; Map p54; www.ajaloomuuseum.ee; Pikk 17; adult/child €5/3; ☉ 10am-6pm, closed Wed Oct-Apr) The Estonian History Museum has filled the striking 1410 Great Guild Hall building with a series of ruminations on the Estonian psyche, presented through interactive and unusual displays. Coin collectors shouldn't miss the display in the old excise chamber, while military nuts should head downstairs. The basement also covers the history of the Great Guild itself.

The major exhibition, Spirit of Survival – 11,000 years of Estonian History, poses such questions as 'Is Estonia the most secular country in the world?' and 'Have Estonians been happy in their own land?' (The answer

LANGUAGE

Hello	*Tere*	*te*-rre
Goodbye	*Head aega*	head *ae*-gah
Yes	*Jah*	yah
No	*Ei*	ay
Thank you	*Tänan*	*ta*-nahn
You're welcome	*Palun*	*pah*-lun
Excuse me/I'm sorry	*Vabandage*	*vah*-bahn-dah-ge
Cheers! (literally 'to your health')	*Terviseks!*	*ter*-vi-seks

54

Central Tallinn

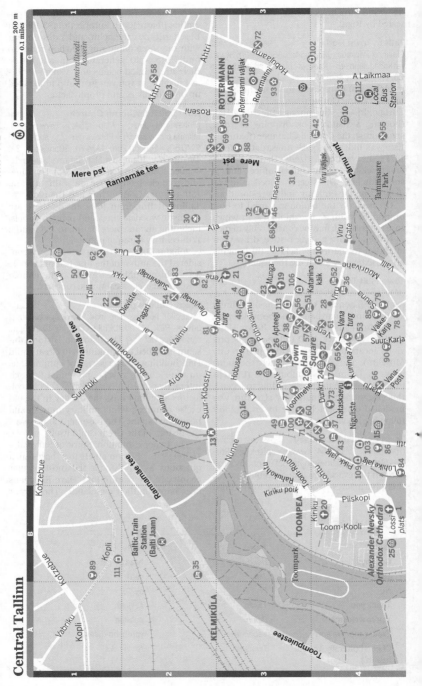

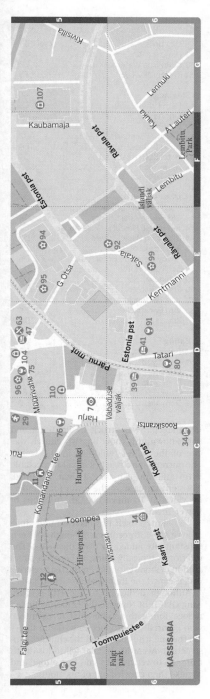

to the latter is no, apparently, backed up with statistics suggesting that they're one of the least happy peoples of Europe.)

Draakoni Gallery
GALLERY

(Map p54; www.eaa.ee/draakon; Pikk 18; ⊙11am-6pm Mon-Sat) **FREE** In among the guilds, behind a fabulous sculpted art nouveau facade, this commercial gallery hosts small, often stimulating, exhibitions of contemporary art.

St Catherine's Cloister
CHURCH

(Map p54; www.kloostri.ee; Vene 16; adult/child €2/1) One of Tallinn's oldest buildings, St Catherine's Monastery was founded by Dominican monks in 1246. In its glory days it had its own brewery and hospital. A mob of angry Lutherans torched the place in 1524 and the monastery languished for the next 400 years until its partial restoration in 1954. Today the ruined complex includes the gloomy shell of the barren church and a peaceful cloister lined with carved tombstones.

Opening hours are sporadic but it can often be accessed from a door in the foyer of the neighbouring Catholic cathedral.

St Peter & St Paul's Catholic Cathedral
CHURCH

(Peeter-Paul katedraal; Map p54; ☑644 6367; www.katoliku.ee; Vene 18; ⊙9.30am-1pm Sun, 5.30-6.30pm Mon, Tue & Thu-Sat, 7.45-9.30am Wed) Looking like it was beamed in from Spain, this handsome 1844 cathedral was designed by the famed architect Carlo Rossi, who left his mark on the neoclassical shape of St Petersburg. It still functions as one of Tallinn's only Catholic churches, largely serving the Polish and Lithuanian communities. The front courtyard is a quiet spot for some respite from the summertime bustle.

City Museum
MUSEUM

(Linnamuuseum; Map p54; www.linnamuuseum.ee; Vene 17; adult/child €4/3; ⊙10.30am-5.30pm Tue-Sun) Tallinn's City Museum is actually split over 10 different sites. This, its main branch, is set in a 14th-century merchant's house and traces the city's development from its earliest days. The displays are engrossing and very well laid out, with plenty of information in English, making the hire of the audioguide quite unnecessary.

The top floor presents an insightful (and quite politicised) portrait of life under Soviet rule and there's a fascinating video of the events surrounding the collapse of the regime.

Central Tallinn

St Nicholas' Orthodox Church CHURCH
(Püha piiskop Nikolause kirik; Map p54; Vene 24; ⊙9.30am-5pm) Built in 1827 on the site of an earlier church, St Nicholas' was the focal point for the Russian traders of Vene street. It's known for its precious iconostasis.

Fat Margaret MUSEUM
(Paks Margareeta; Map p54; www.meremuuseum. ee; Pikk 70; adult/child €5/3; ⊙10am-6pm, closed Mon Oct-Apr) Attached to the Great Coast Gate, this 16th-century cannon tower once protected a major entrance to Old Town. It's now the slimmer, older sister of Lennusadam Seaplane Harbour (p60), displaying model ships and assorted sea-going artefacts from the Estonian Maritime Museum's collection. Combined tickets are available (adult/child €16/10).

St Olaf's Church CHURCH
(Oleviste kirik; Map p54; www.oleviste.ee; Lai 50; tower adult/child €2/1; ⊙10am-6pm Sep-Jun, to 8pm Jul & Aug) From 1549 to 1625, when its 159m steeple was struck by lightning and burnt down, this (now Baptist) church was one of the tallest buildings in the world. The current spire reaches a still respectable 124m and you can take a tight, confined, 258-step staircase up the tower for wonderful views of Toompea over the rooftops of Lower Town.

The church itself has been around since at least the 13th century, although it's been substantially added to over the years. The interior is typically stark, although a small section of stone carvings on the rear exterior wall escaped the Reformation's iconoclasts.

Although dedicated to the 11th-century King Olaf II of Norway, the church is linked in local lore with another Olaf, its architect, who ignored the prophecies of doom to befall the one who completed the church's construction. Accordingly, Olaf fell to his death from the tower, and it's said that a toad and a snake then crawled out of his mouth.

Lower Town Wall
FORTRESS

(Linnamüür; Map p54; Väike-Kloostri 3; adult/child €1.50/0.75; ☉11am-7pm Jun-Aug, to 5pm Fri-Wed Apr, May, Sep & Oct, to 4pm Fri-Tue Nov-Mar) The most photogenic stretch of Tallinn's remaining walls connects nine towers lining the western edge of Old Town. Visitors can explore the barren nooks and crannies of three of them, with cameras at the ready for the red-rooftop views.

Niguliste Museum
MUSEUM

(Map p54; www.nigulistemuuseum.ee; Niguliste 3; adult/student €5/3; ☉10am-5pm Tue-Sun May-Sep, Wed-Sun Oct-Apr) Dating from the 13th century, imposing St Nicholas' Church (Niguliste kirik) was badly damaged by Soviet bombers in 1944 and a fire in the 1980s, but today stands restored to its Gothic glory. It houses a branch of the Estonian Art Museum devoted to religious art. The acoustics are first-rate, and organ recitals are held here most weekends.

The most famous work on display is Berndt Notke's 15th-century masterpiece *Dance Macabre*. The gist of this eerie skeletal conga line is that whether you're a king, a pope or a young slacker, we're all dancing with death. Other artefacts include painted altarpieces (including the church's own extraordinary cabinet-style altarpiece by Herman Rode from Lübeck, dating from 1481), carved tombstones and a chamber overflowing with silverware.

Toompea

Lording it over the Lower Town is the ancient hilltop citadel of Toompea. In German times this was the preserve of the feudal nobility, literally looking down on the traders and lesser beings below. It's now almost completely given over to government buildings, churches, embassies and shops selling amber knick-knacks and fridge magnets.

St Mary's Lutheran Cathedral   CHURCH

(Tallinna Püha Neitsi Maarja Piiskoplik Toomkirik; Map p54; www.toomkirik.ee; Toom-Kooli 6; church/tower €2/5; ⊘9am-5pm daily May-Sep, 10am-4pm Tue-Sun Oct-Apr) Tallinn's cathedral (now Lutheran, originally Catholic) was founded by at least 1233, although the exterior dates mainly from the 15th century, with the tower completed in 1779. This impressive building was a burial ground for the rich and titled, and the whitewashed walls are decorated with the elaborate coats-of-arms of Estonia's noble families. Fit view-seekers can climb the tower.

Toompea is named after the cathedral – the Estonian 'toom' is borrowed from the German word 'dom' meaning cathedral. In English you'll often hear it referred to as the 'Dome Church', despite there being no actual dome.

★ Alexander Nevsky Orthodox Cathedral   CHURCH

(Map p54; Lossi plats; ⊘8am-7pm) The positioning of this magnificent, onion-domed Russian Orthodox cathedral (completed in 1900) at the heart of the country's main administrative hub was no accident: the church was one of many built in the last part of the 19th century as part of a general wave of Russification in the empire's Baltic provinces. Orthodox believers come here in droves, alongside tourists ogling the interior's striking icons and frescoes. Quiet, respectful, demurely dressed visitors are welcome but cameras aren't.

Toompea Castle   HISTORIC BUILDING

(Map p54; Lossi plats) Three towers have survived from the Knights of the Sword's hilltop castle, the finest of which is 14th-century Pikk Hermann (best viewed from the rear). In the 18th century the fortress underwent an extreme makeover at the hands of Russian empress Catherine the Great, converting it into the pretty-in-pink baroque palace that now houses Estonia's parliament (Riigikogu).

Linda Hill   PARK

(Lindamägi; Map p54; Falgi tee) Shaded by 250-year-old linden trees, this small mound near the top of Toompea is named after Linda, wife of Kalev, the heroic first leader of the Estonians. Accorded to legend, Toompea is the burial mound which she built for him. During the Soviet years the statue of the grieving Linda became the unofficial memorial to victims of Stalin's deportations and executions.

🏃 City Walk
Tallinn's Old Town

START FREEDOM SQ
END VIRU GATES
LENGTH 4KM; THREE HOURS

We've designed this walk as an introduction to Tallinn's meandering medieval streets. Starting at ❶ **Freedom Square** (p52), take the stairs up into Toompea and continue to ❷ **Linda Hill**. From here you can see the remaining medieval elements of ❸ **Toompea Castle**; backtrack and turn left onto Lossi plats (Castle Sq) for a view of its baroque facade. Directly across the square is onion-domed ❹ **Alexander Nevsky Orthodox Cathedral**.

Take Toom-Kooli to ❺ **St Mary's Lutheran Cathedral** and cut across Kiriku plats (Church Sq) onto Rahukohtu, where a lane leads to the ❻ **Patkul lookout** (Patkuli vaateplats), offering terrific views across the Lower Town to the sea. Continue winding around the lanes to the ❼ **Court Square lookout** (Kohtuotsa vaateplats).

Cut past the rear of both cathedrals and head through the opening in the wall to the ❽ **Danish King's Garden**, where artists set up their easels in summer to capture the view over the rooftops. Exit to the left and then take the steps up through the ❾ **Short Leg Gate Tower**, which is thought to be the most haunted building in Tallinn. Ghostly apparitions have been reported inside this tower, including a crucified monk and a black dog with burning eyes. Turn right and take the long sloping path known as Long Leg (Pikk jalg) through the red-roofed ❿ **Long Leg Gate Tower** (1380) and into the Lower Town.

Turn left along Nunne and then veer right into Väike-Kloostri where you'll come to the best-preserved section of the ⓫ **Lower Town Wall** (p57), linking nine of the 26 remaining towers; there were once 45. Pass through the gate and turn right for a better view. Wander through the park to the next small gap in the walls and exit onto Aida. At the end of the street, turn left onto Lai (Wide St), which is lined with German merchant's houses. Many of these were built in the 15th century and contain three or four storeys, with the lower two used as living and reception quarters and the upper ones for storage.

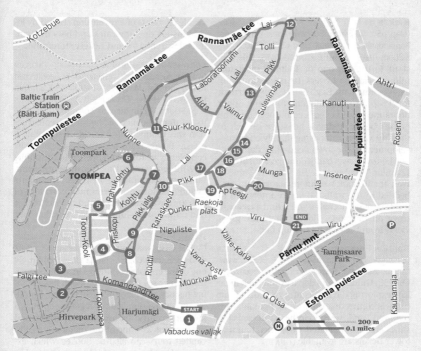

At the very end of Lai, follow the small path to the right alongside the wall to the **12 Great Coast Gate**, the most impressive of the remaining medieval gates. Note the crest on the outside wall and the crucifix in a niche on the town side.

As you head up Pikk (Long St), spare a thought for those that suffered at number 59, the **13 former KGB headquarters**. The building's basement windows were bricked up to prevent the sounds being heard by those passing by on the street. A small memorial on the wall translates as: 'This building housed the headquarters of the organ of repression of the Soviet occupational power. Here began the road to suffering for thousands of Estonians.' Locals joked, with typically black humour, that the building had the best views in Estonia – from here you could see all the way to Siberia.

Further along the street are buildings belonging to the town's guilds, associations of traders and artisans, nearly all German dominated. First up, at number 26, is the **14 Brotherhood of the Blackheads** (Mustpeade maja). The Blackheads were unmarried young men who took their name not from poor dermatology but from their patron, St Maurice (Mauritius), a legendary African-born Roman soldier whose likeness is found on the building facade (dating from 1597), above an ornate, colourful door. Its neighbour, **15 St Olaf's Guild Hall** (Olevi gildi hoone), was the headquarters for what was probably the first guild in Tallinn, dating from the 13th century. Its membership comprised more humble non-German artisans and traders.

Next up is the 1860-built **16 St Canute's Guild Hall** (p80), topped with zinc statues of Martin Luther and its patron saint. A little further down the road is the 1410 headquarters of the **17 Great Guild hall** (p53), to which the most eminent merchants belonged.

Cross the small square to the left, past the photogenic **18 Holy Spirit Church** (p53) and take narrow Saiakang (White Bread Passage – named after a historic bakery) to **19 Town Hall Square** (p52). Continue left to Vene (the Estonian word for Russian, named for the Russian merchants who once resided and traded here) and cut through the arch into **20 Katariina käik** (p81). At the far end, turn right and left again onto Viru, one of Old Town's busiest streets. Finish at the **21 Viru Gate**, which connects Old Town with the commercial centre of the modern city.

Kiek in de Kök
CASTLE, MUSEUM

(Map p54; 644 6686; www.linnamuuseum.ee; Komandandi tee 2; adult/child €5/3; 10.30am-5.30pm Tue-Sun) Built around 1475, this tall, stout fortress is one of Tallinn's most formidable cannon towers. Its name (amusing as it sounds in English) is Low German for 'Peep into the Kitchen'; from the upper floors medieval voyeurs could peer into the houses below. Today it houses a branch of the City Museum, focusing mainly on the development of the town's elaborate defences.

The tower was badly damaged during the Livonian War, but it never collapsed (nine of Ivan the Terrible's cannonballs remain embedded in the walls). If you're interested in military paraphernalia, you'll find a treasure trove on the upper floors. There are great views from the cafe on the top floor.

Bastion Passages
FORTRESS

(Bastionikäigud; Map p54; 644 6686; www.linnamuuseum.ee; Komandandi tee 2; adult/child €6/3.50) Guided tours depart from Kiek in de Kök exploring the 17th-century Swedish-built tunnels connecting the towers. Bookings are required, and warm clothes and sensible shoes are recommended. Combined tour and tower tickets are available (€9).

Museum of Occupations
MUSEUM

(Okupatsioonide muuseum; Map p54; www.okupatsioon.ee; Toompea 8; adult/child €6/3; 10am-6pm Tue-Sun) Displays illustrate the hardships and horrors of five decades of occupation, under both the Nazis (briefly) and the Soviets. The photos and artefacts are interesting but it's the videos (lengthy but enthralling) that leave the greatest impression – and the joy of a happy ending.

The overwhelming majority of the exhibits are focused on the lengthy Soviet period; for more detail on the Nazi occupation, visit Maarjamäe Palace Stables (p66).

Kalamaja

Immediately northwest of Old Town, this enclave of tumbledown wooden houses and crumbling factories has swiftly transitioned into one of Tallinn's most interesting neighbourhoods. The intimidating hulk of Patarei Prison had seemed to cast a malevolent shadow over this part of town, so its transformation over the last few years has been nothing short of extraordinary. Major road projects and the opening of an impressive museum at Lennusadam are only the most visible elements of a revolution started by local hipsters opening cafes and bars in abandoned warehouses and rickety storefronts.

Lennusadam Seaplane Harbour
MUSEUM

(www.lennusadam.eu; Vesilennuki 6; adult/child €14/7, incl Fat Margaret €16/10; 10am-7pm May-Sep, Tue-Sun Oct-Apr; P) When this triple-domed hangar was completed in 1917, its reinforced-concrete shell frame construction was unique in the world. Resembling a classic Bond-villain lair, the vast space was completely restored and opened to the public in 2012 as a fascinating maritime museum, filled with interactive displays. Highlights include exploring the cramped corridors of a 1930s naval submarine, and the icebreaker and minehunter ships moored outside.

Patarei
HISTORIC BUILDING

(504 6536; www.patarei.org; Kalaranna 2; adult/child €3/2, tours €8; noon-7pm May-Sep) Surely one of the creepiest buildings in all of Estonia, this former sea fortress and prison has a chilling history as a place of incarceration, brutality and oppression. Part of it is now open as a kind of eccentric art project, with graffiti and installations in some of the mouldering cells. Guided tours can also be booked which explore other sections of the 4-hectare complex.

Built as a sea fortress in 1840 under the Russian tsars (the name means 'battery'), Paterei initially served as an army barracks – although from the outset it was a damp, uncomfortable place to be stationed. It was first used as a prison in 1920 following Estonian independence, but it gained its notoriety during the Soviet and German occupations. Numerous people were brutally interrogated and executed here, including 250 French Jews killed by the Nazis who are remembered by a simple memorial stone near the southern entrance.

At the other end of the complex a sign points to the 'hanging room', where a hook in the ceiling and trapdoor in the floor are the only explanations necessary. The last execution took place in Patarei in 1991, right at the end of Soviet rule, although the prison remained operational until 2002. Since then it's been left to languish and it's quickly deteriorating.

The current 'cultural park' is perhaps the least offensive attempt thus far to put Patarei to a new use – although one has to question whether the beach bar behind the barbed wire is in good taste.

Kalamaja

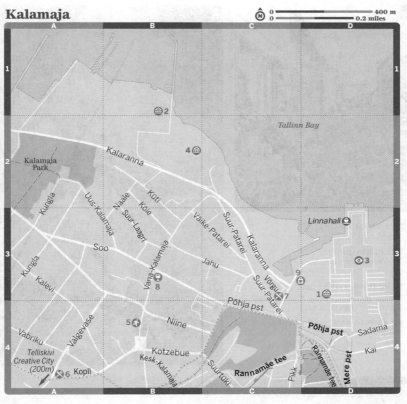

Kalamaja

◎ Sights
1 Estonian Museum of
   Contemporary Art D3
2 Lennusadam Seaplane Harbour B1
3 Linnahall D3
4 Patarei B2

◉ Activities, Courses & Tours
5 Kalma Saun B4

◈ Eating
6 Boheem A4
   Klaus .... (see 9)
7 Moon C3

◎ Drinking & Nightlife
8 Tops B3

◉ Shopping
9 Estonian Design House C3

**Estonian Museum of
Contemporary Art**   GALLERY
(Eesti kaasaegse kunsti muuseum; www.ekkm.ee;
Põhja pst 35; ⊙1-7pm Tue-Sun Apr-Oct) FREE Despite its highfalutin name, this grungy old
warehouse space is more slapped together
than slick. Exhibitions tend to be edgier and
more oddball than anything you'll find at
the more official galleries.

Telliskivi Creative City   AREA
(Telliskivi Loomelinnak; Map p50; www.telliskivi.
eu; Telliskivi 60a; ⊙shops 8.30am-9pm Mon-Sat,
9am-7pm Sun) Once literally on the wrong
side of the tracks, this set of 10 abandoned
factory buildings is now Tallinn's most alternative shopping and entertainment precinct. All the cliches of hipster culture can be
found here: cafes, a bike shop, bars selling
craft beer, graffiti walls, artist studios, food

STEFAN CIOATA/GETTY IMAGES ©

1. Pärnu (p132)
Picturesque Pärnu is Estonia's summer capital

2. Hiiumaa (p157)
This island is peppered with windmills, lighthouses, eerie old Soviet bunkers and empty beaches

3. Old Town, Tallinn (p51)
Picking your way along the narrow, cobbled streets is like strolling into the 15th century

4. Lahemaa National Park (p86)
Erratic boulders, brought from Scandinavia by glacial action, are a feature of this national park

Kadriorg

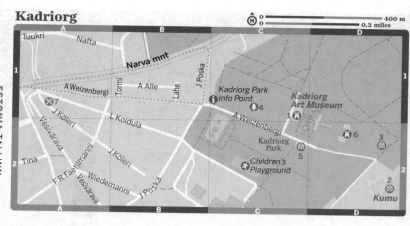

Kadriorg

trucks etc. But even the beardless flock to Telleskivi to peruse the fashion and design stores, sink espressos and rummage through the stalls at the weekly flea market.

◎ City Centre

Hotel Viru & the KGB   MUSEUM
(Map p54; ☑ 680 9300; www.viru.ee; Viru väljak 4; tour €10; ⊙ daily May-Oct, Tue-Sun Nov-Apr) When the Hotel Viru was built in 1972, it was not only Estonia's first skyscraper, it was the only place for tourists to stay in Tallinn – and we mean that literally. Having all the foreigners in one place made it much easier to keep tabs on them and the locals they had contact with, which is exactly what the KGB did from their 23rd-floor spy base. The hotel offers fascinating tours of the facility in various languages; bookings essential.

Rotermann Quarter   AREA
(Rotermanni kvartal; Map p54; www.rotermann.eu) With impressive contemporary architecture wedged between 19th-century brick warehouses, this development has transformed a former factory complex into the city's swankiest shopping and dining precinct.

Architecture Museum   MUSEUM
(Arhitektuurimuuseum; Map p54; www.arhitektuurimuuseum.ee; Ahtri 2; adult/child €4/2; ⊙ 11am-6pm Wed-Sun) A restored limestone warehouse – the former Rotermann Salt Store – houses this modest museum, displaying building and town models, and regular temporary exhibitions.

◎ Kadriorg

Kadriorg Park   PARK
(Kadrioru park; www.kadriorupark.ee) About 2km east of Old Town, this beautiful park's ample acreage is Tallinn's favourite patch of green. Together with the baroque Kadriorg Palace, it was commissioned by the Russian tsar Peter the Great for his wife Catherine I soon after his conquest of Estonia (Kadriorg means Catherine's Valley in Estonian).

Nowadays the oak, lilac and horse chestnut trees provide shade for strollers and picnickers, the formal pond and gardens provide a genteel backdrop for romantic promenades and wedding photos, and the children's playground is a favourite off-leash area for the city's youngsters.

Call into the park's **information centre** (Kadrioru pargi infopunkt; Weizenbergi 33; ⊙ 10am-5pm Wed-Sun), housed in pretty 18th-century cottage near the main entrance, to see a scale model of the palace and its grounds.

Trams 1 and 3 stop right by Kadriorg Park. Buses 1A and 34A (among others) stop at the J Poska stop on Narva mnt, near the foot of the park, while 31, 67 and 68 head to the Kumu end.

★ **Kadriorg Art Museum** PALACE, GALLERY
(Kardrioru kunstimuuseum; www.kadriorumuuse um.ee; A Weizenbergi 37; adult/child €5.50/3.50; ☉10am-6pm Tue & Thu-Sun, to 8pm Wed May-Sep, 10am-8pm Wed, to 5pm Thu-Sun Oct-Apr) Kadriorg Palace, built by Peter the Great between 1718 and 1736, now houses a branch of the Estonian Art Museum devoted to Dutch, German and Italian paintings from the 16th to the 18th centuries, and Russian works from the 18th to early 20th centuries (check out the decorative porcelain with communist imagery upstairs). The building is exactly as frilly and fabulous as a palace ought to be and there's a handsome French-style formal garden at the rear.

Mikkel Museum GALLERY
(Mikkeli muuseum; www.mikkelimuuseum.ekm. ee; A Weizenbergi 28; adult/concession €3.50/2; ☉10am-6pm Tue & Thu-Sun, to 8pm Wed May-Sep, 10am-8pm Wed, to 5pm Thu-Sun Oct-Apr) The Estonian Art Museum's collection spills over into this former kitchen for Kadriorg Palace. It displays a small but interesting assortment of paintings and porcelain, along with temporary exhibitions. Joint admission with the palace is €6.50.

Presidential Palace PALACE
Echoing the style of Kadriorg Palace, this grand building was purpose-built in 1938 to serve as the official residence of the Estonian president – a role it once again fulfills. It's not open to the public, but you can peer through the gates at the honour guards out the front.

Sadly, Estonia's first president, Konstantin Päts, didn't get long to enjoy living here. Following the Soviet takeover in 1940 he spent most of his remaining years incarcerated in psychiatric institutions – he was deemed delusional for continuing to maintain that he was the president of Estonia.

House of Peter I MUSEUM
(Peeter I majamuuseum; www.linnamuuseum.ee; Mäekalda 2; adult/concession €2/1; ☉10am-6pm Tue-Sun May-Sep, 10am-5pm Wed-Sun Oct-Apr) This is the humble cottage Peter the Great occupied on visits to Tallinn while Kadriorg Palace was under construction. The museum is filled with portraits, furniture and artefacts from the era.

★ **Kumu** GALLERY
(www.kumu.ee; A Weizenbergi 34; all galleries adult/ student €6/4, permanent only €4.50/3; ☉11am-6pm Tue & Thu-Sun, to 8pm Wed Apr-Sep, closed Mon & Tue Oct-Apr) This futuristic, Finnish-designed, seven-storey building (2006) is a spectacular structure of limestone, glass and copper, nicely integrated into the landscape. Kumu (the name is short for *kunstimuuseum* or art museum) contains the country's largest repository of Estonian art as well as constantly changing contemporary exhibits.

The permanent collection is split into 'Treasury' (on the 3rd floor, featuring works from the beginning of the 18th century until the end of WWII) and 'Difficult Choices' (on the 4th floor, showcasing art during the Soviet era). Current and cutting-edge exhibitions fill the 5th floor. The complex is wheelchair accessible and has an excellent shop and cafe.

Tallinn Song Festival Grounds AMPHITHEATRE
(Tallinna lauluväljak; Map p50; www.lauluvaljak. ee; Narva mnt 95; ☉lighthouse 8am-4pm Mon-Fri) FREE This open-air amphitheatre is the site of the main gatherings of Estonia's national song festivals and assorted rock concerts and other events. Built in 1959, it's an elegant and surprisingly curvaceous piece of Soviet-era architecture with an official capacity of 75,000 people and a stage that fits 15,000. When there are no events booked it's possible to climb the 42m 'lighthouse' where the festival flame is lit; inside there's a photo display on the history of the song festival.

In September 1988, 300,000 squeezed in for one songfest and publicly demanded independence in what became known as the 'Singing Revolution'. Approximately half a million people, including a large number of Estonian émigrés, were believed to have been present at the 21st Song Festival in 1990, the last major fest before the restoration of independence. An Estonian repertoire was reinstated and around 29,000 performers sang under the national flag for the first time in 50 years.

◉ Maarjamäe

Pirita tee, the coastal road curving northwards alongside Tallinn Bay through Maarjamäe, is a popular route for joggers, cyclists and skaters, offering particularly fine sunset views over Old Town. Buses 1A, 5, 8, 34A and 38 all stop here.

WHEN BIGGER IS JUST BIGGER

Nothing says 'former Soviet' quite like a gigantic public building and Tallinn has two that are quite difficult to miss, both designed by local architect Raine Karp.

Linnahall (City Hall; www.linnahall.ee; Mere pst 20) Built for the 1980 Moscow Olympics and originally christened the Lenin Palace of Culture and Sport, Linnahall contains a vast concert arena within its crumbling, much-graffitied concrete hulk. It's fair to say that the city doesn't know quite what to do with it. The templelike structure has heritage protection but it has decayed considerably since closing its doors in 2009 and it acts as a colossal barricade, cutting off Old Town from the harbour. Recently there's been talk of converting Linnahall into a conference centre. In the meantime, baffled tourists continue to wander its rooftop walkways and take endless photos to show their friends back home their brush with post-Soviet decay.

Estonian National Library (Eesti rahvusraamatukogu; Map p50; www.nlib.ee; Tõnismägi 2; ⊗ noon-6pm Mon-Fri) Construction commenced in 1985 but the Estonian National Library wasn't completed until 1993, making this prime example of Soviet architecture one of independent Estonia's first new public buildings. It's clad in the local dolomite limestone and it's well worth calling into the foyer, if only to check out the pointy red chairs. Frequent exhibitions take place on the upper floors.

Maarjamäe Palace   MUSEUM
(Maarjamäe loss; Map p50; www.ajaloomuuseum. ee; Pirita tee 56; adult/child €4/2; ⊗ 10am-5pm Wed-Sun) North of Kadriorg Park, Maarjamäe is a neo-Gothic limestone manor house built in 1874 for a Russian count. It's now home to the **Estonian Film Museum** and a less-visited branch of the **Estonian History Museum**, detailing the twists and turns of the 20th century. Don't miss the Soviet sculpture graveyard at the rear of the building.

A particularly beautiful Socialist Realist mural entitled *Friendship of Nations* covers the walls of the banqueting hall, featuring triumphant factory workers, peasants, cosmonauts and an apparition of Lenin's face among the red flags. When this was unveiled in 1987, it's clear that nobody foresaw the dramatic events of the following few years.

When we last visited there were ambitious plans afoot to restore the palace and turn the complex into a 'experiential museum', including making use of the dismantled Soviet sculptures and hosting open-air concerts and film screenings. Watch this space.

Maarjamäe Palace Stables   MUSEUM
(Maarjamäe lossi tallihoone; Map p50; www. ajaloomuuseum.ee; Pirita tee 66; adult/child €3/2, with palace €6; ⊗ 10am-6pm Wed-Sun) The lengthy Soviet occupation of Estonia is covered in painstaking detail elsewhere, so this branch of the Estonian History Museum, housed in a 19th-century stable block at Maarjamäe, is devoted solely to the German occupation (1941–1944). Entitled *Castles &*

Pawns, it's a fascinating and at times harrowing exposé of life under the Nazi regime, including interactive displays and videoed interviews with survivors of the concentration camps.

Following on from the horrors of the first Soviet occupation of Estonia in 1940, known as the 'Red Year', many Estonians initially welcomed the German invasion. It's now estimated that the regime executed around 8000 Estonians, including 1000 Estonian Jews (almost the entire Jewish population that hadn't already fled) and 250 to 500 Estonian Roma. In addition, around 12,500 foreign Jews were transported to camps in Estonia, mainly from the other Baltic states but from as far away as France.

If you're interested in exploring this dark episode in the country's history further or paying your respects to the victims, the Estonian History Museum has erected an outdoor exhibition at the site of the Klooga concentration camp, 38km southwest of Tallinn.

The stables are the last major building in the complex, close to the war memorial.

Maarjamäe War Memorial   MEMORIAL
(Map p50; Pirita tee) Perched on the headland next to Maarjamäe Palace, this large Soviet-era monument consists of an elegant bowed obelisk set amid a large crumbling concrete plaza. The obelisk was erected in 1960 to commemorate the Soviet troops killed in 1918 – hardly a popular edifice, as the war was against Estonia and all of the Estonian monuments to their dead were

destroyed shortly after the Soviet takeover (many have since been re-erected).

The remainder of the complex – broad concrete avenues, pointy protrusions and all – was built in 1975 as a memorial to Red Army soldiers killed fighting the Nazis. It was built partly over a war cemetery housing 2300 German dead, dating from 1941. The cemetery was rededicated in 1998 and is now delineated by sets of triple granite crosses in the style common to German WWII military cemeteries throughout Europe.

◉ Pirita

Just past Maarjamäe the Pirita River enters Tallinn Bay and the city's favourite beach begins to unfurl. The area's other claim to fame was as the base for the sailing events of the 1980 Moscow Olympics; international regattas are still held here.

Buses 1A, 8, 34A and 38 all run between the city centre and Pirita.

Pirita Beach   BEACH
(Pirita rand; Map p50) Easily Tallinn's largest and most popular beach, Pirita has the advantage of being only 6km from the city. In summer, bronzed sun-lovers fill the sands and hang out in the laid-back cafes nearby. It's a bleak and windswept place if the weather's not good, but if the conditions are right there are plenty of wind- and kiteboarders providing visual entertainment.

Pirita Convent   RUINS
(Pirita klooster; Map p50; www.piritaklooster. ee; Kloostri tee; adult/student €2/1; ⊙10am-6pm Apr-Oct, noon-4pm Nov-Feb) Only the massively high Gothic stone walls remain of this convent, which was completed in 1436. The rest was destroyed courtesy of Ivan the Terrible during the Livonian War in 1577. In 1996 Bridgettine sisters were granted the right to return and reactivate the convent. Their new headquarters are adjacent to the ruins. Atmospheric concerts are held here in summer.

◉ Kloostrimetsa

Literally 'the convent's forest', this leafy nook spreads out along the north bank of the Pirita River. Bus 34A and 38 from the city head here via Pirita Beach.

Tallinn TV Tower   VIEWPOINT
(Tallinna teletorn; www.teletorn.ee; Kloostrimetsa tee 58a; adult/child €8/5; ⊙10am-7pm) Opened in time for the 1980 Olympics, this futuristic 314m tower offers brilliant views from its 22nd floor (175m). Press a button and frosted glass disks set in the floor suddenly clear, giving a view straight down. Once you're done gawping, check out the interactive displays in the space-age pods. Daredevils can try the open-air 'edge walk' (€20).

The most dramatic moment in the tower's history came on 20 August 1991, the day after Estonia's official declaration of independence, when Soviet troops attempted to take the tower by force. While ordinary people blocked the path of the tank, four men barricaded themselves in the control room to ensure that the tower continued broadcasting. There's a monument to these events on the plaza in front of the tower.

Tallinn Botanic Garden   GARDENS
(Tallinna botaanikaaed; www.botaanikaaed.ee; Kloostrimetsa tee 52; adult/child €5/2.50, with TV Tower €11; ⊙9am-5pm Oct-Apr) Set on 1.2 sq km fronting the Pirita River and surrounded by lush woodlands, this pretty garden boasts 8000 species of plants scattered between a series of greenhouses and various themed gardens and arboretums. Bring a picnic and make an afternoon of it.

◉ Haabersti

The westernmost district of Tallinn is home to over 43,000 people, although the population only started to intensify following the completion of the Väike-Õismäe (Little Flower Hill) development in the 1970s. This intriguing example of Soviet town planning features a giant oval ring of immense apartment blocks gathered around an ornamental lake. Nearby is Estonia's second-largest shopping mall, the Rocca al Mare Kaubanduskeskus.

★ Estonian Open-Air Museum   MUSEUM
(Eesti vabaõhumuuseum; Map p50; www.evm. ee; Vabaõhumuuseumi tee 12, Rocca al Mare; adult/ child May-Sep €7/3.50, Oct-Apr €5/3; ⊙10am-8pm May-Sep, to 5pm Oct-Apr) If tourists won't go to the countryside, let's bring the countryside to them. That's the modus operandi of this excellent, sprawling complex, where historic buildings have been plucked and transplanted among the tall trees. In summer the time-warping effect is highlighted by staff in period costume performing traditional activities among the wooden farmhouses and windmills.

There's a chapel dating from 1699 and an old wooden tavern, Kolu Kõrts, serving traditional Estonian cuisine. Kids love the horse-and-carriage rides (adult/child €5/3) and bikes can be hired (per hour €3). If you find yourself in Tallinn on Midsummer's Eve (23 June), come here to witness the traditional celebrations, bonfire and all.

To get here from the centre, take Paldiski mnt. When the road nears the water, veer right onto Vabaõhumuuseumi tee. Bus 21 (departing from the train station at least hourly) stops right out front. Combined family ticket combos are available including Tallinn Zoo, which is a 20-minute walk away.

Tallinn Zoo   ZOO

(Tallinna loomaaed; Map p50; www.tallinnzoo. ee; Paldiski mnt 145, Veskimetsa; adult/child €7/4; ☺9am-9pm May-Aug, to 7pm Mar, Apr, Sep & Oct, to 5pm Nov-Feb) Boasting the world's largest collection of mountain goats and sheep, plus around 350 other species of feathered, furry and four-legged friends (including lions, leopards and African elephants), this large, spread-out zoo is gradually upgrading its enclosures into modern, animal-friendly spaces as funds allow. It's the best place to see all of the natives (bears, lynx, owls, eagles) you're unlikely to spot in the wild.

However, it poses a bit of a dilemma for the animal-lover: while some of the older enclosures are certainly unsatisfactory (we feel particularly sorry for the poor old bears), things are clearly improving. If people don't visit they'll never have enough funds to complete the work – including a desperately needed new polar bear enclosure, for which they're currently fundraising.

A recent addition to the zoo complex is an **adventure park** (adult/child €17/6) with a high ropes course. Last entry to the zoo is two hours before closing time and all of the indoor enclosures are closed on Mondays. The zoo is best reached by bus 21 or trolleybus 7, which both depart from the train station, or by trolleybus 6 from Freedom Sq.

Stroomi Beach   BEACH

(Map p50) Shallow Stroomi beach is in Pelguranna, a neighbourhood favoured by Tallinn's Russian community. While the backdrop of ports and apartment blocks isn't as pleasant as Pirita, sunlovers swarm to the long stretch of sand. There's a distinct local buzz in summer. It's located 3km due west of Old Town (a 20-minute ride on bus 40 from Viru Keskus or 48 from Freedom Sq).

🏃 Activities

Locals attribute all kinds of health benefits to a good old-fashioned sweat and, truth be told, a trip to Estonia just won't be complete until you've paid a visit to the sauna. You won't have to look far – most hotels have one – but Tallinn also has some good public options.

Club 26   SPA

(Map p50; ☎631 5585; www.club26.ee; Liivalaia 33; private sauna per hour €25-65; ☺7am-10pm) On the top floor of the Radisson Blu Hotel Olümpia, with correspondingly outstanding views, this is one of the most luxurious sauna choices in town. There are two private saunas, each with plunge pool and tiny balcony. Food and drink can be ordered to complete the experience; prices cover up to 10 people.

The complex includes a solarium, a small gym, a massage centre and a 16m swimming pool.

Kalma Saun   SPA

(☎627 1811; www.kalmasaun.ee; Vana-Kalamaja 9a; admission €7.50-10; ☺11am-11pm) In a grand building behind the train station, Tallinn's oldest public sauna still has the aura of an old-fashioned, Russian-style *banya* (bathhouse) – flagellation with a birch branch is definitely on the cards. It has separate men's and women's sections (the women's is slightly cheaper) and private saunas are available (per hour €20; up to six people).

Kalev Spa Waterpark   SWIMMING, SPA

(Map p54; www.kalevspa.ee; Aia 18; 2½hr visit adult/child €13/10; ☺6.45am-9.30pm Mon-Fri, 8am-9.30pm Sat & Sun) For serious swimmers there's an indoor pool of Olympic proportions but there are plenty of other ways to wrinkle your skin here, including waterslides, spa pools, saunas and a kids' pool. There's also a gym, a day spa and three private saunas, with the largest holding up to 15 of your closest hot-and-sweaty mates.

Bell-Marine Boat Rental   BOATING

(Map p50; ☎621 2175; www.bellmarine.ee; Kloostri tee 6a; per hour kayak/rowboat €10/15; ☺10am-10pm Jun-Aug) The Pirita River is an idyllic place for a leisurely paddle, with thick forest edging the water. Rowboats and kayaks are hired from beside the road bridge, close to the convent ruins.

Harju Ice Rink   SKATING

(Harju tänava uisuplats; Map p54; ☎610 1035; www.uisuplats.ee; Harju; per hour adult/child/skate rental €5/3/2.50; ☺10am-10pm Nov-Mar) Wrap up warmly to join the locals at Old Town's outdoor ice rink. You'll have earned a *hõõg-vein* (mulled wine) by the end of it.

Tours

The tourist office and most travel agencies can arrange tours in English or other languages with a private guide; advance booking is required.

Tallinn Traveller Tours TOUR
(📞 5837 4800; www.traveller.ee) Entertaining, good-value tours – including a two-hour Old Town walking tour which departs at midday from outside the tourist information centre (it's nominally free but tips are encouraged). There are also ghost tours (€15), pub crawls (€20), bike tours (from €19) and day trips to as far afield as Rīga (€55).

EstAdventures TOUR
(📞 5308 3731; www.estadventures.ee; tour from €19; ☺May-Sep) Offers themed walking tours of Tallinn ('Old Town & Kalamaja', 'Haunted Tallinn'). Full-day excursions include Lahemaa National Park, Rakvere and Haapsalu.

Estonian Experience TOUR
(📞 5346 4060; www.estonianexperience.com; tour for 1 person/4 people from €80/96) Offers private tours on a wide range of specialist themes ('Medieval Beer Tasting & Legends', 'Jewish Tallinn', 'Family Walking Tour & Marzipan Workshop'), some of which include transport, food and drink. Although they cater to solo travellers, the prices work out much better if you're travelling as part of a small group.

City Bike BICYCLE TOUR
(Map p54; 📞 511 1819; www.citybike.ee; Vene 33; ☺10am-7pm) 'Welcome to Tallinn' tours (€19, two hours) depart at 11am year-round and include Kadriorg and Pirita. 'Other Side' tours take in Kalamaja and Stroomi Beach (from €19, 2½ hours), while 'Countryside Cycling & Old Town Walking' tours head out as far as the Open-Air Museum (from €47, four hours). It also co-ordinates self-guided day trips and longer itineraries.

Tallinn City Tour BUS TOUR
(Map p54; 📞 627 9080; www.citytour.ee; 24hr-pass adult/child €19/16) Runs red double-decker buses that give you quick, easy, hop-on/hop-off access to the city's top sights. A recorded audiotour accompanies the ride. The main stop is on Mere pst, just outside Old Town. Combo tickets are available including museum entries, a boat ride or a balloon ride.

The red line covers the city centre and Kadriorg; the green line travels to Pirita, Tallinn Botanic Gardens and the TV Tower; and the blue line heads west to the zoo and the Estonian Open-Air Museum.

Blue Super Segway SEGWAY
(Map p54; 📞 512 0030; www.bluesupersegway.ee; Viru 7; 1hr rental €30, plus guide per group €60) Motor yourself around town on a two-wheeled posing platform, or arrange a guided tour.

Euro Audio Guide WALKING TOUR
(www.euroaudioguide.com; iPod rental €13) Preloaded iPods are available from the tourist office with commentary on various Old Town sights. If you've got your own iPod,

---

TALLINN FOR CHILDREN

Tallinn's Old Town, with its lively medieval street scene and battlements, is pure eye candy for the under-12 crowd – although those cobblestones can play havoc with pushchair wheels. Kids are welcome almost everywhere; many restaurants have separate children's menus and most larger hotels have play areas and child-minding services.

Children will particularly enjoy the Estonian Open-Air Museum, the zoo, the beaches, Kalev Spa Waterpark and the Harju Ice Rink. There's a large playground in Kadriorg Park and another one in Hirvepark, downhill from Toompea.

Nuku (Map p54; 📞 679 555; www.nuku.ee; Nunne 8; admission €4.80; ☺11am-6pm Tue-Sun) The state puppet museum has lots of historic puppets behind glass but plenty to play with too. There's a Cellar of Horrors full of 'evil and scary puppets' (including a vampiric rabbit), a dress-up room, a shadow theatre and windows into the workshops where the puppets are made. Sadly there aren't any puppet shows in summer, but on the weekends at other times they're included in the price. Performances are in Estonian, but the visual fun is multilingual.

Tschu-Tschu (adult/child €5/3) A favourite of little nippers and footsore adults, this road train takes a 20-minute loop through Old Town in summer.

iPhone or iPad you can download the tour and an ebook for €15.

360° Adventures KAYAKING
(☎ 5686 4634; www.360.ee) Runs three- to four-hour guided kayaking tours on Tallinn Bay on Wednesdays from late June to August (€33). Also offers multiday kayaking, bog walking, snowshoeing and nature excursions.

Reimann Retked KAYAKING
(☎ 511 4099; www.retked.ee) Offers sea-kayaking excursions, including a four-hour paddle out to Aegna Island (€35). Other interesting possibilities include diving, rafting, bog walking, snowshoeing and beaver watching.

★★ Festivals & Events

It seems like there's always something going on in the city in summer. For a complete list of Tallinn's festivals, visit www.culture.ee and the events pages of www.tourism.tallinn.ee.

Jazzkaar MUSIC
(www.jazzkaar.ee) Jazz greats from around the world converge on Tallinn in mid-April during this excellent 10-day festival. Tallinn also hosts smaller events in autumn and around Christmas.

TALLINN UNIVERSITY SUMMER SCHOOL

Tallinn University Summer School (Map p50; ☎ 640 9218; http://summer school.tlu.ee; Narva mnt 25; course €440, cultural program student/nonstudent €350/400) Do you have Estonian heritage or perhaps just a fascination for obscure languages? Tallinn University offers three-week intensive courses in the Estonian language every July, which can be combined with a cultural program including lectures, guided tours and day trips delving into aspects of Estonian culture, history, art, music and traditions.

The language classes take place on weekday mornings while the cultural component is offered in the afternoons and weekends, making it quite possible to undertake one or the other, or both. If Estonian's not for you, other options include Russian and Mandarin Chinese (with instruction in English), and a broad range of creative and technical courses.

Old Town Days CULTURAL
(www.vanalinnapaevad.ee) This week-long festival in late May/early June features themed days (Music Day, Medieval Day, Children's Day etc), with dancing, concerts, costumed performers and plenty of medieval merrymaking on nearly every corner of Old Town.

Baltica International Folklore Festival CULTURAL
(www.folkloorinoukogu.ee) Music, dance and displays focusing on Baltic and other folk traditions. This festival is shared between Rīga, Vilnius and Tallinn; it's Tallinn's turn to play host in June 2016, 2019 and 2022.

Õllesummer BEER, MUSIC
(Beer Summer; www.ollesummer.ee) This extremely popular ale-guzzling, sausage-eating, rock-music extravaganza takes place over four days in early July at the Tallinn Song Festival Grounds. Alongside the cover bands and local singer-songwriters there are usually a few international drawcards (past performers include Placebo, the Cardigans, Pet Shop Boys and Scissor Sisters).

Estonian Song & Dance Celebration CULTURAL, MUSIC
(www.laulupidu.ee) The big one. This immense nationwide gathering convenes in July during the 4th and 9th years of every decade and culminates in a 34,000-strong traditional choir. The youth version slots in during the 2nd and 7th years of the decade.

Medieval Days CULTURAL
(www.folkart.ee) Old Town hosts a parade, a carnival and a jousting tournament, and Town Hall Sq is covered in craft stalls for a week in mid-July.

Tallinn International Organ Festival MUSIC
(www.concert.ee) Ten days of pulling out the stops in the city's churches, starting late July.

Birgitta Festival MUSIC
(www.birgitta.ee) An excellent chance to enjoy the intersection of music and theatre in a variety of genres, including choral, opera, ballet, modern dance and classical concerts held at the atmospheric convent ruins in Pirita over a week in mid-August.

Black Nights Film Festival FILM
(www.poff.ee) Featuring movies from all over the world, Estonia's biggest film festival brings life to cold winter nights for two weeks from mid-November. Subfestivals include animated films, student films and youth films.

🛏 Sleeping

Tallinn's medieval charm is no longer a state secret, so be sure to book well in advance in summer. Prices rise considerably in high season (peaking in July and August) and, irrespective of budget category, it can be extremely difficult to find a bed on the weekend without a couple of weeks' notice.

Tallinn has a good range of accommodation to suit every budget. Most of it is congregated in Old Town and its immediate surrounds, where even backpackers might find themselves waking up in an atmospheric historic building. If you're travelling with a car, you're more likely to find free parking a little further out.

🛏 Old Town

★ Tabinoya
HOSTEL **€**

(Map p54; 🕿 632 0062; www.tabinoya.com; Nunne 1; dm/s/d from €15/30/40; @ 🛜) The Baltic's first Japanese-run hostel occupies the two top floors of a charming old building, with dorms and a communal lounge at the top, and spacious private rooms, a kitchen and a sauna below. Bathroom facilities are shared. The vibe's a bit more comfortable and quiet than most of Tallinn's hostels. Book ahead.

Red Emperor
HOSTEL **€**

(Map p54; 🕿 615 0035; www.redemperor hostel.com; Aia 10; dm/s/d from €12/21/32; @ 🛜) Situated above a wonderfully grungy live-music bar, Red Emperor is Tallinn's premier party hostel for those of a beardy, indie persuasion. Facilities are good, with brightly painted rooms, wooden bunks and plenty of showers, and there are organised activities every day (karaoke, shared dinners etc). Pack heavy-duty earplugs if you're a light sleeper.

Old House Hostel & Guesthouse
HOSTEL **€**

(Map p54; 🕿 641 1281; www.oldhouse.ee; Uus 22 & Uus 26; dm/s/d from €14/29/48; 🅿 @ 🛜) Although one is called a hostel and one a guesthouse, these twin establishments both combine a cosy guesthouse feel with hostel facilities (bunkless dorm rooms, shared bathrooms, guest kitchens and lounges). The old-world decor (antiques, wacky wallpaper, plants, lamps) and the relatively quiet Old Town location will appeal to budget travellers who like things to be nice and comfortable.

Old Town Backpackers
HOSTEL **€**

(Map p54; 🕿 5351 7266; www.tallinnoldtown backpackers.com; Uus 14; dm/s €15/35; @ 🛜) Enter this baroque house and the whole hostel is laid out before you: a large room with half a dozen beds that also serves as the kitchen and living room. Given the tightness, late-night partying isn't encouraged but you'll certainly get to know your fellow guests. Especially as there's a sauna and spa.

Old House Apartments
APARTMENT **€€**

(Map p54; 🕿 641 1464; www.oldhouseapartments. ee; Rataskaevu 16; apt from €89; 🅿 🛜) Old House is an understatement for this wonderful 14th-century merchant's house. It's been split into eight beautifully furnished apartments (including a spacious two-bedroom one with traces of a medieval painted ceiling). There are a further 21 apartments scattered around Old Town in similar buildings, although the quality and facilities vary widely.

Zinc
HOSTEL **€€**

(Map p54; 🕿 5781 0173; www.zinchostel.ee; Väike-Karja 1; tw/tr/f €35/50/60; 🛜) More like a budget guesthouse than a traditional hostel, Zinc doesn't have dorms but its tidy private rooms share bathrooms and a kitchen and TV lounge. Colourful stencils line the halls of the century-old building. It's a quieter option in a noisy neighbourhood.

Bern Hotel
HOTEL **€€**

(Map p54; 🕿 680 6604; www.bern.ee; Aia 10; r from €63; ❄ 🛜) A newer hotel on the outskirts of Old Town, Bern is nothing special from the outside, but rooms are petite and modern, with great attention to detail for the price. Extras include robes and slippers, minibars, hairdryers and air-con.

Villa Hortensia
APARTMENT **€€**

(Map p54; 🕿 504 6113; www.hoov.ee; Vene 6; s/d from €45/65; 🛜) Situated in the sweet, cobbled Masters' Courtyard, Hortensia has four split-level studio apartments with kitchenettes and access to a shared communal lounge, but the two larger apartments are the real treats, with balconies and loads of character. In summer they can get hot and the downstairs cafe is open until midnight, so pack earplugs if you're an early sleeper.

Viru Backpackers
HOSTEL **€€**

(Map p54; 🕿 644 6050; www.virubackpackers. com; 3rd fl, Viru 5; s/d from €28/42; ❄ 🛜) This small, much flasher sibling of Monk's Bunk (p73) offers cosy, brightly painted private rooms, some of which have their own bathrooms. It's a quieter environment than the Monk, albeit in a noisier part of town.

★ Hotel Cru HOTEL €€€

(Map p54; ☑ 611 7600; www.cruhotel.eu; Viru 8; s/d/ste from €88/110/198; ☎) Behind its pretty powder-blue facade, this boutique 14th-century offering has richly furnished rooms with plenty of original features (timber beams and stone walls) scattered along a rabbit warren of corridors. The cheapest are a little snug.

Three Sisters HOTEL €€€

(Map p54; ☑ 630 6300; www.threesistershotel. com; Pikk 71; r/ste from €195/305; ☎) Offering sumptuous luxury in three conjoined merchant houses dating from the 14th century, Three Sisters has 23 spacious rooms, each unique but with uniformly gorgeous details, including old-fashioned bathtubs, wooden beams, tiny balconies and canopy beds. If you've got regal aspirations, the piano suite is the usual choice of visiting royalty.

Hotel Telegraaf HOTEL €€€

(Map p54; ☑ 600 0600; www.telegraafhotel.com; Vene 9; s/d/ste from €165/185/605; P ❋ ☎ ☒) This upmarket hotel in a converted 19th-century former telegraph station delivers with style in spades. It boasts a spa, a pretty courtyard, an acclaimed restaurant, swanky decor and smart, efficient service. 'Superior' rooms, in the older part of the building, have more historical detail but we prefer the marginally cheaper 'executive' rooms for their bigger proportions and sharp decor.

Savoy Boutique Hotel HOTEL €€€

(Map p54; ☑ 680 6688; www.tallinnhotels.ee; Suur-Karja 17/19; s/d/ste from €98/116/278; ☎) Soft cream and caramel tones make these rooms an oasis of double-glazed calm off one of Old Town's busy intersections (request a room on a higher floor for the rooftop views). Nice boutique touches include fruit on arrival and robes and slippers in every room, but what really sets it apart is the welcoming and attentive staff.

Hotel St Petersbourg HOTEL €€€

(Map p54; ☑ 628 6500; www.schlossle-hotels. com; Rataskaevu 7; r/ste from €153/216; ❋ ☎) Imperial Russia meets contemporary bling in this eclectically furnished hotel. The curious mix of styles includes zany light fixtures, mirrored chests of drawers, large-scale photographs of ballerinas and a giant Oscar statuette in the foyer. Rates include breakfast and a complimentary morning sauna.

Schlössle Hotel HOTEL €€€

(Map p54; ☑ 699 7700; www.schlossle-hotels.com; Pühavaimu 13/15; r/ste from €167/275; ❋ ☎) Occupying a clutch of medieval buildings grouped around a courtyard, this boutique hotel has only 23 rooms and a particularly atmospheric vaulted basement bar. Rooms vary widely in size and style; the smaller ones have more historic charm while some of the larger ones are a little lacklustre for the price.

PRIVATE APARTMENTS & ROOMS

Apartment agencies can be an excellent option, especially for midrange travellers who prefer privacy and self-sufficiency. True, you're unlikely to meet other travellers, but you'll usually get much more space than a hotel room, plus a fully equipped kitchen, lounge and often a washing machine. Prices for apartments drop substantially in the low season, and with longer stays. Old House Apartments (p71) has a good range in Old Town.

Romeo Family Apartments (☑ 644 4255; www.romeofamily.ee; apt €55-110; ☎) With a dozen spick-and-span apartments scattered around Old Town, this family-run operation is an extremely good option. Most are spacious and nicely furnished, with kitchens and clothes washing facilities. It also offers an airport pick-up service (€10).

Goodson & Red (☑ 666 1650; www.redgroup.ee; apt from €49) This agency has 22 apartments on its books ranging from modern studios to two-bedroom units. Most have excellent locations with some even overlooking Town Hall Sq. The minimum booking period is two nights and there's an additional €40 cleaning fee payable.

Ites Apartments (☑ 631 0637; www.ites.ee; apt from €80; ☎) A friendly and efficient bunch offering several well-appointed apartments in Old Town and its surrounds. There are significant discounts for stays of more than one night.

☷ City Centre

United Backpackers
HOSTEL **€**

(Map p50; ☑ 5685 0415; www.unitedbackpackers. ee; Narva mnt 9j; dm/d from €14/32; @ 🛜) Hidden in a clump of buildings off a major road, this well-kept, friendly wee hostel has artfully decorated rooms gathered together on one floor. You'll have no problem charging your myriad devices in the spacious dorms; each bed has six electrical sockets. All bathrooms are shared, but there's plenty of them. Plus there's a pool table and a 24-hour bar.

Euphoria
HOSTEL **€**

(Map p54; ☑ 5837 3602; www.euphoria.ee; Roosikrantsi 4; dm/r from €11/35; P @ 🛜) So laid-back it's practically horizontal, this hippyish hostel, just south of Old Town, is an entertaining place to stay with a palpable sense of traveller community – especially if you like hookah pipes and impromptu late-night jam sessions (pack earplugs if you don't).

Monk's Bunk
HOSTEL **€**

(Map p54; ☑ 636 3924; www.themonksbunk. com; Tatari 1; dm €11-14, r €38; @ 🛜) Very much a party hostel, the only monk we can imagine fitting in here is, perhaps, Friar Tuck. There are organised activities every night, including legendary pub crawls seemingly designed for maximum intoxication. The facilities are good, with high ceilings, free lockers and underfloor heating in the bathrooms.

★ Y-residence
APARTMENT **€€**

(Map p50; ☑ 502 1477; www.yogaresidence.eu; Pärnu mnt 32; apt from €80; 🛜) The 'Y' stands for 'yoga', which is a strange name for what's basically a block of very modern, fresh and well-equipped apartments, a short stroll from Old Town. You can expect friendly staff, a kitchenette and, joy of joys, a washing machine. There is a second block in an older building north of Old Town.

Hotell Palace
HOTEL **€€€**

(Map p54; ☑ 640 7300; www.tallinnhotels.ee; Vabaduse Väljak 3; r/ste from €100/170; ✳ 🛜 ☷) A recent renovation has swept through this architecturally interesting 1930s hotel, leaving comfortable, tastefully furnished rooms in its wake. It's directly across the road from Freedom Sq and Old Town. The complex includes an indoor pool, a spa, saunas and a small gym, although they're only free for those staying in superior rooms or suites.

Swissôtel Tallinn
HOTEL **€€€**

(Map p50; ☑ 624 0000; www.swissotel.com; Tornimäe 3; r from €158; ✳ 🛜 ☷) Raising the standards at the big end of town while stretching up 30 floors, this 238-room hotel offers elegant, sumptuous rooms with superlative views. The bathroom design is ultracool (bronze and black tiles; separate freestanding bathtubs and shower stalls) and, if further indulgence is required, there's an in-house spa. Friendly staff, too.

Estoria
HOTEL **€€€**

(Map p54; ☑ 680 9300; www.sokoshotels.ee; Viru väljak 4; r from €134; ✳ 🛜) The design team at Sokos Hotels have done a great job of eradicating any lingering KGB vibes from this block connected to the infamous Hotel Viru. Bright orange and green armchairs, robes and slippers lighten the mood, and each floor has its own little lounge area, set up with a coffee machine, bowls of chocolates and chess sets.

Nordic Hotel Forum
HOTEL **€€€**

(Map p54; ☑ 622 2900; www.nordichotels.eu; Viru väljak 3; r/ste from €119/189; P ✳ @ 🛜 ☷) The Forum shows surprising personality for a large, business-style hotel – witness the stencilled artwork on the facade, the garden path carpet, the floral frosted glass in the bathrooms and the trees on the roof. Facilities include saunas and an indoor pool with an 8th-floor view.

☷ Kassisaba & Kelmiküla

Immediately west of Old Town, at the base of Toompea hill, these small neighbourhoods have a good crop of modern, mid-rise, midprice hotels, handy for the train station. Kassisaba is Estonian for Cat's Tail, referring to the path through the ramparts into Toompea, while Kelmiküla means Rogue's Village, which remains apt as the area around the train station still has a roguish feel.

Go Hotel Schnelli
HOTEL **€€**

(Map p54; ☑ 631 0100; www.gohotels.ee; Toompuiestee 37; s/d/apt from €56/59/117; P ✳ 🛜) Right next to the train station, this modern block has fresh and comfortable rooms in a handy location close to both Kalamaja and Old Town. The free parking makes it a brilliant choice if you've got a car and the street-facing rooms have extraordinary views of the Toompea skyline.

L'Ermitage　　　　　　　　　　HOTEL €€
(Map p54; ☑699 6400; www.lermitagehotel.
ee; Toompuiestee 19; s/d/ste from €67/76/125;
🅿❄🐾) Built in 2004 but looking very
1970s, this love-it-or-hate-it metal-clad building contains unassuming but comfortable
rooms. The interior design has a more contemporary feel, with white walls set off with
splashes of colour. Rear rooms are quieter.

Kreutzwald Hotel Tallinn　　　　HOTEL €€
(Map p50; ☑666 4800; www.kreutzwaldhotel.
com; Endla 23; r from €68; @🐾) Here Scandinavian chic meets Japanese minimalism to
create an excellent midrange place to lay your
head. The pricier 'Zen' doubles have spa baths,
flat-screen TVs and soothing mood lighting.
It's a 15-minute walk from Old Town.

🛏 Kristiine

Valge Villa　　　　　　GUESTHOUSE €€
(Map p50; ☑654 2302; www.white-villa.com;
Kännu 26/2; s/d from €35/45; 🅿🐾) Homely
and welcoming, this three-storey, 10-room
guesthouse in a quiet residential area, 3km
south of the centre, is a good basic option,
particularly if you've got a car to park. All
rooms have fridges and kettles and some
have fireplaces, balconies, kitchenettes and
bathtubs. It's well connected to Old Town by
public transport.

✖ Eating

If your expectations of food in the former
USSR are low, prepare to be blown away
by what's on offer in Tallinn these days. Tal-
linnites are spoilt for choice with an array of
interesting, varied eateries, charging a fraction of what you'd pay for similar quality in
Western European capitals and tourist traps
(although prices are quickly rising). The service can still be hit and miss, but most places
have at least taught their staff to smile as
they rush by.

　While tourist-saturated neighbourhoods
worldwide struggle to offer good-quality,
good-value restaurants, Tallinn's Old Town
has plenty. Plus, the atmosphere is hard to
beat: winters are all about snuggling into
cosy vaulted cellars, while in summer the
streets are covered with temporary terraces
garlanded in flowers or herb boxes.

　If you want to get even better gastronomic bang for your buck, there are some
wonderful local favourites within walking
distance of Old Town in Kalamaja.

✖ Old Town

★V　　　　　　　　　　　　　VEGAN €
(Map p54; ☑626 9087; Rataskaevu 12; mains
€6-9; ⏰noon-11pm; 🍴) Visiting vegans are
spoiled for choice in this wonderful restaurant. In summer everyone wants one of the
four tables on the street but the atmospheric
interior is just as great. The food is excellent;
expect the likes of sweet potato peanut curry,
spicy tofu with quinoa and stuffed zucchini.

III Draakon　　　　　　　　　　CAFE €
(Map p54; Raekoja plats; mains €1-3;
⏰9am-midnight) There's bucketloads of atmosphere at this lilliputian tavern below the
Town Hall, and supercheap elk soup, sausages and oven-hot pies baked fresh on site.
The historic setting is amped up – expect
costumed wenches with a good line in tourist banter, and beer served in ceramic steins.

Chocolats de Pierre　　　　　　CAFE €
(Map p54; ☑641 8061; www.pierre.ee; Vene 6;
mains €5-13; ⏰8am-midnight) Nestled inside
the picturesque Masters' Courtyard and offering respite from Old Town's hubbub, this
snug cafe is renowned for its delectable (but
pricey) handmade chocolates, but it also
sells pastries, sandwiches and quiches, making it a great choice for a light breakfast or
lunch. As the day progresses, pasta finds its
way onto the menu.

Kompressor　　　　　　　　CREPERIE €
(Map p54; Rataskaevu 3; pancakes €5; ⏰11am-
late) Plug any holes in your stomach with
cheap pancakes of the sweet or savoury persuasion. Don't go thinking you'll have room
for dessert. By night, this is a decent detour
for a budget drink – it's low on aesthetics but
high on value.

Must Puudel　　　　　　　　　CAFE €
(Map p54; Müürivahe 20; mains €6.50-11;
⏰9am-11pm Sun-Wed, to 2am Thu-Sat; 🐾)
Mismatched 1970s furniture, an eclectic
soundtrack, courtyard seating, excellent coffee, cooked breakfasts (less than €5), tasty
light meals, long opening hours and a name
that translates as 'Black Poodle' – yep, this is
Old Town's hippest cafe.

Kehrwieder　　　　　　　　　　CAFE €
(Map p54; www.kohvik.ee; Saiakang 1; snacks
€2-6.90; ⏰8am-11pm Sun-Thu, to 1am Fri & Sat)
Sure, there's seating on Town Hall Sq, but
inside the city's cosiest cafe is where the real
ambience is found – you can stretch out on

a couch, read by lamplight and bump your head on the arched ceilings. Foodwise, it offers only pastries, cakes, chocolates and preprepared wraps and salads.

Rimi   SUPERMARKET €
(Map p54; Aia 7; ⊘8am-11pm) Old Town doesn't have convenience stores, making this small but well-stocked supermarket particularly handy.

★Rataskaevu 16   ESTONIAN €€
(Map p54; ✆642 4025; www.facebook.com/ Rataskaevu16; Rataskaevu 16; mains €6.90-15; ⊘noon-11pm; ⊛) If you've ever had a hankering for braised roast elk, this is the place to come. Although it's hardly a traditional eatery, plenty of Estonian faves fill the menu – fried Baltic herrings, grilled pork fillet and Estonian cheeses among them. Finish with a serve of its legendary chocolate cake.

Von Krahli Aed   MODERN EUROPEAN €€
(Map p54; ✆626 9088; www.vonkrahl.ee/aed/; Rataskaevu 8; mains €8.50-17; ⊘noon-midnight; ⊛⊿) You'll find plenty of greenery on your plate at this rustic, plant-filled restaurant (*aed* means 'garden'). The menu embraces fresh flavours and wins fans by noting vegan, gluten-, lactose- and egg-free options.

Pegasus   MODERN EUROPEAN €€
(Map p54; ✆662 3013; www.restoranpegasus. ee; Harju 1; mains €7.80-15; ⊘noon-11pm; ⊛) This hip restaurant occupies three design-driven floors of a very cool Soviet-era building, with porthole-style windows and roughcast walls. There's a lightness of touch to the menu, which encompasses salads, soups and generous serves of greenery accompanying the mains. The homemade bread is perhaps Tallinn's best and the staff are charming.

Vanaema Juures   ESTONIAN €€
(Map p54; www.vonkrahl.ee/vanaemajuures/; Rataskaevu 10/12; mains €12-15; ⊘noon-10pm) Food just like your grandma used to make, if she was a) Estonian, and b) a really good cook. 'Grandma's Place' was one of Tallinn's most stylish restaurants in the 1930s, and still rates as a top choice for traditional, home-style Estonian fare. The antique-furnished, photograph-filled dining room has a formal air.

Elevant   INDIAN €€
(Map p54; ✆631 3132; www.elevant.ee; Vene 5; mains €8.50-22; ⊘noon-11pm; ⊿) Aromas assault your senses as you ascend the wrought-iron staircase to the bright upstairs rooms where diners linger over tasty Indian-inspired cuisine. There's a wide selection of vegetarian dishes and some curiosities (moose korma, wild boar curry, crocodile in mango sauce).

Clayhills Gastropub   PUB FOOD €€
(Map p54; www.clayhills.ee; Pikk 13; mains €12-15; ⊘11am-midnight Sun-Thu, to 2am Fri & Sat) As well as being our favourite Old Town pub – for its live bands, comfy couches, stone-walled upstairs room and sunny summer terrace – Clayhills serves up quality grub. Chow down on pub classics such as (Estonian pork-and-apple) bangers and mash, gourmet burgers and snack platters.

La Bottega   ITALIAN €€
(Map p54; ✆627 7733; www.labottega.ee; Vene 4; mains €10-20; ⊘noon-11pm) Ancient wooden beams and stone pillars contrast with a sweeping pine staircase in the high-ceilinged dining room, providing an atmospheric setting for hearty Sardinian food. Naturally, there's plenty of seafood on the menu (including traditional treats such as stuffed squid) alongside local game meats such as wild boar and rabbit.

★Tchaikovsky   RUSSIAN, FRENCH €€€
(Map p54; ✆600 0610; www.telegraafhotel. com; Vene 9; mains €24-26; ⊘noon-3pm & 6-11pm Mon-Fri, 1-11pm Sat & Sun) Located in a glassed-in pavilion at the heart of the Hotel Telegraaf, Tchaikovsky offers a dazzling tableau of blinged-up chandeliers, gilt frames and greenery. Service is formal and faultless, as is the classic Franco-Russian menu, all accompanied by live chamber music.

★Leib   MODERN ESTONIAN €€€
(Map p54; ✆611 9026; www.leibresto.ee; Uus 31; mains €15-16; ⊘noon-11pm) An inconspicuous gate opens onto a large lawn guarded by busts of Sean Connery and Robbie Burns. Welcome to the former home of Tallinn's Scottish club (really!), where 'simple, soulful food' is served along with homemade *leib* (bread). The slow-cooked meat and grilled fish dishes are exceptional.

Dominic   EUROPEAN €€€
(Map p54; ✆641 0400; www.restoran.ee; Vene 10; mains €15-17; ⊘noon-midnight Mon-Sat, to 9pm Sun) A romantic choice, Dominic is a white linen and candlelight establishment, with a heavily French-accented menu and wine list. Think perfectly cooked duck or a hearty beef bourguignon topped off with a Roquefort and white-chocolate cake for dessert.

Chedi ASIAN €€€
(Map p54; ☑646 1676; www.chedi.ee; Sulevimä-gi 1; mains €12-32; ⓧnoon-11pm) UK-based chef Alan Yau (of London's Michelin-starred Hakkasan and Yauatcha) consulted on the menu of sleek, sexy Chedi, and some of his trademark dishes are featured here. The modern pan-Asian food is exemplary – try the delicious crispy duck salad and the artful dumplings.

Olde Hansa ESTONIAN €€€
(Map p54; ☑627 9020; www.oldehansa.ee; Vana turg 1; mains €15-50; ⓧ10am-midnight) Amid candlelit rooms with peasant-garbed servers labouring beneath large plates of game meats, medieval-themed Olde Hansa is the place to indulge in a gluttonous feast. If it all sounds a bit cheesy, take heart – the chefs have done their research in producing historically authentic, tasty (albeit not particularly sophisticated) fare.

MEKK MODERN ESTONIAN €€€
(Map p54; ☑680 6688; www.mekk.ee; Suur-Karja 17/19; mains €17-22; ⓧnoon-11pm Mon-Sat) The name of the Savoy Boutique Hotel's ground-floor restaurant is a contraction of *Moodne Eesti Köök* (modern Estonian cuisine), which pretty much says it all. It's a great place for a fancy meal and good service in an upmarket environment.

Ribe MODERN EUROPEAN €€€
(Map p54; ☑631 3084; www.ribe.ee; Vene 7; mains €17-19; ⓧnoon-11pm) In a corner position on Old Town's main eat street, with tables spilling outdoors in summer, Ribe has a formal bordering on stuffy ambience and a menu full of fresh, seasonal, Estonian produce.

Bocca ITALIAN €€€
(Map p54; ☑611 7290; www.bocca.ee; Olevimä-gi 9; mains €15-22; ⓧnoon-11pm) Sophistication and style don't detract from the fresh, delectable cuisine served at this much-lauded Italian restaurant. Creative dishes are matched to a strong wine list. Bocca also has a cosy lounge and bar where Tallinn's A-list gathers over evening cocktails.

✕ Kalamaja

F-hoone PUB FOOD €
(Map p50; www.fhoone.ee; Telliskivi 60a; mains €5.50-8.70; ⓧ9am-11pm Mon-Sat, 10am-9pm Sun; ⬥⬥⬥) The trailblazer of the uberhip Telliski-vi complex, this cavernous place embraces industrial chic and offers a quality menu

of pasta, burgers, stews, grilled vegies and felafels. Wash it down with a craft beer from the extensive selection.

Boheem CAFE €
(Kopli 18; mains €5.40-6.50; ⓧ9am-11pm; ⬥) First port of call for Kalamaja hipsters, this local favourite serves up tasty and affordable crepes, wraps, salads, stews, quiches and pasta dishes. Or you can just drop by for a coffee and a beer.

★ Moon RUSSIAN €€
(☑631 4575; www.kohvikmoon.ee; Võrgu 3; mains €12-17; ⓧnoon-11pm Mon-Sat, 1-9pm Sun, closed Jul) The best restaurant in increasingly hip Kalamaja, Moon is informal but excellent, combining Russian and broader European influences to delicious effect. Save room for dessert.

Klaus CAFE €€
(☑5691 9010; www.klauskohvik.ee; Kalasadama; mains €9.50-12; ⓧ9am-11pm; ⬥) There's a fresh, designery feel to this informal cafe down by the water. The menu is full of tasty snacks and more substantial meals, including lamb koftas, pasta and steaks. We wholeheartedly endorse the 'Cubanos' pulled pork sandwich, although we don't suggest tackling this messy beast on a date.

✕ City Centre

Vapiano ITALIAN €
(Map p54; www.vapiano.ee; Hobujaama 10; mains €6-9; ⓧ11am-11pm; ⬥) Choose your pasta or salad from the appropriate counter and watch as it's prepared in front of you. If it's pizza you're after, you'll receive a pager to notify you when it's ready. This is 'fast' food that's fresh, cheap and relatively healthy in a big, bright and buzzing setting. There's a second branch inside the Solaris Centre.

Cafe Lyon CAFE, FRENCH €€
(Map p54; ☑622 9297; www.cafelyon.ee; Viru väljak 4; breakfast €2.80-5.30, mains €5.90-13.90; ⓧ8am-11pm Sun-Wed, to 1am Thu-Sat; ⬥) Facing the park on the edge of the Viru Centre, this spacious cafe has a counter positively groaning under the weight of drool-inducing French-style pastries and cakes. At dinnertime the menu shifts gear to bistro fare.

Sfäär MODERN EUROPEAN €€
(Map p54; ☑5699 2200; www.sfaar.ee; Mere pst 6e; mains €9-15; ⓧ8am-10pm Mon-Wed, to midnight Thu & Fri, 10am-midnight Sat, 10am-10pm Sun) Chic Sfäär delivers an inventive menu

highlighting the best Estonian produce in a warehouse-style setting that's like something out of a Nordic design catalogue. If you just fancy a tipple, the cocktail and wine list won't disappoint. If the lubrication loosens the purse strings sufficiently, there's a pricy fashion store attached.

★ Ö MODERN ESTONIAN €€€

(Map p54; ☑ 661 6150; www.restoran-o.ee; Mere pst 6e; 4-/5-/7-course menu €46/59/76; ⊗ 6-11pm Mon-Sat, closed Jul) Award-winning Ö (pronounced 'er') has carved a unique space in Tallinn's culinary world, delivering inventive degustation menus showcasing seasonal Estonian produce. There's a distinct 'New Nordic' influence at play, and the understated dining room nicely counterbalances the theatrical cuisine.

Neh MODERN ESTONIAN €€€

(Map p50; ☑ 602 2222; www.neh.ee; Lootsi 4; mains €22-24; ⊗ 6pm-midnight Tue-Sat mid-Sep–Feb) Taking seasonal cooking to the extreme, Neh closes completely in summer and heads to the beach – well, Pädaste Manor on Muhu island – where it runs one of Estonia's best restaurants. In the low season it decamps back to the city, bringing the flavours of the Baltic islands with it.

Horisont MODERN EUROPEAN €€€

(Map p50; ☑ 624 3000; www.horisont-restoran. com; 30th fl Swissôtel, Tornimäe 3; mains €17-29; ⊗ 6-10pm Tue-Sat) With excellent service, a creative menu, stylish decor and magnificent views (over most of the city except, sadly, Old Town), Horisont offers a wonderful experience at the swishier end of the scale. Bread, dips, appetisers and palate-cleansing sorbets are liberally scheduled around the courses.

Enzo EUROPEAN €€€

(Map p54; ☑ 607 1150; www.enzocafe.ee; Laeva 2; mains €15-24; ⊗ noon-11pm; ☎) Russia, Estonia, France and Italy form a sophisticated alliance on the menu at this upmarket eatery. If you can drag yourself away from the delicious eclairs in the cafe section, take a seat under the exploding-firework chandeliers in the more formal restaurant and prepare to be pampered with amuse-bouches and palate cleansers between courses.

Kadriorg

NOP CAFE €€

(www.nop.ee; J Köleri 1; mains €7-12; ⊗ 8am-10pm; ▦) Well off the tourist trail, NOP is the kind of neighbourhood deli-cafe that's a magnet for yummy mummies, hipsters and itinerant foodies. White walls, wooden floors and a kids' corner set the scene, while the menu highlights cooked breakfasts, soups, salads and wraps. It's not far from Kadriorg Park.

Pirita

★ NOA INTERNATIONAL €€€

(☑ 508 0589; www.noaresto.ee; Ranna tee 3; mains €12-18, 5/7 courses €59/79; ⊗ noon-11pm; ☑) It's worth the trek out to the far side of Pirita to this elegant eatery which opened in 2014 and was rated the best in Estonia that very year. It's housed in a stylish low-slung pavilion which gazes back over Tallinn Bay to Old Town. Choose between the more informal à la carte restaurant and the dégustation-only Chef's Hall.

🍷 Drinking & Nightlife

Since independence, Tallinn has established a reputation as a party town and while things have cooled off a little, marauding troops of British stag groups and Finnish booze-boys still descend, especially on summer weekends. Given that they tend to congregate around a small nexus of Irish and British pubs in the southeast corner of Old Town (roughly the triangle formed by Viru, Suur-Karja and the city walls), they are easily avoided – or located, if you'd prefer.

ORGANISED INTOXICATION

If getting completely annihilated is your mark of a good night out, Tallinn has a couple of organised options to get you well on your way.

The **Epic Bar Crawl** (☑ 5624 3088; www.ministryofentertainment.ee; tour €15; ⊗ 9.30pm Wed-Sat) bills itself as 'the most fun and disorderly pub crawl in Tallinn' and the price includes a welcome beer or cider, a shot in each of three bars and entry to a nightclub. It also offers particularly ignominious packages designed for stags.

Party hostel Monk's Bunk (p73) ups the inebriation level on its **Mad Monk Pub Crawl** with an hour's unlimited beer or cider in its own bar, followed by a free shot in two different bars and club entry. It's priced at €12 for hostel guests and €15 for everyone else.

Elsewhere you'll find a diverse selection of bars where it's quite possible to have a quiet, unmolested drink.

Old Town

Check out Bocca (p76) for cocktails, Clayhills Gastropub (p75) for live music and a cosy pub atmosphere or head to the wonderfully grungy bar at Red Emperor hostel (p71) for live bands and an edgier up-for-it vibe.

DM Baar
BAR

(Map p54; www.depechemode.ee; Voorimehe 4; ☺noon-4am) If you just can't get enough of Depeche Mode, this is the bar for you. The walls are covered with all manner of memorabilia, including pictures of the actual band partying here. And the soundtrack? Do you really need to ask? If you're not a fan, leave in silence.

Kultuuriklubi Kelm
BAR

(Map p54; Vene 33; ☺5pm-2am Mon-Thu, to 6am Fri, 7pm-6am Sat, 7pm-2am Sun) It may be a 'culture club', but you're unlikely to hear 'Karma Chameleon' blasting out in this artsy rock bar. Expect lots of live music, art exhibitions, ping-pong competitions and movies on Wednesday nights.

Hell Hunt
PUB

(Map p54; www.hellhunt.ee; Pikk 39; ☺noon-2am; 🛜) Billing itself as 'the first Estonian pub', this trusty old trooper boasts an amiable air and a huge beer selection – local and imported. Don't let the menacing-sounding name put you off – it actually means 'gentle wolf'. In summer, it spills onto the little square across the road.

Põrgu
PUB

(Map p54; www.porgu.ee; Rüütli 4; ☺noon-midnight Mon-Thu, to 2am Fri & Sat) While the name may mean 'hell', the descent to this particular underworld is nothing short of heavenly for craft beer fans. There's a good mix of local and imported drops, including 13 beers and two ciders on tap and dozens more by the bottle. The food's good too.

Von Krahli Baar
BAR

(Map p54; www.vonkrahl.ee; Rataskaevu 10; ☺10am-midnight; 🛜) Comfortably grungy Von Krahli has courtyard tables and a barnlike interior which hosts the occasional live band or DJ. It's a great spot for an inexpensive meal or a beer in an indie ambience.

Paar Veini
WINE BAR

(Map p54; www.paarveini.ee; Sauna 1; ☺6-11pm Mon & Tue, to 1am Wed & Thu, to 5am Fri & Sat) The name means 'a couple of wines' and that's exactly what locals head here for. The vibe's relaxed and cosy, with comfy sofas, mismatched chairs and candles on the tables.

Frank
BAR

(Map p54; www.frankbistro.ee; Sauna 2; ☺noon-midnight) Out of all of Old Town's bars, this is a particular favourite of locals, whether for a burger, a cooked breakfast at dinnertime, or just a quiet drink in a relaxed environment.

Drink Bar & Grill
PUB

(Map p54; www.facebook.com/Drinkbaarandgrill; Väike-Karja 8; ☺noon-11pm Mon-Thu, to 2am Fri & Sat) You know a bar means business when it calls itself Drink. The best of Tallinn's British-style pubs, Drink takes its beer and cider seriously (its motto is 'no crap on tap'), and offers pub grub and long happy hours.

Levist Väljas
BAR

(Map p54; www.facebook.com/levistvaljas; Olevimägi 12; ☺3pm-3am Sun-Thu, to 6am Fri & Sat) Inside this cellar bar (usually the last pit stop of the night) you'll find broken furniture, cheap booze and a refreshingly motley crew of friendly punks, grunge kids and anyone else who strays from the well-trodden tourist path.

Clazz
BAR

(Map p54; www.clazz.ee; Vana turg 2; ☺noon-midnight Sun & Mon, to 2am Tue-Sat) Behind the cheesy name (a contraction of 'classy jazz') is a popular lounge bar featuring live music every night of the week, ranging from jazz to soul, funk, blues and Latin.

Beer House
MICROBREWERY

(Map p54; www.beerhouse.ee; Dunkri 5; ☺11am-midnight Sun-Thu, to 2am Fri & Sat) This microbrewery offers up the good stuff (seven house brews) in a huge, tavernlike space where, come evening, the German oompah-pah music can rattle the brain into oblivion. Sometimes raucous, it's for those who have had an overdose of cosy at other venues.

Maiden Tower Museum-Cafe
WINE BAR

(Neitsitorn Muuseum Kohvik; Map p54; www. linnamuuseum.ee/neitsitorn; Lühike jalg 9a; admission €2; ☺noon-9pm) Although it's actually a branch of the City Museum, we wouldn't pay the admission for the scant displays on the history of Estonia's confectionery industry. Neither would we bother with the cafe. But head up to the top of this medieval tower and there's a relaxed wine bar with comfy chairs angled for Old Town views.

St Patrick's
PUB

(Map p54; www.patricks.ee; Suur-Karja 8; ☺11am-2am Sun-Thu, to 4am Fri & Sat) One of a chain of five dotted around town, this lively, good-looking bar has plenty of beer to go round, and attracts a surprising number of Estonians. It's bang in the middle of the stag party triangle, so expect a lagered-up tourist crowd on weekends.

Club Privé
CLUB

(Map p54; www.clubprive.ee; Harju 6; admission from €14; ☺midnight-6am Fri & Sat) Privé occupies an old vaudeville theatre decked out with ornate chandeliers and baroque mirrors. Prices are high and the door policy exacting (scour the suitcase for your coolest clean threads), but a roster of international and local DJs make this Estonia's glitziest clubbing option.

Club Hollywood
CLUB

(Map p54; www.club-hollywood.ee; Vana-Posti 8; ☺11pm-5am Wed-Sat) A multilevel emporium of mayhem, this is the nightclub that draws the largest crowds. Wednesday night is ladies' night (free entry for women), so expect to see loads of guys looking to get lucky. It tends to be the last port of call for the organised pub crawls, so it can get pretty trashy.

🍷 Kalamaja

Tallinn's hipsters tend to leave the pricey bars of Old Town to the tourists and head to Kalamaja. Telliskivi Creative City (p61) is the liveliest nook – especially F-hoone (p76) – but there are cosy local pubs scattered throughout the neighbourhood.

Speakeasy by Põhjala
BAR

(Map p54; www.speakeasy.ee; Kopli 4; ☺6pm-2am Wed-Sat) It's pretty basic – particle-board walls, junk-shop furniture and a courtyard surrounded by derelict buildings – but this hip little bar is a showcase for one of Estonia's best microbreweries. Expect lots of beardy dudes discussing the relative merits of the India Pale Ale over the Imperial Baltic Porter.

Pudel
BAR

(Map p50; www.pudel.ee; Telliskivi 60a; ☺4pm-midnight Sun-Fri, noon-2am Sat) Laid-back and intimate, this friendly puppy offers 13 craft beers on tap and booze-soaking snacks to go with them.

Tops
BAR

(www.kohviktops.ee; Soo 15; ☺4-11pm Tue-Thu, 4pm-2am Fri, noon-2am Sat) All you'd want in a chilled out neighbourhood local: comfy couches, a good beer selection and a mixed crowd of local misfits. If that's sounding too cosy and sedentary, DJs drop by to rev things up on themed nights such as Femme Fatale and Funky Friday.

GAY & LESBIAN TALLINN

Tallinn holds the monopoly on visible gay life in Estonia, with a small cluster of venues south of the Old Town. The main regular celebration is Baltic Pride, which rotates between Tallinn, Rīga and Vilnius every year, usually in June. Tallinn's turn falls in 2017 and 2020. It's possible to download a free *Gay Map* (www.tallinn.gaymap.ee), although it isn't regularly updated.

X-Baar (Map p54; www.xbaar.ee; Tatari 1; ☺4pm-1am Sun-Thu, to 3am Fri & Sat) This long-standing bar is the mainstay of the gay and lesbian scene, attracting a mixed crowd of mainly local men and women. It's a relaxed kind of place, with a snug bar and a large dancefloor.

G-Punkt (Map p54; www.gpunkt.ee; Pärnu mnt 23; admission €5; ☺6pm-1am Tue-Thu, 8pm-6am Fri & Sat) To see what Eastern European gay clubs were like 15 years ago, head to this friendly venue, mainly attracting Russian-speaking lesbians. With no sign advertising itself, it's tricky to locate – as the *g-punkt* (G-spot) is wont to be. It's accessed across a parking lot from Tatari.

Club 69 (Map p50; www.club69.ee; Sakala 24; admission €16; ☺4pm-2am Sun-Thu, to 7am Fri & Sat) Gay men's sauna; push the buzzer by the discreetly located sign at the gate for admittance.

🍷 City Centre

Sfäär (p76) and Enzo (p77) are sophisticated options, or head up to Horisont (p77) for a cocktail in the clouds.

Protest   BAR
(Map p54; www.protest.ee; Mere pst 6a; ⊘2pm-late) Hidden at the bottom of an old building in the flashy Rotermann Quarter, this dimly lit drinking den has a vaulted ceiling and oddball art on every wall that's not spray-painted gold. The music happily vaults the chasm from Tame Impala to Vanilla Ice, attracting a mixed crowd of local hipsters and blow-ins from the neighbouring hostel.

Scotland Yard   BAR
(Map p54; www.scotlandyard.ee; Mere pst 6e; ⊘9am-11pm Sun, 11am-11pm Mon-Thu, 11am-2am Fri, 9am-2am Sat) As themed bars go, this is very well done, right down to the prison-cell toilets and staff dressed as English bobbies. There's a big menu of all-day pub grub, a small outdoor terrace and clubby leather banquettes. The large fish tank and electric-chair loos may not quite fit the theme but neither do the live bands, and they all add to the fun.

☆ Entertainment

It's a small capital as capitals go, and the pace is accordingly slower than in bigger cities, but there's still plenty to keep you stimulated in Tallinn. Events are posted on walls, advertised on flyers found in shops and cafes, and listed in newspapers. Tallinn's best English-language listings guide is *Tallinn in your Pocket* (www.inyourpocket.com), published every two months; buy it at bookshops or the tourist office (€2.50), or download it for free from the website. Despite the name, *Tallinn This Week* is also bimonthly; it's available from the tourist office and venues around town. For performing arts listings, see www.culture.ee, www.concert.ee and www.teater.ee.

Buy tickets for concerts and big events at Piletilevi (www.piletilevi.ee), either online or inside the Viru Keskus shopping centre.

Live Music

Kultuuriklubi Kelm (p78), Clazz (p78), Clayhills Gastropub (p75) and Scotland Yard all host regular live music. Touring international acts usually perform at Tallinn Song Festival Grounds (p65), A Le Coq Arena or Saku Suurhall.

For major classical concerts, check out what's on at the Estonia Concert Hall. Chamber, organ and smaller-scale concerts are held at various halls and churches around town.

Estonia Concert Hall   CLASSICAL MUSIC
(Eesti Kontserdisaal; Map p54; www.concert.ee; Estonia pst 4) The city's biggest classical concerts are held in this double-barrelled venue. It's Tallinn's most prestigious performance venue and houses the **Estonian National Opera and Ballet** (www.opera.ee), and the **Estonian National Symphony Orchestra** (www.erso.ee).

Theatre & Dance

Most theatre performances are in Estonian, or occasionally in Russian.

Tallinn City Theatre   THEATRE
(Tallinna Linnateater; Map p54; www.linnateater.ee; Lai 23) Tallinn's most beloved theatre company performs on seven stages scattered around its main building in Lai St, including a summer stage at the rear. Tickets can be hard to come by.

Estonian Drama Theatre   THEATRE
(Eesti Draamateater; Map p54; ☑680 5555; www.draamateater.ee; Pärnu mnt 5) Flagship company staging mainly classic plays.

Teater No99   THEATRE
(Map p54; ☑660 5051; www.no99.ee; Sakala 3) More experimental productions happen here.

Von Krahli Theatre   THEATRE
(Map p54; ☑626 9090; www.vonkrahl.ee; Rataskaevu 10) Known for its experimental and fringe productions.

St Canute's Guild Hall   DANCE
(Kanuti Gildi Saal; Map p54; ☑646 4704; www.saal.ee; Pikk 20) Tallinn's temple of modern dance also hosts the occasional classical dance performance.

Sport

A Le Coq Arena   FOOTBALL
(Map p50; Asula 4c) About 1.5km southwest of town, this arena is home to the national squad and Tallinn's football team **FC Flora** (www.fcflora.ee).

Saku Suurhall   BASKETBALL
(Map p50; www.sakusuurhall.ee; Paldiski mnt 104b) Basketball ranks as one of Estonia's most passionately watched games, and the big games are held in this arena, west of the centre.

Cinema

Films are generally shown in their original language, subtitled in Estonian and Russian.

Artis   CINEMA

(Map p54; www.kino.ee; Estonia pst 9) Inside the Solaris Centre but somewhat tricky to find, this art-house cinema shows European, local and independent productions.

Kino Sõprus   CINEMA

(Map p54; www.kinosoprus.ee; Vana-Posti 8) Set in a magnificent Stalin-era theatre (be sure to check out the reliefs on the facade), this cinema screens an excellent repertoire of art-house films.

Coca-Cola Plaza   CINEMA

(Map p54; www.forumcinemas.ee; Hobujaama 5) A modern 11-screen cinema, playing the latest Hollywood releases.

🛍 Shopping

The city's glitziest shopping precinct is the Rotermann Quarter (p64), which has dozens of small stores selling everything from streetware to Scandinavian-designed furniture to gourmet food and wine. Telliskivi Creative City (p61) has fewer shops but they're more eclectic. You'll be tripping over *käsitöö* (handicraft) stores in Old Town. Dozens of small shops sell traditional Estonian-made souvenirs, such as linen, knitwear, leather-bound books, ceramics, jewellery (particularly amber), stained glass and household items carved from dolomite or from juniper wood. There are also plenty of antique stores selling everything from objets d'art to Soviet-era nostalgia.

If you're stuck for gift ideas, you can't go wrong with a bottle of Vana Tallinn liqueur.

🏛 Old Town

Masters' Courtyard   HANDICRAFTS

(Meistrite Hoov; Map p54; www.hoov.ee; Vene 6; ⊙10am-6pm) Rich pickings here, with the cobbled courtyard not only home to a cosy cafe but also small stores and artisans' workshops selling quality ceramics, glass, jewellery, knitwear, woodwork and candles.

Katariina käik   HANDICRAFTS

(St Catherine's Passage; Map p54; off Vene 12) This lovely lane is home to the Katariina Gild comprising several artisans' studios where you can happily browse ceramics, textiles, patchwork quilts, hats, jewellery, stained glass and beautiful leather-bound books.

Ivo Nikkolo   FASHION

(Map p54; www.ivonikkolo.ee; Suur-Karja 14; ⊙10am-7pm Mon-Fri, 11am-4pm Sat & Sun) Classic-with-a-twist women's fashion that's a mix of floaty and fun, or muted and professional, but all made with natural, high-quality fabrics. The Old Town address has two floors of womenswear and accessories, or you can find it in the Viru Keskus shopping centre.

Rae Antiik   ANTIQUES

(Map p54; www.oldtimes.ee; Raekoja plats 11; ⊙10am-6pm Mon-Fri, to 4pm Sat) There are plenty of treasures waiting to be unearthed in this crowded shop, in the same building as

---

THE MARKET ECONOMY

Whether you're looking for picnic supplies or a knock-off Lenin alarm clock, Tallinn's markets provide fertile hunting grounds and excellent people watching.

Train Station Market (Jaama Turg; Map p54; Kopli; ⊙8am-6pm) A taste of old-school Russia behind the train station. It's a bit seedy in parts (watch your bag) but there are lots of fascinating junk shops to delve through.

Telliskivi Flea Market (Telliskivi Kirbuturg; Map p50; www.kirbuturg24.ee; Telliskivi 60a; ⊙10am-3pm Sat) Where the cool kids come to sell their cast-offs or to find new treasures. There's a wide range of stuff for sale, including clothing, books and household bits and bobs.

Knit Market (Map p54; Müürivahe) Along the Old Town wall there are a dozen or so vendors praying for cool weather and selling their woollen scarves, sweaters, mittens, beanies and socks.

Central Market (Keskturg; Map p50; Keldrimäe 9; ⊙8am-6pm) Fruit and vegetables are the main game but you'll occasionally luck upon a Soviet-era gem in one of the shady shops around the periphery. To get here, take tram 2 or 4 to the Keskturg stop.

the Town Council Pharmacy. Dive right in – or shop online. Prices aren't cheap.

Nu Nordik
GIFTS, CLOTHING

(Map p54; www.nunordik.ee; Vabaduse väljak 8; ⊘10am-6pm Mon-Sat, noon-6pm Sun) Lots of funky stuff, ranging from homewares to clothes, bags and jewellery.

Galerii Kaks
HANDICRAFTS

(Map p54; www.facebook.com/galeriikaks; Lühike jalg 1; ⊘10am-6pm) Lühike jalg, the alley leading up to Toompea, has a good selection of craft galleries. Galerii Kaks is probably the best of them, selling striking ceramics, jewellery, fabric and glassworks.

Lühikese Jala Galerii
HANDICRAFTS

(Map p54; www.hot.ee/lgalerii; Lühike jalg 6; ⊘10am-6pm) This little gallery is full of floaty textiles, jewellery, glass art and ceramics. Ask to look at the natural spring-fed waterfall that cascades down the back wall.

Zizi
HOMEWARES

(Map p54; www.zizi.ee; Vene 12; ⊘10am-6pm Mon-Sat, to 4pm Sun) Stocks a range of quality, Estonian-made linen napkins, placemats, tablecloths and cushion covers.

Chado
DRINK

(Map p54; www.chado.ee; Uus 11; ⊘noon-6pm Mon-Fri, to 4pm Sat & Sun) These passionate providores specialise in tea in all of its comforting forms, sourcing many of their leaves directly from Asia. Call in to chat chai and to sample brews from the clued-up staff.

🏠 Kalamaja

Estonian Design House
GIFTS

(Eesti Disaini Maja; www.estoniandesignhouse.ee; Kalasadama 8; ⊘noon-6pm Tue-Sat) This slick little store showcases the work of Estonian designers creating everything from shoes to lamps. Keep an eye out for the environmentally friendly Reet Aus label, which creates clothes from the offcuts of fabric left over from mass production processes.

🏠 City Centre

Viru Keskus
SHOPPING CENTRE

(Map p54; www.virukeskus.com; Viru väljak 4; ⊘9am-9pm) Tallinn's showpiece shopping mall is home to fashion boutiques, a great bookshop (Rahva Raamat) and a branch of the Piletilevi event ticketing agency. At the rear it connects to the Kaubamaja department store. The main terminal for local buses is in the basement.

Kaubamaja
DEPARTMENT STORE

(Map p54; www.kaubamaja.ee; Gonsiori 2; ⊘9am-9pm) Established in 1960, this is the most upmarket of Tallinn's department stores. It stocks all manner of high-end international fashion labels for men and women (Hugo Boss, Michael Kors, DKNY etc), along with local clothing brands (Ivo Nikkolo, Bastion, Monton), footwear, kidswear, toys, homewares and beauty products.

Stockmann Kaubamaja
DEPARTMENT STORE

(Map p50; www.stockmann.ee; Liivalaia 53; ⊘9am-9pm) One of the first foreign stores to open after independence, this upmarket Finnish department store helped relegate Soviet shortages to the pages of textbooks and usher in a new era of Western-style rampant consumerism.

Foorum
SHOPPING CENTRE

(Map p54; www.foorumkeskus.ee; Narva mnt 5; ⊘10am-8pm) More like a shopping arcade than a mall, Foorum has a single glitzy avenue of high-end stores. There's also a handy branch of Tele2 if you're after a local SIM for your mobile phone.

Kalev
FOOD

(Map p54; www.kalev.eu; Roseni 7; ⊘10am-8pm Mon-Sat, 11am-6pm Sun) This local legend has been producing delicious chocolate and other confectioneries since 1806. Tallinn's Old Town looks like its was made with the lid of a chocolate box in mind, so why not take one with you?

ℹ️ Information

Benu Apteek (www.benu.ee; Aia 7; ⊘8.30am-8.30pm Mon-Sat, 10am-6pm Sun) One of many well-stocked *apteegid* (pharmacies) in town.

East-Tallinn Central Hospital (Ida-Tallinna Keskhaigla; ☎620 7002; www.itk.ee; Ravi 18) Offers a full range of services, including a 24-hour emergency room.

Post Office (Map p54; Narva mnt 1; ⊘8am-8pm Mon-Fri, 10am-4pm Sat & Sun) Enter from Hobujaama.

Tallinn Dental Clinic (Tallinna Hambapoliklinik; ☎1920; www.hambapol.ee; Toompuiestee 4; ⊘8am-8pm Mon-Fri, 9am-3pm Sat & Sun)

Tallinn Tourist Information Centre (Map p54; ☎645 7777; www.visittallinn.ee; Niguliste 2; ⊘9am-7pm Mon-Fri, to 5pm Sat & Sun May-Aug, 9am-6pm Mon-Fri, to 3pm Sat & Sun Sep-Apr) Brochures, maps, event schedules and other info.

Tõnismäe Südameapteek (☑ 644 2282; www.
sudameapteek.ee; Tõnismägi 5; ⊘24hr) Pharmacy south of Old Town, open 24 hours.

ℹ Getting There & Away

AIR

Tallinn Airport (Tallinna Lennujaam; Map
p50; ☑ 605 8888; www.tallinn-airport.ee;
Tartu mnt 101) is conveniently located within
the heart of Tallinn, 4km southeast of Old Town.
Numerous airlines fly to Tallinn from within the
Baltic region (p178) and from further afield
(p416). Domestic flights are operated by
Avies and are limited to the main islands.

Avies (☑ 630 1382; www.avies.ee) Flies to/
from Kärdla (Hiiumaa) at least daily and Kuressaare (Saaremaa) most days.

BOAT

Ferries head to Tallinn from Helsinki (p191)
and other Baltic ports (p419).

BUS

Regional and international buses depart from
the **Central Bus Station** (Tallinna bussijaam;
Map p50; ☑ 12550; www.bussijaam.ee; Lastekodu 46; ⊘5am-1am), about 2km southeast of
Old Town; tram 2 or 4 will get you there. Services
depart from here for Latvia (p178) and other
European destinations (p418).

The national bus network is extensive, linking
Tallinn to pretty much everywhere you might
care to go. All services are summarised on the
extremely handy T pilet site (www.tpilet.ee).
Some of the main routes:

Haapsalu (€4.35 to €8.50, 1¾ hours, at least
hourly)

Kuressaare (€15 to €17, four hours, 11 daily)

Pärnu (€6.50 to €11, two hours, at least hourly)

Tartu (€7 to €12, 2½ hours, at least every
half-hour)

Viljandi (€9.50 to €11, 2½ hours, 11 daily)

CAR & MOTORCYCLE

Like accommodation, cars book up in summer, so
it pays to reserve. The large international companies are all represented and major players have
desks at Tallinn Airport. If you haven't booked
ahead, enquire at the tourist office about the
smaller local companies – they're usually cheaper.

Advantec (☑ 520 3003; www.advantage.ee)
Summer rates from €39 for a day (cheaper for
longer rentals).

Bulvar (☑ 503 0222; www.bulvar.ee) From €26
for a day (good deals for longer rentals).

Europcar (☑ 605 8031; www.europcar.ee)

Hansarent (☑ 655 7155; www.hansarent.ee)

Hertz (☑ 605 8923; www.hertz.ee)

R-Rent (☑ 605 8929; www.rrent.ee) Single-day
rates from €32.

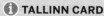

ℹ TALLINN CARD

Tallinn Card (www.tallinncard.ee; 1-/2-/3-
day card adult €31/39/49, child €16/19/24)
Flash a Tallinn Card to get free entry to
most of the city's sights; discounts on
shopping, dining and entertainment;
free public transport; and your choice
of one free sightseeing tour. They work
out to be good value if you were already
planning to take a tour. Otherwise, you'd
need to cram a lot of sights into each
day to make it worthwhile. You can buy
it online, from the tourist information
centre, or from many hotels.

TRAIN

The **Baltic Train Station** (Balti Jaam; Toompuiestee 35) is on the northwestern edge of Old
Town. Despite the name, there are no direct
services to the other Baltic states. **GoRail**
(www.gorail.ee) runs a daily service stopping in
Rakvere (from €6, 1¼ hours) and Narva (€7.90,
three hours) en route to St Petersburg and
Moscow.

Domestic routes are operated by **Elron** (www.
elron.ee) and include the following destinations:

Narva (€11, 2¾ hours, two daily)

Pärnu (€7.60, 2¼ hours, three daily)

Rakvere (€5.50, 1½ hours, three daily)

Tartu (€11, two to 2½ hours, eight daily)

Viljandi (€8.40, 2¼ hours, four daily)

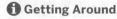

ℹ Getting Around

TO/FROM THE AIRPORT

➡ Bus 2 runs roughly every 20 minutes
(6.30am to around midnight) from the A
Laikmaa stop, opposite the Tallink Hotel, next
to Viru Keskus. From the airport, bus 2 will take
you via six bus stops to the centre and on to
the passenger port. Buy tickets from the driver
(€1.60); journey time depends on traffic but
rarely exceeds 20 minutes.

➡ A taxi between the airport and the city centre
should cost less than €10. The airport suggests
that you use the cabs waiting at the official
rank to avoid being scammed. Coming to the
airport, ask your accommodation provider to
book a reputable firm to collect you.

TO/FROM THE FERRY TERMINALS

There are three main places where passenger
services dock, all a short (less than 1km) walk
from Old Town. Most ferries and cruise ships
dock at the Old City Harbour (Vanasadama).
Eckerö Line, Viking Line and St Peter Line use
Terminals A & B (Map p50; Sadama) while
Tallink uses **Terminal D** (Map p50; Lootsi),

just across the marina. Linda Line ferries dock a little further west at the hulking **Linnahall** (Kalasadama).

Bus 2 runs every 20 to 30 minutes from the bus stop by Terminal A, stopping at Terminal D, the city centre, central bus station and airport; if you're heading to the port from the centre, catch the bus from the A Laikmaa stop, out the front of the Tallink Hotel. Also from the heart of town, trams 1 and 2 and bus 3 go to the Linnahall stop (on Põhja pst, near the start of Sadama), five minutes' walk from all of the terminals.

A taxi between the city centre and any of the terminals should only cost about €5.

BICYCLE

As well as offering tours, City Bike (p69) can take care of all you need to get around by bike within Tallinn, around Estonia or through the Baltic region (city and mountain bikes per three/24 hours €7/15; road and electric bikes €15/20). You can also rent panniers, GPS systems, and kids' bikes, seats and trailers. It also performs repairs and dispenses maps and advice. For longer journeys, it offers one-way rentals, for a fee.

CAR & MOTORCYCLE

Driving in Tallinn provides a few unique challenges, not least as it means sharing the road with trams and trolleybuses. For those streets where the tram stop is in the centre of the road, cars are required to stop until the disembarking passengers have cleared the road.

The central city has a complicated system of one-way roads and turning restrictions, which can be frustrating to the newcomer. Surprisingly, you are allowed to drive in much of Old Town – although it's slow going, parking is extremely limited and you can only enter via a few streets. Frankly, it's easier to park your car for the duration of your Tallinn stay and explore the city by foot or on public transport.

Parking is complicated, even for locals, and often involves paying via your mobile phone (which isn't easy if you don't have a local SIM). Look for signs (not that you'll necessarily make any sense of them) and expect a fine if you don't obey them. The first point for information is your accommodation provider – some will offer parking (rarely free), or will point you in the direction of the nearest parking lot.

PUBLIC TRANSPORT

Tallinn has an excellent network of buses, trams and trolleybuses that run from around 6am to midnight. The major **local bus station** (Map p54; Viru Väljak 4) is on the basement level of the Viru Keskus shopping centre, although some buses terminate their routes on the surrounding

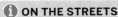

ON THE STREETS

» *maantee* – highway (often abbreviated to mnt)

» *puiestee* – avenue/boulevard (often abbreviated to pst)

» *sild* – bridge

» *tänav* – street (usually omitted from maps and addresses)

» *tee* – road

» *väljak/plats* – square

streets. All local public transport timetables are online at www.tallinn.ee.

Public transport is free for Tallinn residents. Visitors still need to pay, either the driver with cash (€1.60 for a single journey) or by using the e-ticketing system. Buy a plastic smartcard (€2 deposit) and top up with credit, then validate the card at the start of each journey using the orange card-readers. Fares using the e-ticketing system cost €1.10/3/6 for an hour/day/five days.

The Tallinn Card includes free public transport. Travelling without a valid ticket runs the risk of a €40 fine.

TAXI

Taxis are plentiful in Tallinn but each company sets its own fare; prices should be posted prominently. However, if you hail a taxi on the street, there's a chance you'll be overcharged. To save yourself the trouble, order a taxi by phone. Operators speak English; they'll tell you the car number (licence plate) and estimated arrival time (usually five to 10 minutes). If you're concerned you've been overcharged, ask for a receipt, which the driver is legally obliged to provide.

Throughout Old Town you'll find plenty of bicycle taxis driven by nothing but pedal power and enthusiasm; you'll generally find available vehicles lingering just inside the town walls on Viru.

Krooni Takso (1212; www.kroonitakso. ee; base fare €2.50, per kilometre 6am-11pm €0.50, 11pm-6am €0.55)

Reval Takso (1207; www.reval-takso.ee; base fare €2.29, per kilometre €0.49)

Takso24 (1224; flagfall €2.90, per kilometre €0.58)

Tallink Takso (1921; www.tallinktakso.ee; flagfall €3.90, per kilometre 6am-11pm €0.79, 11pm-6am €0.89) If you've got a larger group, book an eight- to 12-seater Maksitakso (flagfall €5.75, per kilometre €1.25).

Tulika Takso (1200; flagfall €3.65, per kilometre 6am-11pm €0.69, 11pm-6am €0.80)

AROUND TALLINN

With Tallinn at its centre, Harju County (Har-jumaa) covers around half of Estonia's north-ern coast and reaches into the hinterland as well. A scattering of sights make for easy day trips from the capital, or as diversions on the way to further-flung destinations.

Keila-Joa

Schloss Fall & Keila-Joa Castle WATERFALL
(www.schlossfall.com; castle adult/child €8/5; ☺cas-tle 10am-6pm) Flat Estonia isn't known for its waterfalls and at 6m, this one isn't all that high. It is, however, particularly picturesque, partly due to its juxtaposition with a little Neo-Gothic manor house, built in 1833 for Count Alexander von Benckendorf. A crenel-ated tower lends it a castle-like aspect, but its pretensions to being a fortress are purely ro-mantic. Two suspension bridges lead through lush countryside to the top of the horseshoe waterfall where rainbows dance in the spray.

Tsar Nicholas I visited Keila-Joa twice and was so impressed that he commissioned its architect, Andrei Stackenschneider, to build several palaces in St Petersburg and to refur-bish part of the Winter Palace. It was during Nicholas I's 1833 visit that the Russian Impe-rial anthem *God Save the Tsar!* had its de-but. A small museum in the basement of the castle recalls this august event, but it's argu-able whether it justifies the admission price.

The building was ransacked in 1917, na-tionalised in 1920, requisitioned by the Red Army in 1940, then by the German Army in 1941 and finally became the home of the Soviet 572nd fighter plane regiment in 1953. Needless to say, it wasn't in a good state when the National Heritage Foundation took it over and its reconstruction has left the floors and plasterwork looking a little too shiny and new.

Still, it's well worth the 30-minute drive west of Tallinn for a picnic by the waterfall. To get here from Tallinn, head west on Pald-iski mnt and, 12km past the zoo, turn right at Kiia onto route 410.

Padise

Padise Monastery RUIN
(Padise klooster; www.padiseklooster.ee) FREE
The great hulking shell of this former mon-astery practically begs exploration. Stairs lead up into the ruins, where you can wan-der around the masonry and climb to the top of the tower for views stretching for miles over the flat countryside. The former church still has its roof and Gothic windows and even in its derelict state it's easy to im-agine how grand it must once have been.

The land was given to the Cistercian or-der in 1220 in gratitude for its role in con-verting the Estonian pagans following the Christian invasion, but construction of the monastery didn't start until 1317. If you're thinking it looks more like a fortress than a place of worship, it's for good reason. Re-lations with the enslaved Estonian populace were shaky, and during the St George's Night Uprising, locals attacked the monastery, kill-ing 28 monks and burning it to the ground.

The monastery was rebuilt and reached the height of its powers in around 1480. In 1558 it was seized by the master of the Livonian Or-der, who turfed out the monks and strength-ened the fortifications. During successive wars it changed hands several times and was further fortified, before being converted into a manor house in the 17th century. A lightning strike in 1766 set it alight once again, and it was finally abandoned, the stones being used to build neighbouring Padise Manor.

Padise Manor HOTEL €€
(Padise Mõis; ☎608 7877; www.padisemois.ee; s/d from €79/84; 🅿🛜) Even though it's close to the main road, this historic manor house hotel has an exceptionally beautiful setting, flanked by lawns, a lake and the enigmatic ruins of Padise Monastery. The rooms are well appointed, with an antique feel, making this a great choice for a countryside escape.

Kaberneeme

Perched at the tip of a spit of land 40km east of central Tallinn, this sleepy little village would be unremarkable if it wasn't for two things: a long, unpeopled stretch of pine-lined sandy beach and a surprisingly good restaurant. Al-though there's a beach right by the marina, you're best to drive southeast along the coast for about 1.5km and look for the designated parking areas within the pine forest.

Activities

Aktiivne Puhkus WATER SPORTS
(☎504 6019; www.aktiivnepuhkus.ee; Sadama tee; ☺10am-9pm mid-Jun–Aug) Operating out of a shed on the sand near the marina, 'Active Hol-iday' rents kayaks (per hour €10), surfbikes (€40), motorboats (€120) and jetskis (€120).

🛏 Sleeping & Eating

OKO
MODERN EUROPEAN €€€

(📞5300 4440; www.okoresto.ee; Sadama tee 1; mains €14-19, r €80; ⏰noon-11pm) Little sister to Estonia's top-rated restaurant NOA, OKO celebrates its position right by Kaberneeme's little harbour with nautical-chic decor, a sunny deck and a menu loaded with seafood. If you don't fancy driving back to Tallinn, there are pleasant rooms with balconies upstairs (although bathrooms could do with an overhaul).

ℹ Getting There & Away

There's no public transport to Kaberneeme. To get here from Tallinn, turn off the main Tallinn–Narva highway (Hwy 1) at Koogi and follow the signs. If you're coming from the east, turn off at Kiiu.

NORTHEASTERN ESTONIA

The crowning glory of Estonia's national parks, Lahemaa occupies an enormous place – literally and figuratively – when talk of the northeast arises. Lahemaa comprises a pristine coastline of rugged beauty, lush inland forests rich in wildlife, and sleepy villages scattered along its lakes, rivers and inlets.

The park lies about one third of the way between Tallinn and the Russian border. Travelling east of the park, the bucolic landscape transforms into an area of ragged, industrial blight. The scars left by Soviet industry are still visible in towns such as Kunda, home to a mammoth cement plant; Kohtla-Järve, the region's centre for ecologically destructive oil-shale extraction; and Sillamäe, once home to Estonia's very own uranium processing plant.

Those willing to take the time will find some rewarding sites here, including the youthful city of Rakvere, the picturesque limestone cliffs around Ontika and the curious spectacle of the seaside city of Sillamäe, a living monument to Stalinist-era architecture. The most striking city of this region is Narva, with its majestic castle dating back to the 13th century.

For those seeking a taste of Russia without the hassle of visas and border crossings, northeastern Estonia makes a pocket-sized alternative. The vast majority of residents here are ethnic Russians, and you'll hear Russian spoken on the streets, in shops and in restaurants. You'll have plenty of opportunities to snap photos of lovely Orthodox churches, communist-bloc high-rises and other legacies left behind by Estonia's eastern neighbour.

Lahemaa National Park

Estonia's largest *rahvuspark* (national park), the 'Land of Bays' is 725 sq km of unspoiled, rural Estonia, making it the perfect country retreat from the nearby capital. A microcosm of Estonia's natural charms, the park takes in a stretch of deeply indented coast with several peninsulas and bays, plus 475 sq km of pine-fresh hinterland encompassing forest, lakes, rivers and peat bogs, and areas of historical and cultural interest.

The landscape is mostly flat or gently rolling, with the highest point just 115m above sea level. Stone fields, areas of very thin topsoil called alvars and large rocks called

Northeastern Estonia

WORTH A TRIP

TO THE MANOR REBORN

The Estonian countryside is littered with the once-grand manors of the long-vanished Baltic German elite. While most lie in ruin due to either war damage or neglect, an ever-increasing number are finding new lives as boutique hotels and restaurants. If you're heading between Tallinn and Tartu, there are some great options to tempt you off Hwy 2.

Once the home of 19th-century explorer Otto von Kotzebue, **Kau Manor** (☑ 644 1411; www.kau.ee; Triigi, Kose Parish; r from €130, mains €14-19; ⊕ restaurant 5-10pm Wed-Fri, 1-10pm Sat, 1-8pm Sun; P ⚡ ⛱) has recently been rescued from dereliction and converted into a fabulously flamboyant hotel and an acclaimed restaurant. Both the decor and menu take their inspiration from von Kotzebue's travels, with historical prints blown up to extravagant sizes on the walls and a veritable menagerie of stuffed animals scattered about.

Rooms in the main house are packed with antiques and vintage upholstery, while those in the coach house are just as comfortable but more restrained. Rates include breakfast and a morning sauna and swim in the indoor pool.

The Eight Legs (Kaheksa Jalga) Restaurant takes its name from a particularly over-the-top octopus chandelier in the dining room. The menu changes monthly to make the most of seasonal produce, with each month's dishes themed around a different place von Kotzebue visited.

Kau Manor is located 50km southeast of central Tallinn, 9km off the Tallinn-Tartu highway (turn off at Kose).

The decayed ambience of **Põhjaka Manor** (☑ 526 7795; www.pohjaka.ee; Mäeküla, Paide Parish; mains €12-15; ⊕ noon-8pm daily Jun-Aug, Wed-Sun Sep-May; ⚡) serves as a blank canvas for a wonderful restaurant showcasing fresh Estonian farm produce, where traditional stomach-fillers such as pork ribs and mash are taken to the next level of culinary excellence. It's well signposted from the Tallinn–Tartu highway, 90km from central Tallinn (95km from Tartu).

---

erratic boulders (brought from Scandinavia by glacial action) are all typically Estonian.

Almost 840 plant species have been found in the park, including 34 rare ones. There are 50 mammal species, among them brown bears, lynx and wolves (none of which you're likely to see without specialist help). Some 222 types of birds nest here – including mute swans, black storks, black-throated divers and cranes – and 24 species of fish have been sighted. Salmon and trout spawn in the rivers, feasting on the multitude of mosquitos that are ever-present in summertime (pack insect repellent).

In winter the park is transformed into a magical wonderland of snowy shores, frozen seas and sparkling black trees.

Visitors are well looked after: there are cosy guesthouses, restored manors and remote camp sites to stay in, and an extensive network of forest trails for walkers, cyclists and even neo-knights on horseback.

Nowadays the main attraction is the water, but from 1945 to 1991 the entire national park's coastline was a military-controlled frontier, with a 2m-high barbed-wire fence ensuring villagers couldn't access the sea.

Loksa, the main town within the park, has a popular sandy beach but is otherwise rather down-at-heel. **Võsu**, the next largest settlement, is much nicer, with its long sandy beach and summertime bars. It fills up with young revellers in peak season, depite being just a somewhat overgrown village.

History

When it was founded in 1971, Lahemaa was the first national park in the Soviet Union. Though protected areas existed before that, the authorities believed that the idea of a national park would promote incendiary feelings of nationalism. Sly lobbying (including a reference to an obscure decree signed by Lenin which mentioned national parks as an acceptable form of nature protection) and years of preparation led to eventual permission. Latvia and Lithuania founded national parks in 1973 and 1974 respectively, but it wasn't until 1983 that the first one was founded in Russia.

Lahemaa National Park

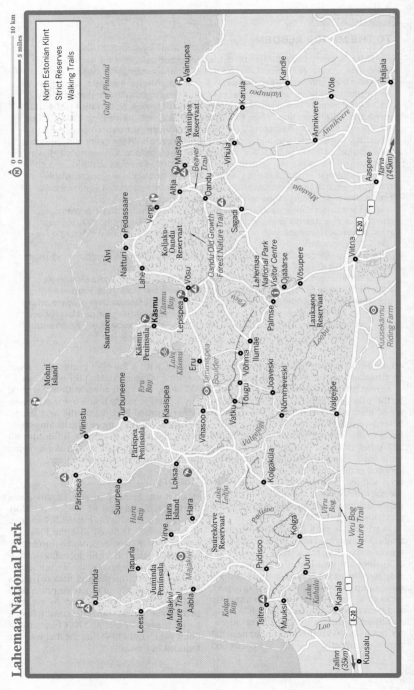

Legend:
- North Estonian Klint
- Strict Reserves
- Walking Trails

0 5 miles
0 10 km

Gulf of Finland

Vainupea
Kandle
Võle
Haljala
Karula
Vainupea Reservaat
Annikvere
Vihula
Mustoja
Altja
Beaver Trail
Oandu
Sagadi
Aaspere
Narva (145km)
Vergi
Pedassaare
Nattur
Ālvi
Koljaku-Oandu Reservaat
Oandu Old Growth Forest Nature Trail
Lahemaa National Park Visitor Centre
Vitna
Saartneem
Lahe
Võsu
Võsupere
Võsupere
Mõhni Island
Kāsmu
Kāsmu Peninsula
Lake Kāsmu
Lepispea
Kāsmu Bay
Eru
Tsirmispea Boulder
Palmse
Ojaäärse
Kuusekânnu Riding Farm
Viinistu
Turbuneeme
Eru Bay
Kasispea
Vihasoo
Ilumäe
Võhma
Võhma
Tõugu
Joaveski
Laukasoo Reservaat
Loobu
Pärispea
Pärispea Peninsula
Loksa
Vatku
Nõmmeveski
Valgejõe
Valgejõgi
Suurpea
Hara Bay
Virve
Hara Island
Hara
Lake Lohju
Kolgaküla
Tapurla
Juminda
Majakivi Nature Trail
Juminda Peninsula
Aabla
Majakivi
Suurekõrve Reservaat
Pudisoo
Padisoo
Kolga
Viru Bog.
Leesi
Pudisoo
Uuri
Viru Bog Nature Trail
Tsitre
Muuksi
Lake Kahala
Kahala
Kolga Bay
Loo
Kuusalu
Tallinn (35km)

Vainupea (river)
Mustoja (river)
Võsu (river)

E-20
E-20
1
1

⊙ Sights

We suggest that you start your explorations at the national park visitor centre at Palmse Manor.

Palmse Manor
HISTORIC BUILDING

(www.palmse.ee; adult/child €7/5; ⊙10am-7pm) Fully restored Palmse Manor is the showpiece of Lahemaa National Park, housing the visitor centre in its former stables. The pretty manor house (1720, rebuilt in the 1780s) is now a museum containing period furniture and clothing. Other estate buildings have also been restored and put to new use: the distillery is a hotel, the steward's residence is a guesthouse, the lakeside bathhouse is a summertime restaurant and the farm labourers' quarters became a tavern.

The wealth of the German land- and serf-owning class is aptly demonstrated by this 52-hectare estate encompassing more than 20 buildings. In the 13th century there was a Cistercian convent here. From 1677 it was owned by a Baltic-German family (the von der Pahlens), who held it until 1923, when it was expropriated by the state – an event celebrated by the simple stone Land Reform Monument, gloating at the manor house from across the ornamental lake and French-style gardens. There are also working greenhouses and an orangery to explore.

Sagadi Manor & Forest Museum
HISTORIC BUILDING

(Sagadi Mõis & Metsamuuseum; ☑ 676 7888; www.sagadi.ee; adult/child €3/2; ⊙10am-6pm May-Sep, by appointment Oct-Apr) Completed in 1753, this pretty pink-and-white baroque mansion is surrounded by glorious gardens (which are free to visit), encompassing a lake, modern sculptures, an arboretum and an endless view down a grand avenue of trees. The house ticket includes admission to the neighbouring Forest Museum, devoted to the forestry industry and the park's flora and fauna.

The Sagadi estate was nationalised during Estonia's first period of independence, although the aristocratic von Focks were permitted to live here until 1939. The outbuildings now have a new lease of life, housing the State Forest Management Centre (Riigimetsa Majandamise Keskus; RMK), its Nature School, a hotel and a hostel.

Altja
VILLAGE

First mentioned in 1465, this fishing village has many restored or reconstructed traditional buildings, including a wonderfully ancient-looking tavern which was actually built in 1976. Altja's Swing Hill (Kiitemägi), complete with a traditional Estonian wooden swing, has long been the focus of Midsummer's Eve festivities in Lahemaa. The 3km circular Altja Nature & Culture Trail starts at Swing Hill and takes in net sheds, fishing cottages and the stone field known as the 'open-air museum of stones'.

There are some good beaches between Altja and Mustoja, to the east. A scenic hiking and biking route runs east along the old road from Altja to Vainupea.

Käsmu
VILLAGE

Known as the Captains' Village, from 1884 to 1931 tiny Käsmu was home to a marine school that churned out ship captains. At one stage it was said that every Käsmu family had at least one captain in their midst. In the 1920s a third of all boats in Estonia were registered in this village.

Käsmu lies in a stone field which boasts the largest number of erratic boulders in Estonia. They can be viewed on the walking trails that start at the very end of the road. The Käsmu Nature & Culture Trail is a 4.2km, 90-minute circuit, taking in the coast and pine forest. A longer trail starts by the chapel and stretches 15km to Lake Käsmu (Käsmu järv).

Käsmu Sea Museum
MUSEUM

(Käsmu Meremuuseum; www.kasmu.ee; Merekooli 1; admission by donation) The former Soviet coastguard barracks at Käsmu now shelters this eclectic museum, displaying artfully arranged marine knick-knacks and charts. It's a private museum, with the owners living on site, so there are no formal opening hours.

Viinistu Art Museum
GALLERY

(Kunstimuuseum; www.viinistu.ee; adult/child €4/2; ⊙11am-6pm Wed-Sun) It's extraordinary that an obscure, remote village near the top of the Pärispea Peninsula should be home to one of the country's best galleries, yet Viinistu houses the remarkable private art collection of Jaan Manitski, reputedly one of Estonia's richest men. This ever-expanding assemblage is devoted entirely to Estonian art and pays particularly strong attention to contemporary painting – although you'll also find sculpture, etchings, drawings and some older, more traditional canvasses.

Manitski was born in Viinistu village but left when he was a baby and went on to make his fortune as the business manager for Swedish superstars ABBA. He's transformed his sleepy birthplace with this gallery and the neighbouring hotel and restaurant, housed in what was once a fish factory on the waterfront. In summertime there's often live music performed here as well.

Tammispea Boulder   LANDMARK
Over the millennia it has split into several pieces, but this gigantic 7.8m-high erratic boulder is still an impressive sight. It's hidden within a lovely stand of forest. To find it, leave the main coastal road and head through Tammispea village, continuing on to the unsealed road. Look for the sign shortly after passing the house with the polar bear sculptures.

Kolga Museum & Manor   MUSEUM
(www.kuusalu.ee; adult/child €2/1; ⊘10am-6pm mid-May–mid-Sep, 9am-4pm Mon-Fri rest of year) FREE The photogenically tumbledown, classical-style manor house at Kolga dates from 1642 but was largely rebuilt in 1768 and 1820. It's once again in the hands of the Stenbock family, who owned it from the 17th to the early 20th century, but attempts to restore it have stalled, due to lack of finance. In a neighbouring building, the small local history museum has limited information in English but there's an interesting display on Bronze Age burials at nearby Lake Kahala.

🏃 Activities

Cycling
Lahemaa's shady backroads are perfect for cyclists and many of the park's accommodation providers have bikes to rent (around €10 per day), including Lepispea Caravan & Camping, Merekalda, Sagadi Manor, Toomarahva Turismitalu and Uustula B&B.

The best off-road route is the 11.6km Käsmu Cycling Trail, which is mainly a loop with a couple of lenghty side tracks. Starting at the end of the road in Käsmu it heads through the forest to the Matsikivi erratic boulder then continues to the tip of the peninsula, down to Lake Käsmu and pops out back in the village, near the church. You can download a map from the Lahemaa section of www.loodusegakoos.ee.

City Bike (p69) coordinates self-guided day tours in the park from Tallinn (from €29, not including train to and from Kadrina), including bike hire.

Hiking
Some excellent hikes course through the park's diverse landscapes. Pick up maps and trail information from the visitor centre.

The Oandu Old-Growth Forest Nature Trail is a 4.7km circular trail, 3km north of Sagadi, that is perhaps the park's most interesting. Note the trees that wild boars and bears have scratched, bark chewed by irascible elk and pines scarred from resin-tapping.

Between Oandu and Altja is the Beaver Trail (Koprarada), a beautiful 1km walkway which passes beaver dams on the Altja River, although you're unlikely to see the shy, nocturnal creatures themselves.

The Viru Bog Nature Trail is a 3.5km trail across the Viru Bog, starting at the first kilometre off the road to Loksa (near Kolga), off the Tallinn–Narva highway; look for the insectivorous sundew (Venus flytrap, Charles Darwin's favourite plant).

The 7km Majakivi Nature Trail starts on the Loksa–Leesi road, near the charmingly old-fashioned coastal village of Virve, and takes in 7m-high Majakivi (House Boulder); at 584 cu metres, it's Lahemaa's largest erratic boulder.

Horse Riding
Kuusekännu Riding Farm   HORSE RIDING
(Kuusekännu Ratsatalu; ☑325 2942; www.kuuse kannuratsatalu.ee; riding per hour €20) Just outside the national park, near Viitna, this riding farm arranges trail rides through Lahemaa. Two-day treks include meals and accommodation, and stop overnight in Käsmu (€295). The three-day option stops overnight in Käsmu and either Atlja or Sagadi (from €390). Call ahead and check the website for directions.

👉 Tours

Both Tallinn Traveller Tours (p69) and EstAdventures (p69) offer excursions to Lahemaa out of Tallinn, starting from around €55. A private tour with the likes of Estonian Experience (p69) ranges from €320 for one person to €460 for four.

🛏 Sleeping

Käsmu, set on a rocky shoreline, has plenty of low-key guesthouses. If you want rowdier beach action, head to Võsu, a popular summertime hang-out for Estonian students. Guesthouses are scattered throughout the region; the visitor centre in Palmse keeps lists of options. It's worth keeping in mind that lots of small guesthouses have dogs (big ones). Keep that in mind before vaulting over fences.

The camping is fantastic in Lahemaa, with lots of free, basic RMK-administered camp sites. You will find them near Tsitre at Kolga Bay, at the northern tip of Juminda and Pärispea Peninsulas, immediately south of Võsu and by the Sagadi–Altja road, 300m south of the Oandu trail. When looking for these sites, keep your eyes peeled for the small wooden signs with the letters 'RMK'. All camp sites (free RMK ones and private ones) are marked on the excellent *Lahemaa Rahvuspark* map available in the visitor centre (€1.90).

Lepispea Caravan & Camping
CAMPGROUND €

(☏ 5450 1522; www.lepispea.eu; Lepispea 3; tent per person €5, caravan €15; ☉ May-Sep; P 🛜 🐾) In Lepispea, 1km west of Võsu, this camping ground is spread over a large field fringed by trees and terminating in a little reed-lined beach. Facilities are good, including a sauna house for rent. It also hires bikes (per day €10).

Uustula B&B & Campsite
GUESTHOUSE, CAMPGROUND €

(☏ 325 2965; www.uustalu.planet.ee; Neeme tee 78a, Käsmu; sites per person €4, caravan €10, s/d €30/45; P) At the end of the Käsmu road, this complex has simple, cheerful rooms on a waterfront property; breakfast is €6 extra. Campers are welcome to pitch a tent on the grassy lawn, although you'll have to pay extra for a shower (€3). Bikes are available to rent at €8 per day.

★ Merekalda
GUESTHOUSE, APARTMENT €€

(☏ 323 8451; www.merekalda.ee; Neeme tee 2, Käsmu; cabin/r €20/45, apt €69-99; ☉ May-Sep; P 🛜) At the entrance to Käsmu, this peaceful retreat is set around a lovely large garden right on the bay. Ideally you'll plump for an apartment with a sea view and terrace, but you'll need to book ahead. If funds are running low, there's a basic but romantic wooden cabin by the water. Boat and bike hire are available.

★ Toomarahva Turismitalu
GUESTHOUSE, CAMPGROUND €€

(☏ 505 0850; www.toomarahva.ee; Altja; tent/hayloft per person €3/5, caravan €10, s/d €25/50, apt €80-110; 🛜) This atmospheric farmstead comprises thatch-roofed wooden buildings and a garden full of flowers and sculptures. Sleeping options include two cute and comfortable rooms which share a bathroom, an apartment which can be rented with either one or two bedrooms – or you can even doss down in the hayloft in summer. Plus there's a traditional sauna for hire.

Sagadi Manor
HOTEL, HOSTEL €€

(☏ 676 7888; www.sagadi.ee; Sagadi; dm €15, s/d from €60/80; @ 🛜) Waking up in the rarefied confines of Sagadi Manor, with its gracious gardens, is a downright lovely experience. There's a tidy 31-bed hostel in the former estate manager's house, while the hotel has fresh and comfortable rooms in the whitewashed stables block across the lawn.

ESTONIAN WILDLIFE

Estonia has 64 recorded species of land mammals, and some animals that have disappeared elsewhere have survived within the country's extensive forests. The brown bear faced extinction at the turn of the 20th century but today there are more than 600 in Estonia. The European beaver, which was also hunted to near extinction, was successfully reintroduced in the 1950s and today the population is around 20,000.

While roe deer and wild boar are present in their tens of thousands, numbers are dwindling, which some chalk up to predators – though these animals are hunted and appear on the menu in more expensive restaurants (along with elk and bear). Estonia still has grey wolves (thought to number around 135) and lynx (more than 750), handsome furry cats with large, impressive feet that act as snowshoes. Lynx, bears, wolves and beavers are just some of the animals that are hunted each year, although a system of quotas aims to keep numbers stable.

Estonia also has abundant birdlife, with 363 recorded species. Owing to the harsh winters, most birds here are migratory. Although it's found throughout much of the world, the barn swallow has an almost regal status in Estonia and is the 'national bird'; it reappears from its winter retreat in April or May. Another bird with pride of place in Estonia is the stork. While their numbers are declining elsewhere in Europe, white storks are on the increase – you'll often see them perched on the top of lamp posts in large round nests. Black storks, on the other hand, are in decline.

Palmse Guesthouse   GUESTHOUSE €€
(✆5386 6266; www.palmse.ee; Palmse Manor; s/d without bathroom €25/50, ste €76-96; P🅿🛜) Housed in Palmse estate's former steward's house (1820), this guesthouse is a more atmospheric option than Palmse's main hotel. Only the junior suites and the suites have their own bathrooms, though.

Viinistu Hotel   HOTEL €€
(✆5373 6446; www.viinistu.ee; Viinistu; s/d/f €40/50/70) There's a fresh nautical flavour to the decor at this bright waterfront hotel next door to Jaan Manitski's private art museum. Family rooms are considerably bigger and contain kitchenettes. Make sure you book a sea-facing room with a balcony.

Vihula Manor   HOTEL €€€
(✆326 4100; www.vihulamanor.com; Vihula; r/ste from €94/164; P🅿🛜🏊) As part of its transformation into a spiffy country club and spa, this estate has converted its manor house and several historic outbuildings into guest rooms, eateries and a day spa. The rooms in the main house, particularly, are slick, elegant places to bed down, with tempting bathtubs. Hire a boat to row on the lake.

✕ Eating & Drinking

You can load up on provisions at Meie (www.meietoidukaubad.ee; Mere 67; ⊘10am-8pm) in Võsu (which has an ATM inside) or at the much bigger Loksa Kauplus (Tallinna 36; ⊘9am-10pm) in Loksa.

★ Altja Kõrts   ESTONIAN €
(www.palmse.ee; Altja; mains €6-8; ⊘noon-8pm) Set in a thatched building with a large terrace, this uber-rustic place serves delicious plates of traditional fare (baked pork with sauerkraut etc) to candlelit wooden tables. It's extremely atmospheric and a lot of fun.

Viinistu Restaurant   EUROPEAN €
(✆5558 6984; www.viinistu.ee; Viinistu; mains €8; ⊘noon-9pm; 🛜) Focusing firmly on seasonal fare, this smart restaurant-bar offers a concise but delicious menu including the likes of squid-ink pasta and fresh salads. There's an inviting deck but if the weather's not great, the sea views are just as good through the restaurant's big picture windows.

Viitna Kõrts   ESTONIAN €
(✆520 9156; www.viitna.eu; Viitna; mains €6-13; ⊘11am-10pm; 🛜) A popular pit stop for families travelling between Tallinn and Narva, this reconstruction of an 18th-century tav-

ern has a huge menu full of tempting traditional offerings such as honey-roasted pork or herring with cottage cheese. Next door is a basic cafe, open from 7am, serving up the essentials (coffee, sandwiches etc), and there's also a kebab counter.

Palmse Kõrts   ESTONIAN €€
(www.palmse.ee; Palmse; mains €7.50-13; ⊘11am-9pm) Just a short walk south of Palmse Manor, housed in the 1831 farm labourers' quarters, this rustic tavern evokes yesteryear under heavy timber beams with a short, simple menu of traditional Estonian fare. The creamy, eggy potato salad is stodgy and delicious, as is 'granny's cake'.

La Boheme   EUROPEAN €€€
(✆326 4100; www.vihulamanor.com; Vihula Manor; mains €18-22; ⊘2-11pm; P🅿🛜) You can dine in the garden or on a balcony, but you'd be missing out on the grand ambience of Vihula Manor's ballroom. The menu showcases local fish and game, and the service is top-notch. Make sure you save room for dessert.

O Kõrts   PUB
(Jõe 3, Võsu; mains €5-10; ⊘11am-midnight Sun-Thu, to 4am Fri & Sat) This tavern has a warm wooden interior and a flower-filled outdoor terrace, perfect for catching the late-afternoon sun. The menu covers plenty of ground from beer-drinking snacks to predictable mains of pork, steak and salmon. On long summer nights there are DJs and live musicians.

ℹ Information

Lahemaa National Park Visitor Centre (✆329 5555; www.loodusegakoos.ee; Palmse Manor; ⊘9am-5pm daily May-Oct, Mon-Fri Oct-Apr) This excellent centre stocks the essential map of Lahemaa (€1.90), as well as information on hiking trails, accommodation and guiding services. It's worth starting your park visit with the free 17-minute film Lahemaa – Nature and Man.

ℹ Getting There & Around

Lahemaa is best explored by car or bicycle as there are only limited bus connections within the park. The main bus routes through the park include the following:

➡ Tallinn to Altja (€6.50, 1¾ hours, daily) via Loksa, Käsmu, Lepispea and Võsu.

➡ Rakvere to Sagadi (€1.55 to €1.95, 45 minutes, one to four daily), Palmse (€1.75 to €2, 50 minutes, one daily), **Altja** (€1.90 to €2.25, one hour, most days), **Võsu** (€1.95 to €2.55, one hour, six daily) and **Käsmu** (€2.20 to €2.55, one hour, four daily).

Rakvere

POP 15,300

Roughly halfway between Tallinn and Narva, Rakvere is a thoroughly pleasant place for a pit stop or an overnight stay. The vibe here is upbeat, youthful and modern – quite unlike Narva.

The city loudly celebrates its connection to Estonia's most famous son, composer Arvo Pärt, who moved here as a child. However, it's also known for a more unusual musical tradition, the **Estonian Punk Song Festival** (www.punklaulupidu.ee). Started as a protest against the conservatism of the national festival, it's held every three or four years and was last staged in August 2015. You just haven't lived until you've heard *Anarchy in the UK* sung by a heavily accented mass choir sporting novelty technicolour mohawks!

◎ Sights & Activities

Rakvere Castle   CASTLE

(Rakvere Linnus; ☑507 6183; www.rakverelinnus. ee; Vallikraavi; adult/child €7/5; ⊙10am-7pm May-Sep, 10am-4pm Wed-Sun Oct-Apr) Rakvere's star attraction differentiates itself from other such mouldering ruins by offering hands-on, medieval-style amusements. While much is aimed towards children (dress-up costumes, a petting zoo), adults will get a kick out of handling the reproduction swords (blunted, thankfully), trying their hands at archery or jousting, and scoffing beer and victuals in the inn. Admission includes alchemy demonstrations, cannon-firing displays and tours of the torture chamber (despite the castle never actually having one; expect red lights, fake skeletons and coffins).

This hillside was the site of the earliest fortifications in Estonia, dating from the 5th and 6th centuries, although the castle itself was built in the 14th century by the Danes. It subsequently served many masters, including the German Livonian Order, the Russians, the Swedes and the Poles. It was badly damaged in a battle between the latter two powers in 1605 and was turned into an elaborate manor house in the late 17th century.

Concerts and plays are held here in summer; enquire at the tourist office.

Tarvas Statue   MONUMENT

Looming large near the castle, this massive 7-tonne, 3.5m-high, 7.1m-long statue was completed by local artist Tauno Kangro to commemorate the town's 700th anniversary in 2002. You might be forgiven for thinking that's a lot of bull, but actually it's an aurochs – a large, long-horned wild ox that became extinct in the 17th century.

The 1226 Chronicle of Livonia included a description of an ancient wooden castle on Rakvere hill, called Tarvanpea. In Estonian, Tarvanpea means 'the head of an aurochs' – hence the statue.

Rakvere Oak Grove   FOREST

(Rakvere tammik) Covering the next hill along from the castle, this 23-hectare expanse of mature oak and lime forest is a wonderful place for a leafy stroll. Although there probably was a sacred oak grove here in ancient times, the forest has been clear-felled on several occasions, most recently in around 1800.

On an expanse of lawn near the southern end is **Okaskroon** (Crown of Thorns), a memorial to locals deported to Siberia during the Soviet era. Deeper within the forest there's a small **German military cemetery** marked by triple sets of crosses set between the trees.

Citizen's House Museum   MUSEUM

(Linnakodaniku majamuuseum; www.svm.ee; Pikk 50; adult/child €1.60/1; ⊙11am-5pm Tue-Sat May-Sep, 11am-5pm Tue-Fri, to 3pm Sat Oct-Apr) There are many historic wooden and stone buildings on Pikk street, including this 18th-century home, kitted out mainly in early-20th-century garb. Displays include a cobbler's workshop, a collection of children's toys and a piano that once belonged to Arvo Pärt.

Holy Trinity Church   CHURCH

(Kolmainu kirik; www.kolmainu.ee; Pikk 17; ⊙10am-6pm Mon-Sat, to 12.30pm Sun Jun-Aug) Dating from the beginning of the 15th century, although it's been damaged and repaired several times since, this rather lovely Lutheran church has a 62m steeple, a carved pulpit with painted panels (1690) and some impressive large canvasses. Every year on 16 September it hosts a concert celebrating Arvo Pärt's birthday.

Market Square   SQUARE

(Turuplats; Lai, Laada & FG Adoffi) For a Soviet-era plaza, Tartu's expansive main square is actually pretty cool. Big yellow steel lamps arch over pebble circles and fountains, and there's a whimsical statue of composer Arvo Pärt pictured as a young boy holding his bicycle. Around its perimeter you'll find cafes and the tourist office.

Church of the Nativity of the Mother of God
CHURCH

(Jumalaema Sündimise kirik; Tallinna 17; ⊙10am-4pm) When we visited a new layer of bling was being added to this cute 19th-century Orthodox church, with its elegant onion domes in the process of being gilded. It contains the relics of Sergius Florinsky, a local priest who was shot in 1918 by local communists, now regarded as a saint by the Russian Orthodox church.

Aqva Waterpark & Sauna Centre
SWIMMING, SPA

(www.aqvahotels.ee; Parkali 4; 2½hr €9-13, incl saunas €12-18; ⊙9am-10pm) An attraction in its own right, Aqva Hotel's pool and sauna complex is one of the best of its kind in the country. Serious swimmers can rack up laps in a 25m covered pool while the kids splash around the wave pool or shoot down the slide. The paddling pool is popular with the under-fives and there's a small outdoor pool and sun terrace.

Each of the changing rooms has a sauna but it's worth investing in the pricier ticket to try out the various dry saunas and steam rooms in the sauna centre, especially the particularly relaxing salt sauna.

🛏 Sleeping

★ Villa Theresa
HOTEL €€

(☑322 3699; www.villatheresa.ee; Tammiku 9; s/d €55/65; ﾟ🅿❋🛰) In a wooded nook on the outskirts of town, 1.5km south of the main square, this wonderful boutique hotel offers a winning combination of peace and quiet, comfort, great food and reasonable prices. An antique ambience carries through seamlessly from the old wooden house at the front to the rooms in the modern extension.

Art Hotell
HOTEL €€

(☑323 2060; www.arthotell.ee; Lai 18; s/d €38/60; 🅿🛰) Under the same ownership as the smart cafe opposite, this little hotel has crisp, understated style – you'd never suspect that at the beginning of the 19th century it was a brothel. Rooms have sloping attic ceilings, frosted glass bathroom partitions and flat-screen TVs.

Aqva Hotel & Spa
HOTEL €€€

(☑326 0000; www.aqvahotels.ee; Parkali 4; s/d/ste from €93/105/215; 🛰🛋) This large architecturally interesting complex includes a day spa and fabulous indoor water park, making it a predictable hit with Finnish families. The water theme is taken to the max here, from the fabulous swirly purple carpet to the aquarium and water wall in the lobby. Standard rooms are on the small size, but they're modern and stylish.

🍴 Eating & Drinking

Art Café
CAFE €

(www.artcafe.ee; Lai 13; mains €5.50-12; ⊙11am-11pm Mon-Sat, to 9pm Sun; 🛰) With a big-city feel, an inviting rear garden and a diverse clientele, this cafe serves as a cool hang-out for food or late-night drinks. Friendly (but slow-moving) staff will help you select from a range of salads, soups, pancakes, pasta and other more creative dishes.

Inglise Pubi
PUB FOOD €

(www.inglisepub.ee; Tallinna 27; mains €6.50-9.90; ⊙11am-midnight; 🛰) Amid antique wallpaper, dark timber and brass bar fixtures, this place does a good impersonation of an English pub, and the beer garden is a great spot in which to sink a pint. The simple, no-surprises menu (Weiner schnitzel, pork chops, grilled salmon) lends authenticity.

Villa Theresa
EUROPEAN €€€

(☑322 3699; www.villatheresa.ee; Tammiku 9; mains €15-19; ⊙noon-10pm) If it's a more upmarket, formal ambience you're after, the restaurant at the Villa Theresa hotel is well worth seeking out. The menu offers creamy pastas and plenty of deliciously rich French-style mains.

ℹ Information

Tourist Office (☑324 2734; www.rakvere.ee; Laada 14; ⊙9am-5pm Mon-Fri year-round, plus 9am-3pm Sat & Sun mid-May–mid-Sep) Your first stop should be this friendly centre, where you can pick up a town map and walking-tour pamphlet.

ℹ Getting There & Away

BUS

The bus station is on the corner of Laada and Vilde, one block south of the tourist office. Major routes include the following:

Narva (€5 to €9, two hours, 10 daily)

Pärnu (€9 to €11, 2¾ to four hours, three daily)

Tallinn (€3.50 to €7, 1½ hours, 19 daily)

Tartu (€7 to €9, three hours, eight daily)

Võsu (€1.95 to €2.55, one hour, six daily)

TRAIN

➡ Elron has three trains daily to Tallinn (€5.50, 1½ hours) and two to Narva (€5.60, 1½ hours).

→ GoRail's Moscow and St Petersburg trains also stop in Rakvere twice daily; other stops include Narva (€4.30, 1½ hours) and Tallinn (from €6, 1¼ hours).

→ The train station is on Jaama pst, 1.2km northeast of the main square.

Ontika & Oru Park Landscape Reserves

Squeezed between a narrow coastal road and the sea, roughly halfway between Rakvere and Narva, these slim reserves protect a section of the limestone escarpment known as the Baltic Klint, where the land falls suddenly into the sea, forming cliffs up to 54m high. The klint extends 1200km, from Sweden to Lake Ladoga in Russia, although 500km of this lies underwater.

The only major settlement on this stretch of coast is **Toila**, a small spa and beach town set between the two reserves.

◉ Sights

Valaste juga　　　　　　　　　　WATERFALL
At Valaste a viewing platform and metal stair faces Estonia's highest waterfall (varying from 26m to 30m), which, depending on the month, may be a torrent, a mere trickle or photogenically frozen.

Oru Park Landscape Reserve　　PARK
(Oru Pargi Maastikukaitseala) Majestic Oru Castle was built in 1899 by notable St Petersburg businessman Grigory Yeliseyev, one of Russia's richest merchants. In 1935 it became the summer palace of the Estonian president but, sadly, it was completely destroyed during the war. Although the building is gone, the surrounding park remains one of Estonia's loveliest.

An avenue of mature trees leads to French-style landscaped gardens and the castle's surviving terrace, which offers views out to sea. Paths meander through the 75-hectare reserve, leading to a grotto with a freshwater spring, a viewing tower, a WWII graveyard and the beach.

⚏ Sleeping & Eating

Saka Manor　　　　HOTEL, CAMPGROUND €€
(☑ 336 4900; www.saka.ee; site per person €3.20, hotel s/d from €60/80, mansion d/ste from €110/230; ⓟ 🛜 🐾) 🍴 In a peaceful clifftop setting, signposted off the highway just east of Varja, this estate encompasses a campground, a low-key spa hotel and an

Italianate manor house (1864) containing guest bedrooms and a basement restaurant (mains €8 to €16). A metal stair leads from the cliff edge to the seashore below.

Valaste Cafe & Accommodation　GUESTHOUSE, CAMPGROUND €€
(☑ 332 8200; www.valaste.eu; Valaste; site/cabin per person €4/17, s/d €30/40) The small, brightly painted guesthouse by Valaste waterfall has a large communal kitchen, well-kept shared bathrooms and a large field for campers. Reception is handled by the cafe, where you can score artery-clogging snacks anytime of the day or night.

Toila Spa Hotell & Camping Männisalu　HOTEL, CAMPGROUND €€
(☑ 334 2900; www.toilaspa.ee; Ranna 12, Toila; site per person €5, cabin €45-70, s/d from €53/78; ⓟ 🛜 🐾) Balancing the needs of young families and mature holidaymakers, this midrange hotel has a large water park, a spa centre, a children's play area, a gym and restaurants. Rooms are modest but tidy. The camping area among the pines (open May to September) is also a good option, with tent and caravan sites and simple wooden cabins.

❶ Getting There & Away

There are no direct bus services from Tallinn or Narva; you'll need to transfer from Jõhvi or Kohtla-Järve.

Sillamäe

POP 14,000

Perhaps destined to be caught perpetually between the USSR (on a good day) and modern Estonia, the coastal town of Sillamäe is an intriguing place and a must for fans of Stalinist neoclassical architecture. Planned by Leningrad architects, its grand buildings include a **town hall** designed to resemble a Lutheran church. In the park opposite there's a wonderful period-piece **sculpture** of a muscle-bound worker holding aloft an atom.

The region's fate was sealed in the post-WWII years upon the discovery that oil shale contains small amounts of extractable uranium. The infamous uranium processing and nuclear chemicals factory was quickly built by 5000 Russian political prisoners, while the town centre was built by 3800 Baltic prisoners of war who had previously served in the German army. By 1946 the city was strictly off limits to visitors; it was known by various spooky code names (Leningrad 1; Moscow 400) and was often omitted from Soviet-era maps. Yet life for the workers who lived here was generally better than in other parts of the Estonian Soviet Socialist Republic.

Only unfinished uranium was processed at the plant, though the eerily abandoned buildings on the city's western border are testament to Soviet plans to process pure, nuclear-reactor-ready uranium. Only the disbanding of the USSR saved Estonia's ecology from this. Uranium processing ceased in 1989 and today the radioactive waste is buried under concrete by the sea. Fears of leakage into the Baltic have alarmed environmentalists; EU funding has been channelled towards ensuring the waste is stable and safe, at enormous cost.

These days the privatised Sillamäe plant is the world's main producer of the rare metals niobium and tantalum, which are used in the manufacture of medical and electronic equipment, among other things.

◉ Sights

Sillamäe Museum   MUSEUM
(www.sillamae-muuseum.ee; Kajaka 17a; adult/child €2/1; ☺10am-6pm Mon-Thu, to 4pm Fri) Until very recently, this little museum was jam-packed with fascinating Soviet-era relics, including uniforms, flags and large portraits of Lenin and Stalin. Now Lenin and his mates have been banished to a branch in the **Sillamäe Cultural Centre** (Kesk 24) and displays of dolls and teddy bears have taken his place. The excellent mineral display remains, alongside some rather dry coverage of the local extractive industry. More interesting is the room set up like a 1950s flat.

The building's a little tricky to find; it's set back between Kajaka and Majakovski streets, a block up from the water.

ⓘ Getting There & Away

St Petersburg buses stop here, but the major domestic destinations include the following:

Narva (€1.47 to €4, 45 minutes, at least hourly)

Pärnu (€15, 4¼ hours, daily)

Rakvere (€5 to €7, 1½ hours, nine daily)

Tallinn (€7 to €12, three hours, 21 daily)

Tartu (€7 to €12, 2¾ hours, seven daily)

Narva

POP 58,400

Estonia's easternmost city is separated from Ivangorod in Russia by the Narva River and is almost entirely populated by Russians. It's quite literally a border town: the bridge at the end of the main street is the country's principal link with Russia and no man's land protrudes right up to the edge of the town square. Aside from its magnificent castle and baroque Old Town Hall, most of Narva's outstanding architecture was destroyed in WWII. The reconstructed city has a melancholy, downtrodden air; the prosperity evident in other parts of the country is visibly lacking. Yet Estonia's third-largest city is an intriguing place for a (brief) visit – you'll find no other place in Estonia quite like it.

History

Inhabited since the Stone Age, Narva sits on an important trade route. After the Christian invasion, it found itself stranded on the edge of civilisations, on the divide between the Western (Catholic) and Eastern (Orthodox) Churches. Unsurprisingly, it has been embroiled in border disputes and wars throughout the centuries. Testimony to this is Hermann Castle's chess-piece face-off with the castle across the river at Ivangorod, built by Ivan III of Muscovy in 1492. In the 16th and 17th centuries Narva changed hands often from Russian to Swede, until finally falling to Russia in 1704.

During WWII Narva was bombed by both the Germans and Russians and was almost completely destroyed in 1944 during its recapture by the Red Army. Afterwards it became part of the northeastern Estonian industrial zone and one of Europe's most polluted towns. Today emissions have been greatly reduced, with investment in cleaner technology well under way.

◉ Sights

Narva Hermann Castle   CASTLE
(Peterburi 2) Built by the Danes at the end of the 13th century and strengthened over successive centuries, this imposing castle, along with Russia's matching Ivangorod Fortress across the river, creates an architectural ensemble unique in Europe. The outer walls enclose the **Castle Yard**, a large expanse of lawn which is open to the public and

contains what must be one of Estonia's last remaining public statues of Lenin. Restored after damage during WWII, Hermann Tower houses the Narva Museum.

The best view of the picturesque stand-off between the two castles is from the popular riverside beach, immediately south of the two.

Narva Museum
MUSEUM

(www.narvamuuseum.ee; Narva Hermann Castle, Peterburi 2; adult/child €6/3; ☺10am-6pm, closed Mon & Tue Sep-May) Museum admission gives you the opportunity to ascend Hermann Tower to a wooden viewing gallery, while checking out exhibits on each level of your climb (of varying degrees of interest and relevance, not all with English labels). Most interesting are the before and after pictures of the city's wartime destruction. In summer the Northern Yard is set up like a 17th-century town, complete with an apothecary, blacksmith, potter and lace workshops. Admission is included in the museum ticket.

Old Town
AREA

The remnants of Narva's war-pummelled Old Town is in the blocks north of the castle. Most impressive is the baroque Old Town Hall on Raekoja plats, built between 1668 and 1671. The striking building next to it is the Narva College of the University of Tartu. A large modern extension angles out and over the lower part of the building, which is a re-creation of the former baroque

stock exchange building which once stood here.

As in Tallinn and Tartu, the Swedes surrounded Old Town with a star-shaped set of bastions and most of the earthen ramparts are still visible. The Dark Park *(Pimeaed)* on the Victoria Bastion is a shady spot offering river views.

Art Gallery
GALLERY

(Kunstigalerii; www.narvamuuseum.ee; Vestervalli 21; adult/child €2/1, with museum €7/3.50; ☺10am-6pm) Spread over three floors of a 19th-century gunpowder storeroom on the Gloria bastion, Narva's art gallery has an interesting collection, the highlight being the historic, pre-WWII items.

Alexander Church
CHURCH

(Aleksandri kirik; www.narvakirik.ee; Kiriku 9) Named after the Russian tsar assassinated while it was being built (1881–1884), this Lutheran church is the largest religious building in Estonia. It was badly damaged in both of the world wars and the hefty octagonal belltower was only rebuilt post independence from the USSR. It now serves as Narva's Lutheran cathedral.

Orthodox Cathedral of the Resurrection
CHURCH

(Voskresensky sobor; www.narvasobor.ee; Bastrakovi 4) Hidden, in typical Soviet atheist style, among dingy apartment blocks northwest of

---

DON'T MISS

KUREMÄE

Originally a site of ancient pagan worship, the peaceful hilltop village of Kuremäe, 20km southeast of Jõhvi, is now home to a magnificent Russian Orthodox convent. Local lore has it that in the 16th century, Mary, the Mother of Jesus, appeared to a shepherd in an oak grove in these parts (conveniently echoing pre-Christian Estonian beliefs in divine beings living in holy groves). An icon of the Dormition of the Mother of God was subsequently found under one of the oaks; it now belongs to the convent, which has become a place of pilgrimage for believers. There is also a revered 'holy spring' here that is said to never freeze.

To get here by bus, you'll usually need to transfer at Jõhvi or Kohtla-Järve, although there are two direct buses per week from Tallinn (€8.60, 3½ hours) and Rakvere (€6.70, two hours).

Pühtitsa Convent (☑337 0715; www.orthodox.ee; ☺7am-7pm) Built between 1885 and 1895, the five green onion-domed towers of the impressive main church of Pühtitsa Convent are visible for miles around. Murals by the convent gate depict Mary, the Mother of Jesus, to whom the complex is dedicated. The community of Russian Orthodox nuns work the surrounding land and are self-sufficient; they will give tours to visitors for a small fee. Otherwise you're welcome to enter the gate and visit the church as long as you're dressed modestly.

the train station, this 1896 cathedral has an attractive red-brick exterior and a glittering core. Check out the frescoes inside the dome and the wonderful carved iconostasis.

🛏 Sleeping & Eating

King Hotel   HOTEL €€
(📞357 2404; www.hotelking.ee; Lavretsovi 9; s/d €28/36, mains €5-17; 🛜) Within Old Town, not far from the castle, King has snug modern rooms in a 1681 building and an excellent, atmospherically gloomy restaurant with a shady terrace. Try the local speciality, lamprey fished from the Narva River.

Elektra Külalistemaja   GUESTHOUSE €€
(📞716 6651; www.elektra.nev.ee; Kerese 11; s/d €40/45; 🅿🛜) That this odd little guesthouse, attached to the crumbling hulk of a power station, is one of the best places in the city to stay says a lot about Narva. Rooms are clean and have kitchenettes but they can get hot in summer and the flimsy drapes sure are ugly. On the upside, there's a sauna and spa pool.

100% China House   CHINESE €
(📞357 5099; www.chinahouse.ee; Tallinna mnt 6b; mains €5-13; ⊙noon-11pm) It may not be the best Chinese food you'll ever eat but it's likely to be the best you eat in Estonia. Located in a big yellow house set back from the main road, China House has a lengthy picture menu (including some Korean appetisers) and a suitably kitsch interior resplendent with bedazzled dragons and lanterns. What's not to like?

Antalya Kebab House   TURKISH €
(Aleksander Puškini 15; mains €4-8; ⊙11.30am-11pm) Fine dining it's not, but if you're in the mood for delicious pide (Turkish-style pizza), kebab, shashlik (barbecued skewers) or black-as-death coffee, this humble eatery will sort you out. It's around the corner and across the road from the tourist office.

🛍 Shopping

Aleksandr Antiques   ANTIQUES
(Aleksander Puškini 13; ⊙11am-6pm Tue-Fri, to 3pm Sat) Pop in for Russian memorabilia: Lenin busts, medals, jewellery and religious icons. There's a fair bit of modern tat as well.

ℹ Information

Tourist Office (📞359 9087; http://tourism. narva.ee; Peetri plats 3; ⊙10am-5.30pm) You can get maps and city information from friendly and efficient English-speaking staff at this excellent information centre. There are interesting interactive displays as well.

ℹ Getting There & Away

The train and bus stations are next to each other on Vaksali 2, at the southern end of the main street, Aleksander Puškini.

BUS

Buses head from here to Rīga and St Petersburg. Domestic routes include the following:
Narva-Jõesuu (€2, 30 minutes, roughly hourly)
Pärnu (€15, 4¾ hours, daily)
Sillamäe (€1.47 to €4, 45 minutes, at least hourly)
Tallinn (€7 to €13, 3¼ hours, roughly hourly)
Tartu (€7 to €12, three hours, nine daily)

TRAIN

Elron runs domestic services to and from Tallinn (€11, 2¾ hours) and Rakvere (€5.60, 1½ hours) twice daily. GoRail's Moscow and St Petersburg trains (p419) also stop in Narva twice daily en route to Rakvere (€4.30, 1½ hours) and Tallinn (€7.90, three hours).

Narva-Jõesuu

POP 2630

About 13km north of Narva, the holiday resort of Narva-Jõesuu (literally 'Narva River mouth') is a pretty but ramshackle town, popular since the 19th century for its long, golden-sand beach backed by pine forests. Impressive early-20th-century wooden houses and villas are scattered around, along with half a dozen hotels and spas – making this a good base for exploring Narva. There's plenty of new development going on, largely catering to holidaying Russians. The busiest area is centred on the Meresuu hotel.

🛏 Sleeping

Meresuu Spa & Hotel   RESORT €€
(📞357 9600; www.meresuu.ee; Aia 48a; s/d/ste from €88/99/176; 🅿🛜♨) This shiny 11-storey hotel offers service with a smile and attractive rooms, alongside a roll-call of extras: sea views, an 'aqua centre' (seven pools!), saunas, a gym, a wellness centre, a kids' playroom, bike yacht rental, and the requisite restaurant, serving up buffets and à la carte dining.

Noorus Spa Hotel   RESORT €€€
(📞356 7100; www.noorusspahotel.com; L Koidula 19; s/d/ste from €132/149/229; 🅿@🛜♨) With a name meaning 'youth' it's not clear wheth-

er this large new complex is aiming to attract young people or those seeking the eternal variety. Rooms are modern and comfortable and the facilities are top-notch, including indoor and outdoor pools, a spa centre with eight different types of sauna, a gym, a restaurant, a bar and even a bowling alley.

❶ Getting There & Away

Bus 31 runs about hourly to connect Narva with Narva-Jõesuu (€2, 30 minutes). There are also direct services to and from Tallinn (€7 to €14, 4¼ hours, three daily), Rakvere (€7 to €9.40, three hours, two daily) and Sillamäe (€3 to €3.60, one hour, three daily).

SOUTHEASTERN ESTONIA

With rolling hills, picturesque lakes and vast woodlands, the southeast boasts some of Estonia's most attractive countryside. It also contains one of Estonia's most important cities, the vibrant university centre of Tartu.

No matter which direction you head from Tartu, you'll find resplendent natural settings. In the south lie the towns of Otepää and Võru, the gateway to outdoor adventuring: hiking and lake-swimming in summer and cross-country skiing in winter. Quaint towns set on wandering rivers or in picturesque valleys add to the allure. For a serious dose of woodland, head to the crisp lakes and gently rolling hills of Haanja Nature Park or Karula National Park.

To the east stretches Lake Peipsi, one of Europe's largest lakes. Along its shores are beautiful sandy beaches and a surprisingly undeveloped coastline. Aside from swimming, boating, fishing and soaking up the scenery, you can travel up its western rim

stopping at roadside food stands and in tiny villages.

One of Estonia's most intriguing regions is also among its least visited. In the far southeast, clustered in villages near Lake Pihkva, live the Setos, descendents of Balto-Finnic tribes who settled here in the first millennium.

If you plan only to dip into the region, then you'll be fine getting around by bus. For more in-depth exploring – particularly around Haanja Nature Park, Setomaa and Lake Peipsi – services are infrequent and you'll save loads of time by renting a car.

Lake Peipsi

Straddling the Estonia–Russia border, Lake Peipsi (Chudskoe Ozero in Russian) is the fifth-largest lake in Europe (3555 sq km) – though its maximum depth is only 15m. There are some good, uncrowded beaches to be found on its sandy, 42km-long, northern coast. This area had popular resorts during Soviet times but many of them have been left to crumble and very few new developments have taken their place.

On the northeastern corner of the lake is Vasknarva, an isolated fishing village with about 100 residents and an evocative Orthodox monastery that, according to some, once held a KGB radio surveillance centre. The Narva River starts here, draining the lake and forming the border with Russia as it rushes to the Baltic. Also in Vasknarva, the scant ruins of a 1349 Teutonic Order castle stand by the shore.

The village of Alajõe has the area's main Orthodox church. Kauksi, where the main road from the north reaches the lake, has the most beautiful and popular beach.

RUSSIAN OLD BELIEVERS

Between 1652 and 1666 Patriarch Nikon introduced reforms to bring Russian Orthodox doctrine into line with the Greek Orthodox Church. Today, these liturgical reforms may seem trivial (including changes to the way the sign of the cross is made, the direction of a procession and the number of times that 'alleluia' should be said) but they were held to be vitally important by many believers. Those who rejected the reforms suffered torture or were executed, and many homes and churches were destroyed.

Over the next few centuries, thousands fled to the western shores of Lake Peipsi, where they erected new villages and worship houses. Although they escaped persecution, they were still governed by tsarist Russia and weren't allowed to openly practise their religion until Estonia gained its independence in 1918. Today there are around 2600 Russian Old Believers in Estonia, living in 11 congregations, primarily along the shore of Lake Peipsi.

With a population of 1320, **Mustvee** is the largest lakeside town, with a little harbour and a sandy beach. A little further south along the lake a forlorn WWII memorial, *The Grieving Girl* (1973), stands by the shore with her head bowed. It commemorates the 264 Red Army soldiers buried here in a mass grave. There's also a pretty Old Believers church nearby, dating from 1927.

In the 18th and 19th centuries Russian Old Believers *(Starovyery)* – a breakaway Orthodox sect who were persecuted for refusing to accept liturgical reforms carried out in 1666 – took refuge on the western shores of the lake. This intriguing community survives in several coastal villages which they founded, the largest of which is **Kallaste**.

A settlement of Old Believers has existed in Kallaste since 1720, when the area was known as Krasniye Gori (Red Mountains) because of the red sandstone cliffs, up to 11m high, that surround the town. Most of its 819 inhabitants are Russian-speaking. It's worth stopping to visit the Old Believers' cemetery at the southern end of town, and the sandy beach with small caves.

Kolkja is a village of Russian Old Believers with a dainty, green wooden church and a tiny Old Believers' Museum in what seems like a private house. Other places settled by

Southeastern Estonia

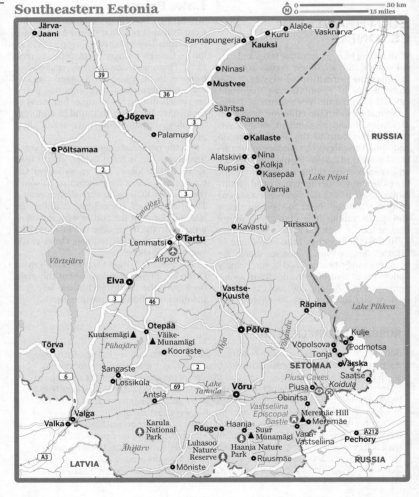

the Old Believers include Kasepää, Varnja and the island of Piirissaar.

◎ Sights & Activities

Alatskivi Castle   HISTORIC BUILDING
(Alatskivi loss; ☑5303 2485; www.alatskiviloss.ee; adult/child €5/3; ⏰11am-7pm daily Jun-Aug, 11am-6pm Wed-Sun May, Sep & Oct, 10am-4pm Mon-Fri Nov-Apr) Signposted off the main Kallaste–Tartu road, Alatskivi Castle channels the Scottish Highlands into a particularly verdant slice of Estonia – its white turrets and stepped baronial-style roofline inspired by the British queen's favourite abode, Balmoral Castle. Upstairs, five rooms are devoted to the life of Eduard Tubin (1905–82), an important Estonian composer and conductor; all signs are in Estonian. The surrounding estate encompasses 130 hectares of publicly accessible parkland filled with oaks, ashes, maples, alders and a linden-lined lane.

There's been a manor here for centuries, but the current neo-Gothic centrepiece dates from 1885. After nationalisation in 1919, the building was used as a school, a cavalry barracks, a state farm, council offices, a cinema and a library, but it's now been restored to its former grandeur based on old photos provided by descendents of the original aristocratic occupants.

As well as the Tubin museum, the house contains a restaurant and a set of four guest suites (€80 per night, including breakfast).

Liiv Museum   MUSEUM
(www.muusa.ee; Rupsi; adult/child €2/1; ⏰10am-6pm Jun-Aug, 10am-4pm Tue-Sat Sep-May) This museum is devoted to Juhan Liiv (1864–1913), a celebrated writer, poet and nationalist figure, of sorts. Even if you haven't heard of him (and let's face it, if you're not Estonian, you're not likely to have), it's a lovely rural setting and the 19th-century farm buildings where the Liiv family once lived are interesting in themselves. Occasional concerts and poetry competitions are held here.

Old Believers Museum   MUSEUM
(www.hot.ee/k/kolkjamuuseum/; Kolkja; adult/child €3/1; ⏰11am-6pm Wed-Sun Apr-Sep, 11am-5pm Sat & Sun Oct-Mar) There's not much in this little private museum in Kolkja village but it's interesting to read about the seemingly minor liturgical changes that caused such bloodshed. It's tricky to find – turn left at the Estonian flag, continue past the blue-painted restaurant and turn right at the lake.

Peipsirent   BOATING, CYCLING
(☑504 1067; www.peipsirent.eu; Narva 9c, Mustvee) Operating out of the Kalamesteemaja hotel in Mustvee, Peipsirent has motorboats (per day €35 to €120) and bikes (per day €10) for hire. In winter they'll take you out on the lake in a snowmobile sledge.

🛏 Sleeping

Don't forget to pack the mosquito repellent if you're staying by the lake.

Hostel Laguun   GUESTHOUSE €
(☑505 8551; www.hostel-laguun.ee; Liiva 1a, Kallaste; site/r per person €4/17) In a prime lakeside spot in Kallaste, Laguun is a small (10-bed) guesthouse offering simple rooms with shared bathroom, plus space for campers. There's a large garden and barbecue area, plus a communal kitchen. Try for a room with lake views.

Kuru Puhkemajad   CAMPGROUND €
(☑529 5088; www.kurupuhkemajad.ee; Kuru; s/d €12/24, cabin €30-48, campervan per person €10; 🅿) At Kuru, just a couple of kilometres east of Kauksi (off the secondary road from the lake to Iisaku), this complex offers rooms in barnlike buildings and wooden cabins – all sharing a communal kitchen and rudimentary bathrooms. The pretty grounds have barbecues and kids' play equipment and you can rent a bike (per hour €2) or motorboat (per hour €100).

Aarde Villa   B&B €€
(☑518 3617; www.aardevilla.ee; Sääritsa; sites per person €5, s/d/ste €26/52/56; 🅿🅰) Halfway between Mustvee and Kallaste, this lakeside estate offers comfy ensuite rooms in a stone building dating from 1711, set by its own beach. It's a wonderful, peaceful retreat with a plethora of activities on offer, including boats (with fishing equipment) and bikes for rent. Camping is possible within the leafy grounds.

🍴 Eating

Locally caught and smoked fish (trout or salmon) is a speciality of the area; some would say the delicious catch alone warrants the journey. Look for *suitsukala* (smoked fish) stands scattered all along the main road curving around the lake. There are supermarkets in Mustvee and Kallaste, and a *pood* (grocery store) in Kuru.

Kivi Kõrts ESTONIAN €
(☑ 745 3872; www.kivikorts.ee; Tartu mnt 2, Alatskivi; mains €2.70-7.90; ⏰ 10am-8pm Mon-Wed, to 10pm Thu-Sun) The most atmospheric place in the region for a cheap, hearty meal, this cosy, dimly lit tavern has taken an antique-shop-meets-junkyard approach to decor (much of what you see is for sale). The menu has patchy English translations and is very pork-heavy, but there are also fish and chicken dishes.

Fish & Onion Restaurant RUSSIAN €
(Kala-Sibula Restoran; ☑ 745 3445; www.hot.ee/k/kolkjarestoran; Kolkja; mains €6-8; ⏰ noon-6pm daily, by appointment in winter) This simple, blue-painted restaurant offers you the chance to try the Old Believer cuisine, largely based around locally caught fish and onions grown in the villagers' gardens. If you speak Russian, it's worth calling ahead to confirm opening hours.

ℹ Information

Kallaste Tourist Office (☑ 745 2705; www.kallaste.ee; Oja 22; ⏰ 10am-6pm Mon-Fri, 10am-4pm Sat & Sun Jun-Aug)

ℹ Getting There & Around

Getting to and around the lakeside villages is tricky without your own wheels. From Mustvee there are buses to the following destinations:

Alatskivi (€3.40, 40 minutes, daily)
Kallaste (€2.80, 30 minutes, two daily)

THE BLUE, BLACK & WHITE

Estonia's tricolour dates back to 1881, when a theology student named Jaan Bergmaan wrote a poem about a beautiful flag flying over Estonia. The only problem, for both Jaan and his countrymen, was that no flag in fact existed. Clearly, something had to be done about this. This was, after all, the time of the national awakening, when the idea of independent nationhood was on the lips of every young dreamer across the country.

In September of that year, at the Union of Estonian Students in Tartu, 20 students and one alumnus gathered to hash out ideas for a flag. All present agreed that the colours must express the character of the nation, reflect the Estonian landscape and connect to the colours of folk costumes. After long discussions, the students came up with blue, black and white. According to one interpretation, blue symbolised hope for Estonia's future; it also represented faithfulness. Black was a reminder of the dark past to which Estonia would not return; it also depicted the country's dark soil. White represented the attainment of enlightenment and education – an aspiration for all Estonians; it also symbolised snow in winter, light nights in summer and the Estonian birch tree.

After the colours were chosen, it took several years before the first flag was made. Three young activist women – Emilie, Paula and Miina Beermann – carried this out by sewing together a large flag made out of silk. In 1884 the students held a procession from Tartu to Otepää, a location far from the eyes of the Russian government. All members of the students' union were there as the flag was raised over the vicarage. Afterwards it was dipped in Pühajärv (a lake considered sacred to Estonians) and locked safely away in the student archive.

Although the inauguration of the flag was a tiny event, word of the flag's existence spread, and soon the combination of colours appeared in unions and choirs, and hung from farmhouses all across Estonia. By the end of the 19th century the blue, black and white was used in parties and at wedding ceremonies. Its first political appearance, however, didn't arrive until 1917, when thousands of Estonians marched in St Petersburg demanding independence. In 1918 Estonia was declared independent and the flag was raised on Pikk Hermann in Tallinn's Old Town. There it remained until the Soviet Union seized power in 1940.

During the occupation the Soviets banned the flag and once again it went underground. For Estonians, keeping the flag on the sly was a small but hopeful symbol of one day regaining nationhood. People hid flags under floorboards or unstitched the stripes and secreted them in bookcases. Those caught with the flag faced severe punishment – including a possible sentence in the Siberian gulags. Needless to say, as the Soviet Union teetered on the brink of collapse, blue, black and white returned to the stage. In February 1989 the flag was raised again on Pikk Hermann. Independence was about to be regained.

Narva (€5, two hours, five daily)
Tallinn (€13, three hours, daily)
Tartu (€4 to €5, one hour, 10 daily)

Palamuse

This sleepy little town, 35km north of Tartu, is a major drawcard for Estonian tourists due to its role as the setting for Oskar Luts' coming-of-age novel *Spring (Kevade)* and, even more so, as the location for the 1969 movie adaptation of the same. Trotted out every year for a television rerun at Christmas, it's unquestionably the nation's favourite family flick. Even if *Spring* has passed you by, Palamuse makes for a pleasantly rural pit stop.

◉ Sights

O Luts Parish School Museum   MUSEUM
(O Lutsu kihelkonnakoolimuuseum; www.palamuse um.ee; Köstri allee 3; admission €1.50, slingshot €0.90; ⊙ 10am-6pm May-Sep, 10am-5pm Mon-Fri Oct-Apr) The future novelist Oskar Luts attended school in this rustic building from 1895 to 1899, as immortalised in his most famous book *Spring*. The subsequent film adaptation was shot here and the schoolhouse now features displays on all three: the film, the book and the writer.

Spring's primary audience is Estonian, so it's not surprising that English captions are limited. However, it's still fun to potter around the re-created classroom, dorm and teacher's bedroom, and to look at the black-and-white stills of the movie and various stage productions.

Best of all, you can hire a slingshot and attempt to re-create a scene in the movie by breaking a window in a neighbouring building. Museum staff assure us that kids have a much better success rate at this than their parents do – and in any case, the window is quickly replaced.

**St Bartholomew's
Lutheran Church**   CHURCH
(Püha Bartholomeuse kirik; Köstri allee 2; ⊙ 10am-5pm May-Sep) Another star of the movie adaptation of *Spring*, this lovely Gothic church has its roots in the 13th century, although it has been substantially altered over time. Its most interesting feature is a carved wooden pulpit from 1696, festooned with saints and angels.

❶ Information

Jõgevamaa Tourist Information Centre (☑776 8520; www.visitjogeva.com; Köstri allee 1;

⊙ 10am-5pm Mon-Fri, to 3pm Sat & Sun mid-May–mid-Sep, 10am-5pm Mon-Fri rest of year)

❶ Getting There & Away

Public transport is limited, with only one bus per day to and from Tartu (one hour).

Tartu

POP 98,000
Tartu lays claim to being Estonia's spiritual capital, with locals talking about a special Tartu *vaim* (spirit), created by the time-stands-still feel of its wooden houses and stately buildings, and by the beauty of its parks and riverfront.

Small and provincial, with the tranquil Emajõgi River flowing through it, Tartu is Estonia's premier university town, with students making up nearly a seventh of the population. This injects a boisterous vitality into the leafy, historic setting and grants it a vibrant nightlife for a city of its size. On long summer nights, those students that haven't abandoned the city for the beach can be found on the hill behind the Town Hall, flirting and drinking.

Tartu was the cradle of Estonia's 19th-century national revival and it escaped Soviet town planning to a greater degree than Tallinn. Its handsome centre is lined with classically designed 18th-century buildings, many of which have been put to innovative uses. Aside from its own attractions – including some interesting galleries and museums – Tartu is a convenient gateway to exploring southern Estonia.

History

By around the 6th century there was an Estonian stronghold in Tartu and in 1030 Yaroslav the Wise of Kyiv is said to have founded a fort here called Yuriev. The Estonians regained control, but in 1224 were defeated by the Knights of the Sword, who placed a castle, cathedral and bishop on what henceforth became known as Toomemägi (Cathedral Hill). The surrounding town became known as Dorpat – its German name – until the end of the 19th century.

Throughout the 16th and 17th centuries Dorpat suffered repeated attacks and changes of ownership as Russia, Sweden and Poland-Lithuania fought for control of the Baltic region. Its most peaceful period was during the Swedish reign, which coincided with the university's founding in 1632 – an

ESTONIA TARTU

Tartu

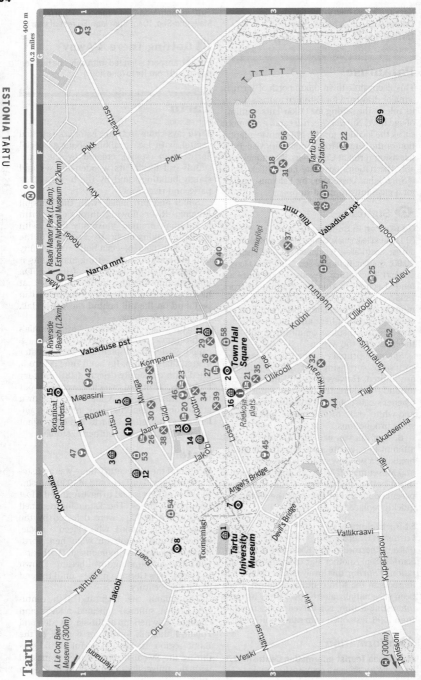

A Le Coq Beer Museum (300m)

Raadi Manor Park (1.6km);
Estonian National Museum (2.2km)

Riverside Beach (1.2km)

Narva mnt

Vabaduse pst

Botanical Gardens

Town Hall Square

Tartu University Museum

Angel's Bridge

Devil's Bridge

Toomemägi

Vallikraavi

Tartu Bus Station

Rila mnt

Vabaduse pst

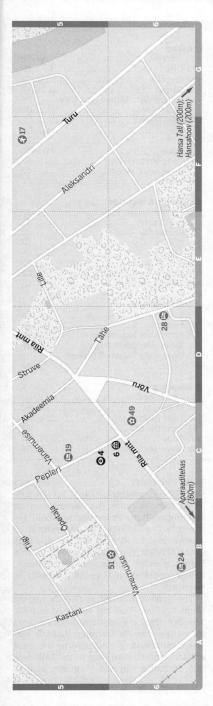

event that was to have an enormous impact on the city's future. This peace ended in 1704, during the Great Northern War, when Peter the Great took Tartu for Russia. In 1708 his forces wrecked the town and most of its population was deported to Russia.

In the mid-1800s Tartu became the focus of the Estonian national revival. The first Estonian Song Festival was held here in 1869, and the first Estonian-language newspaper was launched here – both important steps in the national awakening.

The peace treaty that granted independence to Estonia (for the first time in its history) was signed in Tartu between Soviet Russia and Estonia on 2 February 1920. Tartu was severely damaged in 1941 when Soviet forces retreated, blowing up the grand 1784 Kivisild stone bridge over the river, and again in 1944 when they retook it from the Nazis. Both occupying forces committed many atrocities. A monument now stands on the Valga road where the Nazis massacred 12,000 people at Lemmatsi.

◉ Sights

Tartu, as the major repository of Estonia's cultural heritage, has museums devoted to an eclectic array of subjects. The tourist office will be able to help you out if your interests extend to, say, farm machinery.

◉ Old Town

★ Town Hall Square   SQUARE

(Raekoja plats) Tartu's main square is lined with grand buildings and echoes with the chink of glasses and plates in summer. The centrepiece is the Town Hall itself, fronted by a statue of students kissing under a spouting umbrella. On the south side of the square, look out for the communist hammer-and-sickle relief that still remains on the facade of number 5.

Town Hall   HISTORIC BUILDING

(Raekoja plats) Built between 1782 and 1789, this graceful building was designed by German architect JHB Walter, who modelled it on a typical Dutch town hall. It's topped by a tower and weather vane, and a clock was added to encourage students to be punctual for classes. As well as the council offices, it contains the tourist information centre and a pharmacy.

Tartu Art Museum   GALLERY

(Tartu Kunstimuuseum; www.tartmus.ee; Raekoja plats 18; adult/student €4/3; ⊙ 11am-6pm Wed

Tartu

& Fri-Sun, to 9pm Thu) If you're leaving one of the plaza's pubs and you're not sure whether you're seeing straight, don't use this building as your guide. Foundations laid partially over an old town wall have given a pronounced lean to this, the former home of Colonel Barclay de Tolly (1761–1818) – an exiled Scot who distinguished himself in the Russian army. It now contains an engrossing gallery spread over three levels, the bottom of which is given over to temporary exhibitions.

Paintings comprise the bulk of the permanent collection, along with some sculpture, photography, video art and mixed media work, including some truly wonderful 20th-century portraiture.

Tartu University   UNIVERSITY
(Tartu Ülikool; www.ut.ee; Ülikooli 18) Fronted by six Doric columns, the impressive main building of Tartu University was built between 1803 and 1809. The university itself was founded in 1632 by the Swedish king Gustaf II Adolf (Gustavus Adolphus) to train Lutheran clergy and government officials. It was modelled on Uppsala University in Sweden.

The university closed in 1710 during the Great Northern War but reopened in 1802, later becoming one of the Russian Empire's foremost centres of learning. Its early emphasis on science is evidenced by the great scholars who studied here in the 19th century, including physical chemistry pioneer and Nobel prize winner for chemistry, Wilhelm Ostwald; physicist Heinrich Lenz; and the founder of embryology, natural scientist Karl Ernst von Baer.

Tartu University Art Museum   MUSEUM
(Tartu Ülikooli kunstimuuseum; www.kunstimuuseum.ut.ee; Ülikooli 18; adult/child €3/2; ☺10am-6pm Mon-Sat May-Sep, 11am-5pm Mon-Fri Oct-Apr) Within the main university building, this collection comprises mainly plaster casts of ancient Greek sculptures made in the 1860s and 1870s, along with an Egyptian mummy. The rest of the collection was evacuated to Russia in 1915 and has never returned. Admission includes entry to the graffiti-covered attic lock-up, where students were held in solitary confinement for various infractions.

In the 19th century, failing to return a library book on time could net you two days in the lock-up; insulting a lady, four days; insulting a (more sensitive?) porter, five days; duelling, up to three weeks.

St John's Lutheran Church   CHURCH
(Jaani kirik; www.jaanikirik.ee; Jaani 5; steeple adult/child €2/1.50; ☺10am-7pm Mon-Sat Jun-Aug, 10am-6pm Tue-Sat Sep-May) Dating to at least 1323, this imposing red-brick church is unique for the rare terracotta sculptures placed in niches around its exterior and interior (look up). It lay in ruins and was left derelict following a Soviet bombing raid in 1944 and wasn't fully restored until 2005. Climb the 135 steps of the 30m steeple for a bird's-eye view of Tartu.

Tartu Toy Museum   MUSEUM
(Tartu mänguasjamuuseum; www.mm.ee; Lutsu 8; adult/child €5/4; ☺11am-6pm Wed-Sun) A big hit with the under-eight crowd (and you won't see too many adults anxious to leave), this is a great place to while away a few rainy hours. Set in a late-18th-century building, this excellent museum showcases dolls, model trains, rocking horses, toy soldiers and tons of other desirables. It's all geared to be nicely interactive, with exhibits in pull-out drawers and a kids' playroom.

The adjacent courtyard house is home to characters and props from Estonian animated films and TV shows. Also included in the admission price is the small museum in the basement of the Theatre House, two doors down, showcasing theatre puppets.

Citizen's Home Museum   MUSEUM
(Linnakodaniku muuseum; http://linnamuuseum.tartu.ee; Jaani 16; adult/child €2/1; ☺11am-5pm

Wed-Sat, 11am-3pm Sun Apr-Oct, 10am-3pm Wed-Sun Nov-Mar) This old wooden house is furnished to show how a burgher from the 1830s lived. There are only a few rooms but it's still quite interesting.

**Tartu University
Botanical Gardens**   GARDENS
(Tartu Ülikooli botaanikaaed; ☎737 6180; www.botaanikaaed.ut.ee; Lai 38; greenhouse adult/child €3/2; ☺gardens 7am-7pm, to 9pm Jun-Aug, greenhouses 10am-5pm) **FREE** Founded in 1803, these gardens nurture 6500 species of plants including a large collection of palms in the greenhouse. In summer it's always full of local families wandering the paths and strolling around the ornamental lake.

Estonian Sports Museum   MUSEUM
(Eesti Spordimuuseum; www.spordimuuseum.ee; Rüütli 15; adult €2.30/1.60; ☺11am-6pm Wed-Sun) Chronicling more than just Estonian Olympic excellence (although the glittering medal display serves that purpose admirably), this offbeat museum has a real sense of fun. While the photos of puffed-up early-20th-century bodybuilders in posing pouches suggest that they took themselves tremendously seriously, nobody's suggesting that you should. If you're feeling inspired, take a spin on the exercise bikes or test your strength on the interactive tug-of-war.

Postal Museum   MUSEUM
(Postimuuseum; www.erm.ee; Rüütli 15; admission €1.20; ☺11am-6pm Wed-Sun) Sharing a building with the Sports Museum, the Postal Museum is rather more staid but still quietly fascinating. The stamp displays lay bare Estonia's recent history, with the swastika appearing in 1941, giving way to the hammer and sickle in 1945.

◉ Toomemägi

Rising to the west of the Town Hall, Toomemägi (Cathedral Hill) is the original reason for Tartu's existence, functioning on and off as a stronghold from around the 5th or 6th century. It's now a tranquil park, with walking paths meandering through the trees and a pretty-as-a-picture rotunda which serves as a summertime cafe.

The approach from Town Hall Sq is along Lossi, which passes beneath the Angel's Bridge (Inglisild), which was built between 1836 and 1838 – follow local superstition and hold your breath and make a wish as you cross it for the first time. A bit further up the hill is Devil's Bridge (Kuradisild).

★ Tartu University Museum   MUSEUM
(Tartu Ülikool muuseum; www.muuseum.ut.ee; Lossi 25; adult/child €4/3; ⊙10am-6pm Tue-Sun May-Sep, 11am-5pm Wed-Sun Oct-Apr) Atop Toomemägi are the ruins of a Gothic cathedral, originally built by German knights in the 13th century. It was substantially rebuilt in the 15th century, despoiled during the Reformation in 1525, used as a barn for a period, and partly rebuilt between 1804 and 1809 to house the university library, which is now a museum. Inside there are a range of interesting exhibits chronicling student life.

Start by taking the historic 1920s lift to the top and working your way down. Morgenstern Hall retains the appearance of the historic library and is lined with statues of the Ancient Greek muses. Kids will love the Cabinet of the Crazy Scientist, where they take part in some hand's on science themselves. Other highlights include the beautiful White Hall and the Treasury, which houses eclectic items such as the death mask of Russian poet Aleksandr Pushkin, a 1504 Dürer print, a human hand once used for anatomy lessons and a set of elaborate cheat-sheet scrolls extracted from students in the 1980s.

From May to September the museum ticket also includes entrance to the viewing platform on top of the cathedral tower.

Sacrificial Stone   SHRINE
In pagan times, offerings used to be left in the cup-shaped depressions carved into this stone and the hundreds like it that are scattered throughout the country. Actually, offerings are still left; you'll often find coins or flowers, even on those stones that have made their way into museums, and on this particular stone, students leave burnt offerings of their lecture notes.

Nearby is a natural parapet known as the Kissing Hill, where Russian newlyweds affix padlocks with their names scratched into them.

◉ City Centre

Science Centre AHHAA   MUSEUM
(Teaduskeskus AHHAA; www.ahhaa.ee; Sadama 1; adult/child €12/9, planetarium €4, flight simulator €1, 4D theatre €2; ⊙10am-7pm) Head under the dome for a whizz-bang series of interactive exhibits which are liable to bring out the mad scientist in kids and adults alike. Allow at least a couple of hours for button pushing, water squirting and knob twiddling. And you just haven't lived until you've set a tray of magnetised iron filings 'dancing' to Bronski Beat's *Smalltown Boy*. Upstairs there's a nightmarish collection of pickled organs and deformed fetuses courtesy of the university's medical faculty.

KGB Cells Museum   MUSEUM
(KGB kongide muuseum; http://linnamuuseum. tartu.ee; Riia mnt 15b, enter from Pepleri; adult/

TARTU'S SCULPTURES

Hidden in parks, proudly displayed in squares and skulking in lanes, Tartu's sculptures are often surprising and sometimes plain bizarre. Here are some to look out for:

Everybody's favourite The snogging students in front of the Town Hall.

Most whimsical Oscar Wilde and Estonian writer Eduard Vilde, sharing both a surname and a park bench in front of Vallikraavi 4. Of course, they never actually met.

Creepiest The man-sized naked baby holding hands with the baby-sized naked man on Küüni. It's actually a self-portrait of the artist with his son.

Most clever The fountain at the corner of Vanemuise and Struve which at first glance looks like a tangle of steel tubes with water shooting out the back, but turns into a caricature of famed professor Yuri Lotman (1922–93) when viewed from certain angles.

Most likely to put you off your chops The pig standing on a barrel outside the market, with one side already marked up by the butcher. This little piggy went to market; it didn't end well.

Best 1970s flashback *Women From The Countryside* in front of the art gallery. The younger woman's flared jeans and obvious lack of a bra would date it to 1978, even if there wasn't a plaque to that effect.

child €4/2; ⊙11am-4pm Tue-Sat) What do you do when a formerly nationalised building is returned to you with cells in the basement and a fearsome reputation? In this particular case, the family donated the basement to the Tartu City Museum, which created this sombre and highly worthwhile exhibition. Chilling in parts, the displays give a fascinating rundown on deportations, life in the gulags, the Estonian resistance movement and what went on in these former KGB headquarters, known as the 'Grey House'.

Cornflower Monument   MEMORIAL
In 1990 this metallic monument was erected near the KGB headquarters in memory of the victims of Soviet repression; the blue cornflower is Estonia's national flower. Sadly, it's badly in need of maintenance.

◉ Karlova & Vaksali

Aparaaditehas   AREA
(www.aparaaditehas.ee; Kastani 42) It was still part abandoned building, part construction site when we last visited, but this old factory complex could be well worth checking out. Plans are afoot to turn it into a hip dining, drinking, shopping and cultural hub akin to the extremely popular Telliskivi Creative City (p61) development in Tallinn.

◉ Tähtvere

A Le Coq Beer Museum   MUSEUM
(☑744 9726; www.alecoq.ee; Laulupeo 15; adult/child €5/2; ⊙tours 2pm Thu, 10am, noon & 2pm Sat) Located at the famous brewery, this museum briefly covers the history of beer making but tours focus mainly on the machinery and brewing techniques, with free samples at the end. A Le Coq has churned out its trademark beverage since 1879.

◉ Raadi-Kruusamäe

★ Estonian National Museum   MUSEUM
(Eesti rahva muuseum; www.erm.ee; Narva mnt 177) When we last visited, the immense, low-slung, architectural showcase built to house the Estonian National Museum had yet to open its doors. Built on a Soviet airstrip on the grounds of Raadi Manor (the museum's original prewar home), the new building has a floor space of nearly 34,000 sq metres and will contain a cafe, restaurant and displays on august themes such as 'Estonian Dialogues' and 'Echo of the Urals'. Check the website for details.

Raadi Manor Park   PARK
(Raadi Mõisapark; www.erm.ee; Narva mnt 177; ⊙7am-10pm) FREE On the main road heading north out of town stands the sad remains of Raadi Manor. It was once a beautiful baroque-style building but WWII bombing has left only a red-brick shell. In the 19th century the manor grounds were considered to be one of Estonia's most beautiful parks and, while they're a shadow of their former selves, locals still come to stroll around and swim in the lake.

🏃 Activities

Pegasus   CRUISE
(☑733 7182; www.dorpat.ee; adult/child €8/6; ⊙noon & 2pm Tue-Sun, plus 4pm Sat) Ninety-minute riverboat cruises, departing from the quay by Hotel Dorpat.

Riverside Beaches   BEACH
If the sun's beating down and you can't make it to Pärnu there are a pair of pleasant beaches on opposite banks of the Emajõgi, about a 1km walk northwest of the Kroonuaia bridge.

Aura Veekeskus   WATER PARK
(www.aurakeskus.ee; Turu 10; pool €3-6, water park €6-8; ⊙10am-10pm, closed Jul) A 50m indoor pool and family-friendly water park with all the trimmings.

✦✦ Festivals & Events

Tartu regularly dons its shiniest party gear and lets its hair down; check out www.kultuuriaken.tartu.ee for more.

Tartu Student Days   CARNIVAL
(Tartu Tudengipäevad; www.studentdays.ee) Catch a glimpse of modern-day student misdeeds at the end of April, when they take to the streets to celebrate term's end (and the dawn of spring) in every way imaginable. A second, smaller version occurs in mid-October.

Hanseatic Days   CARNIVAL
(Hansapäevad; www.hansapaevad.ee) Tartu's medieval membership of the Hanseatic League is celebrated over a weekend in mid-July, with craft workshops, markets, family-friendly performances and a street parade.

tARTuFF   FILM
(www.tartuff.ee) A big outdoor cinema takes over Town Hall Sq for a week in August. Screenings (with art-house leanings) are

free, plus there are docos, poetry readings and concerts.

Christmas City Tartu CHRISTMAS
(Jõululinn Tartu; www.joululinntartu.ee) Choirs sing as Advent candles are lit in a ceremony in Town Hall Sq at 4pm on each of the four Sundays preceding Christmas. It's a chance to see the square at its most magical: decorated with fairy lights and Christmas trees, and sprinkled with snow.

🛏 Sleeping

🏠 Old Town

Terviseks HOSTEL €
(☑ 565 5382; www.terviseksbbb.com; top fl, Raekoja plats 10; dm €15-17, s/d €22/44; @ �?) Occupying a historic building in a perfect main-square location, this excellent 'backpacker's bed and breakfast' offers dorms (maximum four beds, no bunks), private rooms, a full kitchen and lots of switched-on info about the happening places in town. It's like staying in your rich mate's cool European pad. Cheers (*terviseks!*) to that.

★Domus Dorpatensis APARTMENTS €€
(☑ 733 1345; www.dorpatensis.ee; Raekoja plats 1; s €40-69, d €55-84; �?) Run by an academic foundation, this block of 10 apartments offers an unbeatable location and wonderful value for money. The units range in size but all have writing desks (it's run by scholars, after all) and almost all have kitchenettes. The staff are particularly helpful – dispensing parking advice and directing guests to the communal laundry. The entrance is on Ülikooli.

Tampere Maja GUESTHOUSE €€
(☑ 738 6300; www.tamperemaja.ee; Jaani 4; s/d/tr/q from €48/79/99/132; P ✳ @ �?) With strong links to the Finnish city of Tampere (Tartu's sister city), this cosy guesthouse features six warm, light-filled guest rooms in a range of sizes. Breakfast is included and each room has access to cooking facilities. And it wouldn't be Finnish if it didn't offer an authentic sauna (one to four people €13; open to nonguests).

Wilde Guest Apartments APARTMENTS €€
(☑ 511 3876; www.wildeapartments.ee; Vallikraavi 4; apt €60-90; �?) The people behind the Eduard Vilde Restaurant also have five beautiful self-contained apartments for rent.

Four of them are near the restaurant, either on Vallikraavi or Ülikooli street, with the last one in the striking highrise tower by the river. All of them have a separate bedroom and a sofa bed in the lounge.

★Antonius Hotel HOTEL €€€
(☑ 737 0377; www.hotelantonius.ee; Ülikooli 15; s/d/ste from €88/108/196; ✳ �?) Sitting plumb opposite the main university building, this first-rate 18-room boutique hotel is loaded with antiques and period features. Breakfast is served in the 18th-century vaulted cellar, which in the evening morphs into a top-notch restaurant.

London Hotell HOTEL €€€
(☑ 730 5555; www.londonhotel.ee; Rüütli 9; s/d from €79/99; P @ ☔) After the glitzy lobby, with its brass trim and water feature, the decor of the rooms at this upmarket hotel is quite lacklustre. Still, you can't fault the prime location.

🏠 City Centre

Academus Hostel HOSTEL €
(☑ 5306 6620; www.academus.ee; Pepleri 14; s/tw/f €30/40/50; P ☔) The university runs three hostels but only this one is open to nonstudents, year-round. Rooms are clean, bright and reasonably large, and have private kitchenettes and bathrooms. Despite being a tad institutional, they're excellent value for money. Advance reservations are a must.

Hotel Tartu HOTEL €€
(☑ 731 4300; www.tartuhotell.ee; Soola 3; s/d €49/68, without bathroom €33/44; P ✳ @ ☔) In a handy position across from the bus station and Tasku shopping centre, this hotel offers rooms from the Ikea school of decoration – simple but clean and contemporary. As well as the regular rooms there's a small hostel wing, offering cheaper rooms with shared bathrooms. A sauna's available for hire (per hour €25).

Pallas Hotell HOTEL €€
(☑ 730 1200; www.pallas.ee; Riia mnt 4; s/d €60/80; P @ ☔) The Pallas occupies the site of a former art college and has attempted to channel some of that creativity into its decor. The rooms are bright and airy; request a city-facing room on the 3rd floor, for space, views and artworks. British-themed Big Ben Pub juts out the side of the building in its own glass mushroom.

Karlova & Vaksali

Looming
HOSTEL €

(☑ 5699 4398; www.loominghostel.ee; Kastani 38; dm €15-17, s/d €32/39; @ 🛈) 🥾 Run by urban greenies with a commitment to recycled materials and sustainable practices, Looming ('creation' in Estonian) offers smart bunk-free dorms and private rooms in a converted art nouveau factory building. There's an appealing roof terrace and bikes for rent (per day €10).

Villa Margaretha
BOUTIQUE HOTEL €€

(☑ 731 1820; www.margaretha.ee; Tähe 11/13; s/d/ste from €50/60/150; P 🛈) Like something out of a fairy tale, this wooden art nouveau house has a sweet wee turret and romantic rooms decked out with sleigh beds and artfully draped fabrics. The cheaper rooms in the modern extension at the rear are bland in comparison. It's a little away from the action but still within walking distance of Old Town.

✗ Eating

✗ Old Town

Werner
CAFE €

(www.werner.ee; Ülikooli 11; baked items €2-3; ⊙ 7.30am-11pm Mon-Thu, 8am-1am Fri & Sat, 9am-9pm Sun) Upstairs there's a proper restaurant serving pasta and meaty mains, but we prefer the buzzy cafe downstairs. The counter positively groans under a hefty array of quiches and tempting cakes, plus there's a sweet little courtyard at the back.

Noir
EUROPEAN €

(☑ 744 0055; www.cafenoir.ee; Ülikooli 7; mains €7-8; ⊙ 11am-11pm Mon-Sat, to 6pm Sun; 🌐) Definitely a place to impress a date, this sexy, black-walled restaurant-cum-*vinothèque* is a fine place for wining, dining and reclining. It's tucked away in a courtyard off Ülikooli, with outdoor tables and a well-priced menu of salads and pasta.

Crepp
CREPERIE €

(www.crepp.ee; Rüütli 16; mains €4.50-8.50; ⊙ 11am-11pm) Locals love this place. Its warm, stylish decor belies its bargain-priced crêpes (of the sweet or savoury persuasion, with great combos such as cherry-choc and almonds). It serves tasty salads too.

Cafe Truffe
MODERN EUROPEAN €€

(☑ 742 8840; www.truffe.ee; Raekoja plats 16; mains €7.50-15; ⊙ 11am-11pm Sun-Thu, to 1am Fri & Sat) Truffe calls itself a cafe, although it feels more like an upmarket bar and the food is absolutely restaurant quality. One thing's for certain, it's the best eatery on Town Hall Sq and one of Tartu's finest. In summer, grab a seat on the large terrace and tuck into a steak with truffle sauce or a delicately smoked duck breast.

Polpo
MODERN EUROPEAN €€

(☑ 730 5566; www.polpo.ee; Rüütli 9; mains €9.50-17; ⊙ 11am-11pm Mon-Sat; 🛈) Despite being slightly below street level, Polpo's vaulted space beneath the London Hotell is surprisingly bright and modern. And despite the name, the menu isn't particularly Italian. Expect hearty mains such as beef cheek, roast lamb and smoked pork alongside some simple but creative pasta and risotto dishes.

La Dolce Vita
ITALIAN €€

(☑ 740 7545; www.ladolcevita.ee; Kompanii 10; mains €7-15; ⊙ 11.30am-11pm) Thin-crust pizzas come straight from the wood-burning oven at this cheerful, family-friendly pizzeria. It's the real deal, with a lengthy menu of bruschetta, pizza, pasta, grills etc and classic casual decor (checked tablecloths, Fellini posters – tick).

Pierre
CAFE €€

(☑ 730 4680; www.pierre.ee; Raekoja plats 12; mains €6.50-18; ⊙ 8am-11pm Mon-Thu, to 1am Fri, 10am-1am Sat, to 10pm Sun) Tallinn's favourite chocmeister has set up on Tartu's main square, offering a refined atmosphere, old-world decor and all-important truffles. This is a prime spot for coffee and a sugar fix at any time of day, and there's a full bistro-style menu too.

Eduard Vilde
Restaurant & Cafe
MODERN EUROPEAN €€

(☑ 734 3400; www.vilde.ee; Vallikraavi 4; mains €8-19; ⊙ 11.30am-9pm Mon-Wed, to 11pm Thu, noon-1am Fri & Sat, to 5pm Sun) Choose healthy fare in the cafe downstairs or, better still, head up to the restaurant for a pasta, elk cutlet or Caesar salad – or just for a tipple on the very pleasant terrace.

University Cafe
CAFE €€

(Ülikooli Kohvik; ☑ 737 5405; www.kohvik.ut.ee; Ülikooli 20; mains €7-16; ⊙ 11.30am-9pm Mon-Wed, to midnight Thu-Sat) This venerable institution inhabits a labyrinth of elegantly decorated rooms. It's simultaneously grand and cosy, with serves to sate the most ravenous of scholars. In the evening the Tartu Jazz Club takes over the bottom floor.

Antonius EUROPEAN €€€
(☑737 0377; www.hotelantonius.ee; Ülikooli 15; mains €18-24; ⏰6-11pm) Tartu's most upmarket restaurant is within the romantic, candlelit nooks and crannies of the Antonius Hotel's vaulted cellar, which predates the 19th-century building above it by several centuries. Expect a concise menu of meaty dishes, prepared using French techniques from the finest Estonian produce.

Meat Market STEAKHOUSE €€€
(☑653 3455; www.meatmarket.ee; Küütri 3; mains €15-22; ⏰noon-11pm Mon-Thu, to 1am Fri & Sat, to 9pm Sun) The name says it all, with dishes ranging from elk carpaccio to nose-to-tail Livonian beef, to smoky Azeri-style shashlik (skewered meat, delivered flaming to the table). The vegie accompaniments are excellent too. It's open late for cocktails.

✖ City Centre

Dorpat BUFFET €
(www.dorpat.ee; Soola 6; buffet €4-6.50; ⏰buffet noon-2pm Mon-Fri) The elegant restaurant at the Dorpat also has a reputable a la carte menu, but it's the weekday lunch buffet that we're particularly keen on. For €4 you'll get a bottomless bowl of your choice of soup and salad, while for €6.50 you get the full bain-marie as well.

Tartu Market Hall MARKET €
(Tartu Turuhoone; www.tartuturg.ee; Vabaduse pst 1; ⏰7.30am-5pm Mon-Fri, to 3pm Sat & Sun) Tartu's riverside market hall is mainly devoted to meat, although you will find stalls selling fruit and vegetables, cheese and baked goods. The fishmongers have a stinky section all to themselves.

✖ Karlova & Vaksali

Hansa Tall ESTONIAN €€
(www.hansahotell.ee; Aleksandri 46; mains €9.50-16; ⏰7am-10pm Sun-Thu, 8am-midnight Fri & Sat; 📶) If you want to look at a menu and really know you're in Estonia, head to this super-rustic, barnlike tavern southeast of the centre. You need not try the smoked pig's ears or blood sausage to enjoy the diverse, hearty menu, live music and even livelier locals.

 Drinking & Nightlife

In summer the bars are quiet, unless they've got outside seating. You'll find most of the nonholidaying students on the designated drinkers' hill behind the Town Hall. During term, Wednesday is the traditional scholars' party night.

Genialistide Klubi BAR, CLUB
(www.genklubi.ee; Magasini 5; ⏰noon-3am Mon-Sat) The Genialists' Club is an all-purpose, grungy 'subcultural establishment' that's simultaneously a bar, a cafe, an alternative nightclub, a live-music venue, a cinema, a specialist Estonian CD store and, just quietly, the hippest place in Tartu.

Naiiv BAR
(www.naiiv.ee; Vallikraavi 6; ⏰6pm-1am Tue-Thu, to 3am Fri & Sat) An imperious white cat holds court at this very cool craft beer and cocktail bar. The selection is extensive, so ask the clued up staff for suggestions on good local brews, then find a comfy sofa to sink into or head out to the small rear courtyard.

Püssirohukelder PUB
(www.pyss.ee; Lossi 28; mains €7-17; ⏰noon-2am Mon-Sat, to midnight Sun) Set in a cavernous 18th-century gunpowder cellar built into the Toomemägi hillside, this boisterous pub serves beer-accompanying snacks and meaty meals under a soaring 10m-high vaulted ceiling. There's regular live music and a large beer garden out front.

Vein ja Vine WINE BAR
(www.veinjavine.ee; Rüütli 8; ⏰5pm-1am Tue-Sat) Serving wine and excellent deli snacks, this little bar attracts a slightly older crowd (postgraduates, perhaps) but it still gets jammed and overflows onto the street in summer.

Zavood PUB
(www.zavood.ee; Lai 30; ⏰7pm-5am) This battered cellar bar attracts an alternative, down-to-earth crowd with its inexpensive drinks and lack of attitude. Student bands sometimes play here.

Club Tallinn CLUB
(www.facebook.com/ClubTallinn; Narva mnt 27; admission €5-7; ⏰11pm-3am Wed-Sat) Tartu's best dance club is a multifloored extravaganza with many nooks and crannies. Some top-notch DJs spin here, drawing a fashionable, up-for-it crowd.

Illusion   CLUB
(www.illusion.ee; Raatuse 97; admission €3-6; ⊙11pm-4am Wed, Fri & Sat) Occupying a grand Stalin-era movie theatre north of the river, Illusion has a lavish interior and draws a blinged-up crowd. It shuts up shop during the university summer holidays.

Atlantis   CLUB
(www.atlantis.ee; Narva mnt 2; admission €3-7; ⊙11pm-4am Tue-Sat) Overlooking the Emajõgi River, Atlantis is a popular, mainstream place that's pretty short on style. The riverside setting, however, is nice if you're in the mood for a cheesy good time.

☆ Entertainment

For information on classical performances, see www.concert.ee.

Vanemuine Theatre & Concert Hall THEATRE
(☑744 0165; www.vanemuine.ee; Vanemuise 6) Named after the ancient Estonian song god, this venue hosts an array of theatrical and musical performances. It also puts on shows at its small stage (Vanemuise 45) and Sadamateater (Harbour Theatre; Soola 5b). The latter has a prime location on the banks of the Emajõgi and tends to stage the most modern, alternative productions.

Hansahoov   LIVE MUSIC
(☑737 1802; www.hansahoov.ee; Aleksandri 46) Concerts and theatre productions are regularly staged in the large rustic courtyard of the Hansa Tall tavern.

Cinamon   CINEMA
(www.cinamon.ee; Turu 2) For Hollywood blockbusters, head to the multiplex above the Tasku shopping centre.

Ekraan   CINEMA
(www.forumcinemas.ee; Riia 14) This smaller cinema complex screens a mix of popular features and more art-house offerings.

🛍 Shopping

Antoniuse Gild   HANDICRAFTS
(Lutsu 5; ⊙noon-6pm Tue-Fri) Here you'll find 16 artisans' studios set around St Anthony's Courtyard, where local craftspeople make ceramics, stained glass, jewellery, textiles, woodcarvings, dolls etc. It's well worth a visit.

Tartu Kaubamaja   SHOPPING CENTRE
(www.kaubamaja.ee; Riia 1; ⊙9am-9pm Mon-Sat, 10am-7pm Sun) Tartu's biggest and flashest shopping centre has as its anchor tenant a branch of Tallinn's Kaubamaja department store. Expect plenty of top fashion and much more.

Tasku   SHOPPING CENTRE
(www.tasku.ee; Turu 2; ⊙10am-9pm Mon-Sat, to 6pm Sun) A big, glitzy mall with a Rimi supermarket on the bottom floor, a cinema multiplex on the top and a branch of the excellent Rahva Raamat bookstore chain in between.

Nukumaja   TOYS
(www.facebook.com/Nukumaja; Lai 1a; ⊙11am-5pm Thu & Fri, to 3pm Sat) On the side of Toomägi, next to Tartu's version of the Addams Family house, this sweet, small store sells handmade dolls and toys for the young and young-at-heart.

Tartu Open Market   MARKET
(Tartu avaturg; www.tartuturg.ee; Soola 10; ⊙7am-5pm, to 3pm Sat & Sun) Near the bus station, locals come here seeking fresh flowers, cheap clothes, nonbranded sunglasses and other bargains.

University Bookshop   BOOKS
(Ülikooli raamatupood; Raekoja plats 11; ⊙10am-6pm Mon-Fri) Stocks a great selection of

---

SOUTHERN ESTONIAN LANGUAGES

Visitors may notice a quite different, choppier-sounding language spoken in the southeastern corner of Estonia. Until the end of the 19th century, the northern and southern Estonian languages flourished quite independently of each other. Then, in the interests of nationalism, a one-country, one-language policy was adopted, and the dominant northern Estonian became the country's main language.

Within the southern Estonian strand there are several distinct language groupings, the largest by far of which is Võro, spoken by around 75,000 native speakers, most of whom live in Võrumaa (Võru County). It's very closely related to Seto, which has an additional 12,600 speakers. Other variants include the Mulgi and Tartu dialects, with 9700 and 4100 speakers respectively.

To learn more about the unique Võro language, contact the **Võro Institute** (www.wi.ee).

books, along with university T-shirts, ties, scarves and mugs.

❶ Information

Raekoja Apteek (☑ 742 3560; www.apotheka. ee; Raekoja plats 1a; ⊙ 24hr) Twenty-four-hour pharmacy within the town hall.

Tartu Tourist Information Centre (☑ 744 2111; www.visittartu.com; Town Hall, Raekoja plats; ⊙ 9am-6pm mid-May–mid-Sep, 9am-5pm Mon-Fri, 10am-2pm Sat & Sun rest of year) Stocks local maps and brochures, books accommodation and tour guides, and has free internet access.

❶ Getting There & Away

AIR

Tartu Airport (TAY; ☑ 605 8888; www.tartu-airport.ee; Lennu tn 44, Reola küla) is 9km south of the city centre but the only scheduled flights are daily Finnair services to and from Helsinki (p178).

BUS

Regional and international (p178) buses depart from **Tartu Bus Station** (Tartu Autobussijaam; ☑ 12550; Turu 2, enter from Soola; ⊙ 6am-9pm), which is attached to the Tasku shopping centre.

Major domestic routes:

Kuressaare (€18, 5½ hours, two daily)

Otepää (€2 to €3.50, one hour, 10 daily)

Pärnu (€9.60 to €12, 2¾ hours, 12 daily)

Tallinn (€7 to €12, 2½ hours, at least every half-hour)

Viljandi (€5.80, 1¼ hours, 14 daily)

CAR & MOTORCYCLE

The tourist office keeps up-to-date lists of car-hire agencies with prices.

Avis (☑ 744 0360; www.avis.ee; Tartu Airport)

Budget (☑ 605 8600; www.budget.ee; Tartu Airport)

City Car (☑ 523 9669; www.citycar.ee; Tartu Bus Station)

Europcar (☑ 605 8031; www.europcar.ee; Tartu Airport)

Hertz (☑ 506 9065; www.hertz.ee; Tartu Bus Station)

TRAIN

Tartu's beautifully restored wooden **train station** (☑ 673 7400; www.elron.ee; Vaksali 6), built in 1877, is 1.5km southwest of Old Town at the end of Kuperjanovi street. Four express (2½-hour) and four regular (two-hour) services head to Tallinn daily (both €11), and there are also three trains a day to Sangaste (€3.70, one hour) and Valga (€4.40, 70 minutes).

❶ Getting Around

TO/FROM THE AIRPORT

Tartaline (☑ 505 4342; www.tartaline.ee; tickets €5) runs an airport shuttle, departing the terminal 10 minutes after each flight and from outside Tartu Kaubamaja 80 minutes before every flight. Hotel pick-ups can be prebooked in advance. Taxis cost around €10.

BICYCLE

Bikes can be rented from **Jalgratas** (☑ 742 1731; www.kauplusjalgratas.ee; Laulupeo 19; per day €14; ⊙ 10am-6pm Mon-Fri, 10am-3pm Sat) or from Looming hostel.

BUS

Tartu is easily explored on foot but there is also a local bus service. You can buy a single-use ticket from any kiosk (€0.83) or from the bus driver (€1), and be sure to validate the ticket once on board or risk a fine. Kiosks also sell day passes (€2.50).

CAR

Parking in the city is metered from 8am to 6pm Monday to Friday and through the weekends in July; buy a day ticket from www.parkimine.ee (€7.50) or pay by the hour at a machine (€0.50 to €1.50). There's a free lot by Atlantis nightclub at Narva mnt 2.

TAXI

Local taxi companies include **Takso Üks** (☑ 742 0000; www.taksod.ee; flagfall €2.80, per kilometre €0.60) and **Tartu Taksopark** (☑ 730 0200; www.gotaksopark.ee; flagfall €2.95, per kilometre €0.69).

Setomaa

In the far southeast of Estonia lies the politically unrecognised area of Setomaa, stretching over the border into Russia. Culturally it's quite distinct from the rest of Estonia, making it an interesting place for a short stop.

Värska, the biggest town in Estonian Setomaa (population 1170), has been inhabited for 5000 years. It's known for its mineral water, sold throughout Estonia, and its healing mud. There's plenty of rural charm here, including a picturesque 1907 stone church and a leafy cemetery surrounding it.

The tiny village of **Podmotsa**, sitting at the tip of a peninsula northeast of Värska, was once closely linked to the Seto village of Kulje, which stands just across the inlet in what is now Russia. Kulje's beautiful Orthodox church, which was once Podmotsa's parish church, is clearly visible from the shoreline – as is the border-guard watchtower. It's a surreal experience to gaze across the water, with Russia surrounding you on three sides, and wonder whether you're being watched. The Podmotsa cemetery contains three ancient stone crosses; in pagan times, a holy grove stood nearby.

A few kilometres north of Värska, on the west side of Värska Bay, are a pair of classic Seto villages. There's not much to see here, but these back roads make for a very pleasant cycle. In **Võpolsova** there's a monument to folk singer Anne Vabarna, who is said to have known 100,000 verses by heart. Võpolsova's homesteads typically consist of a ring of outer buildings around an inner yard. The houses in the neighbouring village of **Tonja** face the lake from which its people get their livelihood.

THE SETO WAY

Setomaa's native people, the Setos, have a culture that incorporates a mix of old Estonian and Russian traditions. Like the Estonians they are of Finno-Ugric origin, but the people became Orthodox, not Lutheran, because this part of the country fell under the subjugation of Novgorod and later Pihkva (Russian: Pskov) and was not controlled by German barons, like the rest of Estonia was.

They never fully assimilated into Russian culture and throughout the centuries retained their language, many features of which are actually closer in structure to old Estonian than the modern Estonian language (Seto is the spelling in the local language; northern Estonians use Setu). The same goes for certain pagan traditions that linger, for instance, leaving food on a relative's grave; this was a common Estonian practice before the German crusaders brought Christianity on the point of a sword.

All of Setomaa was contained within independent Estonia between 1920 and 1940, but the greater part of it is now in Russia. The town of Pechory (Petseri in Estonian), 2km across the border in Russia and regarded as the 'capital' of Setomaa, is famed for its fabulous 15th-century monastery, considered one of the most breathtaking in Russia.

Today the Seto culture looks to be in a slow process of decline. While efforts have been made to teach and preserve the language, and promote customs through organised feasts, the younger generation is being quickly assimilated into the Estonian mainstream. The impenetrable border with Russia that has split their community since 1991 has further crippled it.

There are 12,600 Seto speakers in Estonia, with only around 3000 of these still residing in Estonian Setomaa. As Setos on the Russian side of the border are entitled to Estonian citizenship based on the pre-USSR border, almost all of the Russian Setos have chosen to move to Estonia. It's estimated that less than 200 remain on the Russian side of the border, meaning that many now require a passport to visit the churches and graves of their ancestors.

A cursory look at the Seto landscape illustrates how unique it is in the Estonian context. Notably, their villages are structured like castles, with houses facing each other in clusters, often surrounded by a fence. This is in stark contrast to the typical Estonian village where farmhouses are positioned as far as possible from each other. Here, the Orthodox tradition has fostered a tighter sense of community and sociability.

Aside from the large silver breastplate that is worn on the women's national costume, what sets the Seto apart is their singing style. Setomaa is particularly known for its female folk singers who improvise new words each time they chant their verses. Seto songs, known as *leelo,* are polyphonic and characterised by solo, spoken verses followed by a refrain chanted by a chorus. There is no musical accompaniment and the overall effect evokes great antiquity.

A cult of Peko, a pagan harvest god, has managed to coexist alongside the Orthodox religion, although the Seto tend to refer to him more as a kingly figure. The 8000-line Seto epic *Pekolanõ* tells the tale of this macho god, the rites of whom are known only to men. The epic dates back to 1927 when the Setos' most celebrated folk singer, Anne Vabarna, was told the plot and spontaneously burst into song, barely pausing to draw breath until she had sung the last (8000th) line.

Information on the region can be found at www.setomaa.ee and www.visitsetomaa.ee.

The village of Obinitsa is a pleasant place to stop for lunch. A sculpture of the Seto 'Song Mother' stares solemnly over little Lake Obinitsa, which is dammed at one end and has a swimming platform.

👁 Sights & Activities

Seto Farm Museum   MUSEUM
(Seto talumuuseum; www.setomuuseum.ee; Pikk 56, Värska; adult/child €2/1; ⏺10am-6pm Tue-Sun Jun-Aug, 10am-4pm Tue-Sat Sep-May) Presided over by a wooden carving of the god/king Peko, this museum consists of a 19th-century farmhouse complex, with stables, a granary and the former workshops for metalworking and ceramics. Don't bypass the charming restaurant here or the excellent gift shop – Setomaa's best – selling handmade mittens, socks, hats, dolls, tapestries, books and recordings of traditional Seto music.

Piusa Caves   MINE
(Piusa Koopad; www.piusa.ee; ⏺11am-6pm daily May–mid-Sep, noon-4pm Sat & Sun rest of year) 🚶 Sitting on a band of sandstone nearly 500m thick, Piusa was the site of a major quarry from 1922 to 1966 when it was discovered that the stone contained 99% quartz and was perfect for glass production. The result is a 22km network of cathedral-like hand-hewn caves. Tours into the cave entrance are included in the flash turf-roofed visitor centre's entry fee.

The centre screens films about the history and ecology of the site, allows you to explore the depths via an interactive computer simulation and lets you set in motion a large pendulum which carves graceful arcs in the sand laid on the floor. There's also a cafe and a playground.

The caves form the Baltic region's largest winter holiday resort for bats, including several rare species. About 3500 gather here from October to May, drawn from a 100km radius. Tours only lead you to the opening of the main cavern and not into the caves proper – both for safety reasons and to avoid bat-bothering. The subterranean temperatures remain at a steady four to five degrees even on the coldest or hottest days, so bring warm clothes.

This is also the starting point for the **Piusa Nature Trail**, a tranquil 1.4km loop through pine forests and past WWII trenches. A series of ponds have been created here to provide a home for the rare great crested newt.

If you're heading south from Piusa to Obinitsa, the road to the caves is signposted on the left, close to the railway bridge.

Obinitsa Seto Museum House   MUSEUM
(Obinitsa Seto muuseumitarõ; ☑785 4190; www. obinitsamuuseum.ee; adult/child €2/1; ⏺11am-6pm daily mid-May–mid-Sep, 11am-4pm Mon-Fri rest of year) This one-room museum has folk costumes, tapestries, cookware and some old photos – but no explanations in English. It's a good place to pick up tourist brochures.

Meremäe Hill   VIEWPOINT
In such a flat country, even a modest 204m hill can become a high point. This one has a four-storey wooden viewing tower. It's right next to Setomaa Tourist Farm, a conference and group accommodation complex which is often booked up for weddings.

Vastseliina Episcopal Castle   CASTLE
(Vastseliina piiskopilinnus; www.vastseliina.ee/lin-nus; Vana-Vastseliina; museum & castle adult/child €4/3, castle only €1; ⏺10am-6pm daily Jun-Aug, Wed-Sun Sep) With a pretty setting high on a bluff above the gurgling Piusa River, right on the edge of Setomaa, these evocative ruins maintain a state of picturesque decrepitude. Only a section of wall and three crumbling towers remain standing, all of which are popular nesting sights for oversized storks. A neighbouring 17th-century tavern has been converted into a museum devoted to the castle's history and general medieval concerns (pilgrimages, torture, executions, alchemy, surgery, death etc).

Founded in 1342 by the German Livonian knights on the then border with Russia, Vastseliina (or Neuhausen, as it was then known) was once the strongest castle in Old Livonia. It prospered from its position on the Pihkva–Rīga trade route and as an important pilgrimage site due to the presence of a miraculous white cross which conveniently materialised in the chapel. The castle was finally destroyed after falling to the Russians in 1700, early in the Great Northern War.

Museum admission includes entry to the castle grounds where you can clamber over the fallen masonry and climb one of the towers. You can also visit a small chapel, just outside the castle walls. Opposite the museum a **handicrafts store** shares an old stone building with a small **cafe** which only serves soup, cake and pancakes.

The castle is also the starting point for a 15km **hiking trail** which heads across country to the village of Lindora.

Buses head to Vana-Vastseliina from Võru (€1.70, one hour, four daily) and Obinitsa (€0.80, 20 minutes, three daily).

Festivals & Events

Seto Kingdom Day   CULTURAL

(www.visitsetomaa.ee) According to tradition, the Seto god/king Peko sleeps night and day in his cave of sand near Pechory. So on Seto Kingdom Day – proclaimed on the first Saturday in August – the Seto people gather in a different part of their district each year to appoint an *ülemtsootska* (regent). This colourful event is as fascinating as it is kooky.

Contenders for regent must be fluent in the Seto language, nominated by 10 of their peers and have their case sung for them by a traditional Seto *leelo* choir. They then must stand on a stump while their compatriots line up in front of their favourite.

Just as important as choosing this de facto cultural ambassador is preserving traditional Seto folk industries, so competitions are held to select the best mitten and belt knitters, and bread, beer, wine and cheese makers. There's also a strongman contest.

And so the royal court is completed. Amid the day's celebrations, traditional Seto songs and dances are performed and customary good wishes exchanged. The women are adorned with traditional Seto lace and large silver breastplates and necklaces, said to weigh as much as 3kg each. Later in the day respects are paid to the dead and everyone joins in the parade of the 'Seto army', wielding farm implements and the like.

Feast of the Transfiguration   RELIGIOUS

Every year on 19 August hundreds of Setos come to Obinitsa for a procession from the church to the neighbouring cemetery, which has been a place of burial for over 1800 years (long before the Christian invasion). It ends with a communal graveyard picnic featuring lots of apples and honey, and the leaving of food on graves for the departed souls.

Sleeping & Eating

Hirvemäe Holiday Centre   GUESTHOUSE €€

(Hirvemäe puhkekeskus; 797 6105; www.hirvemae.ee; Silla 6; s/d from €33/57; P) Set on a pretty lake by the bridge leading into Värska, this attractive guesthouse has comfy, wood-floored rooms. Camping is possible too. The extensive grounds encompass a tiny beach, tennis courts, minigolf, a sauna and a playground. The on-site café's menu is short, simple and cheap (soup, salad, meat – you know the drill).

Seto Teahouse   SETO CUISINE €

(Seto tsäimaja; www.setomuuseum.ee; Pikk 56, Värska; mains €4.70-7; 11am-7pm Tue-Sat, to 5pm Sun mid-May–mid-Sep, 11am-5pm Tue-Sat rest of year;) Next door to the Seto Farm Museum, this atmospheric log cabin makes an unbeatable setting for a traditional home-cooked meal. The fare is nothing fancy – cold Seto soup, smoked or stewed pork, herring with sour cream, fried chicken – but it's a real gem nonetheless.

Taarka Tarõ Köögikõnõ   SETO CUISINE €

(www.taarkatare.com; Obinitsa; mains €2-2.50; 10am-8pm May-Sep;) Occupying Obinitsa's Seto community centre, this casual place serves up a range of traditional Seto dishes, such as milky cold soup with tomatoes, gherkins, lettuce and cucumber (it's surprisingly nice). The staff speaks little English.

ⓘ RUSSIAN BORDER

The official crossing point with Russia in this area is at Koidula, immediately north of Pechory (Estonian: Petseri), but Setomaa is littered with abandoned control points, seemingly unguarded wooden fences and creepy dead ends with lonely plastic signs. One road, from Värska to Saatse, even crosses the zigzagging border into Russian territory for 2km; you're not allowed to stop on this stretch.

Be aware that crossing the border at any unofficial point (even if you have a Russian visa) is illegal and could lead to your arrest. It was in this vicinity that an Estonian security officer was controversially arrested by Russian troops in late 2014 and sentenced to 15 years in prison for spying. Estonia maintains that he was kidnapped from the Estonian side of the border, while Russia insists he was arrested on the Russian side. In light of the current tensions, you shouldn't take any risks.

❶ Information

Värska Tourist Office (📞 512 5075; www.
verska.ee; Pikk 12; ⏱11am-5pm Tue-Fri, to 4pm
Sat & Sun mid-May–mid-Sep, 11am-5pm Mon-
Fri rest of year)

❶ Getting There & Away

This is an area that is much more profitably explored by car or bike. There are, however, buses
to Värska from Tartu (€6.60, 1¾ hours, eight
daily) and Tallinn (€14, 4¼ hours, twice weekly).
From Võru there are buses to both Obinitsa (€2,
one hour, four daily) and Meremäe (€2, one hour,
three daily).

Võru

POP 12,500

Set on Lake Tamula, Võru has a mix of wood-
en 19th-century buildings (many of which
are quite rundown) and some painfully ugly
Soviet-era ones. The sandy shoreline is the
town's best feature; it's been spruced up
with a new promenade and attracts plenty
of beachgoers in summer.

Võru was founded in 1784 by special
decree from Catherine the Great, though
archaeological finds here date back several
thousand years. Its most famous resident,
however, was neither a tribesman nor a
tsarina, but the writer Friedrich Reinhold
Kreutzwald (1803–82), who is known as
the father of Estonian literature for his folk
epic *Son of Kalev (Kalevipoeg)*.

◉ Sights

**Dr F R Kreutzwald Memorial
Museum**   MUSEUM
(Dr Fr R Kreutzwaldi memoriaalmuuseum; www.
lauluisa.ee; Kreutzwaldi 31; adult/child €2/1; ⏱10am-
5pm Wed-Sun) Võru's most interesting museum
is set in the house where the great man lived
and worked as a doctor from 1833 to 1877.
Built in 1793, it's one of the oldest houses in
town and there's a lovely garden at the rear.
Displays cover the doctor's life and career focusing, naturally, on his lasting achievement:
the publication of the *Son of Kalev* epic, based
on in-depth research of Estonian folk tales.

One of the outbuildings is devoted to editions of *Son of Kalev* published in a surprising
variety of languages (including Mandarin
Chinese and Hindi), alongside book illustrations and other art inspired by the story.

There's also a monument to the writer in
the park at the bottom of Katariina allee,
near the lake.

Võru County Museum   MUSEUM
(Võrumaa muuseum; Katariina allee 11; adult/child
€1.30/0.70; ⏱11am-5pm Wed-Sun) Housed
in one of the town's ugliest buildings, this
museum has mildly interesting exhibits on
regional history and culture. Captions are in
Estonian and Russian but an English translation booklet is provided. There's also a gallery which displays temporary exhibitions of
mainly local art.

St Catherine's Lutheran Church   CHURCH
(Katariina kirik; Jüri 9) Dedicated to the early
Christian martyr Catherine but named in
honour of Tsarina Catherine the Great, Võru's main Lutheran church was completed
in 1793, only nine years after the town was
founded. The pyramid over the lintel is a
symbol of the Holy Trinity. On the neighbouring square there's a granite monument
to 17 locals who lost their lives in the 1994
Estonia ferry disaster (p162).

St Catherine's Orthodox Church   CHURCH
(Ekaterina kirik; Lembitu 1a; ⏱4-7pm Sat, 7-11am
Sun May-Sep) Like it's Lutheran cousin, Võru's main Orthodox church is dedicated to
St Catherine as a nod to the town's founder
Catherine the Great. Completed in 1804, its
elegant neoclassical design is topped with
distinctly Russian-looking curved steeples.
Inside there's a beautiful iconostasis and
the remains of Nikolai Bežanitski, a priest
killed by the Bolsheviks, who is now hon-
oured as a martyr by the Russian Orthodox
church.

✦ Festivals & Events

Võru Folklore Festival   CULTURAL
(Võru folkloorifestival; www.vorufolkloor.ee) This
mid-July festival is the biggest and brightest
event on the local calendar – five days full of
dancers, singers and musicians decked out
in colourful traditional dress.

🛏 Sleeping & Eating

Kubija   HOTEL €€
(📞 786 6000; www.kubija.ee; Männiku 43a; s/d/
ste €69/79/129; 🅿🛜❄) Tucked away on the
forested shores of a lake on Võru's southern fringes, this older hotel may look a little former-Soviet from the outside but the
rooms have been freshened up, and the
refurbished spa centre is one of the best in
Estonia. Brave locals socialise in the outdoor sauna houses before taking a bracing
dip in the lake.

Ränduri GUESTHOUSES, PUB €€
(☑786 8050; www.randur.ee; Jüri 36; s/d €45/55,
mains €6-9; ☺pub 8am-midnight; Ⓟ☜) Above
this rustic, timber-lined pub there's a pleasant set of 10 rooms, each decorated around
a different motif and colour scheme (Japanese, Egyptian, Russian etc). It's also one of
the better places in Võru for a simple hearty
meal: you want pork or chicken, you've got it.

Spring Cafe CAFE €
(www.springcafe.ee; Petseri 20; mains €6-13;
☺11am-9pm Mon-Sat) If you're hankering for
something a little less pubby, a little more
cafe-bar, this slick lakeside spot should do
more than satisfy. It has a pretty terrace, a
brick-and-timber dining room, and a loun-
gey 2nd floor with big windows. The food's
great too, with barbecued pork and chicken a
speciality, alongside salads and more typical
cafe fare.

☕ Drinking & Entertainment

Õlle 17 PUB
(www.olle17.ee; Jüri 17; ☺11am-midnight Sun-Thu,
to 2am Fri & Sat) This convivial sports pub is a
popular meeting place and drinking hole for
locals, with a pool table, big-screen TV, back
terrace and comprehensive pub-grub menu.

Võru Kannel CINEMA, THEATRE
(www.vorukannel.ee; Liiva 13) The garden behind this cultural centre hosts occasional
concerts and folk festivals, while the centre
itself acts as the town's cinema and theatre.
Check with the tourist office to see if anything's on while you're in town.

🛍 Shopping

Karma ANTIQUES
(www.antiques.ee; L Koidula 14; ☺10.30am-4pm
Tue-Fri, 10am-2pm Sat) One of Estonia's best
antiques stores and a fun place to browse,
even if you already have enough WWII helmets, scythes, sleigh bells, Soviet match-
books and wooden beer steins.

ℹ Information

Tourist Office (☑782 1881; www.visitvoru.ee;
Jüri 12, entrance on L Koidula; ☺10am-5pm
Mon-Sat mid-May–mid-Sep, Mon-Fri rest of
year) A good place to pick up a map and get
information about festivals, attractions and
tourist farms throughout Võru County.

ℹ Getting There & Away

Major services stopping at **Võru Bus Station**
(Võru bussijaam; ☑782 1018; Vilja 2):

Pärnu (€14, 2¾ hours, daily)
Rõuge (€0.75 to €3, 25 minutes, eight daily)
Tallinn (€10 to €14, four hours, 10 daily)
Tartu (€2 to €5.60, 1½ hours, 16 daily)
Valga (€4.50, two hours, twice daily)

Haanja Nature Park

With 169 sq km of thick forests, sparkling
lakes and meandering rivers, this protected
area south of Võru encompasses some of the
most pleasant scenery in the country.

The charming village of Rõuge sits
among gently rolling hills on the edge of the
gently sloping Ööbikuorg (Nightingale Valley), named for the birds that gather here
in the spring for the avian version of the
songfest. Seven small lakes are strung out
along the ancient valley floor, including Estonia's deepest lake, Suurjärv (Great Lake,
38m), in the middle of the village; it's said to
have healing properties. Linnamägi, the hill
above Linnjärv (Town Lake), was an Estonian stronghold during the 8th to 11th centuries. In the 13th century the ailing travelled
from afar to see a healer called Rõugetaja,
who lived here. There's a good view across
the valley from the hill (accessed from behind the Nightingale Valley Centre).

Stock up on maps and information
about the park's multifarious hiking and
cross-country skiing opportunities from the
Nightingale Valley Centre in Rõuge or the
tourist offices in Võru, Otepää or Tartu.

◎ Sights & Activities

Suur Munamägi VIEWPOINT
(www.suurmunamagi.ee; entry via stairs adult/child
€4/3, elevator €6; ☺tower 10am-8pm Apr-Aug, to
5pm Sep & Oct, noon-3pm Sat & Sun Nov-Mar) At
a less-than-overwhelming 318m, Suur Munamägi (literally Great Egg Hill) still manages to be the highest peak in the Baltic. In fact,
the tree-covered 'summit' is easy to miss if
you're not looking out for it. Crack the Great
Egg with an ascent of its 29m observation
tower, built in 1939. On a clear day you can
see Tartu's TV towers, the onion domes of the
Russian town of Pihkva (Pskov) and lush forests stretching out in every direction.

There's a pleasant indoor-outdoor cafe on
the ground floor, and another selling burgers
and fudge back on the main road.

Stairs lead up the hill from the Võru–
Ruusmäe road, about 1km south of the
otherwise uninspiring village of Haanja
(which in turn is 13km south of Võru).

ESTONIA HAANJA NATURE PARK

DON'T MISS

KARULA NATIONAL PARK

Fairies, ghosts and witches abound in the 123 sq km of wooded hills, small lakes and ancient stone burial mounds that form Karula National Park, at least according to local folklore. At its centre is **Ähijärv**, a beautiful lake ringed with trees and reeds which has been considered holy since pagan times.

The park's lakeside **visitor centre** (786 8360; www.keskkonnaamet.ee; Ähijärve village; ⊘10am-6pm mid-May–mid-Sep) distributes information and maps for various walking trails. It takes about 90 minutes to loop along the northern end of the lake and through forest and meadows on the blissful 4km-long **Ähijärv Trail**; keep an eye out for woodpeckers and native orchids.

The park is accessed by a partly unsealed road leading from Mõniste village in the south to the town of Antsla in the north.

St Mary's Lutheran Church   CHURCH

(Maarja kirik; Haanja mnt 10, Rõuge; ⊘9am-3pm Thu-Sun Jun-Aug) Rõuge's whitewashed stone church dates from 1730, replacing a 16th-century church destroyed in the Great Northern War. Inside, the focal point is the altar painting *Christ on the Cross* (1854), framed by a neoclassical relief. Outside there's a monument to the local dead of the 1918–20 independence war. The memorial was buried in someone's backyard throughout the Soviet period to save it from destruction.

Luhasoo Nature Reserve   NATURE RESERVE

(Luhasoo maastikukaitseala) Set in untouched swampland on the border with Latvia (just outside the boundaries of Haanja Nature Park), this reserve provides a fascinating glimpse into Estonia's primordial past. A well-marked 4.5km trail passes over varied bogs and along a velvety black lake, with Venus flytraps and water lilies among the foliage. You might spot elk and deer but the most you're likely to see of wolves, bears and lynx is their tracks.

To get there, take the Krabi road from Rõuge and, after the Pärlijõe bus stop, turn left towards Kellamäe.

Haanja Hikes   OUTDOORS

(Haanjamatkad; 511 4179; www.haanjamatkad.ee; per day bike/canoe €10/32) This Võru-based crew has canoes and bikes for rent and leads canoeing (three to six hours, adult/child €20/10) and rafting (four to six hours, 10-person raft €200) excursions, or two-day cycling and hiking adventures.

🛏 Sleeping & Eating

If you want to base yourself in the park, Rõuge is your best bet. Eating options are limited, although there's a small supermarket in the village, and the Nightingale Valley Centre stocks some delicious traditional produce and baked goods.

Ööbikuoru Puhkekeskus   CAMPGROUND €

(509 0372; www.visit.ee; Ööbikuoru 5, Rõuge; sites per adult/child €4/2, cabins per person €9-15, house €115) Set in a lovely spot overlooking Nightingale Valley, this outfit offers lodging in simple wooden cabins and self-contained houses (sleeping up to six). Rowboat (per hour €4), canoe (€4) and bike (€2) rental is available and there's a sauna for hire (two hours €30). It's located 600m from the main road, signposted as you head south.

★ Ööbikuoru Villa   HOTEL, CAFE €€

(509 9666; www.oruvilla.ee; Tiida küla; r from €58, mains €8-12; P 🛜) Spread between two neighbouring buildings overlooking a small lake, this is our top pick in Rõuge for both a bed and a bite. Don't be fooled by the fussy antique-style furniture, it's basically brand new – and the rooms are as comfortable and modern as you could wish for. Downstairs, Cafe Andreas serves up tasty bistro-style lunches and dinners.

Rõuge Suurjärve Külalistemaja   GUESTHOUSE €€

(524 3028; www.maremajutus.ee; Metsa 5, Rõuge; s/d €25/35, without bathroom €11/22; P) A great place to unwind in lovely surrounds, this big, yellow, family-run guesthouse has views over the valley from its pretty garden and a range of fuss-free rooms (most with private bathroom, some with TV, a few with balcony). The turn-off to the guesthouse is opposite St Mary's Lutheran Church. There's not much English spoken.

ℹ Information

Nightingale Valley Centre (Ööbikuorg Keskus; 785 9245; ⊘10am-6pm mid-May–Aug) Signposted about 1.5km east from Rõuge's church, on the road to Haanja, this excellent centre has an information desk dispensing details on local walking trails. There's also a handicrafts store and a shop selling locally made food (snacks €1.50).

ⓘ Getting There & Away

There are buses from Võru to Haanja village (€0.70 to €1.40, 25 minutes, five daily) and Rõuge (€0.75 to €3, 25 minutes, eight daily).

Valga

POP 12,400

If you thought that Narva's central-city border crossing was odd, wait until you see Valga. This town was the only place that was seriously contended between Estonia and Latvia after WWI. A British mediator had to be called in to settle the dispute and suggested the current border, splitting the town in two. As a result, as you wander around the town centre you'll find yourself passing in and out of Valga and Valka (as the Latvian side is known). Mercifully there are no longer checkpoints (cheers, Schengen!), although you should really carry your passport with you. The local authorities cooperate on important stuff such as tourist information and bus services.

Valga is enjoying a slow process of gentrification, but its old wooden houses and parks are still skirted by some grim industrial areas. Its bloody wartime history makes it an interesting place for a brief stop before moving on. Although there are some large military bunkers and war cemeteries on the Valka side, most items of interest are on the Estonian side of the border.

◎ Sights

Valga Museum   MUSEUM
(www.valgamuuseum.ee; Vabaduse 8; museum adult/child €2/1, gallery €1/0.50; ⊙11am-6pm Wed-Fri, 10am-3pm Sat & Sun) Housed in an art nouveau building which was once a theatre and bank, this museum focuses on the local area, with displays on natural history, archaeology, Soviet-era deportations, everyday Soviet life and local hero Alfred Neuland, winner of the gold for weightlifting at the 1920 Olympic Games. Most captions are in Estonian, but there are booklets with English translations. Before visiting the attached gallery, it's worth peering through the streetside windows to see whether the exhibition takes your fancy.

St John's Lutheran Church   CHURCH
(Jaani kirik; Kesk 23) Close to the tourist office, this oddly shaped church was built in 1816 and holds the distinction of being the only oval church in Estonia. It's other claim to fame is a rare 19th-century organ.

World War II Memorial   MEMORIAL
(Roheline) An estimated 29,000 Russians died at the Nazi POW camp Stalag-351, which was located in converted stables at Priimetsa on Valga's outskirts. Most died of starvation, cold and disease. Nothing remains of the camp, but a simple, moving monument known as the *Mourning Mother* is located close by. The Soviets took over the camp and held German POWs here, 300 of whom are buried among the firs in an official war cemetery nearby.

🛏 Sleeping & Eating

Metsis   HOTEL €€
(☑766 6050; www.hotellmetsis.com; Kuperjanovi 63; s/d from €53/65, mains €8.50-13; P🐕) Set on large lawns, this 1912 hotel is Valga's best sleeping option, with pleasant rooms, some of which have their own sauna and jacuzzi. If you can ignore the hunting trophies, the downstairs restaurant is also very good.

Voorimehe Pubi   PUB FOOD €
(☑767 9627; www.voorimehepubi.ee; J Kuperjanovi 57; mains €6-8.50) An atmospheric dark-wood pub serving filling salmon, schnitzel, pork and the like. DJs spin on the weekend.

ⓘ Information

Tourist Office (☑766 1699; www.valgamaa.ee; Kesk 11; ⊙10am-5pm daily mid-May–mid-Sep, 10am-5pm Mon-Fri, 10am-2pm Sat & Sun rest of year) Town maps and information for both sides of the town divide.

ⓘ Getting There & Away

Valga Bus & Railway Station (☑512 0295; Jaama pst 10) is a couple of blocks southeast of the town centre.

BUS

International coaches head here from Russia and Latvia. Major domestic destinations:

Otepää (€3.30, one hour, four daily)

Pärnu (€10, 2½ hours, daily)

Tallinn (€14, four hours, six daily)

Tartu (€5.50 to €7, 1¾ hours, five daily)

Viljandi (€6.50 to €7.20, 1¾ hours, six daily)

TRAIN

Valga's historic station is the terminus for both the Estonian and Latvian rail systems; you'll have to change trains here if you're heading, say, between Tartu and Rīga (p179). On the Estonian side there are three direct services a day to and from Tartu (€4.40, 70 minutes).

Sangaste

POP 228

There are two good reasons to stop at this small village on the road between Valga and Otepää, and they both have a lot to do with rye. Sangaste is known as the 'Rye Capital of Estonia', which in such a rye-crazy nation is quite an honour. This is largely due to the efforts of the local Baltic German nobleman Friedrich Georg Magnus von Berg (1854–1938), who became known as the 'Rye Count' due to his successful efforts in developing a strain which is now grown throughout the world.

◉ Sights

Sangaste Castle   HISTORIC BUILDING

(Sangaste Loss; www.sangasteloss.ee; adult/child €3/2; ⊙10am-6pm) British travellers might experience déjà vu gazing on this majestic red-brick manor house, as the influence of Windsor Castle on the architecture is unmistakeable. Completed in 1881 as the home of the 'Rye Count' Friedrich von Berg, it's regarded as one of the prime examples of Gothic Revival architecture in the Baltics. History has taken its toll, but visitors can explore the impressive octagonal ballroom and head up a precarious set of stairs to the roof of the tower.

While most manor houses were nationalised during the first period of Estonian independence, the popular count dropped the noble 'von' from his name and was allowed to continue living here as plain old Friedrich Berg until his death at the age of 93. Subsequently the house was used as a Red Army barracks, a German army hospital and, following the war, as a cinema and a Soviet Pioneers youth camp. The hotel and cafe that are here now haven't quite managed to shake off an institutional feel, but gradually the building is being restored, as funds allow.

Sangaste Castle is located in Lossiküla (castle village), 3.5km southeast of the main Sangaste village.

St Andrew's Lutheran Church   CHURCH

(⊙noon-1.30pm Sun May-Aug) It's thought that the name Sangaste might derive from the Latin phrase *Sanguis Christi* (Blood of Christ), referring to a relic kept in Sangaste's original 13th-century church. The current building dates from 1742, with its baroque gable tower added in 1873. The interior is relatively plain, although it's worth noting the starry sky over the sanctuary and the calvary scene above the altar, painted in Munich in 1883.

🛏 Sleeping & Eating

Sangaste Rye House   ESTONIAN €

(Sangaste Rukki Maja; ☑766 9323; www.rukki maja.ee; Valga mnt 13; mains €7-8, s/d €35/45; P❄🌐👪) This cosy restaurant celebrates Sangaste's 'Rye Capital' designation with a menu devoted to the grain. Alongside delicious rye bread it serves a surprising array of traditional soups, pork, salmon and chicken dishes. If you feel like settling in for the night, there are tidy rooms upstairs, available at a very reasonable price.

ℹ Getting There & Away

There's no bus station, but there are daily buses to and from the following destinations:

Otepää (€1.70, 30 minutes, six daily)

Tallinn (€13, four hours, daily)

Tartu (€5, 1¼ hours, three daily)

Valga (€2.20, 35 minutes, seven daily)

Otepää

POP 1900

The small hilltop town of Otepää, 44km south of Tartu, is the centre of a picturesque area of forests, lakes and rivers. The district is beloved by Estonians for its natural beauty and its many possibilities for hiking, biking and swimming in summer, and cross-country skiing in winter. It's often referred to as Estonia's winter capital, and winter weekends here are busy and loads of fun. Some have even dubbed the area (tongue firmly in cheek) the 'Estonian Alps' – a reference not to its peaks but to its excellent ski trails. The 63km Tartu Ski Marathon kicks off here every February but even in summer you'll see professional athletes and enthusiasts hurtling around on roller skis.

The main part of Otepää is on the intersection of the Tartu, Võru and Valga highways, where you'll find the main square, shops and some patchy residential streets. A small swath of forest separates it from a smaller settlement by the lakeshore, 2km southwest.

⊙ Sights

Pühajärv
LAKE

According to legend, 3.5km-long, 8.5m-deep Pühajärv (Holy Lake) was formed from the tears of the mothers who lost their sons in a battle of the *Son of Kalev* epic. Its five islands are said to be their burial mounds. Pagan associations linger, with major Midsummer festivities held here every year. The popular sandy beach (Ranna tee) on the northeastern shore has water slides, a swimming pontoon, a cafe and lifeguards in summer.

The lake was blessed by the Dalai Lama when he came to Tartu in 1991; a wheel-shaped monument near the beach commemorates his visit.

A 13km trail encircles the lake, but much of it follows the road, so it's not the most interesting walk. Much more worthwhile is the 3.5km Murrumetsa walking trail, which starts near the Pühajärve Spa Hotel and loops counterclockwise along the lakeshore, through a marshy meadow and then into a blissful stand of birch, alder and spruce forest.

Energy Column
MONUMENT

(Energiasammas; Mäe) If energy levels are low, recharge at this odd bear-covered totem pole. It was erected in 1992 to mark the long-held belief of psychics that this area resounds with positive energy.

Otepää Winter Sports Museum
MUSEUM

(Otepää talispordimuuseum; www.spordimuuseum. ee; Tehvandi Stadium House, Valga mnt 12; adult/child €1.50/1; ⊙11am-4pm Wed-Sun) Big, flash Tehvandi Stadium, used for football and ski events, is a testimony to Otepää's obsession with sport. Within the bowels of the main stand, this two-room museum displays equipment, costumes and medals belonging to some of Estonia's most famous winter athletes. If the displays inspire you to sporting greatness, you can hire a frisbee (€4) from the counter for a round of 'disk golf' in the nearby course.

Linnamägi
RUINS

The pretty tree-covered hill south of the church was an ancient Estonian stronghold for around 800 years before it was topped by an episcopal castle in 1224. Known as the 'Bear's Head' *(oti pää)*, it's from this that the town takes its name. Remnants of the fortifications remain on the top along with wonderful views of the surrounding valleys. The castle was largely destroyed in 1396 in a battle between the Bishop of Tartu and the Livonian Order.

St Mary's Lutheran Church
CHURCH

(Maarja Luteri kirik; Võru mnt; ⊙10am-7pm Tue-Sat mid-May–mid-Sep) Otepää's Gothic hill-top church dates from 1671, although it was largely reconstructed in 1890. Inside there's intricate woodwork, low-hanging chandeliers and an impressive crucifixion scene (1880) above the altar. It was here in 1884 that the Estonian Students' Society consecrated its new blue, black and white flag, which later became the flag of independent Estonia. Bas-reliefs flanking the gates and doors celebrate the occasion; they were originally erected in 1934, destroyed during the Soviet era and re-erected in 1989.

Facing the church's main door is a small mound with a monument to those who died in the 1918–20 independence war. The memorial's top section was buried from 1950 to 1989 to prevent its destruction.

🏃 Activities

The tourist office has maps and information on hiking, cycling and skiing trails, which range from short and kid-focused to a 20km track. Staff can also provide information on the numerous activities on offer in the region, including horse riding, frisbee golf, regular golf, snowtubing, sleigh rides and snowmobile safaris.

For cross-country skiing, the closest trails start on the edge of town near Tehvandi Sports Centre. You can also find some good trails near Lake Kääriku.

If you're considering a canoeing or rafting trip, call at least a day or two ahead of time. Operators will pick you up from your hotel, take you to the river and drop you back afterwards.

Otepää Forest Adventure Park
ADVENTURE SPORTS

(Otepää seikluspark; ☑504 9783; www.seikluspark. ee; Tehvandi 3; ⊙10am-7pm May-Oct) Explore the treetops on a high ropes course (adult/child €20/10) or the shrubbery on the kid's adventure trail (must be 90cm to 120cm tall, €5). Alternatively hurtle all the way to Linnamägi on a zip line (adult/child €8/6) or up into the air on the reverse-bungy catapult (€6).

Tehvandi Sports Centre
SKIING, CYCLING

(Tehvandi spordikeskus; ☑766 9500; www.tehvandi. ee; Tehvandi; ski training track per day €6, incl ski-jumping €12, shooting €12) A former training centre for the Soviet Union's Winter Olympics team, this large turf-covered hobbit hole

Otepää

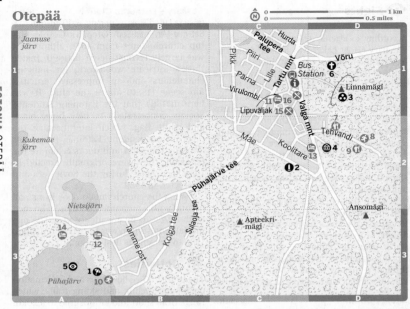

Otepää

⊙ Sights
1 Beach	A3
2 Energy Column	C2
3 Linnamägi	D1
4 Otepää Winter Sports Museum	D2
5 Pühajärv	A3
6 St Mary's Lutheran Church	D1

⊕ Activities, Courses & Tours
7 Fan-Sport	D2
8 Otepää Forest Adventure Park	D2
9 Tehvandi Sports Centre	D2
10 Veesõidukite Laenutus	A3

⊟ Sleeping
11 Edgari Külalistemaja	C1
12 GMP Clubhotel	A3
13 Murakas	D2
14 Pühajärve Spa & Holiday Resort	A3

⊗ Eating
Edgari Pood	(see 11)
15 l.u.m.i.	C1
16 Oti Pubi	C1
Pühajärve Pub	(see 14)
Pühajärve Restaurant	(see 12)

of a hotel is a hub for all manner of winter and summer activities, including Nordic skiing, ski jumping, shooting, cycling, roller skiing and skating. There's also a 34m climbing wall and viewing platform attached to the ski-jump tower (entry by lift/stairs €2/3).

Kuutsemäe   SKIING
(☎ 766 9007; www.kuutsemae.ee; day pass Mon-Fri €17, Sat & Sun €20) While cross-country skiing is the area's drawcard, this resort operates six modest downhill runs, ranging from 214m to 476m in length. It's the area's most developed ski centre, with a tavern, accommodation and a skiing and snowboarding

school. It's located 14km west of Otepää at Kuutsemägi.

VeeTee   CANOEING, RAFTING
(☎ 506 0987; www.veetee.ee) Offers a range of canoeing and rafting trips along the Ahja and Võhandu Rivers and around the small lakes of the Kooraste River valley (per person €20). It also rents skis and snowboards and offer lessons.

Toonus Pluss   CANOEING, SKIING
(☎ 505 5702; www.toonuspluss.ee) Specialises in canoeing trips through the Ahja River valley; tailor-made expeditions can combine

canoeing with hiking and mountain biking. It also rents skis and offers instruction.

Fan-Sport   SNOW SPORTS
(☑507 7537; www.fansport.ee; Tehvandi) Operating out of the Karupesa Hotel in winter, this outfit rents cross-country skis (three hours/day €7/13), downhill skis (€10/13) and snowboards (€10/13). It can also arrange ski lessons.

Veesõidukite Laenutus   BOATING
(☑5343 6359; Ranna tee 5; ☉10am-7pm Jun-Aug) Rents rowboats (€10), canoes (€8), kayaks (€8) and pedalos (€8) from the beach on the northeastern shore of Pühajärv; all prices per hour.

Paap Kõlar's Safari Centre   SNOW SPORTS
(Paap Kõlari Safarikeskus; ☑505 1015; http://safarikeskus.paap.ee/; Nüpli village; intro €25, per hour €90; ☉Jan-Mar) Explore the winter wonderland in a two-person snowmobile; bookings required. It's operated by the same adventurers who run Surf Paradiis on Hiiumaa.

✮ Festivals & Events

Tartu Ski Marathon   SPORTS
(www.tartumaraton.ee) Otepää is the starting point for this famous 63km cross-country race every February (it finishes in Elva), attracting around 10,000 participants. The same organisation hosts a range of sporting events (cycling road races, mountain-bike races, running races) in and around Tartu throughout the year.

🛏 Sleeping

The low seasons here are April to May and September to November; during these months prices are about 10% to 15% cheaper. Higher rates are charged on weekends in high season.

Murakas   HOTEL €€
(☑731 1410; www.murakas.ee; Valga mnt 23a; s/d €45/50; P☎) With only 10 bedrooms, Murakas is more like a large friendly guesthouse than a hotel. Stripey carpets, blonde wood and balconies give the rooms a fresh feel and there's a similarly breezy breakfast room downstairs.

Pühajärve Spa & Holiday Resort RESORT €€
(☑766 5500; www.pyhajarve.com; Pühajärve tee; s/d/ste from €60/75/125; P@☎❄) The best thing about this large white complex is its location, set on sprawling lawns right on the lakeside. The wonderful glassed-in pool overlooking the lake comes a close second. Otherwise, there's still a vaguely Soviet vibe about the place, and the rooms, although large enough, are somewhat spartan.

Edgari Külalistemaja   GUESTHOUSE €€
(☑766 6550; http://edgari.otepäält.ee; Lipuväljak 3; s/d €25/50; ☎) Edgar's occupies the upstairs levels of an attractive brick building, right in the centre of town, with a deli and cafe below. Some rooms are tiny while others are larger and have balconies; they're all priced identically, so ask for a bigger one when you're booking.

GMP Clubhotel   APARTMENT €€€
(☑799 7000; www.clubhotel.ee; Tennisevälja 1; apt from €120; P☎) This superslick lakeside block is decked out with kitchenettes, funky furniture, comfy beds and oversized photos. The icing on the cake is the luxurious pair of single-sex saunas on the top level, open in the evenings for those who fancy a sunset sweat.

🍴 Eating & Drinking

l.u.m.i.   CAFE €
(☑742 4020; www.lumikohvik.ee; Munamäe 8; mains €5.50-13; ☉noon-8pm Mon-Thu, to 11pm Fri & Sat, to 6.30pm Sun) The hippy manifesto at the start of the menu informs us that *lumi* means snow, and among all the talk of good energy, there's a fairly traditional list of pasta, fish, pork, lamb and chicken dishes. The groovy vibe comes with the requisite mismatched furniture and some cool cutlery lampshades. An excellent choice.

Edgari Pood   BAKERY, DELI €
(http://edgari.otepäält.ee; Lipuväljak 2; pastries €0.80; ☉8am-6pm Mon-Fri, 9am-3pm Sat) Stock up on sliced meat and vodka or grab some pastries for a cheap and tasty breakfast.

Oti Pubi   PUB FOOD €€
(www.otipubi.ee; Lipuväljak 26; mains €7-13; ☉10am-midnight; ☎) In an octagonal building draped in ski memorabilia in the centre of town, the 'bear pub' has a loyal local following. It's a good spot for a drink and a meal, so long as you're not expecting any surprises from the menu (soup, pasta, pizza, grills etc).

Pühajärve Restaurant   MODERN EUROPEAN €€
(☑799 7000; www.clubhotel.ee; Tennisevälja 1; mains €9-18; ☉noon-10pm) From the 1960s to 1980s this was Otepää's most famous restaurant, but when the Soviet Union went down the gurgler it followed in its wake.

The opening of the attached Clubhotel has given Pühajärve a new lease of life and it now offers a tasty menu on a terrace above its namesake.

Pühajärve Pub PUB FOOD **€€**
(☑766 5500; www.pyhajarve.com; Pühajärve tee; mains €6-19; ☺11am-11pm Sun-Thu, to 1am Fri & Sat) The lakeside hotel's casual, all-day pub caters to everyone (kids, vegetarians, et al) with an extensive menu. The sunny outdoor terrace is the place to be, but the brick-lined interior, with its pool tables and open fire, is not a bad wet-weather option.

⭐**Mr Jakob** MODERN ESTONIAN **€€€**
(☑5375 3307; www.otepaagolf.ee; Mäha küla; mains €14-18; ☺noon-9pm; ☜) Otepää's best restaurant is hidden away at the golf club, 4km west of Pühajärv. The menu is as contemporary and playful as the decor, taking the old Estonian classics such as pork ribs and marinated herring fillets and producing something quite extraordinary. Added to that is charming service and blissful views over the course and surrounding fields.

ℹ️ Information

Otepää Tourist Information Centre (☑766 1200; www.otepaa.eu; Tartu mnt 1; ☺10am-5pm Mon-Fri, to 3pm Sat & Sun mid-May–mid-Sep, 10am-5pm Tue-Fri, to 3pm Sat rest of year) Well-informed staff distribute maps and brochures, and make recommendations for activities, guide services and lodging in the area.

ℹ️ Getting There & Around

The **bus station** (Tartu mnt 1) is next to the tourist office. Destinations include the following:

Narva (€10, 4¼ hours, twice weekly)

Sangaste (€1.70, 30 minutes, six daily)

Tallinn (€13, 3½ hours, daily)

Tartu (€2 to €3.50, one hour, 10 daily)

Valga (€3.30, one hour, four daily)

SOUTHWESTERN ESTONIA

The big drawcard of this corner of the country is the beach. Set on a long stretch of sand, Pärnu attracts legions of holidaymakers during the summer. Young partygoers appear from Tallinn and Tartu heading to the sands and nightclubs, just as busloads of elderly out-of-towners arrive seeking spa treatments and mud cures.

East of Pärnu stretches Soomaa National Park, a biodiverse region of meandering meadows and swamps. Viljandi lies just beyond Soomaa; it's a laid-back regional centre and a focus for things folk, especially music.

Viljandi

POP 17,600

One of Estonia's most charming towns, Viljandi overlooks a picturesque valley with a tranquil lake at its centre. The Knights of the Sword founded a castle here in the 13th century. The town that grew around it later joined the Hanseatic League, but subsequently was subject to the comings and goings of Swedes, Poles and Russians. It's now a relaxed kind of place, perfect for time-travelling ambles, with some evocative castle ruins, historic buildings and abundant greenery.

If you visit in late July, make sure your accommodation is sorted – the four-day Viljandi Folk Music Festival is the biggest annual music festival in Estonia.

◉ Sights

The old part of town in the blocks immediately north of the castle is full of handsome wooden buildings with finely wrought details, but things get scrappier as you head further out.

⭐**Viljandi Teutonic Order Castle** CASTLE
(Viljandi ordulinnus; Lossimäed) **FREE** Set within a lush park, the scant remains of Viljandi's hilltop castle form a picturesque set of ruins and offer sweeping views over the valley and the lake below. Built in 1224 by the German Knights of the Sword on a series of three small hills divided by ravines, it replaced an Estonian hill fort which had stood here since the 9th century. It finally fell into disrepair after the 17th century Polish-Swedish wars.

Only scant sections of wall and crumbling foundations remain but there are interesting display panels describing the castle's layout. One of the approaches to the fortress is spanned by an elegant 50m suspension foot-

---

ℹ️ VILJANDI TRIPLE TICKET

A combination ticket (adult/child €5/3) is available incorporating the Viljandi Museum, Kondas Centre and Old Water Tower.

Southwestern Estonia

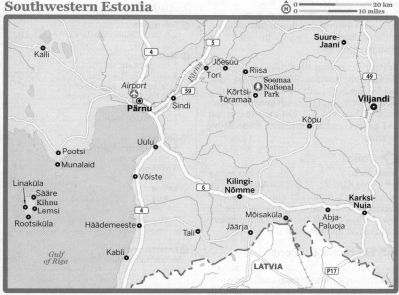

bridge which was built in 1879 for another set of castle ruins at Tarvastu and was only moved to this site in 1931.

A small cemetery to the rear of the castle park is the final resting place of German soldiers killed here during WWII.

St John's Lutheran Church   CHURCH
(Jaani Kirik; Pikk 6; ⊙11am-6pm Mon-Sat, 9am-6pm Sun mid-May–mid-Sep) This medieval church looks like it's been given a Cape Cod *Better Homes* makeover, with pale-grey walls and a stone altar – rescuing it from its Soviet incarnation as a furniture warehouse. It was originally part of a 15th-century Franciscan abbey (hence the stained-glass image of the saint to the right of the altar) and if you look closely you can spot the remains of pre-Reformation frescoes over the arch leading from the porch into the church proper.

Kondas Centre   GALLERY
(Kondase keskus; www.kondas.ee; Pikk 8; adult/student €2/1; ⊙10am-5pm Wed-Sat Jan-Mar, Wed-Sun Apr & Sep-Dec, 11am-6pm daily May-Aug) Housing vibrantly colourful works by local painter Paul Kondas (1900–85) and other self-taught artists working outside the mainstream, this is Estonia's only gallery dedicated to naïve and outsider art. It's not hard to find – in a marvellously

oblique reference to the artist's 1965 work *Strawberry Eaters,* the stalks of all the giant strawberries scattered around town point here.

Viljandi Museum   MUSEUM
(📇 433 3316; www.muuseum.viljandimaa.ee; Laidoneri plats 10; adult/child €2/1; ⊙10am-5pm Tue-Sat Apr & Sep-Dec, 11am-6pm daily May-Aug) Facing the old market square, this modest two-storey museum has displays tracing Viljandi's history from the Stone Age to the mid-20th century. There are folk costumes, stuffed animals, old photos of the city, Viking-era jewellery and a mock-up of what the original castle probably looked like. English translations are limited.

Old Water Tower   VIEWPOINT
(Vana veetorn; www.sakalakeskus.ee; Laidoneri plats 5; adult/child €2/1; ⊙11am-6pm May-Aug, 10am-5pm Tue-Sat Sep) One of Vijlandi's most distinctive landmarks, this odd 30m red-brick water tower topped with a hexagonal wooden structure offers fine views over the countryside.

Viljandi järv   LAKE
Accessed by a steep path leading down from Pikk street, the lake is a popular place for a swim on warm summer days. All the usual

hallmarks of the Estonian beach are here (volleyball court, cafes, boat rental) and there's a swimming platform just offshore. Come Midsummer's Eve, it's the site of the main celebrations.

St Paul's Lutheran Church CHURCH
(Pauluse kirik; Kiriku 5; ☺10am-3pm Tue-Fri, to 1pm Sun Jun-Aug) Built in the Tudor Gothic style in 1866, this big, castlelike, stone-and-brick Lutheran church has a wooden pulpit and gallery, and a crucifixion scene above its altar.

☞ Tours

Town Walk WALKING TOUR
(adult/child €1/0.50; ☺1pm Jun-Aug) In summer, a bargain-priced one-hour guided walking tour departs daily from outside the tourist office. Pay at the office; commentary is in English and Estonian.

✪ Festivals & Events

Hanseatic Days CULTURAL
(www.hansa.viljandi.ee; Hansapäevad) Celebrating the town's past over a long weekend in early June.

Viljandi Old Music Festival MUSIC
(Viljandi vanamuusika festival; www.vivamu.ee) Archaic instruments and musical forms are showcased in the town's churches and concert halls over a week in mid-July.

Viljandi Folk Music Festival MUSIC
(Viljandi pärimusmuusika festival; www.folk.ee) Easily the biggest event on the calendar, this hugely popular, four-day music festival is renowned for its friendly, relaxed vibe and impressive international line-up. It sees Viljandi's population double in size around the last weekend of July, with over 20,000 attendees at over 100 concerts.

⌂ Sleeping

Hostel Ingeri GUESTHOUSE €€
(☏433 4414; www.hostelingeri.ee; Pikk 2c; s €29, d €40-45; P☎) On one of Viljandi's nicest streets, this six-room guesthouse offers seriously good value with its bright, comfortable rooms, all with TVs and bathrooms. Plant life and a kitchen for guest use make it a good home-from-home, while the parkside location couldn't be better.

Grand Hotel Viljandi HOTEL €€
(☏435 5800; www.ghv.ee; Tartu 11; s/d €76/98; P☎) In the heart of the old part of town,

this moderately chi chi hotel has art deco–styled rooms with dark-wood trim, satiny chairs, large windows and wildly patterned carpets. There's a pleasant summertime cafe in front, as well as a smart à la carte restaurant. Look out for the sign for 'EVE', the name of the 1938 building housing the hotel.

Villa Hilda GUESTHOUSE €€
(☏433 3710; www.hildavilla.ee; Valuoja pst 7; r €46-84; P☎) While Hilda's a plain Jane from the outside, this homely guesthouse has plenty of 1930s period features inside, including polished wooden floors, antique stoves and some nanna-fabulous furniture. There are only three rooms, one of which has a balcony overlooking the park.

Endla GUESTHOUSE €€
(☏433 5302; www.reinup.ee; Endla 9; s/d from €30/35; @☎) There's a vaguely Swiss feel to this little guesthouse, set on a quiet backstreet north of the bus station. The rooms are simple but smartly furnished and as spick and span as you could ask for.

✖ Eating & Drinking

Dining options in Viljandi are quite limited for a town of its size and status, but there are some appealing pubs.

Viljandi

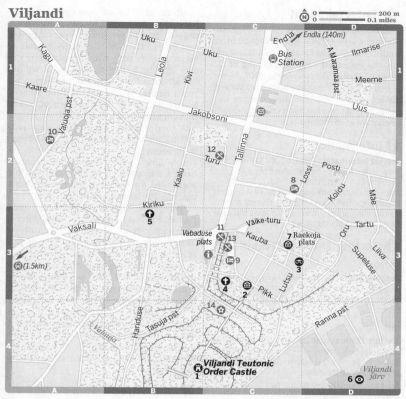

Aida

CAFE €

(📞434 2066; www.aidakohvik.ee; Tasuja pst 6; mains €7.80-9.60; ⏰11am-11pm Mon-Sat, to 7pm Sun) The cafe in the Traditional Music Centre has the best views of any eatery in town, overlooking Castle Park through floor-to-ceiling windows and from its roof terrace. Hearty, skilfully cooked Estonian food is on offer along with pasta, Asian-style vegie stir-fry and a good salad selection.

Suur Vend

PUB FOOD €

(www.suurvend.ee; Turu 4; mains €4.50-9; ⏰noon-10pm Sun & Mon, to midnight Tue & Wed, to 3am Thu-Sat; 🛜📶) Friendly service, big portions, a pool table and boppy music from the jukebox create a cheerful mood at this cosy pub, with an outdoor deck and lots of dark wood inside. The wide-ranging menu offers few surprises and there are plenty of snacks perfect for beer-drinking. Later on, disco and karaoke nights keep the locals entertained.

Tegelaste Tuba

PUB FOOD €

(www.facebook.com/TegelasteTuba; Pikk 2b; mains €3.50-9; ⏰11am-midnight Sun-Thu, to 2am Fri & Sat; 🛜📶📶) The terrace overlooking the park is one drawcard of this tavern but so is the comfy interior on cold, rainy days. Estonian handicrafts enliven the walls, and a diverse crowd enjoys the wide-ranging menu of soups, salads and Russian and Estonian comfort food (dumplings and lots of pork and chicken).

Fellin

CAFE €€

(📞435 9795; www.kohvikfellin.ee; Kauba 2; mains €9-16; ⏰11am-8pm Sun & Mon, to 10pm Tue-Sat) 'Local food and live music' is the mantra at this very cool cafe-bar, which stands head and shoulders above Viljandi's other eating and drinking options. The menu ranges from light snacks, salads and soups to more substantial meals (duck breast, smoked pork, steamed fish), or you can just call in for wine and a song.

☆ Entertainment

Traditional Music Centre   LIVE MUSIC
(Pärimusmuusika ait; www.folk.ee; Tasuja pst 6) Viljandi's reputation as Estonia's folk-music capital was cemented with the opening of this very unfolksy modern centre in 2007. As well as being a place for study, it has two state-of-the-art concert halls and an upmarket cafe; call in to find out what's on performance-wise or enquire at the tourist office.

ⓘ Information

Tourist Information Centre (☑ 433 0442; www.visitestonia.com; Vabaduse plats 6; ◷10am-6pm Mon-Fri, to 3pm Sat & Sun mid-May–mid-Sep, 10am-5pm Mon-Fri rest of year) Local maps and information on Viljandi and surrounding areas (including Soomaa National Park) in loads of languages.

ⓘ Getting There & Around

BICYCLE
Joosepi Jalgrattapood (☑ 434 5757; www.jalgrattad.eu; Kaalu 9; per hour/day €4.50/10; ◷9am-6pm Mon-Fri, to 3pm Sat) Bike hire and service.

BUS
The **bus station** (bussijaam; ☑ 433 3680; www.bussireisid.ee; Ilmarise 1; ◷6.15am-8pm Mon-Sat, 8am-8pm Sun) is 500m north of the tourist office. Major destinations:

Kuressaare (€18, five hours, two daily)
Pärnu (€6 to €6.80, 1½ hours, 11 daily)
Tallinn (€9.50 to €11, 2½ hours, 11 daily)
Tartu (€5.80, 1¼ hours, 14 daily)
Valga (€6.50 to €7.20, 1¾ hours, six daily)

TRAIN
The **train station** (raudteejaam; ☑ 434 9425; www.elron.ee; Vaksali 44) is 1.6km southwest of the tourist office. Four trains run daily to and from Tallinn (€8.40, 2¼ hours).

Soomaa National Park

Embracing Estonia's largest area of swamps, meadows and waterside forests, 390-sq-km Soomaa National Park (Soomaa literally means 'bogland') is primarily made up of four bogs – Valgeraba, Öördi, Kikepera and Kuresoo – the peat layer of which measures 7m in places. The bogs are split by tributaries of the Pärnu River, the spring flooding creating a 'fifth season' in March and April for the inhabitants of this swampy land, when the waters can rise to 5m.

Up to 43 different mammal species inhabit the surrounding forests, among them wolves, lynx, brown bears, elks, wild boars and otters. Thousands of birds migrate to Soomaa every year, with 180 observed species. The best time to visit for a wildlife encounter is from September to May, when you'll be able to see tracks in the snow at least – and avoid the blitzkrieg of insects that comes with summer.

A good way to explore the national park and its numerous meandering waterways is by canoe or by *haabja*, a traditional Finno-Ugric single-tree boat that is carved from a single log of aspen wood and has been used for centuries for fishing, hunting, hauling hay and transportation.

Bogs have historically provided isolation and protection to Estonians. Witches were said to live here, although traditional healers were sometimes stuck with that label. According to folklore, it is the mischievous will-o'-the-wisp who leads people to the bog, where they are forced to stay until the swamp gas catches fire, driving the grotesque bog inhabitants out for all to see. Closer to reality, bogs were also hiding places for partisans escaping from outside invaders who couldn't penetrate their murky depths as easily as they could the forests (perhaps they were scared of the gremlins).

⚗ Activities & Tours

The 1.8km **Beaver Trail** starts at the Sooma Nature Centre and leads past beavers' dams. Another good, easy path is the **Riisa Nature Trail**, a 4.8km loop on a well-maintained boardwalk through the Riisa bog (1.2km of which is currently wheelchair accessible). Before hitting the paths, especially in winter, it's best to let the centre know what you plan to do, either by email or in person.

Soomaa.com   OUTDOORS
(☑ 506 1896; www.soomaa.com) Offers an extensive range of activities, such as guided and self-guided canoe trips, beaver watching by canoe, bog walking and mushroom-picking tours, and in winter, kick sledding, cross-country skiing and snowshoe excursions. The **Wilderness Day Trip** includes bog walking and canoeing (€50 per person, minimum two people; runs from May to September, add €20 for a Pärnu pick up).

THE FOREST BROTHERS

Today the sleepy marshes and quiet woodlands of Estonia are a haven only for wildlife, but between 1944 and 1956 much of what is now national park and nature reserve was a stronghold of the Metsavennad (or Metsavendlus; Forest Brothers) proindependence movement. The Forest Brothers fiercely resisted the Soviet occupation. Many resorted to an underground existence in the woods and some remained there for years. They knew their terrain well and used this knowledge to their advantage both for their own survival and in the fight to restore the republic.

The Soviets claimed Estonia in the Molotov-Ribbentrop Pact of 1939 and, after the Germans retreated from a difficult three-year occupation, secured this claim by advancing on Tallinn in 1944. The early resistance, believing this latest occupation would not be recognised in accordance with the British-US Atlantic treaty of 1941 (which states that sovereignty and self-governance should be restored when forcibly removed), rallied support for what some thought would be a new war. As international assistance did not eventuate, the independence cause remained Estonia's own.

Resistance action began with isolated attacks on Red Army units that claimed the lives of around 3000 soldiers. Tactical expertise and secure intelligence networks resulted in damaging offensives on Soviet targets. At the height of the resistance there were more than 30,000 Forest Brothers and their supporters, which included women, the elderly, young people and a network of 'Urban Brothers'. The impact of resistance activity is found in Soviet records from the time, which detail incidents of sabotage on infrastructure such as railways and roads that hindered early attempts at moulding Estonia into a new Soviet state.

In the years that followed, the Metsavennad suffered high casualties, with varied and increasing opposition. The NKVD/KGB (Soviet secret police) provided incentives to some of the local population who were able to infiltrate the resistance. The Soviets coordinated mass deportations of those suspected to be sympathetic to the resistance cause, and some Metsavennad supporters were coerced into acting against the resistance. By 1947 15,000 resistance fighters had been arrested or killed. The greatest blow to the Metsavennad came in 1949 with the deportation of 20,000 people – mainly women, children and the elderly – many of whom had provided the support base and cover for resistance activities.

The movement continued for some years but was greatly impeded by the strength of the Soviets and the loss of local support due to ongoing deportations and the clearing of farmhouses for collectivisation. Some of the Forest Brothers who were not killed or imprisoned escaped to Scandinavia and Canada.

There are many heroes of the Metsavennad, most of whom came to a violent end. Kalev Arro and Ants Kaljurand (*hirmus*, or 'Ants the Terrible' to the Soviets) were famous for their deft disguises and the humour with which they eluded the Soviets. It was only in 1980 that the final Forest Brother, Oskar Lillenurm, was found – shot dead in Lääne county.

Much work has been done to compile a history of the movement by recording accounts of local witnesses. Surviving members are regarded as national heroes and are awarded some of the country's highest honours. For more details on the resistance, a good reference is former Estonian prime minister (and historian) Mart Laar's *War in the Woods: Estonia's Struggle for Survival, 1944–1956*.

ESTONIA SOOMAA NATIONAL PARK

🛏 Sleeping

There are 10 designated sites for free, basic camping in the park, including one near the nature centre. Each has a long-drop toilet, a fire ring and (usually) firewood, but no running water.

ⓘ Information

Soomaa Nature Centre (☏ 435 7164; www. keskkonnaamet.ee; ☉ 10am-6pm mid-Apr–mid-Sep, 10am-4pm Mon-Fri rest of year) Park information is available from this welcoming, highly professional outfit in Kõrtsi-Tõramaa. It distributes hiking maps and, with advance notice, can arrange accommodation and guides.

ⓘ Getting There & Away

BUS

There's a daily bus from Pärnu to Riisa (€2.20, one hour), which is 6km from the Nature Centre.

CAR & MOTORBIKE

It's easiest to access the park from the Pärnu (western) side, heading through Tori and Jõesuu. Viljandi's actually closer, but the 23km road from the village of Kõpu to the visitor centre is largely unsealed.

Pärnu

POP 39,800

Local families, hormone-sozzled youths and German, Swedish and Finnish holidaymakers join together in a collective prayer for sunny weather while strolling the beaches, sprawling parks and picturesque historic centre of Pärnu (*pair*-nu), Estonia's premier seaside resort. In these parts, the name Pärnu is synonymous with fun in the sun; one hyperbolic local described it to us as 'Estonia's Miami', but it's usually called by its slightly more prosaic moniker, the nation's 'summer capital'.

In truth, most of Pärnu is quite docile, with leafy streets and expansive parks intermingling with turn-of-the-20th-century villas that reflect the town's fashionable, more decorous past. Older visitors from Finland and the former Soviet Union still visit, seeking rest, rejuvenation and Pärnu's vaunted mud treatments.

Pärnu

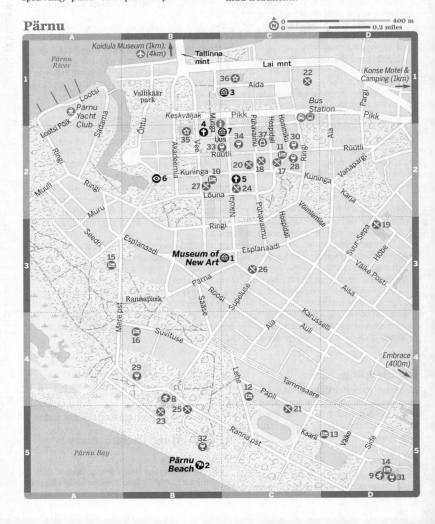

History

There was a trading settlement at Pärnu before the German crusaders arrived, but the place entered recorded history in 1234 when the Pärnu River was fixed as the border between the territories of the Ösel-Wiek bishop (west and north) and the Livonian knights (east and south). The town, joined by rivers to Viljandi, Tartu and Lake Peipsi, became the Hanseatic port of Pernau in the 14th century (sinking water levels have since cut this link).

Pernau/Pärnu had a population of German merchants from Lübeck until at least the 18th century. It withstood wars, fires, plagues, and switches between German, Polish, Swedish and Russian rule, and prospered in the 17th century under the Swedes until its trade was devastated by Europe-wide blockades during the Napoleonic Wars.

From 1838 Pärnu gradually became a popular resort, with mud baths as well as the beach proving a drawcard. Only the resort area was spared severe damage in 1944 as the Soviets drove out the Nazis, but many parts of Old Town have since been restored.

◉ Sights

Pärnu straddles both sides of the Pärnu River at the point where it empties into Pärnu Bay. The south bank contains the major attractions, including Old Town and the beach. The main thoroughfare of the historic centre is Rüütli, lined with splendid buildings dating back to the 17th century.

★ Pärnu Beach   BEACH

Pärnu's long, wide, sandy beach – sprinkled with volleyball courts, cafes and changing cubicles – is easily the city's main drawcard. A curving path stretches along the sand, lined with fountains, park benches and an excellent playground. Early 20th-century buildings are strung along Ranna pst, the avenue that runs parallel to the beach. Across the road, the formal gardens of **Rannapark** are ideal for a summertime picnic.

★ Museum of New Art   GALLERY

(Uue kunstimuuseum; ☑ 443 0072; www.mona.ee; Esplanaadi 10; adult/child €3/1.50; ◷ 9am-9pm) Pärnu's former Communist Party headquarters now houses one of Estonia's edgiest galleries. As part of its commitment to pushing the cultural envelope, it stages an international nude art exhibition every summer. Founded

Pärnu

by film-maker Mark Soosaar, the gallery also hosts the annual Pärnu Film Festival.

There's also a great little gift shop and a cafe with an internet terminal (per hour €2).

Tallinn Gate GATE
(Tallinna Värav) The typical star shape of the 17th-century Swedish ramparts that once surrounded Old Town can easily be spotted on a colour map as most of the pointy bits are now parks. The only intact section, complete with its moat, lies to the west of the centre. Where the rampart meets the western end of Kuninga, it's pierced by this tunnel-like gate that once defended the main road which headed to the river-ferry crossing and on to Tallinn.

St Elizabeth's Lutheran Church CHURCH
(Eliisabeti kirik; www.eliisabet.ee; Nikolai 22; ☉noon-6pm Tue-Sat, 9am-noon Sun Jun-Aug) Named after John the Baptist's mum but also the Russian empress at the time it was built (1747), this baroque church has low dangling chandeliers, a Gothic-style carved wooden pulpit and a wonderful altarpiece of the Resurrection from Rotterdam (1854).

St Catherine's Orthodox Church CHURCH
(Ekatarina Kirik; Vee 8) Built in 1768, this superb baroque church is named after Russian empress Catherine the Great, while also name-checking the early Christian martyr.

Town Hall HISTORIC BUILDING
(Nikolai 3) This 1797 neoclassical building now houses the tourist office and a small gallery space. Also note the half-timbered house, dating from 1740, diagonally opposite across Nikolai.

Pärnu Museum MUSEUM
(✏️443 3231; www.parnumuuseum.ee; Aida 3; adult/child €4/2; ☉11am-6pm Tue-Sun) This museum covers 11,000 years of regional history, from prehistoric archaeological relics, right up to a reconstruction of a Soviet-era apartment. Pride of place goes to the star exhibit, an 8000-year-old 'Stone-Age Madonna'.

Koidula Museum MUSEUM
(www.parnumuuseum.ee; Jannseni 37; adult/child €2/1; ☉10am-6pm Tue-Sun Jun-Aug, 10am-5pm Tue-Sat Sep-May) The memory of one of Estonia's poetic greats, Lydia Koidula (1843–86), is kept alive in this six-room museum in her former home/schoolhouse. The old classroom and the antique-strewn living room and bedrooms are moderately interesting, even if you're not all that enthused about the Estonian cultural renaissance.

 Activities

Hedon Spa SPA
(✏️449 9011; www.hedonspa.com; Ranna pst 1; treatments from €25; ☉9am-7pm Mon-Sat, to 5pm Sun) Built in 1927 to house Pärnu's famous mud baths, this handsome neoclassical building has recently been fully restored and opened as a day spa. All manner of pampering treatments are offered, only some of which involve mud.

Tervise Paradiis Veekeskus WATER PARK
(www.terviseparadiis.ee; Side 14; adult/child 3hr €13/9, day €20/15; ☉10am-10pm) At the far end of the beach, Estonia's largest water park beckons with pools, slides, tubes and other slippery fun. It's a big family-focused draw, especially when bad weather ruins beach plans. The large resort also offers spa treatments, fitness classes and ten-pin bowling.

Festivals & Events

The tourist office distributes *Pärnu This Week*, which lists events happening around town.

Grillfest Good Food Festival FOOD
(Hea Toidu Festival; www.grillfest.ee) Over the second weekend in June, around 45,000 people wend their way around the 200 food vendors in Vallikäär Park, enjoying the best of Estonian cuisine.

Pärnu Hanseatic Days CULTURAL
(Pärnu Hansapäevad; http://hansa.parnu.ee) Pärnu goes medieval for a weekend in late June, with a knightly tournament, market stalls, performances and a poultry and livestock fair.

Pärnu Film Festival FILM
(Pärnu Filmifestival; www.chaplin.ee) This increasingly prestigious international festival has been showcasing documentary films since 1987. It's held at the Museum of New Art and other venues in town over two weeks in early July.

Sleeping

You'll need to book ahead in summer, especially if you're planning to stay on the weekend. Outside of high season you should be able to snare yourself a good deal – perhaps even half the rate.

Konse Motel & Camping
CAMPGROUND €
(☑5343 5092; www.konse.ee; Suur-Jõe 44a; sites €9-15, r with/without bathroom from €52/40; P@🛜) Crammed beside the river about 1km from the centre, Konse offers camping and a variety of rooms, all with kitchen access. It's not an especially charming spot but there is a sauna (per hour €15), and bike (per day €10) and rowboat (per hour €10) rental.

Embrace
B&B, APARTMENTS €€
(☑5887 3404; www.embrace.ee; Pardi 30; r from €75; P✳🛜) Snuggle up in an old wooden house in a suburban street, close to the beach and water park. Rooms strike a nice balance between antique and contemporary, and there's a set of four modern self-contained apartments in a neighbouring annex.

Inge Villa
GUESTHOUSE €€
(☑443 8510; www.ingevilla.ee; Kaarli 20; s/d/ste €56/70/82; ✳🛜) Describing itself as a 'Swedish-Estonian villa hotel', low-key and lovely Inge Villa occupies a prime patch of real estate near the beach. Its 11 rooms are simply decorated in muted tones with Nordic minimalism to the fore. The garden, lounge and sauna seal the deal.

Villa Johanna
B&B €€
(☑443 8370; www.villa-johanna.ee; Suvituse 6; s/d/ste €50/80/100; P🛜) Decorated with hanging flowerpots and planter boxes, this pretty old-fashioned wooden house offers comfy pine-lined rooms on a quiet street near the beach. One room has its own balcony. Not much English is spoken.

Hotell Legend
HOTEL €€
(☑442 5606; www.legend.ee; Lehe 3; s/d/ste from €50/70/90; P@🛜✳) The Tiffany-style lamps, model ships and wooden panelling lend an old-world feel to the lobby, which is quite a contrast to the boxy exterior. Tidy rooms, charming staff and proximity to the beach make this a good midrange option.

Hommiku Hostel
GUESTHOUSE €€
(☑445 1122; www.hommikuhostel.ee; Hommiku 17; s/d from €25/35; P🛜) Located in a prime central position, Hommiku is far more like a budget hotel than a hostel. Rooms have private bathrooms, TVs and kitchenettes; some also have old beamed ceilings.

Villa Ammende
HOTEL €€€
(☑447 3888; www.ammende.ee; Mere pst 7; s/d/ste from €165/210/400; P✳🛜) Luxury abounds in this refurbished 1904 art nouveau mansion, which lords it over handsomely manicured grounds. The gorgeous exterior – looking like one of the cooler Paris metro stops writ large – is matched by an elegant lobby and individually antique-furnished rooms. Rooms in the gardener's house are more affordable but lack a little of the wow factor.

Frost Boutique Hotel
HOTEL €€€
(☑5303 0424; www.frosthotel.ee; Kuninga 11; r/ste from €140/210; P🛜) Tucked behind an old burnt-out building, this surprisingly chic set of rooms has the most over-the-top decor in Pärnu: rustic wooden walls, chandeliers, metallic bathroom tiles, fur throws, cowhide poofs, teddy bears and all. Breakfast costs an additional €12.

Tervise Paradiis
RESORT €€€
(☑445 1600; www.terviseparadiis.ee; Side 14; s/d/ste from €91/104/153; P🛜✳) Big (120-odd rooms) and *busy* in summer, this hotel near the water has slick rooms, all with balconies and beach views (ask for a room on a higher floor). Here, happy-holiday facilities are laid on thick: bowling alley, kids' playroom, spa, fitness club, water park, restaurants, bar. It's very popular with Swedish and Finnish guests, so book ahead in summer.

✖ Eating

★ Piccadilly
CAFE, VEGETARIAN €
(www.wine.kohvila.com; Pühavaimu 15; mains €4.50-7.50; ☺9am-11pm Mon-Sat, 10am-8pm Sun; ☑) Piccadilly offers a down-tempo haven for wine-lovers and vegetarians and an extensive range of hot beverages. Savoury options include delicious salads, sandwiches and omelettes, but really it's all about the sweeties, including moreish cheesecake and handmade chocolates.

Steffani
PIZZA €
(www.steffani.ee; Nikolai 24; mains €6.10-8.30; ☺11am-midnight Sun-Thu, to 2am Fri & Sat; 🖭) The queue out front should alert you – this is a top choice for thin-crust and pan pizzas, particularly in summer when you can dine alfresco on the big, flower-filled terrace. The menu also stretches to pasta and, oddly, burritos. During summer it also operates out of a **beach branch** (Ranna pst 1; mains €7.10-9.90).

Port Arturi Konsum
SUPERMARKET €
(Lai mnt 11; ☺9am-10pm) The most central supermarket is inside the Port Artur shopping centre.

Old Market
MARKET €

(Vana Turg; Suur-Sepa 18; ⊙ 7am-4.30pm Tue-Sat, 7am-3pm Sun) Covered market; good for fruit and vegetables.

Piparmünt
MODERN EUROPEAN €€

(☑ 442 5736; www.kurgovilla.ee; Papli 13; mains €11-17; ⊙ noon-11pm) Despite its low-key feel and tucked-away location (it's attached to a small hotel on a side street near the beach), Piparmünt is easily one of Pärnu's best restaurants. The menu changes constantly, but you can expect dishes which are interesting, artfully arranged and liberally loaded with flavour.

Supelsaksad
CAFE €€

(☑ 442 2448; www.supelsaksad.ee; Nikolai 32; mains €10-18; ⊙ 8am-10pm Sun-Thu, 9am-midnight Fri & Sat) Looking like it was designed by Barbara Cartland on acid (bright pink and a riot of stripes and prints), this fabulous cafe serves an appealing mix of salads, pastas and meaty mains. If you eat all your greens, make a beeline for the bountiful cake display.

Mahedik
CAFE €€

(☑ 442 5393; www.mahedik.ee; Pühavaimu 20; breakfast €5-6, mains €8-15; ⊙ 10am-7pm Sun, 9am-9pm Mon-Thu, 10am-11pm Fri & Sat) The name roughly translates as 'organic-ish', and local, seasonal fare is the focus of this cosy all-day cafe. There are cooked breakfasts, locally caught fish dishes and a divine array of cakes.

★ Lime Lounge
INTERNATIONAL €€€

(☑ 449 2190; www.limelounge.ee; Hommiku 17; mains €12-21; ⊙ noon-midnight Mon-Sat, to 9pm Sun; 🛜🍴) Bright and zesty Lime Lounge feels more like a cocktail bar than a restaurant, although the food really is excellent. The well-travelled menu bounds from Russia (borscht) to France (duck breast), Italy (delicious pasta) and all the way to Thailand (*tom kha gai* soup).

Raimond
MODERN EUROPEAN €€€

(☑ 5556 2686; www.hedonspa.com; Ranna pst 1; lunch €8, dinner €19-25; ⊙ 1pm-midnight) Facing the water at the rear of the Heddon Spa & Hotel, Raimond delivers light lunches to a beachy crowd on its large terrace (soups, salads and a legendary beef tartare). In the evening the well-heeled slink in to the glitzy interior to enjoy more substantial dishes such as venison sirloin, beef tenderloin or fresh fish.

Trahter Postipoiss
RUSSIAN €€€

(☑ 446 4864; www.trahterpostipoiss.ee; Vee 12; mains €13-22; ⊙ noon-11pm) Housed in an 1834 postal building, this rustic tavern has excellent Russian cuisine (ranging from simple to sophisticated), a convivial crowd and imperial portraits watching over the proceedings. The spacious courtyard opens during summer and there's live music on weekends.

🍷 Drinking & Nightlife

Veerev Õlu
PUB

(Uus 3a; ⊙ 11am-1am Mon-Sat, 1pm-1am Sun) Named after the Rolling Stones, the 'Rolling Beer' wins the award for the friendliest and cosiest pub by a long shot. It's a tiny rustic space with good vibes, cheap beer and the occasional live folk-rock band (with compulsory dancing on tables, it would seem).

Sweet Rosie
PUB

(www.sweetrosie.eu; Munga 2; ⊙ 11am-midnight Sun-Thu, to 2am Fri & Sat) Revellers jam into the warm, dark-wood interior of this fun Irish pub for a huge beer menu, tasty pub grub, occasional live music and a raucous good time.

Puhvet APTEK
BAR, CLUB

(www.aptek.ee; Rüütli 40; ⊙ 10pm-2am Wed & Thu, to 4am Fri & Sat) Drop by the old 1930s pharmacy to admire the clever restoration that has turned it into a smooth late-night haunt. Fabulous decor (including original cabinets, vials and bottles) competes for your attention with cocktails and DJs.

Pärnu Kuursaal
PUB

(www.kuur.ee; Mere pst 22; mains €3.50-5.50; ⊙ noon-10pm Sun-Wed, to midnight Thu, to 4am Fri & Sat) This late-19th-century dance hall has been transformed into a spacious countrified beer hall with a large terrace at the back. An older mix of tourists and locals come for the draft beer and the live music, and a menu that takes its meat and beer snacks seriously.

Citi
PUB

(Hommiku 8; mains €5-13; ⊙ 10am-11pm Mon-Sat, 11am-9pm Sun) When the sun's shining, the outdoor tables at this lively pub are jam-packed with a diverse crowd, while the rustic interior matches the simple menu of beery snacks and inexpensive meaty mains (salmon fillet, grilled chicken, pork roast). It's popular with visitors and locals, and the owner's a local character.

Romantic Bar
BAR

(www.terviseparadiis.ee; 8th fl Tervise Paradiis, Side 14; ⏱2pm-midnight) Despite the cheesy name and bland hotel-bar vibe, the superb sea views from this venue make it the perfect setting for a sundowner cocktail or a nightcap, either inside on the white, podlike leather chairs, or on the small terrace.

Sunset
CLUB

(www.sunset.ee; Ranna pst 3; ⏱11pm-6am Fri & Sat Jun-Aug) Pärnu's biggest and most famous summertime nightclub has an outdoor beach terrace and a sleek multifloor interior with plenty of nooks for when the dance floor gets crowded. Imported DJs and bands keep things cranked until the early hours.

Rock Club Volume
CLUB

(www.rockclubvolume.ee; Mere pst 22; admission €7-12; ⏱hours vary) Attached to the Kuursaal pub, this heavy rock club attracts an eager crowd of young metalheads with a mixture of live bands and DJ sets.

☆ Entertainment

In summer, concerts are held at traditional venues such as the concert hall and Kuursaal, as well as in parks, the town hall, churches and the grounds of the beautiful Ammende Villa.

Pärnu Concert Hall
CLASSICAL MUSIC

(Pärnu konserdimaja; ☑445 5810; www.concert.ee; Aida 4) This striking riverside glass-and-steel auditorium with first-rate acoustics is considered the best concert venue in Estonia.

Endla Theatre
THEATRE

(☑442 0667; www.endla.ee; Keskväljak 1; ⏱closed Jun) Pärnu's best theatre stages a wide range of performances (usually in Estonian). It also houses an art gallery, a jazz club and an open-air cafe.

🔒 Shopping

Maarja-Magdaleena Gild
CRAFTS

(www.maarjamagdaleenagild.ee; Uus 5; ⏱10am-6pm Mon-Fri, to 3pm Sat) The artisans associated with this local guild sell their wares (leather, glass, paper, weaving, felt, jewellery, pottery) from the main shop downstairs and from their various little studios scattered throughout the building.

ℹ Information

Pärnu Central Library (Pärnu keskraamatukogu; www.pkr.ee; Akadeemia tänav 3; ⏱10am-

7pm Mon-Fri, to 3pm Sat) Call into this spiffy modern library for free internet access.

Pärnu Tourist Information Centre (☑447 3000; www.visitparnu.com; Uus 4; ⏱9am-6pm mid-May–mid-Sep, 9am-5pm Mon-Fri & 10am-2pm Sat & Sun rest of year) A very helpful centre stocking maps and brochures, booking accommodation and rental cars (for a small fee), and providing a left-luggage service (per day €2). There's a small gallery attached as well as a toilet and showers.

ℹ Getting There & Away

AIR

Pärnu Airport (Pärnu lennujaam, EPU; ☑447 5000; www.parnu-airport.ee; Lennujaama tee, Eametsa) lies on the northern edge of town, west of the Tallinn road, 4km from the town centre. It's only used by one small airline, Luftverkehr Friesland-Harle (LFH), for flights to the islands of Kihnu and Ruhnu, and then only in winter when sea travel is impossible. Bus 23 runs from the bus station to the airport twice a day (15 minutes), or a taxi should cost no more than €3.

BOAT

Pärnu Yacht Club (Pärnu jahtklubi; ☑447 1750; www.jahtklubi.ee; Lootsi 6) has a marina with a customs point, along with a restaurant and accommodation.

BUS

Buses stop at the corner of Pikk and Ringi, but the main **bus station ticket office** (Ringi 3; ⏱6.30am-7.30pm) is about 100m away, across Ringi (look for the red 'bussijaam' sign). International coaches head from here to as far afield as St Petersburg and Vilnius (p178). The main domestic destinations include the following:

Haapsalu (€5.05, 2½ hours, daily)

Kuressaare (€13, 3½ hours, four daily)

Tallinn (€6.50 to €11, two hours, at least hourly)

Tartu (€9.60 to €12, 2¾ hours, 12 daily)

Viljandi (€6 to €6.80, 1½ hours, 11 daily)

CAR & MOTORCYCLE

Rental options include **Avis** (☑667 1515; www.avis.ee; Rüütli 44), which is based at the Hotel Pärnu.

TRAIN

Three daily trains run between Tallinn and Pärnu (€7.60, 2¼ hours), but this isn't a great option given that **Pärnu station** (Liivi tee) is an inconvenient 5km east of the town centre in a difficult to find and to access spot on a major road. There's no station office; buy tickets on the train. Note, if you're coming from Tallinn, make sure you get in the right carriages as part of the train unhooks at Lelle and continues on a different track to Viljandi.

ℹ️ Getting Around

BICYCLE

In summer, **Tõruke Rattarent** (📞 502 8269; www.bicyclerentalparnu.eu; Ranna pst 1a; bike per hr/day/week €2.50/10/43; ⏱ 9am-7pm Jun-Aug) rents bikes from a stand near the beach, on the corner of Ranna pst and Supeluse. Otherwise, you can get a bike delivered to your accommodation for an extra €1.

BUS

There are local buses but given that all the sights are within walking distance of each other, you probably won't need to bother with them. Tickets for local journeys are €0.64 if prepurchased or €1 from the driver.

TAXI

Taxis line up near the bus station on Ringi. Local companies include **E-Takso** (📞 443 1111; www. etakso.ee; flagfall €2.90, per kilometre €0.96) and **Pärnu Takso** (📞 443 9222; www.parnutakso.ee; flagfall €2.88, per kilometre €0.96).

Kihnu

POP 502

Kihnu island, 40km southwest of Pärnu in the Gulf of Rīga, is a living museum of Estonian culture. Many of the island's women still wear their traditional, colourful striped skirts nearly every day. There are four villages on the 7km-long island and long, quiet beaches line the western coast.

In December 2003 Unesco declared the Kihnu Cultural Space 'a Masterpiece of the Oral and Intangible Heritage of Humanity'. This honour is a tribute to the rich cultural traditions that are still practised, in song, dance, the celebration of traditional spiritual festivals and the making of handicrafts. In part, the customs of Kihnu have remained intact for so many centuries thanks to the island's isolation.

Many of the island's first inhabitants, centuries ago, were criminals and exiles from the mainland. Kihnu men made a living from fishing and seal hunting, while women effectively governed the island in their absence. The most famous Kihnuan was the sea captain Enn Uuetoa (better known as Kihnu Jõnn), who was said to have sailed on all the world's oceans. He drowned in 1913 when his ship sank off Denmark on what was to have been his last voyage before retirement. He was buried in the Danish town of Oksby but in 1992 his remains were brought home to Kihnu.

After WWII a fishery collective was established here, and fishing and cattle herding continue to be the mainstay of employment for Kihnu's inhabitants.

👁 Sights

Kihnu Museum   MUSEUM
(📞 446 9983; www.kihnu.ee; Linaküla; adult/child €3/1.50; ⏱ 10am-5pm May-Aug, 10am-2pm Tue-Sat Sep, 10am-2pm Tue-Fri Oct-Apr) You can learn more about Kihnu Jõnn and life on Kihnu at this museum, near the picturesque Orthodox church.

St Nicholas' Orthodox Church   CHURCH
(Nikolaose kirik; Linaküla; ⏱ 10am-3pm May-Sep) The islanders are among the minority of ethnic Estonians who adhere to the Russian Orthodox religion. This pretty little church at the centre of the island dates from 1786, with some additions from 1862.

Kihnu Lighthouse   LIGHTHOUSE
(Kihnu Tuletorn; adult/child €3/1.50; ⏱ 10am-6pm Jun-Aug, 10am-3pm Sat & Sun May & Sep) Constructed from parts shipped from England in 1864, this 29m-high lighthouse flashes at passing ships from the southern extremity of the island. In summer you can climb to the top to enjoy the views.

🛏 Sleeping & Eating

Homestays are popular as they provide an opportunity to interact with locals and experience home cooking. See www.visitestonia. com for options; chances are your hosts won't speak English.

Rock City   GUESTHOUSE €
(📞 446 9956; www.rockcity.ee; Sääre; sites per person €4, s/d from €15/30; ⏱ May-Aug) Near the port, this place offers simple, wood-floored rooms with shared bathroom. Services include bike rental, a sauna, excursions and a restaurant serving hearty country fare.

Tolli Tourist Farm   GUESTHOUSE €€
(📞 527 7380; www.kihnukallas.ee; Sääre; sites per person €6, s/d €32/40; ⏱ May-Sep) Located about 2km north of the port, Tolli offers rooms in the main farmhouse, in the barn or in a rustic log cabin, or you can pitch a tent. Other services include a sauna and boating excursions, and guests can order meals. They can even arrange to sail you over from the mainland.

ℹ Information

Kihnurand Travel Agency (☑ 525 5172; www. kihnurand.ee; Sääre) Arranges day trips and tours.

ℹ Getting There & Away

AIR

In winter (usually from December or whenever the boats stop), **LFH** (☑ 512 4013; www. lendame.ee) flies to and from Pärnu.

BOAT

➡ As long as ice conditions allow (from at least mid-May to the end of October), there are ferries to Kihnu operated by **Veeteed** (☑ 443 1069; www.veeteed.com) departing from Munalaid (adult/child/car/bike €3/1.50/12/1, 50 minutes, two to four daily), 40km southwest of Pärnu.

➡ Buses from Pärnu to Munalaid are theoretically timed to meet the ferries.

➡ At the time of writing there were also ferries departing from central Pärnu (adult/child/car/bike €5/2.50/15/free, 2½ hours, Thursday to Sunday only). However, these services were under review and may be stopped permanently. Even if you catch the bus, the journey is considerably quicker from Munalaid.

➡ Tickets can be purchased at any of the ports.

➡ The Pärnu tourist office keeps updated ferry timetables.

➡ On Kihnu, the ferry dock is halfway between the villages of Sääre and Lemsi.

ℹ Getting Around

The best way to get around the island is by bicycle. Various places hire bikes, including most accommodation providers.

WESTERN ESTONIA & THE ISLANDS

One of the Baltic's most alluring regions, the west coast of Estonia encompasses forest-covered islands, verdant countryside and quiet seaside villages slumbering beneath the shadows of picturesque medieval castles.

Pine forests and juniper groves cover Saaremaa and Hiiumaa, Estonia's largest islands. Dusty roads loop around them, passing desolate stretches of coastline, with few signs of development aside from 19th-century lighthouses and old wooden windmills – both emblems of the islands. Here you'll find peaceful settings for hiking, horse riding or simply touring through the countryside in search of hidden stone churches and crumbling fortresses – ruins left behind by pagan Estonian warriors, German knights and Soviet military planners.

Saaremaa, the largest and most visited of the islands, boasts spa resorts, a magnificent castle and a pretty 'capital' that comes to life during the summer months. It's also the departure point for the wildlife-rich islands of Vilsandi National Park.

On the mainland, Haapsalu is an enchanting but ragged town that was once a resort for 19th-century Russian aristocrats. The jewel of its Old Town is a 14th-century bishop's castle, today the setting for open-air festivals and summer concerts.

Muhu

POP 1560

Connected to Saaremaa by a 2.5km causeway, the island of Muhu has the undeserved reputation as the 'doormat' for the bigger island – lots of people passing through on their way from the ferry, but few stopping. In fact, Estonia's third-biggest island offers plenty of excuses to hang around, not least one of the country's best restaurants and some excellent accommodation options. There's no tourist office on the island, but there's lots of good information online at www.muhu.info.

⊙ Sights & Activities

Muhu Museum   MUSEUM
(www.muhumuuseum.ee; Koguva; adult/concession €3/2; ⊙ 9am-6pm mid-May–mid-Sep, 10am-5pm Tue-Sat rest of year) Koguva, 6km off the main road on the western tip of Muhu, is an exceptionally well-preserved, old-fashioned island village, now protected as an open-air museum. One ticket allows you to wander through an old schoolhouse, a house displaying beautiful traditional textiles from the area (including painstakingly detailed folk costumes) and a farm which was the ancestral home of author Juhan Smuul (1922–71). You can poke around various farm buildings, one of which contains a collection of Singer sewing machines.

The village is still very much lived in, mainly by the families that have resided here for generations, so respect their privacy by sticking to the designated museum areas.

Koguva Kunstitall
GALLERY

(Koguva; ⊘noon-5pm Jun-Aug) **FREE** If you're in Koguva, it's well worth calling into this handsome modern art gallery and cafe.

Eemu Tuulik
WINDMILL

(adult/child €1/0.50; ⊘10am-6pm Wed-Sun mid-May–mid-Sep) On the main road at Nautse, this working windmill has a display board and sells bread made from its milled flour.

Muhu Stronghold
FORTRESS

(Muhu Maalinn) Immediately southwest of the Eemu windmill, this earthen ring draped in greenery is where in 1227 the pagan Estonians made their last stand, holding off a 20,000-strong force led by the Knights of the Sword for six days before surrendering. A stone obelisk remembers the massacre that followed when all 2500 warriors were slaughtered by the Christians.

Muhu Ostrich Farm
FARM

(Muhu Jaanalinnufarm; www.jaanalind.ee; adult/child €3.50/2.50; ⊘10am-6pm mid-May–mid-Sep) The quirky ostrich owners will give you an earful about these strange creatures and let you feed them (mind your fingers). There's also a minimenagerie of kangaroos, wallabies, emus and ponies (for kids to ride). A small shop sells feathers, eggs, purses and shoes made from ostrich leather – it is a farm, after all. The signposted turn-off is 200m east of the Eemu windmill (to which it's no relation).

Cycling Routes
CYCLING

(www.muhu.ee/Activities-on-Muhu/) Muhu's quiet backroads are perfect for two-wheeled exploration. Two cycling routes have been set out: the 52.5km northern route and the 26km southern route. Both start from the ferry and end at the causeway to Saaremaa, meaning they can be combined into one big loop. Download a map from the website.

🍃 Courses

Nami Namaste
COOKING COURSE

(www.naminamaste.com; Simisti; per person €245; ⊘May-Sep) Finnish TV personality Sikke Sumari offers bespoke cooking classes including meals and accommodation in her rustic-chic farmhouse lodge in Muhu's south. Most ingredients are seasonal and local (many are home-grown), and classes are given in various languages, including English. It's also possible to stay or to dine here without taking the class, although numbers are limited.

🛏 Sleeping

Vanatoa Turismitalu
GUESTHOUSE €€

(☎454 8884; www.vanatoa.ee; Koguva; s/d from €30/60; ⓟ🛜) On the edge of lost-in-time Koguva village, family-run Vanatoa has renovated rooms with slick little en suite bathrooms (gotta love that underfloor heating) in a thatched-roof farm complex. The attached restaurant serves up perfunctory Estonian stomach-fillers such as pork fillet and herring. It's often snapped up for weddings or school groups, so book ahead.

★ Pädaste Manor
HOTEL €€€

(☎454 8800; www.padaste.ee; Pädaste; r/ste from €159/265; ⊘Mar-Oct; ⓟ🛜) If money's no object, here's where to part with it. This manicured bayside estate encompasses the restored manor house (14 rooms and a fine-dining restaurant), a stone carriage house (nine rooms and a spa centre) and a separate stone 'sea house' brasserie. The attention to detail is second-to-none, from the pop-up TVs to the antique furnishings and Muhu embroidery.

🍴 Eating

Muhu Kalakohvik
SEAFOOD, ESTONIAN €

(☎459 8551; Liiva; mains €5.50-7.50; ⊘noon-8pm summer) Set slightly back from the main road at Liiva, this humble 'fish cafe' serves up first-rate seafood in what is basically a family dining room. If we're a bit vague about opening hours, it's only because it's a very informal operation. Call ahead to ensure it's open or take your chances if you're passing through.

Alexander
MODERN EUROPEAN €€€

(☎454 8800; Pädaste; 3/5/7/9 courses €67/80/103/119; ⊘1-2.30pm Mar-May & Sep, 7-10.30pm Mar–mid-Oct) If you're not interested in a culinary adventure, go elsewhere. Although a set three-course dinner is offered, the focus here is on multicourse *dégustation* (tasting) menus. Expect New Nordic cuisine of the highest calibre, including elements of molecular gastronomy and plenty of fine island produce. From June to August a lighter lunch is served on the Sea House Terrace.

ⓘ Getting There & Away

BOAT

➔ Car ferries run by **SLK** (☎4524 4444; www.tuulelaevad.ee; adult/child/car €2.60/1.30/7.40) make the 25-minute crossing between Virtsu on the mainland and Kuivastu on Muhu.

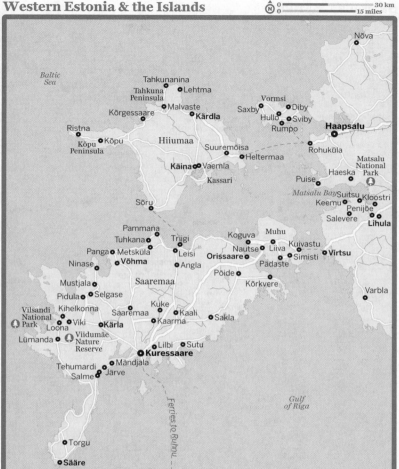

➡ Boats depart Virtsu from roughly 5.35am until midnight, with at least one or two sailings per hour up until 10.15pm.

➡ A 50% surcharge applies to vehicles heading to the island after 1pm on Fridays and departing the island after 1pm on Sundays.

➡ Up to 70% of each boat's capacity is presold online; the website has a real-time indicator showing what percentage has already been sold. The remaining 30% is kept for drive-up customers and offered on a first-in, first-on basis. You should definitely consider prebooking at busy times, particularly around weekends in summer.

➡ Tickets purchased online must be printed or loaded as an electronic ticket onto a smartphone.

➡ If you miss your prebooked boat, your ticket will be valid for the regular queue on subsequent boats for up to 48 hours.

BUS

Buses take the ferry from the mainland and continue through to Saaremaa via the causeway, stopping along the main road. Some Kuressaare–Kuivastu services also divert to Koguva and Pädaste on weekdays. Major destinations:

Kuressaare (€5 to €5.60, one hour, 18 daily)

Pärnu (€8.80, 2½ hours, four daily)

Saaremaa & Muhu

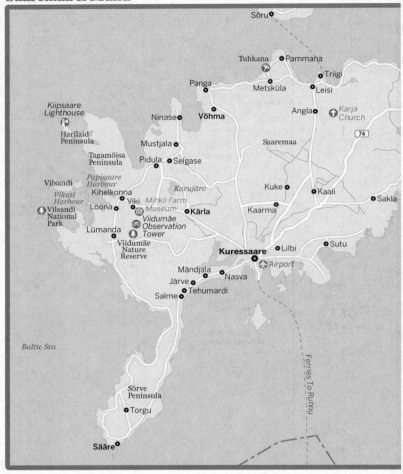

Tallinn (€12 to €14, three hours, 11 daily)
Tartu (€17, five hours, two daily)
Viljandi (€15, four hours, two daily)

Saaremaa

POP 31,600

Saaremaa (literally 'island land') is synonymous to Estonians with space, spruce and fresh air – and bottled water, vodka and killer beer. Estonia's largest island (roughly the size of Luxembourg) is still substantially covered in forests of pine, spruce and juniper, while its windmills, lighthouses and tiny villages seem largely unbothered by the passage of time.

During the Soviet era the entire island was off limits to visitors (due to an early-radar system and rocket base stationed there), even to 'mainland' Estonians, who needed a permit to visit. This resulted in a minimum of industrial build-up and the unwitting protection of the island's rural charm.

This unique old-time setting goes hand-in-hand with inextinguishable Saaremaan pride. Saaremaa has always had an independent streak and was usually the last part of Estonia to fall to invaders. Its people have

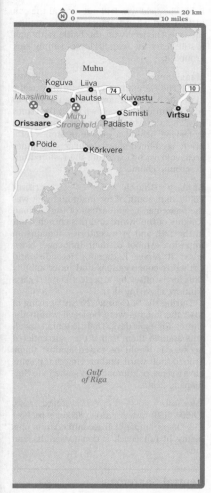

More information is available online at www.saaremaa.ee.

History

Saaremaa's earliest coastal settlements (dating from the 4th millennium BC) now lie inland because the land has risen about 15m over the last 5000 years. In the 10th to 13th centuries Saaremaa and Muhu were the most densely populated parts of Estonia. Denmark tried to conquer Saaremaa in the early 13th century; however, in 1227 it was the German Knights of the Sword who subjugated it. The island was then carved up between the knights, who took Muhu and the eastern and northwestern parts of Saaremaa, and the Haapsalu-based bishop of Ösel-Wiek, who made Kuressaare his stronghold.

Saaremaa rebelled against German rule many times between 1236 and 1343, when the knights' castle was destroyed and the Germans were expelled. However the islander's gains were always short-lived and in 1345 the Germans reconquered the island.

In the 16th century Saaremaa became a Danish possession during the Livonian War, but by 1645 the Swedes had their turn, compliments of the Treaty of Brömsebro. Russia took over in 1710 during the Great Northern War and Saaremaa became part of the Russian province of Livonia, governed from Rīga.

❶ Getting There & Away

Most travellers reach Saaremaa by taking the ferry from Virtsu to Muhu and then crossing the 2.5km causeway connecting the islands.

AIR

Kuressaare Airport (Kuressaare Lennujaam; ☑ 453 0313; www.kuressaare-airport.ee; Roomassaare tee 1) is at Roomassaare, 3km southeast of the town centre.

Buses 2 and 12 connect it with the bus station at Kuressaare.

Avies (p83) flies to/from Tallinn twice-daily on weekdays and once on Sundays.

BOAT

Additional to the Muhu ferry, **SLK Ferries** (☑ 4524 4444; www.tuulelaevad.ee) runs two boats a day between Sõru on Hiiumaa and Triigi on the north coast of Saaremaa (adult/child/car €2.60/1.30/7.40, 65 minutes); from mid-September to mid-May there are no sailings on Tuesdays, Thursdays or Saturdays. Tickets can be purchased at the harbour or prebooked

their own customs, songs and costumes. They don't revere mainland Estonia's *Son of Kalev* legend, for Saaremaa has its own hero, Suur Tõll, who fought many battles around the island against devils and fiends.

Kuressaare, the capital of Saaremaa, is on the south coast (75km from the Muhu ferry terminal) and is a natural base for visitors. It's here among the upmarket hotels that you'll understand where the island got its nickname, 'Spa-remaa'. When the long days arrive, so too do the Finns and Swedes, jostling for beach and sauna space with Estonian urban-escapees.

online, but you'll need to be able to print out the ticket in advance.

Saaremaa is very popular with visiting yachties. The best **marina** (⌨ 503 1953; www. kuressaare.ee/sadam/en; Tori 4) facilities are at Kuressaare. Visit www.sadamaregister.ee for details of this and other harbours on Saaremaa.

BUS

Buses from the mainland take the Muhu ferry and continue to Saaremaa via the causeway, terminating in Kuressaare. The major routes:

Muhu island (€5 to €5.60, one hour, 18 daily)
Pärnu (€13, 3½ hours, four daily)
Tallinn (€15 to €17, four hours, 11 daily)
Tartu (€18, 5½ hours, two daily)
Viljandi (€18, five hours, two daily)

❶ Getting Around

There are over 400km of paved roads on Saaremaa and many more dirt roads. Hitching is not uncommon on the main routes but you'll need time on your hands; there's not much traffic on minor roads.

BICYCLE

Flat Saaremaa is well suited to exploring by pedal power. Apart from the main highway leading from Muhu to Kuressaare, most of the roads have only light traffic and there are lots of side routes to explore.

Many accommodation providers rent bikes. In Kuressaare, **Bivarix** (⌨ 455 7118; www.bivarix. ee; Tallinna mnt 26; per 1hr/4hr/day €4/6/10; ◷10am-6pm Mon-Fri, to 2pm Sat) rents bicycles and touring gear such as trailers for kids or luggage. It can also advise on interesting routes.

BUS

Local buses putter around the island, but not very frequently. The main terminus is **Kuressaare bus station** (Kuressaare Bussijaam; ⌨ 453 1661; Pihtla tee 2) and there's a route planner online at www.bussipilet.ee.

Eastern Saaremaa

Apart from the town of Orissaare, which faces Muhu over the channel between the two islands, the eastern end of Saaremaa is sparsely populated and pleasantly rural.

❂ Sights & Activities

Orissaare Oak   LANDMARK
(Kuivastu mnt) Even in a nation where people still leave offerings in sacred groves, Orissaare's most famous landmark is, well, a little weird. Winner of the 2015 'European Tree of the Year' award, this 150-year-old oak stands right in the middle of a football field. The field was laid out around the oak in 1951 and when tractors came to remove the tree, the tree won the battle (although it still bears the scars). Players simply kick around it.

Maasilinnus   CASTLE
FREE The German knights built this castle, 4km north of Orissaare, during the 14th to 16th centuries. It was blown up by the Danes in 1578 to prevent the Swedes from taking it, leaving behind a jumble of stones by a pretty reed-lined shore. Indulge your inner archaeologist by exploring the restored underground chamber.

St Mary's Church   CHURCH
Pöide, 3km south of the main highway, was the Saaremaa headquarters of the German Knights of the Sword and this church, built in the 13th and 14th centuries, remains an imposing symbol of their influence. Nowadays it serves Lutheran, Methodist and Orthodox congregations and its crumbling exterior is offset by a perfect stained-glass window above the altar.

During the St George's Night Uprising of 1343 the knights were besieged within the church for eight days. Their Estonian assailants assured them that if they surrendered no swords would be raised against them. True to their word, and proving that pagans have a sense of humour, they stoned the Germans to death.

Tika Talu   HORSE RIDING
(⌨ 504 4169; www.tikatalu.ee; Körkvere; per hour €12) Offers simple B&B accommodation plus plenty of horseback action for adults and kids.

Central Saaremaa

If you're arriving by ferry from Hiiumaa, the first settlement you'll hit is **Leisi**, a pretty village of old wooden houses, 3.5km from the harbour of Triigi. There are some interesting sights scattered around this section of the north coast, along with plenty of others on either side of the main road heading south to Kuressaare.

❂ Sights

Tuhkana   BEACH
Tucked away within pine forest, Tuhkana is one of Saaremaa's best sandy beaches, due in large part to its remoteness. To get here from Leisi, head west for 11km to Metsküla and

turn right onto the unsealed road. After about 3km, look for a parking area on your left.

Panga Pank
VIEWPOINT

Saaremaa's highest cliffs run along the northern coast near Panga for 3km. The highest point (21.3m) was a sacred place where sacrifices were made to the sea god; gifts of flowers, coins, vodka and beer are still sometimes left here. It's a pretty spot, looking down at the treacherous waters below.

Angla Windmill Hill
WINDMILLS

(Angla Tuulikumägi; adult/child €3.50/1.50; ⊘9am-8pm May-Aug, to 5pm Sep-Apr) Charge up those camera batteries: this is the site of the largest and most photogenic grouping of wooden windmills on the islands. By the early 16th century there were already nine windmills on this hill. Now there are four small ones, mainly dating from the 19th century, and one large Dutch-style one, built in 1927. There are excellent (free) views from the road, but the modest admission charge allows you to poke around in their innards.

There's also a collection of old tractors and ploughs, and an excellent tavern-style cafe where peasant-dressed staff dispense homemade bread, cakes and beer.

St Catherine's Lutheran Church, Karja
CHURCH

(Karja Katariina kirik; Linnaka village; ⊘10am-5.30pm Mon-Sat, 12.30-5.30pm Sun mid-May-mid-Sep) The pagan and Christian meet in this fortresslike 14th-century church. Outside there's an interesting panel about pre-Christian symbols with particular reference to some of the 13th- and 14th-century trapezoidal gravestones found here. Inside, oak leaves curl along the top of the columns and there are some interesting symbols painted on the walls.

There's also an unusual carved crucifixion scene above the exterior door on the right-hand side, showing Jesus between the two thieves. The good thief's soul (in mini-me form) is exiting through his mouth into the arms of an angel, ready to whisk him off to heaven. A similar-looking devil is awaiting the other.

Kaali Crater
LAKE

Perhaps proof of its powers of attraction, Estonia has one of the world's highest concentrations of documented meteor craters. At Kaali, 18km north of Kuressaare, is a 100m-wide, 22m-deep, curiously round lake formed by a meteorite at least 4000 years ago. There are a further eight collateral craters in the vicinity, ranging from 12m to 40m in diameter, formed from the impact of fragments of the same meteorite. In Scandinavian mythology, the site was known as the sun's grave.

A tourist village of sorts has sprung up here – there's a small **museum** (www.kaali. kylastuskeskus.ee; adult/child €1.50/0.70; ⊘9am-7pm), handicrafts stores and a hotel, as well as an old-style tavern offering Estonian fare and locally brewed beer.

GoodKaarma
FARM

(☑5348 4006; www.goodkaarma.com; Kuke; ⊘10am-6pm Jun-Aug, other times by arrangement) 🌿 Run by an English-Estonian couple from their farm outside the village of Kaarma, about 15km north of Kuressaare, GoodKaarma makes organic soaps from local ingredients such as juniper, pine and sea-buckthorn berries. If you're interested in getting your hands dirty (or should that be clean), you can book into a 75-minute soap-making workshop (adult/child €7.50/4; minimum four people).

There's also a pretty garden terrace and cafe-bar, with homemade snacks, organic teas, local beers etc. Besides soap, the shop sells local arts and crafts.

ISLAND BREW

Saaremaa has a long history of beer home-brewing and even its factory-produced brew has a great reputation. Tuulik, with its distinctive windmill branding, is the most popular, but don't mention that it's now brewed in Tartu (the popular Saaremaa vodka also has a windmill on its label and it's not distilled there either).

For a classier drop, try Pöide (especially the dark version), which is produced in a microbrewery in the village of the same name. It's available at the pubs in Kuressaare and in craft beer stockists nationwide.

Beer-lovers should be sure to try any homemade beer wherever it's offered. A longtime island tradition, the brew features the traditional malt, yeast and hops, but comes off a bit sour on the palate. It's light and refreshing, best quaffed from a wooden tankard on a warm summer's day.

❶ Information

Leisi Tourist Office (☎ 457 3073; ⏱1-7pm Jun-Aug; 🔊) If you're arriving from Hiiumaa via the Sõru–Triigi ferry, pick up maps and get general Saaremaa information at the tiny Leisi tourist office, inside the pretty, vine-covered restaurant, Sassimaja.

Kuressaare

POP 13,000

What passes for the big smoke in these parts, Kuressaare has a picturesque town centre with leafy streets and a magnificent castle rising up in its midst, surrounded by the usual scrappy sprawl of housing and light industry. The town built a reputation as a health centre as early as the 19th century, when the ameliorative properties of its coastal mud were discovered and the first spas opened. Now they're a dime a dozen, ranging from Eastern Bloc sanatoriums to sleek and stylish resorts.

Kuressaare exists because of its castle, which was founded in the 13th century as the Haapsalu-based Bishop of Ösel-Wiek's stronghold in the island part of his diocese. The town became Saaremaa's main trading centre, developing quickly after passing into Swedish hands in 1645. From 1952 to 1988 Kuressaare was named Kingisseppa, after Viktor Kingissepp, an Estonian communist of the 1920s.

Apart from the castle, the best of Kuressaare's historic buildings are grouped around the central square, Keskväljak. The tourist office is housed in the town hall (1670), a baroque building guarded by a fine pair of stone lions. Directly across the square the Vaekoja pub inhabits a former weigh-house, also from the 17th century.

❍ Sights

★ Kuressaare Castle   CASTLE

Majestic Kuressaare Castle stands facing the sea at the southern end of the town, on an artificial island ringed by a moat. It's the best-preserved castle in the Baltic and the region's only medieval stone castle that has remained intact. The castle grounds are open to the public at all times but to visit the keep you'll need to buy a ticket to Saaremaa Museum.

A castle was founded in the 1260s, but the mighty dolomite fortress that stands today was not built until the 14th century, with some protective walls added between the 15th and 18th centuries. It was designed as an administrative centre as well as a stronghold. The more slender of its two tall corner towers, Pikk Hermann to the east, is separated from the rest of the castle by a shaft crossed only by a drawbridge, so it could function as a last refuge in times of attack.

Outdoor concerts are held in the castle yard throughout the summer and you can also try your hand at archery. There's a memorial on the eastern wall to 90 people killed within the castle grounds by the Red Army in 1941. Its grim companion piece lies beyond the castle wall on one of the island ramparts – a large memorial to 300 people executed during the Nazi German occupation.

The shady park around the castle moat was laid out in 1861 and there are some fine wooden resort buildings in and around it, notably the Spa Hall (Kuursaal) dating from 1899, which is now a restaurant, and the neighbouring bandstand from 1920. If the weather's nice, you can hire rowboats (per hour €10) or bikes (per hour €4) from the Spa Hall.

Saaremaa Museum   MUSEUM

(www.saaremaamuuseum.ee; adult/concession €5/2.50; ⏱10am-7pm May-Aug, 11am-6pm Wed-Sun Sep-Apr) Occupying the keep of Kuressaare Castle, this museum is devoted to the island's nature and history. A large part of the fun is exploring the warren of chambers, halls, passages and stairways, apt to fuel anyone's *Game of Thrones* fantasies. One room near the bishop's chamber looks down to a dungeon where, according to legend, condemned prisoners were dispatched to be devoured by hungry lions (recorded growls reinforce the mental image).

Legend also tells of a knight's body found when a sealed room was opened in the 18th century, which has given rise to varying accounts of how he met his tragic fate. Upon discovery the knight's body dissolved into dust but don't worry, it's since been re-created to creepy effect.

In the museum proper, there's not a lot of signage in English until you hit the EU-sponsored post-WWII section, when suddenly the Estonian/Russian captions change to Estonian/English. There's some interesting coverage of daily life under the USSR, including the interior of a typical apartment, but some of the captions are quite propagandist (you have to admire the irony of a photo labelled 'a prejudiced pro-Soviet crowd').

On the top floor, the museum has a cafe boasting fine views over the bay and surrounding countryside.

Kuressaare Beach
BEACH

(Raiekivi tee 1) Although the best beaches are out of town, this small sandy bay behind Kuressaare Castle fills up with sunbathers, paddlers and volleyball players during the summer.

Suur Töll & Piret
STATUE

Estonia's jauntiest statue enlivens the waterfront near the Spa Hotel Meri. It features Saaremaa's legendary gigantic hero, Suur (meaning 'the great') Töll and his wife Piret carrying a boat laden with fish on their very naked shoulders.

St Nicholas' Orthodox Church
CHURCH

(Püha Nikolai kirik; Lossi 8; ⊙10am-1pm Mon-Fri & Sun, 4.30-6.30pm Sat) Dating from 1790, Saaremaa's oldest Orthodox church has twin steeples and an impressive dolomite and wrought-iron gate. A faint image of its name saint has survived on the exterior wall facing the street, while inside there are some lovely icons, including one featuring the church itself.

St Lawrence's Lutheran Church
CHURCH

(Laurentiuse kirik; Tallinna 13; ⊙10am-5pm Tue-Fri, to 2pm Sat Jun-Aug) Although this large church only dates from 1836, its prized feature is considerably older: a medieval stone baptismal font, probably from the early 15th century, carved with dragonlike creatures. Also worth noting are the grey wooden box pews, low-hanging chandeliers and the fine vaulted roof above the sanctuary painted with an interesting trompe l'œil effect.

Johannes & Joosep Aavik's Memorial Museum
MUSEUM

(Johannes & Joosep Aaviku majamuuseum; www.saaremaamuuseum.ee; Vallimaa 7; adult/child €1/0.50; ⊙11am-5pm Wed-Sun) The Aavik family home is now a small museum dedicated to the life and works of linguist Johannes Aavik (1880–1973), who introduced major reforms to the Estonian language, and his musically talented cousin, Joosep Aavik (1899–1989).

🏃 Activities

Spa Hotel Rüütli
WATER PARK

(www.saaremaaspahotels.eu; Pargi 16; adult/child €7/4; ⊙7am-9pm) If the weather means an indoor splash is best, bring the kids to this hotel water park to make use of the pools and 52m slide. Mum and Dad might like to book a spa treatment while they're at it.

Saare Golf
GOLF

(☎453 3502; www.saaregolf.ee; Merikotka 35; 9/18 holes €35/60, club hire €20) This 18-hole championship course is immediately west of Kuressaare's town centre.

✨ Festivals & Events

Kuressaare's dance card is certainly full over the summer. As well the high-profile festivals, there are regular summer concerts held in the castle grounds and park; find out what's up at the tourist office.

Saaremaa Opera Festival
MUSIC

(Saaremaa ooperipäevad; www.saaremaaopera.eu) For a week in late July, about 2000 people pack into the grounds of Kuressaare Castle to watch productions from an international guest company.

Kuressaare Chamber Music Days
MUSIC

(Kuressaare kammermuusika päevad; www.kammerfest.ee) Concerts take place all over town during five days in late July/early August.

Kuressaare Maritime Festival
CULTURAL

(Kuressaare merepaevad; www.merepaevad.ee) Stalls line the beach behind the castle selling food, drink and handicrafts, while performers entertain the crowds. It's held over a weekend in early August.

🛏 Sleeping

The tourist office can organise beds in private apartments and farms across the island. Hotel prices are up to 50% cheaper from September through April. Most hotel spa centres are open to nonguests.

Hotell Mardi
HOSTEL, HOTEL €

(☎452 4633; www.hotelmardi.eu; Vallimaa 5a; hostel s/tw €20/30, hotel s/d from €44/67; ℗🛜) These simple, fuss-free rooms are attached to a college. The hostel rooms have bunk beds and share bathrooms; they're a little institutional, but probably Kuressaare's best cheapies.

★Georg Ots Spa Hotel
HOTEL €€

(Gospa; ☎455 0000; www.gospa.ee; Tori 2; r/apt/ste from €75/149/194; ℗❄🛜🏊) Named after a renowned Estonian opera singer, Gospa has modern rooms with wildly striped carpet, enormous king-sized beds and a warm but minimalist design. Most rooms have

Kuressaare

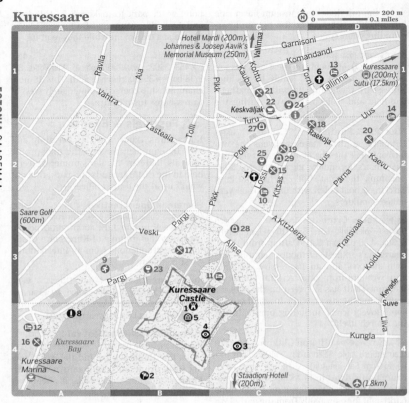

Kuressaare

⊙ **Top Sights**
1 Kuressaare Castle B4

⊙ **Sights**
2 Kuressaare Beach B4
3 Memorial to Victims of the Nazis C4
4 Memorial to Victims of the Red
  Army B4
5 Saaremaa Museum B4
6 St Lawrence's Lutheran Church........... D1
7 St Nicholas' Orthodox Church............. C2
8 Suur Tõll & Piret................................ A4

🏃 **Activities, Courses & Tours**
9 Spa Hotel Rüütli A3

🛏 **Sleeping**
10 Arensburg C2
11 Ekesparre C3
12 Georg Ots Spa Hotel........................... A4
13 Grand Rose Spa Hotel........................ D1
14 Karluti Hostel D2

🍽 **Eating**
15 Classic Cafe C2
16 Gospa Restaurant A4
17 Ku Kuu.. B3
18 Rae Konsum D2
19 Retro C2
20 Saaremaa Trahter.............................. D2
21 Vanalinna C1

🍷 **Drinking & Nightlife**
22 Chameleon C1
23 John Bull.. B3
24 Vaekoja Pubi C1
25 Vinoteek Prelude............................... C2

🛍 **Shopping**
26 Central Market C1
27 GoodKaarma C2
28 Lossi Antiik C3
29 Saaremaa Kunstistuudio..................... C2

balconies, and there's a fitness centre and excellent spa centre, including a pool and multiple saunas. Separate freestanding 'residences' are also available, and families are very well catered to.

Staadioni Hotell   HOTEL €€

(☑ 453 3556; www.staadionihotell.ee; Staadioni 4; s/d €44/56; ☉ mid-May–early Sep; P ◉ 🛜) Good-value spacious and bright rooms are available at this pleasant, secluded spot, south of the castle. It's surrounded by parkland and sports facilities. Bikes can be hired here (per day €8) and there's a sauna available.

Karluti Hostel   GUESTHOUSE €€

(☑ 501 4390; www.karluti.ee; Pärna 23; tw/tr without bathroom €38/55; ◉ 🛜) A charming older couple run this cheerful mustard-coloured guesthouse, set on large lawns on a quiet residential street close to the centre. If you work up an appetite on the volleyball court, you can always sate it in the guest kitchen. There are only a handful of bright, spotless rooms available, so you'll need to book ahead – especially in summer.

★Ekesparre   BOUTIQUE HOTEL €€€

(☑ 453 8778; www.ekesparre.ee; Lossi 27; r from €125; P 🛜) Holding pole position on the castle grounds, this elegant 10-room hotel has been returned to its art nouveau glory. Period wallpaper and carpet, Tiffany lamps and a smattering of orchids add to the refined, clubby atmosphere, while the 3rd-floor guests' library is a gem. As you'd expect from the price, it's a polished operator.

Arensburg   BOUTIQUE HOTEL €€€

(☑ 452 4700; www.arensburg.ee; Lossi 15; s €115, d €130-185, ste €250; P 🛜 ⌨) Arensburg is almost two hotels in one, with a severe case of old versus new. Our vote goes to the bold and sexy charcoal-painted rooms in the slick 2007 extension (standard rooms in the historic wing are OK but unremarkable). A spa and two restaurants round things out nicely.

Grand Rose Spa Hotel   HOTEL €€€

(☑ 666 7000; www.grandrose.ee; Tallinna 15; s/d/ste from €130/135/205; 🛜 ⌨) Floral and frilly is the theme of this hotel, from the baroque black velvet chairs, chandeliers and water feature in the rose-filled lobby to the rose carpet throughout. Deluxe rooms have a balcony, separate bathtub and shower stall, and over-the-top beds, but feel more crammed than the standard rooms. The spa centre and restaurant are both very good.

✖ Eating

★Retro   CAFE €

(☑ 5683 8400; www.kohvikretro.ee; Lossi 5; mains €7.50-8.50; ☉ noon-10pm Mon-Thu, to midnight Fri & Sat, to 8pm Sun; 🛜 🚼) The menu at this hip little cafe-bar is deceptively simple (pasta, burgers, steak, grilled fish), but Retro takes things to the next level, making its own pasta and burger buns, and using the best fresh local produce. Desserts are delicious too. There's also a great selection of Estonian craft beer, perfect for supping on the large rear terrace.

Vanalinna   BAKERY, CAFE €

(☑ 455 5309; www.vanalinna.ee; Kauba 8; snacks €1-2; ☉ 7.30am-7pm Mon-Sat, 8am-4pm Sun) There's an attractive vibe to this bakery-cafe, with its timber-and-stone interior and black-and-white photos hanging from orange walls. The counter has an appealing selection of sandwiches, salads, pastries and ice cream.

Rae Konsum   SUPERMARKET €

(Raekoja 10; ☉ 9am-9pm) Behind the tourist office.

Ku Kuu   MODERN EUROPEAN €€

(☑ 453 9749; www.kuressaarekuursaal.ee; Lossi-park 1; mains €6-15; ☉ 11am-midnight May–mid-Sep; 🛜) Occupying the elegant spa hall from which it takes its name (Ku Kuu is short for Kuressaare Kuursaal), this is Saaremaa's loveliest dining room. The wood panelling and panes of coloured glass provide an atmospheric backdrop for a tasty menu of seafood and island produce, prepared with a strong French accent.

Saaremaa Trahter   ESTONIAN €€

(☑ 453 3776; www.saaremaaveski.ee; Pärna 19; mains €9-12; ☉ 11am-10pm Sun-Thu, to midnight Fri & Sat; 🚼) How often can you say you've dined inside a 19th-century windmill? Without being too touristy, this place keeps quality and ambience at a premium, with plenty of hearty local fare – including wild boar hotpot, beetroot soup and Saaremaa cheeses.

Classic Cafe   CAFE, PIZZA €€

(Lossi 9; mains €5-16; ☉ 9am-10pm) You can order meaty bistro-style dishes, but the fresh salads, soups, pasta and, especially, the pizza are much better value. Despite the stylish decor, it's a laid-back and relaxed kind of place.

Gospa Restaurant
EUROPEAN €€€

(455 0000; www.gospa.ee; Tori 2; mains €12-20; noon-11pm) Picture windows make the most of the marina views in the Georg Ots Spa Hotel's bright and airy dining room. The food is light, fresh and creative, making good use of local produce.

Drinking & Nightlife

Vinoteek Prelude
WINE BAR

(453 3407; www.prelude.ee; Lossi 4; mains €11-12; 4pm-midnight;) A sculpted bunch of grapes heralds the entrance to this cosy, dimly lit wine bar in an 18th-century building. Climb the staircase to sofas under the eaves and choose from a menu of international wines (plenty by the glass), antipasti-style snacks and bistro meals.

John Bull
PUB

(Lossipark 4; 11am-10pm) Despite the name, this pub in the castle park isn't particularly English. In fact, there's more of a Soviet vibe going down; the bar is made from an old Russian bus and there's even a 'red corner' hung with portraits of Lenin. Sit on the deck for great views looking over the moat to the castle.

Chameleon
CAFE, BAR

(www.chameleon.ee; Kauba 2; mains €7.50-14; 11am-11pm Sun-Thu, to 1am Fri & Sat;) Chameleon is indeed a changeable creature, morphing from cafe to cocktail bar as the sun goes down, but it's the latter incarnation that suits it best. The sleek black and grey decor (with pink lighting) adds an air of city-slick, but the kids' playroom ably demonstrates that it's not trying too hard to be cool.

Vaekoja Pubi
PUB

(www.vaekoda.ee; Tallinna 3; 10.30am-11pm Sun-Wed, to 5am Thu, to 6.30am Fri & Sat;) The name means 'weigh-house' and this is one of Kuressaare's most significant historic buildings, built in 1663 to measure goods so that they could be taxed. These days it's a relaxed, no-nonsense pub with tables spilling onto the street. For hardened local drinkers, it's the last stop of the night.

Shopping

Lossi Antiik
ANTIQUES

(www.lossiantiik.eu; Lossi 19; 10am-4pm Mon-Sat) Towards the castle, this jam-packed little store sells all sorts of antiques, from 19th-century farm tools to Soviet memorabilia. It's a fun place to browse.

Central Market
MARKET

(Tallinna 5; 9am-5pm) Set back within the same block as the Vaekoja pub, this outdoor market has stalls selling all kinds of Saaremaa treats and tat: dolomite canisters, woollen sweaters, honey, strawberries etc.

Saaremaa Kunstistuudio
ART

(453 3748; www.kunstistuudio.ee; Lossi 5; 11am-7pm Mon-Fri, noon-5pm Sat) This bright gallery contains a variety of works by Estonian artists, including covetable textiles, ceramics, sculptures and paintings.

GoodKaarma
BEAUTY

(www.goodkaarma.com; Kauba 3; 10am-6pm Mon-Sat) If you don't make it to the Saaremaa farm where it's produced, you can always buy GoodKaarma's organic soap here.

Information

Kuressaare Tourist Office (453 3120; www.kuressaare.ee; Tallinna 2; 9am-6pm Mon-Fri, 10am-4pm Sat & Sun mid-May–mid-Sep, 9am-5pm Mon-Fri rest of year) Inside the old town hall, it sells maps and guides, arranges accommodation and has information on boat trips and island tours.

Getting There & Around

Kuressaare Takso (453 0000; www.kuressaaretakso.ee; day/night flagfall €2.20/2.40, per kilometre €0.80/0.95) is a reliable local taxi firm.

Southwest Coast

The long stretch of pine-lined sand from **Mändjala** to **Järve**, west of Kuressaare, is Saaremaa's main beach resort. The shallow beach curves languidly towards the south, where the 32km **Sõrve Peninsula** takes over. This beautiful but sparsely populated finger of land comes to a dramatic end at **Sääre**, with a lighthouse and a narrow sand spit extending out to sea.

The peninsula saw heavy fighting during WWII, and the battle scars remain. Various abandoned bunkers and battlements, and the remnants of the Lõme-Kaimri antitank defence lines, can still be seen.

Sights

Tehumardi Night Battle Monument
MEMORIAL

On the night of 8 October 1944 a gruesome battle took place in the coastal village of Tehumardi between retreating German troops and a Soviet Estonian Rifle Division. The horror defies belief: both armies fought blindly, firing on intuition or finding the enemy by touch. This large Soviet-era monument takes the form of a sword with the stylised reliefs of faces set into it. The Estonian dead lie buried in double graves nearby.

Sõrve Military Museum & Natural History Museum
MUSEUM

(Sõrve militaarmuuseum & loodusmuuseum; Sääre; adult/child €4/2; ⊙9am-8pm Jun-Aug, 10am-5pm Sep-May) Based in the old Soviet border guard barracks, this ramshackle museum showcases military detritus, much of which was gathered from the surrounding battlefield. Arguably more interesting than the collection itself are the ruins of a massive gun embankment and various other bits of masonry littered around the garden. Included on the same ticket, a nearby cottage is jam-packed with an eclectic array of bugs, butterflies, feathers, skulls, mosses and stuffed critters.

Sõrve Visitor Centre
MUSEUM

(Sõrve külastuskeskus; www.sorvekeskus.ee; Sääre; adult/child €4/2; ⊙10am-7pm daily May-Aug, 11am-6pm Thu-Sun Sep-Apr) For all the money that's clearly been spent on this whiz-bang centre in Sääre's old lighthouse-keeper's residence, it's not particularly interesting – for non-Estonian speakers at least. Displays are split over several floors and include a lighthouse room, a nature room and a sea room (devoted to shipwrecks and the rescue service). There's also a children's playroom. The first lighthouse was built here in 1646, although the current black-painted incarnation only dates to 1960.

🛏 Sleeping & Eating

Tehumardi Camping
CAMPGROUND €

(⊉457 1666; www.tehumardi.ee; Tehumardi; tent/caravan site €5/15, r & cabin €50; 🅿🛜) The best of the camping grounds on the beach stretch, Tehumardi has a leafy site by a little lake. As well as basic four-person wooden cabins there are little hotel-style rooms (with their own bathrooms) and larger houses and bunkrooms for families or groups.

★ Piibutopsu
APARTMENT €€

(⊉5693 0288; www.piibutopsu.ee; Ülejõe 19a, Nasva; d/tr/q €60/90/120; 🅿🛜) Set on the ample lawn of a private residence down a side street in Nasva (the first little settlement west of Kuressaare), Piibutopsu offers four well-equipped holiday apartments in a new

custom-built block. The units are grouped around a central lounge with a wood fire, and there's even a mini spa centre on site. All in all, an excellent option.

Sääre Paargu
SEAFOOD €€

(⊉5624 5585; www.saarepaargu.ee; Sääre; mains €9-13; ⊙10am-10pm Sun-Thu, to 4am Fri & Sat May-Sep; 🛜) Paargu means 'summer house' and this slick little pavilion near the tip of the Sõrve Peninsula only kicks off in the warmer months. Grilled fish fills most of the slots of the menu, freshly caught by local fisherfolk. As the evening progresses the heavy rock gets turned up a notch and there's more of a pub vibe.

Western Saaremaa

Even in summer, it's easy to beat the tourist hordes down this end of the island. The main settlement is sleepy Kihelkonna, which is more an oversized village than a town. It's the gateway to Vilsandi, the most remote of Estonia's national parks.

⦿ Sights

Viidumäe Nature Reserve
NATURE RESERVE

(Viidumäe looduskaitseala) Founded in 1957, Viidumäe Nature Reserve covers an area of 26 sq km, with a 22m **observation tower** on Saaremaa's highest point (54m). The tower (about 2km along a dirt road off the Kuressaare–Lümanda road at Viidu) offers a panoramic view of the forest and the wonders of the island itself. The view is particularly memorable at sunset. There are two **nature trails** (2.2km and 1.5km), marked to highlight the different habitats of the area.

Viidumäe is a botanical reserve, its favourable climate and conditions making it home to rare plant species. At the reserve's headquarters, near the tower, you can see a small exhibition on the subject.

Mihkli Farm Museum
FARM

(Talumuuseum; www.saaremaamuuseum.ee; Viki; adult/child €1.50/1; ⊙10am-6pm daily mid-May-Aug, Wed-Sun early May & Sep-mid-Oct) In a pretty setting southeast of Kihelkonna, this early-18th-century farm has been preserved in its entirety, complete with thatched-roof wooden farmhouses, a sauna (for rent at €30 per hour), a windmill and a traditional village swing.

St Michael's Lutheran Church
CHURCH

(Mihkli kirik; Kiriku 4; ⊙10am-5pm May-Aug) Kihelkonna's tall, austere, early-German church dates from before 1280. It's dark and gloomy inside, partly due to the wooden supports holding up the roof, but it's worth noting the Renaissance *Last Supper* triptych (1591) above the altar and the carved pulpit (1604). The church didn't get its steeple until 1899. Before that the bells were rung from the freestanding **belfry** (1638) about 100m away; once common, it's the only one of its kind remaining in Estonia.

Tagamõisa Peninsula   AREA
Much of the beautiful and rarely visited western coast of the Tagamõisa Peninsula is protected as part of Vilsandi National Park, including the Harilaid Peninsula. At its northwestern tip (accessible only on foot) is the striking **Kiipsaare lighthouse**, which due to beach erosion now sits about 30m out to sea. The erosion has caused the lighthouse to develop a visible lean, although it periodically corrects itself as the sands shift.

🛏 Sleeping & Eating

Loona Manor   GUESTHOUSE €€
(☑ 454 6510; www.loonamanor.ee; Loona; sites per person €5, r/ste €75/85; ☺ Apr-Oct; P 🤶) Loona may be a 16th-century manor house but it's more homely than palatial, with simple, clean rooms and roomier suites. Vilsandi National Park's visitor centre is within the grounds and you can also hire bikes (per day €10), two-person canoes (€26), inflatable boats (four hours €32) and skis (€7).

Söögimaja   ESTONIAN €
(☑ 457 6493; www.soogimaja.planet.ee; Lümanda; mains €5-11; ☺ 10am-10pm) 🍴 This rustic farmhouse eatery provides a unique snapshot into island life via its cuisine. The menu features the kind of food eaten by the island's forefathers – fish soup, boiled pork with turnips and carrots, and cabbage rolls. It's on the main road in Lümanda, right next door to the village church.

Matsalu National Park

A twitcher's paradise, Matsalu National Park (Matsalu Rahvuspark) is a prime bird-migration and breeding ground, both for the Baltic and for Europe. Some 282 different bird species have been counted here. Encompassing 486 sq km of wetlands (including 20km-long Matsalu Bay, the deepest inlet along the west Estonian coast), it was first protected as a reserve in 1957 before being declared a national park in 2004.

Spring migration peaks in April/May, but swans arrive as early as March. Autumn migration begins in July and can last until November. **Birdwatching towers**, with views of resting sites over various terrain, have been built at Keemu, Suitsu, Penijõe, Kloostri and Rannajõe. There are also marked **nature trails** at Penijõe (3.2km to 7km), Salevere (1.5km) and Suitsu (1km). Bring reliable footwear, as the ground is wet and muddy.

WORTH A TRIP

VILSANDI

Vilsandi, west of Kihelkonna, is the largest of 161 islands and islets off Saaremaa's western coast protected as **Vilsandi National Park** (which also includes parts of Saaremaa itself, including the Harilaid Peninsula). The park covers 238 sq km (163 sq km of sea, 75 sq km of land) and is an area of extensive ecological study. The breeding patterns of the common eider and the migration of the barnacle goose have been monitored very closely here. Ringed seals can also be seen in their breeding season and 32 species of orchid thrive in the park.

Vilsandi, 6km long and in places up to 3km wide, is a low, wooded island. The small islets surrounding it are abundant with currant and juniper bushes. Around 250 bird species are observed here, and in spring and autumn there is a remarkable migration of waterfowl: up to 10,000 barnacle geese stop over on Vilsandi in mid-May, and the white-tailed eagle and osprey have even been known to drop by.

The **National Park Visitor Centre** (☑ 5301 2772; www.loodusegakoos.ee; ☺ 10am-6pm daily Jun-Aug, 9am-5pm Mon-Fri rest of year) is on Saaremaa, at Loona Manor. Staff can provide information on the park's four basic free camp sites and the two private 'tourist farms' offering accommodation and boat transfers.

Islander (☑ 5667 1555; www.islander.ee; ☺ May-Sep) offers speedboat water taxis to the island, as well as diving, waterskiing, tubing and seal-spotting trips.

The reserve's headquarters is 3km north of the Tallinn–Virtsu road at Penijõe, an early-18th-century manor house near Lihula. Here you'll find a **nature centre** (☏472 4236; www.loodusegakoos.ee; ⊙9am-5pm daily mid-Apr–Sep, Mon-Fri rest of year) with a permanent exhibition and a free 20-minute film. With advance notice, the centre can hook you up with guides offering tours of the reserve, from two-hour canoe trips around the reed banks to several days of birdwatching. It can also recommend lodging in the area. **Estonian Nature Tours** (☏5349 6695; www.naturetours.ee), based in nearby Lihula, employs naturalist guides who have a wealth of knowledge about Matsalu's avian, mammalian and botanic riches. Check its website for a calendar of its specialist tours.

Haapsalu

POP 10,200

Set on a fork-shaped peninsula that stretches into Haapsalu Bay, this quaint resort town (100km from Tallinn) makes a fine stopover en route to the islands. Haapsalu has a handful of museums and galleries, and a few rather modest spa hotels, but the town's biggest attraction is its striking castle. A bit rough around the edges, Haapsalu's Old Town is more rustic than urban, with wooden houses set back from the narrow streets, a slender promenade skirting the bay and plenty of secret spots for watching the sunset.

Those seeking mud or spa treatments might opt for Haapsalu over Pärnu or Kuressaare, though the centres here are a bit more proletarian. Nevertheless, Haapsalu lays claim to superior mud, which is used by health centres throughout Estonia.

History

Like other Estonian towns, Haapsalu has changed hands many times since its founding. The German Knights of the Sword conquered this region in 1224, and Haapsalu became the bishop's residence, with a fortress and cathedral built soon afterwards. The Danes took control during the Livonian War (around 1559), then the Swedes had their turn in the 17th century, but they lost it to the Russians during the Great Northern War in the 18th century.

The city flourished under the tsars, mostly because of mud. Once the curative properties of its shoreline were discovered in the 19th century, Haapsalu transformed into a spa centre. The Russian composer Tchaikovsky and members of the Russian imperial family visited the city for mud baths. A railway that went all the way to St Petersburg was completed in 1907. In Soviet times, Haapsalu was closed to foreigners.

⊙ Sights & Activities

Haapsalu Episcopal Castle   CASTLE
(Haapsalu piiskopilinnus; www.haapsalulinnus.ee; Lossiplats 3; adult/child €4/3; ⊙10am-6pm May-Sep, 11am-4pm Fri-Sun Oct-Apr) Haapsalu's unpolished gem is its bishop's castle, which was western Estonia's centre of command from the 13th to 16th centuries but now stands in partial but very picturesque ruins. A turreted tower, most of the outer wall and some of the moat still remain. Entry to the grounds is free year-round, but a ticket is required to enter the castle proper, where there's a **museum** devoted to its history, including some creepy tunnels and dramatically displayed medieval weaponry.

Accessed from within the museum is the striking **Dome Church** (or, more officially, St Nicholas' Cathedral), built in a mix of the Romanesque and Gothic styles, with three inner domes. It's the largest such structure in the Baltic and its acoustics are said to be phenomenal; concerts are regularly held here. Inside the church, keep your eyes peeled for the ghost of the White Lady.

In summer, the park within the outer walls is used for concerts. There's a wonderful **children's playground** complete with a pirate ship, and a **viewing platform** within one of the towers. You can also try your hand at archery just outside the main gate (€5).

Town Hall Museum   MUSEUM
(Raekoda muusem; www.salm.ee; Kooli 2; adult/child €3/2; ⊙10am-6pm May-Aug, 11am-5pm Wed-Sun Sep-Apr) Built in 1775, Haapsalu's former town hall now houses a charming little museum with displays on the history of the resort town, regional history, a re-created pharmacy and the well-preserved Mayor's office.

Ilon's Wonderland   GALLERY
(Iloni Imedemaa; www.ilon.ee; Kooli 5; admission €6; ⊙11am-6pm May-Aug, 11am-5pm Wed-Sun Sep-Apr) Showcasing the works of Estonian-Swedish illustrator Ilon Wikland, who spent her childhood in Haapsalu and is best known for her illustrations for the Pippi Longstocking books, this gallery is

fabulously set up for kids, with many artworks hung at their viewing level.

St John's Lutheran Church CHURCH
(Jaani Kirik; Kooli 4; ⏰10am-2pm Fri & Sat, 1-4pm Sun mid-May–Aug) Although it has its roots in the 16th century, the exterior of this whitewashed church owes much to a renovation in 1858. Inside, look out for the sculpted reliefs above the altar (dating from 1630) and the carved pulpit.

Birdwatching Tower VIEWPOINT
Haapsalu Bay is one of the key habitats for migrating waterfowl in Estonia and is listed as a **Ramsar Wetland of International Importance** (www.ramsar.org). During their spring and autumn migrations as many as 20,000 birds descend. If you know your gadwalls from your grebes and fancy a gander at a goosander, head up the birdwatching tower, just south of Africa Beach. Keep an eye out for circling white-tailed eagles.

Africa Beach BEACH
(Aafrikarand) People still take to the waters at this pint-sized beach, despite the water being murky and full of weeds. It earned its name from the statues of wild animals which used to grace the shoreline (and which were sadly used as firewood by Soviet soldiers in the 1940s). There's an excellent children's playground here.

Promenaadi WATERFRONT
Nineteenth-century Russian toffs, like their counterparts in Victorian England and Paris' belle époque, liked nothing more than a good see-and-be-seen promenade, and the premier strolling route was along the waterfront. Sculptures dating from Haapsalu's fashionable era are scattered along the promenade, including a sundial and a bust commemorating mud-cure pioneer Dr Karl Abraham Hunnius, and the symphony-playing **Tchaikovsky Bench**, erected in 1940.

Haapsalu Kuursaal HISTORIC BUILDING
(www.haapsalukuursaal; Promenadi 1; ⏰noon-8pm May–mid-Sep) This fairy-tale wooden confection painted pale-green and white sits plumb on the waterfront, surrounded by rose gardens. Stepping into the cavernous spa hall (1897) is like stepping back into a more genteel time, with a small stage at one end (used for concerts) and a summertime restaurant at the other. The ambience trumps the food but it's certainly worth checking out.

Museum of the Estonian Swedes MUSEUM
(Rannarootsi muuseum; www.aiboland.ee; Sadama 32; adult/child €2/1.50; ⏰10am-4pm Sun & Mon, to 6pm Tue-Sat) This quaint museum has relics, photos, old fishing nets and a marvellous tapestry tracing the history of Swedes in Estonia from the 1200s to their escape back to Sweden on the *Triina* in 1944.

Estonian Railway Museum MUSEUM
(Eesti raudteemuuseum; www.jaam.ee; Raudtee 2; adult/child €3/2; ⏰10am-6pm May-Aug, 11am-4pm Fri-Sun Sep-Apr) Haapsalu's colourful former train station, with its wooden lace ornamentation and grand colonnade, was opened in 1907 to transport the Russian nobility to the spa resort. Designed to keep the royals dry, its 214m-long covered platform was then said to be the longest in the Russian Empire. This boxcar-sized museum records the golden years of train travel and there are old locomotives to explore nearby. In summer, a road train runs between here and Old Town (€2).

Paralepa Forest Park BEACH, FOREST
(☎rowboat rental 5660 3144; Ranna tee; rowboat per hour €8) On the western edge of town, beyond the train station, this shady park has a popular beachfront which, despite being a bit swampy, attracts plenty of sunseekers. In summer there's a cafe and a kiosk which rents rowboats. To get to the beach, follow the signs towards Fra Mare Thalasso Spa and keep going.

Fra Mare Thalasso Spa SPA
(☎472 4600; www.framare.ee; Ranna tee 2; 20min mud treatment €37) If you want to experience Haapsalu's magic mud, this spa hotel offers a variety of treatments (massage, baths etc), along with a pool, a sauna and a gym.

🎭 Festivals & Events

Haapsalu has a packed calendar of concerts and festivals, with the action concentrated between June and August.

Haapsalu Horror & Fantasy Film Festival FILM
(Haapsalu õudus-ja fantaasiafilmide festival; www.hoff.ee) The town is overtaken by zombies during this creepy, kooky four-day festival, held to coincide with the April full moon.

Haapsalu Early Music Festival MUSIC
(Haapsalu vanamuusika festival; www.haapsalu.ee) Held in early July and making full use of the magnificent acoustics of the Dome Church.

Haapsalu

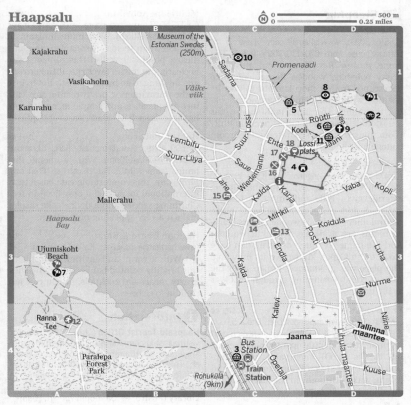

Haapsalu

◎ Sights
1 Africa Beach	D1
2 Birdwatching Tower	D1
3 Estonian Railway Museum	C4
4 Haapsalu Episcopal Castle	C2
5 Haapsalu Kuursaal	C1
6 Ilon's Wonderland	D2
7 Paralepa Forest Park	A3
8 Promenaadi	D1
9 St John's Lutheran Church	D2
10 Tchaikovsky Bench	C1
11 Town Hall Museum	D2

۞ Activities, Courses & Tours
12 Fra Mare Thalasso Spa	A4

⊜ Sleeping
13 Endla Hostel	C3
14 Kongo Hotell	C3
15 Lahe Maja	C2

✪ Eating
16 Hapsal Dietrich	C2
17 Müüriääre Kohvik	C2

◍ Drinking & Nightlife
18 Herman Bistro & Bar	C2

August Blues　　　　　　　　　　MUSIC
(Augustibluus; www.augustibluus.ee) Over two days in early August, this is Estonia's biggest blues festival.

White Lady Festival　　　　　　CULTURAL
(Valge daami päevad; www.valgedaam.ee) A big event with a ghostly theme, held over three days in August.

🛏 Sleeping

Lahe Maja
B&B €€

(☑ 516 3023; www.lahemaja.com; Lahe 7; r/cottage/house from €70/130/700; P 🛜) The name means 'Bay House' and this very pretty pale-blue wooden house looks like it's escaped from a chocolate box to take its position within manicured lawns overlooking the water. The large main house has four double rooms and a four-person family room, plus there's a separate two-bedroom cottage for rent at the rear.

Kongo Hotell
HOTEL €€

(☑ 472 4800; www.kongohotel.ee; Kalda 19; s/d/ste from €68/87/150; 🛜) The unassuming exterior gives little indication of Kongo's stylish, Scandi-chic decor – off-white walls, neutral linens and pale wooden floors. Larger rooms are available, with kitchenettes. And the name? A rough drinking den once stood on this spot, known for its brawling. The place was nicknamed 'Kongo' after the African country suffering through civil war at the time.

Endla Hostel
HOSTEL €€

(☑ 473 7999; www.endlahostel.ee; Endla 5; s/d €30/40; 🛜) Very little English is spoken and it's more than a little institutional-feeling, but this is an OK moderately priced option on a quiet street. Rooms are small and bright, with bathrooms in the hallway and a guest kitchen. No dorms.

🍴 Eating & Drinking

If you're self-catering there's a cluster of supermarkets in the newer part of town, near the intersection of the Tallinna highway and Posti street. For fresh fruits and vegetables visit the open-air market on Jaama street, a few blocks east of the bus station. It's a great spot to pick up fresh strawberries in summer.

Müüriääre Kohvik
CAFE €

(☑ 473 7527; www.muuriaare.ee; Karja 7; mains €3-8; ⊘ 10am-10pm) With more umlauts in its name than seems reasonable (the name means 'beside the walls'), this gorgeous cafe is clearly the town's favourite, if the crowds are anything to go by. And what's not to love in the warm interior, pretty rear terrace, cabinet full of cakes, and simple menu of fresh, light meals such as salads, pasta and quiche.

Hapsal Dietrich
CAFE €€

(☑ 509 4549; www.dietrich.ee; Karja 10; mains €7-14; ⊘ 9.30am-10pm) With a menu that jumps from wild garlic risotto to Thai *tom yum* soup, this comfortable cafe has a tasty international menu and a cosy lived-in feel. Charming service and a divine cake display make it a very appealing proposition.

Herman Bistro & Bar
BAR

(www.hermanhaapsalu.ee; Karja 1a; mains €3-8; 🛜) With a warm and inviting atmosphere, this brightly painted bar serves sandwiches, hearty meals and cocktails, or you can just slink in for a beer.

ℹ Information

Haapsalu Tourist Office (☑ 473 3248; www.visithaapsalu.com; Karja 15; ⊘ 9am-5pm mid-May–mid-Sep, 10am-5pm Mon-Fri rest of year; 🛜) This friendly, well-staffed office has loads of info about Haapsalu and the surrounding area.

Library (Posti 3; ⊘ 10am-6pm Tue-Fri, 10am-3pm Sat) The library, which shares a striking iron and limestone complex with the town art gallery (Linnagalerii), offers free internet access.

ℹ Getting There & Away

The **bus station** (Jaama 1) is at the pretty but defunct train station. Major destinations include Tallinn (€4.35 to €8.50, 1¾ hours, at least

---

A GHOSTLY VIGIL

Haapsalu's biggest annual event, the **White Lady Festival** (p155), coincides with the August full moon. The day begins with merriment – storytelling for the kids, theatre for the adults – and culminates with a ghastly apparition. During the full moon every August and February, moonlight at a precise angle creates a ghostly reflection upon a cathedral window.

According to legend, the shadow is cast by a young girl who, in the 14th century, was bricked up alive inside the walls. Back then the castle was an all-male enclave, and the archbishop got pretty worked up when he heard that a young woman, disguised in monastic vestments, sneaked in to be close to her lover-monk. In August excited young crowds stay out late to see a play recounting the story in the castle grounds, after which everyone gathers around the wall to await the shadow.

hourly), Tartu (€12, 4¼ hours, daily) and Pärnu (€5.05, 2½ hours, daily). For Hiiumaa, there are two daily buses to Kärdla (2¾ hours) and a daily bus to Käina (2¼ hours).

Ferries to Hiiumaa and Vormsi leave from Rohuküla, 9km west of Haapsalu.

❶ Getting Around

➔ You can rent bicycles at **Vaba Aeg Rattad** (☑ 521 2796; Karja 22; bikes per hour/day/24hr €2.50/10/16).

➔ Bus 1 runs regularly between Lossi plats, the bus station and Rohuküla (the ferry wharf, 9km west); timetables are posted at Lossi plats and the bus station.

Hiiumaa

POP 8590

Hiiumaa, Estonia's second-biggest island (1000 sq km), is a peaceful and sparsely populated place with some agreeable stretches of coast and a forest-covered interior. The island has less tourist development than Saaremaa, with considerably fewer options for lodging and dining. There's also less to do and see, but most visitors that come here are content simply to breathe in the fresh sea air and relax.

Scattered about Hiiumaa you'll find picturesque lighthouses, eerie old Soviet bunkers, empty beaches and a nature reserve with over 100 different bird species. Those seeking a bit more activity can hike, horse ride or indulge in various water sports. And the good news is that, thanks to the island's microclimate, the weather here is considerably warmer than on the mainland, 22km away.

Given their relative isolation from mainland Estonia, it's not surprising that the islanders have a unique take on things, and a rich folklore full of legendary heroes, such as Leiger, who had nothing to do with the Son of Kalev (the hero over on the mainland). People who move onto the island must carry the name *isehakanud hiidlane* (would-be islanders) for 10 years before being considered true residents. Hiiumaa is also said to be a haven for creatures like fairies and elves, ancestors of those born on the island. Modern-day Hiiumites rarely discuss this unique aspect of their family tree, however, as this can anger their elusive relatives.

For further information about the island, see www.hiiumaa.ee.

❶ Getting There & Away

AIR

There are two Avies (p83) flights a day between **Kärdla Airport** (Kärdla Lennujaam; ☑ 463 1381; www.kardla-airport.ee; Hiiessaare) and Tallinn on weekdays and one on weekends. The airport is 5km east of the centre of Kärdla; buses are timed to meet all flights (€1).

BOAT

➔ Most people arrive in Hiiumaa on the **SLK Ferries** (☑ 4524 4444; www.tuulelaevad.ee) service from Rohuküla to Heltermaa (adult/child/car/bike €3/1.50/8.80/3.70, 1½ hours, seven to nine daily).

➔ The busiest boats are those heading to Hiiumaa on a Friday and returning after 1pm on a Sunday afternoon. A 50% surcharge for vehicles applies during these periods.

➔ Up to 70% of each boat's capacity is presold online; the website has a real-time indicator showing what percentage has already been sold. The remaining 30% is kept for drive-up customers and offered on a first-in, first-on basis. You should consider prebooking at busy times, particularly around weekends in summer.

➔ Tickets purchased online must either be printed out or loaded as an electronic ticket on a smart phone.

➔ If you miss your prebooked boat, your ticket will be valid for the regular queue on subsequent boats for up to 48 hours.

➔ Ferry services also operate between Hiiumaa and Saaremaa (p143).

BUS

There are two daily buses between Kärdla and Tallinn (€13, 3¾ hours) and one between Käina and Tallinn (€12, two hours), all of which stop in Suuremõisa, Heltermaa, Rohuküla and Haapsalu.

❶ Getting Around

Paved roads circle Hiiumaa and cover several side routes; the rest are unsealed. Like many of the quiet nooks of rural Estonia, Hiiumaa is a good place to explore by bike. It's relatively flat and none of its roads are particularly busy – unless you happen to hit a queue of traffic coming off the ferry.

There are petrol stations at Kärdla and Käina. Many accommodation providers can arrange car or bike hire, as can **Jaanus Jesmin** (☑ 511 2225; www.carrent.hiiumaa.ee) in Kärdla, which rents out cars from €20 per day.

Buses, nearly all radiating from Kärdla but some from Käina, get to most places on the island, though not very often. Schedules are posted inside the bus station in Kärdla and online at www.peatus.ee.

Hiiumaa & Vormsi

Rohuküla

Diby
Sviby
Vormsi
Hullo
Rumpo

Saxby
Saxby
Lighthouse

Heltermaa

Suuremõisa

Airport
80

Kassari
Chapel
Hiiumaa
Museum
Kassari
Hiiumaa
Museum.

Kärdla

Vaemla
Käina
Orjaku
Sääre
tirp

Lehtma

Tahkuna Lighthouse
Military
Museum
Mihkli Farm
Museum
Hill of
Crosses

Hiiumaa

Tahkuna
peninsula
Malvaste

Kõrgessaare

Sõru

Kõpu
Lighthouse
Kõpu

Kõpu
Peninsula

Baltic Sea

Ristna
Lighthouse

Saaremaa

0   10 miles
0   20 km

N

Suuremõisa

Meaning 'great estate', Suuremõisa village is spread out around a blocky 18th-century **manor house** (Suuremõisa loss) which once belonged to the rich baronial Ungern-Sternberg family. It's certainly seen better days and is now looking very unkempt, with many of its windows painted over, but the leafy grounds are pleasant enough in an untidy kind of way.

More interesting is **St Lawrence's Lutheran Church** in nearby Pühalepa, the oldest building on Hiiumaa, dating from the 13th century. Twentieth-century stained glass enlivens the simple whitewashed structure and if you like poking around graveyards, there are some rare circular crosses to be spotted.

Kärdla

POP 3009

Hiiumaa's 'capital' grew up around a cloth factory founded in 1829 and destroyed during WWII. It's a green town full of gardens and tree-lined streets, with a sleepy atmosphere and few diversions. Still, it's Hiiumaa's centre for services of all kinds and if you need to stock up on provisions, it has a couple of supermarkets.

The town sits on the edge of the world's 'best-preserved Palaeozoic meteorite crater', not that you'd know it as, despite being 4km in diameter, it's barely visible. It's fair to say that you wouldn't want to have been visiting here 455 million years ago when the impact occurred.

◉ Sights

Pikk Maja MUSEUM
(www.muuseum.hiiumaa.ee; Vabrikuväljak 8; adult/child €3/2; ⊙10am-6pm May-Sep, 10am-5pm Mon-Fri Oct-Apr) The 'Long House' was once home to the cloth-factory bigwigs but now has displays related to the factory, including a reconstructed worker's cottage. Also featured is work by local artists and upstairs there's a collection of Estonian military and civil service medals.

Kärdla Beach BEACH
(Lubjaahju) While not spectacular, Kärdla's extremely shallow beach is pleasant enough, with a sandy shoreline edged by Rannapark. This expanse of lawns and forest was partly built on the site of a Swedish cemetery.

🛏 Sleeping

Kivijüri Külalistemaja B&B €€
(☑526 9915; www.kivijuri.ee; Kõrgessaare mnt 1; s/d €40/55; ℗ 🤶) This cosy, bright-red country house has only four pleasant rooms, each one with TV and bathroom. Breakfast is excellent (one of the best we had in Estonia) and there's a backyard patio and a lawn to unwind on. Campers are welcome, and the hospitable, multilingual owners can help arrange bike and car rental. A fine choice.

Padu Hotell HOTEL €€
(☑463 3037; www.paduhotell.ee; Heltermaa mnt 22; s/d/apt from €40/55/65; ℗ 🤶) If you're staying here you may feel like you're sleeping inside a sauna, with the pleasant pine motif taken to extremes: walls, floors, ceilings, doors, furniture. The rooms are cosy and decently equipped, all with balconies, but the apartments are quite a bit bigger and some have their own saunas. There's also a communal sauna and an on-site cafe.

🍴 Eating & Drinking

Gahwa Cafe CAFE €
(Põllu 3; snacks €1-2; ⊙10am-6pm Mon-Fri, to 3pm Sat & Sun; 🤶) A pretty pit stop with indoor and outdoor seating, this cafe offers light meals such as soup or quiche. Make sure you save room for the sensational chocolate cake.

Linnumäe Puhkekeskus EUROPEAN €
(☑462 9244; www.linnumae.ee; Heltermaa mnt; mains €5.50-13; ⊙11.30am-7pm; 🤶) The outdoor deck at this restaurant-bar holds plenty of appeal for an afternoon beer, or you can opt to enjoy a meal inside. The menu holds few surprises but it's well priced and well executed, with big portions the name of the game. Try the tasty trout with Béarnaise sauce. It's on the outskirts of town, 500m past Padu Hotell.

★ Kuur MODERN EUROPEAN €€
(www.restokuur.ee; Sadama 28; mains €11-12; ⊙11am-11pm May-Sep; 🌱) The name means 'shed', but with two glass walls and one fashioned from artfully stacked firewood, this summer-only, harbourside pop-up is much slicker than that. The food's extraordinary: only three starters and mains, but everything's beautifully presented, inventive and totally delicious. Add to that great service and a sunny deck and you've got Hiiumaa's top eatery by a long shot.

Rannapaargu CLUB
(www.rannapaargu.ee; Lubjaahju 3; ⊙10pm-4am Fri & Sat) This pyramid-shaped restaurant has large windows overlooking the beach. The food isn't up to much but come the weekend around 300 people descend to party along to the island's best DJs and visiting live bands. It doesn't kick off until well after midnight.

ⓘ Information

Hiiumaa Tourist Office (☑ 462 2232; www. hiiumaa.eu; Hiiu 1; ⊙10am-5pm Mon-Fri year-round, plus 10am-2pm Sat & Sun mid-May–mid-Sep) This friendly centre distributes maps and can help arrange accommodation and guides. It also sells the *Lighthouse Tour*, a 40-page driving tour of the island in English (€3). The office is housed in an old fire tower.

Western Hiiumaa

The western half of Hiiumaa is sparsely populated, even for Estonia. Knobbly **Tahkuna Peninsula** was the scene of a vicious battle between German and Soviet troops during WWII. On the road leading to the lighthouse you'll see deserted Soviet military installations, including a complete underground bunker which you can wander through; bring a torch (flashlight).

The island ends at the narrow **Kõpu Peninsula**, stretching due west like an index finger pointing straight at Stockholm. If you've been to a few Estonian beaches and refuse to believe that anyone could surf here, be prepared to be proved wrong. At Ristna, where the peninsula protrudes out into the Baltic currents, waves of up to 10m have been seen. It's a dangerous stretch with rips that will do their darnedest to deliver you on the doorstep of Finland, but for experienced surfers it's a blast.

Sõru, where the ferries leave for Saaremaa, is quite a beautiful spot, with a reed-lined forested shore stretching out in both directions.

◉ Sights & Activities

Hill of Crosses MEMORIAL
(Ristimägi) Northern Hiiumaa had a population of free Swedish farmers until they were forced to leave on the orders of Catherine the Great, with many ending up in the Ukraine on the false promise of a better life. This mound (only in flat Estonia could it be called a hill) beside the main road, 7km west of Kärdla, marks the spot where the last 1000 Swedes living on Hiiumaa performed their final act of worship before leaving the island in 1781.

It has become a tradition for first-time visitors to Hiiumaa to brave the mosquitoes to lay a homemade cross here.

Mihkli Farm Museum FARM
(Mihkli talumuuseum; www.muuseum.hiiumaa.ee; adult/child €2/1.50; ⊙10am-6pm Tue-Sat mid-Jun–mid-Aug) Hidden away in the forest at Malvaste, 2km north of the Kärdla–Kõrgessaare road, this (originally Swedish) farm complex gives an authentic taste of early rural life. The working smoke sauna (€90 for up to 10 people) is a unique, old-fashioned experience but not recommended for sensitive eyes; book ahead, as it takes a day to heat it.

Hiiumaa Military Museum MUSEUM
(Hiiumaa Militaarmuuseum; www.militaarmuuseum. ee; adult/child €3/1.50; ⊙10am-6pm mid-May–mid-Sep) Despite limited English captions, this

---

HIIUMAA HANDICRAFTS

Handicraft hunters will find fertile ground in Hiiumaa, where traditional crafts are experiencing a minor resurgence. One of the best outlets is the museum shop in Kassari (p162), which carries top-quality woven woollen rugs, among other things. The following are also worth checking out:

Heltermaa Crafts House (Heltermaa käsitöömaja; www.heltermaakasitoomaja.voog.com; Heltermaa; ⊙10.30am-7pm Mon-Fri, to 5.30pm Sat Jun-Aug) If you've got time to kill before the ferry docks, stop in here for knitted socks, honey, wooden salad servers or the ubiquitous woven cloth rugs.

Hiiu Wool Factory (Hiiu villavabrik; www.hiiuvill.ee; Vaemla; ⊙9am-6pm Mon-Sat, 10am-4pm Sun mid-May–Aug, 9am-6pm Mon-Fri, 10am-4pm Sat rest of year) This small woollen mill, 4km east of Käina, still uses 19th-century weaving and spinning machines to produce traditional knitwear. You can rug up in the sweaters and mittens for sale, or stock up on wool to knit your own. In summer there's a cafe on site.

small museum in the former Soviet border guard station on the Tahkuna Peninsula is quite engrossing. There are big items of military hardware to peruse in the yard, while inside there are uniforms, photographs, posters, weapons and medals.

Tahkuna Lighthouse
LIGHTHOUSE

(Tahkuna Teletorn, adult/child €2/1; ⏱10am-7pm Tue-Sun May–mid-Sep) Dating from 1874, this 43m lighthouse watches over Tahkuna Peninsula's northwest tip. Beyond the lighthouse stands an eerie memorial to the victims of the *Estonia* ferry disaster. Facing out to sea, the 12m-tall metal frame encases a cross from the bottom of which a bell with sculpted children's faces is suspended; it only rings when the wind blows with the same force and in the same direction as it did on that fatal night in September 1994, when the *Estonia* went down.

Between the memorial and the lighthouse is a curious low stone labyrinth, a replica of an ancient one found on the island. The idea is that you follow the path between the stones as a form of meditation.

According to Soviet military lore concerning the battle that raged in this vicinity during the Nazi invasion of 1941, the Red Army fought to the bitter end, their last man climbing to the top of the lighthouse and flinging himself off while still firing at the Germans.

Kõpu Lighthouse
LIGHTHOUSE

(Kõpu Tuletorn; adult/child €2/1; ⏱10am-8pm May–mid-Sep) With its pyramid-like base and stout square tower, the inland Kõpu Lighthouse is the best-known landmark on Hiiumaa and some claim it to be the oldest continuously operational lighthouse in the world. A lighthouse has stood on this raised bit of land since 1531, though the present white limestone tower was rebuilt in 1845. At 37m high, it can be seen 55km away.

The neighbouring cafe (delicious cake, terrible coffee) shares the same hours as the lighthouse, and concerts are staged on the lawns in summer.

Ristna Lighthouse
LIGHTHOUSE

(Ristna Tuletorn; adult/child €2/1; h10am-7pm Tue-Sun May–mid-Sep) Kõpu Peninsula's second lighthouse stands in all its blazing red glory at the western tip of the peninsula (Stockholm is just over 200km west of here). In 1874 it was brought to Hiiumaa by freighter from Paris where it was made, together with the lighthouse at Tahkuna. There's a small bar here serving drinks and snacks.

ℹ️ LIGHTHOUSE COMBO

If you're planning on climbing all three of Hiiumaa's lighthouses, a combined ticket is available (adult/child €5/2). Buy it at the first lighthouse you visit.

Sõru Museum
MUSEUM

(adult/child €2/1; ⏱11am-5pm Wed-Sun Jun-Aug, 11am-4pm Wed-Fri Sep-May) If you've got time to kill before the Saaremaa ferry, this little community museum is worth a look. Downstairs you might find art from the village schoolkids or locally made feltwork, while upstairs there's a permanent display containing the usual black-and-white photos of fisherfolk and farmers, interspersed with old nets and tools. At the very top you can scan the horizon on a heavy-duty set of Soviet border guard binoculars.

Surf Paradiis
WATER SPORTS

(☑505 1015; http://surfparadiis.paap.ee/; adult/child €40/20; ⏱May-Nov) Set on a stretch of sandy beach about 1km down an extremely rough road from Ristna (the turn-off is just before you reach the lighthouse), this outfit offers all manner of wet and wild activities. A day pass for the 'water park' includes use of surfboards, boogie boards, water trampoline, kayaks, rowboats, snorkelling equipment, a sauna and sun lounges, often accompanied by live music.

Add-ons include windsurfing, jetskiing, banana-boat rides, fishing and archery. There's also accommodation available.

It's a good idea to call ahead, as all activities are weather-dependent, and the place is sometimes booked solidly by groups.

Ristna is a surprisingly demanding surfing spot, so don't attempt to go it alone without first coordinating with the centre, which operates a lifeguard and first-aid service.

Käina
POP 1880

Hiiumaa's second-largest settlement is a nondescript kind of place, its most interesting feature being the hulking ruins of St Martin's Church (c 1500), which was wrecked by a WWII bomb.

◉ Sights

Rudolf Tobias House Museum
MUSEUM

(Rudolf Tobiase Majamuuseum; www.muuseum.hiiumaa.ee; Hiiu mnt; adult/child €2/1.50; ⏱11am-5pm

Wed-Sun mid-May–mid-Aug) On the western edge of Käina, the humble 1840 wood-and-thatch home of Rudolf Tobias (1873–1918), composer of some of Estonia's first orchestral works, has been preserved in his memory. There's no English signage but the staff do their best to point things out. There's a windmill out the back.

🛏 Sleeping

Hotell Liilia HOTEL €€
(📞 463 6146; www.liiliahotell.ee; Hiiu mnt 22; s/d €42/48; 🌐) Set in a two-storey building next to the church ruins, Liilia offers tasteful, well-kept rooms with pale wooden floors and ceilings. There's also a large restaurant downstairs with a pleasant terrace but it only opens when demand requires it.

Kassari

POP 300

Covered with mixed woodland and boasting some striking coastal scenery, this 8km-long island is linked to Hiiumaa by two causeways that virtually cut off Käina Bay from the open sea. The bay is an important bird reserve, serving as a breeding ground for about 70 different species. You can get a good view of the avian action from the **birdwatching tower** north of Orjaku, where you'll also find a short walking trail. During the hot summer months a large part of the bay dries up and becomes not much more than a muddy field.

👁 Sights & Activities

Hiiumaa Museum MUSEUM
(www.muuseum.hiiumaa.ee; adult/child €3/2; ⊙10am-6pm May-Sep, 10am-5pm Wed-Sun Oct-Apr) Located in Kassari village's old post office, this small museum has a collection of artefacts and exhibits on Hiiumaa's history and biodiversity. Among the curiosities: a 1955 Russian-made TV, the jewel-like prism of the 1874 Tahkuna lighthouse and the stuffed body of the wolf that allegedly terrorised the island until its 1971 demise. It also sells excellent handicrafts and special island postal stamps.

Sääre Tirp AREA
Southern Kassari narrows to a promontory with some unusual vegetation and ends in a thin 3km spit of land, the tip of which juts out into the sea. It's a beautiful place for a

---

MS ESTONIA: CONSIGNED TO MYSTERY

About 30 nautical miles northwest of Hiiumaa's Tahkuna Peninsula lies the wreck of the ferry *Estonia*, which sank during a storm just after midnight on 28 September 1994, en route from Tallinn to Stockholm. Only 137 people survived the tragedy, which claimed 852 lives in one of Europe's worst maritime disasters.

The cause of the tragedy remains the subject of contention and conspiracy theory. In 1997 the final report of the Joint Accident Investigation Commission (JAIC), an official inquiry by the Estonian, Swedish and Finnish governments, concluded that the ferry's design was at fault and the crew were probably underskilled in emergency procedures. The report claimed the bow gate was engineered inadequately for rough sailing conditions and that during the storm the visor was torn from the bow, exposing the car deck to tonnes of seawater that sank the *Estonia* completely within one hour. Escape time for the 989 people on board was estimated at only 15 minutes and they were denied access to lifeboats due to the sudden list and sinking of the ferry. For those who did escape, the freezing conditions of the water that night reduced survival time to only minutes.

The integrity of the report was questioned after dissent within the JAIC became public. In 2000 a joint US-German diving expedition and new analyses of the *Estonia's* recovered visor prompted theories of an explosion on board. Conspiracy theorists claim that the *Estonia* was transporting unregistered munitions cargo, as an illicit trade in weapons was to be curtailed with new export laws about to come into effect. Claims of a cover-up have been bolstered by the alleged disappearance of eight crew members, initially listed as survivors.

Unexplained interference with the wreck, along with the Swedish government's dumping of sand to stabilise it in 2000, further fuelled conspiracy claims and calls for a new inquiry. The governments of Estonia, Finland and Sweden are resolute that the ferry will remain where it sank as a memorial to the dead; an estimated 700 people are thought to be inside.

walk and there's a small but surprisingly popular reedy beach on the way.

Legend has it that the rocky outcrop is the remains of an aborted bridge that local hero Leiger started to build to Saaremaa, to make it easier for his brother, Saaremaa's hero Suur Tõll, to visit and join in various heroic acts. As for Leiger, there's a statue of him at the Sääre Tirp fork, carrying a boulder on his shoulder.

Kassari Lutheran Chapel   CHURCH

(Kassari kabel; ⊙ 11am-4pm mid-Jun–Aug) There's no electricity supply to this pretty, whitewashed, thatch-roofed chapel (1801) at the east end of Kassari island, meaning that services are still held in enchanting candlelight. The main distinguishing feature of the interior is an unusual pulpit positioned above the altar. It's a good destination for a drive, walk or ride; follow the sign down the dirt road from the easternmost point of the island's sealed road.

From the chapel, a path continues nearly 2km to a small bay in Kassari's northeastern corner.

Kassari Ratsamatkad   HORSE RIDING

(⌨ 5342 3346; www.kassari.ee; trail ride per hour/day €13/40) On the road to Kassari Chapel, Hiiumaa's largest horse farm offers a range of excursions including multiday treks through forests and along untouched coastline.

🛏 Sleeping & Eating

Dagen Haus   B&B €€

(⌨ 518 2555; www.dagen.ee; Orjaku; r €65-89; P ⊗) One of Hiiumaa's most attractive options, this restored former granary has rough-hewn walls, timber beams and five stylish modern bedrooms, all set in big green grounds. The gorgeous communal areas will have you plotting to move in permanently. The owners have appealing holiday houses on offer too, sleeping up to 12 people (€99 to €219). Book well ahead.

Kassari Puhkekeskus   HOTEL €€

(⌨ 469 7169; www.kassarikeskus.ee; Kassari village; d €70, apt €85-105; P ⊗) Abandoned factories are a dime a dozen in Estonia, but cool conversions like this one are scarce. The decor is fresh and modern, and even the standard rooms have a microwave and a little astroturfed balcony. Apartments have a separate living area and a proper kitchenette, and open onto a large shared terrace with a spa pool.

Lest & Lammas Grill   ESTONIAN €

(⌨ 469 7169; www.kassarikeskus.ee; Kassari village; mains €7.50-11; ⊙ noon-9pm Jun-Aug; ⊗) The name means 'flounder and sheep' and the emphasis is on grilled fish and (beautifully marinated) lamb, along with barbecued sausages, pork and chicken. Or you can just share a bottle of wine under a thatched shelter on one of the landscaped terraces. It's part of the Kassari Puhkekeskus complex.

Vetsi Tall   ESTONIAN €

(⌨ 462 2550; www.vetsitall.ee; mains €4.50-6, site per person €4, cabin s/d/tr €30/40/55, apt €100; ⊙ 10am-11pm Jun-Aug; P) On the main road between the villages of Orjaku and Kassari, this dark atmospheric tavern (dating from 1843) offers massive serves of good simple food. Tiny barrel-shaped wooden cabins are set amid the surrounding apple orchard and camping is also possible, although bathroom facilities are rudimentary (a hosepipe shower, for instance). There's also a two-bedroom apartment above the tavern.

Vormsi

POP 277

Vormsi, Estonia's fourth-biggest island (93 sq km), rose from the sea around 3000 years ago and continues to rise at a rate of 3mm per year (its highest point is a modest 13m above sea level and is said to be a hiding place for trolls). Except for its voracious mosquitoes, the island has only ever been sparsely inhabited and as a consequence its forests, coastal pastures and wooded meadows have remained relatively undisturbed. Swedes arrived in the 13th century and before WWII they formed the overwhelming majority of the island's then 2500 residents. They fled back to Sweden en masse during WWII and few have returned.

The island, 16km from east to west and averaging 6km from north to south, is a good place to tour by bicycle; there is about 10km of paved road. From the ferry it's 1.5km to the village of Sviby. The cheerfully named Hullo, Vormsi's largest village, lies about 3km west of here. You'll spot ruins of a Russian Orthodox church within an old collective farm, right by the Hullo turn-off. Two kilometres south of here is the much smaller Rumpo (these people really do have a way with names!), sitting on an attractive juniper-covered peninsula jutting into Hullo Bay. Much of the island, including the 30 islets in Hullo Bay, is protected as part of the

Vormsi Landscape Reserve (Vormsi Maastikukaitseala). It's a haven for rare lichens and coastal birds, as well as large critters such as elk, roe deer, lynx and boar.

◉ Sights

The island doesn't have a tourist office but there are information boards near the ferry wharf.

Vormsi Farm Museum   FARM

(Vormsi talumuuseum; www.talumuuseum.vormsi.ee; Sviby; adult/child €2.50/1; ☉10am-5pm Wed-Sun Jun-Aug) The island's Swedish heritage is kept alive in this restored farmstead, including the inhabitants' distinctive fashion sense (the women wore chunky red socks to emphasise their ankles as strong legs were a sex symbol; nobody wanted a wife who couldn't perform heavy manual work).

St Olaf's Lutheran Church   CHURCH

(Püha Olavi kirik; ☉10.30am-12.30pm Sun May-Sep) There's a colourful little statue of the saint with his trusty axe in the niche above the door of this blocky, whitewashed 14th-century church, just out of Hullo. It has a fine baroque painted pulpit (1660) and medieval ceiling paintings.

Saxby Lighthouse   LIGHTHOUSE

Built in 1864, this 24m lighthouse is a short walk from Saxby, the island's westernmost settlement, which is itself 7km from Hullo.

Church Rock   BOULDER

(Kirikukivi) This 5.8m-high erratic boulder stands near Diby in the northeast.

⊨ Sleeping & Eating

You can find accommodation options online (www.vormsi.ee) or at the tourist office in Haapsalu. Both Rumpo Mäe Puhketalu and Elle-Malle Külalistemaja rent out bicycles and boats, and include breakfast in the price. The only eatery on the island is Kõrts Krog No14, a brand new tavern on the outskirts of Hullo.

Rumpo Mäe Puhketalu   B&B €€

(☏5342 9926; www.rumpomae.ee; d/tr €55/75; ☏) Just a few steps from the coast at Rumpo, this handsome thatched-roof farmhouse has en suite rooms with an old-style ambience. More basic accommodation is offered in a rustic sauna house (per person/whole house €45/220) and the eight-bed 'small house' (whole house €135 to €205), and there's also a field for campers. A single-night surcharge applies.

Elle-Malle Külalistemaja   B&B €€

(☏5647 2854; ellemalle@gmail.com; Hullo; per person €24) In a peaceful location between Hullo and St Olaf's Lutheran Church, this friendly guesthouse has tidy pine-lined rooms in the main house and a romantic double loft room in a separate wooden cottage (with a private bathroom below). Meals can be arranged (three-course dinner €9) and the owner also sells a small but high-quality selection of local antiques.

Hullo Kauplus   SELF-CATERING €

(Hullo; ☉10am-8pm Mon-Sat, to 5pm Sun; ☏) Stock up on victuals in Hullo's small general store; there's a post office and internet point attached.

❶ Getting There & Around

Vormsi lies just 3km off the Estonian mainland. **SLK Ferries** (☏4524 4444; www.tuulelaevad.ee) plies the 10km route between Rohuküla and Sviby three to five times daily (return ticket per adult/child/car/bike €6.40/3.20/14/2, 45 minutes). There's a 50% surcharge for boats departing Rohuküla after 1pm on Fridays and departing Sviby after 1pm on Sundays. If you're taking a vehicle in the summer, reserve a place in advance online (€1.60 extra).

By the ferry, **Sviby Bike & Boat Rental** (☏517 8722; www.vormsi.ee/sviby; ☉late May-Sep) doesn't just rent bikes (per ½/8/24 hours €5/10/15) and rowboats (per hour €5), it also runs a water-taxi service and tours around the island. Accommodation providers generally offer these services too.

UNDERSTAND ESTONIA

Estonia Today

The long, grey days of Soviet rule are well behind Estonia. Today, first-time visitors are astonished by the gusto with which the country has embraced the market economy. Entrepreneurship is widespread, and the economy has diversified considerably since 1991.

It's in the digital sphere where Estonia has excelled, earning it the nickname 'e-Stonia' in the tech world. Various innovations have originated from Estonian software designers, most notably Skype, which allows free voice and video calls to be made over the internet. Estonian citizens can vote, lodge their taxes and affix a digital signature to documents online, and in 2014 Estonia

ESTONIA ESTONIA TODAY

became the first country to offer a virtual 'e-Residency' to nonresidents.

Estonia has been lauded as the outstanding economic success story of the former USSR. It has joined the EU, NATO, Organisation for Economic Co-operation and Development (OECD) and the eurozone.

Having politically and economically shaken off the Soviet era, Estonia's gaze is very much to the West and the north. Its people view themselves as having more in common (linguistically and culturally) with their Finnish neighbours than they do with Latvia and Lithuania to their south, and see the 'Baltic States' label as a handy geographic reference but not much more. There's even been talk of further cementing ties with Finland by building a tunnel under the Gulf of Finland to connect the two countries, but the cost of such a venture is likely to be prohibitive.

Meanwhile, if Estonia is increasingly facing West, it's also nervously looking over its shoulder to the Great Bear to the east. The Russian annexation of Crimea and the armed conflict in the Ukraine (widely believed in these parts to have been fomented by the Kremlin) have rattled the nerves of many in this newly independent country. People here are painfully aware of the fleeting nature of the first Estonian independence in the interwar decades. That the current period of statehood has now lasted longer than the first offers only limited assurance.

Estonia's response to the Ukrainian crisis has been to enthusiastically support sanctions against the Russia Federation and to simultaneously strengthen ties with NATO, with president Toomas Ilves calling for a permanent base to be stationed on Estonian soil.

Tensions with Russia escalated in 2015 when an Estonian security officer was sentenced by a Russian court to 15 years in prison for spying; the Russians insist that they arrested him on their side of the border while the Estonians (and the EU) claim that he was kidnapped on the Estonian side. Estonia has now declared that it is planning to build a 110km-long, 2.5m-high fence on its land border with Russia (much of the rest of the border is defined by Lake Peipsi and the Narva River).

At the same time, the Estonian government is increasingly aware of the need to improve relations with its own large ethnic Russian minority, a substantial chunk of which have yet to gain Estonian citizenship (p171). While the average Russian living in Estonia has a higher standard of living than the average Russian living in Russia, they still lag behind their Estonian compatriots. A 2015 Amnesty International report noted that Estonia's ethnic minorites, of which Russians are by far the largest, are disproportionately affected by unemployment and poverty.

A drive through some of the crumbling towns of the northeast, where both work and hope are in short supply, gives some clue to the Russian plight. Russian speakers are over-represented in the prison population, HIV infection rates and drug-addiction statistics, and the greater social problems in the Russian community in turn feed the negative stereotypes that some Estonians have about Russians.

While instances of overt hostility based on ethnicity or race are infrequent, they do occasionally occur. The tension, and ultimately violence, that was sparked by the government's decision in 2007 to move a Soviet-era war memorial from the centre of Tallinn demonstrated that fissures remain between the country's ethnic Russians and the rest of the population, and there are regular complaints (from the Russian media, in particular) that Russian-speaking minorities in Estonia are being discriminated against. One strategy from the Estonian side has been to attempt to curb the influence of the Russian media by promoting Russian-language news services from within Estonia.

History

Beginnings

Estonia's oldest human settlements date back 10,000 years, with Stone Age tools found near present-day Pärnu. Finno-Ugric tribes from the east (probably around the Urals) came centuries later – most likely around 3500 BC – mingling with Neolithic peoples and settling in present-day Estonia, Finland and Hungary. They took a liking to their homeland and stayed put, spurning the nomadic ways that characterised most other European peoples over the next four millennia.

The Christian Invasion

By the 9th and 10th centuries AD, Estonians were well aware of the Vikings, who seemed more interested in trade routes to Kyiv (Kiev) and Istanbul than in conquering the land. The first real threat to their freedom came from Christian invaders from the south.

Following papal calls for a crusade against the northern heathens, Danish troops and German knights invaded Estonia, conquering the southern Estonian fortress of Otepää in 1208. The locals put up a fierce resistance and it took well over 30 years before the whole territory was conquered. By the mid-13th century Estonia was carved up between the Danes in the north and the German Teutonic Order in the south. The Order, hungry to move eastward, was powerfully repelled by Alexander Nevsky of Novgorod on frozen Lake Peipsi (marvellously imagined in Sergei Eisenstein's film *Alexander Nevsky*).

The conquerors settled in at various newly established towns, handing over much power to the bishops. By the end of the 13th century cathedrals rose over Tallinn and Tartu, around the time that the Cistercian and Dominican religious orders set up monasteries to preach to the locals and (try to) baptise them. Meanwhile, the Estonians continued to rebel.

The most significant uprising began on St George's Night (23 April) in 1343. It started in Danish-controlled northern Estonia when Estonians pillaged the Padise Cistercian Monastery and killed all of the monks. They subsequently laid siege to Tallinn and the bishop's castle in Haapsalu and called for Swedish assistance to help them finish the job. The Swedes did indeed send naval reinforcements across the gulf, but they came too late and were forced to turn back. Despite Estonian resolve, by 1345 the rebellion was crushed. The Danes, however, decided they'd had enough and sold their part of Estonia to the Livonian Order (a branch of the Teutonic Order).

The first guilds and merchant associations emerged in the 14th century, and many towns – Tallinn, Tartu, Viljandi and Pärnu – prospered as trade members of the Hanseatic League (a medieval merchant guild). However, it was mainly German merchants who lived in these towns while the native Estonians were relegated to toiling as peasants in the countryside.

Estonians continued practising nature worship and pagan rites for weddings and funerals, though by the 15th century these rites became interlinked with Catholicism and they began using Christian names. Peasants' rights disappeared during the 15th century, so much so that by the early 16th century most Estonians became serfs (enslaved labourers bought and sold with the land).

The Reformation, which originated in Germany, reached Estonia in the 1520s, with Lutheran preachers representing the initial wave. By the mid-16th century the church had been reorganised, with churches now under Lutheran authority and monasteries closed down.

The Livonian War

During the 16th century the greatest threat to Livonia (now northern Latvia and southern Estonia) came from the east. Ivan the Terrible, who crowned himself the first Russian tsar in 1547, had his sights clearly set on westward expansion. Russian troops, led by ferocious Tatar cavalry, attacked in 1558, around the region of Tartu. The fighting was extremely cruel, with the invaders leaving a trail of destruction in their wake. Poland, Denmark and Sweden joined the fray, and intermittent fighting raged throughout the 17th century. Sweden emerged the victor.

Like all wars, this one took a heavy toll on the inhabitants. During the two generations of warfare (roughly 1552 to 1629), half the rural population perished and about three-quarters of all farms were deserted,

---

THE SOURCE OF EESTI

In the 1st century AD the Roman historian Tacitus described a people known as the 'Aestii'. In rather crude fashion he depicted them as worshipping goddess statues and chasing wild boars with wooden clubs and iron weaponry. These people were also known as traders of amber. Although Tacitus was describing the forerunners to the Lithuanians and Latvians, the name 'Aestii' was eventually applied specifically to the Estonians, who call themselves Eesti to this day.

with disease (such as plague), crop failure and the ensuing famine adding to the war casualties. Except for Tallinn, every castle and fortified centre in the country was ransacked or destroyed – including Viljandi Castle, once among northern Europe's mightiest forts. Some towns were completely obliterated.

The Swedish Era

Following the war, Estonia entered a period of peace and prosperity under Swedish rule. Although the lot of the Estonian peasantry didn't improve much, cities, boosted by trade, grew and prospered, helping the economy speedily recover from the ravages of war. Under Swedish rule, Estonia was united for the first time in history under a single ruler. This period is regarded as an enlightened episode in the country's long history of foreign oppression.

The Swedish king granted the Baltic-German aristocracy a certain degree of self-government and even generously gave them lands that were deserted during the war. Although the first printed Estonian-language book dates from 1535, the publication of books didn't get under way until the 1630s, when Swedish clergy founded village schools and taught the peasants to read and write. Education received an enormous boost with the founding of Tartu University in 1632.

By the mid-17th century, however, things were going steadily downhill. An outbreak of plague, and later the Great Famine (1695–97), killed off 80,000 people – almost 20% of the population. Peasants, who for a time enjoyed more freedom of movement, soon lost their gains. The Swedish king, Charles XI, for his part wanted to abolish serfdom in Estonian crown manors (peasants enjoyed freedom in Sweden), but the local Baltic-German aristocracy fought bitterly to preserve the legacy of enforced servitude.

The Great Northern War

Soon Sweden faced serious threats from an anti-Swedish alliance of Poland, Denmark and Russia – countries seeking to regain lands lost in the Livonian War. The Great Northern War began in 1700 and after a few successes (including the defeat of the Russians at Narva), the Swedes began to fold under the assaults on multiple fronts. By 1708 Tartu had been destroyed and all of its survivors shipped to Russia. By 1710 Tallinn capitulated and Sweden had been routed.

The Enlightenment

Russian domination was bad news for the native Estonian peasants. War (and the 1710 plague) left tens of thousands dead. Swedish reforms were rolled back by Peter I, destroying any hope of freedom for the surviving serfs. Conservative attitudes towards Estonia's lower class didn't change until the Enlightenment, in the late 18th century.

Among those influenced by the Enlightenment was Catherine the Great (1762–96), who curbed the privileges of the elite while instituting quasi-democratic reforms. It wasn't until 1816, however, that the peasants were finally liberated from serfdom. They also gained surnames, greater freedom of movement and even limited access to self-government. By the second half of the 19th century the peasants started buying farmsteads from the estates, and earning an income from crops such as potatoes and flax (the latter commanding particularly high prices during the US Civil War and the subsequent drop in American cotton exports to Europe).

National Awakening

The late 19th century was the dawn of the national awakening. Led by a new Estonian elite, the country marched towards nationhood. The first Estonian-language newspaper, *Perno Postimees,* appeared in 1857. It was published by Johann Voldemar Jannsen, one of the first to use the term 'Estonians' rather than *maarahvas* (country people). Other influential thinkers included Carl Robert Jakobson, who fought for equal political rights for Estonians; he also founded *Sakala,* Estonia's first political newspaper.

Numerous Estonian societies formed, and in 1869 the first song festival was held. Estonia's rich folklore also emerged from obscurity, particularly with the publication of *Son of Kalev,* Friedrich Reinhold Kreutzwald's poetic epic that melded together hundreds of Estonian legends and folk tales. Other poems, particularly works by Lydia Koidula, helped shape the national consciousness – one imprinted with the memory of 700 years of slavery.

Rebellion & WWI

The late 19th century was also a period of rampant industrialisation, marked by the development of an extensive railway network linking Estonia with Russia and by the rise of large factories. Socialism and discontent accompanied those grim workplaces, with demonstrations and strikes led by newly formed worker parties. Events in Estonia mimicked those in Russia, and in January 1905, as armed insurrection flared across the border, Estonia's workers joined the fray. Tension mounted until autumn that year, when 20,000 workers went on strike. Tsarist troops responded brutally by killing and wounding 200.

Tsar Nicholas II's response incited the Estonian rebels, who continued to destroy the property of the old guard. Subsequently, thousands of soldiers arrived from Russia, quelling the rebellions; 600 Estonians were executed and hundreds were sent off to Siberia. Trade unions and progressive newspapers and organisations were closed down and political leaders fled the country.

More radical plans to bring Estonia to heel – such as sending thousands of Russian peasants to colonise the country – were never realised. Instead, Russia's tsar had another priority: WWI. Estonia paid a high price for Russia's involvement – 100,000 men were drafted, 10,000 of whom were killed in action. Many Estonians went off to fight under the notion that if they helped defeat Germany, Russia would grant them nationhood. Russia had no intention of doing so. But by 1917 the matter was no longer the tsar's to decide. In St Petersburg, Nicholas II was forced to abdicate and the Bolsheviks seized power. As chaos swept across Russia, Estonia seized the initiative and on 24 February 1918 it effectively declared its independence.

The War of Independence

Estonia faced threats from both Russia and Baltic-German reactionaries. War erupted as the Red Army quickly advanced, overrunning half the country by January 1919. Estonia fought back tenaciously, and with the help of British warships and Finnish, Danish and Swedish troops, it defeated its long-time enemy. In December Russia agreed to a truce and on 2 February 1920 it signed the Tartu Peace Treaty, which renounced forever Russia's rights of sovereignty over Estonian territory. For the first time in its history, Estonia was completely independent.

Fleeting Independence

In many ways, the independence period was a golden era. The mainly Baltic-German nobility were given a few years to sort their affairs before their manor houses were nationalised and their large estates broken up, with the land redistributed to the Estonian people. For the very first time many peasant farmers were able to own and work their own land.

The economy developed rapidly, with Estonia utilising its natural resources and attracting investment from abroad. Tartu University became a university for Estonians, and the Estonian language became the lingua franca for all aspects of public life, creating new opportunities in professional and academic spheres. Secondary education also improved (per capita the number of students surpassed most European nations) and an enormous book industry arose, with 25,000 titles published between 1918 and 1940 (again surpassing most European nations in books per capita).

On other fronts – notably the political one – independence was not so rosy. Fear of communist subversion (such as the failed 1924 coup d'état supported by the Bolsheviks) drove the government to the right. In 1934 Konstantin Päts, leader of the transitional government, along with Johan Laidoner, commander-in-chief of the Estonian army, violated the constitution and seized power, under the pretext of protecting democracy from extremist factions. Thus began the 'era of silence', a period of authoritarian rule that dogged the fledgling republic until WWII.

The Soviet Invasion & WWII

Estonia's fate was sealed when Nazi Germany and the USSR negotiated a secret pact in 1939, essentially handing Estonia over to Stalin. The Molotov-Ribbentrop Pact, a nonaggression pact between the USSR and Nazi Germany, secretly divided Eastern Europe into Soviet and German spheres of influence. Estonia fell into the Soviet sphere. At the outbreak of WWII, Estonia declared itself neutral, but Moscow forced Estonia to sign a mutual assistance pact. Thousands of Russian soldiers subsequently arrived, along with military, naval and air bases. Estonia's Communist Party orchestrated a sham rebellion whereby 'the people' demanded to be part of the USSR. President Päts, General Laidoner and other leaders were sacked and sent off to Russian prison camps. A puppet government was installed and on 6 August 1940 the Supreme Soviet accepted Estonia's 'request' to join the USSR.

Deportations and WWII devastated the country. Tens of thousands were conscripted and sent not to fight but to work (and usually die) in labour camps in northern Russia. Thousands of women and children were also sent to gulags.

When Russia fled the German advance, many Estonians welcomed the Nazis as liberators; 55,000 Estonians joined home-defence units and Wehrmacht Ost battalions. The Nazis, however, did not grant statehood to Estonia and viewed it merely as occupied territory of the Soviet Union. Hope was crushed when the Germans began executing communist collaborators (7000 Estonian citizens were shot) and those Estonian Jews who hadn't already fled the country (around 1000). To escape conscription into the German army (nearly 40,000 were conscripted), thousands fled to Finland and joined the Estonian regiment of the Finnish army.

In early 1944 the Soviet army bombed Tallinn, Narva, Tartu and other cities. Narva's baroque Old Town was almost completely destroyed. The Nazis retreated in September 1944. Fearing the advance of the Red Army, many Estonians also fled and around 70,000 reached the West. By the end of the war one in 10 Estonians lived abroad. All in all, Estonia had lost over 280,000 people in the war (a quarter of its population). In addition to those who emigrated, 30,000 were killed in action and others were executed, sent to gulags or exterminated in concentration camps.

Back in the USSR

After the war, Estonia was immediately incorporated back into the Soviet Union. This began the grim epoch of Stalinist repression, with many thousands sent to prison camps and 19,000 Estonians executed. Farmers were forced into collectivisation and thousands of immigrants entered the country from other regions of the Soviet Union. Between 1945 and 1989 the percentage of native Estonians fell from 97% of the population to 62%.

Resistance took the form of a large guerrilla movement calling themselves the Metsavennad, or 'Forest Brothers'. Around 14,000 Estonians armed themselves and went into hiding, operating in small groups throughout the country. The guerrillas had little success against the Soviet army, and by 1956 the movement had been effectively destroyed.

Although there were a few optimistic periods during the communist years (notably the 'thaw' under Khrushchev, where Stalin's crimes were officially exposed), it wasn't until the 1980s when Soviet leader Mikhail Gorbachev ushered in an era of *perestroika* (restructuring) and *glasnost* (openness) that real change seemed a possibility.

The dissident movement in Estonia gained momentum and on the 50th anniversary of the 1939 Molotov-Ribbentrop Pact, a major rally took place in Tallinn. Over the next few months, more and more protests were held, with Estonians demanding the restoration of statehood. The song festival was one of Estonia's most powerful vehicles for protest. The biggest took place in 1988 when 300,000 Estonians gathered in Tallinn's Song Festival Grounds and brought much international attention to the Baltic plight.

In November 1989 the Estonian Supreme Soviet declared the events of 1940 an act of military aggression and therefore illegal. Disobeying Moscow's orders, Estonia held free elections in 1990 and regained its independence in 1991.

TALLINN'S CHECHEN HERO

In January 1991 Soviet troops seized strategic buildings in Vilnius and Rīga, and soldiers were ordered to do the same in Tallinn. The commander of the troops at the time, however, disobeyed Moscow's orders, and refused to open fire upon the crowd. He even threatened to turn the artillery under his command against any attempted invasion from Russia. That leader was Dzhokhar Dudayev, who would go on to become the president of Chechnya and lead its independence movement. He was killed by the Russian military in 1995. In Estonia he is fondly remembered for his role in bringing about Estonian independence.

Independent Estonia Mark Two

In 1992 the first general election under the new constitution took place, with a proliferation of newly formed parties. The Pro Patria (Fatherland) Union won a narrow majority after campaigning under the slogan 'Cleaning House', which meant removing from power those associated with communist rule. Pro Patria's leader, 32-year-old historian Mart Laar, became prime minister.

Laar set to work transforming Estonia into a free-market economy, introducing the Estonian kroon as currency and negotiating the complete Russian troop withdrawal. (The latter was a source of particular anxiety for Estonians, and the country breathed a collective sigh of relief when the last garrisons departed in 1994.) Despite Laar's successes, he was considered a hothead, and in 1994 he was dismissed when his government received a vote of no confidence by the Riigikogu (National Council).

Following a referendum in September 2003, approximately 60% of Estonians voted in favour of Estonia joining the EU. The following spring, the country officially joined both the EU and NATO. This was followed by membership of the OECD in December 2010 and adoption of the euro in place of the short-lived kroon at the beginning of 2011.

Recurring post-EU-accession themes are the economy, increasing income inequality and strained relations with Russia, particularly with regards to Estonia's large Russian-speaking community.

WAGE INEQUALITY & SALMON SANDWICHES

According to Eurostat, Estonian men earn an average of 30% more than Estonian women, which is the largest gender income gap in the EU. In a creatively obscure protest to highlight this gap (lõhe), participating cafes and restaurants on Equal Pay Day sell sandwiches made from salmon (which is also lõhe in Estonian) at a 30% surcharge when served with dill (in Estonian till, which doubles as a slang word for penis).

The People

Despite (or perhaps because of) centuries of occupation by Danes, Swedes, Germans and Russians, Estonians have tenaciously held onto their national identity and are deeply, emotionally connected to their history, folklore and national song tradition. The Estonian Literary Museum in Tartu holds over 1.3 million pages of folk songs, the world's second-largest collection (Ireland has the largest), and Estonia produces films for one of the world's smallest audiences (only Iceland produces for a smaller audience).

According to the popular stereotype, Estonians (particularly Estonian men) are reserved and aloof. Some believe it has much to do with the weather – those long, dark nights breeding endless introspection. This reserve also extends to gross displays of public affection, brash behaviour and intoxication – all frowned upon. This is assuming that there isn't a festival under way, such as Jaanipäev, when friends, family and acquaintances gather in the countryside for drinking, dancing and revelry.

Estonians are known for their strong work ethic, but when they're not toiling in the fields, or putting in long hours at the office, they head to the countryside. Ideal weekends are spent at the family cottage, picking berries or mushrooms, walking through the woods, or sitting with friends soaking up the quiet beauty. Owning a country house with a sauna is one of the national aspirations.

Of Estonia's 1.3 million people, 69% are ethnic Estonians, 25% Russians, 2% Ukrainians, 1% Belarusians and 1% Finns. Ethnic Russians are concentrated in the industrial cities of the northeast, where in some places (such as Narva) they make up the vast majority of the population. Russians also have a sizable presence in Tallinn (37%). These figures differ markedly from 1934, when native Estonians comprised over 90% of the population. Migration from other parts of the USSR occurred on a large scale from 1945 to 1955 and, over the next three decades, Estonia had the highest rate of migration of any of the Soviet republics.

One of the most overlooked indigenous ethnic groups in Estonia are the Seto people, who number up to 15,000, split between southeastern Estonia and neighbouring Russia.

EESTI CITIZENSHIP

When Estonia regained independence in 1991, not every resident received citizenship. People who were citizens of the pre-1940 Estonian Republic and their descendants automatically became citizens. Those who moved to Estonia during the Soviet occupation (mostly Russian speakers, many of whom didn't learn the local language) could choose to be naturalised, an ongoing process that required applicants to demonstrate knowledge of Estonia's history and language to qualify. For these people, one alternative was to apply for Russian citizenship, as all citizens of the former USSR were eligible, and another was to remain in Estonia as noncitizen residents. However, only citizens may vote in parliamentary elections.

The naturalisation process and the perceived difficulty of the initial language tests became a point of international contention as the Russian government, the EU and a number of human rights organisations (including Amnesty International) objected on the grounds that many Russian-speaking inhabitants were being denied their political and civil rights. As a result, the tests were somewhat altered and the number of stateless persons has steadily decreased. In 1992 32% of residents lacked any form of citizenship while today the UNHCR estimates that this figure has reduced to around 6.7% of the population.

One consequence of this policy is that only 84% of the population of Estonia holds Estonian citizenship. Nearly 9% of the population holds the passport of another state, mostly the Russian Federation, Ukraine or Finland.

According to a 2009 Gallup poll, Estonia was the least religious country in the world (they've subsequently lost pole position to China), although many consider themselves spiritual, with a nature-based ethos being popular. Since the early 17th century, Estonia's Christians have been predominantly Lutheran, although the Orthodox church gained a foothold under the Russian Empire and has experienced a resurgence in recent years. Today only a minority of Estonians profess religious beliefs, with 16% identifying as Orthodox and 10% as Lutheran; no other religion reaches over 1% of the population.

Jews arrived in Estonia as early as the 14th century and by the early 1930s the population numbered 4300. Three-quarters escaped before the German occupation and of those that remained, nearly all were killed. Today the Jewish population stands at around 2000 and in 2007 the Jewish community celebrated the opening of its first synagogue since the Holocaust, a striking modern structure at Karu 16, Tallinn.

The Arts

Music

On the international stage, the area in which Estonia has had the greatest artistic impact is in the field of classical music.

Estonia's most celebrated composer is Arvo Pärt (b 1935), the intense and reclusive master of hauntingly austere music many have misleadingly termed minimalist. Pärt emigrated to Germany during Soviet rule and his *Misererie Litany, Te Deum* and *Tabula Rasa* are among an internationally acclaimed body of work characterised by dramatic bleakness, piercing majesty and nuanced silence. He's now the world's most performed living classical-music composer.

The main Estonian composers of the 20th century remain popular today. Rudolf Tobias (1873–1918) wrote influential symphonic, choral and concerto works as well as fantasies on folk song melodies. Mart Saar (1882–1963) studied under Rimsky-Korsakov in St Petersburg but his music shows none of this influence. His songs and piano suites were among the most performed pieces of music in between-war concerts in Estonia. Eduard Tubin (1905–82) is another great Estonian composer whose body of work includes 10 symphonies. Contemporary composer Erkki-Sven Tüür (b 1959) takes inspiration from nature and the elements as experienced on his native Hiiumaa.

Estonian conductors Tõnu Kaljuste (who won a Grammy in 2014 for a Pärt recording), Anu Tali and Paavo Järvi are hot tickets at concert halls around the world.

Hortus Musicus is Estonia's best-known ensemble, performing mainly medieval and

Renaissance music. Rondellus, an ensemble that has played in a number of early music festivals, performs on medieval period instruments and isn't afraid of experimentation. Its well-received album *Sabbatum* (2002) is a tribute album of sorts to Black Sabbath – the only difference being the music is played on medieval instruments, and the songs are sung in Latin!

Rock and punk thrives in Estonia with groups such as Vennaskond and the heavy but timelessly Estonian Metsatöll, whose song titles and lyrics make heavy use of archaic Estonian language and imagery. The more approachable Ultima Thule and Smilers are among the country's longest-running and most beloved bands.

The pop- and dance-music scene is strong in Estonia, exemplified by Estonia's performances in that revered indicator of true art, the Eurovision Song Contest. Tanel Padar won the competition for Estonia in 2001, making Estonia the first former Soviet republic to win. The tough-girl band Vanilla Ninja hit the charts throughout central Europe early in the millennium with various English-language tracks. Stig Rästa of local hitmakers Outloudz teamed up with reality TV contestant Elina Born to represent Estonia at Eurovision 2015 with *Goodbye To Love,* which subsequently entered the charts in 10 countries.

Eccentric dance diva Kerli Kõiv, better known by her first name alone, has notched up two Billboard US Dance number ones since 2011. Another one to watch is the youthful DJ and producer Rauno Roosnurm (aka Mord Fustang), whose remixes have garnered him a following with international clubbers.

See www.estmusic.com for detailed listings and streaming samples of Estonian musicians of all genres.

Literature

Estonian was considered a mere peasants' language by its foreign overlords rather than one with full literary potential, and as a result the history of written Estonian is little more than 150 years old. Baltic Germans published an Estonian grammar book and a dictionary in 1637, but it wasn't until the national awakening movement of the late 19th century that the publication of books, poetry and newspapers began.

Estonian literature grew from the poems and diaries of a young graduate of Tartu

---

CAN I BUY A VOWEL, PLEASE?

Intrigued by the national language? Fancy yourself a linguist? If you're keen to tackle the local lingo, bear in mind that Estonian has 14 cases, no future tense, and no articles. And then try wrapping your tongue around the following vowel-hungry words:

➡ *jäääär* – edge of the ice

➡ *töööö* – work night (can also be *öötöö*)

➡ *kuuuurija* – moon researcher

➡ *kuuüür* – monthly rent

And then give this a go: '*Kuuuurijate töööö jäääärel*', or 'a moon researcher's work night at the edge of the ice'!

University, Kristjan Jaak Peterson. Also a gifted linguist, he died when he was only 21 years old in 1822. His lines 'Can the language of this land/carried by the song of the wind/ not rise up to heaven/and search for its place in eternity?' are engraved in stone in Tartu and his birthday is celebrated as Mother Tongue Day (14 March).

Until the mid-19th century Estonian culture was preserved only by way of an oral folk tradition among peasants. The national epic poem *Son of Kalev (Kalevipoeg)*, written between 1857 and 1861 by Friedrich Reinhold Kreutzwald (1803–82), made use of Estonia's rich oral traditions; it was inspired by Finland's *Kalevala*, a similar epic created several decades earlier. Fusing hundreds of Estonian legends and folk tales, *Son of Kalev* relates the adventures of the mythical hero, which ends with his death and his land's conquest by foreigners, but also a promise to restore freedom. The epic played a major role in fostering the national awakening of the 19th century.

Lydia Koidula (1843–86) was the poet of Estonia's national awakening and first lady of literature. Anton Hansen Tammsaare (1878–1940) is considered the greatest Estonian novelist for *Truth and Justice (Tõde ja Õigus)*, written between 1926 and 1933. A five-volume saga of village and town life, it explores Estonian social, political and philosophical issues.

Eduard Vilde (1865–1933) was an influential early-20th-century novelist and playwright who wrote *Unattainable Wonder (Tabamata Ime,* 1912). It was due to be the first play performed at the opening of the Estonia Theatre in 1913 but was substituted with *Hamlet,* as Vilde's scathing critique of the intelligentsia was deemed too controversial. In most of his novels and plays, Vilde looked with great irony at what he saw as Estonia's mad, blind rush to become part of Europe. For Vilde, self-reliance was the truest form of independence.

Paul-Eerik Rummo (b 1942) is one of Estonia's leading poets and playwrights, dubbed the 'Estonian Dylan Thomas' for his patriotic pieces, which deal with contemporary problems of cultural identity. His contemporary, Mati Unt (1944–2005), played an important role in cementing the place of Estonian intellectuals in the modern world, and wrote, from the 1960s onwards, quite cynical novels (notably *Autumn Ball; Sügisball,* 1979), plays and articles about contemporary life in Estonia.

The novelist Jaan Kross (1920–2007) won great acclaim for his historical novels in which he tackled Soviet-era subjects. His most renowned book, *The Czar's Madman (Keisri hull,* 1978), relates the story of a 19th-century Estonian baron who falls in love with a peasant girl and later ends up in prison. It's loosely based on a true story, though the critique of past- and present-day authoritarianism is the crux of his work.

Jaan Kaplinski (b 1941) has had two collections of poetry, *The Same Sea In Us All* and *The Wandering Border,* published in English. His work expresses the feel of Estonian life superbly. Kross and Kaplinski have both been nominated for the Nobel Prize in Literature.

Tõnu Õnnepalu's *Border State (Piiri Riik,* 1993, published under the pseudonym Emil Tode) is about a young Estonian man who travels to Europe and becomes a kept boy for an older, rich gentleman. This leads him down a tortuous road of self-discovery. Not a mere confessional, *Border State* is a clever and absorbing critique of modern Estonian values. In popular fiction, Kaur Kender's *Independence Day (Iseseisvuspäev,* 1998) tells the misadventures of young and ambitious entrepreneurs in postindependence Estonia.

The most acclaimed Estonian novel of recent times is *Purge (Puhastus,* 2008) by Sofi Oksanen, a harrowing tale weaving together Stalin's purges and modern-day people-trafficking and sex slavery. A bestseller in Estonia and Finland, it's won six major awards and has been published in 36 languages (including English). It was initially created as a play and it's subsequently been made into a feature film and an opera.

Cinema

The first moving pictures were screened in Tallinn in 1896, and the first cinema opened in 1908. Estonia's cinematographic output has not been prolific, but there are a few standouts. It's also worth noting that Estonia produces films for one of the world's smallest audiences – far more than the output of the neighbouring Baltic countries, and with domestic films capturing an impressive 14% of the filmgoing market share.

The nation's most beloved film is Arvo Kruusement's *Spring (Kevade,* 1969), an adaptation of Oskar Luts' country saga. Its sequel, *Summer (Suvi,* 1976), was also popular though regarded as inferior. Grigori Kromanov's *Last Relic (Viimne Reliikvia,* 1969) was a brave and unabashedly anti-Soviet film that has been screened in 60 countries.

More recently Sulev Keedus' lyrical *Georgica* (1998), about childhood, war, and life on the western islands, and Jaak Kilmi's

KIIKING

From the weird and wacky world of Estonian sport comes *kiiking.* Invented in 1997, it's the kind of extreme sport that, frankly, we're surprised the New Zealanders didn't think of first. *Kiiking* sees competitors stand on a swing and attempt to complete a 360-degree loop around the top bar, with their feet fastened to the swing base and their hands to the swing arms. The inventor of *kiiking,* Ado Kosk, observed that the longer the swing arms, the more difficult it is to complete a 360-degree loop. Kosk then designed swing arms that can gradually extend, for an increased challenge. In competition, the winner is the person who completes a loop with the longest swing arms – the current record stands at a fraction over 7m! If this concept has you scratching your head, go to www.kiiking.ee to get a more visual idea of the whole thing and to find out where you can see it in action (or even give it a try yourself).

Pigs' Revolution (Sigade Revolutsioon, 2004), about an anti-Soviet uprising at a teenagers' summer camp, have made the rounds at international film festivals. Veiko Õunpuu's 2007 film Autumn Ball (Sügisball), based on the novel by Mati Unt, won awards at seven festivals from Brussels to Bratislava.

In 2014 Tangerines (Mandariinid), an Estonian-Georgian coproduction, became the first Estonian film to be nominated for the Academy Award for Best Foreign Language Film. Set in Georgia, it tells the story of two Estonian farmers who get caught in the crossfires of the war in Abkhazia.

One of Estonia's most popular locally made films is Names in Marble (Nimed Marmortahvlil, 2002), which tells the story of a group of young classmates and their decision to fight in the fledgling nation's War of Independence against the Red Army in 1918–20. It was directed by acclaimed Estonian stage director Elmo Nüganen and it's based on the book of the same name (by Albert Kivikas) that was banned during Soviet times.

Theatre

Many of the country's theatres were built solely from donations by private citizens, which gives an indication of the role theatre has played in Estonian cultural life. The popularity of theatre is also evidenced in theatregoing statistics: in 2013 Estonia came third in the EU for theatre attendance in the Eurobarometer survey of cultural participation (behind Sweden and the Netherlands). The results showed that 45% of Estonians attend the theatre at least once a year (the EU average is 28%). Travellers, however, will have trouble tapping into the scene without any knowledge of the local language.

Food & Drink

Quite simply, Tallinn is a wonderful city for food lovers. Cuisines from all over the world are represented in its many atmospheric eateries and the prices are generally much lower than you'd pay for a similar meal in most other European capitals. Several restaurants are strongly influenced by New Nordic cuisine, a food trend emphasising the pure, seasonal flavours of the north

EATING PRICE RANGES

The following Estonian price ranges refer to a standard main course.

€ less than €10

€€ €10 to €15

€€€ more than €15

exemplified by Copenhagen's world-topping Noma restaurant.

Finally the rest of Estonia has started to catch up with the capital, with some fantastic restaurants springing up in recent years in Pärnu, Tartu, Otepää and various manor houses scattered around the countryside.

However, many areas still offer visitors little variety beyond what type of meat they'd like with their potatoes. This owes much to Estonia's roots. For centuries native Estonians were relegated to the role of serfs working the fields. Heavy nourishment was required to fuel their long days. Food preparation was simple and practical, using whatever could be raised, grown or gathered from the land. Daily fare was barley porridge, cheese curd and boiled potatoes. On feast days and special occasions, meat made an appearance. Coastal dwellers also garnered sustenance from the sea, mainly cod and herring. To make foods last through the winter, people dried, smoked and salted their fish.

Restaurants have turned humble traditions and historic locations to their advantage, offering table-straining feasts served by young folk in medieval peasant garb. The best example of this is Tallinn's Olde Hansa, but the trend has extended to historic taverns scattered throughout the countryside.

Eesti Specialities

Did someone say 'stodge'? Baltic gastronomy has its roots planted firmly in the land, with livestock and game forming the basis of a hearty diet. The Estonian diet relies on sealiha (pork), other red meat, kana (chicken), vurst (sausage) and kapsa (cabbage). Potatoes add a generous dose of winter-warming carbs to a national cuisine often dismissed as bland, heavy and lacking in spice. Sour cream is served with everything but coffee, it seems.

Kala (fish), most likely *heeringas* (herring), *forell* (trout) or *lõhe* (salmon), appears most often as a smoked or salted starter. Lake Peipsi is a particularly good place for tracking down *suitsukala* (smoked fish); look for roadside stands along the shore road. A more aquired taste is *kilu,* pickled Baltic sprat, often served in sandwiches or as part of a breakfast buffet.

Another favourite is *kama,* a thick milkshakelike drink made from a powdered mixture of boiled, roasted and ground peas, rye, barley and wheat mixed together with buttermilk or *kefir* (fermented milk). It's often served as a dessert, with the addition of berries and sugar.

At Christmas time *verivorst* (blood sausage) is made from fresh blood and

EAT YOUR WORDS

Don't know your *kana* from your *kala*? Your *maasikas* from your *marjad*? Get a head start on the cuisine scene by learning the words that make the dish.

Useful Phrases

May I have a menu?	*Kas ma saaksin menüü?*	*kas* mah *saahk*-sin me*nüü*
I'd like...	*Ma sooviksin...*	ma *saw*-vik-sin...
The bill, please.	*Palun arve.*	*pah*-lun *ahrr*-ve
I'm a vegetarian.	*Ma olen taimetoitlane.*	mah *o*-len *tai*-me-toyt-lah-ne
Bon appetit!	*Head isu!*	head *i*-su
To your health! (when toasting)	*Terviseks!*	*ter*-vi-seks
breakfast	*hommikusöök*	*hom*-mi-ku-serrk
lunch	*lõuna*	*lyu*-na
dinner	*õhtusöök*	*er*-tu-serrk

Food Glossary

berries	*marjad*	*mahrr*-yahd
cabbage	*kapsas*	*kahp*-sahs
caviar	*kaaviar, kalamari*	*kaa*-vi-ah, ka-la-*mah*-rri
cheese	*juust*	*yoost*
chicken	*kana*	*kah*-nah
fish	*kala*	*kah*-lah
fruit	*puuviljad*	*poo*-vil-yahd
grilled 'chop'	*karbonaad*	*kah*-bo-noahd
herring	*räim, heeringas*	*rraim, heh*-rrin-gahs
meat (red)	*liha*	*li*-hah
mushrooms	*seened*	*seh*-ned
pancake	*pannkook*	*pahn*-kawk
pork	*sealiha*	*sea*-li-ha
potato	*kartul*	*kahrr*-tul
rye bread	*leib*	layb
salmon	*lõhe*	*ly*-he
sausage	*vorst*	vorrst
sprats	*kilud*	*ki*-lud
vegetables	*köögivili*	*kerrg*-vi-li
white bread	*sai*	sai

wrapped in pig intestine (joy to the world indeed!). Those really in need of a culinary transfusion will find *verivorst, verileib* (blood bread) and *verikäkk* (balls of blood rolled in flour and eggs with bits of pig fat thrown in for taste) available in most traditional Estonian restaurants year-round. *Sült* (jellied meat) is likely to be served as a delicacy as well.

The seasons continue to play a large role in the Estonian diet. When spring arrives, wild leek, rhubarb, fresh sorrel and goat's cheese appear, and the spring lambs are slaughtered. During summer there are fresh vegetables and herbs, along with berries, nuts and mushrooms gathered from the forests – still a popular pastime for many Estonians. Be sure to take advantage of the local *turg* (market) and load up on superbly flavoured strawberries (check you're buying the local stuff, not imports).

Autumn was always the prime hunting season and although many species are now offered some protection through hunting quotas, you'll often see elk, boar, deer and even bear making their way onto menus, year-round. In winter, Estonians turn to hearty roasts, stews, soups and plenty of sauerkraut.

Given Estonia's rustic origins, it's not surprising that bread is a major staple in the diet, and that Estonians make a pretty good loaf. Rye is by far the top choice. Unlike other ryes you may have eaten, here it's moist, dense and delicious (assuming it's fresh), and usually served as a free accompaniment to every restaurant meal.

Terviseks!

The traditional Estonian toast translates as 'your health' (it's much easier to remember if you think 'topsy-turvy sex'). Beer is the favourite tipple in Estonia and the local product is very much in evidence. The biggest brands are Saku and A Le Coq, which come in a range of brews. In recent years the craft beer revolution that's overtaken the world has found fertile ground in Estonia, with dozens of microbreweries producing tasty drops, many with a surprisingly high alcohol percentage (Põhjala's brews are well worth looking out for). On Saaremaa and Hiiumaa you'll also find homemade beer, which is flatter than lager but still the perfect refreshment on a hot day. In winter Estonians drink mulled wine, the antidote to cold wintry nights.

Estonia's ties to Russia have led to vodka's enduring popularity. Viru Valge is the best brand, and it comes in a range of flavours, which some Estonians mix with fruit juices (try the vanilla-flavoured vodka mixed with apple juice).

Vana Tallinn is in a class of its own. No one quite knows what the syrupy liqueur is made from, but it's sweet and strong and has a pleasant aftertaste. It's best served neat, in coffee, over ice with milk, over ice cream, or in champagne or dry white wine.

Even without any vineyards to call their own, wine bars are quite fashionable, especially in the larger cities. However, few offer an extensive range by the glass. The capital also boasts the largest wine cellars in the Baltic and plenty of medieval settings in which to imbibe.

Where, When & How

Meals are served in a *restoran* (restaurant) or a *kohvik* (cafe), *pubi* (pub), *kõrts* (inn) or *trahter* (tavern). Nearly every town has a *turg* (market), where you can buy fresh local fruit and vegetables, as well as meats and fish.

Estonian eating habits are similar to other parts of northern Europe. Either lunch or dinner may be the biggest meal of the day. Cooked breakfasts aren't always easy to find but many cafes serve pastries and cakes throughout the day. Tipping at top restaurants is fairly commonplace but not essential, with 10% the norm. For reviews of the country's culinary best, see www.eestimaitsed.com.

If invited for a meal at an Estonian home you can expect abundant hospitality and generous portions. It's fairly common to bring flowers for the host. Just be sure to give an odd number (even-numbered flowers are reserved for the dead).

SURVIVAL GUIDE

ℹ Directory A–Z

ACCOMMODATION

If you like flying by the seat of your pants when you're travelling, you'll find July and August in Estonia very problematic. The best accommodation books up quickly and in Tallinn, especially on weekends, you might find yourself scraping for anywhere at all to lay your head. In fact, Tallinn gets busy most weekends, so try to book about a month ahead anytime from May through to September (midweek isn't anywhere near as bad).

High-season in Estonia means summer. Prices drop off substantially at other times. The exception is Otepää, when there's also a corresponding peak in winter.

CUSTOMS REGULATIONS

If arriving from outside the EU, there are the usual restrictions on what can be brought into the country; see www.emta.ee for full details, including alcohol and tobacco limits.

EMBASSIES & CONSULATES

For up-to-date contact details of Estonian diplomatic organisations as well as foreign embassies and consulates in Estonia, check the website of the Ministry of Foreign Affairs (www.vm.ee).

Australian Consulate (☑ 650 9308; www.sweden.embassy.gov.au; Marja 9, Mustjõe, Tallinn) Honorary consulate; embassy in Stockholm.

Canadian Embassy Office (☑ 627 3311; www.canada.ee; Toom-Kooli 13, Toompea, Tallinn) An office of Canada's Baltic embassy, which is in Rīga.

Dutch Embassy (☑ 680 5500; www.netherlandsembassy.ee; Rahukohtu 4-I)

Finnish Embassy (☑ 610 3200; www.finland.ee; Kohtu 4, Toompea, Tallinn)

French Embassy (☑ 616 1610; www.amba-france-ee.org; Toom-Kuninga 20, Uus Maailm, Tallinn)

German Embassy (☑ 627 5300; www.tallinn.diplo.de; Toom-Kuninga 11, Tõnismägi, Tallinn)

Irish Embassy (☑ 681 1888; www.embassyofireland.ee; Rahukohtu 4-II, Toompea, Tallinn)

Latvian Embassy (☑ 627 7850; www.mfa.gov.lv; Tõnismägi 10, Tõnismägi, Tallinn)

Lithuanian Consulate (☑ 737 5225; http://ee.mfa.lt; Jakobi 2-434, Tartu)

Lithuanian Embassy (☑ 616 4991; http://ee.mfa.lt; Uus 15, Tallinn)

Russian Consulate (☑ 356 0652; www.rusemb.ee; Kiriku 8, Narva)

Russian Consulate (☑ 740 3024; www.rusemb.ee; Ülikooli 1, Tartu)

Russian Embassy (☑ 646 4175; www.rusemb.ee; Pikk 19, Tallinn)

Swedish Embassy (☑ 640 5600; www.sweden.ee; Pikk 28, Tallinn)

UK Embassy (☑ 667 4700; www.ukinestonia.fco.gov.uk; Wismari 6, Kassisaba, Tallinn)

US Embassy (☑ 668 8100; http://estonia.usembassy.gov/; Kentmanni 20, Tatari, Tallinn)

GAY & LESBIAN TRAVELLERS

Hand-in-hand with its relaxed attitude to religion, today's Estonia is a fairly tolerant and safe home to its gay and lesbian citizens – certainly much more so than its neighbours. Unfortunately, that ambivalence hasn't translated into a wildly exciting scene (only Tallinn has gay venues).

Homosexuality was decriminalised in 1992 and since 2001 there has been an equal age of consent for everyone. In 2014 Estonia became the first former Soviet republic to pass a law recognising same-sex registered partnerships, coming into effect in 2016.

INTERNET ACCESS

Wireless internet access (wi-fi) is ubiquitous in 'E-stonia' (you may find yourself wondering why your own country lags so far behind this tech-savvy place). You'll find literally hundreds of hot spots throughout the country. We're talking on city streets, in hotels, hostels, restaurants, cafes, pubs, shopping centres, ports, petrol stations, even on long-distance buses and in the middle of national parks! Keep your eyes peeled for orange-and-black stickers indicating availability. In most places connection is free.

If you're not packing a laptop or smartphone, options for getting online are not as numerous as they once were. Some accommodation providers offer a computer for guest use and there are a few internet cafes with speedy connections. Plus public libraries have web-connected computers that can usually be accessed free of charge (you may need photo ID). Most small communities will have a well-signed public internet point, often connected to the general store.

MAPS

If you're just going to major cities and national parks, you'll find the maps freely available in tourist offices and park centres more than adequate. If, however, you're planning on driving around and exploring more out-of-the-way places, a good road atlas is worthwhile and easy to find. **Regio** (www.regio.ee) produces a good, easy-to-use road atlas, with enlargements for all major towns and cities. **EO Map** (www.eomap.ee) has fold-out sheet maps for every Estonian county and city, as well as a road atlas.

MONEY

On 1 January 2011 Estonia joined the eurozone, bidding a very fond farewell to its short-lived kroon. ATMs are plentiful and credit cards are widely accepted. Travellers cheques have gone the way of the dinosaurs; most banks will still exchange them but commissions can be high. Tipping in restaurants has become the norm; round the bill up to something approaching 10% (or less).

PUBLIC HOLIDAYS

New Year's Day (Uusaasta) 1 January

Independence Day (Iseseisvuspäev) Anniversary of 1918 declaration on 24 February

Good Friday (Suur reede) March/April

Easter Sunday (Lihavõtted) March/April

Spring Day (Kevadpüha) 1 May

Pentecost (Nelipühade) Seventh Sunday after Easter (May/June)

Victory Day (Võidupüha) Commemorating the anniversary of the Battle of Võnnu (1919) on 23 June

St John's Day (Jaanipäev, Midsummer's Day) Taken together, Victory Day and St John's Day on 24 June are the excuse for a week-long midsummer break for many people

Day of Restoration of Independence (Taasiseseisvumispäev) On 20 August, marking the country's return to independence in 1991

Christmas Eve (Jõululaupäev) 24 December

Christmas Day (Jõulupüha) 25 December

Boxing Day (Teine jõulupüha) 26 December

TELEPHONE SERVICES

There are no area codes in Estonia; if you're calling anywhere within the country, just dial the number as it's listed. All landline phone numbers have seven digits; mobile (cell) numbers have seven or eight digits and begin with 5. Estonia's country code is 372. To make a collect call dial ☏ 16116, followed by the desired number. To make an international call, dial ☏ 00 before the country code.

Almost all of Estonia is covered with digital mobile-phone networks, and every man and his dog has a mobile. To avoid the high roaming charges, you can get a starter kit (around €5), which will give you an Estonian number, a SIM card and around €5 of talk time (incoming calls are free with most providers). You can buy scratch-off cards for more minutes as you need them. SIM cards and starter kits are widely available from post offices, supermarkets and kiosks.

Public telephones accept chip cards, available at post offices, hotels and most kiosks. For placing calls outside Estonia, an international telephone card with a pin, available at many kiosks and supermarkets, is better value. Note that these cards can only be used from landlines, not mobile phones.

TOURIST INFORMATION

In addition to the info-laden, multilingual website of the **Estonian Tourist Board** (www. visitestonia.com), there are tourist offices in most cities and many towns and national parks throughout the country. At nearly every one you'll find English-speaking staff and lots of free material.

ⓘ Getting There & Away

AIR

Eleven European airlines have scheduled services to Tallinn year-round, with additional routes and airlines added in summer (see p416). The main Baltic services:

airBaltic (www.airbaltic.com) Multiple daily flights between Tallinn and Rīga.

Estonian Air (www.estonian-air.ee) Flies between Tallinn and Vilnius four times per week.

Finnair (www.finnair.ee) Four to six flights a day between Helsinki and Tallinn, and daily flights between Helsinki and Tartu.

BUS

The following bus companies all have services between Estonia and the other Baltic states:

Ecolines (☏ 606 2217; www.ecolines.net) Major routes: Tallinn–Pärnu–Rīga (seven daily), two of which continue on to Vilnius; Tallinn–St Petersburg (four daily); Tartu–Valga–Rīga (daily); Vilnius–Rīga–Tartu–Narva–St Petersburg (daily).

Lux Express & Simple Express (☏ 680 0909; www.luxexpress.eu) Major routes: Tallinn–Pärnu–Rīga (10 to 12 daily), six of which continue on to Panevėžys and Vilnius; Tallinn–Rakvere–Sillamäe–Narva–St Petersburg (six to nine daily); Tallinn–Tartu–Võru–Moscow (daily); Rīga–Valmiera–Tartu–Sillamäe–Narva–St Petersburg (nine to 10 daily).

UAB Toks (www2.toks.lt) Two daily Tallinn–Pärnu–Rīga–Panevėžys–Vilnius buses, with one continuing on to Kaunas and Warsaw.

CAR & MOTORCYCLE

The three Baltic countries are all part of the Schengen agreement, so there are no border checks when driving between Estonia and Latvia. There's usually no problem taking hire cars across the border but you'll need to let the rental company know at the time of hire if you intend to do so; some companies will charge an additional fee.

TRAIN

Valga is the terminus for both the Estonian and Latvian rail systems, but the train services don't connect up. From Valga, Estonian trains operated by **Elron** (www.elron.ee) head to Tartu, while Latvian trains operated by **Pasažieru vilciens** (www.pv.lv) head to Valmiera, Cēsis, Sigulda and Rīga. There are also direct trains to Tallinn from St Petersburg and Moscow (p419).

ℹ️ Getting Around

BICYCLE, CAR & MOTORCYCLE

➡ Estonian roads are generally very good and driving is easy.

➡ Touring cyclists will find Estonia mercifully flat.

➡ In rural areas, particularly on the islands, some roads are unsealed but they're usually kept in good condition.

➡ Winter poses particular problems for those not used to driving in ice and snow.

➡ Car and bike hire is offered in all the major cities.

BUS

➡ The national bus network is extensive, linking all the major cities to each other and the smaller towns to their regional hubs.

➡ All services are summarised on the extremely handy **T pilet** (www.tpilet.ee) site.

➡ Don't presume that drivers will speak English.

➡ Concessions are available for children and seniors.

TRAIN

Train services have been steadily improving in recent years. Domestic routes are run by **Elron** (www.elron.ee) but it's also possible to travel between Tallinn, Rakvere and Narva on the Russian-bound services run by **GoRail** (www.gorail.ee)

The major domestic routes:

Tallinn–Rakvere (three daily), with two continuing to Narva

Tallinn–Tartu (eight daily)

Tallinn–Viljandi (four daily)

Tallinn–Pärnu (three daily)

Tartu–Sangaste–Valga (three daily)

Helsinki Excursion

Best Places to Stay

➡ Hotelli Helka (p186)

➡ GLO Hotel Kluuvi (p186)

➡ Hotel Finn (p186)

➡ Hostel Academica (p186)

Best Places to Eat

➡ Olo (p187)

➡ A21 Dining (p187)

➡ Skiffer (p187)

Why Go?

At the neck of the Gulf of Finland bottle (for that's how it looks on the map), two capitals – Helsinki and Tallinn – face each other like two old mates who need no one else for company. The 90km separating them can be covered in two hours and an armada of boats is ready to assist you in this not-so-daring accomplishment.

In every respect as Baltic as the three east Baltic capitals, Helsinki boasts an exceptionally scenic setting. It is an archipelago as much as a city, so sea views will accompany you wherever you go when exploring this modern, stylish megalopolis, obsessed with design and hovering at the top of the world's urban livability index.

It is also an interesting historical comparison, for Finland had every chance of repeating the fate of Baltic states, but unlike them it repelled the Soviet invasion in 1939 and stayed free. Now you can see the difference it has made.

When to Go

➡ Helsinki has year-round appeal; there's always something going on.

➡ The summer kicks off in June, when terraces sprout outside every cafe and bar, and the nights seem never to end.

➡ There's a bit of a lull in July when Finns head off to their summer cottages, but in August the capital is repopulated and plenty of activities are on offer.

➡ If you feel like seeing the wintry side of town, go in December, when you can ice skate and absorb the Christmassy atmosphere before temperatures get too extreme.

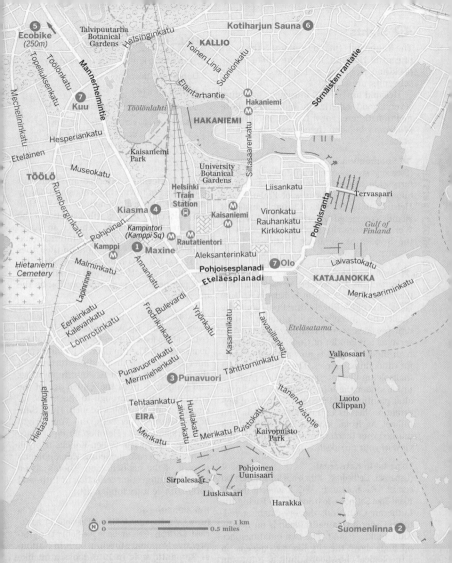

Helsinki Highlights

1 After a few sundowners at **Maxine** (p188), descend into the weekend maelstrom of Helsinki's pubs and bars.

2 Grab a picnic and explore the fortress island of **Suomenlinna** (p182), which guarded Helsinki harbour.

3 Browse the huge range of design shops in **Punavuori** (p189).

4 Select from the city's huge range of museums and galleries such as **Kiasma** (p182) for great contemporary art.

5 Check out **Ecobike** (p190) and take advantage

of the network of cycle paths to explore on two wheels.

6 Sweat out your cares in the traditional, atmospheric **Kotiharjun Sauna** (p183).

7 Dine on traditional Finnish food such as meatballs or liver and mash, or experiment with Modern Suomi cuisine at **Olo** (p187) or **Kuu** (p187).

◉ Sights

The Kauppatori (market square) is the heart of central Helsinki; it's where urban ferries dock and fresh fish and berries, as well as souvenirs, are sold.

Helsinki has over 50 museums, including several good galleries in addition to those mentioned here. For a full list, pick up the *Museums* booklet (free) from the tourist office.

★ Suomenlinna   FORTRESS

(Sveaborg; www.suomenlinna.fi) Just a 15-minute ferry ride from the Kauppatori, a visit to Suomenlinna, the 'fortress of Finland', is a Helsinki must-do. Set on a tight cluster of islands connected by bridges, the UNESCO World Heritage site was originally built by the Swedes as Sveaborg in the mid-18th century.

★ Tuomiokirkko   CATHEDRAL

(Lutheran Cathedral; www.helsinginseurakunnat.fi; Unioninkatu 29; ⊘ 9am-6pm, to midnight Jun-Aug) **FREE** One of CL Engel's finest creations, the chalk-white neoclassical Lutheran Cathedral presides over Senaatintori. Created to serve as a reminder of God's supremacy, its high flight of stairs is now a meeting place for canoodling couples. The spartan, almost mausoleum-like interior has little ornamentation under the lofty dome apart from an altar painting and three stern statues of Reformation heroes Luther, Melanchthon and Mikael Agricola, looking like they've just marked your theology exam and taken a dim view of your prospects.

Uspenskin Katedraali   CATHEDRAL

(Uspenski Cathedral; http://hos.fi/uspenskin-katedraali; Kanavakatu 1; ⊘ 9.30am-4pm Tue-Fri, 10am-3pm Sat, noon-3pm Sun) **FREE** Facing the Lutheran Cathedral, the eye-catching red-brick Uspenski Cathedral stands on nearby Katajanokka island. The two buildings face off high above the city like two queens on a theological chessboard. Built as a Russian Orthodox church in 1868, it features classic onion-topped domes and now serves the Finnish Orthodox congregation. The high, square interior has a lavish iconostasis with the Evangelists flanking panels depicting the Last Supper and the Ascension.

★ Kiasma   GALLERY

(www.kiasma.fi; Mannerheiminaukio 2; adult/child €10/free; ⊘ 10am-5pm Sun & Tue, 10am-8.30pm Wed-Fri, 10am-6pm Sat) Now just one of a

---

series of elegant contemporary buildings in this part of town, curvaceous and quirky metallic Kiasma, designed by Steven Holl and finished in 1998, is still a symbol of the city's modernisation. It exhibits an eclectic collection of Finnish and international modern art and keeps people on their toes with its striking contemporary exhibitions. The interior, with its unexpected curves and perspectives, is as invigorating as the outside.

★ Ateneum   GALLERY

(www.ateneum.fi; Kaivokatu 2; adult/child €12/free; ⊘ 10am-6pm Tue & Fri, 9am-8pm Wed & Thu, 10am-5pm Sat & Sun) The top floor of Finland's premier art gallery is an ideal crash course in the nation's art. It houses Finnish paintings and sculptures from the golden age of the late 19th century through to the 1950s, including works by Albert Edelfelt, Hugo Simberg, Helene Schjerfbeck, the Von Wright brothers and Pekka Halonen. Pride of place goes to the Akseli Gallen-Kallela triptych from the *Kalevala* depicting Väinämöinen's pursuit of the maiden Aino. There's also a small but interesting collection of 19th- and early-20th-century foreign art.

Kansallismuseo   MUSEUM

(www.kansallismuseo.fi; Mannerheimintie 34; adult/child €8/free; ⊘ 11am-6pm Tue-Sun) The impressive National Museum, built in National Romantic style in 1916, looks a bit like a Gothic church with its heavy stonework and tall square tower. This is Finland's premier historical museum and is divided into rooms covering different periods of Finnish history, including prehistory and archaeological finds, church relics, ethnography and changing cultural exhibitions. It's a very thorough, old-style museum – you might have trouble selling this one to the kids – but provides a comprehensive overview.

Helsingin Kaupunginmuseo MUSEUM
(Helsinki City Museum; www.helsinkicitymuseum.
fi; Sofiankatu 4; ⊙9am-5pm Mon-Fri, to 7pm Thu,
11am-5pm Sat & Sun) FREE A group of small
museums scattered around the city centre
constitute this city museum: all have free
entry and focus on an aspect of the city's
past or present through permanent and
temporary exhibitions. The must-see of the
bunch is the main museum, just off Senaatintori. Its excellent collection of historical
artefacts and photos is backed up by entertaining information on the history of the
city, piecing together Helsinki's transition
from Swedish to Russian hands and into
independence.

⭐**Temppeliaukion Kirkko** CHURCH
(☑09-2340 6320; www.helsinginseurakunnat.fi;
Lutherinkatu 3; ⊙10am-5.45pm Mon-Sat, 11.45am-
5.45pm Sun Jun-Aug, to 5pm Sep-May) The Temppeliaukion church, designed by Timo and
Tuomo Suomalainen in 1969, remains one
of Helsinki's foremost attractions. Hewn
into solid stone, it feels close to a Finnish
ideal of spirituality in nature – you could be
in a rocky glade were it not for the stunning
24m-diameter roof covered in 22km of copper stripping. There are regular concerts,
with great acoustics. Opening times vary
depending on events, so phone or search for
its Facebook page updates. There are fewer
groups midweek.

⭐**Seurasaaren Ulkomuseo** MUSEUM
(Seurasaari Open-Air Museum; www.seurasaari.
fi; adult/child €8/2.50; ⊙11am-5pm Jun-Aug,
9am-3pm Mon-Fri, 11am-5pm Sat & Sun late May
& early Sep) West of the city centre, this ex-

cellent island museum has a collection of
historic wooden buildings transferred here
from around Finland. There's everything
from haylofts to a mansion, parsonage and
church, as well as the beautiful giant rowboats used to transport churchgoing communities. Prices and hours refer to entering
the buildings themselves, where guides in
traditional costume demonstrate folk dancing and crafts. Otherwise, you're free to
roam the picturesque wooded island, where
there are several cafes.

🏃 Activities

One of the joys of Helsinki is grabbing a
bike and taking advantage of its long water-
fronts, numerous parks, and comprehensive
network of cycle lanes.

Finnair Sky Wheel FERRIS WHEEL
(www.finnair-skywheel.com; Katajanokanlaituri 2;
adult/child €12/9; ⊙10am-10pm Mon-Thu, 10am-
11pm Fri & Sat, 10am-8pm Sun) Rising over the
harbour, this Ferris wheel gives good perspectives over the comings and goings of
central Helsinki. If you fancy forking out
€195, you get the VIP gondola, with glass
floors below, leather seats and a bottle of
champagne.

⭐**Kotiharjun Sauna** SAUNA
(www.kotiharjunsauna.fi; Harjutorinkatu 1; adult/
child €12/6; ⊙2-8pm Tue-Sun, sauna to 9.30pm)
This traditional public wood-fired sauna
in Kallio dates back to 1928. This type of
place largely disappeared with the advent
of shared saunas in apartment buildings,
but it's a classic experience, where you can

HELSINKI IN...

One Day

Finns are the world's biggest coffee drinkers so, first up, it's a caffeine shot with a *pulla*
(cinnamon bun) at a classic **cafe** in the city centre. Then to the **Kauppatori** (market
square) and the adjacent **Kauppahalli** market building. Put a picnic together and boat out
to the island fortress of **Suomenlinna**. Back in town, check out the **Lutheran Cathedral**
on Senaatintori (Senate Sq) and nearby **Uspenski Cathedral**. Take the metro to legendary **Kotiharjun Sauna** for a predinner sweat. Eat traditional Finnish at **Kuu** or **Olo**.

Two Days

With a second day to spare, investigate the art and design scene. Head to the **Ateneum**
for the golden age of Finnish painting, then see contemporary works at still-iconic
Kiasma. Feet tired? Catch **tram 3** for a circular sightseeing trip around town, before
browsing **design shops** around Punavuori. In the evening, head up to **A21 Cocktail
Lounge** for a chic evening out or to Kaurismäki brothers' **Mockba** for a wilder kind of
alcohol-infused fun.

Helsinki

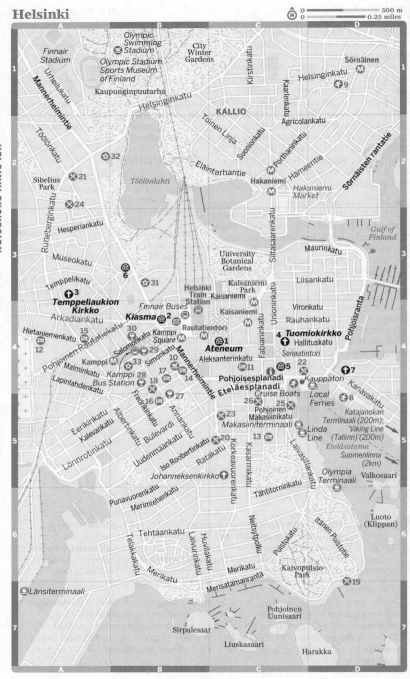

Helsinki

also get a scrub down and massage. There are separate saunas for men and women; bring your own towel or rent one (€3). It's a short stroll from Sörnäinen metro station. Closes Sundays June to mid-August.

Yrjönkadun Uimahalli SWIMMING
(www.hel.fi; Yrjönkatu 21; swimming €5-5.40, swimming plus saunas €14; ⊙ open Sep-May, men 6.30am-8pm Tue & Thu, 8am-8pm Sat, women noon-8pm Sun & Mon, 6.30am-8pm Wed & Fri) For a sauna and swim, these art deco baths are

a Helsinki institution – a fusion of soaring Nordic elegance and Roman tradition. There are separate hours for men and women. Nudity is compulsory in the saunas; bathing suits are optional in the pool.

Cruises CRUISE
Numerous summer cruises leave from the Kauppatori. A 1½-hour jaunt costs €17 to €20; dinner cruises, bus–boat combinations and sunset cruises are all available. Most go past Suomenlinna and weave between other islands. Cruises run from May to September; there's no need to book, just turn up and pick the next departure.

☞ Tours

An excellent budget option is to do a circuit of the city on **Tram 2** or **Tram 3**; pick up the free *Sightseeing on Tram* brochure as your guide around the city centre and out to Kallio.

Natura Viva KAYAKING
(☑ 010-292 4030; www.naturaviva.fi; Ramsinniementie 14; ⊙ Jun-Aug) Located at the Rantapuisto hotel on Vuosaari, east of the city centre, these guys run daily three-hour paddling excursions around the Helsinki archipelago. It's beginner-friendly and they'll pick you up from the centre of town. You can rent kayaks at the paddling centre here, which is also open in May and most of September.

Happy Guide Helsinki WALKING, CYCLING
(☑ 0445 020066; www.happyguidehelsinki.com) Runs a range of original, light-hearted but informative bike and walking tours around the city. There are a lot of options, so study its website.

✾ Festivals & Events

Helsinki Päivä CITY
(Helsinki Day; www.helsinkipaiva.fi) Celebrating the city's anniversary, Helsinki Day brings many free events to Esplanadi on 12 June.

Helsingin Juhlaviikot PERFORMING ARTS
(Helsinki Festival; www.helsinginjuhlaviikot.fi) From late August to early September, this arts festival features chamber music, jazz, theatre, opera and more.

Flow Festival MUSIC
(www.flowfestival.com) An August weekend festival that sees indie, hip hop, electronic and experimental music rock the suburb of Suvilahti.

Baltic Herring Fair FOOD

(www.portofhelsinki.fi) In the first week of October fisherfolk and chefs gather at the Kauppatori to sell delicious salted and marinated herring. It's been going since 1743.

🛏 Sleeping

Accommodation is expensive in Helsinki. From mid-May to mid-August, bookings are strongly advised.

⭐**Hostel Academica** HOSTEL €

(☑ 09-1311 4334; www.hostelacademica.fi; Hietaniemenkatu 14; dm/s/d €28.50/63/75; ☉ Jun-Aug; 🅿 @ 🛜 🛁) 🖉 Finnish students live well, so in summer take advantage of this residence, a clean busy spot packed with features (pool and sauna) and cheery staff. The modern rooms are great, and all come with bar fridges and their own bathrooms. Dorms have only two or three berths so there's no crowding. It's also environmentally sound. Breakfast available. HI discount.

⭐**Hotelli Helka** HOTEL €€

(☑ 09-613 580; www.helka.fi; Pohjoinen Rautatiekatu 23; s €110-132, d €142-162; 🅿 @ 🛜) One of the centre's best midrange hotels, the Helka has competent, friendly staff and excellent facilities, including free parking if you can bag one of the limited spots. Best are the rooms, which seem to smell of pine with their Artek furniture, ice-block bedside lights and print of a rural Suomi scene over the bed, backlit to give rooms a moody glow.

Hotel Finn HOTEL €€

(☑ 09-684 4360; www.hotellifinn.fi; Kalevankatu 3; s €59-119, d €109-199; 🅿 🛜) High in a central-city building, this friendly two-floor hotel is upbeat with helpful service and corridors darkly done out in sexy chocolate and red, with art from young Finnish photographers on the walls. Rooms all differ but are bright, with modish wallpaper and tiny bathrooms. Some are furnished with recycled materials. Rates vary widely – it can be a real bargain.

SLEEPING PRICE RANGES

The following price ranges refer to price of a double room.

€ less than €70

€€ €70 to €160

€€€ more than €160

Omenahotelli HOTEL €€

(☑ 0600 18018; www.omenahotels.com; r €70-130; 🛜) This good-value staffless hotel chain has two handy Helsinki locations: **Lönnrotinkatu** (www.omena.com; Lönnrotinkatu 13); **Yrjönkatu** (www.omena.com; Yrjönkatu 30). As well as a double bed, rooms have fold-out chairs that can sleep two more, plus there's a microwave and minifridge. Book online or via a terminal in the lobby. Windows don't open, so rooms can be stuffy on hot days.

⭐**Hotel Fabian** HOTEL €€€

(☑ 09-6128 2000; www.hotelfabian.fi; Fabianinkatu 7; r €200-270; ❄ @ 🛜) Central, but in a quiet part without the bustle of the other designer hotels, this place gets everything right. Elegant standard rooms with whimsical lighting and restrained modern design are extremely comfortable; they vary substantially in size. Higher-grade rooms add extra features and a kitchenette. Staff are super-helpful and seem very happy to be here.

GLO Hotel Kluuvi HOTEL €€€

(☑ 010-344 4400; www.glohotels.fi; Kluuvikatu 4; s €234-269, d €249-284; ❄ @ 🛜) There are no starched suits at reception at this laidback designer joint, and the relaxed atmosphere continues through the comfortably modish public areas to the rooms. Beds: exceptionally inviting. Facilities: top notch and mostly free. Location: on a pedestrian street in the heart of town. Cute extra: a stuffed tiger toy atop the covers.

🍴 Eating

Helsinki has a great range of restaurants, whether for Finnish classics, Modern Suomi cuisine or international dining. Restaurant food is on the pricey side, but cafes offer good lunch options and Helsinki's famous love of coffee means there are always great places to grab a cup and a traditional pastry.

A good resource is the website www.eat.fi, which plots restaurants on a map of town: even if you can't read all the reviews, you'll soon spot which ones are the latest favourites.

Zucchini VEGETARIAN €€

(Fabianinkatu 4; lunch €8-12; ☉ 11am-4pm Mon-Fri; 🖉) One of the city's few vegetarian cafes, this is a top-notch lunchtime spot; queues out the door are not unusual. Piping-hot soups banish winter chills, and fresh-baked quiche on the sunny terrace out the back is a summer treat. For lunch, you can choose soup or salad/hot dish or both.

Skiffer
PIZZA €€

(www.skiffer.fi; Erottajankatu 11; pizzas €12-17; ⊙11am-9.30pm Mon-Thu, 11am-11pm Fri, 2-11pm Sat, 2-8pm Sun; 🛜) Crusty goodness and great-tasting fresh ingredients combine to excellent effect in this popular, out-of-the-ordinary pizza joint. Nautical-themed art exhibitions brighten the darkish interior; it's a popular meeting spot, so be prepared to wait a wee bit for a table.

Fafa's
KEBAB €€

(www.fafas.fi; Iso Roobertinkatu 2; meals €7-11; ⊙11am-9pm Mon-Wed, 11am-4am Thu-Fri, noon-4am Sat) A cut above the usual kebab places, this serves delicious falafel until late. Opening hours are a bit variable depending on how much has been sold.

Tin Tin Tango
CAFE €€

(www.tintintango.info; Töölöntorinkatu 7; light meals €7-10; ⊙7am-midnight Mon-Fri, 9am-midnight Sat, 10am-midnight Sun; 🛜) This buzzy neighbourhood cafe decorated with prints from the quiffed Belgian's adventures has a bit of everything. There's a laundry and a sauna, as well as lunches, brunches, and cosy tables where you can sip a drink or get to grips with delicious rolls absolutely stuffed full. The welcoming, low-key bohemian vibe is the real draw, though.

Café Ursula
CAFE €€

(www.ursula.fi; Ehrenströmintie 3; lunches €10-16; ⊙9am-9pm Sun-Tue, 9am-10pm Wed-Sat; 🛜) Offering majestic sea views, this cafe looks over the Helsinki archipelago and has marvellous outside seating. In winter you can sit in the modern interior and watch the ice on the sea. It's a posh lunch stop with good if pricey daily specials, elaborate open sandwiches, tasty cakes and glasses of fizz. It opens until midnight in summer, when Sunday brunch (€22) is a great option.

★Kuu
FINNISH €€€

(☎09-2709 0973; www.ravintolakuu.fi; Töölönkatu 27; mains €19-30; ⊙11.30am-midnight Mon-Fri, 2pm-midnight Sat, 2-10pm Sun) Tucked away on a corner behind the Crowne Plaza hotel on Mannerheimintie, this is an excellent choice for both traditional and modern Finnish fare. The short menu is divided between the two; innovation and classy presentation drive the contemporary dishes, while quality ingredients and exceptional flavour are

keys to success throughout. Wines are very pricey, but at least there are some interesting choices.

★Olo
MODERN FINNISH €€€

(☎010-320 6250; olo-ravintola.fi; Pohjoisesplanadi 5; lunch €53, degustations €89-137, with drinks €224-292; ⊙11.30am-3pm Mon, 11.30am-3pm & 6pm-midnight Tue-Fri, 6pm-midnight Sat) Thought of by many as Helsinki's best restaurant, Olo occupies smart new premises in a handsome 19th-century harbourside mansion. It's at the forefront of Modern Suomi cuisine, and its memorable degustation menus incorporate both the forage ethos and a little molecular gastronomy. The shorter 'journey' turns out to be quite a long one, with numerous small culinary jewels. Book a few weeks ahead.

★A21 Dining
MODERN FINNISH €€€

(☎040-171 1117; www.a21.fi; Kalevankatu 17; 5-/7-course menu €65/79, cocktail flight €49-63; ⊙5pm-midnight Tue-Sat) A very out-of-the-ordinary experience is to be had here, with a blinding white interior and innovative degustation menu accompanied by a mood-setting intro to each course. The idea is to transport you into Finland's natural world, and it works, with stunning flavour combinations accompanied by unusual cocktails.

🍷 Drinking & Nightlife

Finns don't mind a drink and Helsinki has some of Scandinavia's most diverse nightlife. In winter locals gather in cosy bars, while in summer early-opening beer terraces sprout up all over town.

The centre's full of bars and clubs, with the Punavuori area around Iso-Roobertinkatu one of the most worthwhile for trendy alternative choices.

Helsinki has a dynamic club scene that's always changing. Some club nights have age limits (often over 20) so check event details on websites before you arrive.

★ **Teerenpeli**   PUB

(www.teerenpeli.com; Olavinkatu 2; ☺noon-2am Mon-Thu, noon-3am Fri & Sat, 3pm-midnight Sun; ☏) Get away from the Finnish lager mainstream with this excellent pub right by Kamppi bus station. It serves very tasty ales, stouts and berry ciders from its microbrewery in Lahti, in a long, split-level place with romantic low lighting, intimate tables and an indoor smokers' patio. The highish prices keep it fairly genteel for this zone.

A21 Cocktail Lounge   COCKTAIL BAR

(www.a21.fi; Annankatu 21; ☺6pm-midnight Wed, 6pm-1am Thu, 6pm-2am Fri & Sat) You'll need to ring the doorbell to get into this chic club but it's worth the intrigue to swing with Helsinki's arty set. The interior is decorated in sumptuous gold, but the real lushness is in the cocktails, particularly the Finnish blends that toss cloudberry liqueur and rhubarb to create the city's most innovative tipples.

Bar Loose   CLUB

(www.barloose.com; Annankatu 21; ☺4pm-2am Tue, 4pm-4am Wed-Sat, 6pm-4am Sun; ☏) The opulent blood-red interior and comfortably cosy seating seem too stylish for a rock bar, but this is what this is, with portraits of guitar heroes lining one wall and an eclectic mix of people filling the upstairs, served by two bars. Downstairs is a club area, with live music more nights than not and DJs spinning everything from metal to mod/retro classics.

THE OLD MARKET HALL

In summer there are food stalls, fresh produce and expensive berries at the Kauppatori, but the real picnic treats are in the **Vanha Kauppahalli** (www.vanhakauppahalli.fi; Eteläranta 1; ☺8am-6pm Mon-Sat; ✏) ⚓ nearby. Built in 1889, some of it is touristy these days (reindeer kebabs?), but it's still a traditional Finnish market, where you can get filled rolls, cheese, breads, fish and an array of typical snacks and delicacies. Here you'll also find **Soppakeittiö** (www.sopakeittio.fi; soups €8-10; ☺11am-3.30pm Mon-Fri, 11am-3pm Sat), a great soup bar with famously good bouillabaisse.

Corona Baari & Kafe Mockba   BAR

(www.andorra.fi; Eerikinkatu 11-15; ☺Corona 11am-2am Mon-Thu, 11am-3am Fri & Sat, noon-2am Sun, Kafe Mockba 6pm-2am Mon-Thu, 6pm-3am Fri & Sat; ☏) Those offbeat film-making Kaurismäki brothers are up to their old tricks with this pair of conjoined drinking dens. Corona plays the relative straight man with pool tables, no doorperson, an island bar and a relaxed mix of people. Mockba is back in the USSR with a bubbling samovar and Soviet vinyl. At closing they clear the place out by playing Brezhnev speeches.

Downstairs in Corona, Dubrovnik Lounge and Lobby is open for events: cinema screenings and album launches.

Maxine   BAR, CLUB

(www.maxine.fi; 6th fl, Kamppi; admission €3.50; ☺4pm-4am Tue-Sat, shorter hours winter; ☏) On the top of Kamppi shopping centre, this refurbished venue makes the most of the inspiring city views from its high perch. It's divided into three sections, with a bar area – a great spot for a sundowner – and two dance floors, one of which (the name, Kirjasto, meaning Library, gives it away) is quieter and aimed at an older crowd.

☆ Entertainment

As the nation's big smoke, Helsinki has the hottest culture and nightlife. Music is particularly big here, from metal clubs to opera. The latest events are publicised in *Helsinki This Week*, which is available at tourist offices, shopping centres, the airport, the railway station and the ferry terminal.

For concerts and performances, see *Helsinki This Week,* enquire at the tourist office, or check the website of ticket outlet **Lippupiste** (☎0600 900 900; www.lippu.fi).

★ **Musiikkitalo**   CONCERT VENUE

(www.musiikkitalo.fi; Mannerheimintie 13) As cool and crisp as a gin and tonic on a glacier, this striking modern building is a great addition to central Helsinki. The interior doesn't disappoint either – the main auditorium, visible from the foyer, has stunning acoustics. There are regular classical concerts, and prices are kept low, normally around €20. The bar is a nice place to hang out for a drink.

Oopperatalo OPERA, BALLET
(Opera House; ☑ 09-4030 2211; www.opera.fi; Helsinginkatu 58; tickets from €14) Opera, ballet and classical concerts are held here, though not during summer. Performances of the Finnish National Opera are surtitled in Finnish.

Tavastia LIVE MUSIC
(www.tavastiaklubi.fi; Urho Kekkosenkatu 4; ⊙8pm-1am Sun-Thu, 8pm-3am Fri, 8pm-4am Sat) One of Helsinki's legendary rock venues, this attracts both up-and-coming local acts and bigger international groups. There's a band every night of the week. Also check out what's on at Semifinal, the venue next door.

🛍 Shopping

Known for design and art, Helsinki is an epicentre of Nordic cool, from fashion to the latest furniture and homewares. The further you wander from Pohjoisesplanadi, the main tourist street in town, the lower prices become. The hippest area is definitely Punavuori, which has several good boutiques and art galleries to explore. The whole of that side of town is bristling with design shops and studios. A couple of hundred of these are part of **Design District Helsinki** (www.designdistrict.fi), whose invaluable map you can find at the tourist office.

ℹ Information

Packed your phone? Helsinki has a cut-down version of its tourism website designed to be delivered to your mobile at www.helsinki.mobi.

Internet access at various public libraries is free. Large parts of the city centre have free wifi, as do many bars and cafes – some also have terminals for customers' use. Public telephones are nonexistent.

City of Helsinki (www.hel.fi) Helsinki City website, with links to copious information.
General Emergency (☑112)
Helsinki City Tourist Office (☑ 09-3101 3300; www.visithelsinki.fi; Pohjoisesplanadi 19; ⊙9am-8pm Mon-Fri, 9am-6pm Sat & Sun mid-May–mid-Sep, 9am-6pm Mon-Fri, 10am-4pm Sat & Sun mid-Sep–mid-May) Busy multilingual office with a great quantity of information on the city. Also has an office at the airport (www.visithelsinki.fi; Terminal 2, Helsinki-Vantaa airport; ⊙10am-8pm May-Sep, 10am-6pm Oct-Apr).
HSL/HRT (www.hsl.fi) Public-transport information and journey planner.
Visit Helsinki (www.visithelsinki.fi) Excellent tourist board website full of information.

ℹ **HELSINKI CARD**
....

If you plan to see a lot of sights, the **Helsinki Card** (www.helsinkiexpert.com; adult per 24/48/72hr €36/46/56, child €15/18/21) gives you free travel, entry to more than 50 attractions in and around Helsinki, and discounts on day tours. It's cheaper to buy it online; otherwise get it at the tourist office, hotels, the ubiquitous R-kioskis shops and transport terminals.

UNDERSTAND HELSINKI

Helsinki Today

Regularly featuring at the top of world's most liveable cities ratings, Helsinki has long graduated from a shy provincial wannabe to a global lifestyle icon lauded by trendsetting publications such as *Monocle*. The economy might be going up and down with the rest of the euro zone, but overall the place feels as stable and confident as Switzerland, with Zurich-level prices to back up the impression. As in the rest of Europe, the political debate revolves around immigration, refugees and how much power should be delegated to Brussels. The local Euroskeptic party, now simply called the Finns, made serious gains in the 2011 election and joined the government coalition after emerging as the country's second most important party as a result of 2015 election.

Russia is another hot issue. For two decades the city has benefited from its proximity to St Petersburg, serving as a weekend shopping destination for rich and middle class Russians (whereas the Finns head across the border for cheap booze). But deteriorating relations between the Kremlin and the West has renewed the debate about Finnish neutrality that has been a political sacred cow since the end of WWII. More people now argue in favour of Finland joining NATO, but it's still a long way before they'll become a majority.

History

Founded in 1550 by the Swedish king Gustav Vasa, Helsinki was to be a rival to the Hansa trading town of Tallinn. For more than 200 years it remained a backwater, suffering from various Russian incursions until the Swedes built their fortress named Sveaborg in 1748 to protect this eastern part of their empire. Once the Russians took control of Finland in 1809, a capital closer to St Petersburg was required to keep a closer eye on Finland's domestic politics. Helsinki was chosen – in large part because of the sea fortress (now called Suomenlinna) just outside the harbour – and so in 1812 Turku lost its longstanding status as Finland's capital and premier town.

In the 19th and early 20th centuries Helsinki grew rapidly in all directions. German architect CL Engel was called on to dignify the city centre, which resulted in the neoclassical Senaatintori (Senate Sq). The city suffered heavy Russian bombing during WWII, but in the postwar period Helsinki recovered and went on to host the Summer Olympic Games in 1952.

These days, the capital is so much the centre of everything that goes on in Finland that its past as an obscure market town is totally forgotten.

SURVIVAL GUIDE

Getting There & Away

AIR

Helsinki's **airport** (www.helsinki-vantaa.fi) is at Vantaa, 19km north of Helsinki. Direct flights are available to Tallinn, Rīga, Vilnius and Tartu. There are an ever-growing number of direct flights from other European, American and Asian destinations. It's also served by various budget carriers from several European countries, especially Ryanair, Air Baltic and Blue1. Most other flights are with Finnair or Scandinavian Airlines (SAS).

BOAT

International ferries link Helsinki with Stockholm (Sweden), Tallinn (Estonia), St Petersburg (Russia) and destinations in Germany and Poland. Ferry tickets may be purchased at the terminal, from a ferry company's office (and often its website) or, in some cases, from the city tourist office. Book well in advance during the high season (late June to mid-August) and at weekends. There is also a regular catamaran and hydrofoil service from Tallinn.

There are five main terminals, three close to the centre:

Katajanokka terminal Served by bus 13 and trams 2, 2V and 4.

Olympia and Makasiini terminals Served by trams 3B and 3T.

Länsiterminaali (West Terminal) Served by bus 15.

Hansaterminaali (Vuosaari) Further afield; can be reached on bus 90A.

BUS

Purchase long-distance and express bus tickets at **Kamppi Bus Station** (www.matkahuolto.fi) or on the bus itself. Long-distance buses depart from here to all of Finland.

TRAIN

Helsinki's **train station** (Rautatieasema; www. vr.fi) is central and easy to find your way around. It's linked by subway to the metro (Rautatientori stop), and is a short walk from the bus station.

The train is the fastest and cheapest way to get from Helsinki to major Finnish centres. There are also daily trains (buy tickets from the international counter) to the Russian cities of Vyborg, St Petersburg and Moscow.

ⓘ Getting Around

TO/FROM THE AIRPORT

Train will become the main transport option for the airport, once the airport train station (already operational at the time of writing) is connected with the terminal. The construction of the terminal exit was due to be completed by the beginning of 2016. The train journey to Helsinki train station takes 30 minutes and costs €5, if you buy tickets from machines located on the platform.

The good old bus 615, which used to ferry passengers between the airport and the city, will ply a longer route with less frequency after the train exit is operational. Check routes and prices once the announcement is made.

There are also door-to-door **airport taxis** (☎ 0600 555 555; www.airporttaxi.fi; 2/4 passengers €29.50/39.50), which need to be booked the previous day, before 6pm, if you're leaving Helsinki (one to two people €27). A normal cab should cost €45 to €65.

BICYCLE

With a flat inner city and well-marked cycling paths, Helsinki is ideal for cycling. Get hold of a copy of the Helsinki cycling map at the tourist office.

The city of Helsinki provides distinctive green 'City Bikes' at stands within a radius of 2km from the Kauppatori. The bikes are free: you deposit a €2 coin into the stand that locks them, then reclaim it when you return it to any stand.

For something more sophisticated, **Ecobike** (☎ 040-084 4358; www.ecobike.fi; Savilankatu

FERRIES TO TALLINN

Eckerö Line (☎0600 4300; www.eckeroline.fi) Sails daily to Tallinn year-round (adult from €19, car from €19, 2½ hours) from Länsiterminaali.

Linda Line (☎0600 066 8970; www.lindaline.fi; Makasiiniterminaali; ☀ Apr-Oct) The fastest. Small passenger-only hydrofoil company ploughing the waters to Tallinn (from €19, 1½ hours) from Makasiini terminal eight times daily when ice-free.

Tallink/Silja (☎0600 15700; www.tallinksilja.com) Runs eight Tallinn services daily (one way adult €26 to €44, vehicle from €25, two hours), from Länsiterminaali.

Viking Line (☎0600 41577; www.vikingline.fi; Katajanokan Terminaali) Operates car ferries (adult €21 to €39, vehicle plus two passengers €60 to €100, 2½ hours) from Katajanokka terminal.

1b; ☀1-6pm Mon-Thu) rents out bicycles with prices starting at €10.

PUBLIC TRANSPORT

The city's public transport system, **HSL** (www.hsl.fi), operates buses, metro and local trains, trams and a ferry to Suomenlinna. A one-hour flat-fare ticket for any HSL transport costs €3 when purchased on board, €2.50 when purchased in advance. The ticket allows unlimited transfers but must be validated in the stamping machine on board when you first use it. A single tram ticket is €2.20 full fare. And because it's Nokialand you can order any of these tickets for the same prices using your mobile: send an SMS to ☎16355 texting A1. Day or multiday tickets for up to seven days (24/48/72 hours €7/10.50/14) are the best option if you're in town for a short time.

TAXI

Hail cabs off the street or join a queue at one of the taxi stands located at the train station, the bus station or Senaatintori. You can phone for a taxi on ☎010-00700.

Latvia

📞 371 / POP 2.2 MILLION

Best Places to Eat

➜ Istaba (p221)
➜ Aragats (p221)
➜ 36.Line (p232)
➜ 3 Pavaru (p219)
➜ Fazenda Bazārs (p220)

Best Places to Stay

➜ Rumene Manor (p243)
➜ Hotel Bergs (p217)
➜ Kārlamūiža (p265)
➜ Art Hotel Laine (p216)
➜ Fontaine Royal (p241)

Why Go?

A tapestry of sea, lakes and woods, Latvia is best described as a vast unspoilt parkland with just one real city – its cosmopolitan capital, Rīga. The country might be small, but the amount of personal space it provides is enormous. You can always secure a chunk of pristine nature all for yourself, be it for trekking, cycling or dreaming away on a white-sand beach amid pine-covered dunes. Having been invaded by every regional power, Latvia has more cultural layers and a less homogenous population than its neighbours. People here fancy themselves to be the least pragmatic and the most artistic of the Baltic lot. They prove the point with myriad festivals and a merry, devil-may-care attitude – well, a subdued Nordic version of it.

When to Go

➜ Spend the holidays in the birthplace of the Christmas tree, and try some bobsledding if you dare during the frigid weeks of December and January.

➜ The all-night solstice in June rings in the warmer months as locals flock to their coastal cottages for beach-lazing and midnight sun.

➜ Refusing to let summer go, Rīgans sip lattes under outdoor heat lamps as the cool September air blows through at the season's last alfresco cafes.

RĪGA

POP 703,500

Gothic spires that dominate Rīga's cityscape might suggest austerity, but it is the flamboyant art nouveau that forms the flesh and the spirit of this vibrant cosmopolitan city, the largest of all three Baltic capitals. Like all northerners, it is quiet and reserved on the outside, but there is some powerful chemistry going on inside its hip bars and modern art centres, and in the kitchens of its cool experimental restaurants. Standing next to a gulf named after itself, Rīga is a short drive from jetsetting sea resort Jūrmala, which comes with a stunning white-sand beach. But if you are craving solitude and a pristine environment, gorgeous sea dunes and blueberry-filled forests, begin right outside the city boundaries.

History

If Rīga were a human, it would be keeping a stack of expired passports issued in its name by a dozen states and empires.

It was born German in 1201. Bishop Albert von Buxhoeveden (say that fast three times) founded Rīga as a bridgehead for the crusade against the northern 'heathens' – the Balts, the Slavs and Finno-Ugric people. Thus Rīga became a stronghold for the Knights of the Sword and the newest trading junction between proto-Russia and the West. When Sweden snagged the city in 1621, it grew into the largest holding of the Swedish empire (even bigger than Stockholm!). Then the Russians snatched Latvia from Sweden's grip and added an industrial element to the bustling burg. By the mid-1860s Rīga was the world's biggest timber port and Russia's third city after Moscow and St Petersburg. The 20th century also saw the birth of cafes, salons, dance clubs and a thriving intellectual culture, which acquired a distinct Latvian flavour after the country became independent in 1918. All of that ended with the Soviet occupation in 1940 followed by WWII, which left the city

LATVIA AT A GLANCE

Currency
Euro (€)

Language
Latvian, Russian (unofficial)

Capital
Rīga

Area
64,589 sq km

bombed out and without its two large communities – the Germans, who resettled into Germany, and the Jews, who were slaughtered in the Holocaust. But somehow, Rīga's indelible international flavour managed to rise up from the rubble, and even as a part of the USSR, Rīga was known for its forward thinking and thriving cultural life.

Today, Rīga's cosmopolitan past has enabled the city to effortlessly adjust to a global climate, making it more than just the capital of Latvia – it's the cornerstone of the Baltic.

◎ Sights

Rīga quietly sits along the Daugava River, which flows another 15km north before dumping into the Gulf of Rīga. Old Rīga (Vecrīga), the historic heart of the city, stretches 1km along the river's eastern side and 600m back from its banks. This medieval section of town is mostly pedestrian, containing a flurry of curving cobbled streets and alleys.

Kaļķu iela heads away from the river and turns into Brīvības bulvāris (Freedom Boulevard) when it hits the thin, picturesque ring of parkland that protects the medieval centre from the gridiron of grand boulevards just beyond. The copper-topped Freedom Monument, in the middle of Brīvības bulvāris, is the unofficial gateway into Central

LANGUAGE

Hello (good day)	Labdien	lab-dee-in
Hi (informal)	Sveiki	svay-kee
How are you?	Kā jums klājas	kah yooms klah-yus
Thank you	Paldies	paul-dee-iss
Please/You're welcome	Lūdzu	lood-zoo

Map labels

Kihnu

Baltic Sea

Rīga to Stockholm

Saaremaa

Nynashamn, Sweden

Lübeck to Rīga (Latvia)

Ruhnu

Ainaž

Salacgrīva

3 Cape Kolka

Mazirbe

Lübeck to Ventspils
Rostock to Venstpils

Ovīši • Miķeltornis

Dundaga
Kaltene

Valdemarpils

Mērsrags

Gulf of Rīga

Ventspils

Vārve

Ugāle

KURZEME

Talsi

Stende

Sku

Saulkras

Baltic Sea

Teranda

Jūrkalne

Sabile
Kandava

Plienciems

5 Ventas Rumba

Alsunga

Kuldīga

Kabile

Jūrmala **8** Old Rīga

Pāvilosta

Pedvāle
Zemite

Tukums

Kalnciems

Rīga **1** **2**

Salasp

Aizpute

Dzukste

Baldc

Skrunda

Saldus

Dobele

Jelgava

7 Liepāja

Lecava

Priekule

Ezere

Auce

Kalnāmuiza

Pirunsdāle **Bausk**

Kiburi

Klampji

Eleja

Zeimelis

6 **Rundāle Palace**

Krumini

Mažeikiai

Alsiai
Zabarė

Saločiai

Skuodas

Seda

Naujoji Akmenė

Joniškis

Linkuva

Pasval

Salantai

Lake Plateliai

Papilė

Gruzdziai

Darbėnai

Plateliai • Plokštinė

Tryškiai

Kuršėnai

Pampenai

Plungė • Telšiai

Palanga

Zarenai

Šiauliai

Radviliškis

Kretinga

Seduva

Smilgiai

Klaipėda

Rietavas
Varniai

Lake Lūkstas

Laukuva

LITHUANIA

Panevėžy

Juodkrantė

Kvėdarna

Kelmė

Priekule • Sveksna

Grinkiškis

Šilalė

Latvia Highlights

1 Click your camera at the nightmarish menagerie of devilish gargoyles, mythical beasts and twisting vines that inhabits the art nouveau architecture in **Rīga** (p193).

2 Lose yourself in the maze of cobblestones, church spires and gingerbread trim that is Unesco-protected **Old Rīga** (p196).

3 Listen to the waves pound the awesomely remote **Cape Kolka** (p248), which crowns the desolate Kurzeme coast.

4 Launch raids into **Gauja National Park** (p256) from the fortress in **Cēsis** (p264).

5 Join swarms of fish jumping over **Ventas Rumba** (p245), the widest (and possibly shortest) waterfall in Europe.

6 Sneak away from the capital and indulge in aristocratic decadence at **Rundāle Palace** (p252).

7 Wander past gritty Soviet tenements and gilded cathedrals in the Karosta district of **Liepāja** (p239).

8 Hobnob with Russian jetsetters in the heart of the swanky spa scene of **Jūrmala** (p229).

Rīga (Centrs). This part of the city, constructed in the 19th and 20th centuries, sports wide avenues, luxurious apartment blocks and plenty of art nouveau architecture. At the outer edges of the city centre, the European grandeur begins to fade into Soviet block housing and *microrajons* (microregions, or suburbs).

👁 Old Rīga (Vecrīga)

The curving cobbled streets of Rīga's medieval core are best explored at random. Once you're sufficiently lost amid the tangle of gabled roofs, church spires and crooked alleyways, you will begin to uncover a stunning, World Heritage–listed realm of sky-scraping cathedrals, gaping city squares and crumbling castle walls.

Rātslaukums

Touristy Rātslaukums is a great place to start exploring the old city. There's a tourist information centre (p227) stuffed to the gills with brochures and maps; it's located in the Blackheads House.

⭐ Blackheads House   HISTORIC BUILDING

(Melngalvju nams; Map p198; www.melngalvjunams. lv; Rātslaukums 7) Built in 1344 as a veritable fraternity house for the Blackheads guild of unmarried German merchants, the original house was decimated in 1941 and flattened by the Soviets seven years later. Somehow the original blueprints survived and an exact replica of this fantastically ornate structure was completed in 2001 for Rīga's 800th birthday.

At the time of writing the house was serving as the temporary home of Latvia's president and off limits for travellers – apart from the tourist office located inside it.

Town Hall   HISTORIC BUILDING

(Map p198; Rātslaukums) Rīga's historic town hall was destroyed in WWII and rebuilt from scratch in 2003. A statue of St Roland, the city's patron, takes pride of place on the square in front of it. It, too, is a replica of the original, erected in 1897, which now stands

RĪGA IN...

Two Days

Start your adventure in the heart of the city with a stop at the much-loved **Blackheads House** in Rātslaukums. Pick up some handy brochures at the in-house information centre, then spend the rest of the morning wandering among the twisting cobbled lanes that snake through medieval **Old Rīga**. After a leisurely lunch, wander beyond the ancient walls, passing the **Freedom Monument** as you make your way to the grand boulevards that radiate away from the city's castle core. Head to the **Quiet Centre**, where you'll find some of Rīga's finest examples of art nouveau architecture. Don't miss the **Rīga Art Nouveau Museum**.

On your second day, fine-tune your bargaining skills during a visit to the **Central Market**, where you can haggle for anything from wild berries to knock-off T-shirts. Have a walk through the small **Spīķeri** district then take a relaxing **boat ride** along the Daugava and the city's inner canals. For a late lunch, wander through the Quiet Centre all the way up to **Miera iela** to enjoy the city's emerging hipster cafe culture near the sweet-smelling Laima chocolate factory. In the evening, if the opera is in season, treat yourself to some of the finest classical music in Europe.

Four Days

After completing the two-day itinerary above, spend day three in your swimsuit along the silky sands in **Jūrmala**, Latvia's uber-resort town. Rent a bike in the afternoon and roam around the stunning wooden cottages near the sea. End the day with a relaxing spa treatment, then return to Rīga to party all night at one of the city's notorious clubbing venues.

Your fourth day can be spent exploring some of Rīga's lesser-known nooks, or you can make tracks to **Gauja National Park** for an action-packed day of castle-ogling mixed with adventure sports. Start in **Sigulda** and get the blood rushing on the Olympic bobsled track, swing through **Turaida** before making your way to the secreted Soviet bunker in **Līgatne**, then finish the day at the fortress ruins in **Cēsis** before returning to the capital.

O CHRISTMAS TREE

Rīga's Blackheads House was known for its wild parties; it was, after all, a clubhouse for unmarried merchants. On a cold Christmas Eve in 1510, the squad of bachelors, full of holiday spirit (and other spirits, so to speak), hauled a great pine tree up to their clubhouse and smothered it with flowers. At the end of the evening they burned the tree to the ground in an impressive blaze. From then on, decorating the 'Christmas tree' became an annual tradition, which eventually spread across the globe (as you probably know, the burning part never really caught on).

An octagonal commemorative plaque, inlaid in cobbled Rātslaukums, marks the spot where the original tree once stood.

in St Peter's. You can walk in, if only to see a mildly interesting exhibition of presents given by visiting delegations of partner cities.

Latvian Riflemen Monument MONUMENT
(Latviešu Strēlnieku laukums; Map p198) Latvian Riflemen Sq, on the other side of the Occupation Museum, was once home to Rīga's central market. Today the square is dominated by the controversial statue honouring Latvia's Riflemen, who formed the core of Russia's Red Army in 1918. Some of them served as Lenin's personal bodyguards. Yet, most returned to the newly independent Latvia.

Mentzendorff's House HISTORIC BUILDING
(Mencendorfa nams; Map p198; ☎ 6721 2951; www.mencendorfanams.com; Grēcinieku iela 18; adult/child €2.85/1.14; ⓧ 10am-5pm daily May-Sep, 11am-5pm Wed-Sun Oct-Apr) Built in 1695 as the home of a wealthy German glazier, this sparsely furnished house offers an insight into everyday life for Rīga's successful merchants. There's a permanent exhibition of contemporary glass art downstairs and temporary exhibitions are held in the attic.

Pēterbaznīca Laukums

St Peter's Church CHURCH
(Sv Pētera baznīca; Map p198; www.peterbaznica. riga.lv; Skārņu iela 19; adult/child under 7 yr €9/free; ⓧ 10am-6pm Tue-Sat, noon-6pm Sun) Forming the centrepiece of Rīga's skyline, this Gothic church is thought to be around 800 years old, making it one of the oldest medieval buildings in the Baltic. Its soaring red-brick interior is relatively unadorned, except for heraldic shields mounted on the columns. A colourful contrast is provided by the art exhibitions staged in the side aisles. At the rear of the church, a lift whisks visitors to a viewing platform 72m up the steeple.

The church's austere Gothic outlook is softened by baroque sculptures, added in the 17th century, along with the spire

that instantly became a signature element of Rīga's skyline. In 1721 the spire was destroyed in a blaze despite Russian emperor Peter I personally rushing to the scene to extinguish the fire. A legend says that when it was re-erected in 1746, builders threw glass from the top to see how long the spire would last; a greater number of shards meant a very long life. The glass ended up landing on a pile of straw and broke into just two pieces. The spire ended up being destroyed again in WWII. When it was resurrected again, the ceremonial glass chucking was repeated, and this time it was a smash hit.

Museum of Decorative Arts & Design MUSEUM
(Dekoratīvi lietišķās mākslas muzejs; Map p198 ☎ 6722 7833; www.lnmm.lv; Skārņu iela 10/20; adult/ child €4.27/2.13; ⓧ 11am-5pm Tue & Thu-Sun, to 7pm Wed) The former St George's Church houses a museum devoted to applied art from the art nouveau period to the present, including an impressive collection of furniture, woodcuts, tapestries and ceramics. The building's foundations date back to 1207 when the Livonian Brothers of the Sword erected their castle here. Since the rest of the original knights' castle was levelled by rioting citizens at the end of the same century, it is the only building that remains intact since the birth of Rīga.

Rīga Porcelain Museum MUSEUM
(Map p198; ☎ 6750 3769; www.porcelanamuzejs. riga.lv; Kalēju iela 9/11; adult/student €2.50/1; ⓧ 11am-6pm Tue-Sun) This quirky museum houses the collection of porcelain assembled in Soviet times by the now-defunct Rīga Porcelain & Faience Factory, itself an heir of two factories that existed before WWII. One was run by Russians hailing from the famous Gzhel factory near Moscow, the other by local Germans. As a result, the Rīga style of porcelain-making grew as a fusion of these two schools.

Old Rīga (Vecrīga)

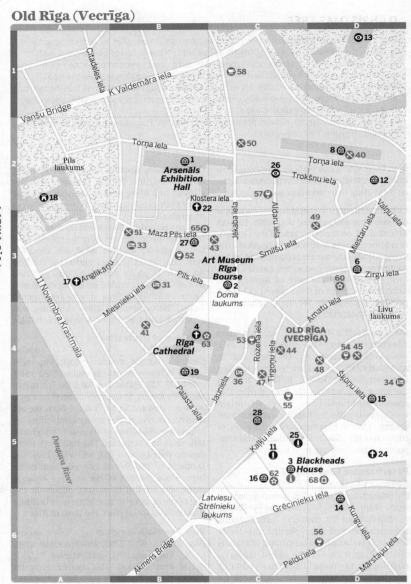

St John's Church CHURCH
(Jāņa baznīca; Skārņu iela 24; Map p198) A 13th-
to 19th-century amalgam of Gothic and baroque styles, it was first mentioned when the
citizens installed catapults on its roof and
successfully dispersed attacking Livonian
knights. Initially run by Dominican monks,
it was pillaged during the Reformation.
After a stint as stables and granary, it was
handed over to the Lutherans, who remain
in control. Next to the church, an archway
leads into **Jāņa sēta** (St John's courtyard),

comes to mind. Note the curving lines above the red-brick gates – they are said to depict the back of the donkey that Jesus rode into Jerusalem. The gist of it is – follow the Christ.

Kalēju iela & Mārstaļu iela

Zigzagging Kalēju iela and Mārstaļu iela are dotted with poignant reminders of the city's legacy as a wealthy northern European trading centre. Several of the old merchants' manors have been transformed into museums.

Latvian People's Front Museum MUSEUM
(Latvijas Tautas Frontes muzejs; Map p198; ☑6722 4502; Vecpilsētas iela 13-15; ☺2-7pm Tue, noon-5pm Wed-Fri, noon-4pm Sat) FREE A branch of the National History Museum, this exhibition, involving modern interactive multimedia technology, goes through the period of the 3rd Atmoda (national awakening), that is the struggle for independence in the years of Soviet perestroika. Led by environmental campaigner Dainis Ivans, the Latvian People's Front was an umbrella organisation that united pro-democracy forces and was responsible for such poignant actions as the Baltic Chain, when Latvians, Estonians and Lithuanians built a human chain that went through all three countries.

Latvian Photography Museum MUSEUM
(Latvijas fotogrāfijas muzejs; Map p198; ☑6722 2713; www.fotomuzejs.lv; Mārstaļu iela 8; adult/child €3.55/1.42; ☺10am-5pm Wed & Fri-Sun, noon-7pm Thu) Occupying a historic merchant's house, this little museum displays early images from Rīga along with changing exhibitions of contemporary photography. There's also a camera obscura and an interesting display on local lad Valters Caps (1905–2003), the inventor of the miniature Minox camera so loved by Cold War spies.

Rīga Synagogue SYNAGOGUE
(www.jews.lv; Peitavas iela 6/8; Map p198) Built in 1905, this art-nouveau-style synagogue was the only one to survive the Nazi occupation – to torch it in the tightly packed Old Town would have put neighbouring buildings at risk. It reopened for worship during the Soviet period but was damaged by bomb attacks by neo-Nazis in 1995 and 1998, following independence. It was only fully restored in 2009 after an infusion of EU money.

Livu Laukums

Lively Livu laukums, near the busiest entrance to Old Rīga along Kaļķu iela, features several beer gardens during summer.

which contains the preserved remains of 13th-century monastery wall.

It was here that Bishop Albert von Buxhoeveden, who founded Rīga in 1201, set up his residence. So if you are looking for the city's exact birthplace, it is about the first spot that

Old Rīga (Vecrīga)

A colourful row of 18th-century buildings lines the square – most of which have been turned into restaurants.

Cat House HISTORIC BUILDING
(Kaķu māja; Miestaru iela 10/12; Map p198) The spooked black cats mounted on the turrets of this 1909 art-nouveau-influenced building have become a symbol of Rīga. According to local legend, the building's owner was rejected from the Great Guild across the street and exacted revenge by pointing the cats' butts towards the hall. The members of the guild were outraged, and after a lengthy

court battle the merchant was admitted into the club on the condition that the cats be turned in the opposite direction.

Doma Laukums

★ **Rīga Cathedral** CATHEDRAL
(Rīgas Doms; Map p198; ☑ 6721 3213; www.doms. lv; Doma laukums 1; admission €3; ☺ 9am-5pm) Founded in 1211 as the seat of the Rīga diocese, this enormous (once Catholic, now Evangelical Lutheran) cathedral is the largest medieval church in the Baltic. The architecture is an amalgam of styles from the 13th to the 18th centuries: the eastern end, the

oldest portion, has Romanesque features; the tower is 18th-century baroque; and much of the rest dates from a 15th-century Gothic rebuilding.

During Soviet times services were forbidden, but the building, along with its huge 6768-pipe organ, built in 1884, underwent a careful reconstruction. It was used as a classical-music venue, which it very much remains now (p224), although services have been resumed since the Lutheran archbishop of Latvia moved in.

The floor and walls of the huge interior are dotted with old stone tombs – note the carved symbols denoting the rank or post of the occupant. Eminent citizens would pay to be buried as close to the altar as possible. In 1709 the cholera and typhoid outbreak that killed a third of Rīga's population was blamed on a flood that inundated the tombs, whereupon new burials were banned.

★ Art Museum Rīga Bourse   MUSEUM

(Mākslas muzejs Rīgas Birža; Map p198; www. lnmm.lv; Doma laukums 6; adult/child €6.40/2.85; ⊙10am-6pm Tue-Thu, Sat & Sun, to 8pm Fri) Rīga's lavishly restored stock-exchange building is a worthy showcase for the city's art treasures. The elaborate facade features a coterie of deities that dance between the windows, while inside, gilt chandeliers sparkle from ornately moulded ceilings. The Oriental section features beautiful Chinese and Japanese ceramics and an Egyptian mummy, but the main halls are devoted to Western art, including a Monet painting and a scaled-down cast of Rodin's *The Kiss*.

Rīga History & Navigation Museum   MUSEUM

(Rīgas vēstures un kuģniecības muzejs; Map p198; www.rigamuz.lv; Palasta iela 4; adult/child €4.27/0.71; ⊙10am-5pm daily May-Sep, 11am-5pm Wed-Sun Oct-Apr) Founded in 1773, this is the oldest museum in the Baltic, situated in the old cathedral monastery. The permanent collection features artefacts from the Bronze Age all the way to WWII, ranging from lovely pre-Christian jewellery to preserved hands removed from Medieval forgers. A highlight is the beautiful neoclassical Column Hall, built when Latvia was part of the Russian empire and filled with relics from that time.

Three Brothers   HISTORIC BUILDING

(Trīs brāļi; Mazā Pils iela 17, 19 & 21; Map p198) Tallinn has its Three Sisters, so Rīga, not to be outdone, has dubbed three of its old stone houses the Three Brothers. These architectural gems conveniently line up in a photogenic row and exemplify Old Rīga's diverse collection of architectural styles. No 17 is over 600 years old, making it the oldest dwelling in town. The 17th-century neighbour houses temporary exhibitions, providing access to the courtyard, where decorations from lost Old Town buildings are exhibited.

Note the tiny windows on the upper levels – Rīga's property taxes during the Middle Ages were based on window size.

St James' Cathedral   CATHEDRAL

(Sv Jēkaba katedrāle; Map p198; Klostera iela; ⊙7am-6pm, to 7pm in summer) Built in 1225, this church has ping-ponged many times between Catholic and Protestant, as well as many languages and communities, including Germans, Swedes, Poles and Estonians. Most notably, it was here that Latvians heard a mass in their own tongue during its Lutheran stint in 1523. Exactly 400 years later it was handed back to the Catholics to be used as their cathedral, which is the role it is playing now.

Pils Laukums

Rīga Castle   CASTLE

(Rīgas pils; Map p198; Pils laukums 3) Built in 1330 as the headquarters of the grand master of the Livonian Order, this building has been much mutated over the years and now only looks properly castley from certain angles. Until it was badly damaged in a fire in 2013 it was the official residence of the Latvian president, a role it will resume once it's fully restored.

★ Arsenāls Exhibition Hall   GALLERY

(Izstāžu zāle Arsenāls; Map p198; www.lnmm. lv; Torņa iela 1; adult/child €3.56/2.13; ⊙noon-5pm Tue, Wed & Fri-Sun, to 8pm Thu) Behind a row of spooky granite heads depicting Latvia's most prominent artists, the imperial arsenal, constructed in 1832 to store weapons for the Russian tsar's army, is now a prime spot for international and local art exhibitions, which makes it worth a visit whenever you are in Rīga. Also check out the massive wooden stairs at the back of the building – their simple yet funky geometry predates modern architecture.

Torņa iela

From Pils laukums, photogenic Torņa iela makes a beeline for City Canal (Pilsētas kanāls) at the other end of Old Rīga. Almost the entire north side of the street is flanked by the custard-coloured **Jacob's Barracks** (Jēkaba Kazarmas; Map p198; Torņa iela 4), built as an enormous warehouse in the 16th century. Tourist-friendly cafes and boutiques now inhabit the refurbished building.

Swedish Gate
GATE

(Zviedru vārti; map p198; Torņa iela 11) Built into the city's medieval walls in 1698 while the Swedes were in power, this is the only remaining gate to Old Rīga, set in the largest surviving section of the town walls. It leads into Trokšņu iela, Old Rīga's narrowest and most atmospheric street.

Latvian War Museum
MUSEUM

(Latvijas kara muzejs; Map p198; www.kara muzejs.lv; Smilšu iela 20; ⊙10am-6pm Apr-Oct, to 5pm Nov-Mar) **FREE** The cylindrical Powder Tower dates back to the 14th century and is the only survivor of the 18 original towers that punctuated the old city wall. Nine Russian cannonballs from 17th- and 18th-century assaults are embedded in its walls. In the past it has served as a gunpowder store, a prison, a torture chamber and a frat house. It now houses a museum which details the political and military history of Latvia from medieval times to the present day.

◉ Central Rīga (Centrs)

As Kaļķu iela breaks free from the urban jumble of turrets and towers, it turns into Brīvības bulvāris (Freedom Blvd), and continues to neatly cut the city centre into two equal parts. An emerald necklace of lush parks acts as a buffer between the medieval walls and the large-scale gridiron of stately boulevards. Central Rīga's hodgepodge of memorable sights includes the flamboyant art nouveau district, a sprawling Central Market housed in mammoth Zeppelin hangars and the iconic Freedom Monument.

Along City Canal

Pilsētas Kanāls (City Canal)
PARK

(Map p204) Pilsētas kanāls, the city's old moat, once protected the medieval interior from invaders. Today, the snaking ravine has been incorporated into a thin belt of stunning parkland splitting Old and Central Rīga. Stately Raiņa bulvāris follows the rivulet on the north side, and used to be known as 'Embassy Row' during Latvia's independence between the world wars.

Raiņa has once again assumed its dignified status, with the stars and stripes fluttering in front of No 7, and *bleu blanc rouge* installed at No 9. Additional diplomatic estates face the central park and moat on Kronvalda bulvāris and Kalpaka bulvāris.

Humble **Bastion Hill** (Bastejkalns) lies along the banks of Pilsētas kanāls near Brīvības, and is the last remnant of medieval Rīga's sand bulwark fortifications. Beneath Bastejkalns, five red stone slabs lie as **memorials to the victims of 20 January 1991** (they were killed here when Soviet troops stormed the nearby Interior Ministry).

On 18 November 1918 Latvia declared its independence at the baroque **National Theatre** (Nacionālais teātris; Map p204), at the junction of the canal and K Valdemāra iela. The beloved Latvian National Opera (p224), which resembles Moscow's Bolshoi Theatre, sits at the other end of the park near K Barona iela.

Freedom Monument
MONUMENT

(Brīvības bulvāris) Affectionately known as 'Milda', Rīga's Freedom Monument towers above the city between Old and Central Rīga. Paid for by public donations, the monument was designed by Kārlis Zāle and erected in 1935 where a statue of Russian ruler Peter the Great once stood.

At the base of the monument there is an inscription that reads *'Tēvzemei un Brīvībai'* (For Fatherland and Freedom), accompanied by granite friezes of Latvians singing and fighting for their freedom. Among the figurines, you may recognise that of Lāčplēsis – the half-man, half-bear who symbolises Latvians' struggle for independence (see p223).

A copper Liberty tops the soaring monument, holding three gold stars in her hands. The three stars represent the three original cultural regions of Latvia: Kurzeme, Vidzeme and Latgale. (Latvia's fourth cultural region, Zemgale, is dismissed as a part of Kurzeme.)

Surprisingly, during the Soviet years the Freedom Monument was never demolished. It helped that one of its authors, Ernests Štālbergs, designed Rīga's main Lenin statue, which stood further up Brīvības until it was removed in 1991. However, all through the Soviet period, Milda was strictly off limits, and people seen placing flowers at the base were persecuted.

Two soldiers stand guard at the monument throughout the day and perform a modest changing of the guards every hour on the hour from 9am to 6pm.

Park Belt

Esplanāde
PARK

(Map p204) The expansive Esplanāde is a large park dotted with tall trees, wooden benches and open-air cafes. The Latvian National Museum of Art graces it on one side, while the cupolas of the Russian Orthodox cathedral majestically rise on the other. The park used to be teeming with Soviet-era sculpture. The monument to Jānis Rainis, Latvia's most celebrated writer, is the only vestige of that era.

He is now accompanied by two military men. The Oskar Kalpak memorial celebrates the man who in 1918 assembled the core of what later became the Latvian army, fighting against the pro-Bolshevik Latvian riflemen. The bronze figure of a man in a cocked hat, standing next to the cathedral, is the monument to Michael Barklay de Tolli. A Rīga native hailing from a German-speaking family of Scottish origin, he led the Russian army in the war against Napoleon and authored the scorched-earth tactics that ensured the ultimate victory for the Russians.

Latvian National Museum of Art
GALLERY

(Latvijas Nacionālā mākslas muzeja; Map p204; www.lnmm.lv; K Valdemāra iela 10a) At the time of writing, Latvia's main gallery was expected to reopen after a thorough restoration. Sitting within the Esplanāde's leafy grounds, this impressive building was purpose-built in a baroque-classical style in 1905. Check online for opening hours and prices.

Nativity of Christ Cathedral
CATHEDRAL

(Kristus Piedzimšanas katedrāle; Map p204; www.pravoslavie.lv; Brīvības bulvāris 23; ⊘7am-7pm) With gilded cupolas peeking through the trees, this Byzantine-styled Orthodox cathedral (1883) adds a dazzling dash of Russian bling to the skyline. During the Soviet period the church was converted into a planetarium but it's since been restored to its former use. Mind the dress code – definitely no shorts; women are asked to cover their heads.

Vērmanes dārzs (Vērmanes Garden)
PARK

(Map p204) From Brīvības, pass the swirls of colour at the 24-hour flower market (p226) along Tērbatas iela to find the inviting Vērmanes dārzs frequented by locals. During the summer months, local bands perform in the small outdoor amphitheatre, and artisans set up shop along the brick walkways.

Quiet Centre

Just when you thought that Old Rīga was the most beautiful neighbourhood in town, the city's audacious art nouveau district (focused around Alberta iela, Strēlnieku iela and Elizabetes iela) swoops in to vie for the prize. Rīga boasts over 750 art nouveau buildings, making it the city with the most art nouveau architecture in the world (see p208).

★ Alberta Iela
ARCHITECTURE

It's like a huge painting, which you can spend hours staring at, as your eye detects more and more intriguing details. But in fact this must-see Rīga sight is a rather functional street with residential houses, restaurants and shops. Art nouveau, otherwise known as Jugendstil, is the style, and the master responsible for most of these is Mikhail Eisenstein (father of filmmaker Sergei Eisenstein). Named after the founder of Rīga, Bishop Albert von Buxhoeveden, the street was the architect's gift to Rīga on its 700th anniversary.

At Alberta iela 2a, constructed in 1906, serene faces with chevalier helmets stand guard atop the facade, which noticeably extends far beyond the actual roof of the structure. Screaming masks and horrible goblins adorn the lower sections amid clean lines and surprising robot-like shapes. Most noticeable are the two stone satyr phoenix-women that stand guard at the front. The facade of the building next door is in much better condition. The three heads on Alberta iela 4, two doors down from 2a, will surely capture your attention. If you look carefully, you'll see a nest of snakes slithering around their heads, evoking Medusa. All six eyes all transfixed on some unseen horror, but only two of the faces are screaming in shock and fear. Two elaborate

---

RĪGA FOR CHILDREN

The Unesco-protected streets of Old Rīga can feel like a magical time warp for the 12-and-under bunch. During the summer months, take the tykes to the **zoo** (p212) in forested Mežaparks or let the little ones cool off on the beach in nearby Jūrmala. Here, between spirited sessions of wave-jumping and sandcastle-building, try **Līvu Akvaparks** (p230), Latvia's largest indoor water park, which features a wave pool and a tangle of waterslides.

Central Rīga (Centrs)

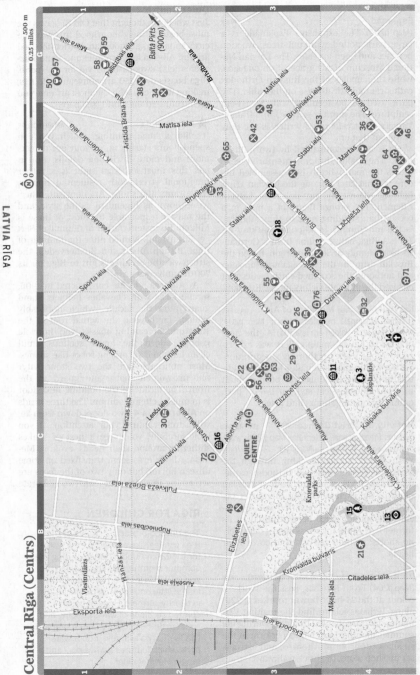

LATVIA RĪGA

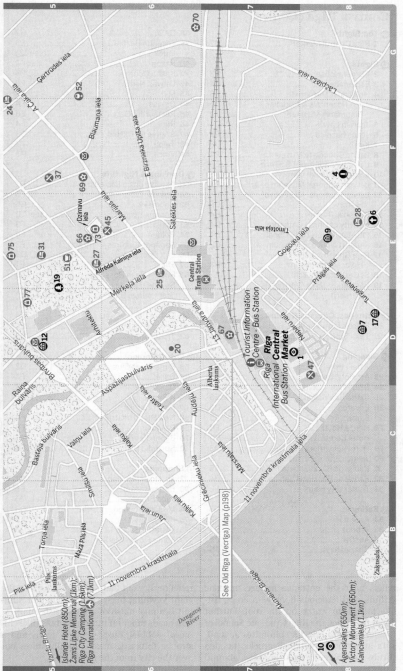

See Old Riga (Vecrīga) Map (p198)

Rīga
Central
Market

Riga
International
Bus Station

Tourist Information
Centre - Bus Station

Central
Train Station

Raina
bulvāris

Basteja bulvāris

Brīvības bulvāris

Aspāzijas bulvāris

Alberta
laukums

Pils
laukums

Pils iela

Torņa iela

Maza Pils iela

Smilšu iela

Valņu iela

Kaļķu iela

Teātra iela

Audēju iela

Jauna iela

Grēcinieku iela

Mārstaļu iela

Merķeļa iela

Arhitektu iela

13. Janvāra iela

Alfrēda Kalniņa iela

Elizabetes iela

Dzirnavu iela

Mārijas iela

Satekles iela

E Birznieka-Upīša iela

Blaumaņa iela

Ģertrūdes iela

A Čaka iela

Gogoļa iela

Prāgas iela

Turgeņeva iela

Timoteja iela

Lāčplēša iela

Nēģu iela

11 novembra krastmala

11 novembra krastmala iela

Akmens Bridge

Daugava
River

Zaķusala

Vanšu Bridge

Islande Hotel (850m);
Žanis Lipke Memorial (1km);
Riga City Camping (1.6km);
Riga International (7.1km)

Āgenskalns (650m);
Victory Monument (650m);
Kalnciemiela (1.1km)

LATVIA RĪGA

Central Rīga (Centrs)

reliefs near the entrance feature majestic griffins, and ferocious lions with erect, fist-like tails keep watch on the roof. Further down the street, the Rīga Graduate School of Law at **Alberta iela 13** epitomises Jugend-stil's attention to detail. Peacocks, tangled shrubs and bare-breasted heroines abound while cheery pastoral scenes are depicted in

relief on Erykah Badu–like turbans atop the giant yawning masks. The triangular summit is a mishmash of nightmarish imagery: lion heads taper off into snake tails (like chimera), sobbing faces weep in agony and a strange futuristic mask stoically stares out over the city from the apex.

Rīga Art Nouveau Museum
MUSEUM

(Rīgas jūgendstila muzejs; Map p204; www.jugend stils.riga.lv; Alberta iela 12; adult/child May-Sep €6/4, Oct-Apr €3.50/2.50; ☉10am-6pm Wed-Sun) If you're curious about what lurks behind Rīga's imaginative art nouveau facades, then it's definitely worth stopping by here. Once the home of Konstantīns Pēkšēns (a local architect responsible for over 250 of the city's buildings), the interiors have been completely restored to resemble a middle-class apartment from the 1920s. Enter from Strēlnieku iela; press No 12 on the doorbell.

Note the spectacular staircase, geometric stencils, rounded furniture, original stained glass in the dining room and the still-functioning stove in the kitchen. There's also a free 10-minute video detailing the city's distinct decor.

Check out the centre's website for details about art nouveau walking routes around town.

Janis Rozentāls & Rūdolfs Blaumanis Museum
MUSEUM

(Map p204; ☑6733 1641; Alberta iela 12; admission €1.42; ☉11am-6pm Wed-Sun) Follow the wonderfully lavish stairwell up to the 5th floor to find the former apartment of Janis Rozentāls, one of Latvia's most celebrated painters, who lived here with his wife, Elli Forssell (a famous Finnish singer), and his friend Rūdolfs Blaumanis (a famous Latvian writer). Enter from Strēlnieku iela; press No 9 on the doorbell.

Jews in Latvia
MUSEUM

(Map p204; www.jewishmuseum.lv; admission by donation; ☉11am-5pm Sun-Thu) This small and rather informal space briefly recounts the city's history of Jewish life until 1945 through artefacts and photography. Rīga's Jewish population (unlike that of Vilnius) was very much integrated into the rest of society. You'll find a teeny kosher cafe in the basement (entrance on Dzirnavu iela) selling traditional treats like challah bread and gefilte fish.

Corner House
MUSEUM

(Former KGB compound; Stūra Māja; Map p204; www.okupacijasmuzejs.lv/en/kgb-building; Brīvības iela 69; adult/student €5/2; ☉10am-5.30pm Mon, Tue, Thu & Fri, 12-7pm Wed, 10am-4pm Sat & Sun) The epitome of a haunted house, this imposing fin de siècle building is remembered by generations of Latvians as the local headquarters of the notorious Soviet secret police, the NKVD/KGB. Arbitrary arrests, torture, executions – it saw it all. These days it houses

an exhibition dedicated to the victims of the 1940–41 political repression, which directly affected around 26,000 Latvian people. An English-language tour of torture dungeons is available daily at 10.30am, except Wednesdays, when it starts at noon.

The courtyard often houses art exhibitions, one of which sparked controversy in 2015, when an installation that included a crucified effigy of Vladimir Putin was vandalised by local fans of the Russian president.

Latvian National Museum of History
MUSEUM

(Latvijas Nacionālais vēstures muzejs; Map p204; ☑6722 1357; www.lnvm.lv; Brīvības bulvāris 32; adult/student €3/1.50; ☉10am-5pm Tue-Sun) If you want to make sense of Latvian history, this museum traces it all the way from the Stone Age to the hipster age.

St Gertrude Church
CHURCH

(Svētās Ģertrūdes baznīca; Map p204; Ģertrūdes iela 8) This gracious red-brick neo-Gothic church is dedicated to you, dear travellers, for its patron – St Gertrude – answers the prayers of those on the road. This is why the church in her name was erected at what was once the edge of the city and where the road started. Now surrounded by art nouveau architecture, it is one of Rīga's best meeting points and a photographer's darling, making a perfect match for the city's trademark scarlet-cloud sunsets in summer.

Just like Rīga's cathedral, St Gertrude's is half-church, half-musical venue. Its organ, built in 1906, is one of the city's best, and classical-music concerts take place all the time.

Miera Iela

Old factory meets olfactory along Miera iela, an industrial district that's home to the Laima chocolate maker just beyond the scatter of stunning art nouveau facades in the Quiet Centre. Walk down the main street to find a charming assortment of cafes, craft shops and bookstores. The street abuts in Aristida Briāna iela, which hosts a cluster of popular drinking and dancing venues.

Laima Chocolate Museum
MUSEUM

(Map p204; www.laimasokoladesmuzejs.lv; Miera iela 22; adult/student/child €7/5/3; ☉10am-7pm Tue-Sun) Your sweet tooth might come to life blocks away from the historic Laima chocolate factory as the sweet cocoa smell permeates the entire area. Founded in 1921 by Vilhelms Kuze, it turned the entire nation

RĪGA ART NOUVEAU

If you ask any Rīgan where to find the city's world-famous art nouveau architecture, you will always get the same answer: 'Look up!' More than 750 buildings in Rīga (more than any other city in Europe) boast this flamboyant and haunting style of decor; and the number continues to grow as myriad restoration projects get under way. Art nouveau is also known as Jugendstil, meaning 'Youth Style', named after a Munich-based magazine called *Die Jugend*, which popularised the design in its pages.

Art nouveau's early influence was Japanese print art disseminated throughout Western Europe, but as the movement gained momentum, the style became more ostentatious and freeform – design schemes started to feature mythical beasts, screaming masks, twisting flora, goddesses and goblins. The turn of the 20th century marked the height of the art nouveau movement as it swept through every major European city from Porto to St Petersburg.

The art nouveau movement in Rīga can be divided into three pronounced phases. The first phase was called 'Eclectic Decorative Art Nouveau'; it occurred during the first five years of the 20th century. During this time, the primary focus was the facade rather than the interior, as highly ornate patterns were imported from Germany by the local architects who studied there. The intricate sculpture work was also locally designed, mostly by August Volz, who did his apprenticeship in Germany as well. This design phase is the most pronounced in Central Rīga because the prevalence of the style coincided with the opening of a local architectural faculty.

After the failed Russian revolution of 1905, however, this art nouveau style was quickly phased out as local architects furiously dabbled with the notion of establishing a design scheme with nationalistic flair. The so-called 'National Romanticism' was born out of this idea, and reflected Latvian ethnographic motifs. An affinity for natural materials flourished as urban facades were left unpainted to show the greys and browns of the building materials. Facades were meant to act as windows, so to speak, into the layout of the structure within. Although this rather un-art-nouveau style was only popular for four years, it coincided with a boom in the city's trading wealth, and thus a lot of structures exhibit this style, even today.

The final phase was known as 'Perpendicular Art Nouveau' – it flourished from around 1908 to 1912. The style was a hybrid design between the existing art nouveau traits and a return to classical motifs (presented in a heavily stylised fashion). An accentuation on verticality was pronounced, as was the penchant for balconies and bay windows.

In Rīga, the most noted Jugendstil architect was Mikhail Eisenstein, who flexed his artistic muscles on **Alberta iela** (p203).

into hopeless chocolate addicts. The modest on-site museum is mostly geared to children, who learn the process of chocolate-making and then blackmail their parents in the adjacent chocolate shop.

Maskavas Forštate

Separated from the Old Town by the Central Railway Station, Rīga's 'Moscow Suburb' is in fact one of its oldest central districts, though unlike the rest of the centre it looks like it has never got over the economic hardships of the 1990s. The place also feels haunted because of its dark history – it was the site of the Jewish ghetto during the Nazi occupation of Latvia. Yet today, it is also the site of Rīga's lovely main market and the city's first gentrified industrial space.

Latvian Academy of Science
HISTORIC BUILDING

(Latvijas Zinātņu Akadēmija; Map p204; www. panoramariga.lv; Akadēmijas laukums 1; panorama €4; ☉8am-10pm) Rising above the Moscow Suburb, this Stalinesque tower is in fact a not-so-welcome present from the Russian capital, which has seven towers like it, only bigger. Construction of what is often dubbed 'Stalin's birthday cake' commenced in 1951 but wasn't completed until 1961, by which time Stalin had run out of birthdays. Those with an eagle eye will spot hammers and sickles hidden in the convoluted facade. The wonderful viewing terrace on floor 17 is Rīga's best vantage point.

★ **Rīga Central Market**   MARKET
(Rīgas Centrāltirgus; Map p204; www.centraltirgus. lv; Nēģu iela 7; ⊙8am-5pm) Haggle for your huckleberries at this vast market, housed in a series of WWI Zeppelin hangars and spilling outdoors as well. It's an essential Rīga experience, providing bountiful opportunities both for people-watching and to stock up for a picnic lunch. Although the number of traders is dwindling, the dairy and fish departments, each occupying a separate hangar, present a colourful picture of abundance that activates ancient foraging instincts in the visitors.

In operation since 1570, the riverside market flourished during the mid-1600s when the city outgrew Stockholm to become the largest stronghold of the Swedish empire. Laden with goods, boats travelling down the Daugava would meet here those traversing the Baltic Sea for a mutually beneficial exchange.

In 1930 the market moved to its current location on the border of Central Rīga and the Russified Maskavas neighbourhood ('Little Moscow') to make use of the railway, which replaced the river as the principal trade route. Confronted with the market's ever-growing size, the city of Rīga decided to bring in five enormous German-built Zeppelin hangars from the town of Vainode in western Latvia. These hangars – each 35m high – added 57,000 sq metres of vending space, allowing an additional 1250 vendors to peddle their goods.

Spīķeri   NEIGHBOURHOOD
(www.spikeri.lv) The shipping yard behind the Central Market is the latest district to benefit from a generous dose of gentrification. These crumbling brick warehouses were once filled with swinging slabs of hanger meat; these days you'll find hip cafes and start-up companies. Stop by during the day to check out **Kim?** (Map p204; ☑6722 3321; www.kim.lv; Maskavas iela 12/1; admission €3; ⊙ noon-8pm Tue, to 6pm Wed-Sun) – an experimental art zone that dabbles with contemporary media – or come in the evening to peruse the surplus of farm produce at the night market.

Rīga Ghetto & Latvian Holocaust Museum   MUSEUM
(Map p204; www.rgm.lv; Maskavas iela 14A; ⊙10am-6pm Sun-Fri) **FREE** The centrepiece of this rather modest museum is a wooden house with a reconstructed flat, like those Jews had to move into when in 1941 the Nazis established a ghetto in this area of Rīga. Models of synagogues that used to stand in all major Latvian towns are exhibited in the ground floor of the house. Outside, there is a photographic exhibition detailing the Holocaust in Latvia.

Jēzus baznīca   CHURCH
(Map p204; www.jezusdraudze.lv; Elijas iela 18) It would be a classical-style Lutheran church like many other, if it wasn't made entirely of wood, which makes it a unique architectural gem and an eye-pleasing sight that dominates an astoundingly pretty square. Definitely worth the extra mile, if only for a brief moment of aesthetic delight.

Holocaust Memorial   MONUMENT
(Map p204) Don't miss the moving Holocaust Memorial, sitting a block behind Akadēmijas laukums in a quiet garden. A large synagogue occupied this street corner until it was burned to the ground during WWII, tragically with the entire congregation trapped inside. No one survived. Today the concrete monument standing in its place is dedicated to the brave Latvians who risked their lives to help hide Jews during the war.

○ **Outlying Neighbourhoods**

Those who venture beyond Rīga's inner sphere of cobbled alleyways and over-the-top art nouveau will uncover a burgeoning artists' colony, a couple of excellent museums, and a handful of other neighbourhoods that help paint a full picture of this cosmopolitan capital.

Pārdaugava

Beyond the river Rīga becomes markedly lower and quieter, with old wooden houses keeping parity with newer ones made of stone.

Latvian National Library   LIBRARY
(Castle of Light; Map p204; ☑22022920; www. lnb.lv; Mūkusalas iela 3; ⊙9am-8pm Mon-Fri, 10am-5pm Sat & Sun) Looking like a ski-jump ramp designed by Swarovski, this new Rīga landmark is in fact a prophecy fulfilled. A feature of many Latvian fairy tales, the Castle of Light was drowned when the age of darkness came, but it would rise again from the waters of the Daugava in the new golden age of enlightenment and freedom. Architect Gunnars Bikkerts made it happen in 2014. The new library now stores

heaps of books and periodicals, including many English titles.

Kalnciema Kvartāls
AREA
(www.kalnciemaiela.lv; Kalnciema iela 35) A lovingly restored courtyard with several wooden buildings has become the location of a very popular weekend market, where Rīgans hawk their local produce – fresh meats, cheeses, vegetables and even local spirits. But there is more to it, with live concerts, performances and art exhibitions taking place outside the market days. But even if nothing is going on, sipping coffee in one of the on-site cafes and soaking in the atmosphere of an old Rīga suburb is worthwhile.

Check the website for upcoming events.

Victory Monument
MEMORIAL
A sprawling green space (now mostly used as a soccer field) is home to the Victory Monument, which was built by the Soviets to commemorate the heroism of their soldiers in WWII. This is a divisive symbol, with members of the Russian community gathering here in their dozens of thousands every 9 May to celebrate what they see as the victory over fascism. But for most ethnic Latvians, it is the symbol of Soviet occupation.

Mežaparks
Woodsy Mežaparks (literally 'Forest Park' in Latvian), along Lake Ķīšezers, 7km north of the centre, is Europe's oldest planned suburb. Built by the Germans in the 20th century, this 'garden city', originally called Kaiserwald, was the go-to neighbourhood for wealthy merchants looking to escape the city's grimy industrial core. The atmosphere hasn't changed all that much over the last 100 years – tourists will find prim country homes, gorgeous art nouveau facades and lazy sailboats gliding along the lake.

The park itself is a huge woodsy area crisscrossed by cycling paths, with a large lake inviting for a swim and all forms of procrastination on the beach. Outlets selling *shashlyk* (Caucasus-styled grilled meat on skewers) and *chebureky* (Tatar meat-filled pastry) are scattered around. There are also a couple of nice lakeside restaurants.

To reach Mežaparks, take tram 11 from K Barona iela to the 'Mežaparks' stop; get off at the 'Brāļu Kapi' stop for the Brothers' Cemetery.

City Walk
Albert to Alberta

START FREEDOM MONUMENT
END ALBERTA IELA
DISTANCE 3KM; TWO HOURS

Bishop Albert von Buxhoeveden is the man who founded Rīga in 1201 and Alberta iela is a street that bears his name. There is seven centuries dividing the two, which you can cover in one leisurely stroll.

Starting at the ❶ **Freedom Monument** (p202), the glorious Milda, cross the tram lines into the Old Town and turn left into Vaļņu iela. It is a commercial street lined with shops, but you'll soon escape the hubble and bubble of modernity by sneaking into the little cobblestoned Gleznotāju iela.

Now you are slicing through medieval Rīga. Walk towards Kalēju iela and turn left. After about 30m, you'll approach a red-brick wall with a gate. It leads into ❷ **Jāņa sēta** (p198), the courtyard of St John's church, where Bishop Albert set up his residence when he founded the city in 1201.

Now we are into a bit of a quest. A narrow passage that was on your right, when you went through the gates, leads into the next medieval courtyard – ❸ **Konventa Sēta** (p215), dominated by the namesake hotel, formerly a retirement home for widows of rich merchants.

Now follow the blue arrow sign pointing towards Georga zale. On the left side of the tiny lane you'll find the wall of the former ❹ **St George's Church** (p197), the only building in Rīga left largely intact since the birth of Rīga in the 13th century.

Turn right to get into the parallel little nameless lane that abuts the touristy ❺ **Black Magic bar**. You might now feel an urge to down a shot of the black magic, aka Rīga balsam, before getting into the busy Kaļķu iela on the other side of the bar. If not, walk around it through a green-coloured passage on your left.

Turn into Šķūņu iela and walk all the way to Dome Sq. ❻ **Rīga Cathedral** (p200) is, of course, a building Bishop Albert embarked on constructing as soon as he set foot here. Follow Jēkaba iela towards ❼ **St James' Cathedral** (p201). This is where the Protestants held the first

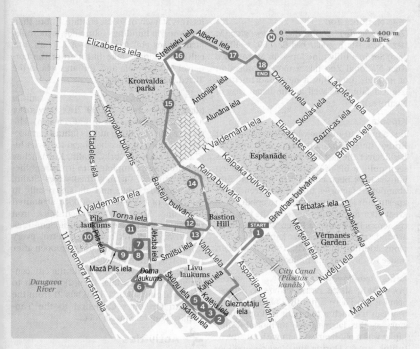

Lutheran-styled mass in 1523, ushering in the epoche of Reformation.

Find a little passage on the left side of the church and sneak into ⑧ **Hobbywool** (p226). Marvel at this little repository of knitted treasures – shawls, hats and socks – before walking out into Mazā Pils iela.

Here, you are in for a date with the ⑨ **Three Brothers** (p201) The three cute old houses carry you from the 15th century all the way into the 17th century, as the oldest of them waited 200 years for the youngest to emerge. German knights were succeeded first by the Poles, then by the Swedes during this period.

Continue along Mazā Pils iela towards ⑩ **Rīga Castle** (p201). Its current outlook was shaped by Polish and Swedish rulers. But as soon as you turn into Torņa iela, you'll find a legacy of the Russians who embarked on massive construction as soon as they took over the city in 1710. Pass the ⑪ **Arsenāls** (p201; now a great art centre) and ⑫ **Jacob's Barracks** (p201; now a restaurant row), built in the present shape on the orders of tsar Peter the Great.

Nod to the ⑬ **Powder Tower** (p202; we are back to Swedish times again), then cross the tram lines and the canal bridge, usually guarded by street musicians. The ⑭ **monument to writer Rūdolfs Blaumanis** will greet you on the other side.

Cross Krišjāņa Valdemāra iela and head towards the pleasant ⑮ **Kronvalda parks**, wasting no time on the yawning Soviet piazza in between. The art nouveau district is now a stone's throw away. Let the ornate building of the ⑯ **Stockholm School of Economics** at Strēlnieku iela 4a serve as an introduction to the style. We are in the 1900s now.

A whole gallery of masterpieces is waiting around the corner at ⑰ **Alberta iela** (p203) As – hopefully dazzled and speechless – you reach the other side of the street, turn into Dzirnavu iela and enter the Albert Hotel. Take the elevator all the way to the ⑱ **Star Lounge Rīga Bar** (p223) on the upper floor. Order a drink, walk onto the balcony and enjoy a bird's-eye view of Rīga, now intimately yours.

Rīga National Zoo ZOO

(Zoologiskais dārz; ☑ 6751 8669; www.rigazoo.lv; Meža prospekts 1; adult/child €2/1.50; ⊙10am-4pm) Set in a hilly pine forest in Mežaparks, Rīga National Zoo has a motley collection of animals, including a new assortment of tropical fauna, as well as the usual cast of Noah's ark.

Ķīpsala

Just a quick 10-minute walk west over Vanšu Bridge, quiet Ķīpsala is Rīga's veritable Left Bank. Over the last five years the island has seen quite a bit of gentrification – wooden houses have been completely restored, and abandoned factories turned into trendy loft apartments. The tree-lined riverside is a great spot for taking photos of the city centre across the Daugava River. While walking around, try to spot a bronze kangaroo, a frivolous addition to a newly restored wooden house by its Australia-linked owner.

Žanis Lipke Memorial MUSEUM

(www.lipke.lv; Mazais Balasta dambis 8; ⊙noon-6pm Tue-Sat) There is hardly a place in Latvia that can tell such a poignant and optimistic story as this labyrinthine memorial. Žanis Lipke was a big-hearted man with an adventurous streak. During the Nazi occupation, he found a job with the German air force, which allowed him to smuggle 56 people out of the Rīga ghetto under the pretext of using them as labourers. He hid them in his own house – now the site of the memorial.

Lipke was helped by his wife and a whole network of volunteers, some of whom played with death by walking into the ghetto to pose as the runaways during the headcount. A tree dedicated to him grows right next to Oscar Schindler's in the Garden of the Righteous inside Jerusalem's Holocaust Memorial.

Northern Neighbourhoods

The Rīga Motor Museum and the Latvian Ethnographic Open-Air Museum orbit Rīga's central core several kilometres out.

Latvian Ethnographic Open-Air Museum MUSEUM

(Latvijas etnogrāfiskais brīvdabas muzejs; www.brivdabasmuzejs.lv; Brīvības gatve 440; adult/child May-Oct €4.27/1.42, Nov-Apr €2.13/0.71; ⊙10am-5pm) If you don't have time to visit the Latvian countryside, a stop at this open-air museum is a must. Sitting along the shores of Lake Jugla just northeast of the city limits, this stretch of forest contains more than 100 wooden buildings (churches, windmills, farmhouses etc) from each of Latvia's four cultural regions. Take bus 1 from the corner of Merķeļa iela and Tērbatas iela to the 'Brīvdabas muzejs' stop.

Rīga Motor Museum MUSEUM

(Rīgas Motormuzejs; ☑ 6709 7170; www.motormuzejs.lv; Eizenšteina iela 6; ⊙10am-6pm) The stars of the collection at this fantastic museum are cars that once belonged to Soviet luminaries such as Gorky, Stalin, Khrushchev and Brezhnev, complete with irreverent life-sized figures of the men themselves. Stalin, pockmarked cheeks and all, sits regally in the back of his 7-tonne, 6005cc armoured limousine. The car has 1.5cm-thick iron plating everywhere except on the 8cm-thick windows. It drank a litre of petrol every 2.5km. The museum was due to reopen after reconstruction in late 2015.

The location is 8km outside the city centre along Brīvības iela, then 2km south to the Mežciems suburb. Take bus 21 from the Russian Orthodox Cathedral to the 'Pansionāts' stop on Šmerļa iela.

🏃 Activities

For an intense adrenaline fix, such as bungee jumping, bobsledding, mountain biking and skydiving, head to the town of Sigulda (p256) in Gauja National Park. Water-sports enthusiasts should spend the day in Jūrmala (p229). Cyclists will be glad to know that there are dozens of routes around town; bicycles for rent (p228) are available at two dozen locations around the city and four more in Jūrmala.

You don't have to run all the way to Jūrmala to see some serious spa action. Rīga has a few standout places to get pampered in traditional Latvian style: being whipped by dried birch branches while sweating it out in temperatures beyond 40°C (over 100°F). Visit www.spa.lv for additional options and details. Sounds relaxing...

Baltā Pirts SPA

(☑ 6727 1733; www.baltapirts.lv; Tallinas iela 71; sauna from €10; ⊙8am-8pm Wed-Sun) Frequented mostly by locals rather than tourists, Baltā Pirts combines traditional Latvian relaxation techniques (the name means 'white birch') with a subtle, oriental design scheme. Take a tram heading north along A Čaka until you reach Tallinas iela.

TOP DAY TRIPS FROM RĪGA

Leave Rīga's jumble of art nouveau goblins and swirling church spires behind and explore Latvia's other gems: flaxen shorelines, rambling palaces, quaint provincial villages and forests full of shady trees.

Jūrmala The Soviet Union's ultimate beach destination still teems with the Russian elite. Take Rīga's suburban train bound for Skola or Tukums, get off at Majōri station, and you'll be smack in the middle of spa-land in 30 minutes flat. (p229)

Saulkrasti If you're looking for a quieter stretch of sand undisturbed by the tanned glitterati, try quaint Saulkrasti, only an hour by train up the Vidzeme coast. (p254)

Sigulda It's hard not to be enchanted by Turaida Castle, hidden deep within the pine forests of Gauja National Park. Adrenaline junkies will get their fix with an endless array of activities, including bobsledding and bungee jumping from a moving cable car. Sigulda is only 1¼ hours away by bus or train. (p256)

Rundāle Palace Latvia's miniature version of Versailles (but without the crowds) is a stunning, 138-room homage to aristocratic ostentatiousness. Try a bus tour (from €25) or rent a car to navigate the 75km trek; public buses only run to Bauska, where you must switch to a local route to complete the last 12km. (p252)

Abava River Valley The quiet valley along the murmuring Abava River starkly contrasts Rīga's bustling urban core. Wander through charming three-street villages and an organic farmstead, and picnic under looming sculptures at the awesome Pedvāle Open-Air Art Museum. A rental car is the best mode of transport. (p243)

LATVIA RĪGA

Taka Spa SPA
(Map p204; ☎ 6732 3150; www.takaspa.lv; Kronvalda bulvāris 3a; treatments from €28; ⏰10am-9pm Mon-Fri, to 7pm Sat & Sun) High-end Taka Spa offers massages, wraps, scrubs and sauna treatments. Try the signature 'opening ritual' in which clients move between saunas and plunge pools while drinking herbal teas.

☞ Tours

Swarms of operators offer tours around Rīga as well as day trips to popular sights nearby.

Amber Way BUS TOUR, WALKING TOUR
(☎6727 1915; www.sightseeing.lv; tours from €15) A smorgasbord of city tours, either on a bus or walking. Tours depart at 11am, noon, 1pm and 3pm. Ask about a walking-bus-lunch combo for €29. Day trips depart at 11am from the Opera House to Rundāle Palace (every Saturday), to Sigulda (every Friday) and to Jūrmala (every Sunday). Most midrange and top-end hotels can book these tours.

Rīga Bike Tours BICYCLE TOUR
(☎28225773; www.rigabikerent.com; Riharda Vagnera iela 14; ⏰10am-6pm) These folks run daily bicycle tours of Rīga that last for three hours and cost €15 (€10 with your own bike). Longer cycling tours of Latvia are also on offer. The useful office operates under Rīga Explorers Club brand.

E.A.T. Rīga WALKING TOUR
(☎22469888; www.eatriga.lv; tours from €12) Foodies may be initially disappointed to discover that the name stands for 'Experience Alternative Tours' and the focus is on off-the-beaten-track themed walking tours (Old Rīga, Art Nouveau, Alternative Rīga, Retro Rīga). But don't fret – Rīga Food Tasting is an option. It also offers a cycling tour of Jūrmala.

Riga Culture Free Tour CULTURAL TOUR
(☎20338877; www.rigaculturefreetour.lv) FREE A daily English-language walk conducted by local cultural experts. It lasts for two hours and begins at noon from the Jānis Rainis monument on Esplanāde.

Retro Tram CULTURAL TOUR
(Map p204; ☎6710 4817; www.rigassatiksme.lv/en/services/retro-tram; tickets €2) Two routes, aboard a restored tram, meander through the art nouveau district and on to Mežaparks. Free guided walking tours of the art nouveau district are available on weekends and public holidays, departing five times a day from the Ausekļa tram stop.

Rīga by Canal BOAT TOUR
(☎25911523; www.kmk.lv; adult/child €18/9; ⏰10am-8pm) Enjoy a different perspective of the city aboard the century-old *Darling*, a charming wooden canal cruiser that belonged

to the family of ABBA producer Stig Anderson and saw the entire band on board. There are three other boats in the fleet that paddle along the same loop around the City Canal and Daugava River.

Rīga City Tour
BUS TOUR

(☎ 26655405; www.citytour.lv; tours €15) A hop-on, hop-off double-decker bus that wends its way through Rīga, stopping at 15 spots on both sides of the Daugava River. Buses leave from Rātslaukums on the hour between 10am and 3pm.

✿✿ Festivals & Events

Rīgans will find any excuse to celebrate, especially when the sun comes out during the summer months. Check out www.rigatourism. lv for a complete list of local events.

International Baltic Ballet Festival
DANCE

(www.ballet-festival.lv) This three-week festival starts in late April, with performances by Latvian and international companies.

Rīga Opera Festival
MUSIC

(Rīgas Operas festivāls; www.opera.lv) The Latvian National Opera's showcase event takes place over two weeks in June and includes performances by world-renowned talents.

Midsummer Celebration
CULTURAL

Latvians return to their pagan roots while celebrating the solstice on 23 June. Crowds gather along the embankment and public transport is free.

Rīgas Ritmi
MUSIC

(www.rigasritmi.lv) 'Rīga's Rhythms' is the capital's international music festival, held at the beginning of July.

Summer Sound
MUSIC

(www.summersound.lv) Latvia's capital of music hosts this festival in July, which showcases the best of Latvian pop music as well as prominent international headliners.

Piens Fest
MUSIC

(http://piens.nu) Rīga's best nightclub has a festival of its own in August that involves circus acts and poetry readings as well as lots of music.

Future Shorts
FILM

The popular festival of short documentaries by Latvian and international directors is currently held at Kalnciema Kvartāls (p210) in August.

Baltā Nakts
ART

(www.baltanakts.lv) Sponsored by the Latvian Centre for Contemporary Art, this 'white night' event in September mirrors Paris' night-long showcase of artists and culture in various city locations.

Survival Kit
ART

This annual event, held in September, showcases some of the best Latvian contemporary artists and guests from the EU and ex-USSR countries.

Arēna New Music Festival
MUSIC

(www.arenafest.lv) Contemporary music festival held at venues throughout Rīga during the last two weeks of October.

Festival of Light
LIGHT SHOW

(www.staroriga.lv) Held around National Day celebrations in November, this festival of lights lifts spirits as Rīga begins to face the long winter ahead. Myriad civic buildings and public objects are lit up during the long nights.

Christmas Tree Path
CHRISTMAS

Rīga claims to be the city that originated the Christmas tree (p197), and thus at Christmas each year, locals decorate an ornate tree in Rātslaukums amid much ado.

🛏 Sleeping

When considering where to stay in Rīga, your first choice will be whether you want to stay in Old Rīga or Central Rīga – both are excellent options for different reasons. The city lends itself well to pedestrians, so staying in either neighbourhood will not be limiting. If you're only in town for a day it's probably best to stay in Old Rīga as you're within arm's reach of most of the city's main attractions. Those who are in town for a bit longer might find Central Rīga to be a better option. The prices are slightly lower and you'll feel more like a local. Besides, in summer noise can be an issue in the Old Town, as street bands keep playing until late and party animals enjoy the sound of their loud voices.

The summer months are also very busy, so whatever your choice, try to book a room in advance from June through August.

Hostels dominate the budget accommodation scene in Rīga, and the competition can be rather fierce in the summer months. Soaring real-estate prices mean that the mainstream backpacker scene is always in flux – some places close their doors for the winter and never reopen when high season rolls around.

Virtually every hostel has free internet and wi-fi; you can count on price hikes on weekends.

At the opposite end of the spectrum, Rīga's crème de la crème can be sharply divided into two categories: flamboyant throwbacks to the city's aristocratic past (think sumptuous antiques and gushing drapery) or avant-garde gems ripped straight from the latest Scandinavian interior design magazine.

Old Rīga (Vecrīga)

Rīga Old Town Hostel   HOSTEL €
(☑ 6722 3406; www.rigaoldtownhostel.lv; Vaļņu iela 43; dm from €17; ❋ 🛜) The Aussie pub on the ground floor doubles as the hostel's hang-out space. If you can manage to lug your suitcase past the faux bookshelf door and up the twisting staircase, you'll find spacious dorms with chandeliers and plenty of sunlight.

★ Naughty Squirrel   HOSTEL €
(☑ 6722 0073; www.thenaughtysquirrel.com; Kalēju iela 50; dm from €18; ❋ @ 🛜) Slashes of paint and cartoon graffiti brighten up the city's capital of backpackerdom, which buzzes with travellers rattling the foosball table and chilling out in the TV room. Sign up for regular pub crawls, adrenaline-charged day trips to the countryside and summer BBQs.

Radi un Draugi   HOTEL €€
(☑ 6782 0200; www.draugi.lv; Mārstaļu iela 1; s/d from €50/60; @ 🛜) Initially built to host Latvian emigrants coming to see their homeland after decades of exile, this a reliable (and soundproof) option in the heart of the Old Town's nightlife quarter. Interior design is slightly on the bland side, but we prefer to regard it as a stylish understatement.

★ Ekes Konvents   HOTEL €€
(☑ 6735 8393; www.ekeskonvents.lv; Skārņu iela 22; r from €60; 🛜) Not to be confused with Konventa Sēta next door, the 600-year-old Ekes Konvents oozes wobbly medieval charm from every crooked nook and cranny. Curl up with a book in the adorable stone alcoves on the landing of each storey. Breakfast is served down the block.

Konventa Sēta   HOTEL €€
(☑ 27087501; www.konventa.lv; Kalēju iela 9/11; s/d from €71/76; 🅿 🛜) The location, inside a 15th-century convent in the heart of medieval Rīga, is unbeatable. Rooms are as small and prim as a nun's cell (which is indeed what they are, since the last nuns only left in 1938).

Wellton Centra   HOTEL €€€
(☑ 6721 2012; www.centra.lv; Audēju iela 1; r from €84; @ 🛜) Centra is a great choice for comfort in the heart of Old Rīga. Rooms are spacious and sport loads of designer details such as swish LCD TVs, porcelain basin sinks and minimalist art on the walls. Rooms on the 5th and 6th floors have lower ceilings but better views of the medieval streets below.

★ Neiburgs   HOTEL €€€
(☑ 6711 5522; www.neiburgs.com; Jauņ iela 25/27; s/d from €170/185; ❋ 🛜) Occupying one of Old Rīga's finest art nouveau buildings, Neiburgs blends preserved details with contemporary touches to achieve its signature boutique-chic style. Try for a room on one of the higher floors – you'll be treated to a view of a colourful clutter of gabled roofs and twisting medieval spires.

Grand Palace Hotel   HISTORIC HOTEL €€€
(☑ 6704 4000; www.grandpalaceriga.com; Pils iela 12; s/d from €195/209; @ 🛜) You'll find no better place to be pampered than the lavish Grand Palace. Rooms have period furnishings that feel classy rather than cluttered, and the friendly staff wax nostalgic about the various luminaries who have stayed here, including Catherine Deneuve and REM – but it's actually more fit for royalty than rock stars.

★ Dome Hotel   HOTEL €€€
(☑ 6750 9010; www.domehotel.lv; Miesnieku iela 4; r from €237; 🛜) It's hard to imagine that this centuries-old structure was once part of a row of butcheries. Today a gorgeous wooden staircase leads guests up to a charming assortment of uniquely decorated rooms that sport eaved ceilings, wooden panelling, upholstered furniture and picture windows with city views.

Central Rīga (Centrs)

★ Cinnamon Sally
HOSTEL €

(Map p204; ☑22042280; www.cinnamonsally. com; Merķeļa iela 1; dm from €12, r €45; @ 🛜) Convenient for the train and bus stations, Cinnamon Sally comes with perfectly clean rooms, very helpful staff and a common area cluttered with sociable characters. It might feel odd to be asked to take off your shoes at the reception, but it's all part of its relentless effort to create a homey atmosphere.

Riga City Camping
CAMPGROUND €

(☑6706 5000; www.rigacamping.lv; Ķīpsalas iela 8; sites per adult/child/tent €3/1.5/6; ☉mid-May–mid-Sep; @ 🛜) Located on Ķīpsala across the river from Old Rīga, this large camp site is surprisingly close to the city centre and offers plenty of room for campers and campervanners. Discounts are available for stays of more than three nights.

Albert Hotel
HOTEL €€

(Map p204; ☑6733 1717; www.alberthotel.lv; Dzirnavu iela 33; s/d from €74/79; P✴@🛜) Albert's boxy, modernist facade starkly contrasts with the surrounding art nouveau buildings, but its interior design is pleasantly oddball and pays tribute to the hotel's namesake, Albert Einstein. The patterned carpeting features rows of atomic-energy symbols and the 'do not disturb' doorknob danglers have been replaced with red tags that say 'I'm thinking'.

Hanza Hotel
HOTEL €€

(Map p204; ☑6779 6040; www.hanzahotel.lv; Elijas iela 7; s/d from €46.5/52; @ 🛜) Just beyond the Central Market, this newer addition to Rīga's lodging scene is a former apartment building transformed into six floors of tidy rooms, many with views of Jēzus baznīca.

★ Art Hotel Laine
HOTEL €€

(Map p204; ☑6728 8816; www.laine.lv; Skolas iela 11; s/d from €34/44; P🛜) Embedded into an apartment block, with an antiquated lift taking guests to the reception on the 3rd floor, this place brings you closer to having your own home in Rīga than most hotels can or indeed wish to do. Dark green walls and armchair velvet, art on the walls, yesteryear bathtubs and furniture only complement the overall homey feeling.

Edvards
HOTEL €€

(Map p204; ☑6743 9960; www.hoteledvards.lv; Dzirnavu iela 45/47; s/d €65/75; 🛜) Tucked in a quiet courtyard at the heart of Rīga's commercial centre, Edvards is equidistant from all major sights and a stone's throw from some of the best cafes and restaurants. Room design matches the laconic no-nonsense elegance of the house, built in 1890.

Hotel Valdemārs
HOTEL €€

(Map p204; ☑6733 4462; www.valdemars. lv; K Valdemāra iela 23; s/d from €59/67; ✴🛜) Hidden within an art nouveau block, this Clarion Collection hotel is an excellent choice for those happy to trade fancy decor for reasonable rates. Most surprisingly, the hotel lays on breakfast, afternoon snacks and a simple dinner buffet for all guests.

Islande Hotel
HOTEL €€

(☑6760 8000; www.islandehotel.lv; Ķīpsalas iela 20; s/d €74/80; @ 🛜) The location on Ķīpsala island feels almost rural, but the views of the Old Town across the river are unbeatable and it only takes 20 minutes to get there on foot. If you ask us, this is better than being surrounded by its noise all through the night.

Jakob Lenz
INN €€

(Map p204; ☑6733 3343; www.guesthouselenz. lv; Lenču iela 2; s/tr €55/64, d/tr with shared bathroom €40/45; @ 🛜) Tucked away along a random side street on the fringes of the art nouveau district, this great find offers 25 adorable rooms and a gut-busting breakfast in the morning.

Teater City Hotel
HOTEL €€

(Map p204; ☑6731 5140; www.cityhotel.lv; Bruņinieku iela 6; r from €60; 🛜) Deep in the Quiet Centre, Teater has a stylish covered patio for a lobby, a view of the palatial art nouveau Stradiņš hospital building from the top-floor breakfast area, and large comfortable rooms that smell a tiny bit chemically, which we optimistically attribute to fresh paint.

B&B Rīga
APARTMENT €€

(Map p204; ☑6727 8505; www.bb-riga.lv; Ģertrūdes iela 43; r from €55; P🛜) Snug, apartment-style accommodation comes in different configurations (suites with lofted bedrooms are particularly charming), and are scattered throughout a residential block. It's just a shame that the beds and pillows aren't more comfortable.

★ Europa Royale
HOTEL €€€

(Map p204; ☑6707 9444; www.europaroyale. com; K Barona iela 12; r from €85; ✴@🛜) Once the home of media mogul Emīlija Benjamiņa

(Latvia's version of Anna Wintour), this ornate manse retains much of its 19th-century opulence with sweeping staircases, high ceilings, and a grand bar and breakfast room. Not all of the bedrooms are as grand, but the bay-window rooms don't disappoint.

Hotel Bergs HOTEL €€€
(Map p204; ☑ 6777 0900; www.hotelbergs.lv; Elizabetes iela 83/85; ste from €187; P ✷ 🛜 😺) A refurbished 19th-century building embellished with a Scandi-sleek extension, Hotel Bergs embodies the term 'luxury'. The spacious suites are lavished with high-quality monochromatic furnishings and some have kitchens. There's even a 'pillow menu', allowing guests to choose from an array of different bed pillows based on material and texture.

Radisson Blu Elizabete Hotel HOTEL €€€
(Map p204; ☑ 6778 5555; www.radissonblu.com/elizabetehotel-riga; Elizabetes iela 73; r from €109; P ✷ 🛜) This flash address was designed by an up-and-coming London architectural firm. The facade is an eye-catching mix of chrome, steel and giant sheets of glass, and the interior continues to impress: stylish furnishings and clever floor plans give the rooms a cosy yet trendy feel.

Radisson Blu Hotel Latvija HOTEL €€€
(Map p204; ☑ 6777 2222; www.radissonblu.com/latvijahotel-riga; Elizabetes iela 55; r from €120; P ✷ 🛜 🏊) During the Soviet era, the Hotel Latvija was a drab monstrosity in which several floors were devoted to monitoring the various goings-on of the hotel's guests. Today, after a much-needed facelift, the era of espionage is long gone; it's all eclectic art and smiley service now. Don't miss the views from the 26th-floor Skyline Bar (p223).

Eating

For centuries in Latvia, food equalled fuel, energising peasants as they worked the

---

RULE, BRITON!

Strolling by the Rīga Opera House, you might bump into an old-fashioned bronze couple walking an – also bronze – chao-chao dog. At first glance they may look like some generic residents of fin de siècle Rīga cast in bronze to remind the contemporaries about their great-grandparents. But in reality the couple (and the dog) were not only real, but important enough for Queen Elizabeth to come over and unveil this monument in 2006.

That's because the man is George Armitstead, who presided over Rīga's belle èpoche (1901–1912), when the city acquired its present cosmopolitan elegance. As it happens, Rīga's best mayor of all ages was a Brit, born into a family of local jute traders hailing from Yorkshire.

So what is Armitstead's legacy? Well, just about everything you can now see outside the Old Town came to life on his watch, starting with 680 art nouveau buildings that now form the architectural face of the Latvian capital. But also: the grandiose Latvian National Museum of Art; the modern outlook of the city's main street, Brīvības bulvāris; parks surrounding the Old Town; the electric tram; the still-functioning water supplies system; the Central Market; and dozens of other things.

Most importantly, it was during his stint as mayor that Rīga acquired its atmosphere of a quirky global megalopolis that embraces modernity and cares about its past.

Although the men of the Armitstead house kept marrying into the Baltic German aristocracy and strove to be loyal citizens of the Russian empire, they remained staunchly British. It was their clan that built Rīga's **Anglican Church** (www.anglicanriga.lv; Anglikāņu iela 2), while the architecture of George Armitstead's countryside residence at Jaunmoku Castle (p235) is full of nostalgia for the land of ancestors. The family's obsession with dogs was also seen as a quite British peculiarity at the time.

So who is the mayor of Rīga in 2015? Also a larger-than-life multicultural character. Former journalist Nils Ushakovs is the only ethnic Russian in charge of an EU capital. Fully bilingual, he appeals to both Russians and Latvians in a city where the two equally sized ethnic communities live still quite separate lives.

Can you spot him walking a dog? No, Ushakovs is a cat man. He keeps at least three cats, which you may see wandering around the Town Hall if you come inside. Does it spell anything for Rīga? Nothing, we hope. Even when it comes to the uneasy inter-ethnic relations, the 'cats and dogs' metaphor is far from applicable.

fields, and warming their bellies during bone-chilling Baltic winters. Today, the era of boiled potatoes and pork gristle has faded away as food becomes a sensorial experience rather than a necessary evil. Although it will be a while before globetrotters stop qualifying local restaurants as being 'good for Rīga', the cuisine scene has improved by leaps and bounds over the last decade. Please note, however, that as Rīga's dining scene expands, there's a great deal of turnover – especially during these uncertain economic times – and dining options can come and go with the seasons.

Lately the Slow Food movement has taken the city's high-end dining scene by storm. Seasonal menus feature carefully prepared, environmentally conscious dishes using organic produce grown across Latvia's ample farmlands. Beyond the sphere of trendy eats, most local joints embrace the literal sense of the term 'slow food' with turtle-speed service.

As Rīga's dining scene continues to draw its influence from a clash of other cultures, tipping *(apkalpošana)* is evolving from customary to obligatory. A 10% gratuity is common in the capital, and many restaurants are now tacking the tip onto the bill.

✗ Old Rīga (Vecrīga)

If you're self-catering, there's a branch of **Rimi** (www.rimi.lv; Audēju iela 16; ◷8am-10pm), a reputable supermarket chain, in Old Rīga's Galerija Centrs shopping mall.

Šefpavārs Vilhelms   FAST FOOD €
(Šķūņu iela 6; pancakes €0.60-0.90; ◷9am-9pm) Join the queue to serve yourself a plateful of stuffed or unstuffed pancakes and then smother them in toppings. They make a quick and easy backpacker breakfast.

LIDO Alus Sēta   LATVIAN €
(www.lido.lv; Tirgoņu iela 6; mains around €5; 🛜) The pick of the LIDO litter (Rīga's ubiquitous smorgasbord chain), Alus Sēta feels like an old Latvian brew house. It's popular with locals as well as tourists – everyone flocks here for cheap but tasty traditional fare and homemade beer. Seating spills onto the cobbled street during the warmer months.

V Ķuze   CAFE €
(www.kuze.lv; Jēkaba iela 20/22; snacks €4; ◷10am-9pm; 🛜) Step into the 1930s in this *dahling* little cafe, where the cabinet positively groans under the weight of cakes and chocolate truffles. It's named after chocolatier Vilhelms Ķuze, who didn't survived his

---

EAT LIKE A LATVIAN

These are the pillars of Lavtian gastronomy:

Black Balzām The jet-black, 45%-proof concoction is a secret recipe of more than a dozen fairy-tale ingredients including oak bark, wormwood and linden blossoms. A shot a day keeps the doctor away, so say most of Latvia's pensioners. Try mixing it with a glass of cola to take the edge off.

Mushrooms A national obsession; mushroom-picking takes the country by storm during the first showers of autumn.

Alus For such a tiny nation there's definitely no shortage of *alus* (beer) – each major town has its own brew. You can't go wrong with Užavas (Ventspils' contribution).

Smoked fish Dozens of fish shacks dot the Kurzeme coast – look for the veritable smoke signals rising above the tree line. Grab 'em to go; they make the perfect afternoon snack.

Kvass Single-handedly responsible for the decline of Coca-Cola at the turn of the 21st century, Kvass is a beloved beverage made from fermented rye bread. It's surprisingly popular with kids!

Rye bread Apart from being tasty and arguably healthier than their wheat peers, these large brown loafs have aesthetic value too, matching nicely the dark wood of Latvia's Nordic interiors.

Berries If you count the total square of blackberry bushes and cranberry marshes, it will likely cover a large chunk of Latvia. Berries are sold at markets all over the country, so you needn't go deep into the woods to collect a jar of them yourself.

post-WWII deportation to Siberia. Today Ķuze Chocolates is up and running once more.

Pelmeņi XL
RUSSIAN €

(Kaļķu iela 7; mains around €2.50; ⊙9am-4am) A Rīga institution for backpackers and after-hours drunkards, this extra-large self-serve eatery stays open extra-late, offering tasty *pelmeņi* (Russian-style dumplings stuffed with meat) amid Flintstones-meets-Gaudí decor (you'll see). Serves are priced by weight but even a big bowl isn't about to break the bank.

Index
SANDWICHES €

(Map p204; www.indexcafe.lv; Brīvības iela 32; sandwiches & salads €2.80; ⊙7am-10pm Mon-Fri, 10am-10pm Sat & Sun) Latvia's trendier version of Pret a Manger is a step up from ready-made sandwiches at the grocery store. Black-and-yellow stencil art rocks the walls and large picture windows open up onto busy Brīvības – the perfect spot for some serious people-watching. There's a second (and slightly cosier) location in the heart of Old Rīga at Šķūņu iela 16.

Vecmeita ar kaki
INTERNATIONAL €€

(Spinster & Her Cat; Mazā Pils iela 1; mains €5-12; ⊙11am-11pm; 🖋) Across from Rīga Castle, this somewhat gloomy restaurant specialises in moderately priced tummy fillers. In warmer weather patrons dine outside on converted sewing-machine tables.

Ķiploku Krogs
EUROPEAN €€

(Garlic Pub; www.kiplokukrogs.lv; Jēkaba iela 3/5; mains €7-14; ⊙noon-11pm) Vampires beware – *everything* at this joint contains garlic, even the ice cream. The menu is pretty hit-and-miss, but no matter what, it's best to avoid the garlic pesto spread – it'll taint your breath for days (trust us). Enter from Mazā Pils.

★ 3 Pavaru
MODERN EUROPEAN €€€

(☑20370537; www.3pavari.lv; Torņa iela 4; mains €23-27; ⊙noon-11pm) The stellar trio of chefs who run the show have a jazzy approach to cooking, with improvisation at the heart of the compact and ever-changing menu. The emphasis is on experiment (baked cod with ox-tail stew, anyone?) and artful visual presentation that could have made Mark Rothko or Joan Miró gasp in admiration.

Le Dome Fish Restaurant
SEAFOOD €€€

(☑6755 9884; www.zivjurestorans.lv; Miesnie-ku iela 4; mains €22-30; ⊙8am-11pm; 🖢) The Dome Hotel's restaurant quickly reminds diners that Rīga sits near a body of water that's full of delicious fish. Service is impeccable and dishes (including some meat and vegetarian options) are expertly prepared, reflecting the eclectic assortment of recipes in the modern Latvian lexicon.

Indian Raja
INDIAN €€€

(Sue's Indian Raja; ☑6722 3240; www.indianraja.lv; Skārņu iela 7; mains €12-17; 🖢) Who knew the Baltic had such brilliant Indian food?! Tucked away down a medieval alley you'll find a welcome antedote to the bland ingredients that rule most Latvian fare – here it's all about savoury curries that incorporate spices directly from the subcontinent.

Gutenbergs
LATVIAN €€€

(www.gutenbergs.eu; Doma laukums 1; mains €15-20; ⊙May-Oct) Go one better than dining with a view – dine *in* the view! The Hotel Gutenbergs' rooftop terrace in the heart of Old Rīga squats between sky-scraping spires and gingerbread trim. Potted plants, cherubic statues and trickling fountains contribute to a decidedly Florentine vibe, although the menu focuses on local favourites.

Tēvocis Vaņa
RUSSIAN €€€

(Uncle Vanya; ☑27886963; www.unclevanya.lv; Smilšu iela 16; mains €14-21; ⊙11am-11pm) Russia puts on its friendly Chekhovian hat in this quaint restaurant that dishes out a fairy-tale-ish assortment of *bliny* (pancakes), *pelmeņi* (dumplings) and *kholodets* – jellied meat that, together with a plate of pickles, is an inseparable aspect of any competent *samogon* (village vodka) drinking experience.

Rozengrāls
LATVIAN €€€

(☑25769877; www.rozengrals.lv; Rozena iela 1; mains €15-27; ⊙noon-midnight) Remember 500 years ago when potatoes weren't the heart and soul of Latvian cuisine? We don't, but Rozengrāls does – this candlelit haunt takes diners back a few centuries, offering medieval game (sans spuds) served by costume-clad waiters.

✗ Central Rīga (Centrs)

Self-caterers should try **Rimi** (Map p204; www.rimi.lv; K Barona iela 46; ⊙8am-11pm) in the Barona Centrs shopping mall, or check out the Central Market (p209).

★ Miit
CAFE €

(Map p204; www.miit.lv; Lāčplēša iela 10; mains €5; ⊙7am-9pm Mon, to 11pm Tue & Wed, to 1am

Thu, to 3am Fri, 9am-1am Sat, 10am-6pm Sun) Rīga's hipster students head here to sip espresso and blog about Nietzsche amid comfy couches and discarded bicycle parts. The two-course lunch is a fantastic deal for penny-pinchers – expect a soup and a main course for under €5 (dishes change daily).

Arbooz
DESSERTS €

(Map p204 www.facebook.com/arbooz.lv; Dzirnavu iela 34a; macarons €2, cupcakes €3.85; ⊗10am-8pm Mon-Fri, 11am-6pm Sat) We'd call this tiny place sweet even if it didn't make these light fruity cupcakes and meringues – just for its looks. You might be able to occupy one of only four tables, otherwise opt for beautifully packaged takeaway and enjoy your coffee on a park bench.

Austra
INTERNATIONAL €

(Map p204; www.facebook.com/cafe.austra; Krišjāna Barona iela 41/43; mains €5-8; ⊗noon-9pm Mon & Tue, to 10pm Wed, to 11pm Thu, to midnight Fri, 1-11pm Sat) The inventive fusion food served in this small unpretentious place achieves the quality of a fashionable upmarket restaurant, but goes for the price of a cafeteria. The €5 two-course lunches are one of the best deals in town.

Lauvas Nams
CAFETERIA €

(Map p204; ☑6731 2661; Brīvibas iela 82; meals €3-5; ⊗24hr) Generations of hungry party animals have stopped for a bite at this round-the-clock cafeteria, strategically located on the route from the centre to the bars in the Miera iela area. Displayed at the counter, the simple Latvian fare – think pork stew and potatoes – comes in large portions, accompanied by traditional dairy and fruity drinks, such as *kefir* and *mors*.

DAD
CAFE €

(Map p204; www.dadcafe.lv; Miera iela 17; mains €5; ⊗10.30am-11pm; 🛜) DAD are the three initials of the owners, who proudly explain that DAD stands for so much more (you'll have to ask them what else DAD means). Couches, chairs and an upright piano are loosely tossed around the modest storefront; several tables spill out onto the street during the warmer months. It's a casual and unpretentious place to gather with friends, and maybe make some new ones.

LIDO Atpūtas Centrs
LATVIAN €

(LIDO Recreation Centre; www.lido.lv; Krasta iela 76; mains around €5; ⊗11am-11pm) If Latvia and Disney World had a love child it would be this enormous log cabin dedicated to the country's coronary-inducing cuisine. Servers dressed like Baltic milkmaids bounce around as patrons hit the rows of buffets. Outside there's a fun park with pony rides and ice-skating.

It's 3.5km southeast of the Rīga Central Market; take tram 3, 7 or 9, get off at the 'LIDO' stop and make for the giant windmill.

★ Fazenda Bazārs
MODERN EUROPEAN €€

(Map p204; www.fazenda.lv; Baznīcas iela 14; mains €7-12; ⊗9am-10pm Mon-Fri, 10am-10pm Sat, 11am-10pm Sun) Although right in the centre, this place feels like you've gone a long way and suddenly found a warm tavern in the middle of nowhere. Complete with a tiled stove, this wooden house oozes megatonnes of charm and the food on offer feels as homey as it gets, despite its globalist fusion nature.

★ Kasha Gourmet
MODERN EUROPEAN €€

(Map p204; ☑20201444; www.kasha-gourmet.com; Stabu iela 14; mains €9-14; ⊗9am-10pm) It might be that it does succeed in making the food feel tastier by turning the plate into a piece of modern art, or perhaps it's the post-modernist mix of ingredients, but this is one of the most unusual and undervalued restaurants in Rīga. We are particularly fond of its set breakfasts beautifully laid out on wooden slabs.

Silķītes un Dillītes
SEAFOOD €€

(Map p204; www.facebook.com/SilkitesUnDillites; Centrāltirgus iela 3; mains €7-10; ⊗8am-6pm) Having explored fish stalls at the Rīga Central Market, one might ask: Where do I get it cooked? Well, Herring & Dill, as the name of this grungy kitchen cum bar translates, is right here and will do the cooking for you. Pick your fish and some minutes later it will be fried and served with veggies and chips.

The place is located in the passage between the fish and vegetable departments of the market.

Telpa
MODERN EUROPEAN €€

(Map p204; www.ecocatering.lv; Matīsa ielas 8; lunch €9; ⊗noon-6pm) The all-you-can-eat buffet lunch comes with Indian-influenced vegetarian options, great salads and a view of the Vidzeme market from the large open terrace. The grungy location above a bicycle repair shop in the courtyard of a former brewery adds a sense of adventure to the culinary experience.

Osīriss CAFE €€

(Map p204; K Barona iela 31; mains €8-15; ⊗8am-11pm Mon-Sat, 10am-11pm Sun; 🖘) Despite Rīga's mercurial cafe culture, Osīriss continues to be a local mainstay. The green faux-marble tabletops haven't changed since the mid-'90s and neither has the clientele: angsty artsy types scribbling in their Moleskines over a glass of red wine and a large plate of Latvian comfort food.

Aragats GEORGIAN €€

(Map p204; 🖉6737 3445; Miera iela 15; mains €7-18; ⊗1-10pm Tue-Sun) Ignore the plastic shrubbery – this endearingly old-fashioned place is all about sampling some killer cuisine from the Caucasus. Start with an appetiser of pickled vegetables – the perfect chaser for your home-brewed *chacha* (Georgian vodka). Then, make nice with the owner as she dices up fresh herbs at your table to mix with the savoury lamb stew.

★ **Istaba** CAFE €€€

(Map p204; 🖉6728 1141; K Barona iela 31a; mains €17; ⊗noon-11pm) Owned by local chef and TV personality Mārtiņš Sirmais, 'The Room' sits in the rafters above a gallery and occasional performance space. There's no set menu – you're subject to the cook's fancy – but expect lots of free extras (bread, dips, salad, veggies), adding up to a massive serving.

★ **Vincents** EUROPEAN €€€

(Map p204; 🖉6733 2830; www.restorans.lv; Elizabetes iela 19; mains €24-35; ⊗6-10pm Mon-Sat) 🖋 Rīga's ritziest restaurant has served royalty and rock stars (Emperor Akihito, Prince Charles, Elton John) amid its eye-catching Van Gogh–inspired decor. The head chef, Martins Ritins, is a stalwart of the Slow Food movement and crafts his ever-changing menu mainly from produce sourced directly from small-scale Latvian farmers.

Restaurant Bergs INTERNATIONAL €€€

(Map p204; 🖉6777 0957; Elizabetes iela 83/85; mains €20-35; ⊗7.30am-11am & noon-11pm Mon-Sat, to 4pm Sun) The short-but-sweet menu reads like a poem: spring salmon fillet with an orange and fennel salad, rack of lamb with wholegrain mustard and minted aubergine stew. If you seek culinary finesse in Rīga, it's one of the places that shouldn't be missed.

Charlestons INTERNATIONAL €€€

(Map p204; 🖉6777 0573; www.charlestons. lv; Blaumaņa iela 38/40; mains €9-21; ⊗10am-

11pm; 🖘) If you're up to your elbows in pork tongue, Charlestons is a sure bet to get rid of the meat sweats. Lounge around the terraced courtyard in the heart of a residential block and feast on delicious platters of Norwegian salmon, sautéed duck and the best Caesar salad in the Baltic.

🍷 Drinking & Nightlife

If you want to party like a Latvian, assemble a gang of friends and pub-crawl your way through the city, stopping at colourful haunts for rounds of beer, belly laughter and, of course, Black Balzām. On summer evenings, nab a spot at one of the beer gardens in Old Rīga.

Rīga's nightclubs are always brimming with bouncing bodies – usually Russians. Latvians tend to prefer pub-crawling across town and tossing back vodka shots with friends. After dark, a lot of bars and cafes in Rīga transform, like a superhero, into a grittier venue with pumping beats.

Some of the city's nightspots have a bit of an edge and cater to an unsavoury clientele. Check the 'Culture & Events' chapter of *Rīga in Your Pocket* for a list of businesses blacklisted by the American Embassy.

🍺 Old Rīga (Vecrīga)

Cuba Cafe BAR

(www.cubacafe.lv; Jaun iela 15; ⊗noon-2am Sun-Tue, to 5am Wed-Sat; 🖘) An authentic mojito and a table overlooking Doma laukums is just what the doctor ordered after a long day of sightseeing. On colder days, swig your caipirinha inside amid dangling Cuban flags, wobbly stained-glass lamps and the murmur of trumpet jazz.

Egle BEER GARDEN

(www.spogulegle.lv; Kaļķu iela 1a; ⊗11am-1am) Split between a noisier half with live music most nights (everything from folk to rockabilly), and a quieter half (which generally closes early), this is the best of Old Rīga's open-air beer gardens. It shuts up shop when the weather gets really horrible.

★ **Folksklub Ala Pagrabs** BEER HALL

(www.folkklubs.lv; Peldu iela 19; ⊗12pm-1am Sun-Tue, to 3am Wed, to 4am Thu, to 6am Fri & Sat) A huge cavern filled with the bubbling magma of relentless beer-infused joy, folk-punk music, dancing and Latvian nationalism, this is an essential Rīga drinking venue, no matter what high-browed locals say about it. The

bar strives to reflect the full geography and diversity of Latvian beer production, but there is also plenty of local cider, fruit wine and *šmakouka* moonshine.

DJ Bar
BAR

(www.djbar.lv; Mazā Jaunavu iela 5; ☺6pm-1am) Specialising in electronic underground, this tiny bar hiding in a tiny lane lets young DJs master their talent under the condition that the music is quiet enough to encourage rather than prevent a conversation over cocktails and wine.

Aptieka
BAR

(Pharmacy Bar; www.krogsaptieka.lv; Mazā Miesnieku iela 1; ☺4pm-1am Sun-Wed, to 4am Thu-Sat) Antique apothecary bottles confirm the subtle but stylish theme at this popular drinking haunt run by a Latvian American. The music is usually excellent and it does a good line in American bar food (burgers etc).

I Love You
BAR

(Aldaru iela 9; ☺noon-late) The three words everyone loves to hear is a chill joint tucked away down one of Old Rīga's wobbly streets. Sneak downstairs for a sea of comfy couches. DJs spin alternative beats on Thursday nights and there's plenty of outdoor seating in the warmer months.

Kama Tea Hub
TEAHOUSE

(www.facebook.com/KamaTeaHub; Jēkaba iela 26/28; ☺noon-midnight) Kama (as in Kama Sutra) stands for 'love' in Sanskrit and this place rewards those who love tea and procrastination with a vaguely Indian new-age environment that contrasts sharply with the classic old-world scenery outside. Come here to enjoy a pot of masala chai and let your dreams carry you away to the Taj Mahal and the tea plantations of Kerala.

Nabaklab
CLUB

(www.nabaklab.lv; ZA Meierovica bulvāris 12; ☺noon-midnight Mon-Wed, to 4am Thu & Fri, 5pm-4am Sat) Imagine if your favourite alternative radio station opened a nightspot that played its signature blend of experimental tunes and electronica. Well, look no further – Naba's (93.1FM) club space attracts the city's boho hobos with its DJ'd beats and cheap beer in a century-old basement.

🍷 Central Rīga (Centrs)

Piens
BAR, CLUB

(Milk; Map p204; www.klubspiens.lv; Aristida Briāna iela 9; ☺noon-midnight Sun-Tue, to 4pm Wed-Sat) Located up in the Miera iela area, this bar-club hybrid occupies a large chunk of industrial land. There's an appealing mix of eclectic decor, old sofas and sunny terraces.

Rocket Bean Roastery
COFFEE

(Map p204; www.facebook.com/pages/Rocket-Bean-Roastery; Miera iela 29/31; ☺8am-9pm Mon, to 10pm Tue-Thu, to 11pm Fri & Sat, to 6pm Sun) 'What kind of Colombian coffee would you like?' Yeah, these people are a bit too academic about the brew, but this airy hipster-ridden place with bare brick walls and a large bar makes for a great pit stop in the progressive neighbourhood of Miera iela. Good food, too.

Trusis Kafe
CAFE

(Map p204; ☎26582462; www.trusiskafe.lv; Dzirnavu iela 43; ☺10am-10pm Mon-Fri, 10am-8pm Sat) This sweet unassuming hipster den (its name translates as 'Rabbit') has an impressive array of Latvian-produced drinks – from Malduguns craft beer and cider to Sabile wines and rhubarb 'champagne'. The right place to drink and chat with friends without needing to shout over music to be heard, but also good for a quick coffee meditation during the day.

Garage
WINE BAR

(Map p204; www.vinabars.lv; Berga Bazārs, Elizabetes iela 83/85; ☺10am-midnight) Apart from a semi-industrial fit-out (polished concrete floors, metal chairs) there's nothing even vaguely garagey about this chic little place. It's equal parts wine bar and cafe (the coffee's excellent), serving tapas and a limited selection of mains.

Gauja
BAR

(Map p204; Tērbatas iela 56; ☺noon-11pm) Step off the street and into time-warped Gauja – a small bar decked out in Soviet-style decor. Hunker down amid period furnishings for a rousing duel on the retro chessboard, or link together the set of wooden dominoes while unique beats soar above (the owners have their own recording studio).

Terrace Riga
BEER GARDEN

(Map p204; Gallerija Riga, Dzirnavu iela 67; ☺10am-11pm) Soaring high over the grand boulevards of Central Rīga, Terrace Riga, on the roof of the Gallerija Riga shopping mall, is an enormous open-air space that attempts to give off a Miami South Beach vibe, where umbrellas act as palm trees and heartier spirits replace daiquiris and pina coladas.

THE BEAR SLAYER

There is a thriller in Latvia that Hollywood has thoughtlessly overlooked, and it is so close to the surface that one can only wonder why. It usually doesn't take more than a few days here before you pass a Lāčplēša street (there is one in virtually every town) or drink a glass of Lāčplēša beer. Latvia's greatest military award is called the Order of Lāčplēsis.

So what's in the name? A liberation leader, a military hero, a popular president? Nothing so banal. In fact, Lāčplēsis was a superhuman of X-people variety, whose story derives from ancient sagas and the imagination of 19th-century Latvian writer Andrejs Pumpurs. He is Latvia's main national hero, chosen by ancient gods to save the land from invaders.

The son of a man and a she-bear, Lāčplēsis inherited his mother's ears, which serve as a secret source of supernatural faculties. Secret – because they are always covered by his modestly hippyish hairdo.

As a young man, he slaughtered an aggressive bear (no offence, Mum) by ripping its mouth apart with his bare (human) hands. This is when people started calling him Lāčplēsis. The word means 'bear slayer' and contains enough letters with diacritic signs to look quintessentially Latvian. You can find a sculpture of him (and the slaughtered bear) at this poignant moment of their lives at the bottom of the Freedom Monument (p202).

Lāčplēsis starts his superhero career by defeating an Estonian giant, but his main nemeses are the Germans – depicted as dark infernal characters who are trying to impose their evil religion (Christianity) on a Latvia that prays to the old gods. The story turns into a bit of an odyssey when Lāčplēsis sails across the Baltic Sea to release his lover from German captivity.

Having succeeded, he throws a wedding party, but the Germans upset the celebration. Their most potent fighter, the Dark Knight, cuts off Lāčplēsis' bear ears, depriving him of his magic power. The hero keeps fighting and the two men tumble into the Daugava – never to be seen again.

If you want to learn more, stop at **Andrejs Pumpurs Museum** (☑ 6505 3759; E.Kauliņa aleja 20; ☺ 10am-5pm Tue-Sat, 10am-3pm Sun) in Lielvārde on the road to Latgale. Or even better – tell Hollywood producers to shoot a sequel.

It's popular with Russian tourists but you'll find just about everyone up here on warmer, windless evenings in summer.

Taka
BAR
(Map p204; Miera iela 10; ☺ 2pm-midnight Mon-Wed, to 2am Thu & Fri, noon-2am Sat, 7-11pm Sun; ☎) An old-timer in the hipsterish Miera iela area, Taka sports bright murals on the walls and extra-comfy couches. A good place to try more unusual beers and listen to underground music.

Skyline Bar
COCKTAIL BAR
(Map p204; www.skylinebar.lv; Elizabetes iela 55; ☺ 5pm-1am Sun-Thu, 3pm-3am Fri & Sat; ☎) A must for every visitor, Skyline Bar sits on the 26th floor of the Radisson Blu Hotel Latvija. The sweeping views are the city's best (even from the toilets!), and the mix of glam spirit-sippers makes for great people-watching.

Star Lounge Bar Riga
BAR
(Map p204; www.alberthotel.lv; Dzirnavu iela 33; ☺ 3pm-1am Sun-Thu, to 2am Fri & Sat) Outside of winter months, Rīga surprises visitors with its long breathtaking sunsets, and the best place to watch the sky go orange and scarlet is the huge balcony on the top of the Albert Hotel. Sip your Rīga balsam cocktail, while observing the spires of the Old Town and distant suburbs beyond the Daugava.

Apsara
TEAHOUSE
(Map p204; Elizabetes iela 74; ☺ 10am-10pm) A charming wooden pagoda set within Vērmanes dārzs (p203), Apsara is a veritable library of rare teas imported from beyond the Himalaya. Daintily sip your imported brews while relaxing on the floor amid a sea of pastel pillows.

Chomsky
BAR

(Map p204; www.facebook.com/chomskybar; Lāčplēša iela 68; ⊗4pm-midnight) Don't get spooked (or over-excited) by the controversial philosopher in the name. The only philosophy patrons share is that of sinking the question of life and universe in a pool of beer or surprisingly good Georgian vodka. Comfy couches and a large open-air area invite long alcohol-infused deliberations with philosophy and art students who comprise a large part of the crowd.

★ Kaņepes Kultūras Centrs
BAR

(Map p204; Skolas iela 15; ⊗2pm-1am) The crumbling building of a former musical school, which half of Rīgans over 40 seem to have attended, is now a bar with a large outdoor area filled with an artsy studenty crowd. Wild dancing regularly erupts in the large room, where the parents of the patrons once suffered through their violin drills.

Left Door Bar
COCKTAIL BAR

(Map p204; Antonijas iela 12; ⊗4pm-midnight) Rīga's grand lodge of cocktail masters masquerades as an unassuming bar in the art nouveau district. Never satisfied with past achievements, the award-winning prodigies in charge are constantly experimenting with the aim to impress globetrotting connoisseurs, not your average Joe. Each cocktail comes in specially shaped glasses.

Try the rum-based Belgium Avenue, which took its author Juris Ķēniņš to the Bacardi Legacy world final in Sydney in 2015.

Alus darbnīca Labietis
BEER HALL

(Map p204; www.facebook.com/AlusDarbnica Labietis; Aristida Briāna iela 9A-2; ⊗1pm-1am) Its minimalist design making it feel a bit like a Gothic church, this place is on a mission to promote more obscure Latvian breweries and local craft beer. A great addition to the gradually gentrifying old factory area at the end of Miera iela.

Golden
GAY & LESBIAN

(Map p204; www.mygoldenclub.com; Ģertrūdes iela 33/35; admission club €10; ⊗4-11pm Tue-Thu, 7pm-5am Fri, 11pm-5am Sat) The golden boy of Rīga's gay scene (admittedly that's not saying much), Golden is a friendly little place with a conservatory-like bar and a weekend-only club.

Teātra Bārs
BAR

(Map p204; Lāčplēša iela 26; ⊗noon-midnight Sun-Thu, to 5am Fri & Sat) Right opposite a popular theatre, this grungy cavern is one of those ancient local institutions, which can afford to look like any other cellar pub in the world, but still attracts some of the best crowds in Rīga. Packed with actors, artists and students, it hosts live-music events and features a smallish dancing area that gets wild in the wee hours.

★ Entertainment

Rīga in Your Pocket and *Rīga This Week* have the most up-to-date listings for opera, ballet, guest DJs, live music and other events around town. The tourist office in the Blackheads House can help travellers book tickets at any concert venue around town. Several trip operators offer bar and club tours if you'd rather have someone else arrange your big night out. Backpackers staying at sociable digs might find hostel-organised pub crawls and parties.

Opera, Ballet & Theatre

Rīga's ballet, opera and theatre season breaks for summer holidays (between June and September).

New Rīga Theatre
THEATRE

(Jaunais Rīgas Teātris; Map p204; ☑6728 0765; www.jrt.lv; Lāčplēša iela 25) Contemporary repertory theatre.

Dailes Theatre
THEATRE

(Map p204; ☑6727 0463; www.dailesteatris.lv; Brīvības iela 75) Rīga's largest modern theatre; it retains a lot of its original architectural elements from the Soviet era.

Latvian National Opera
OPERA, BALLET

(Latvijas Nacionālajā operā; ☑6707 3777; www.opera.lv; Aspazijas bulvāris 3) With a hefty international reputation as one of the finest opera companies in all of Europe, the national opera is the pride of Latvia. It's also home to the Rīga Ballet; locally born lad Mikhail Baryshnikov got his start here.

Concert Venues

Arena Rīga
LIVE MUSIC

(☑6738 8200; www.arenariga.com; Skantes iela 21) This is the main venue for the most popular spectator sports, ice hockey and basketball. The 10,000-seat venue hosts dance revues and pop concerts when it is not being used for sporting events.

Rīga Cathedral
CLASSICAL MUSIC

(Rīgas Doms; ☑6721 3213; www.doms.lv; Doma laukums 1) Short organ concerts are held throughout the week, with lengthier performances on a Friday night.

Great Guild
CLASSICAL MUSIC

([☑]6722 4850; www.lnso.lv; Amatu iela 6) Home to the acclaimed Latvian National Symphony Orchestra.

Sapņu Fabrika
LIVE MUSIC

(Map p204; [☑]6728 1222; www.sapnufabrika.lv; Lāčplēša iela 101) Housed in a former industrial plant, the 'Dream Factory' hosts live bands, hip-hop and electronica.

Palladium
LIVE MUSIC

(Map p204; Marijas iela 21) Built on the grounds of an old movie theatre, the Palladium often attracts international acts.

Daile
CONCERT VENUE

(Map p204; [☑]1189; K Barona iela 31) The former cinema has started a new life as a concert venue, seemingly specialising in acoustic music.

Bites Blues Club
JAZZ

(Map p204; [☑]6733 3123; www.bluesclub.lv; Dzirnavu iela 34a; ⊙11am-11pm Mon-Wed, to 2am Thu-Sat) Try stopping for some grub (mostly French or Italian) an hour or two before the show – you'll skip the cover charge and catch some preconcert riffing. Friday nights see most of the live-music action during the summer; in winter expect tunes on Thursday and Saturday as well.

Cinemas

Catching a movie is a great way to spend a rainy day in Rīga (trust us, there are many). Films are generally shown in their original language – usually English – with Latvian or Russian subtitles. Tickets cost between €4 and €7 depending on the day of the week and venue. Check the cinema websites for show-time details. All theatres (except K Suns) have assigned seating.

Kino Citadele
CINEMA

(Map p204; [☑]1189; www.forumcinemas.lv; 13 Janvāra iela 8) Rīga's multiplex has stadium seating, 14 screens and a cafe on the top floor. Expect the usual Hollywood fare and the occasional Latvian film.

Look at Riga
CINEMA

(www.lookatriga.lv; Latviešu Strēlnieku laukums 1; tickets €8; ⊙11am-7pm Mon-Fri, 10am-7pm Sat & Sun) A 5D flight experience in an impossible aircraft which can go under very small bridges and just above people's heads in busy streets. Films last for 10 minutes and there is almost no waiting time.

RĪGA CARD

If you have a long list of sights and activities on your checklist, we recommend picking up a Rīga Card. Perks include free public transport, free admission to most museums, 10% to 20% discounts on accommodation, a free walking tour of Old Rīga, and a complimentary copy of *Rīga in Your Pocket*. Cards are available for purchase at a variety of locations including the tourist office, the airport and several major hotels. Prices for one-/two-/three-day cards are €25/30/35. Check www.liveriga.com for more information.

Splendid Palace
CINEMA

(Map p204; [☑]6718 1143; www.splendidpalace. lv; Elizabetes iela 61) Obscured from view by Soviet Lego architecture, this art deco gem was the first theatre in Rīga to show sound films. These days it specialises in art house, festival retrospectives and Latvian films.

K Suns
CINEMA

(Ka Suns; Map p204; [☑]6728 5411; www.kino galerija.lv/ksuns.php; Elizabetes iela 83/85, Bergs Bazārs) An artsy cinema that projects mostly indie films on its one screen. Popcorn and soft drinks available.

Shopping

Latvians love their shopping malls (a palpable marker of globalisation), but tourists will be pleased to find a wide assortment of local shops that specialise in all sorts of Latvian items – knits, crafts, spirits and fashion. You'll find a wonderful assortment at **Berga Bazārs** (Map p204; www. bergabazars.lv; Elizabetes iela 83/85), a maze of upmarket boutiques orbiting the five-star Hotel Bergs. Street sellers peddle their wares – amber trinkets, paintings and Russian dolls – outside St Peter's Church on Skārņu iela and along the southern end of Vaļņu iela. Rīga's large crafts fair, the **Gadatirgus**, is held in Vērmanes dārzs (p203) on the first weekend in June. Keep an eye out for the beautiful Namēju rings worn by Latvians around the world as a way to recognise one another.

Madam Bonbon · ACCESSORIES

(Map p204; www.madambonbon.lv; Alberta iela 1-7a; ⊙11am-7pm Mon-Fri, to 3pm Sat) Every surface in this old-school art nouveau apartment features some sort of foot furniture. Squeeze into the stiletto on the baby grand piano, or go for the boot behind the teapot on the kitchen table.

Sakta Flower Market · MARKET

(Map p204; Tērbatas iela 2a; ⊙24hr) Open through the night for those post-midnight mea culpas, when you suspect 'Sorry I'm late, honey' just won't do the trick.

Elina Dobele · SHOES

(www.elinadobele.com; Vaļņu iela 12; ⊙11am-7pm Mon-Sat) Local designer Elīna Dobele specialises in custom-made shoes for men and women. They're true artisanal products, designed and assembled in the studio behind the storefront.

Riija · FASHION

(Map p204; www.riija.lv; Tērbatas iela 6/8; ⊙10am-7pm Mon-Fri, to 5pm Sat) Scandi-sleek design inhabits every polished nook and cranny at this new design enclave in the heart of Centrs. Look out Sweden, Latvian design is on the rise!

Pienene · BEAUTY, HANDICRAFTS

(Kungu iela 7/9; ⊙10am-8pm; ☏) 'The Dandelion' is an airy boutique and cafe in the heart of Old Rīga where visitors can sample locally produced beauty products, try on floaty scarves and sniff scented candles.

Upe · MUSIC

(Vāgnera iela 5; ⊙11am-7pm Mon-Sat) Classical Latvian tunes play as customers peruse traditional instruments and CDs of local folk, rock and experimental music.

Gandrs · OUTDOOR EQUIPMENT

(www.gandrs.lv; Kalnciema iela 28; ⊙10am-8pm Mon-Fri, to 6pm Sat & Sun) If you need to stock up for an outdoor adventure of any variety, head across the Daugava to this excellent shop.

Latvijas Balzāms · DRINK

(www.lb.lv; Audēju iela 8; ⊙9am-10pm) One of myriad branches of a popular chain of liquor stores selling the trademark Latvian Black Balzām.

Hobbywool · HANDICRAFTS

(www.uzadi.lv; Mazā Pils iela 6; ⊙10am-6pm Mon-Sat, 11am-3pm Sun) It feels like walking into a Mark Rothko painting – this little shop is filled from top to bottom with brightly coloured knitted shawls, mittens, socks and jackets.

Robert's Books · BOOKS

(Map p204; www.robertsbooks.lv; Dzirnavu iela 51; ⊙10am-7pm) Robert used to write for the *Economist*; these days he calls Rīga home and tends to his small collection of used English books. Traditional textiles and beeswax candles are also on offer.

Jāņa Sēta · BOOKS

(Map p204; www.mapshop.lv; Elizabetes iela 83/85; ⊙10am-7pm Mon-Fri, to 5pm Sat) The largest travel bookstore in the Baltic overflows with a bounty of maps, souvenir photo books and Lonely Planet guides.

Art Nouveau Rīga · SOUVENIRS

(Map p204; www.artnouveauriga.lv; Strēlnieku iela 9; ⊙10am-7pm) Sells a variety of art-nouveau-related souvenirs, from guidebooks and postcards to stone gargoyles and bits of stained glass.

Kafka · BOOKS

(Vaļņu iela 26; ⊙11am-8pm Mon-Fri, noon-6pm Sat) This modern two-storey shop has a good selection of English-language books, including many Lonely Planet titles. It comes with a little coffee shop where you can read before or after purchasing the books.

ℹ Information

INTERNET ACCESS

Free wi-fi is a standard even in the most obscure hotels, as well as in most cafes and restaurants (but you'll need to ask the waiter for password). The National Library (p209) is unbeatable as a quiet space to work and surf the internet. It only takes a few minutes to get a permanent pass.

Birojnica (www.birojnica.lv; Dzirnavu iela 84 k-2; ⊙10am-6pm Mon-Fri) If you need a working desk away from your working desk (self-hired folks often do), as well as fast internet access and printers, this nicely designed modern co-working space inside Berga Bazārs is the place to go. It's €1.50 per hour (internet access only) or €6 per day (internet, unlimited coffee, printers).

MEDICAL SERVICES

ARS (☑6720 1006; www.ars-med.lv; Skolas iela 5) English-speaking doctors; 24-hour consultation available.

MONEY

There are scores of ATMs scattered around the capital. If for some reason you are having trouble locating a bank, walk down Kaļķu iela (which turns into Brīvības bulvāris) and within seconds you will find a bank or ATM. Withdrawing cash is easier than trying to exchange travellers cheques or foreign currencies; exchange bureaus often have lousy rates and most do not take travellers cheques. For detailed information about Latvian currency and exchange rates visit www.bank.lv.

POST

Those blue storefronts with 'Pasta' written on them aren't Italian restaurants – they're post offices. See www.pasts.lv for more info.

Central Post Office (Map p204; Brīvības bulvāris 32; ⊙7.30am-8pm Mon-Fri, 8am-6pm Sat, 10am-4pm Sun) International calling and faxing services available.

Post Office (Map p204; Elizabetes iela 41/43; ⊙7.30am-7pm Mon-Fri, 9am-3pm Sat)

TOURIST INFORMATION

Tourist Information Centre (☑6730 7900; www.liveriga.com; Rātslaukums 6; ⊙10am-6pm) Dispenses tourist maps and walking-tour brochures; helps with accommodation booking and day trips; and sells concert tickets. It also stocks the Rīga Card (p225), which offers discounts on sights and restaurants, and free rides on public transport. Satellite offices can be found in Livu laukums (May to September only) and at the bus station.

WEBSITES

www.1188.lv Lists virtually every establishment in Rīga and the rest of Latvia. The Latvian language setting yields the most search results.

The search engine also provides up-to-date information on nightlife and traffic.

www.rigaoutthere.com A site managed by a locally run tour operator and featuring a handy travel planner in the right-hand column.

www.zl.lv Another excellent Latvian database offering detailed information about businesses in Rīga and the entire country.

ℹ Getting There & Away

AIR

Rīga International Airport (Starptautiskā Lidosta Rīga; ☑1817; www.riga-airport.com; Mārupe District; ☐22) is in the suburb of Skulte, 13km southwest of the city centre. At the time of writing Rīga was the only city in Latvia with a commercial airport.

BOAT

Rīga's **passenger ferry terminal** (☑6732 6200; www.portofriga.lv; Eksporta iela 3a), located about 1km downstream (north) of Akmens Bridge, offers service to Stockholm aboard **Tallink** (☑6709 9700; www.tallink.lv), three to four times weekly.

BUS

Buses depart from Rīga's **international bus station** (Rīgas starptautiskā autoosta; Map p204; www.autoosta.lv; Prāgas iela 1), located behind the railway embankment just beyond the southeastern edge of Old Rīga. International destinations include Tallinn, Vilnius, Warsaw, Pärnu, Kaunas, St Petersburg and Moscow. Try **Ecolines** (☑6721 4512; www.ecolines.net), **Eurolines Lux Express** (☑680 0909; www.luxexpress.eu) or **Nordeka** (☑6746 4620; www.nordeka.lv).

Baltic services from Rīga include the following (the frequencies cited here refer to the morning period – there is likely to be fewer or no buses in the afternoon):

Aglona (€9, four hours, daily at 4pm and/or 6pm)

Bauska (€3, 1¼ hours, every 30 minutes)

Cēsis (€4.15, two hours, every 30 minutes)

Daugavpils (€9, 3½ to 4¼ hours, every one to two hours)

Dobele (€3.25, 1½ hours, every 30 minutes to one hour)

Jelgava (€2.30, one hour, every 30 minutes)

Kandava (€5, 1½ to two hours, 10 daily)

Kaunas (€20 to €25, four to 5½ hours, three daily)

Kolka (€6.25 to €7.85, 3½ to 4½ hours, five daily)

Kuldīga (€6.40, 2½ to 3¼ hours, hourly)

Liepāja (€8.50, four hours, hourly)

Pärnu (€11, 2¾ hours, hourly)

Pāvilosta (€8.70, 4½ hours, daily)

Sigulda (€2.15, one hour, every 45 minutes)

Tallinn (€14, 4½ hours, hourly)
Ventspils (€7.55, three to four hours, hourly)
Vilnius (€13 to €19, four hours, 13 daily)

TRAIN

Rīga's **central train station** (Centrālā stacija; ☑ 6723 2135; www.pv.lv; Stacijas laukums 2) is convenient to Old and Central Rīga, and is housed in a Soviet-era concrete box (now built into a glass-encased shopping mall), just outside the Old Town.

Found in a large hall to the right of the main entrance, cash offices 1 to 6 sell tickets to international destinations, which now include Moscow (€142, 16 hours, daily), St Petersburg (€107, 15 hours, daily) and Minsk (€66, 12 hours, daily). Domestic tickets are sold in cash offices 7 to 15. The information office (open 7am to 7pm) is located next to the latter.

Most Latvians live in the large suburban and rural ring around Rīga, and commute into the city for work. The city's network of ultrahandy suburban train lines help facilitate commuting, and make day trips to nearby towns a whole lot easier too.

Rīga has six suburban lines. Of most use to travellers is the Dubulti–Sloka–Ķemeri–Tukums Line, which runs through the entire length of Jūrmala, and the Sigulda–Cēsis–Valmiera Line, which can take you into the heart of Gauja National Park. Skulte Line is convenient for Saulkrasti.

In the east, the line goes towards Krustpils, where it divides into two. One goes towards Rēzekne, Ludza and Russia, the other turns south towards Daugavpils and Belarus. Visit www.ldz. lv to view the timetables and prices for long-haul international and domestic trains. Train service is not convenient to any destinations in western Latvia.

The most popular domestic services are listed here. Note that there are no services at night-time, although trains to Jūrmala run until midnight:

Cēsis (€3.50, two hours, four daily)
Daugavpils (€7, 3½ hours, three daily)
Jūrmala (Majori) (€1.40, 30 minutes, two to three per hour)
Ludza (€7.80, four hours, two daily)
Rēzekne (€7.20, 3½ hours, two daily)
Saulkrasti (€2.20, one hour, hourly)

ⓘ Getting Around

For all matters concerning public transport and parking in Rīga, consult the excellent website www.rigassatiksme.lv, run by the municipality.

TO/FROM THE AIRPORT

The cheapest way to get from Rīga airport to the centre is bus 22 (€2, 25 minutes), which runs at least every 30 minutes and stops at several points around town including the Stockmanns complex and on the river side of the Old Town. A taxi ride between the airport and the centre typically costs €12.

BICYCLE

Zip around town with **Sixt Rent a Bicycle** (Sixt velo noma; ☑ 6767 6780; www.sixtbicycle.lv; per 30min/day €0.90/9). A handful of stands are conveniently positioned around Rīga and Jūrmala; simply choose your bike, call the rental service and receive the code to unlock your wheels.

CAR & MOTORCYCLE

Rīga is divided into six parking zones. Municipal parking in the centre of Rīga costs between €2 and €3 per hour. If you need to drop a car in Rīga for longer, consult www.europark.lv – it runs parking lots all around the city and offers more flexibility time- and moneywise.

PUBLIC TRANSPORT

The centre of Rīga is too compact for most visitors even to consider public transport, but trams, buses or trolleybuses may come in handy if you are venturing further out. For routes and schedules, consult www.rigassatiksme.lv. Tickets cost €1.15 (€0.30 for ISIC-holding students). Unlimited tickets are available for 24 hours (€5), three days (€10) and five days (€15). Tickets are available from Narvessen newspaper kiosks as well as vending machines on board new trams and in the underground pass by the train station.

TAXI

Taxis charge €0.60 to €0.80 per kilometre. Insist on having the meter on before you set off. Meters usually start running at around €1.50. It shouldn't cost more than €5 for a short journey (like crossing the Daugava for dinner in Ķipsala). There are taxi ranks outside the bus and train stations, at the airport and in front of a few major hotels in Central Rīga, such as the Radisson Blu Hotel Latvija.

AROUND RĪGA

It's hard to believe that long stretches of flaxen beaches and shady pine forests lie just 20km from Rīga's metropolitan core. Both Jūrmala and Ķemeri National Park make excellent day trips from Rīga.

The highway connecting Rīga to Jūrmala (Latvia's only six-lane road) was known as '10 minutes in America' during Soviet times, because locally produced films set in the USA were always filmed on this busy asphalt strip.

THE EARTH GROANS AT SALASPILS CONCENTRATION CAMP

If you have a taste for Soviet war-themed gigantism, like the iconic Motherland sculpture in Russia's Volgograd, one of the best examples is Salaspils Concentration Camp Memorial, located just beyond Rīga's boundary on the road leading to Latgale. Run by the Nazis during WWII, it wasn't a death camp like Auschwitz, but conditions for inmates – mostly left-wing Latvians and Soviet POWs, as well as a few thousand German Jews – were harsh and many people died here.

The centrepiece is a huge concrete bunker looking like an angled elevator shaft that rises to the skies, symbolising the ascent to eternity through suffering. The inscription on it reads 'Behind this gate the earth groans' – a line from a poem by the Latvian writer Eizens Veveris, who was imprisoned in the camp.

In front of it, seven sorrowful stone figures with names like 'The Undefeated', 'The Humiliated', 'Solidarity' and 'Oath' stand amid a green field in front of it. Inside the bunker a small exhibition recounts the horrors of the camp. In its shadow lies a 6m-long block of polished stone with a metronome inside, ticking a haunting heartbeat, which never stops.

To get there by public transport, take a suburban train on the Ogre–Krustpils Line to Dārziņi (not Salaspils) station. The path from the station to the *piemineklis* (memorial) starts on the barracks side. It's about a 15-minute walk. If you're driving from Rīga on the A6 highway, the hard-to-spot turn-off is on the left, 300m before the A5 junction.

Jūrmala

POP 56,000

The Baltic's version of the French Riviera, Jūrmala (pronounced *yoor*-muh-lah) is a long string of townships with Prussian-style villas, each unique in shape and decor. Even during the height of communism, Jūrmala was always a place to *'sea'* and be seen. These days, Russian tycoons and their glamorous wives comprise a visible part of the population. Wealthy fashionistas flaunt their couture beachwear while worshipping the sun between spa treatments. On summer weekends, vehicles clog the roads when jetsetters and day-tripping Rīgans flock to the resort town for some serious fun in the sun.

Jūrmala's 32km strip of land consists of 14 townships. If you don't have a car or bicycle, you'll want to head straight to the heart of the action – the townships of Majori and Dzintari. A 1km-long pedestrian strip, Jomas iela, connects these two districts and is considered to be Jūrmala's main drag, with loads of tourist-centric venues. Unlike many European resort towns, most of Jūrmala's restaurants and hotels are several blocks away from the beach, which keeps the seashore (somewhat) pristine.

◉ Sights

Besides its Blue Flag beach, Jūrmala's main attraction is its colourful art nouveau **wooden houses**, distinguishable by frilly awnings, detailed facades and elaborate towers. There are over 4000 wooden structures found throughout Jūrmala (most are lavish summer cottages), but you can get your fill of wood by taking a leisurely stroll along **Jūras iela**, which parallels Jomas iela between Majori and Dzintari. The houses are in various states of repair; some are dilapidated and abandoned, others are beautifully renovated and some are brand-new constructions. The tourist office has a handy booklet called *The Resort Architecture of Jūrmala City*, which features several self-guided architectural walking tours – page 8 highlights Majori neighbourhood.

At the other end of the architectural spectrum are several particularly gaudy beachfront Soviet-era sanatoriums. No specimen glorifies the genre quite like the **Vaivari Sanatorium** (Asaru prospekts 61), on the main road 5km west of Majori. It resembles a giant, beached cruise ship that's been mothballed since the Brezhnev era. Surprisingly it still functions, catering to an elderly clientele who have been visiting regularly since, well, the Brezhnev era.

Jūrmala City Museum   MUSEUM
(☑ 6776 4746; Tirgoņu iela 29; ◷ 10am-6pm Tue-Sun) **FREE** After a pricey renovation, this museum now features a beautiful permanent exhibit detailing Jūrmala's colourful history as *the* go-to resort town in the former USSR.

Jūrmala

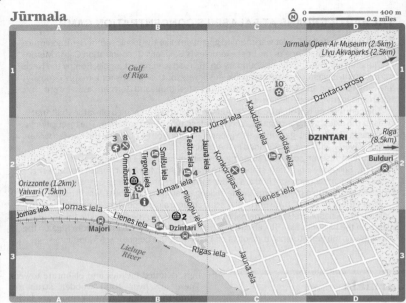

Jūrmala Open-Air Museum   MUSEUM
(6775 4909; Tīklu iela 1a; 10am-6pm Tue-Sun)
In Lielupe, between Jūrmala and Rīga, this
museum preserves 19th-century fishers'
houses and a collection of nautical equipment. If you're lucky, you'll get to try smoked
fish prepared in a traditional Latvian manner.

Art Rezidence 'Inner Light'   GALLERY
(6787 1937; www.jermolajev.lv; Omnibusa iela
19; adult/child €3/1; 11am-5pm) A visit here
will surely cure any rainy-day blues. A local Russian artist runs the studio out of his
home, and dabbles with a secret recipe for
glow-in-the-dark paint by creating portraits
that morph when different amounts of light
strike the painting. Ethereal Enya music
further enhances the trippy experience as
the paintings shine brilliantly in the pulsing
darkness.

🏃 Activities

Jūrmala's first spa opened in 1838, and since
then the area has been known far and wide
as the spa capital of the Baltic. Treatments
are available at a variety of big-name hotels
and hulking Soviet sanatoriums further
along the beach towards Ķemeri National
Park. Many accommodations offer combined spa and sleeping deals.

Baltic Beach Spa   SPA
(6777 1446; www.balticbeach.lv; Jūras iela
23/25; treatments from €15; 8am-10pm) Attached to a beachfront resort, this is the
largest treatment centre in the Baltic, with
three rambling storeys full of massage
rooms, saunas, yoga studios, swimming
pools and spa pools.

The 1st floor is themed like a country barn
and features invigorating hot-and-cold treatments in which one takes regular breaks
from the steam room by pouring buckets of
ice water over one's head à la Jennifer Beals
in *Flashdance*.

Līvu Akvaparks   WATER PARK
(6775 5636; www.akvaparks.lv; Viestura iela
24; 1-day adult/child €29/20; 11am-10pm Mon-
Fri, 10am-10pm Sat & Sun) A massive, family-
friendly water park in Lielupe, located
between Jūrmala and Rīga.

🎊 Festivals & Events

Jūrmala used to host major musical and
comedy festivals geared for the Russian
TV audience, but all of this ended with the
start of war in Ukraine. Yet there is still a
lot going on. Check www.tourism.jurmala.
lv for scheduled events.

Jūrmala

Joma Street Festival   STREET CARNIVAL
(www.jurmala.lv) Jūrmala's annual city festival is held in July; 2009 marked the 50-year anniversary of the unification of Jūrmala's townships. Don't miss the sand-sculpture contest (www.magicsand.lv) along the beach.

🛏 Sleeping

There is no word for 'cheap' in Jūrmalian. If penny-pinching's your game, do a day trip to Jūrmala and sleep in Rīga. The tourist office can assist with booking accommodation in your price bracket. It also keeps a list of locals who rent out private rooms when everything is booked. Summertime prices are the highest; room rates fall dramatically during the low season.

★ Hotel MaMa   BOUTIQUE HOTEL €€
(☑6776 1271; www.hotelmama.lv; Tirgonu iela 22; r from €75; 🖢) The bedroom doors have thick, mattress-like padding on the interior (psycho-chic?) and the suites themselves are a veritable blizzard of white drapery. A mix of silver paint and pixie dust accents the ultramodern furnishings and amenities. If heaven had a bordello, it would probably look something like this.

Parus   HERITAGE HOTEL €€
(☑6776 2391; www.parus.lv; Smilšu iela 2; s/d/tr €65/80/110) One of the Prussian villas that form the face of Jūrmala, this pretty green-coloured wooden house has comfy rooms that come in various shapes and sizes. The beach is just a dune away.

Villa Joma   BOUTIQUE HOTEL €€€
(☑6777 1999; www.villajoma.lv; Jomas iela 90; s/d from €100/110) This inviting boutique hotel sports 15 immaculate rooms that come in quirky configurations. Try for a room with a skylight. Although Villa Joma is several blocks from the beach, there's a lovely garden terrace in the back to catch some rays. Don't miss out on the fantastic food served at the airy ground-floor restaurant.

Hotel Jūrmala Spa   HOTEL €€€
(☑6778 4415; www.hoteljurmala.com; Jomas iela 47/49; r from €80; @🖢🕮) The rooms in this towering black behemoth are on the small side, but they look sparkling new and the ones on the 8th and 9th floor have sweeping views of both the inland river and the sea. Check out the swinging cocktail lounge on the top floor.

🍴 Eating

In summer, stroll down Jomas iela and take your pick from beer tents, cafe terraces and trendy restaurants. If you're not feeling adventurous, almost all of Rīga's popular chain restaurants have a franchise in Jūrmala. Most places are open year-round, catering to beach bums in the summer and spa junkies who pass through for treatments during the winter months. Most hotels also have on-site restaurants.

MaMa   FUSION €€
(http://hotelmama.lv/en/restaurant; Tirgoņu iela 22; mains €10-22; ☺noon-10pm) At MaMa, Italian and Latvian fusion cuisine is served on crisp white-clothed tables surrounded by a mishmash of throne-like chairs. You may notice that some of the seats are particularly tiny – these are reserved for pets (the chef even created a gourmet menu for Fido). Don't miss the technicoloured bathroom with a fun surprise on the ceiling.

Sue's Asia   INDIAN €€
(Jomas iela 74; mains €9-12; ☺noon-11pm) Although it's a bit odd seeing bleach-blonde Baltic women serving pan-Asian platters in

saris, Sue's is worshipped by locals for its almost-authentic cuisine. Enjoy spicy curries or tender butter chicken amid statues of praying deities.

Orizzonte
GOURMET €€

(www.orizzonte.lv; Baznīcas iela 2B; mains €10-20; ⊙11am-11pm) Located directly along the sandy shores in Jūrmala's Dubulti district, Orizzonte is a fantastic place to watch the sun dip below the Gulf of Rīga. After dark it's all white tablecloths, candlelight and gentle strums of the guitar in the corner.

Il Sole
ITALIAN €€€

(Jūras iela 23/25; mains €14-30; ⊙11am-11pm) A romantic restaurant at the Baltic Beach Hotel, Il Sole has fantastic ocean-side seating and a long list of delicious Italian dishes matched with imported wines. The Florentine decor is rather cheesy, but you'll hardly notice while staring out at the setting sun.

★36.Line
MODERN LATVIAN €€€

(☑22010696; www.lauris-restaurant.lv; Līnija 36; mains €12-30; ⊙11am-11pm; ☑) Popular local chef Lauris Alekseyevs delivers modern twists on traditional Latvian dishes at this wonderful restaurant, occupying a slice of sand at the eastern end of Jūrmala. Enjoy the beach, then switch to casual attire for lunch or glam up for dinner. In the evening it's not uncommon to find DJs spinning beats.

🍷 Drinking & Entertainment

Seaside Bar
BAR

(☑6778 4415; Jomas iela 47/49; ⊙3pm-2am, to midnight Sun) This hot dancing spot sits high above the trees on the 11th floor of Hotel Jūrmala Spa. Nurse your cocktail in a space-age bucket seat or get jiggy with it under the disco ball.

Majori Culture House & Cinema
LIVE MUSIC, CINEMA

(Majori Kultūras nams; ☑6776 2403; Jomas iela 35) Hosts films, music concerts and various arts and craft exhibitions.

Dzintari Concert Hall
LIVE MUSIC

(Dzintari Koncertzāle; ☑6776 2092; Turaidas iela 1) The legendary open-air concert hall (there is a roof, but no walls) has been around since 1897, though not in present shape. Dzintari was one of the most sought-out venues for Soviet musicians and comedians and continued to be a home away from home for Russian pop artists until 2015, when Latvia decided to cancel two big Russian festivals

because of the war in Ukraine. As a result, the repertoire is more international and diverse these days. Concerts run from June to August.

ℹ Information

Free internet access is available at the tourist office. The Jūrmala City Museum has free wi-fi access.

Bulduri Hospital (Vienības prospekts 19/21)

Tourist Office (☑6714 7900; Lienes iela 5; ⊙9am-7pm Mon-Fri, 10am-5pm Sat, 10am-3pm Sun) Located across from Majori train station, this helpful office has scores of brochures outlining walks, bike routes and attractions. Staff can assist with accommodation bookings and bike rental. A giant map outside helps orient visitors when the centre is closed.

ℹ Getting There & Around

BICYCLE

Sixt Rent a Bicycle (Sixt velo noma; www.sixtbicycle.lv) Has several locations in Jūrmala. The most useful one is across the square from Majori station. You can also drop its bikes here if you rode them from Rīga.

CAR & MOTORCYCLE

Motorists driving into Jūrmala must pay a €2 toll per day before they cross the Lielupe River, even if they are just passing through. There is plenty of mostly free parking space along Jūras iela.

MINIBUSES

A common mode of transport between Rīga and Jūrmala; take minibuses (30 minutes) in the direction of Sloka, Jaunķemeri or Dubulti and ask the driver to let you off at Majori. These vans depart every five to 15 minutes between 6am and midnight and leave opposite Rīga's central train station. Catch the bus at Majori train station for a lift back. These regularly running minibuses can also be used to access other townships within Jūrmala's long sandy stretch. From 9am to midnight, minibuses also connect Jūrmala to Rīga International Airport.

SLOW BOAT

Slow Boat (☑29237123; www.pie-kapteina.lv; adult/child €15/10) Departs from Rīga's Riflemen Sq and docks in Majori near the train station. The journey takes one hour, and only runs on weekends.

TRAIN

Two to three trains per hour link the sandy shores of Jūrmala to Central Rīga. Take a suburban train bound for Sloka, Tukums or Dubulti and disembark at Majori station (€1.50, 30 to 35 minutes). The first train departs Rīga around 5.50am and the last train leaves Majori around

10.45pm. Jūrmala-bound trains usually depart from tracks 3 and 4, and stop six or seven times within the resort's 'city limits' if you wish to get off in another neighbourhood. Visit www.pv.lv or www.1188.lv for the most up-to-date information.

Ķemeri National Park

Beyond Jūrmala's chic stretch of celebrity homes and seaside bar huts lies a verdant hinterland called Ķemeri National Park (Ķemeru nacionālais parks; ☑ 6673 0078; www.kemerunacionalaisparks.lv). Today, the park features sleepy fishing villages tucked between protected bogs, lakes and forests, but at the end of the 1800s, Ķemeri was known for its curative mud and spring water, attracting visitors from as far away as Moscow. Note that the park's land is 'open' year-round, but the infrastructure for the park only works from June to August.

Ķemeri's **park information centre** (☑ 6714 6819; www.kemeri.lv; ⊙ 10am-6pm Jun-Aug) is located in an old barnlike hotel and restaurant called the 'Funny Mosquito'. Although most of the info is in Latvian, you can rent bikes and sign up for lectures and programs such as bat- and bird-watching. A scenic 600m **trail** starts at the info centre and circles through a slice of flat plain forest.

The pungent smell of rotten eggs wafts through the air at the national park's spa resort, also called Ķemeri (pronounced kyeh-meh-ree or *tyeh*-meh-ree, depending on who you ask), known for its sulphurous springs. Ķemeri's first mud bath opened in the late 1800s, and until WWII the resort had a widespread reputation as a healing oasis. The area's spring water is perfectly potable and apparently quite healthy. Try filling your water bottle at the **Lizard**, a stone sculpture at the mouth of a spring that trickles into the river. Sip your pungent brew while meandering past faded mint-green gazebos and small wrought-iron bridges with romantic names such as Bridge of Sighs or Bridge of Caprices – everything remains exactly as it was during the height of the resort's popularity in the 1930s.

It's hard to miss **Hotel Ķemeri**. Known as the 'White Ship', it was built during Latvia's brief period of independence in the 1930s and has one of the most impressive facades outside of Rīga. At the moment, only the exterior can be appreciated due to a lack of renovation money. Have a wander across the park and take a look at **St Peter-Paul Orthodox Church**. Built in 1893, it is the oldest place of worship in Ķemeri and, if you look closely, you'll notice that this large wooden structure was constructed entirely without nails.

Fish smoking and canning remain traditional occupations in the villages further afield along the coastal road leading north towards Cape Kolka. Nowhere smells fishier than **Lapmežciems**, overlooking Lake Kaņieris, 3km west of Jūrmala. Sprats are canned in the factory on the right at the village's eastern entrance. The village market sells freshly smoked eel, sprat, salmon and tuna, as does the market in **Ragaciems**, 2km north.

ℹ Getting There & Away

Ķemeri National Park is easily accessible from Rīga, as it sits just beyond Jūrmala along the capital's west-bound suburban rail line. Trains between Rīga and Jūrmala's Majori station run 15 times per day. The park can also be accessed by bus 11 from Majori station, or directly from Rīga.

WESTERN LATVIA (KURZEME)

The Shire of the Latvian Middle Earth, Kurzeme generates the true Latvian spirit which cosmopolitan Rīgans feel the urge to connect to in times of celebration and despair. Nationalism apart, Kurzeme is miles and miles of jaw-dropping natural beauty. The region's sandy strands of desolate coastline are tailor-made for an off-the-beaten-track adventure. A constellation of coastal towns – Kolka, Ventspils, Pāvilosta and Liepāja – provide pleasant breaks between the large stretches of awesome nothingness.

Kurzeme wasn't always so quiet; the region used to be run by the namesake Cours, a rebellious tribe known for teaming up with the Vikings for raids and battles. During the 13th century, German crusaders ploughed through, subjugating the Cours, alongside the other tribes living in Latvia. When the Livonian Order collapsed under assault from Russia's Ivan the Terrible in 1561, the Order's last master, Gotthard Kettler, salvaged Courland and neighbouring Zemgale as his own personal fiefdom.

Duke Jakob, Courland's ruler from 1640 to 1682, really put the region on the map when he developed a fleet of navy and merchant ships, and purchased two far-flung

Western Latvia (Kurzeme)

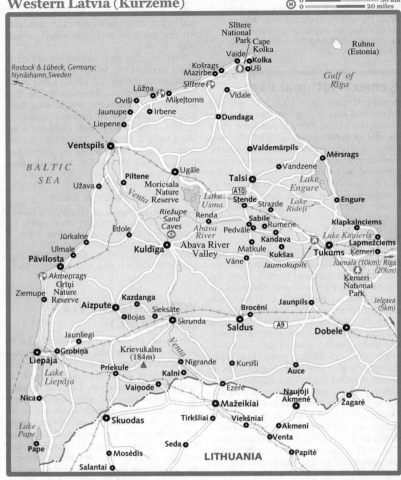

(and totally random) colonies: Tobago, in the Caribbean, and an island in the mouth of Africa's Gambia River. He even had plans to colonise Australia! The Courland empire didn't live for long, but US and Canadian Latvians still gather for reunions on Tobago, although the tropical island is hardly a substitute for the Nordic melancholy of their ancestral land.

Ventspils Road

There are three main roads leading to the Kurzeme coast from Rīga. The Ventspils route is the shortest, with many peculiar sights along the way.

Route A10 branches off the Jūrmala highway and skirts Jūrmala before entering the deep forest of Ķemeri National Park. Soon after the turn to Ķemeri village, look out for the brown sign on your left pointing towards Lielā Ķemeru tīreļa laipa – the **Great Ķemeri Marsh trail**. The 3km boardwalk circuit takes you through the otherworldly landscape of multicoloured moss and infernally dark deep puddles, looking like a suitable habitat for mermaids. There is a watchtower, where selfie-obsessed idlers mingle with serious birders who try to spot the rare black stork.

Around 65km from Rīga, before Tukums, you'll see a signposted turn to Cinevilla (Kinopilsēta Cinevilla; ☑ 6774 4647; www.cinevilla. lv; adults/children €3/1; ⊙10am-7pm) – a theme park that grew out of a set built for Aigars Grauba's 2007 film *Rīgas sargi* and continues to be used by film-makers. Over the years a 'faux' Rīga embankment, complete with a boat, was joined by a bogus 'little town' and a 'railway station' with a real steam train. A 'medieval port' was under construction when we visited. Tourists can play with movie props, try on costumes and even shoot their own movie. There's an on-site restaurant.

After you pass Tukums, you'll be able to spot the red-brick towers of Jaunmoku Castle (☑ 26187442; www.jaunmokupils.lv; museum adult/student €2.50/1.50; ⊙9am-5pm) on your right. Built as a hunting palace by Latvia's most celebrated Englishman, Rīga mayor George Armitstead (p217), the place looks like a fantasy themed on his father's native Yorkshire. There is an interesting small museum, a nice park and a not-so-great hotel on the premises.

A bit further on, Pure chocolate factory is your chance to stock up on sweets for beach picnics on the Kurzeme coast.

Set amid nine little hills, Talsi, 120km from Rīga, is a very pretty lakeside town with nothing much to do, apart from having a meal at the classy Martinelli (mains €10-20) – a secret gem favoured by people in-the-know for its impressive wine list and lovingly and inventively prepared European meals. There is a neat guesthouse upstairs with only two rooms.

Another gem, of natural origin this time, is to be found 30km further west. Lake Usma is a large expanse of water that is polka-dotted with seven islands and backed by leafy forests. Spend a night on the lake at Usma Spa Hotel & Camping (☑ 6367 3710; www.usma.lv; Priežkalni; dm/d from €9/€58; ⊙May-Oct), the perfect getaway-from-it-all option for those who seek peace. You can fish, sail, row, swim and enjoy a full array of spa treatments at this lakeside site, 1km south of Rte A10 on the road to Usma village.

The distance between Rīga and Ventspils is around 190km.

Ventspils

POP 42,500

Fabulous amounts of oil and shipping money have turned Ventspils into one of Latvia's most beautiful and dynamic cities. The air is brisk and clean, and the well-kept buildings are done up in an assortment of cheery colours – even the towering industrial machinery is coated in bright paint. Latvia's biggest and busiest port wasn't always smiles and rainbows, though – Ventspils' strategic ice-free location served as the naval and industrial workhorse for the original settlement of Cours in the 12th century, the Livonian Order in the 13th century, the Hanseatic League through the 16th century and finally the USSR in recent times. Although locals coddle their Užavas beer and claim that there's not much to do, tourists will find a weekend's worth of fun in the form of brilliant beaches, interactive museums and winding Old Town streets dotted with the odd boutique and cafe.

◉ Sights & Activities

The Venta River separates Old Town from the colourful port on the opposite riverbank. When strolling in the centre, take notice of Feldbergs' Seven Mental Meteorites and the monument to Krišjānis Valdemārs, the Latvian writer and educator who empowered thousands of Latvian peasants by setting up the first naval school. On the way from the centre to the beach, take a walk through the Ostgals neighbourhood for a glimpse at simpler days when the town was merely a humble fishing village dotted with wooden abodes. No matter where you go in Ventspils, you'll keep bumping into cow-themed sculptures. A vestige of the long-gone global craze known as Cow Parade, Ventspils' cows were just too surreal, funny and artful to be removed.

Ventspils Beach   BEACH

For Ventspils, the wide stretch of dazzlingly white sand south of the Venta River is what the Louvre is for Paris – its main treasure. During the warmer months, beach bums of every ilk – from nudist to kiteboarder – line the sands to absorb the sun's rays. Backed by a belt of dunes and a lush manicured park, the Blue Flag beach feels as pristine and well cared for as an urban beach can get.

At its northern end, the beach abuts the warehouse area that further on becomes the **Southern Pier**, the city's newest promenade with a watchtower, from which you can observe the harbour and photograph cruise liners on their way in and out.

Open-Air Museum of the Coast MUSEUM
(Ventspils jūras zvejniecības brīvdabas muzejs; ☑ 6322 4467; Riņķu iela 2; adult/child €1.40/0.60; ☉10am-6pm May-Oct) For centuries, life in Kurzeme revolved around seafaring and fishing. Occupying a vast parkland territory, this museum features a collection of fishing crafts, anchors and traditional log houses, brought from coastal villages north and south of Ventspils. A bonus attraction is a narrow-gauge railway, built by the occupying Germans in 1916. The current circuit that runs through the city's maritime park is just a tiny part of the now-defunct network that connected villages along the coast.

But two original German locomotives are still in operation. The station, adjacent to the museum's cash office, is a copy of the one from the village of Mazirbe, north of Ventspils.

Livonian Order Castle CASTLE, MUSEUM
(Livonijas ordeņa pils; ☑ 6362 2031; www.ventspils muzejs.lv; Jāņa iela 17; adult/child €2.10/1.10; ☉10am-6pm Tue-Sun) This blocky building doesn't look obviously castle-like from the outside, but the 13th-century interior is home to a cutting-edge interactive local history and art museum. During Soviet rule the castle was used as a prison and an exhibit in the stables recounts its horrors (in Latvian only). An adjacent Zen rock garden will soothe your soul afterwards.

House of Crafts MUSEUM
(Amatu māja; ☑ 6362 0174; Skolas iela 3; admission €0.90; ☉10am-6pm Tue-Fri, to 3pm Sat) Visitors can learn about the handicrafts of Kurzeme here and watch local artisans spin yarns (literally), before purchasing something to take home with them.

Housed in a wooden structure built during the reign of the dukes of Courland, it was used as a boys' school during Soviet times before being converted into an exhibition hall. English is pretty scarce, so call ahead if you are interested in watching ceramics demonstrations, or if you would like a guided explanation about the history of the building (a classroom still remains intact with desks and chalk slates) and the town.

Hecogs Jēkabs Boat BOAT TOUR
(☑ 26353344; cnr Ostas iela & Tirgus iela; adult/child €1.40/0.60) From April to November the Hecogs Jēkabs boat sails around the mouth of the Venta River. The 45-minute excursions depart six times daily from dock 18.

Churches

Two churches soar above the clutter of prim wooden architecture: the onion-domed **St Nicholas Russian Orthodox Church** (Sv Nivolaja pareizticīgo baznīca; Plosu iela 10), built near the modern ferry pier in 1901, and the **Nicholas Evangelical Lutheran Church** (Nikolaja luterāņu baznīca; Tirgus iela 2), built in 1835 on stately Rātslaukums. Note that the church actually isn't 'St Nicholas', because the house of worship was named for Tsar Nicholas II when he donated loads of cash to the local Lutherans.

I-SPY

The Soviets designed a mammoth 32m-diameter radio telescope in Irbene to eavesdrop on Western satellite communications during the Cold War. Today scientists use it to gaze at the stars, moon and sun.

Hidden in the forest 24km north of Ventspils, Irbene's superpowerful antenna was one of three used to spy on the world by the Soviet army at the USSR Space Communication Centre. When the last Russian troops left in 1994, they took one antenna with them but left the remaining two behind (they were too large to move).

The R-32, a 600-tonne dish mounted on a 25m-tall concrete base, was built by the USSR in the 1980s and is the world's eighth-largest parabolic antenna. Since 1994 the former military installation has belonged to the **Ventspils International Radio Astronomy Centre** (VIRAC, Ventspils Starptautiskais Radioastronomijas Centrs; ☑ 29230818; http://virac.venta.lv), which is part of the Latvian Academy of Sciences. The reconstruction of an antenna was preventing guided tours at the time of writing, but they were due to resume in spring 2016.

Ventspils

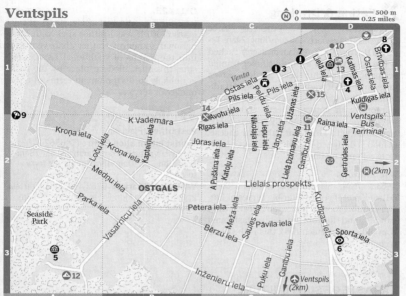

🛏 Sleeping

Piejūras Kempings   CAMPGROUND €
(☏ 6362 7925; Vasarnīcu iela 56; tent sites per person €5, 4-person cottage from €40; @) This charming campus of grassy tent grounds and pine cottages is a full-service operation with an on-site laundrette, bicycle rental, and tennis, volleyball and basketball courts.

Kupfernams   B&B €€
(☏ 6362 6999; www.hotelkupfernams.lv; Kārļa iela 5; s/d €39/59; 🖳) Our favourite spot to spend the night, this charming wooden house at the centre of Old Town has a set of cheery upstairs rooms with slanted ceilings, opening onto a communal lounge. Below, there's a cafe and a hair salon (which doubles as the reception).

Viesu Nams Zītari   GUESTHOUSE €€
(☏ 28160018; www.facebook.com/KrogsZitari; Tirgus iela 11; d from €50) If you don't mind stuffed animals in the common room, there are several well-appointed rooms in the timber-framed house of Zītari beer garden. The location at the market square can't be more central. Rooms have wood

plank floors and lots of wooden furniture, but the design is modern.

✖ Eating & Drinking

Krogs Zītari EASTERN EUROPEAN €€
(☑25708337; www.facebook.com/KrogsZitari; Tirgus iela 11; mains €7-12; ⊙11am-midnight) Tucked in the courtyard of a pretty timber-framed German house, this beer garden serves large portions of traditional (or not so traditional) Latvia fare. But whether it is herring rollmops with cottage cheese and boiled potatoes or – more exotically – oven-baked vegetables with Georgian suluguni cheese, all food is designed to make a perfect match for excellent Latvian beer.

Skroderkrogs LATVIAN €€
(☑6362 7634; Skroderu iela 6; mains €6-13; ⊙11am-10pm) If you're after big serves of Latvian comfort food in a pleasant local setting (candles and flowers on tables fashioned from old sewing machines), this is the place to come.

Ostas 23 MODERN EUROPEAN €€
(☑22015754; http://ostas23.lv; Ostas iela 23; mains €7-10) If you'd rather stick with international standards, rather than venturing into the depths of traditional Latvian cuisine, this slick modern place by the castle is unlikely to disappoint in terms of either quality or service.

❶ Information

Post Office (Platā iela)
Tourist Information Centre (☑6362 2263; www.visitventspils.com; Dārzu iela 6; ⊙8am-6pm Mon-Sat, 10am-4pm Sun) In the ferry terminal.
Ventspils Library (☑6362 4333; Akmeņu iela 2; ⊙10am-7pm Mon-Fri, to 4pm Sat; 🕾) Free internet and wi-fi.

OFF THE BEATEN TRACK

A TASTE OF SUITI CULTURE

If you find yourself caught in the Ventspils–Kuldīga–Liepāja triangle, head for the middle. It's a special place in several respects. An island of Catholicism in the land of Lutherans that is Kurzeme, it is populated by the Suiti people who speak a distinct dialect and stick to their traditions to a much greater extent than most Latvians do. It is the very last place in Latvia where at least some of the locals show up for the Sunday mass in their centuries-old traditional attire, which includes a kind of tartan poncho worn by women over scarlet-coloured dresses.

But at the very heart of their identity lies singing. What experts call 'many-voiced drone', not unlike the traditional choir music in the Caucasus (only it is women who sing), is interrupted with a kind of rapping, in which the soloist satirises those present in the audience for looking untidy, absent-minded or lazy. The text that they sing is entirely improvisational.

The capital of the Suiti is **Alsunga**, quaint village featuring a small Livonian castle and a sweet little inn **Spēlmaņu Krogs** (☑26179298; www.spelmanukrogs.lv; Pils iela 7; r from €25), where you can sleep and eat delicious local fare, including the *sklandraušis* – sweet cakes with carrots and potatoes. During the weekends the owners organise a party that involves traditional cooking on an open fire and a concert of Suitu Sievas – the famous band of Alsunga grannies who put Suiti Land on the cultural map of Latvia.

Alsunga is 14km from the Ventspils–Liepāja road. The turn-off is at another Suiti village – **Jūrkalne**, famous for its high sandstone cliffs backing a beautiful desolate beach. There are also a couple of nice inns in the area, including **Pilsberģi Krogs** (☑27436888; www.pilsbergi.lv; r from €50).

The reason for the Suiti to be Catholics is not political, but entirely romantic. During the Reformation, they became Lutherans like everybody else in Kurzeme. But in 1623 the lord of Alsunga domain, Johan Ulrich von Schwerin, fell in love with a Polish beauty. In order to get his marriage approved by the king of Poland, he had to convert to Catholicism, together with all his subjects. This resulted in self-isolation, which must have been tough for the locals throughout the centuries, but thanks to it we now have a unique culture, officially recognised by Unesco as 'intangible cultural heritage in need of urgent safeguarding'.

❶ Getting There & Away

Ventspils' **bus terminal** (☎ 6362 4262; Kuldīgas iela 5) is served by buses to/from Rīga (€7.50, 2¾ to four hours, hourly), Kuldīga (€3, 1¼ hours, five daily) and Liepāja (€5.20, 2¼ to three hours, seven daily) via Jūrkalne (€2.50, one hour) and Pāvilosta (€3.25, 1¼ hours).

Scandlines (www.scandlines.com) runs ferries five times weekly to Nynashamn, Sweden (€21, 12 hours, five weekly) and to Travemünde, Germany (€21, 25 hours, twice weekly).

Pāvilosta

This sleepy beach burg, located halfway between Ventspils and Liepāja, casually pulls off a chilled-out California surfer vibe despite its location on the black Baltic Sea. Summer days are filled with windsurfing, kiteboarding, surfing and sailing interspersed with beach naps and beers. Learn how to get involved at the friendly tourist office – the staff can also set you up with traditional boat rides and fishing equipment – and if you're lucky you might get a tutorial on how to smoke fish. Make sure to notify the weather gods when you plan on passing through – dreary weather in Pāvilosta means there's really nothing to do.

🛏 Sleeping & Eating

Vēju Paradize INN €€
(☎ 26446644; www.veju-paradize.lv; Smilšu iela 14; d/tr/q from €49/61/73) 'Wind Paradise' is Pāvilosta's largest sleeping spot, with 17 tidy rooms that are simple yet feel distinctly beachy. The aloe plants are a clever touch, especially after spending one too many hours splashing around in the sea. Veju's on-site restaurant is open during the summer months from 9am to 10pm and specialises in light, international dishes.

The place runs a fleet of traditional wooden boats, available for hire.

Das Crocodill BOUTIQUE HOTEL €€
(☎ 26151333; www.crocodill.lv; Kalna iela 6; r high/low season from €80/40; ❄) Crocodill oozes personality from every mosaic tile and light fixture. The decoration is a delightful mishmash of styles from all over the world: Aboriginal Australia, tribal Africa and a hint of Polynesia as well. Splurge for one of the suites in the back overlooking the inviting blue swimming pool.

Watersports equipment and bicycles are available for rent.

Āķagals LATVIAN €
(Dzintaru iela; mains €5-8; ⊙noon-7pm) Enjoy stacks of delicious Latvian cuisine on varnished picnic tables made from thick logs. There's a large swing set, windswept dunes and a rusty lookout tower out the back to keep you busy while you wait for your nosh (the menu inexplicably refers to its dishes as 'noshes').

Snack Bīčbārs CAFE
(Illy; ⊙Jun-Aug) This modified tiki hut sells coffee and cocktails along the dirt path leading to the beach. Take your beverage to go, or chill out on the trendy wicker furniture and thumb through a weathered copy of the latest fashion mag. Note that the bar changes names each summer, depending on which Rīga institution takes over for the warmer months.

❶ Information

There is a 24-hour ATM right beside the tourist office.
Post Office (Tirgus iela 1; ⊙9am-5pm Mon-Fri)
Tourist Office (www.pavilosta.lv; Dzintaru iela 2; ⊙7.30am-9pm Jun-Aug, to 7.30pm Sep-May) Friendly, English-speaking staff can help arrange accommodation and activities. Located along the main road to the docks, near the bus stop.

❶ Getting There & Away

Intercity buses link Pāvilosta to Liepāja (€2.65, 70 minutes, five daily), Kuldīga (€2.70, 65 minutes, once daily with continued service to Rīga) and Ventspils (€3.25, 1¼ hours, four daily). Buses stop in front of the tourist office.

Liepāja

POP 83,400

Liepāja doesn't fit any cliché – a port city of gritty red-brick warehouses, moored torpedo boats and an old prison for the main attraction, it also boasts one of the country's most beautiful beaches, and it has generated a totally disproportionate number of major Latvian musicians. Its rough-around-the-edges vibe that translates into grungy musical sounds makes Liepāja somewhat akin to Manchester, but in reality its search for identity is only beginning.

Founded by the Livonian Order in the 13th century, Latvia's third-largest city wasn't a big hit until Tsar Alexander III deepened the harbour and built a gargantuan naval port at the end of the 1800s. For

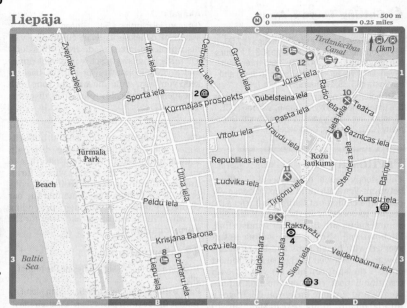

Liepāja

Liepāja

◉ Sights

1 House of Craftsmen D2
2 Liepāja History & Art Museum B1
3 Liepāja Under Occupation
     Museum...D3
4 Peter's Market C3

🛏 Sleeping

5 Fontaine Royal C1
6 Hotel Fontaine C1
7 Promenade Hotel D1
8 Roze...B3

✖ Eating

9 Boulangerie...C3
10 Darbnīca...D1
     Fontaine Delisnack ....(see 12)
11 Pastnieka Māja.......................................C2

🍸 Drinking & Nightlife

12 Fontaine Palace D1
     Prison Bar.....................................(see 5)

years the industrial town earned its spot
on the map as the home to the first Baltic
fleet of Russian submarines, but after WWII
the Soviets occupied what was left of the
bombed-out burg and turned it into a strategic military base.

◉ Sights

Liepāja is light on sights, so why not head
to the **beach** for some R&R. A thin green
belt known as **Jūrmala Park** acts as a buffer between the soft dunes and tatty urban
core.

◉ Karosta

Off limits to everyone during the Soviet
occupation, Karosta, 4km north of central
Liepāja, is a former Russian naval base encompassing about one-third of Liepāja's
city limits. From ageing army barracks to
ugly Soviet-style concrete apartment blocks
(many abandoned), evidence of the occupation still remains. As sights are fairly spread
out, Karosta is best explored by bicycle or by
car. There is a nice beach, so take your swimming suit along on a hot day.

Karosta Prison   HISTORIC BUILDING
(Karostas cietums; ☎ 26369470; www.karostascie
tums.lv; Invalīdu iela 4; adult/child €4.50/3; ⊗9am-
7pm daily Jun-Aug, 10am-6pm daily May & Sep,
noon-3pm Sat & Sun Oct-Apr) Gluttons for punishment will get a bellyful in this creepy old
prison, which operated right up until 1997.
Built in 1900 as an infirmary, it was quickly
turned into a military prison, even before

the building was completed. Tours depart on the hour, detailing the history of the prison, which was used to punish disobedient soldiers. A range of more extreme 'experiences' is also on offer for groups of 10 or more (bookings essential).

If you're craving some serious punishment, or just want to brag that you've spent the night in a Soviet jail, sign up to become a prisoner for the night (€17 per person). You'll be subjected to regular bed checks and verbal abuse by guards in period garb, and forced to relieve yourself in the world's most disgusting latrine (seriously). Try booking the night in cell 26 – solitary confinement – you won't be bothered, but the pitch-blackness will undoubtedly drive you off the edge.

For those wanting a pinch of masochism without having to spend the night, there are one-hour 'reality shows' (adult/child €6/4.50). There are also tours to the once-off-limits northern forts, where you can take part in the *Escape From The USSR* spy game.

⭐ **St Nicholas Maritime Cathedral**　　　　CHURCH
(www.morskoj-sobor.lv; Katedrāles iela 7; ⊙8am-5pm & during evening services) The stunning cathedral, with its bulbous cupolas, shines like a precious stone through the grey concrete of the decrepit Soviet apartment blocks that surround it on all sides. It was built in 1901 in the Russian revival style. During WWI the church was stripped of its intricate interior decorations, and after years as a cinema and sports complex, the cathedral was restored in the 1990s. As with all Russian churches, women are requested to wear headscarves, and no shorts or beach clothes are allowed.

👁 **City Centre**

Liepāja's city centre has a handful of interesting places to visit.

Peter's Market　　　　MARKET
(Kuršu laukums) Vendors have touted their wares here since the mid-17th century. The market expanded in 1910, when a pavilion was constructed adjacent to the square. Today you'll find stalls inside and out at this bustling complex, selling everything from secondhand clothes and pirated DVDs to fresh fruit and veggies.

House of Craftsmen　　　　MUSEUM
(www.saivaart.com; Dārza iela 4/8; ⊙10am-5pm Mon-Fri) **FREE** Check out the largest piece of amber art in the world (an enormous dangling tapestry) here plus legions of women knitting scarves, mittens and blankets available for purchase. The jeweller, based on the 2nd floor, makes unusual (and beautiful) earrings and necklaces.

Liepāja History & Art Museum　　　　MUSEUM
(Liepājas vēstures un mākslas muzejs; ☑29605223; Kūrmājas prospekts 16/18; ⊙10am-6pm) **FREE** Features a variety of impressive displays such as Stone and Bronze Age artefacts unearthed on local archaeological digs, and an interesting collection of old jewellery, weapons and vintage memorabilia from both world wars.

Liepāja Under Occupation Museum　　　　MUSEUM
(K Ukstiņa iela 79; ⊙10am-6pm Wed-Sun) **FREE** Traces the bloody history of the Soviet and Nazi occupations in Latvia, with an emphasis on Liepāja. Captions are in Latvian, but no words are needed to explain the powerful images of the 1939–40 deportations to Siberia (an estimated 2000 people from Liepāja were deported), the genocide committed against Latvian Jews (over 5000 massacred in and around the city) and the 1991 fight for independence.

🛏 **Sleeping**

Hotel Fontaine　　　　HOSTEL **€**
(☑6342 0956; www.fontaine.lv; Jūras iela 24; d with/without bathroom €45/25; @) You'll either adore or abhor this funky hostel set in a charming 18th-century wooden house with lime-green trim. The whole place feels like a secondhand store, from the kitschy knick-knack shop used as the reception to the 20-plus rooms stuffed to the brim with rock memorabilia, dusty oriental rugs, bright tile mosaics, Soviet propaganda and anything else deemed appropriately offbeat. There's a communal kitchen and chill-out space in the basement. Some rooms are located in a second wooden house out the back.

Fontaine Royal　　　　HOTEL **€€**
(☑6348 9777; www.fontaineroyal.lv; Stūrmaņu iela 1; s/d €35/45, s/tw without bathroom €20/25; P🐾) Apart from the rough concrete ceilings, everything is gaudy and gilded at this kooky budget hotel. Strange knick-knacks

and sculptures abound, and the ever-present gold trimming and sparkly spray paint is dazzling – as though guests were sleeping in a framed Renaissance painting.

Roze   INN €€
(☑ 6342 1155; www.parkhotel-roze.lv; Rožu iela 37; s/d from €49/59; ☜) Stylish and comfortable, this pale-blue wooden guesthouse near the sea was once a summer home for the elite, and still has a certain art nouveau styling. Rooms are spacious, and each is uniquely decorated with antique wallpaper and sheer drapery. Extras include satellite TVs, a sauna, and a gazebo-ed garden in the yard.

Promenade Hotel   LUXURY HOTEL €€€
(☑ 6348 8288; www.promenadehotel.lv; Vecā Ostmala 40; r from €89; P @ ☜) The poshest hotel in Kurzeme lives in an enormous harbour warehouse that was once used to store grain.

Eating

The city's drinking and entertainment venues have menus with Latvian and international favourites.

Fontaine Delisnack   FAST FOOD €
(www.delisnack.lv; Dzirnavu iela 4; mains €3-5; ☺24hr) Attached to Fontaine Palace, Liepāja's cheapest chow joint was designed with the inebriated partier in mind: the American-style burgers are a foolproof way to soak up some of those vodka shots downed earlier in the evening. Service is notorious for being glacial-paced.

Boulangerie   BAKERY €
(www.boulangerie.lv; Kuršu ielā 2; pastries €4; ☺10am-7pm Mon-Sat, to 5pm Sun) In the morning you can see croissant and coffee addicts hanging outside the door waiting for this tiny place to open. A queue inevitably forms as staff lay out freshly baked pastries, eclairs and macarons. Pastries are relatively pricey, though €3.50 for an omelette with salad is a good breakfast deal. On a warm day, try to get a seat on the roof terrace that many fail to notice.

Darbnīca   INTERNATIONAL €
(www.darbnicacafe.lv; Lielā iela 8; mains €3-4; ☺8.30am-9pm Mon-Thu, 8.30am-2am Fri, 10am-2am Sat, 10am-8pm Sun) A local hipster hangout, this cafeteria cum bar serves burgers, Asian noodle dishes and not terribly authentic, but perfectly edible, tom yum. At night it turns into a bar with a great

selection of Latvian beers on tap and a good soundtrack.

Pastnieka Māja   LATVIAN €€
(☑ 6340 7521; www.pastniekamaja.lv; Brīvzemnieka iela 53; mains €7-15; ☺11am-11pm) This ultraslick (for Liepāja!) two-level restaurant is housed in the city's old post office (*pastnieka māja* means 'post-office house'). The menu features traditional Latvian favourites, as well as a few very exotic offerings: chase your 'bulls' balls' (you'll see) with a pint of Līvu Alus, Liepāja's local beer.

🍺 Drinking & Nightlife

Liepāja has a reputation throughout Latvia as the centre of the country's rock-music scene, and taking in a concert is a real treat. Even if you can't understand the lyrics, just being a part of the screaming, pulsating masses is a cultural experience you won't soon forget. A new amber-coloured concert hall, in the final stages of construction at the time of research, is set to become one of the nation's hottest musical venues.

Fontaine Palace   BAR
(www.fontainepalace.lv; Dzirnavu iela 4; ☺24hr) A former warehouse, this never-closing rock bar lures loads of live acts through its doors.

Prison Bar   BAR
(Stūrmaņu iela 1; ☺4pm-5am Fri & Sat) Located on the 1st floor of Fontaine Royal, this local haunt is stuffed with cheesy prison-related accoutrements, and the bartender slings drinks from behind bars.

ℹ Information

For extensive, detailed and up-to-date information on pretty much everything in Liepāja, consult the official tourist website www.liepaja.travel. Banks with ATMs can be found along Lielā iela and Kungu iela. Pretty much all restaurants and cafes have wi-fi access – just ask for the password.

Tourist Information Centre (☑ 6348 0808; www.liepaja.travel; Rožu laukums 5; ☺9am-7pm Mon-Sat, 10am-3pm Sun May-Sep, 9am-5pm Mon-Fri Jan-Mar, 9am-5pm Mon-Fri, 10am-3pm Sat Apr & Oct-Dec)

ℹ Getting There & Around

Liepāja Bus Station (☑ 6342 7552; Rīgas iela) is linked by tram 1 with Lielā iela in the downtown. There are convenient daily bus services to/from Rīga (€9, 3½ to 4½ hours, two or three hourly), Kuldīga (€4, 1¾ to three hours, seven daily) and Ventspils (€5 to €6, 2¼ to three hours, seven daily) via Pāvilosta (€2.85, 70 minutes) and Jūrkalne (€3.40, 1½ hours).

Stena Line operates services from Liepāja ferry terminal to Travemünde in Germany (four weekly, 28 hours, from €36) and Nynäshamn in Sweden (weekly, 11 hours, from €21).

Until Liepāja International Airport reopens (scheduled for 2016), visitors and locals use the airport in Lithuania's Palanga (65km away) to get to Scandinavian capitals and Moscow.

Abava River Valley

When the glaciers receded at the end of the last ice age, the crescent-shaped Abava Valley was born. Gnarled oaks and idyllic villages dot the gushing stream, luring city slickers away for a day of unhurried scenery. Most people come here to see Kurzeme's gem, Kuldīga, but the other two towns en route are worth at least a short stopover. This area is best explored by private vehicle. Canoeing down the Abava is another option.

Kandava

Bucolic Kandava, just off the Rīga–Ventspils road on the way to Kuldīga, is a charming collection of stone and wooden houses, a soaring church spire and traces of a fallen empire in the form of Livonian Order **castle ruins**. From the top of the castle mound, there is an excellent view of the fine **stone bridge** (1875) – one of Latvia's oldest – across the Abava River.

Kandava's **tourist office** (⏹63181150; www.kandava.lv; Kūrortu iela 1b; ⏱9am-6pm Mon-Fri, 10am-5pm Sat) is located directly along the route that connects Rīga to Kuldīga. The affable staff can help you sort out bike rental.

Plosti (⏹26130303; www.plosti.lv; Rēdnieki), further along the Abava River towards Sabile, offers bike hire, canoe hire, horse rides and guided paddles down the Abava in addition to accommodation. Another guesthouse nearby, **Plostkrogs**, is a great place to have lunch along the river.

🛏 Sleeping

Kukšu Muiža   HISTORIC HOTEL €€€
(⏹29205188, 25980910; www.kuksumuiza.lv; s/d from €145/160) The owner has poured his heart and soul into turning the once derelict estate into one of the top rural inns in Latvia. The rooms and salons are stuffed with gilded aristocratic heirlooms and flamboyant chandeliers, but the true pièce de résistance is the made-to-order dinner menu, which caters to every guest's whim and only features locally grown organic produce.

The manor's history begins in 1530, but the lakeside peach-coloured mansion you see now is largely a product of 19th-century reconstruction. It is located near the village of Kukšas, 10km south of Kandava.

Rumene Manor   HISTORIC HOTEL €€€
(⏹6777 0966; www.rumene.lv; Rumene; ste from €250; @🖥) This sumptuous manse was originally erected in the 18th century, but had fallen into disrepair until the owners of Hotel Bergs in Rīga lovingly restored the property to its former grandeur. Several new design elements (including the awe-inducing glass ceiling in the kitchen) were added by a noted local architect, and the interior design scheme is nothing short of breathtaking (think hound's-tooth wing-back chairs, and ivory chessboard tables).

If ever you were to consider getting married in Latvia, this would be the ideal location.

Sabile

Sabile would be just another sleepy cobble-stoned Latvian village if its eccentric residents weren't on a mission to find any available method of making it unique. They tend what they claim to be the northernmost open-air vineyard, populate their squares with straw dolls and stage a carnival parade involving hilariously absurdist kinetic installations. A fascinating open-air art space is also located here. There is no particular reason to linger for long, but you can have a few hours of pure joy, especially if you arrive during the wine festival at the end of July.

◎ Sights

Pedvāle Open-Air Art Museum   MUSEUM
(Pedvāles brīvdabas mākslas muzejs; ⏹6325 2249; www.pedvale.lv; adult/child €3/2.50; ⏱10am-6pm May–mid-Oct, to 4pm mid-Oct–Apr) Across the river from Sabile the road climbs to the not-to-be-missed Pedvāle Open-Air Art Museum, located about 1.5km south of the tourist office. Founded in 1991 by Ojars Feldbergs, a Latvian sculptor, the museum showcases over 100 jaw-dropping installations on 100 hectares of rolling hills. Many of the sculptures were created by Feldbergs himself, who often collaborates with other artists from all over the globe. Every year the pieces rotate, reflecting a prevalent theme that permeates the museum's works.

LATVIA'S RARE BLUE COWS

It sounds like your classic old wives' tale: blue cows delivered from the sea by mermaids. Yet at least part of this Liv legend is true – Latvia does indeed have blue cows. About 100 of them, to be exact, making it the world's rarest breed of cow.

These curious ruminants originated in Latvia's Kurzeme region. The first ones appeared in the early 1900s. No one is sure why or how they appeared, which is why the bit about mermaids can't be completely ruled out, but their star quickly waxed as they proved remarkably resistant to cold, rain and wind – three things that Latvia has in great supply.

The blue-cow population dwindled to less than 50 in Soviet times, but began to rebound in the 1990s as geneticists realised the value in cross-breeding with these hearty beasts.

Records show that historically blue cows were found only in Liv households and never in Latvian ones. Today, you might be able to see them grazing on seafront meadows in the village of Mērsrags on the road between Jūrmala and Kolka.

Past themes have included meditations on the Earth's prime elements and time. Standout works include *Muna Muna*, a swirling sphere of TV parts; *Chair*, an enormous seat made from bright blue oil drums; and the iconic *Petriflora Pedvalensis*, a bouquet of flowers whose petals have been replaced with spiral stones. The handy orange *Pedvāle Walk* booklet plots all of the sculptures on a neatly drawn map, and provides simple captions with the artists' names. Additional pieces are on display at Sabile's former synagogue, which Feldbergs transformed into a contemporary art space.

Doll Garden
LANDMARK

Latvia's answer to the Chinese Terracotta Army can barely scare a crow, since it is entirely comprised of straw-filled unarmed civilians. A local granny, Daina Kučera, populated a small roadside garden with over 200 almost-human-sized straw dolls dressed as our contemporaries of all ages and walks of life – from school children to policemen and robbers. The author is around most of the time, guarding her work from vandals and collecting donations, which she spends on designing new dolls.

The garden is located on the main road near the main square, so you'll need a talent to miss it.

Wooden Toy Museum
MUSEUM

(☑ 26542227; Kuldīgas iela 1; ⊗ 11am-5pm Fri-Sun May-Oct) Well, this one is way cooler than just another small collection of toys from around the world. The owner, drawing teacher Andris Millers, makes mind-boggling kinetic wooden sculptures, including vehicles that each year parade during Sabile's wine

festival. With his absurdist sense of humour, Millers and his creations are a bit of a DIY Monty Python show, but you'll need a translator if you don't speak Latvian or Russian.

Some of his works are plain funny, like a device serving as a racecourse for flying snails (yay!), others come with political subtext, like ridiculing Russian president Vladimir Putin's publicity stunts.

Vīnakalns
VINEYARD

Vīnakalns (Wine Hill), located on a tiny mound just 200m from the tourist office, started operating during the 13th century and was resurrected in the 17th century by Duke Jakob of Courland. The duke's vineyard was never very productive and fell into disuse. Although operations resumed in 1936, the vineyard's focus lay in researching hardy strains of vines rather than producing high-quality wines.

The only chance to taste local wine (it's impossible to buy) is at Sabile's wine festival during the last weekend in July.

Sabile Synagogue
ARTS CENTRE

(Strauta iela 4) The modest old synagogue, which hasn't seen any services since the Jewish population perished in the Holocaust, is worth checking out, because it often houses temporary modern art exhibitions curated by the Pedvāle Open-Air Art museum.

🛏 Sleeping & Eating

Firkspedvāle Muiža
HISTORIC HOTEL €

(☑ 6325 2248; r per person €20) The on-site guesthouse at the Pedvāle Open-Air Art Museum has a handful of simply furnished rooms featuring wooden floors and rustic beams. A cafe next door dishes up satisfying food, from simple salads to hearty plates of freshly caught trout. Sit outside on the wooden terrace in summer.

For a truly unique experience, you can camp (sites €2.15 per person, May to mid-October) anywhere within the open-air museum. Uncurl your sleeping bag and watch the midnight shadows dance along the larger-than-life sculptures – we can't think of a better place in Latvia to pitch a tent.

❶ Getting There & Away

Sabile is a stop on the route connecting Kuldīga (€2, 40 minutes, hourly) with Rīga and Liepāja.

Kuldīga

POP 27,000

The lovely old Kuldīga would be a hit even if it didn't have its own Niagara of sorts, with salmon flying over its chute for good measure. Home to what Latvians brand 'the widest waterfall in Europe', Kuldīga is also the place where your immersion into the epoch of chivalry won't be spoiled by day-tripping camera-clickers – the place is simply too far from Rīga.

In its heyday, Kuldīga (or Goldingen, as its German founders called it) served as the capital of the Duchy of Courland (1596–1616), but it was badly damaged during the Great Northern War and never quite able to regain its former lustre. Today, this blast from the past is a favourite spot to shoot Latvian period-piece films.

◉ Sights & Activities

◉ Old Town

Kuldīga's Old Town orbits three town squares: the medieval square, the town-hall square and the 'new' square. The most attractive is the town-hall square, known as **Rātslaukums**; it makes a good place to start your trip. The new **town hall** (Rātslaukums 5), built in 1860 in Italian Renaissance style, is at the southern end of the square, and Kurzeme's **oldest wooden house** – built in 1670, reconstructed in 1742 and renovated in 1982 – stands here on the northern corner of Pasta iela. Further along Baznīcas iela, the unmissable German timber-framed house is known as **Duke Jakob's pharmacy**, although these days it is a residential building. Liepājas iela is Old Town's main commercial drag leading to the

New Town, its margin marked by **Teleports**, Gleb Pantelejev's striking sculpture, which physically depicts the teleportation from the medieval Kuldīga to the 21st century.

Livonian Order Castle RUIN

Cross the teeny Alekšupīte ravine to reach the site of this castle, built from 1242 to 1245, but ruined during the Great Northern War. The **Castle Watchman's House** (Pils iela 4) was built in 1735 to protect the ruins. Legend has it that the house was the site of executions and beheadings, and the stream behind the house ran red with the victims' blood. Today a lovely **sculpture garden** has been set up around the subtle ruins.

From the old castle grounds you'll have a great view of Ventas Rumba (Kuldīga Waterfall). Inside the garden, the **Goldingen Knight open-air cinema** screens fiction films and documentaries on Friday and Saturday nights in summer. For schedules, check www.kuldigasmuzejs.lv

Kuldīga Historic Museum MUSEUM

(Kuldīgas novada muzejs; www.kuldigasmuzejs.lv; Pils iela; adult/child €1/0.70; ☉ noon-6pm Tue, 10am-6pm Wed-Sun) Founded by a local German school director, the newly restored museum is housed in what local legend claims to be a Russian pavilion from the 1900 World Exhibition in Paris. Its 2nd floor has been redesigned as an apartment of a rich early 20th-century local family, which features an international playing cards collection in the 'master's room'. A cluster of Duke Jakob's cannons sits on the front lawn.

Ventas Rumba
(Kuldīga Waterfall) WATERFALL

In a country that is acutely short of verticals but rich on horizontals, landscape features appear to be blatantly two-dimensional – even waterfalls. Spanning 240m, Ventas Rumba is branded Europe's widest, but as it is hardly taller than a basketball player, it risks being dismissed by vile competitors as mere rapid, if it decides to attend an international waterfall congress. That said, it does look like a cute toy Niagara, when observed from the Kuldīga castle hill.

The vaulted arches of the old red-brick bridge make the sight all the more scenic. Now, for several weeks in spring, swarms of vimba come into the picture. In order to procreate further upstream, the fish literally jump over the waterfall in a spectacular show that draws crowds of visitors to Kuldīga. In the warm months you can play jumping

Kuldīga

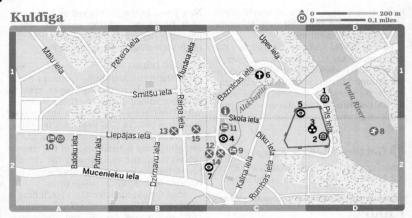

Kuldīga

vimba yourself or just bathe under the waterfalls. Across the bridge, the **Mārtiņsala recreation area** is the town's official Blue Flag beach, complete with changing rooms and sport facilities.

Religious Buildings

The Lutheran **St Katrīna's Church** (Baznīcas iela) is the place of worship for the town's largest religious denomination. Katrina (St Catherine) is Kuldīga's patron saint and protector (she's even featured on the town's coat of arms). The first church on the site was built in the 1200s, and the current incarnation dates back to Duke Jakob's rule in the mid-1600s.

Other religious buildings remain from the times when, like many places in Latvia, Kuldīga was more culturally diverse, with sizable German, Jewish and Russian communities. The opulently decorated **Holy Trinity Church**, also built on the orders of Duke Jakob, is home for a small Catholic congregation The freshly restored **Kuldīga Synagogue**, built in 1875, now houses the town's library and arts centre. Kuldīga's Jewish community was wiped out in the Holocaust. The imposing Russian Orthodox **Church of Virgin's Shroud** caters for a tiny community and only opens for an occasional service.

◎ Around Town

Several attractive **bike routes** wind their way through the dense forests around town (one of them also leads to the caves). Stop by the information centre to rent a bicycle (€7 for 24 hours) and pick up one of the six brochures detailing these trails.

Old Castle Hill   RUIN
The large old castle hill (pilskalns), 2.5km north of town on the western bank of the Venta, was the fortress of Lamekins, the Cour who ruled much of Kurzeme before the 13th-century German invasion. Legend has it that the castle – now ruined beyond recognition – was so staggeringly beautiful (glistening copper pendants hung from the roof) that invaders were reluctant to sack the structure. To get to the hill, follow Ventspils iela then Virkas iela north from the centre, and take a right at the fork in the road.

Riežupe Sand Caves
CAVES
(Smilšu alas; ☑ 6332 6236; tours per person €6; ⏱ 11am-5pm May-Oct) Located 5km outside of town along the unpaved Krasta iela, Riežupe Sand Caves feature 460m of labyrinthine tunnels that can be visited by candlelight. They're a chilly 8°C, so bring a warm sweater. The cave is accessible by car – staff at the tourist office can give directions (like most places in rural Latvia, private transport is a must if you don't want to wait five or so hours for a bus).

🛌 Sleeping

Jēkaba Sēta
GUESTHOUSE €
(☑ 28631122; www.jekabaseta.lv; Liepājas iela 36; s/d from €35/40; ℗ 🛜) This typical Latvian inn, complete with a pub, has standard-looking rooms with wooden furniture. The location is on the main drag near the edge of the Old Town, with plenty of space to park your car, which might be more problematic deeper in the centre.

Metropole
HOTEL €€
(☑ 6335 0588; www.hotel-metropole.lv; Baznīcas iela 11; s/d from €47/63; ℗ ❄ 🛜) It's a little tired and characterless but the bedrooms are clean and spacious, especially the double-decker ones overlooking pedestrian Liepājas iela and Rātslaukums. Black-and-white photos of old Kuldīga are sprinkled throughout.

★ 2 Baloži
GUESTHOUSE €€
(☑ 29152888; www.facebook.com/2balozi; Pasta iela 5; r from €45) Perched above the Alekšupīte stream, this old wooden house has newly refurbished rooms designed in the laconic Scandinavian style with lots of aged wood that creates a pleasant nostalgic ambience. The Goldingen Room restaurant across the square serves as the reception.

🍴 Eating

Kuldīga's hotels also offer decent places to grab grub. Several restaurants in town serve *rupjmaizes kārojums/kārtojums,* which translates as 'black bread mix'. The recipe for the popular dessert is over 1000 years old: Vikings would blend crumbled bread, cream and honey for an after-dinner treat. It tastes a bit like Black Forest gateau.

Stenders
LATVIAN €
(Liepājas iela 3; mains €5; ⏱ lunch & dinner) Looking like the dwelling of a forest witch, this popular bar cum cafe, housed on the 2nd storey of an 18th-century warehouse, specialises in warm potato pancakes and cool pints of Užavas. Its wooden terrace is definitely the best place in town if you want to eat or drink outdoors on a warm day.

Makkabi
CAFE €
(www.facebook.com/cafemakkabi; Liepājas iela 9; mains €4-5; ⏱ 9am-11pm) At least in the name, this smallish, tastefully designed cafe celebrates the times when the area around the synagogue was a thriving Jewish quarter. The main reason to come here is for the superb cakes and strawberry pavlova meringues, but cheapish main courses and the inevitable cold beetroot soup are also available.

★ Pagrabiņš
INTERNATIONAL €€
(Baznīcas iela 5; mains €5-15; ⏱ 11am-11pm Sun-Thu, to 3am Fri & Sat; ☑) Pagrabiņš inhabits a cellar which was once used as the town's prison. Today a combination of Latvian and Asian dishes are served under low-slung alcoves lined with honey-coloured bricks. In warmer weather, enjoy your snacks on the small verandah, which sits atop the trickling Alekšupīte stream out the back.

Goldingen Room
ITALIAN €€
(☑ 6332 0721; www.facebook.com/goldingenroom; mains €6-12; ⏱ 11am-8pm Sun-Thu, to 10pm Fri & Sat) This stylishly designed restaurant – Nordic woodwork with a pinch of Soviet nostalgia – is a reliable source of competently made pizzas and delicious antipasti. Service is patchy, however.

Bangert's
EUROPEAN €€
(☑ 29125228; www.bangerts.lv; Pils iela 1; mains €8-10) Perched on a dramatic clifftop above the Kuldīga waterfall, this upmarket restaurant has a populist penchant for exoticism, with items like deer burger and ostrich steak on the menu. But if you opt for a simple fried trout, you won't be disappointed.

ℹ Information

Post Office (Liepājas iela 34) Near Pilsētas laukums.
Tourist Information Centre (☑ 6332 2259; www.visit.kuldiga.lv; Baznīcas iela 17)

ℹ Getting There & Away

From the **bus station** (☑ 6332 2061; Stacijas iela 2), buses run to/from Rīga (€6.40, 2½ to 3½ hours, every two hours), Liepāja (€3.85 to €4.70, 1¾ hours, seven daily), Ventspils (€3, 1¼ hours, seven daily) and Alsunga (€1.60, 35 minutes, five daily).

Cape Kolka (Kolkasrags)

Enchantingly desolate and hauntingly beautiful, a journey to Cape Kolka (Kolkasrags) feels like a trip to the end of the earth. During Soviet times the entire peninsula was zoned off as a high-security military base, strictly out of bounds to civilians. The region's development was subsequently stunted and today the string of secluded coastal villages has a distinctly anachronistic feel – as though they've been locked away in a time capsule.

Slītere National Park (☑ 6329 1066; www.slitere.gov.lv) guards the last 25km of the cape, right up until Dižjūra (the Great Sea, or Baltic Sea) meets Mazjūra (the Little Sea – the Gulf of Rīga) in a great clash full of sound and fury. The park's administrative offices are in the nearby town of Dundaga (the purported birthplace of the man who inspired the film *Crocodile Dundee*), although information is also available at the Slītere Lighthouse. This towering spire acts as the gatekeeper to the park's rugged, often tundra-like expanse, home to wild deer, elk, buzzards and beaver. In mid-April, during spring migration, the Kolka peninsula sings with the calls of 60,000-odd birds and, during the summer, the park's meagre human population doubles when high-profile Rīgans escape to their holiday retreats.

Gulf Coast Road

Those with a need for speed will prefer taking the inland road through Talsi and Dundaga to reach the tip of the cape, but if you have a little extra time on your hands, try taking the slower scenic coastal road that wanders through dozens of lazy fishing villages along the Gulf of Rīga.

Break up the journey to the horn of the cape with a stop at Lake Engure Nature Park (www.eedp.lv), tucked away on the isthmus between Lake Engure and the sea. Bird-buffs can spy on over 180 types of avian, and lucky visitors might spot a wild horse or an elusive blue cow (p244).

Roja, 36km further north, is an angler's haven, and the last real 'town' (and we use that term lightly) before the quiet ride to Kolka. If you need to spend the night in town (there's that word again), the Roja Hotel (☑ 6323 2227; Jūras iela 6; r from €33), just past the harbour, is a comfortable place with run-of-the-mill motel furnishings.

Kolka

The village of Kolka is nothing to write home about, but the windswept moonscape at the waning edge of the cape (just 1km away) could have you daydreaming for days. It's here that the Gulf of Rīga meets the Baltic Sea in a very dramatic fashion. The raw, powerful effect of this desolate point was amplified by a biblical winter storm in 2005, which uprooted dozens of trees and tossed them like matchsticks onto the sandy beach, where they remain hideously entombed, roots in the air.

A monument to those claimed by treacherous waters marks the entrance to the beach near a small information centre (☑ 29149105) with varying hours. The poignant stone slab, with its haunting anthropomorphic silhouette, was erected in 2002 after three Swedes drowned in the cape's shallow but turbulent waters. One side reads, 'For people, ships and Livian earth'; the other, 'For those the sea took away'. Locals claim the cape's waters are littered with more shipwrecks than anywhere else in the Baltics. For obvious reasons, Cape Kolka's

---

THE LAST OF THE LIVS

Kurzeme is home to some of the last remaining Livs, Finno-Ugric peoples who first migrated to northern Latvia 5000 years ago. Although many Latvians are descended from this fishing tribe, less than 200 Livs remain in Latvia today, clustered in 14 fishing villages along the Baltic coast south of Cape Kolka. Hungary, Finland and Estonia also have small Liv populations, but they consider this area their homeland and return every August for the Liv Festival in Mazirbe, 18km southwest of Kolka.

While the Liv language is still taught in local elementary schools and at Tartu University in Estonia, there are fewer than 20 native speakers remaining in the world. You can learn about the Livs at the small Livonian Centre (☑ 2327 7267; ⊙ 9am-6pm Mon-Fri) behind the library on the main street in Kolka, and in a few other Kurzeme towns.

beauty is best appreciated from the safety of the sand.

Centuries ago, bonfires were lit at the cape's tip to guide sailors around the protruding sandbar. Today, the solar-powered **Kolka Lighthouse** guides vessels to safety. The shimmering scarlet tower, built in 1884, sits on an artificial island 6km offshore.

Next to the information centre, a summer-only field kitchen constantly churns out tonnes of hearty Latvian fare. There is no menu, so your lunch will largely depend on the whims of the cook. The same people run **Laimes Mājas** (☑ 20347286; www.laimesmajas.lv; r €45), which consists of sea-facing barrel-shaped houses on the top of the dune. They are quite charming, but pricey for a place with outside toilets and common showers.

In Kolka village, **Ūši** (☑ 29475692; www.kolka.info; s/d €26/35, sites per person/car €3.50/1.50; ☀) has simple but prim rooms, and a spot to pitch tents in the garden. Look for the brick guesthouse, opposite the onion-domed Orthodox church near the 'Ūši' bus stop. Bike rentals are available.

Don't leave Kolka without stopping by one of the stalls selling smoked fish. With enough charm, persistence and time, you can also arrange to partake in the process of smoking.

Baltic Coast Road

The path stretching south from Kolka towards Ventspils used to be a secret runway for Soviet aircrafts. Today, it's the widest road in Latvia, connecting a quiet row of one-street villages like a string of pearls. Time moves especially slowly here, as very little has changed over many decades. Rusty Soviet remnants occasionally dot the landscape, but they feel more like abstract art installations than reminders of harder times. The beaches' west-facing position offers unforgettable sunsets over the churning sea and stark, sandy terrain.

Elk antlers dangle from a signpost in **Vaide**, 10km southwest of Kolka, where there is little to see or do except wonder at the simple wooden houses. If the antlers spark your curiosity, there are 518 more in the **Museum of Horns & Antlers** (Ragu kolekcija; ☑ 6324 4217; ☺ 9am-8pm May-Oct). The collection, creatively arranged in an attic, is the result of one man's lifetime of work as a forest warden in the region (none are hunting trophies).

Eighteenth-century wooden buildings line the sand-paved streets in pleasant **Košrags**, 6km further along. Spend the night at **Pitagi** (☑ 29372728; www.pitagi.lv; s/d €22/29), a quaint guesthouse with beautifully furnished rooms, an on-site sauna and hearty breakfasts in the morning. Rent a bike for the day and peddle up to the cape's tip.

The gorgeous strip of dune-backed beach in neighbouring **Mazirbe**, another 4km down the coast, is home to the **Livonian People's House** (Livlist rovkuoda in Livonian), which hosts gatherings of Liv descendants and has exhibitions on their culture. An **old fishing boat cemetery** can be found by the windswept beach. It goes back to the times when Soviet border guards banned locals from using their fishing boats, because they thought people would use them to escape to Sweden. They also banned people burning old boats during solstice celebrations in June, or so the legend goes.

About 5km south of Mazirbe you will see a sign for **Slītere Lighthouse** (Slīteres bāka; ☑ 6329 1066; www.slitere.gov.lv; ☺ 10am-6pm Tue-Sun Jun-Aug), 1.4km down an even rougher track. Built in 1849, the lighthouse now functions as an information booth and lookout tower for the park. If the lighthouse is closed, have a wander down the neighbouring nature trail.

ⓘ Getting There & Around

The easiest way to reach Cape Kolka is by private vehicle, but buses are also available. To reach the town of Kolka, buses either follow the Gulf Coast road through Roja, or they ply the route through Talsi and Dundaga (inland). Either way, there are five buses that link Rīga and Kolka town per day between 4.30am and 5.15pm (€6.25, 3½ to 4¾ hours). Those travelling to/from Kuldīga, Ventspils or Liepāja must switch buses in Talsi.

SOUTHERN LATVIA (ZEMGALE)

A long snake-like strip of land between Rīga and the Lithuanian border, southern Latvia has been dubbed the 'bread basket' of Latvia for its plethora of arable lands and mythical forests. The region is known locally as Zemgale, named after the defiant Baltic Semigallian (Zemgallian) tribe who inhabited the region before the German conquest at the end of the 1200s. The Semigallians were

LATVIA SOUTHERN LATVIA (ZEMGALE)

Southern Latvia (Zemgale)

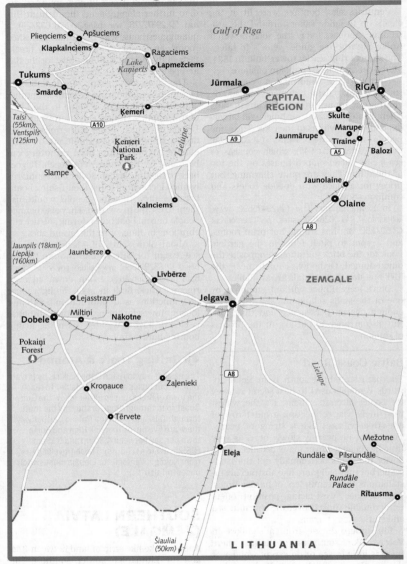

Pliencciems
Apšuciems
Klapkalnciems
Ragaciems
Lake Kanieris
Lapmežciems
Tukums
Smārde
Jūrmala
Ķemeri
Gulf of Rīga
RĪGA
CAPITAL REGION
Skulte
Marupe
Jaunmārupe
Tīraine
Balozi
A9
A5
Talsi (55km); Ventspils (125km)
A10
Ķemeri National Park
Jaunolaine
Slampe
Olaine
Kalnciems
A8
Jaunpils (18km); Liepāja (160km)
Jaunbērze
ZEMGALE
Līvbērze
Jelgava
Lejasstrazdi
Dobele
Miltiņi
Nākotne
Lielupe
Pokaiņi Forest
Kroņauce
Zaļenieki
A8
Tērvete
Mežotne
Eleja
Rundāle
Pilsrundāle
Rundāle Palace
Rītausma
Šiauliai (50km)
LITHUANIA

a valiant bunch, warding off the impending crusaders longer than any other tribe. Before retreating to Lithuania, they burned down all of their strongholds rather than surrendering them to the invaders.

From the 16th to the 18th centuries, the region (along with Kurzeme) formed part of the semi-independent Duchy of Courland, whose rulers set up shop with two mind-boggling palaces in the town of Jelgava

0 ——— 20 km
0 ——— 12 miles

Lake Baltezers
Baltezers
A2
A4
Madona (95km)
Ulbroka
Upeslejas
Saurieši
Salaspils
Ķekava
Daugava
Ogre
Baldone
Avoti
A7
Misa
Vecumnieki
Iecava
Birzes
Bārbele
Bauska
Ceraukste
Mēmele
Uzvara
Panevėžys (70km);
Vilnius (200km)

(also called Mitau) and in Rundāle, just out-side of Bauska. Today, the summer palace at Rundāle is Zemgale's star attraction, and a must-see for art and architecture buffs.

Bauska

POP 27,000

Once an important seat in the Duchy of Courland, these days Bauska is best known as the jumping-off point for the splendid Rundāle Palace. But before you do so, consider checking out the pretty little **Bauska Castle** (Bauskas pils; www.bauskaspils.lv; Pilskalns; admission free, museum adult/student €5/€2.5 May-Oct, €4/€2 Nov-Apr; ⊗9am-7pm May-Sep, to 6pm Oct, to 5pm Nov-Apr). It sits on a picturesue hillock squeezed between two rivers – Mūsa and Mēmele – that flow parallel to each other. It is actually two castles – one from the Livonian Order times, lying in ruins, and the other, built by the Duke of Courland and remaning fully intact. There is a local history exposition inside the latter.

Take a good look at the grey blocks along the facade of the new castle – they appear to be bulging out of the wall, but it's actually an optical illusion – the bottom left corner of each brick has been scraped with a chisel to trick the viewer into thinking that they are seeing a shadow.

During the 18th century an Italian by the name of Magno Cavala moved to Bauska in search of a new business venture. He was something of a casanova (and a conman), and started collecting the water at the junction of the two rivers near the castle. He claimed that the water was a pungent love potion and made a fortune scamming the poor townspeople.

To find the castle ruins from the bus station, walk towards the central round-about along Zaļā iela then branch left along Uzvaras iela for another 800m. Bauska's one-stop shopping mall at the roundabout along Rte A7 has a Rimi supermarket and a couple of decent spots to grab a meal. The **tourist office** (☑6392 3797; www.bauska.lv; Rātslaukums 1; ⊗9am-6pm Mon-Fri, to 3pm Sat) is in the main square.

ⓘ Getting There & Away

Bauska's **bus station** (Slimnīcas iela 11) offers two to three buses per hour between 6.10am and 10.40pm to/from Rīga (€3, 70 minutes to two hours).

LATVIA BAUSKA

Rundāle Palace

Built for Baron Ernst Johann Biron (1690–1772), Duke of Courland and Semigallia, Rundāle Palace (Rundāles pils; ☑ 6396 2197; www.rundale.net; whole complex/house short route/garden/short route & garden €7.20/5/2.85/5.70; ☉ 10am-5pm) is a monument to 18th-century aristocratic ostentatiousness, and rural Latvia's primo architectural highlight.

Ernst Johann started his career as a groom and lover of Anna Ioanovna, the Russian-born Duchess of Courland. She gave him the duchy when she became Russian empress, but he stayed with her in St Petersburg, turning into the most powerful political figure of the empire. In 1736 he commissoned the Italian architect Bartholomeo Rastrelli, of St Petersburg's Winter Palace fame, to construct his summer residence near Bauska.

Russian authors later blamed Biron for ushering in an era of terror, but many historians believe his role in the persecution of the nobility was exaggerated. On her death bed, the empress proclaimed Biron the Regent of Russia, but two months later his rivals arrested him and sentenced him to death by quartering. The sentence was commuted to exile. The unfinished palace stood as an empty shell for another 22 years when, pardoned by Catherine II, Ernst Johann returned home. Rastrelli resumed the construction and in 1768 the palace was finished. Ernst Johann died four years later at the age of 82. A succession of Russian nobles inhabited (and altered) the palace after the Duchy of Courland was incorporated into the Russian Empire in 1795.

The castle is divided into two halves: the East Wing was devoted to formal occasions, while the West Wing was the private royal residence. The Royal Gardens, inspired by the gardens at Versailles, were also used for public affairs. The rooms were heated by a network of 80 porcelain stoves (only six authentic stoves remain) as the castle was mostly used during the warmer months.

The palace was badly damaged in two world wars and what you see now is the result of painstaking restoration started by experts from Leningrad in 1972 and officially finished in 2015. Denifitely spend an extra €2 and opt for the 'long route' option when buying the ticket. Unlike the short route, it includes the duke's and duchess's private chambers, which is your chance to peek into the everyday life of 18th-century aristocrats as well as admire the opulent interior design. Even the duke's chamber pot adorned with a delightful painting of swimming salmon is on display.

Like any good castle, Rundāle has loads of eerie ghost tales, but the most famous spectre that haunts the palace grounds is the 'White Lady'. In the 19th century the royal doctor had a young daughter who was courted by many men, but on her 18th birthday she suddenly grew ill and died. Obsessed with her untimely demise, the doctor kept her corpse in his laboratory to study her and tried to figure out why she was ravaged by illness (or was she poisoned by a lovelorn suitor?). Unable to rest eternally, the daughter's spirit began haunting the castle and cackling wildly in the middle of the night. During Rundāle's restorations, several art historians and masons heard her wicked laughter and brought in a priest to exorcise the grounds.

🛏 Sleeping & Eating

Balta Māja B&B €
(☑ 6396 2140; www.kalpumaja.lv; r from €22) The 'White House' is a quaint B&B and cafe sitting in the palace's Tudor-style servants' quarters near the entrance to the grounds. Salads and meat platters are prepped in the kitchen, and the bedrooms are cluttered with wool duvets and agrarian antiques.

★ Mežotne Palace HISTORIC HOTEL €€€
(☑ 6396 0711; www.mezotnespils.lv; Mežotne; s/d from €72/80) Live like Duke Ernst Johann and check into Mežotne Palace, about 2km from Rundāle. The palace was built in a classical style from 1797 to 1802 for Charlotte von Lieven, the governess of Russian empress Catherine II's grandchildren. After many years in disrepair, it was restored in 2001 and transformed into a hotel and restaurant.

A handful of rooms are open to the public for a small fee, although a visit to Mežotne isn't worth the trek if you aren't sleeping over or eating at the popular restaurant. Rooms are stocked with aristocratic collectibles – think cast-iron bed frames, swinging chandeliers and carefully chosen antiques.

Rundāle Palace Restaurant CAFETERIA €
(mains €3-7) Located in the palace basement, this is a convenient spot for a quick bite. Most of the food is of the Latvian persuasion.

ℹ Getting There & Away

From Bauska (12km away) there are hourly buses to Rundāle Palace (€0.90 to €1.75) between 6am and 7.30pm. Make sure you get off at Pilsrundāle, the villlage before Rundāle.

Dobele & Around

POP 27,000

Provincial Dobele, in the far western corner of Zemgale, is the gateway to a vast acreage of mythical forests and meandering rivers. The town is centred around the impressive Livonian Order castle ruins, which date back to the mid-1330s. This brick bastion was built over the original site of an earlier Semigallian stronghold. In 1289 the Semigallians incinerated their own castle and fled to Lithuania rather than surrendering the structure to the invading crusaders. A monument in town commemorates their departure.

Another attraction that draws throngs of visitors in spring is the massive gardens of the Latvia Institute of Fruit Growing (www.lvai.lv; Graudu St 1; adult/student €2/1.50; ⊙9am-7pm Mon-Fri). Its apricot, cherry and plum orchards, as well the country's largest collection of lilacs, are the legacy of Pēteris Upītis, an outstanding gardener, who founded an experimental farm here in 1945. The gardens come with a museum telling his life story.

Tērvete

Even in its very centre, the town of Tērvete looks like a few buildings scattered around hilly forested terrain. In recent years it grew into a haunt for holidaying families and school excursions. The main pull is the Fairy Tale Forest, populated by whimsical wood-carved figures that almost come alive in the dark shade of ancient fir trees. There are two main clusters. One is dedicated to the characters of Latvian fairy tales, another – the Dwarfs' Town – is a toy village complete with log houses and a mill, where children can play dwarfs (while you can play a busy Snow White).

A witch lives in the park during the summer, entertaining the little ones with games and potions. If weather permits, you can

also go for a swim in a lake at the far end of the forest. The area can be explored on foot, aboard a park train (€0.75 for one stop) or by bicycle, available for rent at the entrance. The Zemgallian fest, which involves a craftsmen fair and lots other fun, is held every second week of August.

The gateway to Fairy Tale Forest doubles as the information centre of its parent organisation, Tērvete Nature Park (☑6372 6212; www.latvia.travel/en/tervete-nature-park; adult/child €3.50/2.50; ⊙9am-7pm), which protects three ancient mounds, including the impressive Tērvete Castle Mound that was abandoned by the Semigallians after several battles with the Livonian Order. Nearby Klosterhill was first inhabited over 3000 years ago by Semigallian ancestors, and Swedish Hill was constructed by the Livonian Order in the 13th century.

There are around seven buses a day from Dobele bus station to Tērvete (€1.15, 30 minutes).

Pokaiņi Forest

Located 16km southwest of Dobele, on the way to Īle, the Pokaiņi Forest Reserve (www.mammadaba.lv; adult/child €2/1.7; ⊙toll booth 10am-7pm) is one of Latvia's biggest unsolved mysteries. In the mid-'90s a local historian discovered subtle stone cairns throughout the park and realised that the rocks had been transported to the forest from faraway destinations. Historians have theorised that Pokaiņi was an ancient sacred ground used in proto-pagan rituals over 2000 years ago. Volunteer efforts have helped create walking trails through the reserve, which is often visited by healers and New Age types. Ask at the toll booth for available tour guides.

Pokaiņi Forest is best reached by car or bicycle. There are two buses daily from Dobele bus station (€0.8, 20 minutes) bound for Īle, which stop at the turn to the visitor centre. Their schedule allows people to spend just over an hour in the forest.

Jaunpils

The small but perfectly medieval Jaunpils Castle (☑6310 7082; www.jaunpilspils.lv; ⊙museum 11am-6pm Mon-Thu, 10am-8pm Fri-Sun) is unique in the fact that it has largely retained its original look since 1301, when it was founded by the master of the Livonian Order, Gotfried von Roga. It also offers a unique chance to dine and sleep in the rooms that saw kings and knights do the same before your great-grandparents were born.

For four centuries until the break-up of the Russian Empire in 1917, it was the home of the German baron family von der Recke. Its walls remember a sword fight between Mathias von der Recke and Swedish king Charles IX. It was a friendly one, apparently, for which the king awarded the baron with a silver helmet and a sword.

Jaunpils Castle Hotel (☑ 29442539; www.jaunpilspils.lv; Jaunpils Pils; r €125) has four rooms, with brick floors, baldachin-covered beds and a real fireplace. They are often booked for weddings during the weekend, so your best chance to get in is on weekdays. The 'medieval tavern' in the castle premises serves quality Latvian fare.

Jaunpils is 20km from Dobele and 8km from the Rīga–Liepāja road, so it's not a problem reaching it by car from any of these three destinations. A single daytime bus to Jaunpils leaves Dobele (€1.70) at 4.40pm (recheck time on www.autoosta.lv). There are no direct buses to Rīga.

❶ Getting There & Away

Dobele is easily accessible by bus to/from Rīga (€3.25, 1½ hours, at least hourly).

NORTHEASTERN LATVIA (VIDZEME)

When Rīga's urban hustle fades into a pulsing hum of chirping crickets, you've entered northeastern Latvia. Known as Vidzeme, or 'the Middle Land', to locals, the country's largest region is an excellent sampler of what Latvia has to offer. Forest folks can hike, bike or paddle through the thicketed terrain of Gauja National Park, ski bums can tackle bunny slopes in the uplands and history buffs will be sated with a generous sprinkling of castles throughout.

Vidzeme Coast

Vidzeme's stone-strewn coast is usually seen from the car – or bus – window by travellers on the Via Baltica (Rte A1) en route to Rīga or Tallinn. Those who stop for a closer look will uncover a desolate strand of craggy cliffs and pebble beaches carved from eons of pounding waves.

Buses north from Rīga to Pärnu and Tallinn travel along Vidzeme's coastal road, usually stopping in Ainaži before touching the border.

Saulkrasti

Saulkrasti, a quick 44km jaunt from the capital, is a closely guarded secret among Latvians. While tourists and Russian jetsetters make a beeline for ritzy Jūrmala, locals gingerly tiptoe up the coast for a day trip in the other direction. They get rewarded with a stunning white-sand beach and sea that, unlike in Jūrmala, gets deep enough to swim before you walk all the way to Sweden. The lack of a tourism infrastructure is as refreshing as the salty breeze, so you'd better come quick before the other tourists catch on.

Like Jūrmala, Saulkrasti is really several holiday villages skewed on the railway line. For the most beautiful stretch of the beach, get off the train at Pabaži station. The word 'Saulkrasti' means Sunny Coast, which makes the place a northern twin of Costa del Sol.

◉ Sights

Baltā Kapā   VIEWPOINT
(White Dune) The striking pine-covered cliff looms above a pristine white-sand beach bisected by a glistening stream. This is one of the most enchanting places along the entire Latvian coast, which famously stunned Russian empress Catherine II, who once stopped here for a swim. Originating here, a trail runs for 3km north through the pine forest along the ridge of the dune. Baltā Kapā is 700m from Inčupe station and 2km from Pabaži station.

Bicycle Museum   MUSEUM
(www.velomuseum.lv; Rīgas iela 44a; ⏱ 10am-6pm) Exhausted by the sun? A good respite from the beach boredom is this lovely collection of retro bicycles, including a 130-year-old specimen assembled in Latvia. Non-retro bikes are available for rent at €10 for 24 hours.

🛏 Sleeping & Eating

A day trip from Rīga with a picnic pack is the best strategy for Saulkrasti. If that's your plan, do stop by the food stall at the end of Stacias ilea that leads from Pabaži station to the beach. Here, elderly ladies sell delicious grilled chicken and blackberries or wild strawberries, depending on seasons. Worthy places to stay and eat are sadly miles away from the best stretch of the beach.

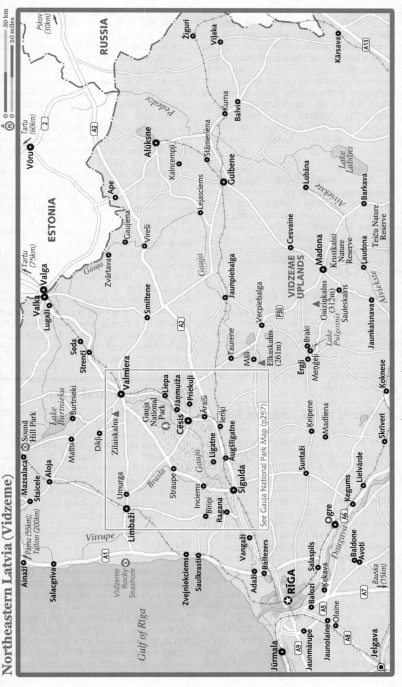

Northeastern Latvia (Vidzeme)

30 km
20 miles

RUSSIA

Pskov
(30km)

Žiguri

Vilaka

Kārsava

A13

ESTONIA

Tartu
(60km)

2

A2

Vōru

Ape

Gaujiena

Kurna

Balvi

Lubāna

Lake
Lubāns

Pēdede

Alūksne

Kalncempji

Stāmeriena

Gulbene

Barkava

Valka

Valga

Tartu
(75km)

Gauja

Zvārtava

Vireši

Lejasciems

Aviekste

Teiču Nature
Reserve

Laudona

Cesvaine

VIDZEME
UPLANDS

Madona

Krustkalni
Nature
Reserve

Gaiziņkalns
(312m)

Saulekalns

Jaunkalsnava

Skrīveri

Smiltene

Gauja

Jaunpiebalga

Vecpiebalga

A2

Taurene

Māli

Elkaskalns
(261m)

Ērgļi

Mengeļi

Braki

Lake
Pulgosnis

P30

Koknese

Seda

Strenči

Valmiera

Liepa

Priekuļi

Jāņmuiža

Cēsis

Āraiši

Ieriķi

Ligatne

Augšligatne

Sigulda

Keipene

Madliena

Suntaži

Lielvārde

Kegums

Ogre

A6

Skrīveri

Lake
Burtnieku

Burtnieki

Matīši

Dikļi

Zilaiskalns

Gauja
National
Park

Gauja

Inciems

Brasla

Straupe

Birini

Ragana

See Gauja National Park Map (p257)

Sound
Hill Park

Mazsalaca

Staicele

Aloja

Umurga

Limbaži

Vangaži

Balte zers

Adaži

RĪGA

Salaspils

Ķekava

Baldone

Avoti

Bauska
(15km)

A7

Vitrupe

Ainaži

Pārnu (55km);
Tallinn (200km)

Salacgrīva

Zvejniekciems

Saulkrasti

A1

Vidzeme
Rocky
Shore

Gulf of Riga

Jūrmala

Jaunmārupe

A9

Jaunolaine

Olaine

A8

Jelgava

A5

Baloži

Porto Resort
RESORT €

(☑ 22722258; www.portoresort.lv; Medzābaki-2, Lilaste, Carnikava novads; r with/without bathroom from €35/25) You have a choice of walking about a kilometre to the sea or plunging into the lake right near your porch in this lovely rustic-styled resort in the village of Lilaste, occupying a picturesque isthmus between a lake and the sea 6km south of Saulkrasti proper. The excellent on-site restaurant is the place to try local lampreys (little eels).

The downside is the location by the main road.

Jūras Priede
CAMPGROUND €

(☑ 27008353; www.juraspriede.lv; Ūpes iela 56a, Zvejniekciems; tent sites per person €5, caravan parking €15, log cabins from €30) Pitch your tent, park your caravan or rent a log house right on the beach in Zvejniekciems, at the northern end of Saulkrasti. There is a cafe on the premises. It's near the main road, but Zvejniekciems railway station is a good 5km away.

ⓘ Getting There & Away

Saulkrasti stretches along the Skulte railway line. Coming from Rīga, the first station is Inčupe, followed by Pabaži (convenient for the beach), Saulkrasti and Zvejniekciems at the northern end. Trains to/from Rīga run at least hourly (€2.20, one hour). Travelling by car, get on the Tallinn highway (Rte E67) and look out for the Saulkrasti exit.

Saulkrasti to the Estonian Border

After Saulkrasti, the Vidzeme coast is a silent stretch of windswept dunes dotted with the occasional lonely guesthouse. The **Vidzeme Rocky Seashore** (☑ 29464686), halfway between Saulkrasti and Salacgrīva, is a scenic spot to stretch your legs. The 14km expanse of protected parkland has rippled sands undulating between tiny capes and caverns. The park's highlight is the **Veczemju Red Cliffs**, a sandstone outcropping crinkled by jagged grottoes. The entire crag has an ethereal reddish hue.

The coast's most substantial town, **Salacgrīva** sits on a harbour at the mouth of the Salaca River. During the summer, one of Latvia's largest music festivals, **Positivus** (www.positivusfestival.lv), takes place among the pines here. It's still a blink-or-you'll-miss-it type of place, but not really worth going out of your way to visit, but if you're hungry on the way to Estonia

it makes a good lunch stop. **Žejnieku Sēta** (☑ 29624153; Rīgas iela 1; mains €7-12; ⏱ 11am-11pm) is a friendly seafood restaurant with a pleasing, old-time nautical vibe – creaky wood floors, a fishing boat moored outside and nets draped across the terrace.

Salacgrīva is also the headquarters for the **North Vidzeme Biosphere Reserve** (☑ 6407 1408; Rīgas iela 10a; ⏱ 8.30am-5pm), a pristine 4500-sq-km domain that is roughly 6% of Latvia's total land share and inscribed in Unesco's 'Man and the Biosphere' program. The vast reserve is best uncovered on a canoeing or cycling adventure. Each year in autumn, visitors can fish from a small bridge for lampreys. The bridge is washed away during the spring thaw and rebuilt each summer. Stop by the **tourist office** (☑ 6404 1254; Rīgas iela 10a; ⏱ 10am-6pm Mon-Fri, 10am-4pm Sat) and ask the friendly staff for details on local outfitters.

The former shipbuilding town of **Ainaži** (derived from the Liv word *annagi*, meaning 'lonely') is 1km south of Estonia. Its only attraction is the old naval academy, now home to the **Naval School Museum** (☑ 6404 3349; Valdemāra iela 45; adult/student €1.14/€0.57; ⏱ 10am-5pm Wed-Sun). This mildly interesting museum exhibits the naval academy's history and the history of shipbuilding along the Vidzeme coast.

Gauja National Park

A stunning stretch of virgin pines, this national park (www.gnp.gov.lv) extends from castle-strewn Sigulda to quiet Valmiera, passing industrial Līgatne and picture-perfect Cēsis along the way. Founded in 1973, Latvia's first national park protects a very leafy hinterland popular for hiking, biking, backcountry camping, canoeing and a slew of offbeat adrenaline sports. There is no entrance fee for Gauja National Park.

Sigulda
POP 17,800

With a name that sounds like a mythical ogress, it comes as no surprise that the gateway to the Gauja is an enchanting spot with delightful surprises tucked behind every dappled tree. Locals proudly call their town the 'Switzerland of Latvia,' but if you're expecting the majesty of a mountainous snow-capped realm, you'll be rather disappointed. Instead, Sigulda mixes its own brew of scenic

Gauja National Park

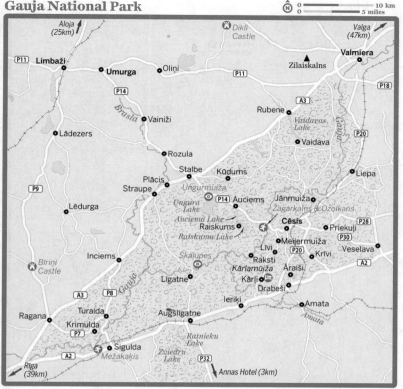

trails, extreme sports and 800-year-old castles steeped in legends.

◉ Sights

Sigulda sprawls between its three castles, with most of the action occurring on the east side of the Gauja River near Sigulda New Castle. Take your own walking tour for an abridged version of Sigulda's greatest hits, and don't forget to take a ride on the **cable car** (☏29212731; Poruka iela 14; one way adult/child €5/4; ⊗10am-6.30pm Jun-Aug, to 4pm Sep-May) across the valley for an awesome aerial perspective.

★ **Turaida Museum Reserve** CASTLE, MUSEUM (Turaidas muzejrezervāts; ☏6797 1402; www. turaida-muzejs.lv; Turaidas iela 10; adult/child €5/1.14; ⊗9am-8pm May-Sep, to 7pm Oct, 10am-5pm Nov-Apr) Turaida means 'God's Garden' in ancient Livonian, and this green knoll capped with a fairy-tale castle is certainly a heavenly place. The red-brick castle with its tall cylindrical tower was built in 1214 on the site of a Liv stronghold. A museum inside the castle's 15th-century granary offers an interesting account of the Livonian state from 1319 to 1561, and additional exhibitions can be viewed in the 42m-high Donjon Tower, and the castle's western and southern towers.

The rest of the reserve features a variety of buildings that have been transformed into small galleries and exhibits. It's worth stopping by the smith house where you can try forging metal. There is a real blacksmith on hand who rents out the space from the reserve – he sells his crafts, and guests can try pounding Liv pagan symbols into small chunks of iron.

In the graveyard of the pretty wooden church (1750) is the grave of Maija Roze (p259), an ill-fated beauty known as the 'Rose of Turaida' and the subject of a romantic

Sigulda

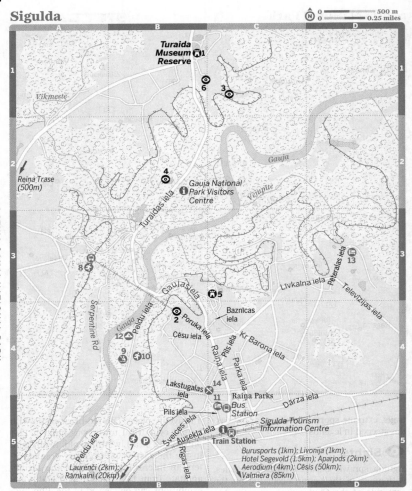

folk story. Look for the onyx headstone bearing the inscription 'Turaidas Roze 1601–1620'.

The nearby **Daina Hill Song Garden** is dotted with sculptures dedicated to epic Latvian heroes immortalised in the *dainas*, poetic folk songs which are a major Latvian tradition.

Sigulda New Castle
CASTLE

(Siguldas jaunā pils; Pils iela 16) This neo-Gothic manor house was built in 1878 as the home of Russian prince Dimitri Kropotkin, the man responsible for turning Sigulda into a tourist haven. It now houses Sigulda district council and is not open to the public, but you can wander through the grounds.

Gūtmaņa Cave
CAVE

The largest erosion cave in the Baltic is most famous for its role in the tragic legend of the Rose of Turaida. Most tourists visit to peruse the inordinate amount of graffiti spread along the walls – some of it dates back to the 16th century – apparently eagle eyes have found the coats of arms of long-gone hunters. Some believe that the stream water flowing out of the cave has a magical blend of minerals that remove facial wrinkles (it didn't work for us).

Sigulda

🏃 Activities

If you're looking to test your limits with a bevy of adrenaline-pumping activities, then you've come to the right place. The bobsled track is for the bravest, but those looking for something more subdued will enjoy hiking and cycling trails through the national park's shady pines, or canoeing down the lazy Gauja River.

High-Adrenaline Sports

Bobsled Track   ADVENTURE SPORTS
(Bob trase; ☎ 6797 3813; www.bobtrase.lv; Šveices iela 13; ☉ noon-5pm Sat & Sun) Sigulda's 1200m bobsled track was built for the Soviet team. In winter you can fly down the 16-bend track at 80km/h in a five-person Vučko **soft bob** (€10 per person, from October to mid-March), or book in for the real Olympian experience on the hair-raising **taxi bob** (€15 per person, from November to mid-March). Summer speed fiends can ride a wheeled **summer bob** (€15 per person, from May to September).

Aerodium   ADVENTURE SPORTS
(☎ 28384400; www.aerodium.lv; 2min weekday/weekend €33/37) The one-of-a-kind aerodium is a giant wind tunnel that propels participants up into the sky as though they were flying. Instructors can get about 15m high, while first-timers usually rock out at about 3m. To find the site, look for the sign along the A2 highway, 4km west of Sigulda.

Even though you will only be airborne for a couple of minutes, there is a brief introductory course, so allow a full hour; book in advance.

Cable Car Bungee Jump   ADVENTURE SPORTS
(☎ 28383333; www.bungee.lv; Poruka iela 14; bungee jump from €40; ☉ 6.30pm, 8pm & 9.30pm Wed-Sun Apr-Oct) Take your daredevil shenanigans to the next level with a 43m bungee jump from the bright-orange cable car that glides over the Gauja River. For an added thrill, jump naked.

Tarzāns Adventure Park   ADVENTURE SPORTS
(Piedzīvojumu Parks Tarzāns; ☎ 27001187; www.tarzans.lv; Peldu iela 1; adult/child combo €32/22, toboggan €3/1.50, ropes course €17/10; ☉ 10am-8pm May-Oct) Head here to swish down a toboggan track or monkey around on the

---

THE ROSE OF TURAIDA

Sigulda's local beauty, Maija Roze (May Rose), was taken into Turaida Castle as a little girl when she was found among the wounded after a battle in the early 1600s. She grew into a famous beauty and was courted by men from far and wide, but her heart belonged to Viktors, a humble gardener at nearby Sigulda Medieval Castle. They would meet in secret at Gūtmaņa Cave, halfway between the two castles.

One day, a particularly desperate soldier among Maija Roze's suitors lured her to the cave with a letter forged in Viktors' handwriting. When Maija Roze arrived, the soldier set his kidnapping plan in motion. Maija Roze pleaded with the soldier and offered to give him the scarf from around her neck in return for her freedom. She claimed it had magical protective powers, and to prove it, she told him to swing at her with his sword. It isn't clear whether or not she was bluffing or if she really believed in the scarf – either way, the soldier duly took his swing and killed the beauty.

The soldier was captured, convicted and hanged for his crime. Court documents have been uncovered, proving that the tale was in fact true. Today, a small stone memorial commemorates poor Maija Roze, the Rose of Turaida.

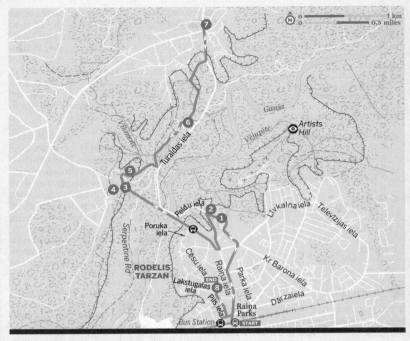

Walking Tour
Castles Day Trip

START SIGULDA TRAIN STATION
END KAĶU MĀJA
DISTANCE 6.6KM; 5½ HOURS

If you're short on time, or visiting Sigulda on a day trip, the town's three main castle reserves and one legendary cave can be easily tackled in an afternoon.

From the train station, walk down Raiņa iela and linden-lined Pils iela until you reach ❶ **Sigulda New Castle** (p258), built on the orders of Russian prince Dimitri Kropotkin, who developed Sigulda as a resort town. He was killed by a revolutionary terrorist in 1879, when the construction commenced. Check out the ruins of ❷ **Sigulda Medieval Castle** around the back, which was constructed in 1207 by the Order of the Brethren of the Sword, but was severely damaged in the 18th century during the Great Northern War. Follow Poruka iela to the rocky precipice and take the ❸ **cable car** (p257) over the scenic river valley to ❹ **Krimulda Manor**,

an elegant estate currently used as a rehabilitation clinic.

After exploring the grounds, check out the crumbling ruins of ❺ **Krimulda Medieval Castle** nearby, then follow Serpentine Rd down to ❻ **Gūtmaņa Cave** (p258). Immortalised by the legend of the Rose of Turaida, it's the largest erosion cave in the Baltic. Take some time to read the myriad inscriptions carved into the walls then head up to the ❼ **Turaida Museum Reserve** (p257). The medieval castle was erected in the 13th century for the Archbishop of Rīga over the site of an ancient Liv stronghold.

Climb the tower for sweeping views of Gauja National Park, then spend some time exploring the grounds, filled with whimsical sculptures depicting Latvian fairy-tale characters. When you are castled out, catch bus 12 back to Sigulda bus station. From there, walk back along Pils iela to ❽ **Kaķu Māja** (p263) for a filling Latvian dinner or coffee with fresh pastry from its on-site bakery.

'Tarzan' ropes course. There's also a chairlift (€1), tube-sliding (€1), reverse bungee (€6), giant swing (€6), climbing wall (€1.50) and archery (€2).

Mežakaķis ADVENTURE SPORTS
(☑6797 6886; www.kakiskalns.lv; Senču iela 1; adult/child €17/9.50; ☺11am-10pm daily Jul & Aug, Tue-Sun May, Jun & Sep, Sat & Sun Apr) This small adventure park has a ropes course with 77 obstacles split into six graded routes, geared towards everyone from children to daredevils and pros. In winter you'll find ski slopes to tackle.

Hiking & Cycling

Sigulda is prime hiking territory, so bring your walking shoes. A popular (and easy) route is the 40-minute walk from Krimulda Castle to Turaida Museum Reserve via Gūtmaņa Cave and Viktors' Cave. Or you can head south from Krimulda and descend to Little Devil's Cave and Big Devil's Cave, cross the river via a footbridge, and return to Sigulda (about two hours). Note the black walls in Big Devil's Cave, which are believed to be from the fiery breath of a travelling demon that took shelter here to avoid the sunlight.

East of Sigulda, try the well-marked loop that joins Peter's Cave, Satezele Castle Mound and Artists' Hill; it starts from behind the Līvkalni hotel and takes about 1½ hours. The panoramic view of Turaida Castle and the Gauja River valley from Artists' Hill is spectacular.

Many outfitters around Sigulda offer bicycle and mountain-bike rentals costing around €15 per day. Try Burusports (☑6797 2051; www.burusports.lv; Mazā Gāles iela 1; ☺noon-8pm Mon, 10am-8pm Tue-Sat), Reiņa Trase (☑29272255; www.reinatrase.lv; Krimulda pagasts; ☺2pm-midnight Mon-Thu, to 1am Fri, 10am-1am Sat, 9am-11pm Sun), Rāmkalni (☑6797 7277; www.ramkalni.lv; nčukalna pagasts; ☺9am-10pm) or Makars Tourism Bureau (p261). Brochures detailing cycling and hiking routes are available at the tourist office.

Canoeing & Boating

Floating down the peaceful Gauja River is a great way to observe this pristine area and have a couple of wildlife encounters (if you're lucky). There are camping grounds all along the stretch of river from Sigulda to Cēsis. Team up with one of the outfitters within the national park that organises boat trips along the Gauja, or you can just head upstream, hop into an innertube, and float back to town.

On the banks of the river in Sigulda, Makars Tourism Bureau (☑29244948; www. makars.lv; Peldu iela 2) arranges one- to three-day water tours in two- to four-person boats from Sigulda, Līgatne, Cēsis and Valmiera, ranging in length from 3km to 85km. Tours cost between €30 and €180 per boat including equipment, transport between Sigulda

LATVIA GAUJA NATIONAL PARK

DON'T MISS

PIRTS

Cast modesty aside and indulge in Latvia's most Latvian tradition, the *pirts*. A *pirts* is Latvia's version of the sauna, and while somewhat similar to the Finnish sauna, there are many elements that set this sweaty experience apart. A traditional *pirts* is run by a sauna master, who cares for her attendees while performing choreographed branch beatings that feel almost shamanistic in nature. Yes, you read that correctly – while lying down in your birthday suit, the sauna master swishes branches in the air to raise the humidity then lightly beats a variety of wildflowers and branches over your back and chest while you rest. *Pirts* also tend to be much hotter and more humid than their Finnish counterparts – a branch-beating session usually lasts around 15 minutes before one exits the sauna to jump in a nearby body of water (lake, pond or sea). The aroma of the sauna is also very important – sauna masters take great care to create a melange of herbs and spices to accent the air. In general, an afternoon at a *pirts* involves multiple sweat sessions interspersed with leaps in cool water – beer, herbal tea and snacks are a must.

All traditional saunas are in the countryside; most can be found at private cottages. If you are interested in trying out one for yourself, then head to Hotel Sigulda or Hotel Ezeri (p263) – they offer private sessions at an elegantly crafted local *pirts*. An afternoon sweat (around three hours) with plenty of tea and snacks costs €100 for two people.

and the tour's starting point, and camp-site fees for up to four people. Tents, sleeping bags and life jackets can also be rented for a nominal fee. Rāmkalni (p261) also rents out boating equipment.

✨ Festivals & Events

Sigulda Opera Festival　　　MUSIC
(www.opersvetki.lv) The romantic Sigulda Castle ruins serve as a backdrop for the country's best opera festival.

🛏 Sleeping

If all of the hotels are full, ask the tourist office about finding a room in a private home or renting your own apartment. Check Sigulda's official website, www.tourism.sigulda.lv, for additional lodging info.

Kempings Siguldas Pludmale　CAMPGROUND €
(☑ 29244948; www.makars.lv; Peldu iela 2; sites per person/tent/car/caravan €5/3/3/6; ☺ mid-May–mid-Sep) Pitch your tent in the grassy camping area beside the sandy beach along the Gauja. The location is perfect; however, there's only one men's and one women's bathroom for the scores of campers. Two-person tents can be hired for €4.50 per day. There's a second camping area up the river in Līgatne that's owned and operated by Makars as well. Ask at this location for directions.

Aparjods　　　　　　HOTEL €€
(☑ 6797 2230; www.aparjods.lv; Ventas iela 1; s/d from €43/57; @ 🛜) Tucked behind the glowing lights of Hesburger on the main road, Aparjods is a rather charming complex of barn-like structures with wooden doors and reed-and-shingle roofing. The rooms aren't

---

DON'T MISS

MUIŽAS OF THE GAUJA

Beyond the park's four main towns, there are plenty of hidden treasures tucked deep within the Gauja region. If you have a little extra time, try checking out these gems, particularly the area's *muižas* (manor houses).

Ungurmuiža (☑ 29424757; www.ungurmuiza.lv; adult/child €3/2; ☺ 10am-6pm Tue-Sun mid-May–Oct) Beautiful Ungurmuiža is one of the best preserved manor houses in all of Latvia. The stately red mansion was created by Baron von Campenhousen, who served under the Swedish king and Russian tsar. Descendants of the baron lived here until WWII, when the government swiftly seized the property. It was, rather miraculously, kept in mint condition and today the delicate mural paintings and original doors are a delightful throwback to aristocratic times. Tours can be easily arranged for €35 per group.

Bīriņi Castle (Bīriņu pils; ☑ 6402 4033; www.birinupils.lv; admission €4) Like a big pink birthday cake sitting on a verdant lawn, Bīriņi Castle governs a scenic tract of land overlooking a tranquil lake. Located on the northwestern edges of the Gauja towards Saulkrasti, the baronial estate has been transformed into an opulent hotel swathed in a Renaissance style focused around the grand foyer staircase. Daytime visitors can still reap the benefits on a guided tour (€15), or by taking in the lovely scenery with a picnic or a boat ride. Operating hours can be erratic (especially in the summer when there's a wedding every week). Call first and make a reservation to avoid difficulties.

Dikli Castle (Diķu pils; ☑ 6402 7480; www.diklupils.lv; d from €60) It was here, in 1864, that a priest organised Latvia's first Song Festival, which gives Dikli Castle an important place in the nation's history. This aristocratic manor has been transformed into a luxurious retreat with hotel rooms and spa services. Visitors can also enjoy strolls in the 20-hectare park and boat rides; tours detailing the history and restoration of the manor are also available.

Annas Hotel (☑ 6418 0700; www.annashotel.com; apt from €115; 🛜) Originally built in the middle of the 18th century as Annas Muiža, Annas Hotel is a modern inn that fuses historical charm with thoroughly modern motifs. There's not much to do around the property, because it's all about relaxation, and the hotel provides just that – spa sessions, and lovely grounds peppered with trees and ponds.

as characterful, but are still among the cosier options in town. The hotel is located 1.5km southwest of town.

Hotel Segevold   HOTEL €€
(☑ 6797 4848; www.hotelsegevold.lv; Mālpils iela 4b; d €50; @ 🛜) After entering the swankified lobby, you'll immediately forget that Segevold is bizarrely located in the heart of an industrial park – the futuristic lighting and giant tentacle-like reliefs starkly contrast the grungy Soviet tractors around the corner. Upstairs, the rooms are noticeably less glam, but they're in mint condition and kept pathologically clean.

Līvkalni   B&B €€
(☑ 22825739; livkalnisigulda@gmail.com; Pēteralas iela 2; r from €45; P ✳ 🛜) No place is more romantically rustic than this idyllic retreat next to a pond on the forest's edge. The rooms are pine-fresh and sit among a campus of adorable thatch-roof manors.

Hotel Sigulda   HOTEL €€
(☑ 6797 2263; www.hotelsigulda.lv; Pils iela 6; d from €50; @ 🛜) Right in the centre of town, this is the oldest hotel in Sigulda – it was built by the Russian baron who had dreams of turning the little hamlet into an exciting tourist destination. While the old stone-and-brick facade is quite charming, the rooms are standard issue and rather plain. The friendly family that owns Hotel Sigulda also runs the more luxurious **Hotel Ezeri** (☑ 6797 3009; www.hotelezeri.com; d from €75) several kilometres outside of town. Ask about their unique sauna experience.

✖ Eating & Drinking

Most of Sigulda's hotels and guesthouses have a small restaurant attached. Options are surprisingly dismal considering this is one of the most popular destinations in Latvia beyond Rīga.

Kaķu Māja   LATVIAN €
(www.cathouse.lv; Pils iela 8; mains around €3; ☺ 8am-11pm) A top spot for a cheap bite, the 'Cat's House' has pick-and-point bain-marie meals and an attached bakery with pastries, pies and cakes. On Friday and Saturday nights, the restaurant in the back busts out the disco ball and morphs into a nightclub until 2am.

Aparjods   INTERNATIONAL €€
(Ventas iela 1; mains €10-28; ☺ noon-10pm) Aparjods' elegant restaurant gets a special mention for its delectable assortment of cuisine served among charming clutters of household heirlooms and gold-embroidered seating. A roaring fire warms the dark-wood dining room in winter, while tables spill out onto the patio during summer. The upmarket atmosphere tends to attract an older clientele.

❶ Information

Sigulda Tourism Information Centre (☑ 6797 1335; www.tourism.sigulda.lv; Ausekļa iela 6; ☺ 9am-6pm; 🛜) Located within the train station, this extremely helpful centre has stacks of information about activities and accommodation.

Gauja National Park Visitors Centre (☑ 26657661; www.gnp.lv; Turaida iela 2a; ☺ 9am-7pm) Sells maps to the park, town and cycle routes nearby.

❶ Getting There & Away

Buses trundle the 50-odd kilometres between Sigulda's bus station and Rīga (€2.15, one hour, every 30 minutes between 8am and 10.30pm).

One train per hour (between 6am and 9pm) travels the Rīga–Sigulda–Cēsis–Valmiera line. Fares from Sigulda include Rīga (€2.35, one or 1¼ hours), Līgatne (€70, 10 minutes) and Cēsis (€2, 40 minutes).

❶ Getting Around

Sigulda's attractions are quite spread out and after a long day of walking, bus 12 will become your new best friend. It plies the route to/from Sigulda New Castle, Turaida Castle and Krimulda Manor hourly during business hours (more on weekends).

Līgatne

Deep in the heart of the Gauja National Park, little Līgatne is a twilight zone of extremes. The town's collection of hideous industrial relics sprouts up from a patchwork of picturesque pine forests and cool blue rivulets. Its two main attractions highlight its bewildering dualism.

◉ Sights

Līgatne Nature Trails   NATURE RESERVE
(☑ 6415 3313; www.gnp.lv; adult/child €3.60/2.10; ☺ 9am-6pm) It's a cross between a nature park and a zoo, where elk, beaver, deer, bison, lynx and wild boar roam in sizable open-air enclosures in the forest (it feels like an open-air zoo). A 5.1km motor circuit and a network of footpaths link a series of

observation points, and there's a 22m lookout tower with a fine panorama. The marked footpaths include a 5.5km nature trail with wild animals, a botanical trail (1.1km) and a wild nature trail (1.3km).

Pension   HISTORIC SITE
([☑]26467747, 6416 1915; www.bunkurs.lv; Skaļupes; guided tours €11.50 noon, 2pm, 4pm Sat & Sun; [☺]tous at noon, 2pm, 4pm Sat & Sun; 3pm Mon-Fri) What poses as a dreary rehabilitation centre is in fact a top-secret Soviet bunker, known by its code name, the Pension. When Latvia was part of the USSR, it was one of the most important strategic hideouts during a time of nuclear threat. In fact, the bunker's location was so tightly guarded that it remained classified information until 2003. Almost all of the bunker's 2000 sq m still look as they did when it was in operation.

It is interesting to note that there is only one bed in the entire bunker even though it was designed for a large crew complement (250 people) – workers were meant to sleep at their stations. Tours last up to 1½ hours and can be translated into English and German. Weekend tours include a (surprisingly tasty) Soviet-style lunch served within the bunker's cafeteria. Note the plastic flowers on the table – they've been adorning the dining hall since 1982.

Vienkoču Parks   SCULPTURE
([☑]29329065; www.vienkoci.lv; adult/child €3/2; [☺]10am-6pm) Rihards, a local wood carver, has filled a 10-hectare park with his unique creations. Small trails snake past bold modern art installations, a classical garden, sundials and a collection of torture instruments. Rent out the park's rustic cabin (25Ls), lit by candles in the evenings, for a 'back to nature' experience.

The park is located near the main Rīga–Cēsis road, immediately after the return to Ligatne.

🛏 Sleeping

Lāču Miga   GUESTHOUSE
([☑]6415 3481; www.lacumiga.lv; Gaujas iela 22; d with/without breakfast €43/37) Built in a large log chalet, the 'Bears' Den' stays true to its moniker with a gargantuan plush teddy bear positioned at the front entrance. Slews of stuffed bears welcome guests in their rooms – there are even ursine pillows that look like a teddy bear that's swallowed a giant Rubik's Cube.

🛈 Getting There & Away

There are hourly buses to Cēsis (€1.40, half an hour) and frequent buses services to Rīga (€3.20, one hour 20 minutes). Trains stop at Ligatne station on their way to/from Rīga (€2.65, one hour 20 minutes) and Cēsis (€1.55, half an hour).

Cēsis

POP 19,500

With its stunning medieval castle, cobbled streets, green hills and landscaped garden, Cēsis is simply the cutest little town in the whole of Latvia. There is a lot of history here, too. The place started eight centuries ago as a Livonian Order stronghold in the land of unruly pagans and saw horrific battles right under (or inside) the castle walls. Although it's an easy day trip from Rīga, Cēsis is definitely worth a longer stay, especially since there is the whole of Gauja National Park around it to explore.

🎯 Sights

★ **Cēsis Castle**   CASTLE
(Cēsu pils; www.cesupils.lv; both castles adult/student €5/2.50, excursions from €33; [☺]10am-6pm daily May-Sep, 10am-5pm Tue-Sun Oct-Apr) It is actually two castles in one. The first is the sorrowful dark-stone towers of the old Wenden castle. Founded by Livonian knights in 1214, it was sacked by Russian tsar Ivan the Terrible in 1577, but only after its 300 defenders blew themselves up with gunpowder. The other is the more cheerful castle-like 18th-century manor house once inhabited by the dynasty of German counts von Sievers. It houses a museum that features original fin de siècle interiors.

After visiting the old and the new castles, take a walk through the landscaped **castle park** with a pond inhabited by the cutest of paddle steamers that takes people around for €2.20. Just as cute is the hilltop **Russian Orthodox church of Transfiguration**, which the von Sievers built at their family cemetery (like many Germans on Russian Orthodoxy they converted to Orthodoxy).

St John's Church   CHRISTIAN
(Svētā Jāņa baznīca; http://cesujana.lelb.lv; [☺]11am-5pm) Switch on your imagination in this 13th-century church where armour-clad Livonian knights prayed and buried their dead in what then was a lonely island of Christianity surrounded by the lands of pagans. Currently the home of the town's

Cēsis

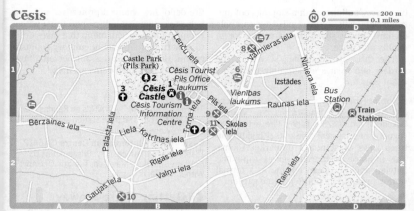

Lutheran community, the church contains tombs of the order's grand masters and top bishops.

🏃 Activities

In winter, skiers and snowboarders pootle down the gentle slopes and cross-country trails at **Žagarkalns** (☎26266266; www.zagarkalns.lv) and **Ozolkalns** (☎26400200; www.ozolkalns.lv; 3hr lift pass €7), the two largest skiing areas in Vidzeme. In summer, they offer bicycle and canoe rentals, and Ozolkalns has a ropes course. If you can't get to either of the ski hills, you can rent a bike at the tourist office.

🎊 Festivals & Events

There are concerts and festivals almost every weekend during the summer.

From mid-July to mid-August, Cēsis comes alive on the weekends with performances ranging from symphonies to storytelling, held at a variety of venues around town as part of the **Mākslas Festivāls** (http://cesufestivals.lv).

🛌 Sleeping

Cēsis has loads of respectable accommodations several kilometres outside of the town centre. Check out www.tourism.cesis.lv for more information and photos.

Glūdas Grava   MOTEL €
(☎27036862; www.gludasgrava.lv; Glūdas iela 6a; r €40) An unusual one. A garage has been transformed into five studios with glassy front walls and individual entrances. Each studio is equipped with a kitchen and sleeps

Cēsis

◎ **Top Sights**
1 Cēsis Castle B1

◎ **Sights**
2 Castle Park (Pils Park) B1
3 Russian Orthodox Church of
   Transfiguration B1
4 St John's Church B2

🛏 **Sleeping**
5 Glūdas Grava A1
6 Kolonna Hotel Cēsis C1
7 Province C1

🍴 **Eating**
8 Izsalkušais Jānis C1
9 Mākslas telpa Mala C1
10 Maxima Supermarket B2
11 Vinetas un Allas Kārumlādes C2

up to four people. There is no reception – book your stay on its website or on www.booking.com and it will come back with instructions about the keys.

Province   B&B €€
(☎26407008; www.province.lv; Niniera iela 6; s/d €50/60; ℗🛜) This cute celery-green guesthouse pops out from the dreary Soviet-era housing nearby. The 11 rooms are simple and spotless, and there's a cafe on the ground floor. English isn't its strong point.

⭐ **Kārlamūiža**   HERITAGE HOTEL €€
(☎26165298; www.karlamuiza.lv; d €45-115) In the village of Kārļi, about 12km away from their Cēsis Castle base, the manor served as a home (not so far) away from home for barons von Sievers, who bought it in 1777. The

two-storey building with a sloping roof and stone-slab walls is surrounded by an apple orchard. Rustic-styled rooms vary a lot in quality and price.

The three-course dinner, served in the garden, is a treat and definitely worth the €18 it goes for.

Kolonna Hotel Cēsis HOTEL €€
(📞 6412 0122; www.hotelkolonna.com; Vienības laukums 1; s/d €44/59; @ 🛜) The exterior is vaguely neoclassical while the inside features rows of standard upmarket rooms. The in-house restaurant serves top-notch Latvian and European cuisine in a formal setting or outdoors in the pristine garden.

✗ Eating

Most of the accommodation in Cēsis has quality restaurants attached. Beyond that, the town has a limited amount of worthwhile eats. Consider swinging by **Maxima Supermarket** (Livu laukums; ⊘ 9am-10pm) to pick up some groceries for a picnic along the rambling stone steps between the castle ruins and the lake.

Mākslas telpa Mala CAFE €
(www.facebook.com/telpamala; Lielā Skolas iela 4; mains €3-4; ⊘ noon-9pm) A truly heart-warming place inside an old wooden house featuring an antiquated tiled wood stove. Cheapish lunch food is on offer, along with craft beer, Latvian cider and fruit wine. We also liked the Latvian rock classics (not something you would hear in your average cafe) for the soundtrack. A small souvenir and cloth shop is attached.

Vinetas un Allas Kārumlādes CAFE €
(Rīgas iela 12; snacks €3-5; ⊘ 9am-7pm) Some 1970s nostalgia is in the air, enhanced by photographic wallpaper and chocolate cartoon characters on sale. This candy shop is primarily targeting local grannies, but anyone will enjoy its blueberry pavlova meringue, as well as cakes and muffins.

2 Locals CAFE €€
(Rīgas iela 24a; mains €7-10; ⊘ 9am-midnight Sun-Thu, to 2am Fri & Sat) A noble attempt at savvy, locally sourced fare, 2 Locals offers a delectable assortment of meat and fish dishes; don't miss the scrumptious homemade desserts!

⭐ **Izsalkušais Jānis** MODERN EUROPEAN €€
(📞 29262001; www.izsalkusaisjanis.lv; Valmieras iela 1; mains €6-17; ⊘ noon-11pm) The town's old fire depot has changed profession and now helps to extinguish hunger and thirst with a compact but powerful menu that takes Cēsis to a metropolitan level of culinary sophistication. Hot trout salad is our personal fave. It also bakes its own delicious bread.

🛈 Information

There are two banks with ATMs on Raunas iela, between the bus and train station and the main square (Vienības laukums).

Cēsis Tourism Information Centre (📞 6412 1815; www.tourism.cesis.lv; Pils laukums 9; ⊘ 10am-5pm daily May-Sep, Tue-Sun Oct-Apr) Within the Cēsis Castle.

🛈 Getting There & Away

Cēsis' bus and train station can be found in the same location, at the roundabout connecting Raunas iela to Raiņa iela. There are up to five trains per day between 6.35am and 9pm linking Cēsis and Rīga (€3.50, two hours). Bikes are allowed on board. Two or three buses per hour between 6.15am and 10.20pm ply the route from Cēsis to Rīga, stopping in Līgatne and Sigulda. Trains also run to Valmiera (€1.55, 30 minutes).

Valmiera

This pleasant, if unremarkable, university town often features as the start or end point of boat trips on the Gauja River. If you happen to be here, check out **St Simon's Church** (Svētā Sīmaņa Baznīca; Bruņinieku iela 2), which dates to 1283 and shelters a fine 19th-century organ. You can climb its tower for a donation. Along the same street you'll find the ruins of **Valmiera Castle** (Bruņinieku iela 2), founded by the Livonian Order in the 13th century.

What the town is really famous for is its beer, which you will have surely tried somewhere by the time you get to Valmiera. The brewery, **Valmiermuiža** (📞 20 264296; www.valmiermuiza.lv; Dzirnavu iela 2; admission €6; ⊘ open every day by appointment), offers visitors a chance to see how the magic is made on its spirited (no pun intended) brewery tours. Expect friendly guides and plenty of grog to go around. Valmiermuiža is just north of the city centre, past Viestura laukums.

If you need need to rent a canoe, a raft or a bicycle for your Gauja National Park adventure head no further than **Eži** (📞 6420 7263; www.ezi.lv; Valdemāra iela; ⊘ 9am-7pm Mon-Sat, to 1pm Sun) – one of the best adventure-sports specialists in the area.

ĀRAIŠI

Āraiši Lake Fortress (Āraišu ezerpils; ☑ 6419 7288; adult/student/child €3/1.50/1; ⊗ 9am-7pm daily Apr-Oct, 9am-4pm Wed-Sun Nov-Mar) Plopped on an islet in the middle of Āraiši Lake, about 10km south of Cēsis, Āraiši Lake Fortress is a reconstruction of a settlement inhabited by Latgallians, an ancient tribe that once called the region home in the 9th and 10th centuries. A wooden walkway leads across the water to the unusual village, which was discovered by archaeologists in 1965.

Peering across the lake are the ruins of **Āraiši Stone Castle** (Āraišu mūra pils), built by Livonians in the 14th century and destroyed by Ivan IV's troops in 1577. From here, a path leads to a reconstructed Stone Age settlement – there are a couple of reed dwellings and earth ovens for roasting meat and fish. The fortress and castle, together with the iconic 18th-century **Āraiši windmill** (Āraišu vējdzirnavas), are signposted 1km along a dirt track from the main road and form the **Āraiši Museum Park** (Āraišu muzejparks).

Valmiera is on the same train line as Cēsis and Sigulda, with at least four trains daily from Rīga (€4.20, 2½ to three hours).

SOUTHEASTERN LATVIA (LATGALE)

Latvia is a maritime nation, but what do you find if you venture deep inland? More water! Latvia's southeast, known as Latgale, is bisected by the mighty Daugava and dotted with scenic lakes hiding in the depths of a thick pristine forest. If staying in a log cabin with no cars and people in sight is your kind of holiday dream, then this is the place to go. German knights failed to capture Latgale at the dawn of Latvia's history, which sent the region along a rather different historical path than the rest of the country. Russian, Polish and Jewish influences are felt much stronger here, while local ethnic Latvians speak a distinct dialect, which many believe should be branded a separate language. As EU money pours in, Latgale's two main cities, Daugavpils and Rēzekne, are slowly shedding their grey Soviet clothes and putting on a modern cosmopolitan outfit.

Daugava River Valley

Latvia's serpentine Daugava River, known as the 'river of fate', winds its way through Latgale, Zemgale and Vidzeme before passing Rīga and emptying out in the Gulf of Rīga. For centuries the river was Latvia's most important transport and trade corridor for clans and kingdoms further east. Today, there is a railway running along its northern bank all the way to Daugavpils, Latvia's second-largest city.

Driving out of Rīga in the eastern direction, you can choose between taking the new E22 road or the much more scenic old road (A6) that passes through riverside towns and villages, with the Daugava in full view most of the time. The two roads merge after Koknese, 95km southeast from Rīga.

Stop at Koknese to admire the **ruins of Kokenhausen**, a 13th-century knights' castle, which lie at the confluence of the Daugava and Perse Rivers. Built by German crusaders in 1209 and surrounded by a beautiful park, the castle ruins lost some of their dramatic cliff-top position after a hydroelectric dam increased the river's water level. Today the twisting ruins appear to be practically sitting in the river, and the sight is enchanting. The next headland down the river is occupied by the **Garden of Destiny**, a project in the making, which – the authors hope – will become a symbol of Latvia, like Milda's statue in Rīga. Designed by acclaimed Japanese gardener cum philosopher Shunmyu Masuno, it is expected to shape up by 2018.

Not long after Koknese and just before the turn to Pļaviņas, stock up on rustic-style bread and pastries – fresh from the oven – at **Liepkalni Maiznīca**, a rest area that boasts a scenic location on the bank of the river. There is a good cafe and a shop selling products made by Latvian craftsmen in the premises.

At Jēkabpils, 140km from Rīga, the A6 road branches off south and follows the Daugava Valley towards Daugavpils and Belarus. The E22 continues east towards Rēzekne and into Russia. If you take the latter, stop at the **watchtower of Teiči Nature**

Southeastern Latvia (Latgale)

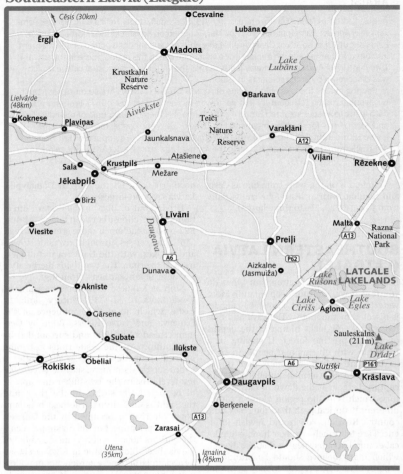

Reserve for sweeping views of the largest moss marsh in the Baltics. The hard-to-miss 27m-tall tower comes after the turn to Atašiene.

Daugavpils

POP 102,500

Latvia's second-largest city is actually so small you can see the surrounding countryside from any of its several vantage points, along with the Daugava River upon which it stands. Predominantly Russian-speaking, Daugavpils has the undeserved reputation of a grim Soviet Gotham City – mostly among Latvians who have never been to it. In reality, it has a fairly well-preserved historical centre and a mighty fortress, reminding of the times when it was a provincial Russian imperial town with a thriving Jewish community. It even has a bit of a cosmopolitan vibe now it is re-inventing itself as an important centre of Russian-language studies in the EU. The city's greatest celebrity, Mark Rothko, went across the ocean to become one of America's most notable 20th-century artists. Bearing his name is the new contemporary art centre, one of the country's best.

Napoleonic Wars, the fortress served as an imperial stronghold during two Polish insurrections in the 19th century and as a home away from home for tsars exploring the western side of their realm.

Although the architecture is rather utilitarian, you can make out Gothic and Egyptian motifs in the decor of its four gates – all named after Russian royals. The fortress itself survived two centuries of wars and revolutions largely intact, but the beautiful 18th-century Jesuit cathedral that stood in the middle was destroyed by WWII bombardment, its ruins later cleared by the Soviets, who instead built a cluster of ugly generic apartment blocks for the military. A plaque outside the main gate states that Tatar poet Musa Jalil languished here from September to October 1942, in what was then the Nazi concentration camp Stalag 340. Inside, a memorial marks the site where local aristocrat Leon Plater was executed by the tsar's soldiers for leading the Polish revolt in the area in 1863.

Daugavpils Mark Rothko Art Centre
ARTS CENTRE

(www.rothkocenter.com; Mihaila iela 3; adult/student €8/4, half-price for people born on 24 Apr & 25 Sep; ⊙11am-7pm Wed-Sat, 11am-5pm Tue & Sun) Russian imperial architects who built the huge arsenal to store weapons inside Dinaburg Fortress would have been surprised to hear that their creation was destined to become an art gallery named after a local Jew who fled to America. Opened in 2011, the ultramodern centre is a new heavyweight on the Latvian art scene, hosting numerous contemporary exhibitions, as well as a team of resident artists.

The 1st floor is dedicated to Daugavpils native Mark Rothko, whose surrealist and abstract works led him to stardom in America, where he emigrated, aged 10. An interactive multimedia exhibition recapping Rothko's biography and explaining the historical context of his childhood years is followed by a small display of Rothko's original works representing 'multiform', the series that he created in the later period of his life. The 2nd floor hosts exhibitions of contemporary Latvian artists.

Church Hill
CHRISTIAN

Celebrating the city's multiculturalism, churches of four main local Christian denominations face each other on a small hill bisected by 18 Novembra iela. While local Lutherans flock into the red-brick

☉ Sights

The city's unsightly centrepiece, Park Hotel Latgola, provides a sweeping 360-degree panorama from its top-floor restaurant and bar – a good place to start exploring Daugavpils.

Dinaburg Fortress
FORTRESS

(⊙24hr) FREE Long-neglected in the post-independence years, the riverside citadel has recently undergone a thorough renovation and is now home to the excellent Mark Rothko Art Centre. Built on the orders of tsar Alexander I on the eve of the

neo-Gothic **Martin Luther Cathedral**, the Catholics congregate at **Holy Virgin Cathedral**. The above two mingle with the Russian Orthodox **Cathedral of Princes Boris & Gleb** and the Old Believer's **Novostroyensky Church of Resurrection, Holy Virgin & St Nikola**.

All except for the latter – Russian dissidents have always been a bit of a secret society – are open for visitors. See how blessed you can get in one go.

Daugavpils Lead Shot Factory   HISTORIC SITE
(☑ 27766655; www.dsr.lv; Varšavas iela 28) Guns and bullets are not to everyone's liking, but it is the near-extinct ancient technology that makes this odd sight worth a visit. It's all about gravitation. Molten lead is poured from the top of an old brick tower. By the time the drops reach the bottom, they solidify into perfectly round balls which subsequently get separated by size, mixed with graphite and packaged into neat boxes. You won't see the actual process – which is both unsafe and unhealthy – but they'll turn on century-old separation machines for you, let you climb the tower and – if you wish – shoot at beer cans from a pneumatic gun.

🛏 Sleeping

**Biplan Guest House
Aleksandria**   GUESTHOUSE **€**
(☑ 27014143; www.biplan.lv/en/guest-house-aleksandria; Stacijas iela 65/67; r from €35) Close to the train station, this guesthouse offers spacious studios, some of which are equipped with a kitchenette and a washing machine. No breakfast is served, but there is a fridge and a microwave in every room. The city's main pedestrian promenade begins around the corner.

**Mark Rothko Art Centre
Residences**   GUESTHOUSE **€€**
(☑ 6543 0278; www.rothkocenter.com; Mihaila iela 3; s/d €30/40) Here is your chance for a real night at the museum. But since the museum is the Mark Rothko Art Centre, the creatures that might come to life after clocks strike midnight would appear quite shapeless, if brightly coloured. Although intended for resident artists, the modestly stylish rooms are often peddled at www.booking.com.

Park Hotel Latgola   HOTEL **€€**
(☑ 6540 4900; www.hotellatgola.lv; Ģimnāzijas iela 46; s/d from €50/60; @🛜) The city's centrepiece and largest building, this Soviet mon-ster sports modern (but overpriced) rooms behind its renovated facade. Check out the views from the hotel's top-storey restaurant and bar.

Villa Ksenija   GUESTHOUSE **€€€**
(☑ 20388008; www.villaks.lv; Varšavas iela 17; s/d from €58/84; P🛜) Occupying a stately mansion built in 1876, this hotel provides a relatively plush if not very central sleeping option in Daugavpils. Their classic style echoing that of the Best Western chain, the rooms are comfortable, but fairly standard. We like the arbors in the garden, where you can have your breakfast on a warm day.

🍴 Eating & Drinking

Gubernators   RUSSIAN **€**
(☑ 6542 2455; www.gubernators.lv; Lāčplēša iela 10; mains €5-8; ⊙ 11am-midnight) Sporting rustic decor with a hint of Soviet nostalgia, this cellar restaurant serves five kinds of Russian *pelmeņi* and many more Eastern European favourites, along with its own brand of beer.

LUNA Café   EUROPEAN **€**
(www.luna.menu; Mihoelsa iela 68-1a; mains €2.50-4; ⊙ 8am-10pm) This cheerful, brightly coloured cafe cum pizzeria is a veritable source of cheap and tasty breakfast and lunch food as well as competently brewed coffee.

★ Artilērijas Pagrabi   BAR
(www.facebook.com/ArtilerijasPagrabi; Rīgas iela 22; ⊙ from 6pm Wed-Sun) Here is the ultimate bar at the end of the universe – the EU universe, that is. This easy-going place sees itself as something of a Latvian cultural bastion in the east, its fire power generated by great local beer and live gigs featuring bands from Latvia and lands beyond the frontier. Easily the best bar outside Rīga.

ℹ Information

Tourist Office (www.visitdaugavpils.lv; Rīgas iela 22a; ⊙ 10am-3pm Mon, to 6pm Tue-Fri, to 5pm Sat, to 4pm Sun) Well stocked with booklets detailing activities in southern Latgale.

ℹ Getting There & Away

Four trains a day depart Daugavpils' **train station** (☑ 6548 7261; Stacijas iela) for Rīga (three to four hours, €7). Other services include St Petersburg in Russia (€49, daily, 10 hours) and Minsk in Belarus (€43, three weekly, nine hours).

From the **bus station** (☑ 6542 3000; www.buspark.lv; Viestura iela 10) buses run to/from

A LONE SURVIVOR

A census conducted in 1897, six years before Mark Rothko was born into the family of a Jewish pharmacist, showed that 46% of Daugavpils (then known as Dvinsk) residents were Jews, which made them the largest, if not the most powerful, community. The city was teeming with Jewish-run businesses, as well as cultural, religious and political institutions. In the streets, Yiddish language could be heard more often than Russian, Latvian or Polish.

There are only several hundred Jews left now. Few if any of them descend from the original Jewish inhabitants. When the Nazis seized Daugavpils in 1941, they drove 13,000 local Jews into a ghetto that was located in an outpost of the Rīga Citadel on the other side of the river. Gradually, nearly all these people were executed, or starved and worked to death. Just about 100 people survived until the Soviet army recaptured the city.

Mark Rothko, who left Daugavpils at the age of 10, is therefore also a survivor, who would have had few chances had his family not emigrated to America.

Having sailed out of Liepāja in 1913, he lived a happy life – first in Portland (Oregon), then in the Yale campus and finally in New York, where he discovered himself as an artist who over decades shifted from figurative surrealism to brightly coloured simple geometrical forms, like those you can admire at Daugavpils Mark Rothko Art Centre (p269). He died in 1970, knowing very well that he'd written more than a page in American art history.

Daugavpils' synagogue hosts a small museum of the city's Jewish history. A visit can be arranged by contacting the affiliated tour guide, Josifs Ročko. Email him at rochko@inbox.lv.

Rīga (€9, 3¾ hours, hourly) and Rēzekne (€4, 1½ to two hours, seven daily), as well as Vilnius in Lithuania (€12, 3½ hours, two daily) and Braslav in Belarus (€3 to €6, 2¼ hours, four daily).

Around Daugavpils

Sventes Muiža

Sventes Muiža MANOR HOUSE €€
(☑ 6542 7822; www.sventehotel.lv; Alejas iela 7, Svente; d from €45; @ 🕲) Count Michael Plater-Ziberg, a scion of Latgale's most prominent aristocratic family, had only two years before WWI broke out to enjoy peace in the portly estate house he built for himself 17km east of Daugavpils. Now it is at your disposal as a fancy-looking, yet affordable, countryside hotel with an acclaimed restaurant and, slightly off-topic, a museum of WWII vehicles on the premises.

Slutišķi

Sitting on the bank of the Daugava, this picturesque hamlet populated by Russian Old Believers served as an unlikely catalyst of Latvia's 'Third Atmoda' (National Awakening), which led to the restoration of independence in 1991. A newspaper article criticising the Soviet government's plan to build a hydropower station and flood Slutišķi generated public outcry that turned its author Dainis Īvans into an instant hero. Soon he was the leader of the Latvian Popular Front, a movement that made the liberation happen. These days, one of the farmsteads has been transformed into a lovely ethnographic museum dedicated to Old Believers. It was undergoing a thorough renovation at the time of research, but was due to reopen soon. Slutišķi is surrounded by the Daugavas Loki nature park, which protects a particularly beautiful stretch of the gracefully bending Daugava. There is an organised picnic area on the river bank, with barbecue facilities, swings for children and a few paths for walking. Slutišķi is located near the village of Markova, 35km from Daugavpils on the road to Krāslava. The turn-off is well signposted. Travelling by bus, get off at Židino, 2.5km away.

Krāslava

Just 6km north of Belarus, sleepy Krāslava is a picturesque town of wooden houses set amid green hills embracing the Daugava. A former domain of the Polish Plater family, Krāslava has always been an intriguing multicultural melting pot. Its coat of arms displays five oars symbolising five local communities: Poles, Latvians, Belarusians, Russians and Jews. The latter used to be the largest group, but virtually all of them perished in the Holocaust.

Occupying a key vantage point, **Plater's castle** is sadly closed for visitors, but on its grounds there is the small **Krāslava museum** and an excellent **tourist information centre**, complete with a shop selling local products, such as *kvass* – a rye-bread drink. If interested, ask about local craft workshops, or just head straight to the **pottery studio** (☑29128695; valdispaulins@inbox.lv; Dūmu iela 8; ⊙9am-7.30pm) of Valdis Paulins for a crash course in traditional Latgale ceramics.

Another hill is topped by the whitewashed **St Ludwig catholic church**, which houses the remains of St Donat, the town's most treasured relic.

For those interested in horseback riding, head to **Klajumi Stables** (☑29472638; www.klajumi.lv; 2-/4-/7-day tours €105/270/515, 1hr trot for 1/2 persons €25/30), 11km southwest of Krāslava near Kaplava. Ilze, the owner, comes from a long line of horse keepers and offers a variety of activities from overnight riding trips to simple countryside afternoon gallops. The adorable guest cottage (from €50) looks like a gingerbread house and comes with a sauna (that doubles as a shower), a kitchenette and a lofted bedroom with satellite TV. The toilet is located in an outhouse nearby.

Krāslava stands on the road leading from Daugavpils to Vitsebsk in Belarus. Buses for Daugavpils leave every two hours (€2.35, 1¼ hours). There are three buses a day to Aglona (€2 to €4, one hour).

Lake Dridži

There seems to be a superlative for every lake in Latvia and this one is simply the deepest – Latvia's Baykal, so to say. About 25km northeast of Krāslava, the gracefully shaped elongated lake features a nice resort. Take Rte P161 leading to Dagda to reach **Dridži** (☑29441221; www.dridzi.lv; tent €7, campervan parking €10, d €30, cottage for 6 €80), the perfect spot for families, featuring volleyball nets, tugboats, rafts and a lovely hillside dotted with wooden gazebos. Each cottage comes with a fully equipped kitchen. It is open year-round.

Aglona

Believe it or not, teeny Aglona, sitting on an isthmus between two large placid lakes, is one of the most visited towns in all of Latvia. But that only becomes apparent for a few days around 15 August, when Catholic pilgrims descend on it in their hundreds of thousands to celebrate Ascension Day in Aglona Basilica.

The pilgrimage commenced over 300 years ago when a group of wandering Dominican monks discovered a healing source hidden among a thicket of spruce trees ('Aglona' means 'spruce tree' in an old dialect). Although the sulphur fount lost its apparent power a century later, the water from the source is still regarded as a product of divine intervention and used in rituals.

Today's basilica is a twin-towered whitewashed cathedral standing in a vast grass courtyard, created for Pope John Paul II's visit in 1993 to bestow the title of 'Basilica Minoris' (Small Basilica) upon the holy grounds. One of the basilica's 10 altars guards a miraculous icon of the Virgin Mary, said to have saved Aglona from the plague in 1708. Mass is held at 7am and 7pm on weekdays, and at 10am, noon and 7pm on Sundays. Rosary is held at noon on weekdays and at 9.30am on Sundays.

While you're in town, consider stopping by the **Bread Museum** (Aglonas maizes muzejs; ☑29287044; Daugavpils iela 7; ⊙9am-6pm Mon-Sat) to learn about the history and traditions surrounding Latgalian dark bread, a local staple. Little English is spoken so it is best to call ahead to arrange a complimentary translator for the one-hour presentation. Even if you don't have time for the presentation, you can still stop by for fresher-than-fresh loaves of bread baked minutes before you walk in the door. Peep through the small window into the kitchen to watch the bakers hard at work.

A small **guesthouse** (☑29287044; Daugavpils iela 7) can be found above the Bread Museum with several cheery dorm rooms swathed in pastels. **Aglonas Cakuli** (☑6537 5465; http://aglonascakuli.lv; Ezera iela 4; d with/without bathroom from €36/24), another adequate sleeping option, sits one block away along Lake Ciriss. Just over 1km south of the basilica, **Aglonas Alpi** (☑29194362; aglonasalpi.lv; s/d €23/42) has wooden cottages clustered on a grassy headland with mesmerising views of Ciriša water reservoir. All guesthouses serve food – terrifyingly huge amounts of it, in fact.

Around 10km south of Aglona lurks Čertoks ezers (Devil's Lake). The Russian word for devil is indeed in the name. For centuries, locals have passed down the tale of a malicious demon that lives at the bottom of the oddly tranquil lagoon. Compasses and sensory equipment never seem to work when activated within the lake's vicinity, which has led scientists to speculate that a magnetic meteor sits below the crystalline surface. To reach Devil's Lake, take Rte P62 towards Krāslava; the turn-off to the lake is not marked (to avoid a deluge of tourists), so you will have to get directions from the friendly staff at the Aglona Tourist Office (☎ 29118597; www.en.aglona.travel; Daugavpils iela 1; ◷ 8.30am-5pm Mon-Fri). To check email, head to the town's library (Daugavpils iela 37; ◷ 10am-6pm Mon-Fri, to 3pm Sat; 🛜), which has free internet access and wi-fi.

❶ Getting There & Around

Aglona is 9km off the main road between Daugavpils and Rēzekne (Rte A13). There are two buses a day to/from Daugavpils (€3, 1½ hours) and three to Krāslava (€2 to €4, one hour). For Rēzekne and Rīga, change at Preiļi (€1.50, 30 minutes, six daily).

Rēzekne

POP 34,500

Rēzekne furtively pokes its head up from a giant muddle of derelict factories and generic block housing. The town took a heavy beating during WWII, when most of its historic buildings were pulverised by artillery fire. Today, there isn't much to keep a tourist in town; however, frequent trains and buses make it a convenient jumping-off point to explore the quiet lakeland further south.

The main street, Atbrīvošanas alejā, runs from Rēzekne II train station (north) to the bus station (south), and crosses the central square en route. In the square's middle stands Māra, a statue twice destroyed by the Soviet authorities in the 1940s and only re-erected in 1992. Its inscription 'Vienoti Latvijai' means 'United Latvia'.

Further down the road you will find a small hillock with the unremarkable remains of Rēzekne castle and the great tourist information centre nearby with a dearth of information on the Latgale lakelands that surround the city.

Across Atbrīvošanas alejā is the new elegant addition to the city's skyline, the Gors (http://latgalesgors.lv; Pils iela 4) – a large cultural centre that brands itself 'The embassy of

LATVIA RĒZEKNE

ON HOME SOIL

Latvians are attached to their land to a much greater extent than most Europeans. That means not just any land, but particular farmsteads owned by their parental families. A staggering number of urbanites still have relatives running a farm, which often comes with fruit gardens, a large chunk of forest and a lake. Summer months spent in the countryside with their grandparents, aunts and uncles is a part of biography for almost any Latvian.

This is explained by the fact that cities and towns were for centuries run by the conquerors – Germans, Russians or Swedes, while the en-masse migration of ethnic Latvians into urbanised areas only began in the 19th century.

If you want to get an idea about traditional rural life, head to Andrupene Farmstead Museum (laukuseta@inbox.lv; Skolas 5, Andrupene), which occupies a farm that remains unaltered since the 1920s, when many Latvians received generous chunks of land in the agrarian reform. It consists of six wooden buildings, including the owners' house, a granary, a smithery and a steam bath. Contact them in advance to arrange a traditional Latgale dinner that comes with delicious bread baked on the spot.

The village of Andrupene is 30km east of Aglona, near Dadga. You really need to be travelling by car or bicycle if you come here, although two to three buses a day stop here on the route between Rēzekne (€2.40, one hour) and Dagda (€1, 20 minutes)

Andrupene Farmstead Museum is a part of the Latgale Culinary Heritage initiative. A list of farms that preserve old recipes and welcome visitors can be found on www.kulinaraismantojums.lv. Tourist information offices in Krāslava and Aglona can also give you some clues.

Latgale'. Concerts, film shows, poetic readings – you name it – take place almost daily.

Continue along Atbrīvošanas alejā and take a walk down Latgales iela, the town's oldest street, which is lined with dozens of charming brick facades constructed by wealthy Yiddish merchants several hundred years ago.

🛏 Sleeping & Eating

Kolonna　　　　　　　　HOTEL €€
(☑ 6460 7820; www.hotelkolonna.com; Brīvibas iela 2; r from €60) If you need to overnight in Rēzekne, this chain hotel has comfortable if bland rooms in a stately art deco building in the very middle of the city. The attached Rozalija restaurant serves European standards as well as Latgale specialities.

Pub Art Salon Mōls　　　　LATGALIAN €
(Latgale iela 22/24; mains €5-8; ☉ 10am-10pm) Sharing space with an art gallery, this little rustic-style place serves meaty calorie-rich Latgalian fare. Service is patchy and cooking may take a while, but after a few shots of Latgale's trademark booze, *šmakouvka*, it all becomes irrelevant.

Ausmeņa Kebabs　　　MIDDLE EASTERN €
(www.ausmena.lv; Rancāna iela 41; mains €2.50-4; ☉ 11am-10pm) It's hard to explain how a kebab shop could have grown into a local institution with a bit of nationalist flavour and a drinking den for bohemians, but there you are. Turkish-style kebabs come in their pita-wrapped takeaway forms as well as served on a plate with chips.

❶ Getting There & Away

The **bus station** (Latgales iela 17) has services to/from Daugavpils (€4, 1¾ to 2¼ hours, four daily), Ludza (€1.70, 30 minutes to one hour, three to five daily) and Rīga (€10, four to 4½ hours, seven daily), among other destinations.

Rēzekne II train station (Stacijas iela) has one train daily each way between Rīga and St Petersburg, and Rīga and Moscow. In all, there are six trains daily to/from Rīga (€7, three to 3¾ hours).

Around Rēzekne

Lake Rāzna Area

A short ride from Rēzekne, Lake Rāzna (Latvia's largest by volume) is an epitome of tranquil beauty. Encircling it, Rāzna National Park is a quiet preserve protecting roughly 600 sq km of Latgale's lakeland. Fishing villages around it were founded by Russian Old Believers, who gave them Slavic-sounding names. The park's **information centre** is located in Lipuški on the southern shore.

Čornaja bay, on the northern side of the lake, 15km from Rēzekne, is the base of **Buruguru** (☑ 29833890; http://buruguru.lv; Dukstigala bay, Čornaja; sailing tours for up to 12 people €300, sleeping per night €100), which is how captain Andris Strutskis brands the operation involving himself and his ocean-going sailing boat. Unless you travel in a large group, it makes sense to enquire in advance about the possibility of sharing the sailing tour price with other tourists. The boat is also available as a romantic floating hotel, which comes way cheaper than sailing.

At the mouth of the bay, you'll find **Ezerkrasti Resort** (☑ 26411207; www.raznasezerkrasti.lv; Dukstigals, Čornajas pagasts; r €30): lush green property dotted with charming wooden cottages offers volleyball, paddleboats, a lake for swimming, and an indoor pool and sauna.

On the other side of the lake, along Rte P56, is **Rāznas Gulbis** (☑ 29994444; www.razna.lv; d from €70), a spacious resort with paddleboats, an on-site restaurant and a small 'aquarium' of corralled fish in the lake. People are also raving about **Būrviga Rāzna** (☑ 27876016; Škrabi, Mākoņkalna pagasts; r from €25), which has rooms that look like an old-school grandmother's home, except they are located inside trailers.

Lake Lubāns

Latvia's largest lake is very shallow, its shores covered in reeds and encircled by a fir tree forest so dark and wild you can shoot films about Siberia in the vicinity. Around 180 species of birds, including swans and eagles, are nesting here and there are six watchtowers in the area for birders to indulge in spotting them.

For information, head to **Bāka** (Lighthouse; baka.rezeknesnovads.lv), a former water-pumping facility transformed into a watersports centre, with windsurfing kits as well as rowing and motor boats available for rent. If you want to spend a night in total solitude amid a sea of reeds, it has one room sleeping two (€30 per night) and another room sleeping four (€40 per night).

Nearby, in the fishing village of Īdeņa, **Zvejnieki** (☑ 29165392, 28301143; www.zvejnieki.lv; Īdeņa, Nagļi pagasts; dm from €8) offers beds in wooden houses scattered around its territory. You can also negotiate renting a whole house, sleeping eight, for yourself. Hearty Latgale food and a wide range of activities, including fishing and birdwatching, are available upon request, but arrangements should be made in advance.

Ludza

POP 15,000

Little Ludza, just a hop from the Russian border, was founded in 1177, making it the oldest town in all of Latvia. Located at the junction of two lakes (known as Big Ludza Lake and Little Ludza Lake), the small village and trading post grew around Ludza Castle, built by German crusaders in 1399 to protect the eastern front of the Livonian Order. The castle has been in ruins since 1775, and today the melange of crumbling crimson brick and smoky grey boulders is both haunting and beautiful, and makes a great place for a picnic overlooking the church spires and rivulets down the hill.

An excellent selection of locally made handicrafts is featured at the Ludza Craftsmen Centre (📞 29467925; www.ludzasamatnieki.lv; Tālavijas iela 27a; ⊙ 9am-5pm Tue-Sat). The centre has three attached workshops in which local artisans perfect their trade. If you ring ahead, you too can try your hand at time-honoured methods of wool spinning, pottery making and sewing. There's a collection of old tools to peruse and a traditional Latgalian costume to try on for picture taking.

❶ Getting There & Around

Ludza is located 26km east of Rēzekne along Rte A12 as it makes its way into Russia. There are three to five buses a day between Ludza and Rēzekne (€1.70, 30 minutes), two of them going all the way to Daugavpils (€5, three hours).

UNDERSTAND LATVIA

Latvia Today

People born after Lenin's monument was dismantled in the main street of Rīga are in their mid-20s now – for them and much of the rest of the population the Soviet past seems so distant that it's almost irrelevant. In a quarter of a century since regaining independence, Latvia has drifted far away from its eastern neighbours, both mentally and politically. Now a member of the EU and NATO, it is a functioning democracy with rule of law standards unthinkable in Russia and Belarus.

Living standards are at least as high, despite Latvia having none of Russia's natural resources or industries. The sheer number of restaurants, cafes, shops and businesses offering all imaginable services puts it in a totally different league. Latvia's cultural pulse is also beating fast – the number of people professionally involved in art, design and philosophy one inevitably befriends in Rīga's trendy bars is astounding. Perhaps most striking of all is the level of environmental protection, as the whole country looks like a giant national park with pristine forests, beaches and lakes.

But Latvia remains divided along the ethnic lines. After the break-up of the USSR, around 700,000 residents (a third of the total population) of primarily Russian origin were denied citizenship. Instead they were given the status of non-citizens, which gave them the same rights, except for the right to vote. The number of non-citizens has now dwindled to 12.5% after an often difficult process of naturalisation, but identity politics prevails with Latvian parties forming the government and the Russian party always in the opposition.

The two communities live fairly separate lives, but tensions never develop beyond mild rhetoric. Rīga, where the number of ethnic Latvians equals that of Russians, feels the most integrated. Most people are bilingual and the mayor is Russian, while society's cultural vanguard does a lot of good work to transcend the divide.

History

The Beginning

The first signs of modern man in the region date back to the Stone Age, although Latvians descended from tribes that migrated north from around Belarus and settled on the territory of modern Latvia around 2000 BC. These tribes settled in coastal areas to fish and take advantage of rich deposits of amber, which was more precious than gold in many places until the Middle Ages.

Eventually, four main Baltic tribes evolved: the Selonians, the Letts (or Latgals), the Semigallians and the Cours. From the latter three derived the names of three of Latvia's four principal regions: Latgale, Zemgale and Kurzeme. The fourth region, Vidzeme (Livland), derived its name from the Livs, a Finno-Ugric people unrelated to the Balts.

During succeeding centuries of foreign rule these tribes merged into one Latvian identity. They were pagan until the 13th century, when German knights forced them into the Christian fold with sword and fire. But pagan traditions linger on, with Midsummer celebrated as the most important national holiday.

Christianity

Arriving in Latvia in 1190, the first Christian missionaries tried to persuade the pagan population to convert. It was an uphill battle: as soon as the missionaries left, the new converts jumped into the river to wash off their baptism. In subsequent years more missionaries would arrive, and more Latvians would submit and then renounce Christianity.

In 1201, at the behest of the pope, German crusaders, led by Bishop von Buxhoeveden of Bremen, conquered Latvia and founded Rīga. Von Buxhoeveden also founded the Knights of the Sword, who made Rīga their base for subjugating Livonia. Colonists from northern Germany followed, and during the first period of German rule, Rīga became the major city in the German Baltic, thriving from trade between Russia and the West and joining the Hanseatic League (a medieval merchant guild) in 1282. Furs, hides, honey and wax were among the products sold westward from Russia through Rīga. Indigenous Baltic inhabitants were sidelined from the regional politics and urbanisation.

Power struggles between the Church, knights and city authorities dominated the country's history between 1253 and 1420. Rīga's bishop, elevated to archbishop in 1252, became the leader of the Church in the German-conquered lands, ruling a good slice of Livonia directly and further areas of Livonia and Estonia indirectly through his bishops. The Church clashed constantly with knights, who controlled most of the remainder of Livonia and Estonia, and with German merchant–dominated city authorities who managed to maintain a degree of independence during this period.

Sweden, Poland & Russia

The 15th, 16th and 17th centuries were marked with battles and disputes about how to divvy up what would one day become Latvia. The land was at the crossroads of several encroaching empires and everyone wanted to secure the area as a means of gaining a strategic upper hand. It was at this time that Martin Luther posted his theses and Lutheran ideals flooded east. Rīga quickly became a centre for the Reformation and merchant elites adopted the doctrine. Fervent religious movements spawned the emergence of written Latvian.

GREY SKIES ARE GONNA CLEAR UP...

Over the last two decades, Latvia's environmental climate has improved by leaps and bounds, largely due to tax reforms and an infusion of EU and private money. When the country gained its independence, the damages to the ecosystem inflicted during the Soviet era were promptly addressed. Since 1990 the amount of factory pollution has decreased by 46%, and waste water has dropped by 44%. Latvia has more than 1300 waste-water treatment plants, which have increased the purity of river waters – the Daugava and Lielupe Rivers are now deemed 'good-quality cyprinid waters'. Pesticides and chemical farming, widely used during Soviet times, have also been monitored and addressed. Today, more than 2750 hectares of farming land (around 200 farms) refrain from using any type of artificial fertilisers, which has helped reduce the number of airborne pesticides by 1000%.

Latvia's water and sewage reforms are restoring the Baltic Sea and Gulf of Rīga to their former swimmable state. The European Blue Flag water safety and purity ranking (with its rigorous criteria) has been awarded to beaches in Jūrmala, Ventspils and Liepāja.

The Latvian Sustainable Development Strategy, a broad-reaching scheme uniting environmental, social and economic structures to increase the longevity and viability of the Latvian land, was conceived in 2002.

For additional information about environmental issues and targeted programs, check out the website for Latvia's Ministry of the Environment (www.vidm.gov.lv).

Western Latvia grew in influence and power under the Duchy of Courland, a semi-autonomous kingdom governed by the capable Duke Kettler, who established far-flung colonies in the Gambia and on Tobago. At this time, southeastern Latvia was grabbed by Poland, and Sweden took Rīga and the northeast. The Russians barged in at the end of the 1620s and gobbled everything up during the Great Northern War (1700–21).

National Awakening

The idea of a cohesive national identity began around the 17th century, when the peasant descendants of the original tribes started to unite under the name 'Latvia'. By the mid-19th century, the sentiment grew stronger as the first newspapers printed their issues in Latvian and the first Song and Dance Festival started up. Farmers flocked to the big city and demanded equal rights. Political parties emerged to organise worker strikes to oust the remaining German aristocracy. Democratic leaders would later call this push for freedom the 'Latvian Revolution'.

A Taste of Freedom

Out of the post-WWI confusion and turmoil arose an independent Latvian state, declared on 18 November 1918. By the 1930s Latvia had achieved one of the highest standards of living in all of Europe. In 1934 a bloodless coup, led by Kārlis Ulmanis, Latvia's first president, ended the power of parliament.

The Soviets were the first to recognise Latvia's independence, but the honeymoon didn't last long. Soviet occupation began in 1939 with the Molotov-Ribbentrop Pact. Nationalisation, killings and mass deportations to Siberia followed. Latvia was occupied partly or wholly by Nazi Germany from 1941 to 1945, when an estimated 175,000 Latvians, mostly Jews, were killed or deported.

Soviet Rule

When WWII ended the Soviets marched back in, claiming to 'save' Latvia from the Nazis. A series of deportations began anew as the nation was forced to adapt to communist ideologies. Smoke-spewing factories were swiftly erected and everyone went to work like bees in a hive. Notions of individuality were stripped away as lovely country cottages and state cosmopolitan buildings were 'nationalised', forcing everyone into drab apartment blocks.

The first public protest against Soviet occupation was on 14 June 1987, when 5000 people rallied at Rīga's Freedom Monument to commemorate the 1941 Siberia deportations. New political organisations emerged in the summer of 1988. The Popular Front of Latvia (PLF) quickly rose to the forefront of the Latvian political scene. Less than two months later, on 23 August 1989, two million Latvians, Lithuanians and Estonians formed a 650km human chain from Vilnius, through Rīga, to Tallinn, to mark the 50th anniversary of the Molotov-Ribbentrop Pact.

Looking Towards Today

When Russian democratic forces led by Boris Yeltsin came out as winners in a standoff known as the August Coup, Latvia was finally free to go its own way. The country declared independence on 21 August 1991, and on 17 September 1991 Latvia, along with Estonia and Lithuania, joined the UN and began taking steps to consolidate its newfound nationhood. Democratic elections were held in 1993 and the new government, headed by Guntis Ulmanis (a farmer and descendant of Kārlis Ulmanis), lurched from crisis to crisis, while a game of prime minister roulette followed the devastating crash of the country's largest commercial bank.

In 1999 Vaira Vīķe-Freiberga, a Latvian by birth but who spent most of her life in Canada, won the presidential election with her promise of propelling the country towards EU membership. It was a tough uphill battle as the nation shook off its antiquated Soviet fetters, and on 1 May 2004 the EU opened its doors to the fledgling nation. Long the Baltic laggard (and the poorest country in the EU), Latvia registered the highest economic growth in the EU in 2004, 2005, 2006 and 2007, even though thousands of Latvians left for jobs in Ireland and elsewhere.

As it turned out, however, much of Latvia's modern economy was built like a house of cards, and thus overspending and borrowing damaged the domestic economy during the global economic crisis that swept across the world at the end of 2008 and the beginning of 2009. The subsequent years were spent clearing the rubble caused by the economic collapse. The crisis in Ukraine affected voting patterns, with the Lavtian nationalists making gains and Saskana losing some seats in the parliamentary election held in the fall of 2014.

In 2015 the parliament elected Raimonds Vējonis the new president of Latvia. Born to a Latvian father, who was a Soviet military officer, and a Russian mother, he represents the Green Party and lists his religious views on Facebook as 'pagan'. He was seen as a compromise figure that satisfied politicians across the spectrum.

The People

Casual hellos on the street aren't common, but Latvians are a friendly and welcoming bunch. Some will find that there is a bit of guardedness in the culture, but this caution, most likely a response to centuries of foreign rule, has helped preserve the unique language and culture through changing times. As Latvia opens up to the world, this slight xenophobia is quickly melting away. Citizens are growing secure with their nation's freedom and the younger generations have access to a more cosmopolitan culture (especially since youths are almost always trilingual and speak Latvian, Russian and English).

Latvian women were traditionally responsible for preserving the hearth and home by passing on traditional songs, recipes, legends and tales. The men, enriched by these closely kept customs, would guard the land. Today, women remain a strong presence in the household but they also have prominent positions in politics and business – although gender equality is still a bit of an uphill battle. Over 41% of the nation's CEOs are women, and Latvia's most noted president was Vaira Vīķe-Freiberga.

Latvians generally adore nature and continue to incorporate their ancient pagan traditions and customs into everyday life, despite being members of the Lutheran church (ethnic Russians are mainly Orthodox or Old Believers). Superstitious beliefs are quite common and often linked to the wildlife that shares the land. In rural Latvia, families will place high wooden beams in their yard to attract storks, which are believed to bring children. Latvians also love flowers; if you go to a birthday party or are invited into someone's home, always bring a bouquet (but make sure it's an odd number of flowers – even numbers are reserved for funerals).

The Arts

Cinema

The Fisherman's Son (Zvejnieka dēls), made in 1940, marked both the beginning and the end of an era in Latvian film-making. It was the nation's first full-length sound film, but it was one of the last major works before WWII and the subsequent years of oppression. At the beginning of the USSR period, the state-owned Rīga Documentary Film Studio created heaps of movies, mostly laden with propaganda. After Stalin's death in 1953, directors earned more freedom, but it wasn't until the 1980s that pastiche and parody became commonplace. Most of the films up until then were adaptations of famous Latvian legends and modern novels.

Latvian director Jānis Streičs has produced a number of films pertinent to Latvia's turbulent past. *Limousine in the Colour of Summer Solstice Night* (1981) and *The Child of Man* (1991) remain popular for their blend of irony and comedy. The latter, about a boy growing up and falling in love in Soviet-occupied Latvia, won the Grand Prix at San Remo in 1992 and was nominated for an Academy Award for best foreign film in 1994. Streičs' more recent film, *The Mystery of the Old Parish Church* (2000), addresses the prickly issue of locals collaborating with Nazi and Soviet occupiers during WWII.

At the end of the Soviet era, the longform documentary film *Is It Easy To Be Young?* by Juris Podnieks became one of the cultural icons of the Soviet perestroika period and broke boxes across the USSR. It focused on taboo issues such as youth subcultures and crime. Podnieks went on documenting the most poignant events of the late Soviet history, such as the Spitak earthquake in Armenia and Chornobyl.

In 2010 Antra Celińska shot a film featuring *Is It Easy To Be Young?* characters, now in their 40s, recapping two decades of their lives after the collapse of the USSR.

Another star of Latvian documentary, Hertz Frank, has moved to Israel, but his *10 Minutes Older* about Izchak Rabin's assassin is an example of quintessentially Latvian film-making, whatever his current citizenship.

Also worth noting is Laila Pakalnina, whose 1998 feature film *The Shoe,* about occupied Latvia, was an official selection at the Cannes 1998 film festival. Pakalnina's 1996 film *The Mail* shows the isolation of Latvia, as symbolised by the lonely delivery of the morning mail.

Fusing folklore with surrealism and satire, Latvian animators produced some powerful films both before and after the restoration of independence. Nils Skapāns claimed Latvia's only Berlinale award with his short film *Let's Fly?!* in 1995.

Rural towns such as Kuldīga are often used to stage period pieces, while other directors prefer to use the synthetic town of Cinevilla (p235), now a major tourist attraction, for filming.

Check out www.latfilma.lv, the official website for the National Film Centre in Latvia, which offers detailed information about directors, festivals, production houses and more.

Latvian Song & Dance

Traditional folk songs have always played an integral role in Latvian culture, although the recognition of music as an established art form did not come about until the mid-19th century. In 1869 Jānis Cimze started cataloguing folk tunes, some dating back 1000 years, and his collection of 20,000 melodies became the basis for Latvia's first song festival, where thousands of singers joined together in huge choirs to celebrate traditional folk music. During the Soviet occupation the song festivals were pivotal in forging a strong sense of national identity and pride, and became part of the battle cry that rallied Latvians to fight for independence. The Song and Dance Festival is held every five years (the next one will be held in 2018) and continues to unite myriad voices in a jaw-dropping display of patriotism.

The Midsummer holiday, Ligo, is the best time to see Latvians get together and sing their favourite old songs. Warning: they will make you sing, too!

The National Opera House is the home of the Rīga Ballet, which produced Mikhail Baryshnikov and Aleksander Godunov during the Soviet years. The opera itself is considered to be one of the finest in Europe and cheap seats have made it accessible to the public, who regard the theatre with the utmost respect.

Latvia struck it big when Prāta Vētra, also known as Brainstorm, finished third at the Eurovision contest in 2000, and then the wee nation hit the jackpot when Marie N (Marija Naumova) took home the grand prize in 2002.

Art & Architecture

Of Latvia's spectrum of visual arts, visitors will be most awestruck by the collection of art nouveau architecture in Rīga (p208). The capital has more Jugendstil buildings than any other European city – 750 buildings and counting (as renovations continue).

Jānis Rozentāls, Latvia's first major painter, lived in Rīga's art nouveau district and his former home has since been transformed into a museum. Mark Rothko, born in Daugavpils, is arguably the most famous Latvian artist around the world. Although he grew up in the USA, a recent interest in the artist and his oeuvre have inspired the construction of a new modern art space, which will hopefully stimulate tourism in the otherwise quiet region of Latgale.

For other Latvian painters, check out the collection of the Latvian National Museum of Art, which includes the strange mesmerising snow and ice landscapes by its first director Vilhelms Purvits and lush expressionist works by Ludolfs Liberts. Also look out for the works of Miervaldis Polls, who was a leading nonconformist underground artist in the Soviet era, but more recently earned

EZERA SKAŅAS FESTIVAL

A romantic setting is a compulsory feature of any classical opera. Some of the world's best artists spend their lives drawing beautiful dawns and sunsets, coasts and castles, sea and mountain views, in order to match the beauty of the singing acts. But what if you take opera out of the city and into a beautiful natural setting? This is exactly what happens at Ezera Skaņas (Sounds of the Lake) Festival.

Each August the audience is taken to a remote and beautiful lake where a performance is staged in its very middle, with spectators watching from rowing boats. For the greatest dramatic effect, the performances take place at dawn.

Start checking www.ezeraskanas.lv and the festival's Facebook page in July for details of the venue and tickets.

a reputation as a 'court artist' by painting post-independence Latvian leaders.

For the latest in Latvian contemporary art, head to Rīga for the Survival Kit festival in September, which showcases the best local artists as well as rising international stars.

Food & Drink

Attention foodies: pack a sandwich if you don't want to pack an artery – traditional food in Latvia is (to put it nicely) very hearty. For centuries, eating has been but a utilitarian task rather than an art and a pleasure, and although things have changed in Rīga, one should still expect greasy menus governed by the almighty pig and ubiquitous potato.

Staples & Specialities

A walk through a Latvian market, such as Rīga's Central Market, will quickly reveal the local faves: roasted meats (including heaps of sausage), smoked fish (herring, pike, trout or salmon), fried potatoes, boiled veggies and loads of pork grease. Dairy products are also a big hit, and *biezpiens* (cottage cheese), *siers* (cheese) and *rūgušpiens* (curdled milk) are main ingredients in many dishes. In fact, during Soviet times dairy products from Latvia were considered a delicacy all over the Union.

During the summer months, picking berries is a national obsession. During autumn, fresh-picked mushrooms, cranberries and nuts replace strawberries and raspberries at the little stalls. Honey is another popular delicacy; Latvians are intrepid beekeepers and many farms have beehives and honey-production facilities.

Those with a sweet tooth won't be disappointed: berries turn into scrumptious fruit pies and *kūka* (tarts). Ancient Cour Viking dessert recipes made from sweet creams and dark breads can still be found in western Latvia. Be sure to try *rupjmaizes kārojums/kārtojums,* which tastes like Black Forest gateau.

Design Your Own Hangover

Not to be missed is Latvia's famous Black Balzām, which Goethe called 'the elixir of life'. This insidious jet-black, 45% proof concoction is a secret recipe created by Rīga druggist Abraham Kunze in the 18th century. Orange peel, oak bark, wormwood and linden blossoms are among some 14 fairy-tale ingredients known to stew in the wicked witch's cooking pot. A shot a day keeps the doctor away, so say most of Latvia's pensioners. Its name originates from *balsamon,* the ancient Greek word for a sweet-smelling medicinal balm or ointment. Its opaque ceramic bottle, labelled with a black-and-gold Rīga skyline, is reminiscent of the clay jars the potent liquid used to be stored in during the 18th and 19th centuries to keep it safe from sunlight.

Alus (beer) has long been a traditional favourite, and for such a small country Latvia has more than its share of breweries. Figure around €2 for a pint in a bar. Try Valmiermuižas Alus, Aldaris Alus or Cēsu Alus brands, and keep an eye out for Bauskas, Piebalgas, Tērvetes and Užavas, each with a distinct taste.

Wine choices are often found on restaurant and bar menus, and tend to be a selection from the usual gamut of celebrated wine-producing nations, as well as lesser regions like the Caucasus.

DO IT YOURSELF: BLACK BALZĀM COCKTAILS

A jug of Black Balzām is the perfect souvenir to bring home to your loved ones. The slender bottle has an attractive antique design, and its contents – a secret concoction of herbs and berries – are delicious. Give your family and friends a little taste of Rīga by mixing them one of the following popular Black Balzām cocktails:

Black Mojito Mix one part Black Balzām with four parts lemon-lime soda, add half of a smashed lime and a drizzle of fruit syrup. Serve over crushed ice.

Innocent Balzām Blend one part Black Balzām, 0.5 parts peach liqueur, three parts peach juice, three parts vanilla ice cream and one canned peach.

Lazybones Add a shot of Black Balzām to a cold glass of cola (our favourite).

EAT YOUR WORDS

These days, most restaurants have English menus, but why not impress your waiter and order your pork gristle in Latvian. We've listed a few of the more useful eating phrases here as well.

Useful Phrases

A table for ... people, please.	Lūdzu galdu ... personām.	loo-dzu gahl-du ...per-so-nahm
Do you have a menu?	Vai jums ir ēdienkarte?	vai yums ir eh-dean-kar-te
I'm a vegetarian.	Es esmu veģetārietis/te. (m/f)	es es-mu ve-gye-tah-reah-tis/te
What do you recommend?	Ko jūs iesakat?	kwo yoos eah-sah-kut
I'd like ...	Es vēlos ...	es vaa-lwos ...
The bill, please.	Lūdzu rēķinu.	loo-dzu reh-kyi-nu

Food Glossary

beefsteak with fried onions	sīpolu sitenis	see-po-luh see-ten-ees
beetroot soup (similar to borscht)	biešu zupa	bee-eh-shu zoo-pa
diced vegetable salad in sour cream and mayonnaise	dārzeņu salāti	dar-zen sa-la-tee
dumplings	pelmeņi	pell-me-nee
fish soup	zivju zupa	zeev-yoo zoo-pah
fresh grated cabbage	kāpostu salāti	kah-post sa-la-tee
fried salmon with potatoes and pickled and fresh vegetables	cepts lasis ar piedevām	tsepts lah-sees ar pee-eh-dev-am
fried pork chop with potatoes and pickled and fresh vegetables	karbonāde ar piedevām	kar-bo-nah-deh ar pee-eh-dev-am
grey peas with pork fat and onions	pelēkie zirņi ar speķi	peh-leh-kee-eh zeer-nee ar speh-kyi
hunter's sausages (pork)	mednieku desiņas	med-nye-kuh deh-see-nyas
meatballs	kotletes	kot-leh-tess
pickled herring with sour cream, egg and beetroot	siļķe kažokā	seel-kye kah-djo-kah
salmon in cream sauce	lasis krējuma mērcē	lah-sis kreh-ma mehr-tse
salmon in mushroom and dill sauce	lasis sēņu un diļļu mērcē	lah-sis seh-nyu oon di-lyu mehr-tse
sausage (usually smoked)	desa	deh-sa

LATVIA FOOD & DRINK

Where to Eat & Drink

Restorāns (restaurants) in Latvia are generally slower, sit-down affairs, while *kafejnīca* (pronounced ka-fay-*neet*-za; cafes) are multipurpose facilities where patrons enjoy a coffee, a faster meal or drinks in the evening. Bars, especially in Rīga and other major cities, often serve a full range of food. For quick, self-service choices, keep an eye out for *pelmeņi* (dumpling) and pancake shops, cafeteria-style venues such as some of the links in the LIDO restaurant chain, and supermarkets, namely Rimi, which sell to-go snacks and meals. Small towns have Latvian restaurants that

EATING PRICE RANGES

We've based the following Latvian price ranges on the average price of a main dish.

€ less than €7

€€ €7 to €14

€€€ more than €14

often offer the occasional international dish (usually pizza).

A Latvian *brokastis* (breakfast), available from sunrise to around 11am, usually consists of bread and cheese, cold meat and smoked fish. *Pusidienās* (lunch) and *vakariņas* (dinner) are more substantial affairs, with heartier Baltic staples. Restaurants serve lunch at midday and daylight patterns often influence dinner times, which can vary from 5pm to midnight.

SURVIVAL GUIDE

ℹ Directory A–Z

ACCOMMODATION

We highly advise booking ahead during the high season (summer). Rates drop significantly in the colder months.

Most rooms are en suite. Smoking in the rooms is normally prohibited.

Visit www.hotels.lv for more info about Latvia's hospitality industry. Check out www.camping.lv for details on pitching a tent.

ACTIVITIES

Latvia's miles of forested acreage are great for hiking, cycling, camping, birdwatching, berry-picking, mushrooming and canoeing during the summer months. The Latvian coast is an almost uninterrupted stretch of wide sand beach backed by pine-covered dunes. Water-sports centres can be found on the Gulf of Rīga and the Kurzeme coast. In winter, skiing and snowshoeing are but some of the uplifting pursuits Latvia has to offer active visitors.

CUSTOMS REGULATIONS

The Latvian Tourism Development Agency (www.latviatourism.lv) posts the latest customs rules on its website.

There are no customs controls at the borders with other EU countries. When travelling within the Schengen zone, tourists (18 years and up) are allowed to move 800 cigarettes, 200 cigars or 1kg of tobacco across the border. For alcohol, the maximum is 110L of beer, 90L of wine (not more than 60L of sparkling wine) and 10L of other alcohol products. When travelling beyond the EU, quantities of cigarettes and alcohol are reduced to 200 cigarettes, 50 cigars, 250g of smoking tobacco and 1L of distilled beverages.

Exporting documents or copies from the state archive also require permits; see www.mantojums.lv.

EMBASSIES & CONSULATES

Most embassies are in Rīga. New Zealand does not have an embassy in Latvia; Australia's is an informal consulate.

Australian Consulate (☑ 6732 0509; Vilandes iela 7)

Belarusian Embassy (☑ 6732 5321; www.latvia.mfa.gov.by; Jēzusbaznīcas 12)

Canadian Embassy (☑ 6781 3945; www.baltic states.gc.ca; Baznīcas iela 20/22)

Estonian Embassy (☑ 6781 2020; www.estemb.lv; Skolas iela 13)

French Embassy (☑ 6703 6600; www.amba-france-lv.org; Raiņa bulvāris 9)

German Embassy (☑ 6708 5100; www.riga.diplo.de; Raiņa bulvāris 13)

Irish Embassy (☑ 6703 9370; www.embassy ofireland.lv; Alberta iela 13)

Lithuanian Embassy (☑ 6732 1519; www.lv.mfa.lt; Rūpniecības iela 24)

Netherlands Embassy (☑ 6732 6147; www.netherlandsembassy.lv; Torņa iela 4)

Russian Consulate (☑ 6721 2579; www.latvia.mid.ru; Dzirnavu iela 57)

Swedish Embassy (☑ 6768 6600; www.sweden abroad.com/riga; Pumpura iela 8)

UK Embassy (☑ 6733 8126; www.ukinlatvia.fco.gov.uk; Alunāna iela 5)

US Embassy (☑ 6710 7000 (emergency number); http://riga.usembassy.gov; Samnera Velsa iela 1)

FESTIVALS & EVENTS

Latvians find any and every excuse to throw a party and larger municipalities try to make sure visitors are entertained at all times, especially during weekends. Check relevant local tourist websites for more information.

INTERNET ACCESS

Almost all accommodation in Rīga offers some form of internet access. Hotels in smaller cities have been doing a good job of following suit. Internet cafes are extinct, but the vast majority of restaurants, cafes and bars now offer wireless connections – just ask for the password.

Lattelecom (Lattelekom; www.lattelecom.lv), Latvia's main communications service provider, has set up wi-fi beacons at every payphone around the city. Users can access the internet from within a 100m radius of these phone booths. To register for a Lattelecom password and username, call ☎ 9000 4111, or send an SMS with the word 'WiFi' to ☎ 1188.

Public libraries across the country are good sources of free wi-fi.

INTERNET RESOURCES

Dear intrepid traveller, meet **www.1188.lv**, your new best friend. Latvia's top search engine is like a genie that grants three wishes...and then 1000 more, answering any questions you might have about bus and train transport, postal services, business listings, traffic reports and taxis. You can even send an SMS to the website service to get listings sent to your phone.

The Latvian Tourism Development Agency (www.latvia.travel) and the Latvia Institute (www.li.lv) both have fantastic websites providing information targeted at foreign visitors.

MAPS

Country, city and town maps of Latvia are available from Rīga-based **Jāņa sēta** (☎ 6724 0894; Elizabetes iela 83-85; ◷ 10am-7pm Mon-Sat, to 5pm Sun). Its town-plan series covers practically every town in Latvia; individual maps range in scale from 1:15,000 to 1:20,000 and cost €3 to €5.

The **Latvian Tourism Development Agency** (www.latvia.travel) has a very detailed map covering each of Latvia's four regions.

MONEY

Latvia abandoned its national currency, the lats, and switched to the euro in January 2014.

POST

The official website of Latvia's postal service (www.post.lv) can answer any of your mail-related questions, including shipping and stamp prices. Service is reliable; mail to North America takes 10 days, and within Europe about a week.

PUBLIC HOLIDAYS

The Latvia Institute website (www.li.lv) has a page devoted to special Latvian Remembrance Days under the 'About Latvia' link.

New Year's Day 1 January

Easter March/April

Labour Day 1 May

Restoration of Independence of the Republic of Latvia 4 May

Mothers' Day Second Sunday in May

Whitsunday A Sunday in May or June

Līgo Eve (Midsummer festival) 23 June

Jāņi (St John's Day and Summer Solstice) 24 June

National Day Anniversary of proclamation of Latvian Republic, 1918, on 18 November

Christmas (Ziemsvētki) 25 December

Second Holiday 26 December

New Year's Eve 31 December

TELEPHONE SERVICES

Latvian telephone numbers have eight digits; landlines start with '6' and mobile numbers start with '2'. To make any call within Latvia, simply dial the eight-digit number. To call a Latvian telephone number from abroad, dial the international access code, then the country code for Latvia (☎ 371) followed by the subscriber's eight-digit number.

Telephone rates are posted on the website of the partly state-owned Lattelecom (www.lattelecom.lv), which enjoys a monopoly on fixed-line telephone communications in Latvia.

Mobile phones are available for purchase at most shopping malls around Rīga and other major cities. If your own phone is GSM900-/1800-compatible, you can purchase a prepaid SIM-card package and top-up credit from any Narvesen *superette* or Rimi grocery store.

Calls on a public phone are made using cardphones called *telekarte*, which come in different denominations and are sold at post offices, newspaper stands and *superettes*.

TOURIST INFORMATION

In recent years, the **Latvian Tourism Development Agency** (☎ 6722 9945; www.latvia.travel) has been streamlining tourist information throughout the country. Try www.tourism.*city name*.lv, or simply www.*city name*.lv for official city websites (English translations are often limited for small destinations). Every city and town in Latvia worth visiting has a tourist office, open during normal business hours (at the very least), with extended hours during the summer. Almost all of the tourist offices have English-speaking staff and oodles of pamphlets and maps.

Check out the website of the Latvia Institute (www.li.lv) for additional information about Latvia.

LATVIA DIRECTORY A–Z

SLEEPING PRICE RANGES

The following price ranges refer to the cost of a double room with private bathroom.

€ less than €40

€€ €40 to €80

€€€ more than €80

ⓘ LIVE LIKE A LOCAL

Planning on sticking around town for a while? Check out Rent In Riga (www.rentinriga.lv) for a detailed listing of available (and red-tape-free!) apartments in town. Click on Vecrīga or Centrs to find a flat in the core of the city.

ⓘ Getting There & Away

AIR

Rīga International Airport (Starptautiskā Lidosta Rīga; ☑ 1817; www.riga-airport.com; Mārupe District; ☑ 22), about 13km southwest of the city centre, houses Latvia's national carrier, **airBaltic** (☑ 9000 1100; www.airbaltic.com), which offers direct flights to over 50 destinations within Europe, including Tallinn and Vilnius.

LAND

In 2007 Latvia acceded to the Schengen Agreement, which removed all border controls between it and both Estonia and Lithuania. We advise carrying your travel documents with you at all times, as random border checks do occur.

Bus

Ecolines (☑ 6721 4512; www.ecolines.net) Routes include Rīga–Pärnu–Tallinn (€17, four to 4¾ hours, seven daily), Rīga–Tartu (€7, four hours, two daily), Rīga–Vilnius (€17, four hours, seven daily), Rīga–Vilnius–Minsk (€24, eight hours, daily) and Rīga–Moscow (€60, 14 hours, daily).

Hansabuss Business Line (www.businessline. ee) Four daily buses between Rīga and Tallinn, three of which stop in Pärnu.

Lux Express & Simple Express (☑ 6778 1350; www.luxexpress.eu) Routes include Rīga–Pärnu–Tallinn (from €13, 4½ hours, 11 daily), Rīga–Tartu–St Petersburg (from €23, 12 hours, four daily), Rīga–Vilnius (from €11, four hours, 10 daily) and Rīga–Kaliningrad (€20, eight hours, daily).

Car & Motorcyle

Rental cars are allowed to travel around the Baltics at no extra fee. We recommend notifying your vehicle renter when you take the car off the lot.

Train

Train travel is convenient for a limited number of destinations, most notably Jūrmala, Gauja National Park and Daugavpils.

SEA

Ferry services from Rīga, Liepāja and Ventspils connect Latvia to Swedish and German ports.

ⓘ Getting Around

BUS

Buses are much more convenient than trains if you're travelling beyond the capital's collection of suburban rail lines. Updated timetables are available at www.autoosta.lv and www.1188.lv.

CAR & MOTORCYCLE

Driving is on the right-hand side. Headlights must be on at all times. Be sure to ask for '*benzene*' when looking for a petrol station – *gāze* means 'air'.

You'll find the usual suspects when it comes to renting a vehicle; however, several small businesses in Rīga offer cheaper options than the international companies at the airport – expect cash-only transactions and free delivery anywhere in the capital. Rentals range from €30 to €60 per day, depending on the type of car and time of year. The number of automatic cars in Latvia is limited. Companies usually allow you to drive in all three Baltic countries, but not beyond.

AddCar Rental (☑ 26589674; www.addcar rental.com)

Auto (☑ 29580448; www.carsrent.lv)

EgiCarRent (☑ 29531044; www.egi.lv)

TRAIN

Most Latvians live in the large suburban ring around Rīga, thus the city's network of commuter rails makes it easy for tourists to reach day-tripping destinations. Latvia's further attractions are best explored by bus. All train schedule queries can be answered at www.pv.lv as well as at www.1188.lv.

Lithuania

Best Places to Eat

➡ Hotel Restaurant Labanoras (p327)

➡ Balzac (p308)

➡ Senoji Kibininė (p321)

➡ Lokys (p309)

➡ Sweetroot (p309)

Best Places to Stay

➡ Miškiniškės (p325)

➡ Bernardinu B&B (p306)

➡ Miško Namas (p370)

➡ Litinterp Guesthouse (p359)

➡ Domus Maria (p306)

Why Go?

A land of wood and water, proud, independent Lithuania (Lietuva) is fast being recognised as one of Europe's gems. Southernmost of the Baltic states, it's a pocket-sized republic that's a nature lover's delight, yet lacks nothing in urban excitement.

Lithuania's foremost attraction is its stunning Baltic coastline, especially the unique sliver of white sand known as Curonian Spit. Lonely coastal wetlands lure migrating birds by the tens of thousands while inland, lush forests watch over burnished lakes.

The capital, Vilnius, is a beguiling artists' enclave, its timeworn courtyards, cobbled streets and baroque churches animated by the vibrant, optimistic culture of today.

Further afield, remnants of Soviet times – a disused nuclear missile site (now a museum to the Cold War) and a Soviet sculpture park – are reminders of a dark recent past, while the Hill of Crosses and Orvydas stone garden stand testament to the land's enduring faith.

When to Go

➡ Lithuania is at its best in high summer, from June to August, when the days are long, the nights are short, and the Baltic Sea's waters are warm – or at least swimmable. Festival season hits high gear: one not to miss is Klaipėda's three-day Sea Festival.

➡ Spring (April and May) is cool and arrives late but is good for canoeing, as the thawing snow feeds the rivers.

➡ Autumn (September to November) can be ideal, with sunny days and chilly nights. Culture reaches a crescendo with classical music festivals and the annual Mama Jazz festival in Vilnius.

Lithuania Highlights

❶ Wander the backstreets of the beautiful baroque capital **Vilnius** (p288), looking for that perfect bar or bistro.

❷ Head to **Curonian Spit** (p363) to spend time cycling, swimming in the Baltic Sea, or exploring hardy human settlements on this thin spit of sand and spruce.

❸ Lose yourself in the whispering rushes, teeming birdlife and perfect serenity of the **Nemunas Delta** (p373).

❹ Stare down the barrel of a disused nuclear missile silo before taking a peaceful

stroll through the woods at **Žemaitija National Park** (p381).

5 Take time out for fishing, boating, bathing and berrying in Lithuania's beloved lakeland, **Aukštaitija National Park** (p323).

6 Stroll, boat or take the waters at **Druskininkai** (p328), Lithuania's leading spa resort.

7 Walk through **Orvydas Garden** (p380), a peaceful rock and statue garden that feels as holy as the Hill of Crosses and as quiet as a national park.

VILNIUS

📱 5 / POP 546,700

Vilnius (vil-nyus), the baroque beauty of the Baltics, is a city of immense allure. It easily tops the country's best-attraction bill, drawing tourists like moths to a flame with an easy, confident charm and a warm, golden glow that makes you wish for long midsummer evenings every day of the year.

The capital may be a long way north and east, but it's quintessentially continental, with Europe's largest baroque Old Town at its heart. Viewed from a hot-air balloon, the skyline – pierced by countless Orthodox and Catholic church steeples – looks like a giant bed of nails. Adding to this heady mix is a combination of cobbled alleys, crumbling corners, majestic hilltop views, breakaway states and traditional artists' workshops – all in a city so small you'd sometimes think it was a village.

It has not always been so happy here, though. There are reminders of loss and pain too, from the KGB's torture cells to the ghettos where the Jewish community was concentrated before being murdered by the Nazis. Yet the spirit of freedom and resistance has prevailed, and the city is forging a new identity, combining the past with a present and future that involves world cuisine, a burgeoning nightlife and shiny new skyscrapers.

History

Legend says Vilnius was founded in the 1320s, when Lithuanian grand duke Gediminas dreamt of an iron wolf that howled with the voices of 100 wolves – a sure sign to build a city as mighty as their cry. In fact, the site had already been settled for 1000 years.

A moat, a wall and a tower on Gediminas Hill protected 14th- and 15th-century Vilnius from Teutonic attacks. Tatar attacks prompted inhabitants to build a 2.4km defensive wall (1503–22), and by the end of the 16th century Vilnius was among Eastern Europe's biggest cities. Three centuries on, industrialisation arrived: railways were laid and Vilnius became a key Jewish city. Occupied by Germany during WWI, it became an isolated pocket of Poland afterwards. WWII ushered in another German occupation and the death knoll for its Jewish population. After the war, Vilnius' skyline was filled with new residential suburbs populated by Lithuanians from other parts of the country, alongside immigrant Russians and Belarusians. In the late 1980s the capital was the focus of Lithuania's push for independence from the USSR.

Vilnius has fast become a European city. In 1994 its Old Town became a Unesco World Heritage Site and 15 years later shared the prestigious title of European Capital of Culture with the Austrian city Linz. Much of Old Town has been sensitively restored.

◉ Sights

Vilnius is a compact city, and most sights are easily reached on foot. Those visiting for a couple of days will scarcely move out of Old Town, where souvenir stalls, folk-artist workshops and designer boutiques jostle for attention with a treasure trove of architectural gems. Stay a couple more days and the New Town beckons, with its museums, shops and riverside action.

Begin your exploration of the city at epicentral Cathedral Sq, with Gediminas Hill rising behind it. Southward lies the cobbled Old Town, bisected by Pilies gatvė. Heading west, Gedimino prospektas drives through the heart of the New Town to parliament, and has several sights worth taking in.

◉ Gediminas Hill

Vilnius was founded on 48m-high Gediminas Hill, topped since the 13th century by a redbrick tower. To reach the top of the hill, clamber up the rocky steps behind the Cathedral's southeastern side or take the funicular.

LANGUAGE

Hello	Sveiki	*svay*-ki
Hi (informal)	Labas	*lah*-bahs
How are you?	Kaip gyvuojate?	*kaip*-gee-vu-aw-*yah*-ta
Goodbye	Sudie	*su*-deah
Thank you	Dėkoju	deh-*kaw*-yu
I'm lost (f/m)	Aš paklyd(usi/ęs)	ahsh-*pah*-klee-d(usi/as)

Gediminas Castle & Museum MUSEUM

(Gedimino Pilis ir Muziejus; Map p294; ☑ 5-261 7453; www.lnm.lt; Arsenalo gatvė 5; adult/child €2/1; ⊙ 10am-7pm daily Apr-Sep, 10am-5pm Tue-Sun Oct-Mar) With its prime hilltop location above the junction of the Neris and Vilnia Rivers, Gediminas Castle is the last of a series of settlements and fortified buildings occupying this site since Neolithic times. This brick version, built by Grand Duke Vytautas in the early 15th century, offers 360-degree views of Vilnius, and an exhibition tracing the history of the castle across the centuries, complete with scale models.

The original tower was a tier higher than the 20m structure that marks the spot today. Its walls were ruined during the Russian occupation (1655–61), but it was restored in 1930 to house the Upper Castle Museum, which contains shiny armour from the 16th to 18th centuries and models of the castle in former times, as well as providing panoramic views of the city.

Funicular to Gediminas Hill CABLE CAR

(Map p294; ☑ 5-261 7453; www.lnm.lt; Arsenalo gatvė 5; adult/student €1.50/1; ⊙ 10am-7pm May-Sep, to 5pm Oct-Apr) This is the quickest and easiest way to the top of Gediminas Hill, with great views en route. The entrance is behind the northeastern side of the Cathedral, inside a small courtyard at the rear of the Museum of Applied Art.

◎ Cathedral Square

Katedros aikštė buzzes with local life. In the 19th century markets and fairs were held here and a moat ran around what is now the square's perimeter so ships could sail to the cathedral door. Within the moat were walls and towers, the only remaining part of which is the 57m-tall **belfry** near the cathedral's western end.

In front of the entrance to the Royal Palace, at the square's eastern end, is an **equestrian statue of Gediminas** (Map p294), built on an ancient pagan site.

Behind the grand old duke, **Bernardinų sodas** leads to **Three Crosses Hill** and **Kalnų Park**.

★ Palace of the Grand Dukes of Lithuania MUSEUM

(Valdovų rumai; Map p294; ☑ 5-212 7476; www.valdovurumai.lt; Katedros aikštė 4; adult/student €2.90/1.45, guided tour €20.27; ⊙ museum 10am-6pm Tue-Thu & Sat, to 8pm Fri, to 4pm Sun) On a

site that has been settled since at least the 4th century AD stands the latest in a procession of fortified palaces, repeatedly remodelled, extended, destroyed and rebuilt over the centuries. What visitors now see is a painstaking restoration of its final grand manifestation, the baroque palace built for the Grand Dukes in the 17th century. While the gleamingly white complex is evidently new, it contains fascinating historical remains, and is a potent symbol of revitalised, independent Lithuania.

Underneath the central courtyard begins a fantastic exposition through two millennia of Lithuanian history. Guided through the strata of the palace's foundations, visitors can see the literal bones of successive episodes in the history of the building, and the nation. A second tour explores the reconstructed ceremonial halls of the Grand Duchy, while planned third and fourth tours will explore Lithuanian and European material culture from the time of the Grand Dukes.

Vilnius Cathedral CATHEDRAL

(Vilniaus Arkikatedra; Map p294; ☑ 5-261 0731; www.katedra.lt; Katedros aikštė 1; ⊙ 7am-7pm) Known in full as the Cathedral of St Stanislav and St Vladislav, this national symbol occupies a spot originally used for the worship of Perkūnas, the Lithuanian thunder god. Seventeenth-century **St Casimir's Chapel**, with its a baroque cupola, coloured marble and frescoes of the saint's life, is the showpiece, while the **crypts** (adult/child €4.50/2.50 ⊙ 10am-4pm Mon-Sat) are the final resting place of many prominent Lithuanians, including Vytautas the Great (1350–1430). The website has details of Mass.

The first wooden cathedral was built here in 1387–88; after several episodes of destruction and reconstruction, the present classical edifice was erected – following the

LITHUANIA VILNIUS

Vilnius

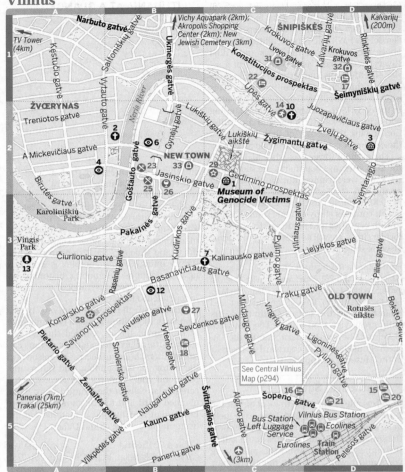

original Gothic floor plan and incorporating St Casimir's and the Valavičius family chapels – in the late 18th century. From 1950 the Soviets used the cathedral as a warehouse, gallery and concert venue, before its reconsecration in 1989.

Cathedral Belfry
HISTORIC BUILDING
(Map p294; ☎8-600 12080; www.bpmuziejus.lt; Katedros aikštė; adult/student €4.50/2.50; ☺10am-7pm Tue-Sat May-Sep, to 6pm Oct-Apr) Once part of the city's 13th-century defences, the belfry in front of Vilnius Cathedral is, at 57m high, one of the tallest towers in the city. There's a small exhibition of historic bells here, but the primary reasons to climb the narrow stairs are priceless views of the city and Gediminas Hill.

National Museum of Lithuania
MUSEUM
(Lietuvos Nacionalinis Muziejus; Map p294; ☎5-262 7774; www.lnm.lt; Arsenalo gatvė 1; adult/child €2/1; ☺10am-6pm Tue-Sun) Building on the collections compiled by the Museum of Antiquities since 1855, this splendid museum shows artefacts from Lithuanian life from Neolithic times to the 20th century. It has special collections devoted to the country's

sacred art. Many pieces were discovered in Vilnius Cathedral in 1985 after being hidden in the walls by Russian soldiers in 1655. Because of fear that they'd be seized by the Soviets, the works, valued at €11 million, remained a secret until 1998, when they were finally displayed to the world.

⊙ Old Town

Eastern Europe's largest Old Town deserves its Unesco status. The area, stretching 1.5km south from Katedros aikštė, was built up in the 15th and 16th centuries, and its narrow winding streets, hidden courtyards and lavish old churches retain the feel of bygone centuries. One of the purest pleasures the city has to offer is aimlessly wandering Old Town backstreets. The main axis is along Pilies, Didžioji and Aušros Vartų gatvė. Its approximate boundary, starting from Katedros aikštė, runs along Stuokos-Gucevičiaus, Liejyklos, Vilniaus, Trakų, Pylimo, Bazilijonų, Šv Dvasios, Bokšto, Maironio, Radvilaitės and Šventaragio streets – an area of roughly 1 sq km.

Pilies Gatvė

Cobbled Pilies gatvė (Castle St) – the hub of tourist action and the main entrance to Old Town from Katedros aikštė – buzzes with buskers, souvenir stalls and the odd beggar. Until the 19th century the street was separated from the square by the lower castle wall, which ran across its northern end. Only a gate in the wall connected the two. Notice the 15th- to 17th-century brickwork of Nos 4, 12 and 16 towards the northern end of the street.

House of Signatories MUSEUM
(Signatarų Namai; Map p294; ☎ 5-231 4437; www.lnm.lt; Pilies gatvė 26; admission €0.58; ⊙ 10am-5pm Tue-Sat) Lithuania's Declaration of Independence was signed here on 16 February 1918. Now, across 14 rooms of this 18th-century house, you'll find a reverent exhibition of materials relating to the National Movement. Independence didn't last long; by 1920 the Poles had retaken Vilnius and the city was only returned to the Lithuanian heartland in 1939 as a 'gift' by Stalin.

Vilnius University

★ **Vilnius University** HISTORIC BUILDING
(Vilniaus Universitetas; Map p294; ☎ 5-268 7298; www.vu.lt; Universiteto gatvė 3; admission to architectural ensemble adult/child €1.50/0.50; ⊙ 9am-6pm Mon-Fri Mar-Oct, 9.30am-5.30pm Mon-Sat Nov-Apr) Founded in 1579 during the Counter-Reformation, Vilnius University was run

different folk traditions, to numismatics (including some of the very first Lithuanian coins) and to burial goods. A statue of Mindaugas, Lithuania's sole king, stands guard over the entrance.

Museum of Applied Art MUSEUM
(Taikomosios Dailės Muziejus; Map p294; ☎ 5-262 8080; www.ldm.lt; Arsenalo gatvė 3a; adult/student €1.74/0.86; ⊙ 11am-6pm Tue-Sat, 11am-4pm Sun) The Old Arsenal, built in the 16th century and restored in the 1980s, houses temporary exhibitions and a permanent collection showcasing 15th- to 19th-century Lithuanian

Vilnius

by Jesuits for two centuries and became one of the greatest centres of Polish learning. It produced many notable scholars but was closed by the Russians in 1832 and didn't reopen until 1919. Today it has 23,000 students and Lithuania's oldest library, shelving five million books (including one of two originals of *The Catechism* by Martynas Mažvydas, the first book ever published in Lithuanian).

The campus's spectacular 'architectural ensemble' features 13 courtyards framed by 15th-century buildings, 300-year-old frescoes, and the Church of Sts Johns.

Sts Johns' Church   CHURCH
(Šv Jonų bažnyčia; Map p294; www.jonai.lt; Šv Jono gatvė 12; campanile €2.50; ☉10am-5pm) The full name is 'Church of St Johns, St John the Baptist and Sts John the Apostle and Evangelist', but 'St Johns' (plural) will do nicely. Founded in 1387, it predates the 16th-century university within which it is situated, although the present late-baroque structure was built following an 18th-century fire. Its freestanding campanile is the tallest structure in Old Town, and contains a Foucault's pendulum demonstrating the rotation of the earth.

Grand Courtyard   UNIVERSITY
(Map p294; Šv Jono gatvė 12; adult/child €1.50/0.50; ☉9am-6pm Mon-Fri Mar-Oct, 9.30am-

5.30pm Mon-Sat Nov-Apr) The gallery of the courtyard – the largest of the 13 that comprise Vilnius University's 'architectural ensemble' – features plaques commemorating the founders, patrons and notaries of the university.

Astronomical Observatory
Courtyard   OBSERVATORY
(Map p294; Universiteto gatvė) Laid over an older garden, the courtyard boasts an 18th-century observatory painted with zodiacal signs.

Central Old Town
Old Town is bisected by Pilies gatvė, which becomes Didžioji gatvė as you head south. This street widens into Rotušės aikštė, the site of the former town hall and effective heart of Old Town. Along this axis, worthwhile sights, museums and churches are spread out on both the eastern and western sides.

St Anne's Church   CHURCH
(Šv Onos Bažnyčia; Map p294; ☎8-698 17731; www.onosbaznycia.lt; Maironio gatvė 8-1; ☉11am-7pm Jun-Aug, from 5pm Sep-May, Mass 6pm Mon-Sat, 9am & 11am Sun) This gorgeous, late 15th-century Gothic church is a tiny confection of red brick, glass and arches, dwarfed by the Bernadine Church outside which it stands. Marrying 33 different kinds of brick into a whole that many regard as the most beautiful in Vilnius, it's reputed that Napo-

leon was so charmed by St Anne's that he wanted to relocate it to Paris.

Bernadine Church & Monastery CHURCH
(Šv Pranciškaus Asyžiečio parapija; Map p294; ☑5-262 6004; www.bernardinuansamblis.lt; Maironio gatvė 10; ⊙7am-7pm Mon-Fri, 8am-7pm Sat & Sun; Mass times on website) The massive buttresses and towering walls of this, one of the most impressive churches in Vilnius, are capable of defence as well as worship. After successive periods of extension and improvement in the 17th and 19th centuries, it came to a prosaic end when the Soviets converted it to a warehouse. The Bernadine community regained its building after independence, restoring it to its former glory, and adding trails for sightseers wishing to explore the complex.

Bernardinų sodas GARDEN
(Bernadine Gardens; Map p294; ☑5-261 1037; Maironio gatvė; ⊙dawn-dusk) Nestled in a crook of the Vilnia River, between Gediminas Hill and the Bernadine Church, these delightful gardens are perhaps Vilnius' prime spot to promenade on a warm afternoon. Formerly known as Sereikiškės Park, it's a harmonious blend of sloping riverbanks, ordered paths and a profusion of trees and flower beds.

Presidential Palace PALACE
(Map p294; ☑5-266 4011; www.president.lt; S Daukanto gatvė 3; ⊙tours 4.30pm Fri, 9am-2.30pm Sat) **FREE** The palace of the bishops of Vilnius in the 16th century, this classical edifice now houses the president and chancellery. It gained its current Russian Empire style early in the 19th century, and was used both by Napoleon (during his advance on Moscow) and his Russian adversary, General Mikhail Kutuzov (chasing him back to Paris). See the ceremonial changing of the guard every day at 6pm, and the flag-hoisting ceremony on Sunday at noon. Visits by guided tour (in Lithuanian, plus English in summer) must be booked in advance.

Shrine of Divine Mercy CHURCH
(Dievo Gailestingumo šventovė; Map p294; www.gailestingumas.lt; Dominikonų gatvė 12; ⊙24hr) Built in the Gothic style in the 15th century, then rebuilt after a fire in the 18th, this single-nave church contains an image of the vision in which Jesus appeared to St Faustina Kowalska. Originally dedicated to the Holy Trinity, it was reconsecrated and devoted to the Divine Mercy in 2004, having been abandoned during Soviet times.

Mickiewicz Memorial Apartment & Museum MUSEUM
(Mickevičiaus memorialinis butas-muziejus; Map p294; ☑5-279 1879; www.mb.vu.lt; Bernardinų gatvė 11; adult/child €1.16/0.58; ⊙10am-5pm Tue-Fri, to 2pm Sat & Sun) 'Lithuania, my fatherland...' is from Poland's romantic masterpiece *Pan Tadeusz*. Its Polish author Adam Mickiewicz (1798–1855) – muse to Polish nationalists in the 19th century – grew up near Vilnius and studied at the university before being exiled for anti-Russian activities in 1824. The rooms where he wrote the well-known poem *Grażyna* (Lithuanian: *Grażia;* a Polish name for a woman with Lithuanian roots meaning 'beauty') are now filled with the poet's letters.

Amber Museum-Gallery MUSEUM
(Gintaro Muziejus-Galerija; Map p294; ☑5-262 3092; www.ambergallery.lt; Šv Mykolo gatvė 8; ⊙10am-7pm) **FREE** Dedicated to Baltic gold and the beautiful things it can be crafted into, this enthusiastic little museum occupies

---

VILNIUS IN...

Two Days
Spend the first day exploring Old Town, not missing the **Cathedral**, **Pilies gatvė**, the **Gates of Dawn** and the **university's 13 courtyards**, followed by lunch on an Old Town terrace. At dusk, hike (or ride the funicular) up **Gediminas Hill** for a city-spire sunset. On the second day, stroll around the **Užupis Republic Constitution**, visit the **Museum of Genocide Victims**, and finish up with an aperitif and Vilnius panorama from the **TV Tower**.

Four Days
Depending on your interests, spend a day discovering **Jewish Vilnius**, marvelling at the religious jewels in the **Museum of Applied Art**, or taking in the collections of any of a number of other museums. Finish up with a spot of **shopping**: scour the city for linen, amber and Lithuanian fashion. You can also squeeze in a day trip by train to **Trakai** and spend a leisurely few hours out on the water.

Central Vilnius

LITHUANIA VILNIUS

NEW TOWN

250 m
0.1 miles

Neris River

Kalnų Park

Bernardinų sodas

7 G

6 Ǫ

Maironio gatvė

39 Ǫ

Olimpiečių gatvė

Arsenalo gatvė

31 🏛

Gediminas Hill

21 🏛

17 ⊙

Radvilaitės gatvė

42 Ǫ

Volano gatvė

Bernardinų gatvė

Tilto gatvė

74 🏛

29 🏛

59 🏛 **68**

3 🏛

Šv. Mykolo

92 ✕

Literatų

Karaliaus Mindaugo Bridge

55 ●

32 🏛

Palace of the Grand Dukes of Lithuania

1 🏛

Katedros aikštė (Cathedral Square)

45 ①

58 🏛

Pilies gatvė

89 ①

26 🏛
Rusų gatvė
144 🏛 **93**

69

Žygimantų gatvė

Radvilų gatvė

Vrublevskio gatvė

53 ①

8 🏛

Tourist Information Office Cathedral Sq

Šventaragio

Vilnius University

46 23 ⊙

141 🏛

Skapo gatvė

① **5** ⊙

Tilto gatvė

61 ⊙

73 🍴

Stuokos-Gucevičiaus gatvė

Universiteto gatvė

Sarbievijus Courtyard

2 🏛

Šv. Jono gatvė

Daukanto aikštė

128 🏛 ✕

78 ✕

Širvydo gatvė

49 ①

96 ✕

Odminių gatvė

120 ✺

115 ①

34 ✕
Sarbievijus

Daukanto aikštė

126 ✺

Vilniaus gatvė

Savivaldybės aikštė

135 🏛

22 ⊙

104 ①

Totorių gatvė

98 ✕

Labdarių gatvė

Tourist Information Office Old Town

35 🏛

Liejyklos gatvė

Šv. Ignoto gatvė

108 ✕
124 ✺

121 ✺

Levelio gatvė

Vienuolio gatvė

125 ✺ **142** 🏛
87

148 ✕

94 ✕
140 🏛

111 ①

79 ✕

Jogailos gatvė

100 ①

Islandijos gatvė

110 ①

41 ①

Benediktinų gatvė

119 ①

Palangos gatvė

Gedimino prospektas

90 ✕

Jakšto gatvė

70 ✺

Stulginskio gatvė

A Smetonas gatvė

138 🏛

Pamėnkalnio gatvė

24 🏛

Jewish Community of Lithuania

16 ⊙

Klaipėdos gatvė

Tauro gatvė

Kalinausko gatvė

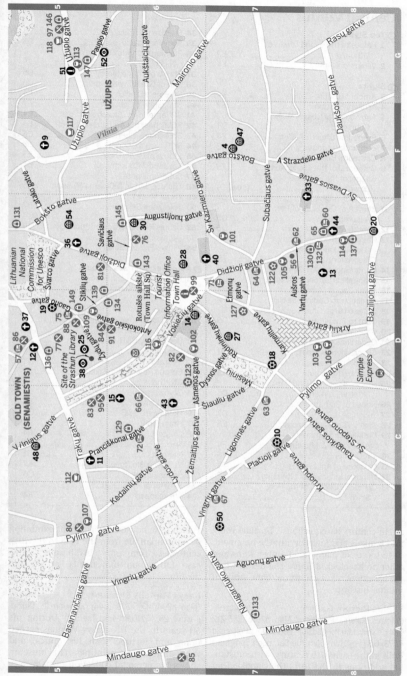

LITHUANIA VILNIUS

UŽUPIS

118 97 146
51
Užupio gatvė
113
147
52 Paupio gatvė

117
Užupio gatvė
9
Vilnia

Maironio gatvė
Aukštaičių gatvė

Rasų gatvė

47
4
Bokšto gatvė
A Strazdelio gatvė
Subačiaus gatvė
Šv Dvasios gatvė
33
Daukšos gatvė

131
Latako gatvė
Bokšto gatvė
54
145
30 Augustijonų gatvė
Savičiaus gatvė
76
36
Didžioji gatvė
101
60
65
44
20
137
114
130
132
13
105
122
62
56
Aušros
Vartų gatvė
64

Lithuanian National Commission for Unesco
Švarco gatvė
19
Gaono gatvė
37
Stiklių gatvė
149
139
81
134
143
Rotušės aikštė (Town Hall Sq)
Tourist Information Office
Town Hall
28
40
Didžioji gatvė
99
71
127
Etmonų gatvė
Kamienių gatvė
Arklių gatvė
Bazilijonų gatvė

57 86
12
136
Site of the Strashun Library
38
Žydų gatvė
25
Antokolskio gatvė
84
91
109
116
Vokiečių gatvė
14
102
82
123
27
18
Rūdninkų gatvė
Mėsinių gatvė
103
106
Simple Express

OLD TOWN (SENAMIESTIS)
48
Vilniaus gatvė
Trakų gatvė
83
95
15
66
43
Ašmenos gatvė
Dysnos gatvė
Šiaulių gatvė
63
Pylimo gatvė
Šv Stepono gatvė

112
Pranciškonai
129
72
11
Kėdainių gatvė
Žemaitijos gatvė
Lydos gatvė
Ligoninės gatvė
Plačioji gatvė
10
Raugyklos gatvė
Knupho gatvė

80
107
Pylimo gatvė
Vingrių gatvė
67
50
Aguonų gatvė

Basanavičiaus gatvė
Vingrių gatvė
Kėdainių gatvė
Nešaiduko gatvė
133
Mindaugo gatvė
Mindaugo gatvė
85

Central Vilnius

a 17th-century baroque house. Upstairs you'll find trinkets and jewellery; in the basement, huge pieces of many-hued amber, kilns and other archaeological finds. The descent into the basement takes you through the strata of Vilnius' history.

Vilnius Picture Gallery MUSEUM
(Vilniaus Galerija Paveikslų; Map p294; ☎5-212 0841; www.ldm.lt; Didžioji gatvė 4; adult/child €1.73/0.87; ◎11am-6pm Tue-Sat, noon-5pm Sun) Built in the early 17th century, with substantial additions in the 19th, the Chodkeviciai

Palace now houses a permanent exhibition of Lithuanian art from the 16th to the 19th centuries. Temporary exhibitions showcase Lithuanian movements, artists and mediums.

Kazys Varnelis Museum MUSEUM
(Map p294; ☎5-279 1644; www.lnm.lt; Didžioji gatvė 26; ◎10am-4pm Tue-Sat) During his 50 years in the US, Kazys Varnelis earned fame and fortune with his optical and three-dimensional paintings. This museum shows his personal collection of paintings,

furniture, sculptures, maps and books, including works by Albrecht Dürer, Francisco Goya and Matteo di Giovanni. Visits are by appointment only, so call beforehand.

MK Čiurlionis House   HISTORIC BUILDING
(Map p294; ☎5-262 2451; www.mkcnamai.lt; Savičiaus gatvė 11; ☉10am-4pm Mon-Fri) FREE Inside the former home of the great artist and composer are a handful of Čiurlionis reproductions, worth seeing if you can't make it to the National Čiurlionis Art Museum in Kaunas.

St Casimir's Church   CHURCH
(Šv Kazimiero Bažnyčia; Map p294; ☎5-212 1715; www.kazimiero.lt; Didžioji gatvė 34; ☉9am-6.30pm Mon-Fri, 8am-1.30pm Sun) This striking church is the city's oldest baroque place of worship. St Casimir's dome and cross-shaped ground plan defined a new style for 17th-century churches when the Jesuits built it between 1604 and 1615. It was destroyed and rebuilt several times over the centuries and has recently emerged from another bout of renovation.

WISH UPON A...

...star? No. Not in Vilnius. Rather, a stone tile bearing the word 'stebuklas' (miracle). It marks the spot on Cathedral Sq where the human chain – formed between Tallinn and Vilnius by two million Lithuanians, Latvians and Estonians to protest Soviet occupation in 1989 – ended. To make a wish, do a clockwise 360-degree turn on the tile. Unfortunately, superstition forbids us from revealing the location of this elusive-but-lucky spot, meaning you have to search for it yourself. Hint, hint...we did tell you it was on Cathedral Sq...

St Michael the Archangel Church CHURCH
(Church Heritage Museum; Map p294; ☑5-269 7803; www.bpmuziejus.lt; Šv Mykolo gatvė 9; adult/child €4.50/2.50; ☺11am-6pm Tue-Sat) This grand early 17th-century chuch, built by the Sapiega family, now houses a wonderful museum of sacral art. The building itself, with its single nave, coloured-marble altar and alabaster statuary, is a rare example of late Renaissance architecture in Vilnius. The exhibition includes religious art, liturgical vessels and rare manuscripts, plus a precious monstrance and reliquaries from Vilnius Cathedral. Combined tickets for the museum and the belfry and crypts at Vilnius Cathedral are €10/5.

Cathedral of the Theotokos CATHEDRAL
(Orthodox Cathedral; Map p294; ☑5-215 3747; Maironio gatvė 14) An Orthodox church has stood here since Lithuania's late pagan days of the 14th century. Over the years it was burned, abandoned, rebuilt, transferred to Catholicisim and even used by Vilnius University as a lecture theatre. Reverting to the Orthodox Church during the Russification campaign of the 19th century, it is now Lithuania's main place of Orthodox worship.

Aušros Vartų Gatvė

Vilnius' oldest street – which leads south out of Didžioji gatvė to the Gates of Dawn – is laden with churches and souvenir shops.

Gates of Dawn HISTORIC BUILDING
(Aušros Vartai; Map p294; ☑5-212 3513; www.ausrosvartai.lt; Aušros Vartų gatvė 12; ☺6am-7pm) **FREE** The southern border of Old Town is marked by the last-standing of five portals that were once built into the city walls. A suitably grand way to enter one of the best-preserved

sections of Old Town, it's also the site of the Gate of Dawn Chapel of Mary the Mother of Mercy and the Vilnius Madonna, a painting of Our Lady said to work miracles.

Chapel of the Gates of Dawn CHAPEL
(Map p294; Aušros Vartų gatvė 12; ☺6am-7pm, Mass in Lithuanian 9am Mon-Sat, 9.30am Sun, in Polish 10am Mon-Sat) Above the Gates of Dawn you'll find this 18th-century chapel, aka the Gate of Dawn Chapel of Mary the Mother of Mercy. Inside is a venerated painting of the Virgin Mary, known as the Madonna of the Gates of Dawn, believed to date from the early 17th century. It is revered equally by the Catholic, Orthodox and Uniate (Greek Catholic) faiths and has evolved into one of Eastern Europe's leading pilgrimage destinations.

Church of the Holy Trinity (Uniates) and Basilian Monastery CHURCH
(Map p294; ☑5-212 2578; Aušros Vartų gatvė 7) Through the elaborate Basilian Gates lie this 16th-century church and monastery, mixing baroque, Gothic and Russian Byzantine styles. The Uniates are an order that sought to unite the Eastern and Western churches, and Mass is held only in Ukrainian.

St Teresa's Church CHURCH
(Šv Teresės Bažnyčia; Map p294; ☑5-212 3513; www.ausrosvartai.lt; Aušros Vartų gatvė 14; ☺7am-7pm) This Carmelite church is early baroque outside and ornate late baroque inside. Underneath its entrance is a chamber for the dead, which contains some fine examples of baroque tombs but is usually locked.

Orthodox Church of the Holy Spirit CHURCH
(Stačiatikių Šv Dvasios Cerkvė; Map p294; ☑5-212 7765; Aušros Vartų gatvė 10; ☺10am-5pm) This pink-domed, 17th-century structure is Lithuania's chief Russian Orthodox church. In a chamber at the foot of a flight of steps in front of the altar (their feet even peep out) lie the preserved bodies of three 14th-century martyrs – Sts Anthony, Ivan and Eustachius. Adjoining are male and female Orthodox monasteries, the only ones in the country.

Artillery Bastion MUSEUM
(Artilerijos bastėja; Map p294; ☑5-261 2149; www.lnm.lt; Bokšto gatvė 20/18; admission €1; ☺10am-6pm Wed-Sun) This 17th-century fortification houses a collection of old weaponry and armour. The building was closed for long-term renovation at the time of research and it wasn't clear when it would reopen.

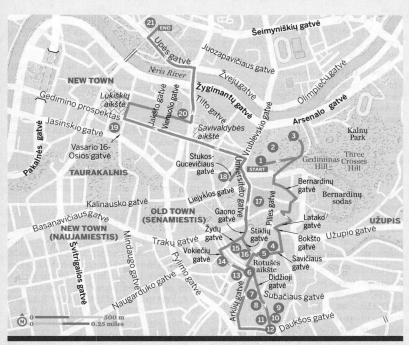

City Walk
The Best of Vilnius

START CATHEDRAL SQ
END SKY BAR
DISTANCE 4.9KM; THREE HOURS

Eastern Europe's largest Old Town is made for meandering.

Begin on Cathedral Sq, taking in its 'magical tile', **1** **Cathedral** (p289) and **2** **Grand Dukes' Palace** (p289) before climbing through the park to the **3** **Castle** (p289) on Gediminas Hill. Survey the city then hike down into Old Town along Pilies gatvė. To get a feel for quaint old Vilnius, cut left onto Bernardinų gatvė and zigzag along Volano gatvė, Literatu gatvė, Rusu gatvė and Latako gatvė to Bokšto gatvė. Midway along Bokšto, turn right onto Savičiaus gatvė for gorgeous handicrafts at **4** **Senujų Amatų Dirbtuvės** (p315) and an introduction to Lithuania's greatest artist at the **5** **MK Čiurlionis House** (p297). Continue along Savičiaus to Didžioji gatvė, turn left and follow the street past the **6** **former town hall**. Continue along Aušros Vartų, past the **7** **National Philharmonic** (p313), **8** **Basilian Gates**, **9** **Orthodox Church of the**

Holy Spirit (p298), **10** **St Teresa's Church** (p298) and **11** **artist workshops** before stopping at the **12** **Gates of Dawn** (p298).

Duck through the Gates of Dawn and turn west on Bazilijonų gatvė before heading north along Arklių gatvė to Rotušes aikštė where the **13** **Contemporary Art Centre** (p300) awaits. Quench your thirst at a cafe or restaurant terrace on **14** **Vokiečių gatvė**, then cut through onto Žydų gatvė for a glimpse of Jewish Vilnius. Browse the **15** **boutiques** heading north along Jewish St, take in **16** **Zoraza** (p314) and other designer stores on Stiklių gatvė then continue north along Gaono gatvė to **17** **Vilnius University** (p291).

Exhausted? Head back to Cathedral Sq and down Stuokos-Gucevičiaus gatvė for refreshments at **18** **Tappo D'Oro** (p311). Still raring to go? Go west along Gedimino prospektas to the **19** **Museum of Genocide Victims** (p303) then cross over into Lukiškių aikštė and head east past the **20** **Opera & Ballet Theatre** (p313). Cross the bridge to Šnipiškės and **21** **Sky Bar** (p312), where grand views await.

Subačiaus gate
HISTORIC BUILDING

(Map p294; Subačiaus gatvė/Bokšto gatvė) This restored section of the city walls gives a sense of their original scope.

Vokiečių Gatvė & Around

Vokiečių gatvė, the wide boulevard running northwest from Rotušės aikštė, is lined with restaurants that sprawl out onto the green parade at its centre.

St Nicholas Church
CHURCH

(Šv Mikalojaus bažnyčia; Map p294; ☑5-262 3069; www.mikalojus.lt; Šv Mikalojaus gatvė 4; ☺1pm-6.30pm Mon-Fri, 7.30am-3pm Sun) Lithuania's oldest church, this red-brick Gothic pile was built by German Christians around 1320, when the country was still pagan. From 1901 to 1939 it was the only church in Vilnius where Mass was held in Lithuanian. It's remarkably well preserved (bar the addition of baroque features) and definitely worth a visit.

Contemporary Art Centre
MUSEUM

(Šiuolaikinio Meno Centras, SMC; Map p294; ☑5-212 1945; www.cac.lt; Vokiečių gatvė 2; adult/child €2.32/1.16; ☺noon-10pm Tue-Sun) With 2400 sq metres of space for photography, video, installations and other exhibits, plus a program of lectures, live music and film screenings, this is the largest centre for contemporary art in the Baltics. There's free entry on Wednesdays, and different pricing for special events.

Russian Orthodox Church of St Nicholas
CHURCH

(Map p294; ☑5-261 8559; Didžioji gatvė 12) Built as a Gothic church in the early 16th century, then restored in the baroque style 300 years later, this church was redecorated in Russian Byzantine style during the Russification of the 19th century. Information is in Russian, and interior photography is strictly forbidden.

Evangelical Lutheran Church
CHURCH

(Evangelikų liuteronų bažnyčia; Map p294; www.augustana.lt; Vokiečių gatvė 20; ☺11am-2pm Mon-Fri) Hidden in a courtyard, this revamped church is home to Vilnius' tiny Protestant community. The church dates from 1555 but displays a mixture of Gothic, baroque and rococo elements in its architecture. Under the Soviets a concrete floor split the church into workshop and basketball court.

Vilniaus Gatvė & Around

At the confluence of Vokiečių gatvė, Vilniaus gatvė and Dominikonų gatvė stand some sizeable church and monastery complexes dating from the 17th and 18th centuries.

Church of the Holy Spirit
CHURCH

(Šv Dvasios bažnyčia; Map p294; Dominikonų gatvė 8; ☺3-7pm) This splendidly ornate late-Baroque church dates to the time of Grand Duke Vytautas, in the early 15th century. The fanciful interior, with its lavish rococo detail and 18th-century organ, is a magnet for wedding parties and fans of devotional kitsch.

St Catherine's Church
CHURCH

(Map p294; ☑5-262 0421; Vilniaus gatvė 30) This twin-towered 18th-century church, rich with baroque and rococo detail, was once part of a Benedictine monastery. Damaged in WWII and used for storage by the unsentimental Soviets, it's now renowned as a classical-music venue.

Church of Our Lady of the Assumption
CHURCH

(Map p294; Trakų gatvė 9/1) Dubbed 'Sands Church' after the quarter in which it stands, this 15th-century Franciscan church has a varied history – it was a hospital for the French army in 1812 and housed the state archives from 1864 to 1934 and 1949 to 1989. Returned to the Franciscans in 1998, it has been the object of years of painstaking restorations.

Theatre, Music & Cinema Museum
MUSEUM

(Teatro, muzikos ir kino muziejus; Map p294; www.ltmkm.lt; Vilniaus gatvė 41; adult/student €2.03/1.45; ☺11am-6pm Tue-Fri, 11am-4pm Sat) Artefacts of Lithuanian song, stage and screen are the stars of this museum. Three centuries of notable instruments – including the *pūslinė* (a primitive Baltic string instrument made from animal bladders) and several *kanklės* (plucked, fretted string instruments) – are exhibited, alongside curios of Lithuanian and Soviet film, and a large collection documenting the national theatre.

Radvilos Palace
MUSEUM

(Radvilų rūmai; Map p294; ☑5-212 1477; www.ldm.lt; Vilniaus gatvė 24; adult/student €1.73/0.87; ☺11am-6pm Tue-Sat, noon-5pm Sun) This 17th-century palazzo houses the foreign fine-arts section of the Lithuanian Art Museum.

Frank Zappa Memorial
MEMORIAL

(Map p294; Kalinausko gatvė 1) West of Vilniaus gatvė, rock 'n' roll legend Frank Zappa is immortalised in a bronze bust atop a 4.2m-high stainless-steel pole. It was the world's first memorial to the offbeat American who died in 1993. Look carefully for it in the parking lot, as it doesn't jump out at you. Also, take a look at the graffiti on the walls surrounding the lot.

LEADING JEWISH HERITAGE SIGHTS

Vilnius' Old Town was once home to a sizable Jewish community that was known around the world for its piety and strength of faith.

With the German invasion of the Soviet Union in 1941, Vilnius fell to the Nazis within days. In the next three months, the Germans (along with many Lithuanians, some willingly and others unwillingly) murdered around 35,000 Jews – almost half those in the city – in the Paneriai Forest. Two ghettos were established to hold the remaining Jews – these were both eventually liquidated. About 6000 Vilnius Jews escaped.

Today the Jewish community in Lithuania numbers around 5000, 80% of whom live in Vilnius. Since independence, a number of notable events have revolved around this small community. In 2001 the **Vilnius Yiddish Institute** (www.judaicvilnius.com) was established in the History faculty at Vilnius University.

Vilnius' main Jewish and Holocaust-related sights are administered by the **Vilna Gaon Jewish State Museum** (www.jmuseum.lt).

Holocaust Museum (Holokausto Muziejus; Map p294; ☑ 5-262 0730; www.jmuseum.lt; Pamėnkalnio gatvė 12; adult/child €2.40/1.20; ☺ 9am-5pm Mon-Thu, 9am-4pm Fri, 10am-4pm Sun) The Holocaust Museum tells the unvarnished account of the destruction of Lithuania's once-vibrant Jewish community, the Litvaks, through a collection of photos, documentation and first-hand accounts. Situated in the so-called 'Green House', the displays lack modern interactive touches but are perhaps all the more moving for it. Many of the items here were donated by survivors and victims' families.

Tolerance Centre (Map p294; ☑ 5-262 9666; www.jmuseum.lt; Naugarduko gatvė 10/2; adult/concession €3/1.10; ☺ 10am-6pm Mon-Thu, to 4pm Fri & Sun) The Tolerance Centre is one of the three main branches of the Vilna Gaon Jewish State Museum. The building, which has been at various stages a refuge, a concert hall and a theatre, exhibits Litvak art and cultural and historical collections. It serves as a helpful adjunct to the Holocaust Museum: its exhibitions focus less on the Holocaust and more on Jewish history and culture over the centuries leading up to WWII.

The explanatory panels in English on the 2nd floor are long but useful guides. Each covers a theme and is balanced and informative. A small permanent exhibit on the Jewish avant-garde in Vilnius between the wars is enlightening.

Choral Synagogue (Choralinė Sinagoga; Map p294; ☑ 5-261 2523; Pylimo gatvė 39; donations welcome; ☺ 10am-2pm Sun-Fri) This synagogue, built in 1903, is the city's only Jewish house of worship to survive WWII intact (the Nazis used it as a medical store). Prayers in the Misnagdim (counter-Hasidic) tradition are heard daily.

Gate to Small Ghetto (Map p294; www.jewishcenter.lt; Stiklių gatvė 12) This was once the entrance to the main Jewish quarter, which lay in the streets west of Didžioji gatvė. Today only street names like Žydų (Jews) and Gaono (Gaon) serve as reminders of those days, while a small plaque marks the site of the gate to the ghetto, liquidated in 1941.

Gate to Large Ghetto (Map p294; Rūdninkų gatvė 18) A plaque and map at No 18 mark the site of the entrance to the Large Ghetto, in which 29,000 Litvaks were imprisoned by the Nazis between 1941 and 1943.

Site of Great Synagogue (Map p294; Žydų gatvė 1-2) The Great Synagogue of Vilna, built in the 1630s on the site of an earlier synagogue, was destroyed by the Soviets in the 1950s, after the Nazis had a go in WWII. There's a Vilna Gaon monument on the site now, and plans are afoot to build a fitting memorial by 2018.

House of Gaon Elijahu Ben Shlomo Zalman (Map p294; Žydų gatvė 5) A plaque marks the former house of the famous 18th-century Talmudic scholar.

Site of New Jewish Cemetery (Map p290) A memorial marks the spot of Vilnius' 19th-century Jewish cemetery, destroyed by the Soviets in the 1960s.

Judenrat (Map p294; Rudninku gatvė 8) The site of the Jewish Ghetto administration during WWII.

East of Gediminas Hill

★**Antakalnis Cemetery**　　CEMETERY
(off Karių kapų gatvė; ⊙9am-dusk) One of Eastern Europe's most beautiful graveyards lies in this leafy suburb, a short stroll east of the centre. Those killed by Soviet special forces on 13 January 1991 are buried here; a sculpture of the Madonna cradling her son memorialises them. Another memorial honours Napoleonic soldiers who died of starvation and injuries in Vilnius while retreating from the Russian army. The remains of 2000 of them were only found in 2002.

Hundreds of Polish soldiers' graves, including many unknown soldiers, are also located here, which gets a mixed reception, especially on All Saints' Day (1 November). Former president Algirdas Brazauskas' grave is a bit abandoned atop a hillslope, in a newer area of the cemetery.

Three Crosses　　MONUMENT
(Trys kryžiai; Map p290) Crosses were first erected in the 17th century, in memory of a group of monks martyred by pagans three centuries earlier. The current crosses replace three bulldozed by the Soviets; their twisted remains can be seen below the current set. Walk up the hill from T Kosciuskos gatvė, and enjoy fabulous views of the city.

St Peter & Paul Church　　CHURCH
(Šv Apaštalų Petro ir Povilo Bažnyca; Map p290; ✆5-234 0229; Antakalnio gatvė 1; ⊙6am-6.30pm) Don't be fooled by the uninspiring exterior of this church. Its baroque interior – a riot of over 2000 stuccoes created by Italian sculptors between 1675 and 1704 – is the finest in the country. The church was founded by Lithuanian noble Mykolas Kazimieras Paca, whose tomb is on the right of the porch.

Užupis

Užupis Republic Constitution　　LANDMARK
(Map p294; Paupio gatvė) The 'Republic' of Užupis' 41-point Constitution is engraved in English, French, Lithuanian and several other languages on plaques running along Paupio gatvė. It guarantees its citizens, among other things, the right to hot water, to be unique, to love, to be free, to be happy (or unhappy) and to be a dog. It ends 'Do not defeat. Do not fight back. Do not surrender.'

Užupis Angel　　MONUMENT
(Map p294; Užupio gatvė) Since its erection in 2002, this statue of a trumpeting angel has come to symbolise Vilnius' quirkiest district.

◉ New Town

The 19th-century New Town (Naujamiestis) stretches 2km west of the cathedral and Old Town. Here the medieval charm of Old Town is replaced by wide boulevards and pockets of lush parkland.

Gedimino Prospektas

Sandwiched between the Roman Catholic cathedral's dramatic skyline and the silver domes of the Russian Orthodox **Church of the Saint Virgin's Apparition** (Znamenskaya Tserkov; Map p290; A Mickevičiaus gatvė 1), fashionable Gedimino is the main street of modern Vilnius. Its 1.75km length is dotted with shops, a theatre, banks, hotels, restaurants, offices, a few park squares and the seats of various official bods, including the Lithuanian **Government Building** (Map p294; www.lrv.lt; Gedimino prospektas 11) and Parliament House. Laid out in 1852, it's had 11 name changes since: the Tsarists named it after St George, the Poles after Mickiewicz, and the Soviet rulers first after Stalin, then Lenin.

REBELS WITH A CAUSE: THE UŽUPIS REPUBLIC

The cheeky streak of rebellion pervading Lithuania flourishes in Vilnius' bohemian heart, where artists, dreamers, drunks and squatters in Užupis have declared a breakaway state.

The Užupis Republic (Užupio Republika) was officially, in an unofficial sense, born in 1998. The state has its own tongue-in-cheek president, anthem and 41-point constitution.

On April Fool's Day, citizens of the Republic of Užupis celebrate their wholly unofficial state. Border guards wearing comical outfits stamp passports at the main bridge and the Užupis president makes speeches in the quarter's small square – the intersection of Užupio, Maluno and Paupio gatvės where the republic's symbol, the **Angel of Užupis**, (302) stands. Increasingly hip, the neighbourhood continues to fill with galleries, restaurants and folk-artist workshops.

A statue of Lenin once stood on **Lukiškių aikštė**, a square that used to bear the name of the levelled statue, now displayed in Druskininkai's Grūtas Park.

★ **Museum of Genocide Victims**   MUSEUM
(Genocido Aukų Muziejus; Map p290; ☑5-249 8156; www.genocid.lt/muziejus; Aukų gatvė 2a; adult/discount €2/1; ☺10am-6pm Wed-Sat, to 5pm Sun) This former headquarters of the KGB (and before them the Gestapo, Polish occupiers and Tsarist judiciary) houses a museum dedicated to thousands of Lithuanians who were murdered, imprisoned or deported by the Soviet Union from WWII until the 1960s. Memorial plaques honouring those who perished tile the outside of the building. Inside, floors cover the harsh realities of Soviet occupation, including gripping personal accounts of Lithuanian deportees to Siberia.

The horror hits home on entering the basement, which contains inmate cells and an execution chamber where, between 1944 and the 1960s, more than 1000 prisoners were shot or stabbed in the skull.

Parliament House   GOVERNMENT BUILDING
(Seimas; Map p290; ☑5-239 6060; www.seimas. lt; Gedimino prospektas 53) This squat, unlovely Soviet-built 'palace', home to the Lithuanian Seimas (Parliament), was the scene of a historic stand-off. On 13 January 1991 barricades were thrown up to deter Soviet troops acting to crush the movement that had passed the Act of the Re-Establishment of the State of Lithuania the previous year. Fourteen people were killed in the disturbances, but the troops ultimately bowed to popular will and quit Vilnius the following December.

Three Muses   STATUE
(Map p294; Gedimino prospektas 4) Striking a theatrical pose atop the Lithuanian National Drama Theatre is the Three Muses statue. The unusual black-robed figures (representing drama, comedy and tragedy) hide behind gold masks and loom over an audience of happy-snapping tourists.

South of Gedimino Prospektas

Vingis Park   PARK
(Map p290; www.vilniausparkai.lt; MK Čiurlionio gatvė 100) At the western end of Čiurlionio gatvė is the wooded Vingis Park, surrounded on three sides by the Neris River. The park has a large open-air amphitheatre used for the Lithuanian Song and Dance Festival (in July). Take trolleybus 7 from the train station or 3 from the Gedimino stop on Vilniaus gatvė to the Kęstučio stop (the second after the bridge over the river), then walk over the footbridge from the end of Treniotos gatvė.

Romanov Church   CHURCH
(Map p290; Jono Basanavičiaus gatvė 27) Formally known as the Orthodox Church of St Michael and St Constantine, this church, with its swelling onion domes and ornate interior, was built to mark 300 years of the Romanov dynasty. Little did they know it would end within four more.

Vilnius Flower Market   MARKET
(Map p290; Basanavičiaus gatvė 42; ☺24hr) If you're ever invited to a Lithuanian home, this always-open Vilnius institution can supply the perfect token of thanks. Haggling expected.

Kenessa   HOUSE
(Map p290; Liubarto gatvė 6) West of Jasinskio gatvė across the Neris is this *kenessa*, a traditional Karaite prayer house, built in 1911.

Šnipiškės
On the north bank of the Neris, the quarter of Šnipiškės has been transformed: the tatty Soviet concrete blocks have gone and in their place is a new skyline of skyscrapers, including the **Europa Tower** (Map p290; Konstitucijos Prospektas 7) on the **Europa Business & Shopping Centre**, which – at 129m – is the Baltics' tallest skyscraper.

This new business district, dubbed 'Sunrise Valley', continues to grow apace, with highrises and construction sites popping up among the relics of Societ architecture. As part of the urban redevelopment project, two new bridges linking the Europa Tower with the centre have been built and the **municipality** (Konstitucijos prospektas 3) has moved here.

Energy and Technology Museum   MUSEUM
(Map p290; ☑5-278 2085; www.emuziejus.lt; Rinktinės gatvė 2; adult/child €3/1.50; ☺10am-5pm Tue, Wed, Fri & Sat, to 7pm Thu) Vilnius' first power station, in operation from 1903 to 2003, now houses exhibitions on energy, technology and their historical development. The original machinery used for power generation has been preserved, and is particularly impressive.

St Raphael's Church   CHURCH
(Šv Rapolo bažnyčia; Map p290; ☑5-272 4164; Šnipiškių gatvė 1; ☺6.30-9am & 5-10pm Sun-Fri) A handsome late-Baroque church, and adjoining monastery, built by the Jesuits.

LITHUANIA VILNIUS

☉ Outside the Centre

TV Tower
TOWER

(Televizijos Bokštas; ☎ 5-252 5333; www.telecentras. lt; Sausio 13-osios gatvė 10; adult/child €6/2.6; ☉ observation deck 11am-11pm Tue-Sat, 11am-9pm Sun & Mon; 🚌 1, 3, 7, 16) It's hard to miss the 326m TV tower on the city's western horizon. This tall needle symbolises Lithuania's strength of spirit: on 13 January 1991 the Soviet army killed 12 pro-Independence resisters here, with Lithuanian TV continuing to broadcast until troops burst through the tower door. There are memorials to the slain near the tower, and a revolving restaurant and observation deck, the Milky Way, at 165m.

🏃 Activities

Aside from walking and cycling, Vilnius isn't blessed with an immensely wild array of outdoor pursuits, but it does, however, offer something you don't find everywhere – hot-air ballooning.

Oreivystės Centras
BALLOONING

(Map p290; ☎ 5-273 2703; www.ballooning. lt; Upės gatvė 5; per person €89-179) Dedicated to the promotion and development of hot-air ballooning in Lithuania, the Ballooning Centre also sells flights over Vilnius, Trakai, Kaunas, and other parts of the country. Hour-long flights can be arranged either early in the morning or in the evening, in suitable weather.

Ryga
BOAT TOUR

(Map p294; ☎ 8-685 01000; www.barta.lt; 1hr tours adult/child €8/4; ☉ 11am-9pm) In summer (May to September), the pleasure craft *Ryga* leaves throughout the day from a small port on the southern side of the Karaliaus Mindaugo Bridge. Minimum group size is 10 people, and children under five sail free.

🧭 Tours

Two-hour walking tours of Old Town in English (€10), starting at 11am on Monday, Wednesday, Friday and Sunday from mid-May to mid-September, are organised by any tourist information office (p315). They also supply audio guides (€10) for self-guided tours and hand out free copies of thematic walking tours, including Jewish Vilnius, Musical Vilnius, and Castles & Palaces of Vilnius.

Senamiesčio Gidas
BUS TOUR

(Old Town Guides; Map p294; ☎ 5-261 5558; www. vilniuscitytour.com; Aušros Vartų gatvė 7; adult/ child one trip €12/6; ☉ 5 buses 10am-3pm) Organises half-day minibus tours of Vilnius and Jewish Vilnius, as well as 'Trace Your Family Roots' tours and day trips to Trakai and Kernavė, Grūtas Park (Soviet sculpture park) and Europe's geographical centre. Prices depend on numbers; see the website for details.

🎊 Festivals & Events

Vilnius is blessed with year-round festivals, many of which are listed online at www. vilnius-events.lt and www.vilnius-tourism.lt. Some of the bigger events:

Užgavėnės
CARNIVAL

Pagan carnival (Mardi Gras) on Shrove Tuesday (usually February).

Kaziukas Crafts Fair
CULTURAL

(www.kaziukomuge.lt) Dating back to the 17th century, this festival of craft and culture comes to Old Town on St Casimir's Day, 4 March.

Vilnius International Film Festival
FILM

(www.kinopavasaris.lt) Also known as Kino Pavasaris ('Cinema Spring') this celebration of celluloid happens every March.

Pavasario Lygiadienis
CULTURAL

Pagan carnival marking the spring equinox, held in March.

New Baltic Dance
DANCE

(www.dance.lt) Contemporary dance festival in early May.

Vilnius Festival
MUSIC

(www.vilniusfestivals.lt) Classical music, jazz and folk concerts in Old Town courtyards in June.

Culture Night
CULTURAL

(Kulturos Naktis; www.kulturosnaktis.lt) Vilnius comes (even more) alive for this wonderful, one-night-only festival in June or July. The city's nooks and squares become a network of stages on which singers, dancers, musicians, actors and performance artists from Lithuania and beyond entertain a party-minded populace. Plan a sleep-in the next day, as it goes all night.

Lithuanian Song and Dance Festival
CULTURAL

(www.dainusvente.lt) This enormous festival of Lithuanian song, dance and folklore, running in various forms since 1923, comes to Vilnius each July.

VILNIUS FOR CHILDREN

Vilnius is generally great for kids: it's welcoming, relatively small-scale and has enough boat tours, hot-air balloons, castles and pizza to keep them satisfied. In cold weather the Akropolis (p315) shopping centre – with a cinema, ice-skating rink and soft-play area for under-12s – has you covered.

Kids will love to splash around at **Vichy Aquapark** (Vandens Parkas; ☑8-700 55118; www.vandensparkas.lt; Ozo gatvė 14c; adult/child full day €22/10; ☉noon-10pm Mon-Fri, to 10pm Sat & Sun), a well-equipped Polynesian-themed water park. The little ones can use up their energy on the adrenaline-pumping water rides and a wave pool, while parents can recharge their batteries in the whirlpools, steam baths and massage salon.

The well-appointed **Akropolis Ice Arena** (☑5-249 2878; www.akropolis.lt; Ozo gatvė 25, Akropolio aikštė I-152; per 45min €2-3; ☉8am-11pm) is a great option for rainy days.

Christopher Summer Festival — MUSIC
(www.kristupofestivaliai.lt) Music festival held in July and August.

Capital Days — PERFORMING ARTS
Music and performing arts in September.

Sirenos — THEATRE
(www.okt.lt) International theatre festival from mid-September to mid-October.

Gaida — MUSIC
(www.vilniusfestivals.lt/EN/gaida) The biggest and most important contemporary music festival in the Baltics, held in late October.

Scanorama — FILM
(www.scanorama.lt) Every November this festival, with its special focus on the film of Northern Europe, comes to Vilnius, then heads on the road to Kaunas and Klaipėda.

Mama Jazz — JAZZ
(www.vilniusmamajazz.lt) Mid-November festival with big-name guests.

🛏 Sleeping

For such a small capital, Vilnius has plenty of accommodation options. Most hotels and guesthouses include private bathrooms.

Filaretai Hostel — HOSTEL €
(Map p290; ☑5-215 4627; www.filaretaihostel. com; Filaretų gatvė 17; dm/s/d/tr per person without bathroom €10/21/15/12; ℗@☎) Affiliated with the Lithuanian Hostels Association, Filaretai occupies a quaint old villa 15 minutes' walk (uphill) from Old Town. Dorms are five- to eight-bedded; bed linen is provided, towels are extra, and there's a communal kitchen and washing machine. To get here take bus 34 from the bus and train stations to the seventh stop.

Hostelgate B&B — B&B €
(Map p294; ☑8-689 60292; www.hostelgate.lt; Šv Mikalojaus gatvė 3; d/f €38/58; @☎) With a great location (just off Vokiečių gatvė), wi-fi, cheery decor, friendly staff, a well-stocked kitchen and some rooms with en suite or balcony, Hostelgate makes a great base for exploring Old Town. The same operation also runs a hostel on **Aušros Vartų gatvė** (Map p294; ☑8-638 32818; Aušros Vartų gatvė 7-1; d/tr €11/39; ☉24hr).

Come to Vilnius — HOSTEL €
(Map p290; ☑8-6202 9390; www.cometovilnius.eu; Šv Stepano gatvė 15; dm/d/tr €16/35/44; @☎) Bright colours, timber furnishings, proximity to transport and free pancakes, hot drinks, towels and wi-fi are the draws at this indie hostel. Prices fall slightly in the low season.

Litwinterp — B&B €
(Map p294; ☑5-212 3850; www.litinterp.lt; Bernardinų gatvė 7-2; s/d/tr €25/40/51; ☉office 8.30am-9pm Mon-Fri, 9am-3pm Sat; ☎) This bright, clean and friendly establishment has a wide range of options in the heart of Old Town. Rooms with shared bathroom can be a little cramped, but those with en suite are generously large. Guests can check in after office hours providing they give advance notice, and mini kitchens and a left-luggage service are available. Breakfast is €3.

Old Town Hostel — HOSTEL €
(Map p290; ☑5-262 5357; www.oldtownhostel. lt; Aušros Vartų gatvė 20-10; dm/d/tr €11/32/42; @☎) This small hostel tucked away in a private courtyard is handy for both Old Town and the bus and train stations. Rooms are basic but accommodating, with a well-stocked kitchen, common area and wi-fi.

Center Stay Hostel
HOSTEL €

(Map p290; ☑5-212 0140; www.centerstayhostel.
com; Aušros Vartų gatvė 16; dm €8; 🛜) Well located (just outside the Gates of Dawn) and
well run, this super-value hostel has wi-fi,
kitchen and living area.

★ Bernardinu B&B
GUESTHOUSE €€

(Map p294; ☑5-261 5134; www.bernardinu
house.com; Bernardinų gatvė 5; d/tr from €60/85;
🅿️❄️🛜) This charming family-owned guesthouse is on one of the most picturesque
lanes in Old Town. The 18th-century townhouse has been sensitively renovated, preserving elements like old timber flooring
and ceilings, and with stripped patches of
brick allowing you to see through the patina
of the years. Breakfast (€4) is brought to
your door on a tray.

Domus Maria
GUESTHOUSE €€

(Map p294; ☑5-264 4880; www.domusmaria.
lt; Aušros Vartų gatvė 12; s/d €50/65; 🅿️😊@🛜)
The guesthouse of the Vilnius archdiocese is
housed in a former monastery dating to the
17th century and oozes charm. Accommodation is in the monks' chambers, but they've
been given a thorough, stylish makeover. Two
rooms, 207 and 307, have views of the Gates of
Dawn and are usually booked far in advance.
Breakfast is served in the vaulted refectory.

Ecotel
BUSINESS HOTEL €€

(Map p290; ☑5-210 2700; www.ecotel.lt; Slucko
gatvė 8; s/d/tr €58/66/81; 🅿️❄️@🛜) This newly
renovated, four-storey hotel is a slick, stylish
operation offering clean and affordable rooms
with everything you need. Some rooms are
designed for people with disabilities (and
those who are tall); beds are 2.1m long.

Panorama Hotel
HOTEL €€

(Map p290; ☑5-233 8822; www.hotelpanorama.lt;
Sodų gatvė 14; s/d from €50/55; 🅿️🅿️🛜) Beneath
the kitsch veneer of this Soviet-era hotel you'll
find well-maintained, good-value accommodation and some fabulous views of Old Town
and surrounding hills. Discounts and special
packages are available on the website.

Grybas House
HOTEL €€

(Map p294; ☑5-264 7474; www.grybashouse.com;
Aušros Vartų gatvė 3a; s/d/ste €67/87/98; 🅿️🛜)
Grybas House – the first family-run hotel
to crop up after Independence – is run with
grace, charm and bags of smiles. Rooms in
this oasis of calm in the centre of Old Town
are old-fashioned but very comfortable, and
some peep at the private courtyard.

Šauni Vietelė
GUESTHOUSE €€

(Map p294; ☑5-212 4110; www.mtr.lt;
Pranciškonai gatvė 3/6; r €27) This three-room
guesthouse in a former Franciscan abbey
is great value for money. Its rooms are
old-fashioned and filled with well-loved
furniture, but they're all spacious and airy.
Breakfast isn't included, but the cafe offers
pancakes and such. The popular bar in the
courtyard – Seven Fridays – hosts live music
that might be a problem for early sleepers.

eLoftHotel
HOTEL €€

(Map p290; ☑5-266 0730; www.elofthotel.lt;
Ševčenkos gatvė 16; d/ste €61/84; 🅿️@🛜) This
pleasant hotel, which boasts 'ecological materials throughout', is a good choice for those
who appreciate the greater quiet (15 minutes'
walk) outside Old Town. Room price includes
Continental breakfast and wi-fi, and there's
even a common kitchen and sauna.

Atrium
HOTEL €€

(Map p294; ☑5-210 7777; www.atrium.lt; Pilies
gatvė 10; d/ste €85/125; 🅿️@🛜) With a plum
Old Town location, services such as laundry
and airport collection, and luxurious rooms
(leather furniture, deep beds, warm lighting
and different decor in each), Atrium may
be the ideal choice if you have only a day or
three in Old Town. Originally a 16th-century
townhouse, Atrium is also well prepared for
travellers with disabilities.

Senatoriai Hotel
HOTEL €€

(Map p294; ☑5-212 6491; www.senatoriai.lt; Tilto gatvė 2a; s/d €78/87; 🅿️@🛜) This small,
homey hotel is so close to the cathedral you
can almost hear Mass. Rooms are generally
spacious and feature heavy leather furniture,
decent beds and free wi-fi. It also offers Lithuanian cooking in its restaurant, a laundry
service, and online discounts in slow periods.

Hotel Rinno
HOTEL €€

(Map p294; ☑5-262 2828; www.rinno.lt; Vingrių
gatvė 25; standard/deluxe r €68/88; 🅿️❄️@🛜)
This charismatic little independent combines lovely rooms (more four-star than
three), and a handy location (between Old
Town and the train and bus stations) at a
good price. Breakfast is served in the pleasant and private back yard.

★ Narutis
HISTORIC HOTEL €€€

(Map p294; ☑5-212 2894; www.narutis.com;
Pilies gatvė 24; s/d €125/145; 🅿️❄️@🛜) Housed
in a red-brick townhouse built in 1581, this
classy pad has been a hotel since the 16th

century. Breakfast and dinner are served in a vaulted Gothic cellar, there's wi-fi access throughout, and free apples at reception add a tasty touch. Booking online can yield substantial savings.

Neringa HOTEL €€€
(Map p294; ☑5-212 2288; www.neringahotel. com; Gedimino prospektas 23; s/superior r/ste €94/109/124; P@🛜🏊) Large swathes of this once-prominent hotel are heritage-listed, and a must for fans of Soviet-era swank. The staircase and landings – with stern non-figurative woodcut decor – and restaurant – with a fabulously kitsch fountain and improving realist mosaics – are particular highlights. What refurbishments have been permitted have left the rooms nicely appointed, with flat-screens, heated floors and decent beds.

Stikliai HOTEL €€€
(Map p294; ☑5-264 9595; www.stikliaihotel.lt; Gaono gatvė 7; s/d/ste €160/190/230; P@🛜🏊) The cream of the crop among Vilnius hotels, this boutique is managed by the Relais & Chateaux chain. Tucked down a picture-postcard cobbled street in the old Jewish quarter, it offers luxurious rooms in a 17th-century building with an abundance of charm.

Shakespeare BOUTIQUE HOTEL €€€
(Map p294; ☑5-266 5885; www.shakespeare.lt; Bernardinų gatvė 8/8; s/d €105/174; P🏶@🛜) This former printing house now accommodates one of the more charismatic high-end hotels in town. More boutique than international five-star, its tasteful eclecticism of decor, touches like naming the rooms for literary and cultural figures, and the switched-on staff give it true distinction. Most importantly, antiques, books and quality furniture make the rooms delightful to spend time in.

Apia Hotel HISTORIC HOTEL €€€
(Map p294; ☑5-212 3426; www.apia.lt; Sv Ignoto gatvė 12; d/ste/tr €100/115/134; P@🛜) This smart, fresh and friendly hotel occupies some prime real estate in the heart of Old Town. Choose from courtyard or cobbled-street views among the hotel's 12 rooms, but if you're after a balcony, reserve room 3 or 4.

Dvaras BOUTIQUE HOTEL €€€
(Map p294; ☑5-210 7370; www.dvaras.lt; Tilto gatvė 3-1; d/ste €104/143; P🏶@🛜) Hospitality began here in the late 18th century, when heritage-listed Dvaras Manor offered five guest rooms and an ale shop. Things have developed since then: it now boasts eight plush

rooms, with wi-fi, satellite TV, minibars and comfy beds. Best of all, you're in easy distance of the cathedral, castle and Old Town sights.

Europa Royale Hotel HOTEL €€€
(Map p294; ☑5-266 0770; www.groupeuropa.com; Aušros Vartų gatvė 6; d/ste €109/239) This beautifully situated four-star hotel boasts plush, colourful rooms and all the conveniences you'd expect. Rooms on the street face the facade of the National Philharmonic building.

Grotthaus HOTEL €€€
(Map p294; ☑5-266 0322; www.grotthusshotel. com; Ligoninės gatvė 7; d/ste €122/207; P@🛜) Step through the red-canopied entrance of this buttercup-yellow boutique townhouse to find Villeroy & Boch bathtubs, 19th-century *Titanic*-style fittings, Italian-made furniture, and curtains allegedly made with the same fabric as that used by the Queen of England! The Old Town location is top-notch, and substantial discounts are available on weekends.

Radisson Blu Royal Astorija HOTEL €€€
(Map p294; ☑5-212 0110; www.radissonblu. com; Didžioji gatvė 35/2; s/d/ste €180/210/360; P🔁@🛜🏊) This excellent splurge or business choice is part of a high-end chain, though the building dates from the early 20th century and exudes character. The central location, overlooking St Casimir's Church, is a plus, as are the popular wintertime Sunday brunches. Mod cons like trouser presses and safes are standard. The superior-class rooms got a thorough makeover in 2014.

Radisson Blu Hotel
Lietuva BUSINESS HOTEL €€€
(Map p290; ☑5-272 6272; www.radissonblu.com; Konstitucijos prospektas 20; r/ste from €159/209; P🏶@🛜) A smart but unexceptional example of the international hotel genre. It is, however, the plushest in the Šnipiškės business district, and offers wonderful views of Vilnius, especially from the top-floor Sky Bar.

🍴 Eating

Whether it's *cepelinai* (parcels of thick potato dough) or *kepta duona* (deep-fried rye bread with garlic) you want, Vilnius has it covered. That said, the Vilnius dining palate is now well used to international cuisine, and the list of restaurants serving food from outside Lithuania's borders grows every month. Most restaurants can be found in Old Town, but getting a meal after midnight is challenging. In summer it's essential to reserve a table for outside evening dining.

Radharanė
VEGETARIAN €

(Map p294; ☑5-240 4720; www.radharane.lt; Gediminio prospektas 32; mains €4; ⊙11am-9pm; 🍴) In a town where light, tasty vegetarian fare isn't thick on the ground, Radharanė's Indian-with-a-Lithuanian-twist fare is a godsend. Try the kofta, paneer with eggplant, channa dahl: all served with rice and salad.

Senoji Kibininė
LITHUANIAN €

(Map p294; www.kibinas.lt; Vilniaus gatvė; mains €3.50; ⊙9am-9pm Mon-Fri, 10am-9pm Sat, 10am-8pm Sun) You can fill up on *cepelinai* or potato pancakes here, but its real thing is *kibinai:* pasties traditional to the country's Turkic Karaite minority that deserve the fame of their Cornish rivals. Whether it's mutton, chicken and mushroom, or spinach and curd you fancy, these toothsome shortcrust pockets are ideal after a few drinks in Old Town.

Pietausim
LITHUANIAN €

(Map p290; ☑8-615 18454; www.pietausim.lt; J Jasinskio gatvė 16; mains €4; ⊙11am-2.30pm) Like a Soviet-era canteen, but with sleek decor and a bustling, youthful clientele, Pietausim bangs out great-value Lithuanian food to the lunchtime cognoscenti. Baked fish, *šaltibarščiai* (cold beetroot soup), salads and more: all gets hoovered up by the early afternoon, so get in quickly.

Pilies kepyklėlė
BAKERY €

(Map p294; ☑5-260 8992; Pilies gatvė 19; mains €3-6; ⊙9am-11pm) This handsome, brick-vaulted creperie-bakery stands out from the crowd on Vilnius' busiest tourist street, mixing old-world charm with a fresh, upbeat vibe. The 9am omelette here is a must, as are the savoury pancakes, stuffed with spinach or ham and cheese and topped with sour cream. The poppyseed cake is reputedly the best on this side of town.

★ Balzac
FRENCH €€

(Map p294; ☑8-614 89223; www.balzac.lt; Savičiaus gatvė 7; mains €12-15; ⊙noon-11pm Mon-Thu, to midnight Fri & Sat, to 9pm Sun) This classic French bistro serves what may be the best French food in Vilnius. Alongside bistro staples like *tournedos de boeuf* and duck confit you'll find a great selection of seafood, some flown fresh from France. While there's a summer terrace, the dining area is small, so book to avoid disappointment.

Sue's Indian Raja
INDIAN €€

(Map p294; ☑5-286 1888; www.suesindianraja. lt; Odminių gatvė 3; mains €10; 🍴) You might not come to Lithuania chasing the heights of Mughal cuisine, but if you fancy a curry, Sue's actually does it very well. The menu doesn't stray from the international Indian-restaurant formula, and the prices reflect the prime location, but there's obvious authenticity in the ingredients and techniques in the kitchen.

Meat Lovers' Pub
PUB FOOD €€

(Map p294; ☑8-652 51233; www.meatloverspub. lt; Šv Ignoto gatvė 14; mains €11; ⊙11.30am-midnight; 🕿) Does what it says on the tin (meat and booze) and does it very well. A mix of Lithuanian, German and other European brews are on tap to wash down hefty T-bones, smoky German sausages and excellent burgers (the budget option, at around €6). Salads, cider and soups balance the menu with a few lighter options.

Vegafe
VEGAN €€

(Map p294; ☑8-659 77411; www.jogosmityba.lt; Totorių gatvė 3; mains €8; ⊙11am-10pm Mon-Fri, from noon Sat & Sun; 🍴) Adhering to vegan and ayurvedic principles (no garlic, no onion), Vegafe is on the swankier end of the conscious-eating spectrum. The room is all calming pastels and clean design, and the food – perhaps a riotous plate of spring greens, or *momos* (Tibetan dumplings) – is as delicious as it is virtuous.

Jurgis ir Drakonas
PIZZA €€

(Map p294; ☑8-600 77977; www.jurgisir drakonas.lt; Pylimo gatvė 22d; mains €6; ⊙11am-10pm Mon-Fri, noon-10pm Sat & Sun) Pizza is easily obtained in Vilnius, but few do it with such fealty to its Neapolitan origins as 'George and the Dragon'. Opened by the husband of Lithuanian TV chef Beata Čičkauskaitė-Nicholson, it flies in tomatoes, cheese, smallgoods and even flour and seafood, to ensure all tastes as it would in Italy.

Fiorentino
ITALIAN €€

(Map p294; ☑5-212 0925; www.fiorentino.lt; Universiteto gatvė 4; mains €10; ⊙11am-11pm; 🕿) Fiorentino backs up its plum position near the Presidential Palace with delicious Italian food, professional service and a convivial atmosphere. Its 'Renaissance-style' courtyard is a great place, in the warmer months, to kick back over Tuscan dishes such as *tagliata* (rare sliced beef with Parmesan and rocket) or ham-and-fontina-stuffed pasta in sage butter.

Kukumuku
CAFE €€

(Map p294; ☑5-261 0630; www.kukumuku.lt; Vokiečių gatvė 6; mains €9-11; ⊙noon-9pm Mon-

Fri, from 10am Sat & Sun; 🛜 👪) Spread over two floors, with bright, cheerful decor, multiple play areas, a small stage and even a 'Lego Room', Kukumuku is a great option if you're travelling with kids. The menu, on which adults will find burgers, beef stroganoff and other cafe fare, thoughtfully caters to those who have allergies, or are yet to grow teeth.

Kitchen   INTERNATIONAL €€

(Map p294; ✆ 8-688 80558; www.inthekitchen.lt; Didžioji gatvė 11; mains €7-12; ⏱ 11.30am-midnight) This stylish, stripped-back place, accessed through a carriageway from bustling Didžioji gatvė, does inventive contemporary food with an emphasis on what's in season locally. That might be cold yoghurt soup with cucumber, or something tasty with the spring's first asparagus. Kitchen operates on reduced hours in summer.

René   INTERNATIONAL €€

(Map p294; ✆ 5-212 6858; www.restoranasrene. lt; Antokolskio gatvė 13; mains €9; ⏱ 11am-11pm; 🛜) René Magritte is the patron saint of this place, which showcases *'La Cuisine de la Biere'*, and wonky, surrealist brickwork. Staff wear bowler hats and patrons are encouraged to draw on paper tablecloths, in between tucking into *moules marinière* and sausages roasted in beer.

★ Lokys   LITHUANIAN €€€

(Map p294; ✆ 5-262 9046; www.lokys.lt; Stiklių gatvė 8; mains €14-16; ⏱ noon-midnight) Track down the big wooden bear to find this Vilnius institution, making merry in the vaulted 16th-century cellars of a former merchant's house since 1972. As a 'hunters' restaurant', it does a strong line in game, including roast venison and boar, game sausages, quail with pear and cowberry, and even beaver stewed with mushrooms. Folk musicians play in summer.

Markus ir Ko   STEAK €€€

(Map p294; ✆ 5-262 3185; www.markusirko.lt; Antokolskio gatvė 11; mains €27) It's not cheap, but it probably has the best steak in Lithuania. Choose classic accompaniments such as *maitre d'hotel* butter, Béarnaise and pepper sauce for your fillet or sirloin, or go off-piste with ginger-honey duck or veal with chanterelles. Look for the sign of the meaty forearm giving the thumbs up, down an alley in the old Jewish quarter.

Bistro 18   INTERNATIONAL €€€

(Map p294; ✆ 8-677 72091; www.bistro18.lt; Stiklių gatvė 18; mains €11-17; ⏱ 11.30am-10pm Tue-Thu, to

---

TOP FIVE VILNIUS PANORAMAS

For a breathtaking cityscape, scale the following:

Gediminas Castle (p289) while sightseeing.

Subačiaus Gate (p300) overlooking the Vilnia.

High over the world's hot-air ballooning capital, with **Oreivystės Centras** (p304).

Sky Bar (p312) with aperitif in hand.

TV Tower (p304) for sunset vistas.

11pm Fri, 1-11pm Sat) Bistro 18 is a breath of fresh air in Vilnius' restaurant scene. The service is friendly, polite and attentive, the decor is minimalist yet comfortable, the food is imaginative, international and flavoursome, and they know how to chill white wine.

Saint Germain   MEDITERRANEAN €€€

(Map p294; ✆ 5-262 1210; www.saintgermain. lt; Literatų gatvė 9; mains €18-22; ⏱ 11am-11pm) Focusing largely on Italian and French fare, with a focus on wine-friendly food, this stylish wine bar–bistro is tucked away on one of Old Town's nicest cobbled streets. If you want to enjoy your Ligurian-style *zander* (pike perch, baked in foil with tomatoes, olives, potatoes and pine nuts) on the summer terrace, think about booking ahead.

Žuvinė   SEAFOOD €€€

(Map p294; ✆ 8-682 19172; www.zuvine.lt; Didžioji gatvė 31; mains €13-18; ⏱ 11am-midnight Mon-Sat, to 10pm Sun) Žuvinė showcases Lithuania's fantastic fresh- and saltwater fish, including *zander*, scallops, smelts and other piscine delights. The location, in the lee of the Town Hall, is ideal for a lingering alfresco dinner when the sun's out.

Sweetroot   LITHUANIAN €€€

(Map p294; ✆ 8-685 60767; www.sweetroot. lt; Užupio gatvė 22; mains €14; ⏱ 4-11pm Tue-Sat) Sweetroot is proof that the (ironically international) trend towards 'locavorism' has reached high-end dining in Vilnius. In a smart if formulaic modern dining room (complete with open kitchen and tattooed chefs) you can enjoy modern dishes using local Lithuanian ingredients such as dock leaves, catmint, snails, beetroot leaves and freshwater fish.

Naked Bite of Contemporary Cuisine
MODERN EUROPEAN €€€
(Map p294; ☑8-623 13455; Stiklių gatvė 12/Žydų gatvė 2; mains €14-16; ☺11am-midnight) This cosy place in the old Jewish quarter brings a touch of New Nordic style to Vilnius. Service is smart and attentive, and the food (such as aged beef with beetroot and shallots, or turbot with pearl barley and scallops) superb. The prix-fixe menus – two or three courses at lunch (€7 or €8), or five at dinner (€23) – are exceptional value.

St Hubertus
MODERN EUROPEAN €€€
(Map p294; ☑8-615 69777; www.st-hubertus.lt; Vokiečių gatvė 24; mains €23; ☺noon-midnight) Named for the patron saint of hunters, Hubertus doesn't tend to attract a lot of vegans. But, alongside all the quadrupedal protein (350g steaks, wild boar, venison) you'll find more easily digested fare, such as cauliflower veloute with tiger prawns, or sea bass with spinach, lentils and cuttlefish ink. There's even a vegetarian option or two!

La Provence
MEDITERRANEAN €€€
(Map p294; ☑8-686 04708; www.laprovence. lt; Vokiečių gatvė 22; mains €26; ☺6pm-midnight Tue-Sat) Not strictly French – it serves Italian and Spanish dishes too – La Provence is a silver-service restaurant with a serious wine list. Carpaccio, bouillabaisse, pastas, game and weighty classics like coq au vin all find their way onto the menu, and you can expect stiff napery, gleaming flatware and walls decked in tapestries.

Self-Catering
Self-catering is a doddle, with a supermarket on every second street corner.

★Senamiesčio Krautuvė
LITHUANIAN €
(Map p294; ☑5-231 2836; www.senamiesciokrau tuve.lt; Literatų gatvė 5; ☺10am-10pm Mon-Sat, 11am-5pm Sun) Look no further than this wonderful, quiet hobbit-hole for the very best Lithuanian comestibles, many unique to the country. Cured meats, fresh sausages, cheeses, fresh fruit and vegetables, honey and preserves, breads and pastries: all are arranged in irresistible profusion around the walls of this snug trove on Literatų gatvė.

Kmyninė
BAKERY €
(Map p290; ☑8-674 47224; Užupio gatvė 38; bread or cookies per kilo €3.50-7; ☺7.30am-8pm Mon-Fri, from 8am Sat; 🐾) This sweet little bakery, named for the caraway seeds so beloved in Central and Eastern Europe, is a great place to pick up moist, sweet rye breads, Lithuanian cookies and *sakotis*, the traditional cake that looks a little like a Christmas tree.

Maxima
SUPERMARKET €
(Map p294; www.maxima.lt; Mindaugo gatvė 11; ☺24hr) The only 24-hour supermarket in town. It has sub-branches all over Vilnius.

Iki
SUPERMARKET €
(Map p290; www.iki.lt; J Jasinskio gatvė 16; ☺8am-10pm) One of the biggest supermarkets in town. Has branches everywhere, including the bus station.

Mini Maxima
SUPERMARKET €
(Map p294; www.maxima.lt; Gedimino prospektas 64; ☺7am-10pm Mon-Fri, 8am-10pm Sat & Sun) Tiny version of the chain supermarket.

Iki Express
SUPERMARKET €
(Map p294; www.iki.lt; Jogailos gatvė 12; ☺7.30am-11pm) A pocket-sized supermarket, handy for emergencies.

🍸 Drinking & Nightlife
Nightlife is a laid-back affair: most places don't hum until late evening, and many double as restaurants. Vokiečių gatvė, lined with wooden-decked terraces in summer, is an obvious starting point; as the night wears on, Totorių or Vilniaus gatvės, with their ever-increasing number of bars, are good bets.

Vilnius has a small but lively clubbing scene that occasionally sees new venues open. It doesn't get going until around midnight and is best experienced in winter, when everyone's around (in summer many go to the seashore to party).

Bukowski
BAR
(Map p294; ☑8-640 58855; Visų Šventų gatvė 7; ☺11am-2am Mon-Wed, to 5am Thu-Sun) The eponymous Barfly is the spiritual patron of this charismatic boho bar in a less-trodden pocket of Old Town. It has a back terrace for finer weather, great beers on tap, a full program of poetry, music and other events, and a welcoming, unpretentious atmosphere. One of Vilnius' best.

Vasaros Terasa
BEER GARDEN
(Map p294; ☑8-633 94995; Vilnius gatvė 39; ☺11am-4am May-Sep) Open only in the warmer months – as the name, 'Summer Terrace', suggests – this big, boisterous courtyard is one of Vilnius' best places to catch a band. Presided over by two ceramic cows, and offering food stalls, flea markets, capoeira and other

distractions for the daylight hours, it's as welcoming as it is bohemian.

Sweet and Sour
COCKTAIL BAR

(Map p294; ☑8-682 27774; Aušros Vartų gatvė 19; ☺4pm-midnight Tue & Wed, to 2am Thu-Sat) You'll get great service and classic cocktails of the pre-Prohibition era at this intimate place on Aušros Vartų gatvė. It's wood-panelled, fire-lit in winter, and classy.

Jamaika
BAR

(Map p294; ☑8-688 76766; Visų Šventųjų gatvė 9; ☺6pm-6am) The slightly scruffy, offbeat front bar of the Jamaika hostel is perhaps one of the friendliest in Vilnius.

Alchemikas
COCKTAIL BAR

(Map p294; ☑8-612 99800; Islandijos gatvė 1; ☺7pm-2am Mon-Thu, to 4am Fri & Sat) Dedicated to serious mixology, 'the Alchemist' turns base materials into golden evenings for many a Vilnius hipster. It's very popular, and the limited space runs out quickly on busier nights.

Soho
GAY & LESBIAN

(Map p290; ☑8-699 39567; www.sohoclub.lt; Švitrigailos gatvė 7/16; admission 11pm-1am €3, 1-4am €6; ☺10pm-7am Fri & Sat) Proud, friendly and party-obsessed, Soho proudly bills itself as Lithuania's 'most popular' LGBTQ club. On a regular night, DJs play house and pop; on special nights, live performers take over.

Exit
CLUB

(Map p290; ☑8-698 59116; J Jasinskio gatvė 16a; admission from €3; ☺11pm-4am Fri & Sat) Probably Lithuania's biggest club, Exit has the sound system, atmosphere and hedonistic crowd to attract big-name internationals to play alongside local DJs.

Špunka
BAR

(Map p294; ☑8-652 32361; Užupio gatvė 9; ☺3-10pm Tue-Sun, from 5pm Mon) This tiny, charismatic little bar does a great line in craft ales from Lithuania and further afield. If you need sustenance to keep the drink and chat flowing, local cheese and charcuterie are on hand.

Būsi Trečias
MICROBREWERY

(Map p294; ☑5-231 2698; www.busitrecias.lt; Totorių gatvė 18; ☺11am-11pm Sun-Fri, 11am-3am Sat) Locals know this microbrewery-pub is a great place to get a cheap, sustaining Lithuanian lunch (mains €3.20). It also offers charismatic wooden decor, 12 varieties of beer (including lime, raspberry and caramel) and courtyard tables for the warmer months.

Opium
CLUB

(Map p294; ☑8-691 41205; www.opiumclub.lt; Islandijos gatvė 4; admission €3-5; ☺10pm-6am Fri, 11pm-5am Sat) This compact venue – which serves food in the daytime – is for serious clubbers. Some of Vilnius' best DJs, and international acts, play electro, techno and house.

LITHUANIA VILNIUS

WHERE TO GO FOR WINE

Vilnius isn't all about the *alus* (beer): plenty of places are dedicated to the joys of the grape.

In Vino/Portobello (Map p294; ☑5-212 1210; www.invino.lt; Aušros Vartų gatvė 7; ☺4pm-2am Sun-Thu, to 4am Fri & Sat) This hugely popular Old Town venue has split: the glamorous wine bar In Vino remains, but has yielded half its space to the English style 'pub' Portobello. On one side of the courtyard you'll find candlelit tables and a fantastic range of wines by the glass; on the other, it's pints of craft beer, red phone boxes and cut-up minis.

La Bohemé (Map p294; ☑5-212 1087; www.laboheme.lt; Šv Ignoto gatvė 4/3; ☺noon-midnight Sun-Wed, to 2am Thu-Sat) Choose between wooden tables below vaulted ceilings and chandeliers, or bypass the main room and grab a comfy couch out the back. Best enjoyed in winter, when the open fire is raging.

Notre Vie (Map p294; ☑8-614 24521; www.notrevie.lt; Stiklių gatvė 10; ☺3pm-midnight; 🛜) Wedged into one of the prime crossroads in the twisting streets of Old Town is this charismatic little wine bar, offering Old and New World wines by the glass, plus cheese, charcuterie, quesadillas and other wine-friendly snacks.

Tappo D'Oro (Map p294; ☑8-686 16866; Stuokos-Gucevičiaus gatvė 7; ☺11am-11pm; 🛜) With an extensive list focusing on Italian varietals, a leafy terrace, a laid-back atmosphere and plenty of wine-friendly snacks, Tappo D'Oro is a sweet spot to refuel when near the cathedral. It also has an outpost geared to the late-drinking crowd, on **Vokiečių gatvė** (Map p294; ☑8-616 74754; Vokiečių gatvė 8; ☺7pm-4am).

GAY & LESBIAN VILNIUS

The scene is low-key and underground. For general information, chat rooms and guides, contact Vilnius-based **Lithuanian Gay League** (📞 5-233 3031; www.gay.lt), which publishes a solid online entertainment guide in English.

There are few clubs in Vilnius that cater exclusively or mostly to a gay clientele. The most popular is Soho (p311).

King & Mouse   BAR

(Map p294; 📞 5-203 2552; www.kingandmouse.lt; Trakų gatvė 2; ☺ 5pm-1am) While a collection of more than 300 whiskies (and whiskeys) from around the world is its forte, this bar also does great cocktails and food. Knowledgeable staff and a welcoming atmosphere make it one of Old Town's sweetest spots to refuel.

Artistai   PUB

(Map p294; 📞 5-212 1268; www.artistai.lt; Šv Kazimiero gatvė 3; ☺ noon-midnight Mon-Thu, to 4am Fri-Sun) Great for live music, this charismatic place also has a terrace in summer, and exhibits the work of local photographers.

Brodvéjus   CLUB

(Map p294; www.brodvejus.lt; Vokiečių gatvė 4/Mėsinių gatvė 4; ☺ 8pm-5am Tue-Sun) Live bands, karaoke, DJs and raucous late nights make this an institution in the heart of Old Town.

Užupio kavinė   CAFE

(Map p294; 📞 5-212 2138; www.uzupiokavine.lt; Užupio gatvė 2; ☺ 10am-11pm; 📶) The plum spot on the Vilnia, next to the main bridge into Užupis, is the best thing about this cafe-bar. In summer, grab a table on the decking overlooking the waving waterweeds (they tend to book up fast) and watch the bohos and tourists stream by. The cosy interior is equally fun in winter, sometimes with impromptu live entertainment.

Sky Bar   BAR

(Map p290; 📞 5-231 4823; Konstitucijos prospektas 20; ☺ 5pm-1am Sun-Thu, to 2.30am Fri & Sat) It may look – and feel – like an airport lounge, but nothing can beat the panoramas of this sky-blue bar on the 22nd floor of the Radisson Blu Hotel Lietuva. DJs spin tunes on Friday and Saturday.

Pinavija   CAFE

(Map p294; 📞 8-676 44422; www.pinavija.lt; Vilniaus gatvė 21; coffee €1.50, pastries €2; ☺ 9am-8pm; 📶) With caramel-striped awnings, flowers throughout, a stunning array of cakes and pastries and good coffee, this smart new bakery-cafe is a lovely place to refuel. There's even a snug kids' area, complete with playhouse and toys, and soothing jazz for the more mature clientele. Try the Lithuanian cookies with cottage cheese and walnuts, or chocolate and nutmeg.

Vaisinė   COFFEE

(Map p294; 📞 8-699 28332; Užupio gatvė 20; coffee €2; ☺ 8am-10pm) With its smart timber interior and general air of expensive good health, Vaisinė is emblematic of the gentrification of Užupis. It's a great place to get elaborate juices, coffee and healthy tidbits.

Skonis ir Kvapas   CAFE

(Map p294; 📞 5-212 2803; www.skonis-kvapas.lt; Trakų gatvė 8; ☺ 10am-10pm Mon-Sat, 11am-8pm Sun) Dedicated to the sensual delights of tea and coffee, 'Taste and Smell' is a stylish courtyard cafe with a talent for the brew. Hot spiced cups for winter, iced tea on the terrace, single-origin coffees, spices, tobacco, sweets, gifts and snacks: it's a bit more than just another coffee shop.

☆ Entertainment

The tourist office publishes events listings, as does the *Baltic Times*.

Cinemas

Find movie listings at www.cinema.lt (in Lithuanian only).

Forum Cinemas Vingis   CINEMA

(Map p290; 📞 1567; www.forumcinemas.lt; Savanorių prospektas 7; ☺ 10.30am-10pm) Mostly popular Hollywood films are screened in English with Lithuanian subtitles at this 12-screen cinema.

Pasaka   CINEMA

(Map p294; 📞 5-261 1516; www.kinopasaka.lt; Šv Ignoto gatvė 4/3) Offers alternative cinema and art-house fare, with films normally screened in their original language.

Forum Cinemas Akropolis   CINEMA

(📞 1567; www.forumcinemas.lt; Ozo gatvė 25) Out of the centre, Forum Cinemas in the Akropolis multiplex shows films in English.

Theatre & Classical Music

Mainstream theatre – from Lithuania and abroad – is performed at several locations in town. Most companies shut for the summer season. Buy tickets at venue box offices.

Small Theatre of Vilnius
THEATRE
(Vilniaus Mažasis Teatras; Map p294; ☑5-249 9869; www.vmt.lt; Gedimino prospektas 22) Founded just before Lithuania achieved legal Independence from the Soviet Union, in March 1990, the Small Theatre has occupied its present premises since 2005. The brainchild of artistic director Rimas Tuminas, it stages productions of classic works (Chekov, Beckett) alongside plays by Lithuanian writers and Tuminas' own repertoire.

Theatre Arena
THEATRE
(Map p290; ☑8-683 77357; www.teatroarena.lt; Olimpiečių gatvė 3) The modern Arena hosts all kinds of acts and assemblies, from guitar gods like Steve Vai to business conventions. It's also the home of the innovative **Oskaras Koršunovas Theatre** (OKT, Oskaro Koršuno Teatro; Map p294; ☑5-212 2099; www.okt.lt; Ašmenos gatvė 8), Lithuania's most progressive company.

Lithuanian National Drama Theatre
THEATRE
(Lietuvos Nacionalinis Dramos Teatras; Map p294; ☑5-262 1593; www.teatras.lt; Gedimino prospektas 4; ☺box office 10am-7pm Mon-Fri, 11am-7pm Sat & Sun, lunch 2-3pm) Operating on this site since 1951, the National Drama Theatre stages national and international productions in Lithuanian.

Lithuanian National Opera & Ballet Theatre
OPERA
(Lietuvos Nacionalinis Operos ir Baleto Teatras; Map p294; ☑8-615 51000; www.opera.lt; Vienuolio gatvė 1; ☺box office 10am-7pm Mon-Fri, to 6.30pm Sat, to 3pm Sun) This stunning (or gaudy, depending on your taste) Soviet-era building, with its huge, cascading chandeliers and grandiose dimensions, is home to Lithuania's national ballet and opera companies. You can see world-class performers for as little as €4 (or as much as €200...)

Youth Theatre
DRAMA
(Jaunimo Teatras; Map p294; ☑5-261 6126; www.jaunimoteatras.lt; Arklių gatvė 5; ☺box office 11am-2pm & 2.30-6pm Tue-Sun) Housed in a handsome classical building, the national youth theatre stages everything from classics to experimental pieces. Closes from mid-July to mid-August.

Vilnius Congress Concert Hall
CONCERT VENUE
(Map p294; ☑5-262 8127; www.lvso.lt; Vilniaus gatvė 6/16; ☺box office noon-7pm Mon-Fri, 11am-4pm Sat) The home of the Lithuanian State Symphony Orchestra, this geometric pile near the Neris hosts symphonies, chamber music, opera and more. Leading Lithuanian and international performers can be seen for a song.

Lithuanian National Philharmonic
CLASSICAL MUSIC
(Lietuvos Nacionalinė Filharmonija; Map p294; ☑5-266 5233; www.filharmonija.lt; Aušros Vartų gatvė 5; ☺box office 10am-7pm Tue-Sat, to noon Sun) Lithuania's premier venue for orchestral, chamber and sacral music. But it's not all classical: prominent international jazz acts often ply their trade here.

Lithuanian Music and Theatre Academy
CLASSICAL MUSIC
(Lietuvos muzikos akademija; Map p290; ☑5-261 2691; www.lmta.lt; Gedimino prospektas 42) Nurturing Lithuania's young musical, dance and theatrical talent, the Academy also stages hundreds of free performances each year. It's spread over four buildings, but the classical pile at No 42 Gedimino prospektas is the main one.

Shopping

Old Town's main thoroughfare, running from Pilies gatvė to Aušros Vartų gatvė, is something of a bustling craft market or tourist trap, depending on your perspective. Traders' stalls are laden with cheap amber trinkets, clothing and small souvenirs; painters sell their wares; and amber and linen shops are a dime a dozen.

Vilnius' main open-air market is the oft-disappointing **Gariūnai**, to the west, off the Kaunas road. Minibuses marked 'Gariūnai' or 'Gariūnų Turgus' ferry shoppers from the train station road to the market every morning. By car it's 11km along Savanorių prospektas from Vilnius centre. Closer to town is the food-driven **Kalvarijų** (☑8-272 2225; www.kalvariju-turgus.lt; Kalvarijų gatvė 61; ☺sunrise-noon Tue-Sun). Both markets open sunrise to noon Tuesday to Sunday.

Old Town

Amber Museum
JEWELLERY
(Map p294; ☑5-212 1988; www.ambergift.lt; Aušros Vartų gatvė 9; ☺10am-6pm Mon-Fri, to 3pm Sat) Displays the wares of top jewellers

working with Baltic Gold in a room itself decorated with more than 500kg of amber.

Lino ir Gintaro Studija HOMEWARES
(Linen & Amber Studio; Map p294; ☑5-261 0213; www.lgstudija.lt; Stiklių gatvė 3; ☺10am-7pm, to 5pm Sun) With additional branches on Pilies (7) and Didžioji gatvės (10 and 11), the Linen and Amber Studio offers lovely gifts and souvenirs in linen, amber and precious metal.

Aušros Vartų Meno Galerija HANDICRAFTS
(Map p294; ☑5-240 5007; www.avmenogalerija. lt; Aušros Vartų gatvė 12; ☺9am-9pm) Good spot to look for locally made souvenirs, including paintings, lace and arts and crafts.

Amatų Gildija CERAMICS
(Craft Guild; Map p294; ☑5-212 0520; www. amatugildija.lt; Pranciškonų gatvė 4; ☺Tue-Sat) Dedicated to preserving and teaching traditional techniques of ceramics, Amatų Gildija is a hive of industry and beautiful handicrafts. It's an open workshop, (commercial) gallery and teaching space set below street level, and always abuzz with quiet, concentrated activity. While it's mainly about pots, it also teaches and displays woodworking, weaving and other crafts.

Dom Bow Ties CLOTHING
(Map p294; ☑8-627 33328; www.ietuviskospete liskes.lt; Stiklių gatvė 6; ☺11am-7pm Tue-Sun) Pop your head through the archway at No 6, take the few steps below the sign of the giant bow tie, and you'll find yourself in what is, perhaps understandably, the only store in Lithuania dedicated to hand-made bow ties. You can even order them to spec.

Ramunė Piekautaitė FASHION
(Map p294; ☑5-231 2270; www.ramunepiekau taite.com; Didžioji gatvė 20; ☺11am-7.30pm Mon-Fri, to 6pm Sat, to 4pm Sun) A swanky boutique showcasing locally designed business, leisure and bridal wear.

Zoraza FASHION
(Map p294; ☑8-640 33588; www.zoraza.com; Stiklių gatvė 9/Gaono gatvė 10; ☺11am-7pm Mon-Sat) Daiva Urbonavičiūtė fronts the fun and funky fashion house where a riot of colours and textures – suede, glitter, beads, felt, crystal, leather and so on – creates an urban, vintage feel.

Aukso Avis FASHION
(Map p294; ☑5-261 0421; www.auksoavis.lt; Pilies gatvė 38; ☺11am-8pm Mon-Fri, to 7pm Sat, to 5pm Sun) This gallery, established by Vilnius fashion designer Julija Žilėniene, sells bags, T-shirts, wall murals and jewellery (think necklaces in felt or wool) made from a rich range of materials.

Gedimino 9 SHOPPING CENTRE
(Map p294; www.gedimino9.lt; Gedimino prospektas 9; ☺10am-7pm Mon-Sat) Housed in a grand mid-Victorian building that has been used by government, newspapers and nightclubs over the years, this swanky development houses international brands like H&M and the Body Shop. It's also out of the price-range of many Vilniusians, and accordingly under-patronised.

Marks & Spencer DEPARTMENT STORE
(Map p294; www.marks-and-spencer.lt; Gedimino prospektas 20/1; ☺10am-9pm Mon-Sat, to 6pm Sun) The popular UK-based purveyor of all things useful, including hard-to-find imported food, alongside Lithuanian staples.

Vinny's WINE
(Map p294; ☑5-269 0013; www.vinnys.lt; Vilniaus gatvė 15; ☺10am-8pm Mon-Thu, 10am-9pm Fri, noon-8pm Sat & Sun) A well-stocked vintner where alongside wines and spirits from across Europe, you can pick up Lithuanian specialities such as mead, Samanė (a brand of legal moonshine that weighs in at a hefty 50% ABV) and Zalgiris (a mead-based spirit that, at 75% ABV, perhaps oughtn't to be legal).

Akademinė Knyga BOOKS
(Map p294; ☑5-266 1680; www.humanitas. lt; Universiteto gatvė 4; ☺10am-6pm Mon-Fri, to 3pm Sat) A scientific and academic book store that also sells fiction, including titles in English.

Humanitas BOOKS
(Map p294; ☑5-262 1153; www.humanitas.lt; Dominikonų gatvė 5; ☺10am-6pm Mon-Fri, to 4pm Sat) Wonderfully stocked with art, design, architecture and gift titles.

Littera BOOKS
(Map p294; ☑5-212 1988; Universiteto gatvė 3; ☺9am-6pm Mon-Fri, 10am-3pm Sat) You'll find the university bookshop, which sells souvenirs too, in MK Sarbievijus courtyard.

Vaga BOOKS
(Map p290; ☑5-249 8392; www.vaga.lt; Gedimino prospektas 9; ☺10am-7pm Mon-Fri, to 4pm Sat) Great map selection and good coffee.

New Town

Juozas Statkevičius   FASHION
(Map p294; www.statkevicius.com; Pamėnkalnio gatvė 2-1) 'Josef Statkus' is a big local name in cutting-edge fashion and costume design, with representatives in Paris, New York and Moscow.

Lino Kopos   FASHION
(Map p290; www.linokopos.com; Krokuvos gatvė 6; ☺10am-7pm Mon-Fri, to 4pm Sat) The local master of linen is Giedrius Šarkauskas. Inspired by life's natural cycle, the designer produces collections sewn solely from linen. Accessories are made from amber, wood and leather.

Lino Namai   HOMEWARES
(Linen House; Map p294; ☑5-212 2322; www.siulas.lt; Vilniaus gatvė 12; ☺10am-7pm Mon-Fri, to 6pm Sat, 11am-5pm Sun) Sells linen from Siūlas, the oldest flax mill in the country, renowned for high-quality table and bed linen. You'll also find accessories and a few pieces to wear. There's another branch on Pilies gatvė 38.

Europa   SHOPPING CENTRE
(Map p290; www.pceuropa.lt; Konstitucijos prospektas 7a; ☺7am-midnight; ☎) Large shopping centre just across the Neris River from Old Town. Three floors of shops and a handful of restaurants and coffee joints.

Akropolis   SHOPPING CENTRE
(☑5-238 7711; www.akropolis.lt; Ozo gatvė 25; ☺10am-10pm; ☎) Massive shopping and entertainment complex with hundreds of stores and restaurants, a multiplex cinema, an ice-skating rink and a children's play area.

ℹ Information

The tourist offices have free maps of central Vilnius that will satisfy most visitors' needs. Otherwise they, along with bookshops, some hotels and supermarkets, sell maps of Vilnius published by **Briedis** (www.briedis.lt; Parodų gatvė 4) and **Jāņa sēta** (www.kartes.lv). Jāņa sēta's *Vilnius*

THE BEST OF FOLK ART IN VILNIUS

Lithuanian folk art is alive and well, as the clutch of enchanting folk-artists' workshops in and around Old Town proves.

Senųjų Amatų Dirbtuvės (Old Crafts Workshop; Map p294; ☑8-613 81889; www.senieji amatai.lt; Savičiaus gatvė 10; ☺11am-7pm Tue-Sun) The tools, materials, processes and final results of a whole range of traditional crafts – weaving, paper-making, book-binding, leather-working, metalworking and more – are lovingly displayed in this fantastic, welcoming little shop. Affiliated with the Fine Crafts Association of Vilnius, it's a wonderful place to learn these time-worn skills, or pick up a beautiful Lithuanian keepsake.

Black Ceramics Centre (BCC; Map p294; ☑8-6994 2456; www.ceramics.w3.lt; Naugarduko gatvė 20) This building contains both the workshop and retail outlet for the Black Ceramics Centre, dedicated to preserving and teaching the ancient Lithuanian art of black ceramics.

Jonas Bugailiškis (Map p294; ☑8-6523 6613; www.bugailiskis.com; Aušros Vartų gatvė 17-10; ☺by arrangement) Lithuanian artist Bugailiškis turns out all manner of weird and beautiful things from his workshop: sculptures, ornate crosses, and even musical instruments.

Sauluva (Map p294; ☑8-686 43906; www.sauluva.lt; Literatų gatvė 3; ☺10am-7pm) A 'Joint Stock Company' selling handicrafts in amber, metal, ceramics, textiles and other materials. Great for unusual and educational toys, it also has branches at Pilies gatvė 21 and 36, and Šv Jono gatvė 12.

Užupis Blacksmith Museum-Gallery (Užupio kalvystės muziejus galerija; Map p294; ☑5-215 3757; www.vilniauskalviai.lt; Užupio gatvė 26; ☺10am-7pm Tue-Fri, to 5pm Sat) Learn about iron-working, see blacksmiths at work, and maybe come away with a piece or two. Demonstrations take place on Tuesday afternoons, or by appointment.

Vilniaus Puodžių Cechas (Vilnius Potters' Guild; Map p294; ☑8-659 99040; Paupio gatvė 2-20; ☺11am-7pm Tue-Fri, noon-6pm Sat) Traditional ceramic manufacturing and handicrafts are on display here.

Vitražo manufaktūra (Map p294; ☑5-212 1202; www.stainedglass.lt; Stiklių gatvė 6-8; ☺11am-8pm Mon-Fri, to 6pm Sat, to 5pm Sun) Exquisite stained-glass sculptures, wall murals and mobiles fill this creative stained-glass workshop; daily demonstrations noon to 4pm.

(1:25,000; €3.50) covers the entire city and includes a 1:10,000 inset of the central city.

INTERNET ACCESS

Most cafes, restaurants and hotels now have free wi-fi zones.

Collegium (Pilies gatvė 22-1; per hour €2; ⊙10am-6pm Mon-Fri) Internet access and telephone. Good location; steep prices.

INTERNET RESOURCES

Vilnius (www.vilnius.lt) Informative city municipality website.

Vilnius Old Town Renewal Agency (www.vsaa. lt) The latest on the Old Town renovation.

Vilnius Tourism (www.vilnius-tourism.lt) Tourist office website; brilliant up-to-the-minute capital guide.

LAUNDRY

Some Vilnius hostels have a washing machine for guests, and a handful of upmarket hotels run a laundry service.

Skalbiu sau (☑ 5-264 8160; www.skalbiusau. lt; Savanorių prospektas 176; ⊙9am-10pm Mon-Fri, 10am-7pm Sat & Sun) Service washes and self-service machines.

LEFT LUGGAGE

Bus Station Left Luggage Service (Map p290; ⊙5.25am-9pm Mon-Fri, 7am-8.45pm Sat & Sun) Bags can be left for €0.87 per piece at the *bagažinė*.

Train Station (Geležinkelio gatvė, central hall basement; ⊙24hr) Luggage lockers are available, from €2 per 24 hours.

LIBRARIES

American Centre (www.vilnius.usembassy.gov; Akmenų gatvė 7; ⊙10am-2pm Mon & Wed-Fri, to 7pm Tue) Housed in the US embassy.

Centre Culturel Français (www.institutfran cais-lituanie.com; Didžioji gatvė 1; ⊙9am-7pm Mon-Fri, 10am-3pm Sat)

MEDIA

Vilnius in Your Pocket (www.inyourpocket. com) Quality city guide published every two months, available as PDF download or in bookshops, tourist offices and newspaper kiosks (€0.58).

MEDICAL SERVICES

Baltic-American Medical & Surgical Clinic (☑ 5-234 2020; www.bak.lt; Nemenčinės gatvė 54a; ⊙24hr) English-speaking health care inside Vilnius University Antakalnis hospital.

Gintarine vaistinė (Geležinkelio gatvė 16; ⊙7am-9pm Mon-Fri, 9am-6pm Sat & Sun) Pharmacy in the central hall of the train station.

University Emergency Hospital (☑ 5-216 9069; www.rvul.lt; Šiltnamių gatvė 29; ⊙24hr) This teaching hospital takes serious and emergency cases.

MONEY

The following all have ATMs accepting Visa and MasterCard. ATMs can also be found throughout the city.

Citadele Bankas (☑ 5-213 5454; www.keitykla. lt; Gedimino prospektas 26; ⊙8am-5pm Mon-Fri) Citadele, Lithuania's Amex representative, exchanges currency.

SEB Vilniaus Bankas (www.seb.lt; Vokiečių gatvė 9; ⊙9am-5.30pm Mon-Fri) Also has a branch on Gedimino (www.seb.lt; Gedimino prospektas 12; ⊙8am-5pm Mon-Fri).

Swedbank (www.swedbank.lt; Gedimino prospektas 56; ⊙9am-5.30pm Mon-Thu, to 4.30 Fri) Cashes Thomas Cook and Amex travellers cheques.

POST

Branch Post Office (Map p294; www.post. lt; Vokiečių gatvė 7-13; ⊙10am-6pm Mon-Fri) Handy for Old Town.

Central Post Office (Centrinis Paštas; Map p294; www.post.lt; Gedimino prospektas 7; ⊙8.30am-7pm Mon-Fri, 9am-2pm Sat) Has the longest hours.

TOURIST INFORMATION

Tourist Information Office Airport (☑ 5-230 6841; www.vilnius-tourism.lt; Rodūnios kelias 2-1; ⊙9am-9pm) Not as extensive as the head office in town, but very useful.

Tourist Information Office Cathedral Sq (Map p294; ☑ 5-262 9660; www.vilnius-tourism.lt; Šventaragio gatvė 2; ⊙9am-1.15pm & 2-6pm) Information kiosk in the heart of Old Town.

Tourist Information Office Old Town (Map p294; ☑ 5-262 9660; www.vilnius-tourism. lt; Vilniaus gatvė 22, LT-01119; ⊙9am-6pm) The head office of Vilnius' tourist information service is great for brochures, advice and accommodation bookings.

Tourist Information Office Town Hall (Map p294; ☑ 5-262 6470; www.vilnius-tourism.lt; Didžioji gatvė 31; ⊙9am-12.30pm & 1.15-6pm) Good for maps, brochures, bike rentals, accommodation booking, advice and more.

TRAVEL AGENCIES

Baltic Travel Service (☑ 5-212 0220; www. bts.lt; Subačiaus gatvė 2; ⊙8am-6pm Mon-Fri, 10am-2pm Sat) Reservations for country farmstays, bus tickets and hotels.

West Express (☑ 5-255 3265; www.westex press.lt; A Stulginskio gatvė 5; ⊙8am-7pm Mon-Thu, to 6pm Fri) Large, nationwide travel agent.

Zigzag (☑ 25-39 7397; www.zigzag.lt; J Basan-avičiaus gatvė 30; ☉9am-6pm Mon-Fri) Cheap fares for International Student Identity Card holders.

❶ Getting There & Away

AIR

There are no domestic flights within Lithuania, unless you detour via another regional capital. Between them, airBaltic and Estonian Air connect Vilnius with Tallinn up to five times daily, and Rīga up to seven times daily.

Major airline offices are at Vilnius airport:
AirBaltic (☑5-235 6010; www.airbaltic.com) For flights within the Baltic states.
Lufthansa (☑5-232 9290; www.lufthansa. com) Opens two hours before, and closes 30 minutes after, Lufthansa flights.

BUS

Vilnius' **bus station** (Autobusų Stotis; Map p290; ☑ information 1661; www.auto busustotis.lt; Sodų gatvė 22) is just south of Old Town. Inside its ticket hall, domestic tickets are sold from 6am to 7.30pm, and information is available. Timetables are displayed on a board here and on the handy website www.autobusu bilietai.lt. Several bus lines run from here to international destinations.

Ecolines (Map p290; ☑5-213 3300; www. ecolines.net; Geležinkelio gatvė 15; ☉8am-7pm Mon-Fri, 9am-5.30pm Sat & Sun) Serves large cities across Europe.
Eurolines (Map p290; ☑5-233 5277; www. eurolines.lt; Sodų gatvė 22; ☉6.30am-9.30pm) Eurolines is a reliable long-distance carrier.
Simple Express (Map p294; ☑5-233 6666; www.simpleexpress.eu; Sodų gatvė 20b1; ☉8am-7pm Mon-Fri, from 9am Sat & Sun) Together with its sister company Lux Express, Simple Express offers arguably the lowest prices to Lithuania from destinations in the Baltics, including daily buses from Vilnius to Rīga (€11) and Tallinn (€23).

Buses to destinations within Lithuania and to Rīga and Tallinn include the following:
Druskininkai (€10, two hours, 15 daily)
Ignalina (€6, 1¾ hours, up to 10 daily)
Kaunas (€6, 1¾ hours, regularly from 5.45am to 11pm)
Klaipėda (€18, four to 5½ hours, 17 daily)
Molėtai (€5, 1¼ to two hours, 17 daily)
Palanga (€18, 4¼ to six hours, 14 daily)
Panevėžys (€10, 1¾ to three hours, regularly from 6am to 10pm)
Rīga (€18, five hours, nine daily)
Šiauliai (€13, three to 4½ hours, 15 daily)
Tallinn (€32, 10½ hours, five daily)
Visaginas (€8, 2½ hours, 12 daily)

CAR & MOTORCYCLE

Twenty-four hour petrol stations are plentiful in Vilnius. If you hire a car and intend to cross a border check you're insured for inter-Baltic travel.
Autobanga (☑5-212 7777; www.autobanga.lt; Rodūnios kelias 2-1) Hire starts from around €25.
Avis (☑5-232 9316; www.avis.com; Rodūnios kelias 2; ☉6am-1.15am) Also has locations in town (☑5-250 7500; B. Radvilaites gatvė 5a; ☉8am-5pm Mon-Fri, 9am-4pm Sat & Sun), and at the railway station (☑5-230 6820; Geležinkelio gatvė 16; ☉8am-5pm Mon-Fri, to 4pm Sat & Sun).
Europcar (☑5-250 3425; www.europcar.com; Rodūnios kelias 2; ☉9am-midnight) Also has a location in town (☑5-250 3420; Slucko gatvė 3; ☉9am-7pm Mon-Fri, from 8am Sat).
Sixt (☑5-239 5636; www.sixt.lt; Rodūnios kelias 2; ☉8am-midnight Mon-Fri, 10am-5pm Sat & Sun) Another big-name option at the airport.

TRAIN

The **train station** (Geležinkelio Stotis; ☑ information 5-233 0088; www.litrail.lt; Geležinkelio gatvė 16) is opposite the bus station and is equipped with ATMs, a supermarket and information desks.

There is no direct or convenient rail link between Vilnius and Rīga or Tallinn. Direct daily services within Lithuania to/from Vilnius:
Ignalina (€4, 1¾ hours, eight daily)
Kaunas (€6, 1½ hours, 14 daily)
Klaipėda (€16, four hours, three daily)
Trakai (€1.70, 40 minutes, up to 10 daily)

❶ Getting Around

TO/FROM THE AIRPORT

Vilnius International Airport (Tarptautinis Vilniaus Oro Uostas; %6124 4442; www.vno.lt; Rodūnios kelias 10a; W; g1, 2) lies 5km south of the centre. The airport is accessible by bus, train or taxi. Bus 1 runs between the airport and the train station; bus 2 runs between the airport and the northwestern suburb of Šeškinė via the Žaliasis bridge across the Neris and on to Lukiskių aikštė. Buy a ticket (€1 from the driver); have small change handy.

Trains run to the central station every 30 minutes between 6am and 11.30pm. On-board tickets cost €0.72 and the trip is only 10 minutes.

Taxi rates vary depending on whether you hail one out the front of the arrivals hall (about €15), or call a reputable firm in advance (around €10).

BICYCLE

Vilnius is becoming increasingly bike-friendly, although bike lanes are rarer outside Old Town and along the banks of the Neris. Orange Cyclocity stations dot the city, the tourist office has free cycling maps, and BaltiCCycle (www.balticcycle.lt) is good for ideas and information.

Cyclocity (☑ 8-800 22008; www.cyclocity.lt; ☺24hr Apr-Oct) Bikes can be easily hired and returned at the 37 orange Cyclocity stations across Vilnius. Either credit cards or Cyclocity Cards (available by advance subscription) can be used to hire a bike. A three-day ticket is €2.90.

Velo-City (☑ 8-674 12123; www.velovilnius.lt; Palangos gatvė 1; per hour/24hr €4/12; ☺10am-9pm Apr-Sep, by appointment Oct-Mar) This well-established bike-hire operation on the edge of Old Town has decent, well-maintained bikes.

CAR & MOTORCYCLE

Vilnius is generally easy to navigate by car, and not too busy, but the traffic burden is getting heavier each year. Street parking around the centre can be hard to find and is expensive: rates (from 8am to 8pm) run to as much as €2 an hour. The rate is identified by a colour code system (blue is the most expensive) and tickets need to be bought from a machine and displayed on the dashboard.

Avoid parking on unlit streets overnight; car break-ins are not unknown. Cars are not permitted in parts of the pedestrian Old Town.

PUBLIC TRANSPORT

The city is efficiently served by buses and trolleybuses from 5.30am or 6am to midnight; Sunday services are less frequent. Single-trip tickets cost: €1 from the driver; €0.64 if you have a Vilniečio Kortelė (an electronic ticket sold at kiosks; see www.vilniusticket.lt for details); or nothing if you have a Vilnius City Card with public transport included (sold in tourist information centres). Fare evaders risk a small fine.

Quicker minibuses shadow most routes. They pick up/drop off passengers anywhere en route (not just at official bus stops) and can be flagged down on the street. Tickets costs €1 from the driver.

Note that much of Old Town is closed to traffic, meaning that very few buses and trolleybuses service this part of town. For destinations within Old Town, you'll normally have to hoof it.

For route details see www.vilniustransport.lt or pick up a transport map from tourist offices.

TAXI

Taxi rates in Vilnius can vary; cabs are generally cheaper if ordered in advance by telephone than if hailed directly off the street or picked up at a taxi stand. Ask the hotel reception desk or restaurant to call one for you. Reliable companies:

Ekipažas (☑1446; www.ekipazastaksi.lt) One of the larger taxi companies in Vilnius.

Martono Taksi (☑ 240 0004) Vilnius taxis.

Mersera (☑ 278 8888) Distinctive yellow cabs.

AROUND VILNIUS

The centre of Europe, a fairy-tale castle and ancient castle mounds lie within easy reach of the capital. Or there is the trip to Paneriai.

Paneriai

Here Lithuania's brutal history is starkly portrayed. As many as 100,000 people – the exact figure is not known – were murdered by the Nazis between July 1941 and July 1944 at this site, 10km southwest of central Vilnius. Around half the city's Jewish population – about 35,000 people – had been massacred here by the end of the first three months of the German occupation (June to September 1941) at the hands of Einsatzkommando 9, an SS killing unit of Nazi troops, and their Lithuanian accomplices.

The Nazis later burnt the exhumed corpses to hide evidence of their crimes. One of the deeper pits, according to its sign, was where they eventually buried those who were forced to dig up the corpses and pulverise the bones.

The forest entrance is marked by a memorial, the Panerių memorialas. The text in Russian, dating from the Soviet period, commemorates the 100,000 'Soviet citizens' killed here. The memorial plaques in Lithuanian and Hebrew – erected later – honour the many Jewish victims.

There are two dozen trains daily (some terminating in Trakai or Kaunas) from Vilnius to Paneriai station (€0.58, 11 minutes). From Paneriai, make a right on leaving the station down Agrastų gatvė and it's a 1km walk southwest from here.

⊙ Sights

Paneriai Museum   MUSEUM
(☑ tours 8-6808 1278; www.jmuseum.lt; Agrastų gatvė 15; ☺9am-5pm Tue-Sun May-Sep, by appointment Oct-Apr) FREE This small museum tells some of the shocking story of Paneriai. There are two monuments here: one is Jewish (marked with the Star of David), the other Soviet (an obelisk topped with a Soviet star). From here paths lead to a number of grassed-over pits where, from July 1941, as many as 100,000 people were murdered.

The Nazis lined up their victims 10 at a time and shot them in the back of the head, allowing the corpses to simply fall into the pits. Several hundred people a day could be killed in this way. The bodies were then covered with sand to await the next layer.

Trakai

📱 528 / POP 5400

With its red-brick, fairy-tale castle, Karaites culture, quaint wooden houses and pretty lakeside location, Trakai is a must-see just 28km from the capital.

Most of the town stands on a 2km-long, north-pointing tongue of land between Lake Luka (east) and Lake Totoriškių (west). Lake Galvė opens out from the northern end of the peninsula and boasts 21 islands.

Gediminas probably made Trakai his capital in the 1320s and Kęstutis certainly based his 14th-century court here. Protected by the 82-sq-km **Trakai Historical National Park** (📱 528-55 776; www.seniejitrakai.lt), Trakai today is a quiet town, outside summer weekends.

◎ Sights

★ Trakai Castle   CASTLE

(Trakų Pilis; www.trakaimuziejus.lt; adult/senior/student & child €6/4/3; ⊙10am-7pm May-Sep, to 6pm Mar, Apr & Oct, to 5pm Nov-Feb; 🖼) The centrepiece of Trakai is its picture-postcard Island Castle atop an island on Lake Galvė. The painstakingly restored red-brick Gothic castle probably dates from around 1400, when Grand Duke Vytautas needed stronger defences than the peninsula castle afforded. The castle closes on Mondays between October and March, and charges €1.16 for photography in its grounds.

A footbridge links it to the shore and a moat separates the triangular outer courtyard from the main tower with its cavernous central court and a range of galleries, halls and rooms. Some house the Trakai History Museum, which charts the history of the castle. The castle's prominence as a holy site is reflected in its collection of religious art. In summer the castle courtyard is a magical stage for concerts and plays.

Church of the Visitation of the Blessed Mary   CHURCH

(Birutės gatvė 5) Founded around the same time as Trakai Castle, and also by Grand Duke Vytautas, this grand, 15th-century parish church has a large collection of ecclesiastical art, including the Trakai Mother of God, a revered image thought to have been donated by Vytautas himself.

Peninsula Castle   RUIN

The peaceful ruins of Trakai's Peninsula Castle, built from 1362 to 1382 by Kęstutis and destroyed in the 17th century, are a little south of the Island Castle. The peninsula itself is dotted with old wooden cottages, many built by the Karaites, and offers great views of the main castle, town and lakes.

Sacred Art Exhibition   MUSEUM

(Sacralineo Meno Muziejus; 📱 528-53 945; www.trakaimuziejus.lt; Kestučio gatvė 4; adult/student €1.16/0.58; ⊙10am-5pm Wed-Sun) This small exhibition space, housed in a former Dominican chapel, displays a range of religious and sacral objects, including altarpieces, crosses, monstrances and chalices.

Karaite Ethnographic Museum   MUSEUM

(Karaimų etnografinė paroda; 📱 528-55 286; www.trakaimuziejus.lt; Karaimų gatvė 22; adult/child €1.16/0.58; ⊙10am-6pm Wed-Sun) The Karaite Ethnographic Museum traces the ancestry of the Karaites, a Judaic sect and Turkic minority originating in Baghdad, which adheres to the Law of Moses. Their descendants – some 380 families – were brought to Trakai from the Crimea around 1400 to serve as bodyguards. Only 12 families (60 individuals) still live in Trakai and their numbers – 280 throughout Lithuania – are dwindling rapidly.

Kenessa   RELIGIOUS SITE

(Karaimų gatvė 30; admission by donation) This well-maintained wooden prayer house, with its interior dome, is a rare surviving example of Karaite architecture. Arrange a visit at the Karaite Ethnographic Museum.

Orthodox Church of the Nativity   CHURCH

(Maironio gatvė 4) A 19th-century Orthodox church that is partly funded by Tsarina Maria Aleksandrovna.

🏃 Activities

The tourist office has information about a plethora of activities, including boating, horse riding, hot-air ballooning and sailing. It also hires out bikes (€3/14 per hour/day) and has maps for a 14km cycling route around the main sights. Winter offers horse-drawn sled rides, skiing and ice-fishing.

Boating   BOATING

(📱 8-609 51305) Pick up a pedalo (€6 per hour) or rowing boat (€5 per hour) near the footbridge leading to the Island Castle. Open during daylight hours, in summer.

Varnikai Cognitive Walking Way   WALKING

For a lovely stroll out of Trakai, head for this botanical-zoological preserve, 4km east of

Trakai

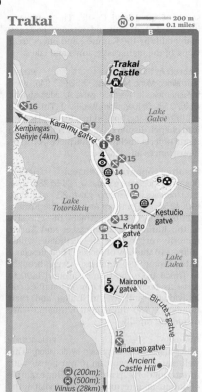

is a modern hotel on the shore of Lake Totoriškių, within walking distance of the centre and the Island Castle. There are 10 well-appointed rooms on the premises and guests have use of the Finnish sauna and pool. Breakfast is €3.

Apvalaus Stalo Klubas　　　HOTEL €€
(☎528-55 595; www.asklubas.lt; Karaimių gatvė 53a; s/d from €73/90; ⊙noon-11pm; P@🖥🌐🏊) This superbly situated lakeside hotel has unrivalled views of the castle, and is perfect for a romantic weekend. Choose a room in either the more elegant French-provincial Ežeras villa, with big comfy furnishings and bold colours on the walls, or the more workaday, modern (and slightly cheaper) digs at the Karaimai villa. There's also an excellent in-house restaurant.

Karaimių 13　　　GUESTHOUSE €€
(☎528-51 911; www.karaimai.lt; Karaimių gatvė 13; d €60; P@🌐) This lovingly renovated, simple Karaite house boasts a cafe that serves Karaite food. The wooden house has been rebuilt in the authentic style of Karaim architecture. The rooms are all simply furnished, but have modern conveniences and internet facilities.

town. To get there, follow the signs marked 'Varnikų Gamtos Takas' across two bridges.

🛏 Sleeping

Trakai is an easy day trip from Vilnius, but it's worth staying overnight to experience the place minus the weekend tourist hordes.

Kempingas Slėnyje　　　CAMPGROUND €
(☎528-53 380; www.camptrakai.lt; Slėnio gatvė 1; sites per adult/car/tent €6/5/5, summer house for 4 people €35) Some 5km out of Trakai in Slėnje, on the northern side of Lake Galvė off the road to Vievis, this campsite has accommodation for all budgets. There are plenty of activities on offer, including a sauna and steam bath, barbecues, bikes and boats for hire, folklore evenings to enjoy and a sandy beach to sprawl on.

Salos　　　HOTEL €
(☎528-53 990; www.salos.lt; Kranto gatvė 5b; s/d/tr €35/47/64; P@🌐🏊) The Salos

✗ Eating

Iki SUPERMARKET €
(Vytauto gatvė 56; ⊙8am-10pm) Stock up for lakeside picnics at this basic supermarket.

Bona Pizzeria PIZZA €€
(✓528-55 595; www.bona.lt; Karaimų gatvė 53a; pizzas €6-8; ⊙11am-11pm) Sitting on the lake, within shutter-snap of the castle, Bona has perhaps the best-located tables in town. Alongside the standard pizzas, salads and pastas, you'll find a smattering of Lithuanian staples, including *cepelinai* and *kibinai*.

Senoji Kibininė KARAITE €€
(✓528-55 865; www.kibinas.lt; Karaimų gatvė 65; mains €4.50-6; ⊙10am-midnight) This traditional Karaite house can be overrun at mealtimes on weekends. Nevertheless, it's worth it to brave the crowds, grab a picnic table when the weather permits, and enjoy excellent Karaite pasties, usually stuffed with pork and served with a bowl of chicken broth.

Markizas LITHUANIAN €€
(✓528-55 859; www.markizas.lt; Karaimų gatvė 25a; mains €6.50-8.50; ⊙11am-11pm) With a cosy interior spilling onto a delightful lakeside terrace in summer, Markizas is ideal for lingering over fish with almond sauce, light summer salads, or outdoor-grilled steak. There's also a kids' menu and occasional live entertainment.

Kybynlar KARAITE €€
(✓8-698 06320; www.kybynlar.lt; Karaimų gatvė 29; mains €7-11; ⊙noon-9pm) The best spot in Trakai to enjoy traditional Karaite cuisine, including the eponymous *kibinai* (pasties stuffed with pork, chicken and other goodies), beef stew and fish pie. Sit inside the pretty interior or grab a lakeside table on the terrace.

Kiubėtė LITHUANIAN €€
(✓528-59 160; www.kiubete.lt; Trakų gatvė 2; mains €6-8; ⊙10.30am-11pm) Offering a mix of Lithuanian and Karaite fare, Kiubėtė has a lovely location opposite Lake Totoriškių, on the quieter side of the Trakai peninsula.

Žejų Namai FISH €€
(✓528-26 008; www.zvejunamai.lt; mains €13; ⊙11am-10pm) If you have your own wheels and a hankering for fresh fish, you'll find Žejų Namai 16km north of Trakai, on the road to Vievis. Rods, bait and buckets are free, and pools teem with live trout and sturgeon. Staff are on hand to weigh, fillet and cook the fish (trout €16.50 per kilogram; sturgeon €19.50).

ℹ Information

Tourist Information Centre (✓528-51 934; www.trakai-visit.lt; Karaimų gatvė 41; ⊙9am-6pm) Lavishly stocked with brochures, staffed by English speakers who can organise everything from boat trips to accommodation, and with an adjoining handicrafts shop, this little office by the lake has everything you need. Closed on weekends between October and April.
Police (✓528-32 230; Vytauto gatvė 57) In the centre of Trakai.

ℹ Getting There & Away

Up to 10 daily trains (€1.48, 30 minutes) travel between Trakai's **train station** (✓51 055; Vilniaus gatvė 5) and Vilnius.

Centre of Europe

In 1989 the French National Geographical Institute pronounced this position – latitude 54° 54', longitude 25° 19' – to be the geographical centre of Europe. It's marked with a boulder inscribed with the points of the compass and the words 'Geografinis Europos Centras'. There's also 27 different EU flags, a wooden decking stage and a white granite obelisk with a crown of gold stars.

◎ Sights & Activities

Europos Parkas Sculpture Park PARK
(✓5-237 7077; www.europosparkas.lt; Europos Parkas gatvė; adult/child €8/4; ⊙10am-sunset) Some 30 minutes north of Vilnius, off the Utena road, is Europos Parkas. Leading contemporary sculptors, including Sol LeWitt and Dennis Oppenheim, show works in wooded parkland (bring mosquito repellent in summer). The exhibitions include the largest sculpture in the world made entirely from TV sets (3000 of them); it's also a maze, leading to a fallen statue of Lenin.

The sculpture park was the brainchild of Lithuanian sculptor Gintaras Karosas, inspired by the 'Centre of Europe' tag. Every year international workshops are held here, attracting artists from all over the world.

European Centre Golf Club GOLF
(✓8-6162 6366; www.golfclub.lt; club hire €23, 18 holes €44; ⊙9am-9pm summer) A well-groomed 18-hole course, suitable for all skill levels. There's also a driving range and restaurant.

ℹ Getting There & Away

Travelling north on the Vilnius–Molėtai road from Vilnius, the Centre of Europe is to the left

STORKS

Eastern Lithuania, indeed the entire country, is prime stork-sighting territory. Lithuania has approximately 13,000 pairs, giving it the highest-density stork population in Europe.

Measuring 90cm in height, this beautiful long-legged, wide-winged creature is breathtaking in flight. Equally marvellous is the catwalk stance it adopts when strutting through meadows in search of frogs to feast on. It sleeps standing on one leg.

The arrival of the stork from Africa each year marks the start of spring. Lithuanians celebrate this traditional protector of the home with Stork Day (25 March), the day farmers traditionally stir their seeds, yet to be planted, to ensure a bigger and better crop.

Storks on their return home usually settle back into the same nest they have used for years. Large and flat, the nest is balanced in a tree or atop a disused chimney or telegraph pole. Some are splayed out across wooden cartwheels, fixed on tall poles by kindly farmers keen to have their farmstead blessed by the good fortune the stork brings.

and marked by the sign 'Europos Centras'. Getting there by public transport requires two bus changes and plenty of patience; the Vilnius tourist offices have more information if you're dead keen.

From Vilnius, bus 146 (marked 'Skirgiskes') leaves from the bus stop on Kalvarijų gatvė for Europos Parkas (€1, 30 minutes) at least three times daily. By car, head north along Kalvarijų gatvė until you reach the Santasriskių roundabout, then bear right towards Žalieji ežerai, following the signs for 'Europos Parkas'.

Kernavė

The quiet town of Kernavė (ker-nar-veh) is home to one of Lithuania's most important historical sites. To get here, follow the road through Dūkštos from Maisiagala on the main road north to Ukmergė, or take a minibus from Vilnius.

◉ Sights & Activities

Kernavė Cultural Reserve ARCHAEOLOGICAL SITE
(Kernavės kultūrinio rezervato; ☑ 382-47 385; www. kernave.org; Kerniaus gatvė) FREE Deemed an 'exceptional testimony to 10 millennia of human settlements in this region' by Unesco, which made it a World Heritage Site in 2004, Kernavė is a must-see. Thought to have been the spot where Mindaugas (responsible for uniting Lithuania for the first time) celebrated his coronation in 1253, this cultural reserve comprises four old castle mounds and the remains of a medieval town.

The sprawling reserve sits on the southern edge of town, facing the Neris River, and gives a good sense of why the site was chosen. While the museum and guided tours are highly worthwhile, there's nothing to stop you simply wandering up and down the hill-forts at your leisure.

**Archaeological &
Historical Museum** MUSEUM
(Archeologijos ir Istorijos Muziejus; ☑ 382-47 385; www.kernave.org; Kerniaus gatvė 4a; admission €2, tours for up to 30 people €20; ⊙ 10am-6pm Tue-Sun Sep, Oct, Apr & May, Wed-Sun Jun-Aug, to 4pm Nov-Mar) This absorbing museum traces the history of the area from 9000 BC to the 13th and 14th centuries AD. There is a wealth of artefacts on display – pottery, Iron Age tools, intricate horn seals – but the highlights are the gilded head decorations, silver jewellery from Russia and cowrie shells from the Indian Ocean that indicate just how far trade had spread during Kernavė's heyday.

✪ Festivals & Events

Rasos Feast CULTURAL
This midsummer festival, on 23 June, brings medieval fun and frolics – axe throwing, catapulting, mead making and so on – to Kernavė.

**International Festival
of Experimental Archaeology** CULTURAL
(☑ 382-47 438) This three-day festival, held annually in July, is lots of fun (despite the deadly name).

EASTERN & SOUTHERN LITHUANIA

The deep, magical forests of Lithuania's eastern and southern corners are a tree-hugger's paradise. Some of the most spectacular scenery in Lithuania is found in these wildernesses, with a lake district that extends into Belarus and Latvia.

Aukštaitija National Park is Lithuania's oldest, framed by the 900-sq-km Labanoras-Pabradė Forest. Outdoor purists will have a ball here, pursuing canoeing, hiking, windsurfing, sailing, birdwatching and, in winter, ice-fishing and even some skiing.

Dzūkija in the far south is the biggest national park, surrounded by the 1500-sq-km Druskininkai-Varėna Forest. Both parks are blessed with an abundant berry crop in early summer, while mushrooms of all shapes and guises sprout by the bucketful from early spring until late autumn.

Close to the Dzūkija National Park is the spa resort of Druskininkai, where rich Lithuanians indulge in winter breaks and the likes of warm honey massages. The Grūtas sculpture park next door, with its busts of Lenin, Stalin and the gang, is a sure nostalgia cure for anyone longing for those 'good old days'.

A few words of warning: mosquitoes are a menace so bring insect repellent; and only pick mushrooms with a local guide and be aware that the stomach of the guide – reared on mushrooms since birth – is substantially more tolerant of certain species than yours.

Aukštaitija National Park

☑ 386

In beloved Aukštaitija (owk-shtai-ti-ya) National Park it's clear where Lithuania's love for nature arose. The natural paradise of deep, whispering forests and blue lakes bewitched this once-pagan country.

Around 70% of the park comprises pine, spruce and deciduous forests, inhabited by elk, deer and wild boar. Its highlight is a labyrinth of 126 lakes, the deepest being **Lake Tauragnas** (60m deep). A footpath leads to the top of 155m **Ice Hill** (Ledakalnis), from where a panorama of some seven lakes unfolds. Particularly pretty is **Lake Baluošas**, ensnared by woods and speckled with islands. White-tailed and golden eagles prey here and storks are plentiful. The **Trainiškis Wildlife Sanctuary** and **Ažvinčiai Forest Reserve**, home to 150- to 200-year-old pine trees, can only be visited with park guides.

Eastern Lithuania

Aukštaitija National Park

N
0 ——————— 5 km
0 ——————— 2.5 miles

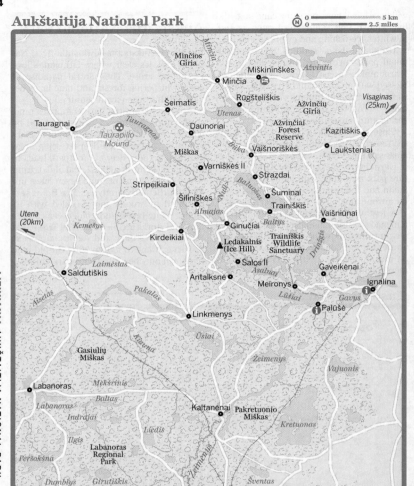

The main jumping-off point for the park is the sleepy town of **Ignalina**, which has a supermarket, a post office, a hotel-restaurant, and one of two information centres that service the park. Nearby **Palūšė**, 3km from Ignalina on the banks of Lake Lūšiai (literally 'Wild Cat Lake'), is home to the park's headquarters and main information centre.

There are around 100 settlements within the park itself: **Šuminai**, **Salos II**, **Vaišnoriškės**, **Varniškės II** and **Strazdai** are protected ethnographic centres.

The park has several ancient *piliakalnis* (fortification mounds), such as the **Tau-** **rapilio mound** on the southern shore of Lake Tauragnas, and some quaint wooden architecture, including a fine **church** and **bell tower** at Palūšė. Around Lake Lūšiai a **wooden sculpture trail** depicts Lithuanian folklore.

◉ Sights & Activities

Boating and trekking are the main activities in the park. Mushroom and berry picking are only permitted in designated forest areas. The National Park Office and Tourist Information Centre are your best sources of information.

Ginučiai Watermill HISTORIC BUILDING
(🖉386-47 478; adult/student €1.20/0.60; ⊙10am-
6pm Tue-Sat May-Sep) This 19th-century mill
in Ginučiai, accessible only with a guided
tour, retains its original mechanism.

Museum of Ancient Beekeeping MUSEUM
(Senorinės Bitininkystės Muziejus; 🖉8-686
12105; Stripeikių kaimas; ⊙10am-6pm Wed-Sun
May–mid-Oct) Stripeikiai's Ancient Beekeeping Museum spins the story of beekeeping
through a merry collection of carved wood-
en statues and hives.

Palūšė valtinė BOATING
(🖉8-650 58515; www.valtine.lt; ⊙8am-8pm May-
Oct) A fibreglass boat for four costs €4 per
hour, or €15 per day.

🛏 Sleeping

Pick up homestay lists from the Palūšė National Park Office or Ignalina Tourist Office.

Žuvėdra HOTEL €
(🖉8-686 09069; www.zuvedra.com; Mokyklos
gatvė 11, Ignalina; s/d/q €26/47/72; 🅿🛜) This
small hotel on the shores of Lake Paplovinis
is an excellent in-town choice, within easy
walking distance of the tourist office in Ignalina. The helpful staff can arrange activities
including bike and boat rental, and the restaurant, serving Lithuanian food (mains €6
to €8), is arguably the best in town.

Tiki Inn GUESTHOUSE €
(🖉8-652 72444; Pašakarvio gatvė 2; d €40) This
quirky slice of Baltic Polynesia is a great option in the sweet town of Palūšė. It's lakeside,
has a kitchen, common area and a beautiful
terrace for watching the sunset, rents kayaks
and paddle-boards, and is as welcoming as
you could possibly hope for. Prices can rise,
depending on the season and demand.

Ginučiai Watermill GUESTHOUSE €
(🖉8-616 29366; www.anp.lt; Ginučių 22; d €35; 🅿)
This 19th-century watermill offers stripped-
back rooms with wood interiors and almost
perfect serenity. Bring your own food to
cook in the kitchen, and end the evening relaxing by the fire or in the sauna. It's open
from April to October, weather-dependent,
and you can book through the National Park
Office.

★Miškiniškės CABIN €€
(🖉8-616 00692; www.miskiniskes.lt; d/apt
€55/140; 🅿🛜) If you've ever harboured
Daniel Boon fantasies – canoeing and hiking

all day among the spruce and pine, eating
heartily then sleeping deeply in a log cabin
– then Miškiniškės is the place. Despite the
forest setting, it's beautifully appointed: the
rooms are snug and attractive, and there's
wi-fi, a sauna and even a gym. You'll need a
car to get here.

Lithuanian Winter Sports Centre HOTEL €€
(Lietuvos žiemos sporto centras; 🖉386-54 193;
www.lzsc.lt; Sporto gatvė 3, Ignalina; d €57; 🅿)
Accommodation (presentable cottages
overlooking the centre's own lake) plays
second fiddle at this Soviet-era sports centre. In winter guests can hire skis, leap on
the ski lift and explore four easy slopes. In
summer there's boating, or rollerblading
along a 7.5km track. From Ignalina centre,
cross the train track and follow Budrių gatvė for 2km.

ⓘ Information

Aukštaitija National Park Office (Aukštaiti-
jos Nacionalinis Parkas; 🖉386-53 135; www.
anp.lt; Lūšių gatvė 16; ⊙9am-5pm Mon-Fri)
Located in Palūšė uphill from the main road
opposite Lake Lūšiai, this office is handy for
park maps and general information. Staff can
arrange treks and backpacking trips by boat,
English-speaking guides (€12 per hour for
groups of up to 20) and even skiing, fishing,
horse riding and sledging.

Tourist Information Centre (🖉386-52 597;
www.ignalinatic.lt; Ateites gatvė 23; ⊙8am-
5pm Mon-Fri year-round, plus 10am-3pm Sat
Jun-Aug) Located in Ignalina's main square,
this centre provides information on the park's
activities and accommodation, and sell maps.

ⓘ Getting There & Away

Hop on a bus (€6, 1¾ hours, 10 daily) or train
(€4, 1¾ hours, eight daily) from Vilnius to Ignalina; there's also at least one bus to/from Kaunas (€7, four hours) via Utena (€2, one hour).
Several buses daily travel between Ignalina and
Palūšė (€1).

Visaginas & Ignalina Nuclear Power Station
🖉386 / POP 28,160
The purpose-built worker-housing town
of Visaginas is as Soviet as you'll get outside the borders of Russia. Built in 1975 for
employees at the former Ignalina Nuclear
Power Station nearby, it's packed with iden-
tical-looking blocks of flats amid forest and

circled by a ring road. Attractive it ain't; bizarre (and fascinating) it is.

In its heyday around 5000 shift workers were shuttled between Visaginas and the former plant, about 3km east of the town centre. A Geiger counter recorded the day's radiation level and Russian was the *lingua franca* on the streets.

The town's future remains uncertain, however, after the nuclear plant was shut down at the end of 2009 as part of Lithuania's agreement to join the EU. Though there's talk of building a new plant, that won't happen until 2018 at the earliest. In the meantime, locals are hoping that increased tourism can bolster the economy.

In mid-August Visaginas bizarrely hosts a bunch of cowboys – hats, boots and all – who ride into town from across Europe for the two-day international country music festival, Visagino Country (www.visagino country.lt).

From Vilnius to Visaginas you can take trains (€5.40, 2¼ hours, six daily) or buses (€8, 2½ hours, 12 daily).

🛏 Sleeping

Hotel Aukštaitija HOTEL €
(☎386-74 858; www.hotel-aukstaitija.lt; Veteranų gatvė 9; s/d/ste €26/38/70; ℗) Those looking for a Soviet experience can overnight in Hotel Aukštaitija, a red-brick high-rise built in the old Soviet tradition. The rooms are not as bleak as the exterior, and several have even been nicely remodelled.

Spa-Hotel Gabriella HOTEL €
(☎386-70 171; www.gabriella.lt; Jaunystės gatvė 21; s/d €40/53; ℗@☀) The Gabriella, as the name suggests, offers massage and spa options, but isn't as fancy as the name implies. There's also a decent restaurant, which is probably the best place in town to have a meal.

Labanoras Regional Park

Southwest of Aukštaitija is 528 sq km of pretty parkland dotted with 285 lakes. At its heart sits the lovely traditional village Labanoras. Canoeing is a grand pastime in the park, particularly on the Lakaja River in the southern section. Cycling is also blissful, weather permitting, but bikes need to be brought in from outside. The national park centre (p325) in Palūšė can help, in season.

Accommodation in the park is limited to a handful of homestays and one delightful hotel-restaurant in Labanoras village.

PULLING THE PLUG AT IGNALINA

In its day the Ignalina Nuclear Power Station near Visaginas was one of the technological wonders of the world. When the Soviets built the plant in the 1980s, its two RBMK 1500 reactors were the most powerful ones commissioned at the time and were capable of generating around 1500MW each of electricity. Unfortunately for Ignalina, the design was similar to the one used at the Chornobyl nuclear plant in Ukraine, which suffered a catastrophic meltdown in 1986. Though Ignalina's second reactor actually came online after the Chornobyl disaster, from the start it was clear the plant's days were numbered.

After Lithuania joined the EU in 2004, the country came under pressure to shut down the two reactors. The EU had no intention of having a Chornobyl-like situation on its hands. Lithuania eventually agreed and decommissioned the first reactor in 2004. The plug was pulled on the second at the end of 2009.

Though power is no longer produced here, the plant is still the subject of some controversy. Foremost is the question of who will bear the prohibitive decommissioning costs, including the billions of euros needed to clean up the reactor site and dispose of redundant radioactive material. Ninety-five per cent of the funds came from the international community, but, while the Lithuanian government found the rest, it has lagged behind expected completion. More information on the decommissioning can be found at www.iae.lt.

Adding to the controversy are plans to build another nuclear power plant here based on a more modern, Western design. In 2006 Lithuania invited neighbours Poland, Latvia and Estonia to collaborate in building a new reactor, and strategic investors such as Japan's Hitachi Corp were taken on board. The project took a big PR hit in 2011 with the Fukoshima nuclear disaster in Japan, though it could be up and running by 2020. Up-to-date news on the project can be found online at www.vae.lt.

🛌 Sleeping & Eating

★ Hotel Restaurant
Labanoras   BOUTIQUE HOTEL €

(☑ 8-655 70918; www.hotellabanoras.lt; s/d €30/45; ℙ) This charming hotel-restaurant takes you to the heart of village Lithuania. The wooden house and outlying cottages are cosy and jammed with bric-a-brac, and the surrounding gardens are peaceful and (in season) watched over by abundant storks. The restaurant, serving whatever's available in the fields and forest, is also delightful (mains around €7 to €9).

ℹ️ Information

Regional Park Information Centre (☑ 387-47 142; www.labanoroparkas.lt; Seniūnijos gatvė 19; ⊙ 8am-5pm Mon-Fri year-round, plus 9am-5pm Sat summer) A trove of information on the flora, fauna and geography of Labanoras, the centre has advice for walkers, bikers, kayakers and foragers. It can also help you find canoes and kayaks for hire (usually around €15 per day).

Molėtai
☑ 383 / POP 6970

A small town 30km southwest of the Aukštaitija National Park, Molėtai (mo-ley-tai) is unstartling apart from its lake surrounds.

The hourly bus from Vilnius (€5, 1¼ to two hours) normally continues on to Utena (€3, 35 minutes). To visit the observatory and museum, catch a bus from Molėtai to Utena, ask to be let off at the *'etnokosmologijos muziejus'* turn-off (signposted 10km north of town) and follow the road to the right for another 4km.

◉ Sights

Molėtai Astronomical
Observatory   OBSERVATORY

(Molėtų astronomijos observatorija; ☑ 383-45 444; www.astro.lt/mao) There are spectacular views of Molėtai's lake-studded landscape and the stars above from the Molėtai Astronomical Observatory on Kaldiniai Hill (193m). The observatory boasts northern Europe's largest telescope; visits must be booked in advance over the phone or online.

Lithuanian Ethnocosmology
Museum   MUSEUM

(Lietuvos etnokosmologijos muziejus; ☑ 383-45 424; www.etnokosmomuziejus.lt; Žvaigždžių gatvė; adult/child €1.40/0.80; ⊙ 8am-4.30pm Mon-Fri) This unusual museum explores the cosmos's connection to cultural ideas of hell, heaven and earth in its bubble-shaped exhibition centre. Dwarfing it are two observation towers housing telescopes providing outstanding views of the surrounding lakeland. Night tours with English-speaking guides (adult/child €1.70/1), two hours after sunset, can be arranged in advance, but note that tour schedules are shortened between October and April.

ℹ️ Information

Tourist Information Centre (☑ 383-51 187; www.infomoletai.lt; Inturkės gatvė 4; ⊙ 8am-6pm Mon-Thu, to 4.45pm Fri, 9am-1pm Sat) All you need to know about Molėtai and the surrounding area. Closes Saturdays and operates reduced hours between September and June.

Utena
☑ 389 / POP 32,480

Utena, 34km north of Molėtai, is a quiet town in the centre of Lithuania's northeastern lakeland region.

From Utena **bus station** (☑ 389-61 735; www.utenosap.lt; A Baranausko gatvė 7) there is one daily bus to/from Ignalina (€3.50, one hour), hourly buses to/from Vilnius (€6, 1½ to two hours), some via Molėtai (€3, 35 minutes), and seven daily buses to/from Kaunas (€8, 2½ hours).

🛌 Sleeping & Eating

Alaušynė   FARMSTAY

(☑ 389-34 317; www.abuva.lt; d/tr €42/68; ℙ) Alaušynė offers log cabins and more modern chalets in rural Sudeikiai village, 12km northeast of Utena. It also has a sauna and pool, hires out boats and quad bikes, and organises fishing excursions. The kitchen makes a mean fish soup – swimming with six different fish (including eel and carp) and served in a brown loaf of bread.

Čili Pica   PIZZA €

(☑ 8-616 11070; www.cili.lt; Aušros gatvė 21; mains €4; ⊙ 10am-11pm) Utena isn't rolling in dining options. If you find yourself near the bus station, and hungry, you could do worse than this branch of the country-wide pizza chain.

ℹ️ Information

Tourist Information Centre (☑ 389-54 346; www.utenainfo.lt; Stoties gatvė 39; ⊙ 9am-6pm Mon-Thu, to 5pm Fri, to 3pm Sat) Occupying the old station house, this centre has all the info on activities and accommodation in and around Utena.

Around Utena

Dusetos, some 34km northeast of Utena, is famous for its annual **horse race** (www. zarasai.lt) held on the first Saturday in February. The race dates from 1865 and attracts horse enthusiasts, musicians and folk artists from all over the region, who pour into the small village to watch the race and slug local Čižo beer. Ideally held on frozen Lake Sartai, it moves to the nearby hippodrome when the ice is thin.

🛏 Sleeping & Eating

Bikėnų Uzeiga   GUESTHOUSE €
(☎ 8-685 44450; www.degesa.lt; d/tr from €15/25; ℗) A fun spot to stay and play is Bikėnų Uzeiga in Bikėnai, on the eastern shore of Lake Antalieptės. There are 'homestead' rooms or log cabins, and the bar hires out rowing boats, kayaks, sailboards and bikes. If you've got more time (and money) you can charter a 10-person speedboat or take a two-day canoe trip on the Šventoji River.

Paukščių Sala   GUESTHOUSE €
(☎ 8-685 44450; www.degesa.lt; s/d from €20/40; ℗) Paukščių Sala sits 1km east of Salakas on the shores of Lake Luodis. The en suite rooms are smallish but clean and good value, and the on-site restaurant will cook your catch from the nearby fish pond (€15 per kilogram). It's activity central here, with bicycles and canoes for hire, plus sailing, wind surfing and, in winter, ice-fishing.

Užeiga Prie Bravoro   LITHUANIAN
(☎ 385-56 653; Dusetų homestead; mains €5-7; ⊙10am-10pm Tue-Sun May-Aug) It's not much to look at, but it's worth stopping by this family-run brewery and restaurant for a meal and a pint or two. Four generations have brewed the light, thirst-quenching Čižo *alus* (beer) here: try the wonderful unfiltered version. Find the brewery on the 178 road to Obeliai, heading north out of Dusetos village.

Druskininkai

☎ 313 / POP 16,450

Nineteenth-century Druskininkai (drus-ki-nin-key) on the Nemunas River is Lithuania's oldest and most chic spa town. Today it attracts plenty of investment and young, hip and wealthy Lithuanians seeking a quick detox from city life. Tourists also come here, mainly for the many excellent spas.

During the days of the USSR, the old and ailing came to this famous health resort in search of miracle cures for all sorts of ailments. While some of these vast dinosaur sanatoriums still remain today, the town is

Southern Lithuania

TOP DRUSKININKAI SPAS

Druskininkai is spa-riddled. But beware, not all are swish. Here's a quick guide to help you make the right decision:

Aqua Park (☑ 313-52 338; www.akvapark.lt; Vilniaus gatvė 13-2; adult/child 2hr water entertainment €9/4.50; ⊙ noon-10pm Mon-Thu, noon-11pm Fri, 10am-11pm Sat, 10am-9pm Sun) Families need look no further than this humid wonderland, which brings together six waterslides (the longest over 200m), spas, saunas, a wavepool, kids' play area and more. Prices rise during summer and on weekends and public holidays.

Grand Spa Lietuva (☑ 313-51 200; www.grandspa.lt; V Kudirkos gatvė 43; ⊙ 9am-4pm Mon-Fri, to 8pm Sat & Sun) Inside Hotel Druskininkai, this upmarket spa offers all sorts of baths (from €6 per 15 minutes) and a bewildering array of massages and other treatments you never realised you needed. A basic relaxing massage is €30 for an hour, but the more exotic options (fancy a body pummel with warm honey, or a volcanic-stone massage?) edge towards the €50 mark.

SpaVilnius (☑ 313-53 811; www.spa-vilnius.lt; K Dineikos gatvė 1; ⊙ 8am-10pm) Located inside an eight-storey hotel, the Druskininkai branch of SpaVilnius is a little tucked away from the centre of things, and all the more relaxing for it. Treatments include amber baths, hydrotherapy, massages and even cosmetic surgery. Double rooms start from €88.

Druskininkai Spa (Druskininkų gydykla; ☑ 313-60 508; www.akvapark.lt; Vilniaus alėja 11; treatments from €13; ⊙ 8am-8pm, to 7pm Sun) Lymph-drainage, hot-stone massage and baths (whirling, herbal, mineral, mud and even vertical) are all on the menu at this well-maintained, vividly green, Soviet-era spa. Some even come seeking treatment for more serious ailments – cardiovascular, cutaneous, vestibular, endocrinal and more.

rapidly renovating and restoring much of the charm that was lost during those times.

⊙ Sights

To see Druskininkai past and present, take a walk around, starting at Laisvės aikštė.

★**Grūtas Park**   STATUE PARK
(Grūto Parkas; ☑ 313-55 511; www.grutoparkas.lt; Grūtas; adult/child €6/3; ⊙ 9am-10pm summer, to 5pm rest of year; ⊕) Both entertaining and educational, the black-humoured Grūtas Park, (aka 'Stalin World') has been an enormous hit since it opened in 2001. The sprawling grounds, built to resemble a concentration camp (complete with loudspeakers bellowing Soviet anthems), feature socialist realist statues of Lenin, Stalin and Lithuanian luminaries and exhibits on Soviet history (with a focus on the oppression of Lithuania). To get there, take bus 2 from Druskininkai, via Viečiūnai, or drive 8km east to Grūtas village.

The park was the idea of Viliumas Malinauskas, a former collective farm head who made a fortune canning mushrooms then won the loan of the hated objects from the Ministry of Culture. It includes a menagerie (where sad-looking bears pay ironic homage to the gulag archipelago), an adventure playground, a library staffed by eerie mannequins and a restaurant, reminiscent of a Soviet-era canteen, where visitors eat vodka-doused sprats and onions with Soviet-made cutlery.

MK Čiurlionis Memorial Museum   MUSEUM
(☑ 313-52 755; MK Čiurlionio gatvė 41; adult/child €1.16/0.58; ⊙ 11am-5pm Tue-Sun) Druskininkai has a strong connection to Lithuania's most talented painter-musician, MK Čiurlionis; he spent his childhood in this residence, which now houses bits and bobs from his life.

Museum of Armed Resistance   MUSEUM
(Vilniaus alėja 24; ⊙ 1-5pm Tue-Sun) FREE On the top floor of the Cultural Centre is the small but worthwhile museum detailing the partisan movement and cultural resistance to Soviet rule. The Cultural Centre plays host to beautiful classical concerts during the Druskininkai Summer with Čiurlionis festival (June to September).

Joy of All Who Sorrow Church   CHURCH
(Laisvės aikštė) The multiple domes of this stunning timber Russian Orthodox church, picked out in sky blue, white and gold, dominate Laisvės aikštė.

Mineralinio Vandens Biuvetė FOUNTAIN
(per cup €0.10; ⊘11am-2pm & 3-7pm) The magical powers of local mineral water can be
tested at the Dzūkija Fountain, inside the
Mineralinio Vandens Biuvetė, a round green
building with mosaic floor and stained-glass
windows on the footpath running along the
Nemunas River. Of particular note is a 1960s
image of Eglė, Queen of Serpents.

Druskininkai Museum MUSEUM
(☑313-51 024; www.druskininkumuziejus.lt; MK
Čiurlionio gatvė 59; adult/child €2/0.85; ⊘11am-
6pm Mon-Sat) Dedicated to the history of the
town and surrounding district, this lakeside
museum shows artworks, old maps and documents and everyday artefacts.

Girios Aidas MUSEUM
(Echo of the Forest; ☑313-53 901; MK Čiurlionio gatvė
116; adult/child €2/1; ⊘10am-6pm Tue-Sun) Two
kilometres east of town, Girios Aidas has been
home to a museum and collection of pagan-
and nature-themed wood carvings since 1972.

🏃 Activities

Bikes and two- or four-seater buggies are the
best way to get around; the tourist office gives
away maps covering three local cycling trails:
the southbound riverside **Sun Path** (Saulės
takas; 24km) goes to the windmill museum,
Stars Orbit (Žvaigzdžių orbita; 24km) snakes
south into the Raigardas Valley, and the forested eastbound **Žilnas Path** (Žilvino takas;
20km) links Druskininkai with Grūtas Park
(8km east). The river and lake are also fun.

Bike Rental BICYCLE RENTAL
(☑8-686 87022; Laisvės alėja 10; bikes per hour/day
€2/9, buggies per 30/60min €5/8; ⊘8am-9pm)
Between May and October bikes and buggies
can be hired from Vilniaus alėja 10, the corner of Vilniaus and Laisvės alėjas, or opposite
the tourist office at MK Čiurlionio gatvė 52.

Boat Hire BOATING
(boats/pedalos per hour €5/6; ⊘9am-9pm Apr-
Oct) Rowing boats and pedalos can be hired
on Lake Druskonis.

Steamboat Druskininkai CRUISE
(☑8-612 26982; www.gelme-druskininkai.lt; ticket
office MK Čiurlionio gatvė 51; adult/child €11/5.50;
⊘2.30pm Tue-Sun May-Oct) Three-hour cruises
for the Liškiava Monastery leave from the
Druskininkai dock.

Snow Arena SKIING
(☑313-59 299; www.snowarena.lt; Nemuno Kelias
2; full day Mon-Fri €14, weekends & holidays €20;

⊘noon-7pm Mon-Thu, to 10pm Fri, 10am-10pm Sat,
to 6pm Sun) If you fancy a spot of skiing in
flat, forested Lithuania, even in the height of
summer, this winter sports complex has you
covered. A drag-lift, carpet and quad-chair
serve the indoor slope, and there's an advanced outdoor track and snowpark. Equipment is rented on-site; if you plan repeat
visits, a loyalty card makes things cheaper.

Gondola SNOW SPORTS
(Vilniaus alėja 13-2) Still getting over teething
troubles at the time of research, this shiny
new folly will link the Aqua Park and Snow
Arena.

🛏 Sleeping

Prices increase on weekends and in July and
August.

Dalija GUESTHOUSE €
(☑313-51 814; www.dalijahotel.lt; Laisvės aikštė 21;
d/tr €40/50; 🛜) This charming, spick-and-
span timber guesthouse is superb value. It's
right in the heart of Druskininkai, rooms
come with satellite TV, mini kitchens and
wi-fi, and there's up to 15% discount on stays
of more than one night.

Druskininkai Camping CAMPGROUND €
(☑313-60 800; camping@druskininkai.lt; Gardino
gatvė 3a; sites for 2 adults/teepees/cabins €18/15/40;
⊘May-Sep; 🅿@) Large, well-organised campground near the tourist office and bus station.
Teepees and cabins sleep up to two people.

Hotel Druskininkai HOTEL €€
(☑313-51 200; www.grandspa.lt; V Kudirkos gatvė
43; s/d/ste from €66/92/147; 🅿@🛜🏊) The
Druskininkai is certainly one of the most stylish hotels in town. Behind its striking glass-
and-wood facade are modern rooms bathed
in subdued light, a Turkish bath, a Jacuzzi
bubbling with Druskininkai mineral water,
and a hotel gym. The location is excellent,
close to the centre, the river and the spas.

Medūna HOTEL €€
(☑313-59 060; www.meduna.lt; Liepų gatvė 2; s/d
€50/65; 🅿🛜) Named for a Lithuanian goddess of surpassing beauty, the Medūna is a
likeable little place set on one corner of leafy
Laisvės aikštė. Rooms are comfortable, clean
and warmly decorated, the in-house restaurant has a great wine cellar, and discounts to
nearby attractions are available.

Aqua Hotel HOTEL €€
(☑313-59 195; www.aquapark.lt; Vilniaus alėja 13-
1; s/d/apt from €54/66/174; 🅿🛜🏊) If you're

Druskininkai

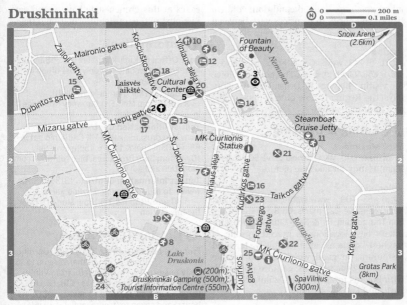

Druskininkai

mainly in Druskininkai for a family romp at the Aqua Park, this may be the place to stay. The rooms are nicely furnished, breakfast and buffet supper are included, you're surrounded by diversions (bowling, spas, the waterpark itself), and excellent packages are available online. Prices rise on Fridays, Saturdays and holidays.

Europa Royale HOTEL €€
(☎ 313-42 221; www.groupeuropa.com; Vilniaus alėja 7; d/tr €75/100; ☜) Housed in a 19th-cen-

tury spa building in the centre of town, the Europa's hospitality is as professional as you'd expect from an international chain. There are distinguishing touches, however, including a children's playroom, and access to the Soviet-era Druskininkai Spa.

Galia HOTEL €€
(☎ 313-60 510; www.galia.lt; Maironio gatvė 3, Dabintos gatvė 3 & 4; s/d €34/58; ℗) Galia surprises with a rainbow of colours. The hotel is spread over three attractive buildings,

all of which are in good condition; confirm before you check in as prices vary between houses.

Regina
HOTEL €€

(📞 313-51 243; www.regina.lt; Kosciuškos gatvė 3; s/d/tr €56/73/91; 🅿 @ 🛜) The hotel of choice for visiting bigwigs in Druskininkai's glory days, the Regina is now quietly dependable as a midrange option.

✖ Eating & Drinking

Mini-Maxima
SUPERMARKET €

(www.maxima.lt; MK Čiurlionio gatvė 50; ⊗ 8am-10pm) Handy for lakeside picnics.

Kolonada
LITHUANIAN €€

(📞 313-53 409; www.sventejums.lt/kolonada; Kudirkos gatvė 22; mains €6-8; ⊗ 11am-11pm Sun-Thu, to 1am Fri & Sat) One of Druskininkai's best locations is graced by one of its best kitchens at this lovely terraced restaurant. In good weather, grab a table overlooking the gardens, get into pork neck with boletus foraged from Dzūkija National Park, and feel the serenity.

Sicilija
ITALIAN €€

(📞 313-51 865; www.sicilia.lt; Taikos gatvė 9; mains €5-7; ⊗ 9am-11pm Sun-Thu, to midnight Fri & Sat) One of the most popular spots in town, and deservedly so – its pizzas and Italian-Lithuanian fare are really good, and its terrace encourages lingering in the warmer months. Now also at MK Čiurlionio gatvė 56.

Forto Dvaras
LITHUANIAN €€

(MK Čiurlionio gatvė 55; mains €4-8; ⊗ 10am-11pm Mon-Thu, to midnight Fri & Sat, to 10pm Sun) The local branch of this chain of countrified restaurants serves very good traditional Lithuanian cooking, and sits right on the lake.

Izumi
JAPANESE €€

(📞 313-51 220; Vilniaus alėja 22-2; mains €5-7; ⊗ noon-midnight; 🛜) If you fancy sushi, yakitori or gyoza, Izumi is the only Japanese restaurant in town.

Beach Bar
BAR

(📞 8-620 88679; Vijūnėlės tvenkinys; pizzas €3; ⊗ 1-9pm Sun-Thu, to midnight Fri & Sat) Open from May to mid-September, this shack by the artificial beach is ideal for a post-swim shandy.

Boulangerie
CAFE

(📞 8-633 35555; www.kepyklele.lt; MK Čiurlionio gatvė 63; ⊗ 9am-7pm) You'll find decent coffee as well as ice cream, Lithuanian cookies and cakes at this French-style bakery and cafe, just next to the tourist information office.

ℹ Information

Post Office (V Kudirkos gatvė 39; ⊗ 8am-6pm Mon-Fri, to 1pm Sat) The only post office in central Druskininkai.

SEB Bankas (MK Čiurlionio gatvė 40; ⊗ 8.30am-5pm Mon-Fri) Currency exchange inside, ATM outside.

Tourist Information Centre (📞 313-51 777; www.info.druskininkai.lt; MK Čiurlionio gatvė 65; ⊗ 10am-1pm & 1.45-6.45pm Mon-Sat, 10am-5pm Sun) Brochures, bike rental, accommodation and advice.

Tourist Information Centre (📞 313-60 800; www.info.druskininkai.lt; Gardino gatvė 3; ⊗ 8.30am-12.15pm & 1-5.15pm Mon-Fri) Near the bus station.

ℹ Getting There & Away

From the **bus station** (📞 313 51 333; Gardino gatvė 1; ⊗ 5.15am-6.50pm) there are up to 15 daily buses (€10, two hours) to/from Vilnius; hourly buses to/from Kaunas (€10, two to three hours); six to/from Panevėžys (€17, 4¼ hours) and seven to/from Šiauliai (€19, 5¼ hours).

Dzūkija National Park
📞 310

The 555-sq-km Dzūkija (dzoo-ki-ya) National Park (Lithuania's largest) is a nature lover's paradise. Four-fifths of it is swathed in pine forest, cover for 48 lakes. The Ūla and Grūda Rivers, perfect for a days' canoeing, flow through it, and an abundance of mushrooms and berries grow here during the season.

Cycling is a wonderful way to explore the park, and bikes can easily be hired in Druskininkai, in season. The tourist information centre also has excellent free maps for cyclists. There are two visitor centres, at Marcinkonys and Merkinė.

In addition to natural reserves, the park houses ethnographic and cultural reserves, plus protected villages such as Zervynos and Liškiava. Merkinė, 10km further down the Nemunas River, is the starting point for a 12km black potters' trail around workshops where pots as black as soot are made from red clay. The extraordinary colour comes from pine-wood resin fired with the pot in an outdoor kiln.

Falling just outside the boundaries of the park, 22km northeast of Marcinkonys and 58km northeast of Druskininkai, is Varėna

MUSHROOMING & BERRYING

Mushrooming is a, well, mushrooming business, particularly in and around the Dzūkija National Park, which in August and September is carpeted with little white and yellow buttons. The forests lining the Varėna–Druskininkai highway (A4) and the Zervynos forests – best known for sand dunes, beehive hollows and substantial *grybas* (mushroom) populations – make rich *grybaula* (mushroom-hunting grounds) too. For mushroom addicts, there's Varėna's September **mushroom festival** (www.varena.lt).

The crinkle-topped, yellow chanterelle and stubby *boletus* are among the edible wild mushroom varieties hunted and exported to other parts of Europe. The less common *baravykas*, with its distinctive brown cap, is a stronger-tasting mushroom that ends up stuffed inside a *cepelinai* (parcels of thick potato dough) or dried and stored until Christmas Eve, when it is served as one of 12 dishes. Lithuania boasts 1200 mushroom species, but only 380 are edible.

Berrying is another trade and tradition. Red bilberries only ripen in August and cranberries in September, but most other berries – wild strawberries, blueberries, buckthorn berries, sloe berries and raspberries – can be harvested whenever they are ripe.

The roadside rate for mushrooms is around €5 to €7 per kilogram. Look for locals selling at roadsides, with glass jam jars overflowing with freshly picked forest goodies lined up on car bonnets. The mushroom season runs from early spring to late autumn.

(www.varena.lt). Founded in the 15th century when Grand Duke Vytautas built a hunting lodge here, it is the birthplace of noted Lithuanian painter and composer MK Čiurlionis. The main road (A4) leading from Varėna to Druskininkai is lined with carved wooden 'totem' poles and sculptures, erected in 1975 in commemoration of the 100th anniversary of his birth.

☉ Sights

**Čepkeliai Strict
Nature Reserve**　　　　NATIONAL PARK
(www.cepkeliai-dzukija.lt) The 112-sq-km Čepkeliai reserve, the largest area of untouched nature in Lithuania, is a glorious wet wilderness of bogs, black alder swamps, Cladinoso-callunosa forest and lakes, home to more than 4000 species of animals and plants (including lynx and wolves). Visits are limited: apply, and pay the necessary fees, at the Marcinkonys Visitor Centre.

Ethnographic Museum　　　　MUSEUM
(Marcinkonių etnografijos muziejus; ☏ 310-39 169; Miškininkų gatvė 6; adult/child €1/0.50; ⏰ 8am-5pm Mon-Fri, to 3.45pm Sat) Housed in an early 20th-century homestead, this exposition explores the everyday life, traditions and material culture of Dzūkian people. There are great examples of woodcarving, weaving, basket-making, beekeeping and more.

Liškiava monastery　　　　MONASTERY
(Liškiava) Commanding a verdant loop of the Nemunas River, 10km north of Druskin-

inkai, this former Dominican monastery is famous for its seven rococo-style altars and its crypt with glass coffins.

🛏 Sleeping

Marcinkonys Visitor Centre　　GUESTHOUSE €
(☏ 310-44 466; www.dzukijosparkas.lt; Šilagėlių gatvė 11; s/d incl breakfast €30/45; ⏰ 8am-5pm Mon-Fri, to 3.45pm Sat; P @) The visitor centre at Marcinkonys has its own simple guesthouse, with en suite rooms, along with a list of homestay accommodation (around €25 per person), but doesn't make bookings. Camping is only allowed in designated areas. The centre closes for lunch between noon and 12.45pm.

ℹ Information

Merkinė Visitor Centre (☏ 310-57 245; www.dzukijosparkas.lt; Vilniaus gatvė 3; ⏰ 8am-5pm Mon-Fri, to 3.45pm Sat) Tons of information on the surrounding environment, plus walks, accommodation, cycling and canoeing. English-speaking guides for mushrooming or berrying can also be arranged at around €15 per hour, or €60 per day. The centre closes for lunch between noon and 12.45pm.

Marcinkonys Visitor Centre (☏ 310-44 466; www.dzukijosparkas.lt; Miškininkų gatvė 61; ⏰ 8am-5pm Mon-Fri, 8am-3.45pm Sat) The visitor centre in Marcinkonys can advise on walking, cycling and canoeing and is the starting point for the 14km Zackagiris Sightseeing Route (Zackagirio Takas) plus shorter (7km and 10.5km) walks. Access to the Čepkeliai Strict Nature Reserve can also be arranged here. A voluntary €1 contribution is levied.

❶ Getting There & Away

In summer a steamboat (p330) makes trips between Druskininkai and Liškiava.

Buses to/from Druskininkai and Vilnius stop at the Merkinė intersection (Merkinės kryžkelė; €2, 25 minutes), 2km east of Merkinė town centre. Three daily trains to/from Vilnius stop at Zervynos (€4, two hours) and Marcinkonys (€4.30, two hours).

CENTRAL LITHUANIA

Most people only give Central Lithuania a quick glance – generally from the seat of their bus or train as they're travelling from capital to coast. This flat land between the country's big attractions is often written off as dull, but such a conclusion would be foolhardy, for here resides Lithuania's most bizarre sight, along with cities of substance and bucolic splendour as far as the eye can see.

Proud Kaunas, the alternative Lithuanian capital between WWI and WWII and the country's perpetual 'number two' city, holds court in the heart of the country. Its Old Town is as intriguing as its mass of museums and art galleries, and there is no better place to base yourself for central-country forays. Within easy reach of Kaunas is Birštonas, a tiny spa town where both jazz and mud treatments are serious business.

Still in the process of reinvention is Šiauliai, once a closed city that sheltered the USSR's largest military base outside Russia. Most tourists make the pilgrimage here for the papal-blessed Hill of Crosses 10km to the north, and leave awed by the strength and devotion of the Lithuanian people.

Kaunas

☎ 37 / POP 353,000

Kaunas (kow-nas), a sprawling city 100km west of Vilnius at the confluence of the Nemunas and Neris Rivers, has a compact Old Town, an abundance of artistic and educational museums, and a fascinating history. A sizeable student population provides plenty of energy, and some rough edges give it that extra bit of spice.

History

Legend has it that Kaunas was founded by the son of tragic young lovers. Beautiful maiden Milda let the Holy Eternal Flame go out while caring for her lover Daugerutis; sentenced to death by vengeful gods they fled to a cave, where Milda gave birth to Kaunas.

Archaeologists believe the city dates from the 13th century and until the 15th century was in the front line against the Teutonic Order in Lithuania's west. Kaunas became a successful river port in the 15th and 16th centuries. German merchants were influential here, and there was a Hanseatic League office. During the interwar period it became the capital of Lithuania, as Vilnius lay in Polish hands. Its strategic position is the main reason it was destroyed 13 times before WWII – when it once again received a battering.

◎ Sights

Rotušės aikštė, the square wedged between the Nemunas and Neris Rivers, is the historic heart. From here pedestrianised Vilniaus gatvė runs east to meet the city's main axis, Laisvės alėja – also pedestrianised.

◎ Old Town

Rotušės Aikštė & Around

This large, open square at the heart of Old Town is lined with pretty 15th- and 16th-century German merchants' houses and is centred on the 17th-century former town hall. In the square's southwestern corner stands a statue of the patriot-poet Maironis.

Kaunas Town Hall   HISTORIC BUILDING
(Kauno rotušė; ☎37-203 572; www.kaunas.lt; Rotušės aikštė 15) Having been co-opted as a theatre, a magazine, a prison and a palace over the years, Kaunas' 17th-century Town Hall is now mainly used for official events. The first two floors also serve as a wedding hall (Saturdays usually see a procession of brides and grooms in their finery) and there's a small ceramics museum in the cellar.

St Francis Xavier Church & Monastery   CHURCH
(☎8-640 52621; www.jesuit.lt; Rotušės aikštė 7-9; tower €1.50; ⊙4-6pm daily, plus 9am-1pm Sun) The southern side of Rotušės aikštė is dominated by the twin-towered St Francis Xavier Church, college and Jesuit monastery complex, built between 1666 and 1720. Take a peek inside and then climb the tower for the best aerial views of Kaunas.

House of Perkūnas   HISTORIC BUILDING
(Perkūno namas; ☎8-641 44614; www.perkuno namas.lt; Aleksoto gatvė 6; adult/child €1.5/0.80; ⊙2-5pm Thu & Fri) This 15th-century Gothic

Central Lithuania

house, built by merchants of the Hanseatic League, is named for the Lithuanian God of Thunder, whose image was found in a wall cavity. It's now owned by the Jesuits, who maintain the cellars, concert hall and exhibit of 19th-century poet Adomas Mickevičius' life and works.

Vytautas Church   CHURCH
(Vytauto bažnyčia; ☑ 37-203 854; www.vytautine. lcn.lt; Aleksoto gatvė 5; ⊙ 2-7pm) Known in full as Vytautas the Great Church of the Accession of the Holy Virgin Mary, this red-brick church is one of the oldest in Kaunas. Built

by Franciscans in the early 15th century, it's been used by the Orthodox church and Napoleon (as an ammunition store) before being returned to Catholicism in 1990.

Holy Trinity Church   CHURCH
(Rotušės aikštė 22) The western side of Rotušės aikštė is filled by the late-Renaissance (1624–34), terracotta-roofed Holy Trinity Church.

**Medicine & Pharmaceutical
History Museum**   MUSEUM
(Medicinios ir farmacijos istorijos muziejus; ☑ 37-201 569; Rotušės aikštė 28; adult/child €1.16/0.58; ⊙10am-5pm Tue-Sat) Dating back to the

Kaunas

LITHUANIA KAUNAS

0   500 m
0   0.25 miles

Kaunas International (10km)

Zemaičių gatvė

GREEN HILL (ŽALIAKALNIS)

Green Hill funicular

Vytautas Park

Vytauto prospektas

Ramybės Park

Sugihara House (700m)

Long-distance

Gedimino gatvė

Miško gatvė

Kęstučio gatvė

Statue of Man

Nepriklausomybės aikštė

Putvinskio gatvė

NEW TOWN

Putvinskio gatvė

Mickevičiaus gatvė

Donelaičio gatvė

Vienybes aikštė

MK Čiurlionis National Museum of Art

Saramorių prospektas

Statue of Vytautas the Great

Ožeškienės gatvė

Laisvės alėja

Daukanto gatvė

Maironio gatvė

Gruodžio gatvė

Nemuno gatvė

City Garden

Kanto gatvė

Sv Gertrūdos gatvė

Kurpių gatvė

Karaliaus Mindaugo prospektas

Birštono gatvė

Jablonskio gatvė

Zamenhofo gatvė

Nemnus River

Jonavos gatvė

Jurbarko gatvė

Jonavos gatvė

Mapu gatvė

Vilniaus gatvė

Daukšos gatvė

OLD TOWN

Sladkevičiaus gatvė

Valančiaus gatvė

St George's Church

Papilio gatvė

Rotušės aikštė

Tlkslto gatvė

Daugrda gatvė

Muziejaus gatvė

Statue of Maironis

Aleksoto gatvė

Multnes gatvė

Aleksoto tiltas

Veiverių gatvė

Veiverių gatvė

Minkovskiu gatvė

Kaunas Botanical Gardens (1km); Birštonas (40km)

Ninth Fort (7km)

Norlis River

Vilnaus gatvė

Nemunas River

Vytauto prospektas

1930s, this unusual little museum details the progress of medical science in Lithuania over the centuries. There are also expositions on Lithuanian and Siberian folk medicine and a reconstructed 19th-century pharmacy.

Maironis Lithuanian Literary Museum   MUSEUM
(Maironio Lietuvos literatūros muziejus; ☑37-207 477; www.maironiomuziejus.lt; Rotušės aikštė 13; adult/child €1.45/0.58; ☉9am-6pm Tue-Sat) This 18th-century mansion was, between 1910 and 1932, the home of Jonas Mačiulis (Maironis), the Kaunas poet-priest who stirred Lithuania's national ambitions in the late 19th and early 20th centuries. It's now a museum dedicated to his life and works, and Lithuanian literature more broadly.

Kaunas

Ceramics Museum MUSEUM

(Keramikos muziejus; ☑ 37-203 572; Rotušės aikštė 15; adult/child €1.16/0.58; ☺ 11am-5pm Tue-Sun, to 7pm Thu) Features Lithuanian ceramics and porcelain from the 20th century and earlier periods, and houses temporary exhibitions.

Communications Development
Museum MUSEUM

(Ryšių istorijos muziejus; ☑ 37-424 920; www.teo. lt/en/node/1449; Rotušės aikštė 19; adult/child €1.40/0.80; ☺ 10am-6pm Wed-Sun) Those with a love of old telephones and big, old analogue technology should take the time to peek inside this museum, housed in the former post office. Outside there's a monument to pioneering cinematographer-puppeteer Vladislovas Starevičius: appropriately, it's two giant insects (an ant and a top-hatted grasshopper) watching one of his films.

Kaunas Castle RUIN

(☑ 37-300 672; www.kaunomuziejus.lt; Papilio gatvė; adult/child €2.32/1.74; ☺ 10am-6pm Tue-Sat, to 4pm Sun) A reconstructed tower, sections of wall and part of a moat are all that remain of 14th-century Kaunas Castle, an important bastion against Teutonic attacks around which the town originally grew. There's an exibition on the history of the castle, and a reconstructed dungeon where you can try out the facilities.

Aleksotas Funicular FUNICULAR

(Aleksoto funikulierius; ☑ 37-391 086; Amerikos Lietuvių 6; tickets €0.58; ☺ 7am-noon & 1-4pm Mon-Fri, from 10am Sat) This historic funicular at the southern end of Aleksoto Tiltas (Aleksoto Bridge) dates from 1935 and affords great rooftop views of Old Town.

Vilniaus Gatvė & Around

Vilniaus gatvė is Old Town's charming main artery.

Presidential Palace of Lithuania PALACE

(Istorinė Lietuvos Prezidentūra; www.istorine prezidentura.lt; Vilniaus gatvė 33; adult/student €1.16/0.58; ☺ 11am-5pm Tue-Sun, to 7pm Thu, gardens 8am-9pm daily) This handsome 19th-century building was the seat of government for the Republic of Lithuania between the wars. Restored to its original grandeur, it now houses an exhibition on independent Lithuania including historic photos, gifts given to past presidents, collections of family silver and presidential awards. Statues of former presidents also stud the palace garden.

Povilas Stulga Lithuanian Folk Music
Instruments Museum MUSEUM

(Lietuvos tautinės muzikos muziejus; www.kau nomuziejus.lt; Zamenhofo gatvė 12; adult/child €1.74/1.16; ☺ 9am-5pm Tue-Fri, to 4pm Sat) This museum shows that almost any raw material can be turned into a musical instrument. Housed in a 16th-century Gothic house, the wonderful 7000-piece collection includes wood and bone flutes, unusual reed pipes, three-string cellos, and both basic and elaborately carved *kanklės* (zithers).

Sts Peter & Paul Cathedral CATHEDRAL

(Šventų Apaštalų Petro ir Povilo Arkekatedra Bazilika; ☑ 37-324 093; www.kaunoarkikatedra.lt; Vilniaus gatvė 1; ☺ 7am-6.30pm) With its single tower, this church owes much to baroque reconstruction, but the original 15th-century Gothic shape of its windows remains. The largest Gothic building in Lithuania, it was probably founded by Vytautas around 1410 and now has nine altars. The tomb of Maironis stands outside the south wall.

☺ New Town

Kaunas expanded east from Old Town in the 19th century, giving birth to the modern centre and its striking 1.7km pedestrian street, Laisvės alėja (Freedom Ave).

Independent Lithuania's first parliament convened in 1920 at the Kaunas State Musical Theatre, the former State Theatre Palace overlooking City Garden (Miestos Sodas) at the western end of Laisvės alėja, which was created in 1892.

Tadas Ivanauskas
Zoological Museum MUSEUM

(Tado Ivanausko zoologijos muziejus; ☑ 37-200 292; www.zoomuziejus.lt; Laisvės alėja 106; adult/ child €2.32/1.45; ☺ 11am-7pm Tue-Sun) With over 250,000 specimens, including an astonishing 13,000 examples of taxidermy, this museum really has the animal kingdom covered. It was founded in 1919 by the eponymous Tadas, a famous Lithuanian naturalist.

St Michael the Archangel Church CHURCH

(Šv Archangelo Mykolo Rektoratas; ☑ 37-226 676; Nepriklausomybės aikštė 14; ☺ 9am-6pm) The Soviets turned this blue neo-Byzantine church, filling the sky so dramatically at the eastern end of Laisvės alėja, into a stained-glass museum. Built for the Russian Orthodox faith in 1893, St Michael's was reopened to Catholic worshippers in 1991.

St Gertrude's Church CHURCH

(☑37-229 965; Laisvės alėja 101a; ⊙10am-7pm Mon-Fri, to noon Sat, 9am-noon Sun) This late 15th-century Gothic gem is tucked in a courtyard off Laisvės alėja. Its red-brick crypt overflows with burning candles, prompting a separate candle shrine to be set up opposite the crypt entrance.

Field of Sacrifice MEMORIAL

(Miesto Sodas) The Field of Sacrifice – a name engraved on paving slabs in front of the City Garden – is a tragic tribute to the young Kaunas hero Romas Kalanta, who, in 1972, set himself alight in protest at Soviet rule.

Choral Synagogue SYNAGOGUE

(Kauno Choralinė Sinagoga; ☑8-614 03100; www.kaunasjews.lt; Ožeškienės gatvė 13; ⊙service 10am Sat) Inside this functioning synagogue, one of the few remnants of Kaunas' once-strong Jewish community, is a remarkable dark-wood and gold *bimah* (raised platform from which the Torah is read); outside there's a memorial to 1600 children killed at the Ninth Fort. The WWII Jewish ghetto was on the western bank of the Neris, in the area bounded by Jurbarko, Panerių and Demokratų streets.

Mykolas Žilinskas Art Gallery MUSEUM

(Mykolo Žilinsko dailės galerija; ☑37-322 788; www.ciurlionis.lt/m-zilinskas-art-gallery; Nepriklausomybės aikštė 12; adult/child €1.74/0.87; ⊙11am-5pm Tue-Sun, to 7pm Thu) This art museum on three floors is based on the private collection of Mykolas Žilinskas, but is now operated by the National Čiurlionis Art Museum. The collection is strongest on European art from the 17th to the 20th centuries and boasts Lithuania's only Rubens.

◉ Vienybės Aikštė & Around

Vienybės Aikštė (Unity Sq) houses **Kaunas Technological University** (Kauno technologijos universitetas; ☑37-300 000; www.ktu.edu; K Donelaičio gatvė 73) and the smaller **Vytautas Magnus University** (Vytauto didžiojo universitetas; ☑37-222 739; www.vdu.lt; K Donelaičio gatvė 58), first founded in 1922 and refounded in 1989 by an émigré Lithuanian.

★MK Čiurlionis National Museum of Art GALLERY

(MK Čiurlionio Valstybinis Dailės Muziejus; ☑37-229 475; www.ciurlionis.lt; Putvinskio gatvė 55; adult/child €2/1; ⊙11am-5pm Tue, Wed & Fri-Sun, to 7pm Thu) In this, Kaunas' leading gallery, you'll find extensive collections of the romantic paintings of Mikalojus Konstantinas Čiurlionis (1875–1911), one of Lithuania's greatest artists and composers, as well as Lithuanian folk art and 16th- to 20th-century European applied art.

Museum of Devils MUSEUM

(Velnių Muziejus; ☑37-221 587; www.ciurlionis.lt; Putvinskio gatvė 64; adult/child €1.74/0.87; ⊙11am-5pm Tue, Wed & Fri-Sun, to 7pm Thu; ⊞) Diabolical is the best word to describe the collection of 3000-odd devils in this museum, collected over the years by landscape artist Antanas Žmuidzinavičius (1876–1966). While the commentary aims for a pseudo-intellectual veneer, linking the devils to Lithuanian folklore, the fun of this museum is all about the spooky masks and stories. Great for kids.

Vytautas the Great War Museum MUSEUM

(Vytauto Didžiojo Karo Muziejus; ☑37-320 765; www.kariuomene.kam.lt/lt/karo_muziejus.html; Donelaičio gatvė 64; adult/child €1.16/0.58; ⊙11am-5pm Tue-Sun) Maintained by the Lithuanian army, this museum keeps exhibitions on the history of weapons, Lithuanian military history, the period of the Grand Duchy and more. Of particular interest is the wreckage of the *Lituanica*, in which Steponas Darius and Stanislovas Girėnas died while attempting to fly nonstop from New York to Kaunas, in 1933.

Kaunas Picture Gallery MUSEUM

(Kauno paveikslų galerija; ☑37-221 779; www.ciurlionis.lt/kaunas-art-gallery; Donelaičio gatvė 16; adult/student €1.74/0.87; ⊙11am-6pm Tue, Wed & Fri-Sun, to 7pm Thu) This underrated gem, another branch of the many-tentacled Čiurlionis museum, exhibits works by late 20th-century Lithuanian artists, with a room devoted to Jurgis Mačiūnas, the father of the Fluxus avant-garde movement.

Christ's Resurrection Basilica CHURCH

(Kauno paminklinė Kristhaus Prisikėlimo bašničia; www.prisikelimas.lt; Zemaicių gatvė 316; ⊙9.30am-7pm) Looking a little like a Soviet-era power station, this truly monumental cathedral took 70 years to build. A Nazi paper warehouse, then a radio factory under the Soviets, it was finally consecrated in 2004.

◉ Outside the Centre

Kaunas is a surprisingly green city, with parks around its fringes. **Vytautas Park** occupies the slope up from the end of Laisvės alėja to the stadium, behind which stretches a large majority of the lovely **Ažuolynas Park**. South

THE HEROES OF KAUNAS

Beloved Lithuanian pilots Steponas Darius and Stanislovas Girėnas died on 15 July 1933, just 650km short of completing the longest nonstop transatlantic flight at the time. Two days after the duo set off from New York, 25,000 people gathered at Kaunas airport for their triumphant return. They never arrived. Their orange plane *Lituanica* crashed in Germany; see the wreckage in the Vytautas the Great War Museum (p339). After being embalmed, then hidden during Soviet occupation, the bodies came to rest at **Aukštieji Šančiai Cemetery** (Ašmenos 1-oji gatvė 1) in 1964.

Kaunas-based Japanese diplomat Chiune Sugihara (1900–86) – with the help of Dutch diplomat Jan Zwartendijk – saved 6000 Jewish lives between 1939 and 1940 by issuing transit visas to stranded Polish Jews who faced the advancing Nazi terror. When the Soviets annexed Lithuania and ordered that all consulates be shut he asked for a short extension. Dubbed 'Japan's Schindler', he disobeyed orders from Tokyo for some 29 days by signing 300 visas per day, and handed the stamp to a Jewish refugee when he left. **Sugihara House** (Sugiharos Namas; ☑ 37-332 881; www.sugiharahouse.com; Vaižganto gatvė 30; adult/child €3/1.50; ☺ 10am-5pm Mon-Fri, 11am-4pm Sat & Sun) tells his life story, and features video installations and stories of those he managed to save.

The small **Museum of Deportation & Resistance** (Rezistencijos ir tremties muziejus; ☑ 37-323 179; Vytauto prospektas 46; adult/child €1.74/1.16; ☺ 9am-5pm Tue-Fri, to 4pm Sat) documents the resistance spirit embodied by the Forest Brothers, who fought the Soviet occupation from 1944 to 1953. Led by Jonas Žemaitis-Vytautas (1909–54), somewhere between 50,000 and 100,000 men and women went into Lithuania's forests to battle the regime. The museum staff estimates that one-third were killed, and the rest captured and deported (in total 150,000 Lithuanians were sent to Soviet territory during this time).

One of the most desperate anti-Soviet actions was the suicide of Kaunas student Romas Kalanta. On 14 May 1972 he doused himself in petrol and set fire to himself in protest at communist rule. A suicide note was found in his diary.

along Vytauto prospektas is **Ramybės Park**, home to the Old City Cemetery until the Soviets tore up all the graves in the 1960s.

Museum of the Ninth Fort MUSEUM
(IX Forto Muziejus; ☑ 37-377 750; www.9fortomuziejus.lt; Žemaičių plentas 73; adult/child €2.30/1.40, catacombs with guide €6; ☺ 10am-6pm Wed-Mon Apr-Oct, to 4pm Nov-Mar) A poignant memorial to the tens of thousands of people, mainly Jews, who were murdered by the Nazis, the excellent Museum of the Ninth Fort, 7km north of Kaunas, comprises an old WWI-era fort and the bunker-like church of the damned. Displays cover deportations of Lithuanians by the Soviets and graphic photo exhibitions track the demise of Kaunas' Jewish community. Take bus 23 from Jonavos gatvė to the 9-ojo Forto Muziejus stop, then cross under the motorway.

Kaunas Botanical Gardens GARDENS
(Kauno botanikos sodas; ☑ 37-295 300; www.botanika.vdu.lt; Ž.E. Žilibero gatvė 6; adult/child €2.32/1.16; ☺ 9am-7pm Apr-Oct) Gardeners from Vytautas Magnus University tend 65 hectares of rare and wonderful plants.

Around 2km south of Old Town; bus 20 or 35 will get you there.

Pažaislis Monastery MONASTERY
(☑ 37-458 868; www.pazaislis.org; Masiulio gatvė 31; adult/child €4/2; ☺ 10am-5pm Tue-Fri, to 4pm Sat) Built by Camaldolese monks in the 17th century, this striking baroque monastery lies 9km east of central Kaunas, on a promontory jutting into the Kauno marios (Kaunas Sea). Given to the Russian Orthodox order by Tsar Alexander in 1831, it's a sumptuous if slightly run-down affair with a 50m-high cupola and luxurious Venetian interior made from pink and black Polish marble. It now has a small museum dedicated to its history.

The monastery has had a chequered past, becoming a psychiatric hospital in the Soviet era, before reverting to its Catholic roots in 1990. It's best to visit during the Pažaislis Music Festival, between June and August. Take trolleybus 9 or 12 from the town centre to the terminus on Masiulio gatvė, a few hundred metres before Pažaislis.

Open-Air Museum of Lithuania MUSEUM
(Lietuvių liaudies buities muziejus; ☑ 34-647 392; www.llbm.lt; L Lekavičiaus gatvė 2; adult/child

€2.90/1.45; ☉ indoor exhibits 10am-6pm May-Oct) The open-air museum consists of re-created 18th- and 19th-century villages representing Lithuania's main regions (Dzūkija, Aukštaitija, Suvalkija, Žemaitija and Lithuania Minor). Potters, weavers and joiners demonstrate their crafts in the museum workshop and, while the indoors exhibits shut for the colder months, tours of the park can be booked throughout the year. The museum is in Rumšiškės, 25km east of Kaunas, 2km off the Kaunas–Vilnius road. It's also accessible by bus from Kaunas (30 minutes, five daily).

✪ Festivals & Events

Music festivals make up many of Kaunas' social highlights.

Kaunas Jazz Festival   JAZZ
(☑ 37-750 146; www.kaunasjazz.lt; Rotušės aikštė 29) Inaugurated just after the departure of the Soviets, this lively festival brings world-class jazz musicians to Kaunas every April, before heading down the road to Vilnius.

Operetta in Kaunas Castle   MUSIC
(☑ 37-203 661; www.operetta.lt; L Zamenhofo gatvė 5a) This open-air festival of opera spends several nights in the ruins of Kaunas Castle before heading on the road, running from May to September.

Pažaislis Music Festival   MUSIC
(☑ 37-203 547; www.pazaislis.lt; T Masiulio gatvė 31) Sprawling across the summer, from May to August, this eclectic festival makes use of the splendid grounds of a 17th-century monastery on the shore of the Kaunas Sea. Expect symphonic and chamber performances, choral work and folk ensembles.

🛏 Sleeping

Plentiful cheap accommodation is another of Kaunas' charms.

Kauno Arkivyskupijos Svečių Namai   GUESTHOUSE €
(☑ 37-322 597; www.kaunas.lcn.lt/sveciunamai; Rotušės aikštė 21; s/d/tr from €15/25/32; P✳@) 🍃 This Catholic archdiocesan guesthouse couldn't have a better location, snuggled between venerable churches and overlooking the Old Town square. Rooms are spartan but spacious, and breakfast is not included. Book well in advance, since it fills up fast.

Apple Economy Hotel   HOTEL €
(☑ 37-321 404; www.applehotel.lt; Valančiaus gatvė 19; s/d from €36/45; P➘@🌐) This simple

hotel in a quiet courtyard on the edge of Old Town is a recommended no-frills option. The rooms are tiny, but bright and cheerful, and the beds are very comfy.

Metropolis   HOTEL €
(☑ 37-205 992; www.metropolishotel.lt; S Daukanto gatvė 21; d/tr €42/56; 🌐) Still redolent of former glories, the Metropolis ('Lietuva' in Soviet times) is a good-value option on a quiet tree-lined street just off Laisvės alėja. Rooms are well fitted out, and time-worn features (such as the sculpted-stone balconies and hefty wooden turnstile leading into the moulded-ceilinged lobby) enhance its charm.

Daugirdas   BOUTIQUE HOTEL €€
(☑ 37-301 561; www.daugirdas.lt; T Daugirdo gatvė 4; s/d/tr €56/63/80; ✳🌐) This stylish boutique hotel, wedged between central Old Town and the Nemunas, is one of the most charismatic in Kaunas. The standard doubles are perfectly acceptable, with good-quality beds and bathrooms (with heated floors), but for something a little out of the ordinary, try the timber ceiling, enormous bed and Jacuzzi of the Gothic Suite.

Kaunas Hotel   BUSINESS HOTEL €€
(☑ 37-750 850; www.kaunashotel.lt; Laisvės alėja 79; s/d/ste from €43/60/64; ✳@🌐✳) Dating back to 1892, but refurbished in 2014, the Kaunas is a slick operation with an eye for business clientele. Glass fronts the top floor where room 512 sports a peek-if-you-dare glass-walled bathroom overlooking Laisvės alėja. There's also two conference rooms and a gym (free with deluxe rooms, otherwise there's a €10 surcharge).

Daniela   HOTEL €€
(☑ 37-321 505; www.danielahotel.lt; Mickevičiaus gatvė 28; s/d/ste from €55/65/120; P@🌐) A retro-chic hotel owned by basketball hero Arvydas Sabonis, Daniela is a fun and bold place, with soft pink chairs, steely mezzanines and extra-large bouncy sofas. Its standard rooms are well above par, and staff do their very best to cater to guests' needs. Online reservations attract a 20% discount.

Kunigaikščių Menė   GUESTHOUSE €€
(☑ 37-320 800; M Daukšos gatvė 28; s/d from €53/75; P@🌐) Atmospheric, family-run guesthouse with an excellent Old Town location. Some of the small rooms have hardwood floors, and there's a decent restaurant in the 16th-century cellar below.

Park Inn by Radisson HOTEL €€

(☑ 37-306 100; www.parkinn.com/hotel-kaunas; K
Donelaičio gatvė 27; s/d from €77/92; P 🖨 🕲 🕙)
This smart business hotel fills eight floors of
a renovated building in the New Town. Service is slick and professional, and rooms are
standard business class, with a few added
extras such as heated bathroom floors and
free tea and coffee. There's a restaurant, a
bar and a conference centre on-site.

✗ Eating

While there's little in the way of top-end dining, options have improved dramatically in
Kaunas in recent years.

Raw Inn VEGETARIAN €

(☑ 8-652 00360; www.rawinn.lt; Vilniaus gatvė
30-1; mains €4-6; ⊙ 10am-9pm Mon-Fri, from
11am Sat, 1-8pm Sun; 🖋) Bursting with cheery
wholesomeness, Raw Inn serves only two
types of food: raw and vegan. If you've had
your fill of *cepelinai,* and can't face anything too challenging, its salads, falafel,
soup and other virtuous treats are well
worth seeking out.

Radharanė VEGETARIAN €

(☑ 37-362 941; www.radharane.lt; Laisvės alėja 40;
mains €4-6; ⊙ 9am-9pm) If you're in the New
Town, and hanker for something meatless,
you can't do much better than the Kaunas
outpost of this Indian-influenced, Hare
Krishna-run restaurant. Curries, giant samo-
sas, soups and salads: order blithely, it's all
good.

Žalias Ratas LITHUANIAN €

(☑ 37-200 050; Laisvės alėja 36b; mains €6;
⊙ 11am-midnight) Tucked away behind the
tourist office, the 'Green Circle' is one of
those pseudo-rustic inns where staff don
traditional garb and bring out the piping-hot Lithuanian fare to eager customers.
It's better than it sounds and a great choice
in summer, when the terrace is buzzing
with diners.

Buon Giorno TAVERNA €

(☑ 8-620 63777; www.buongiorno.lt; Vilniaus gatvė
34; mains €5-7; ⊙ 9am-11pm) The first Buon
Giorno is fantastic for breakfast, with excellent coffee and food. Then, in the evening, it
morphs into a laid-back bistro, with tasteful
tunes and good Italian food. Try any of the
homemade pastas, or the pizza with Parma
ham and rocket. The owners have also opened
a trattoria and grocery (p344).

Buon Giorno TRATTORIA €

(☑ 8-610 63777; www.buongiorno.lt; Daukanto
gatvė 14; mains €5-7; ⊙ 9am-11pm) A newer outpost of the Old Town original this is more
of a full-blown restaurant than its parent.
With further connections to Buon Giorno
grocery, you can bank on the authenticity
of the Italian produce and the quality of the
pasta, salads and mains.

Motiejaus Kepyklėlė BAKERY €

(☑ 8-616 15599; Vilniaus gatvė 7; ⊙ 8am-10pm
Mon-Sat, 9am-6pm Sun) Perhaps the best bakery in Kaunas, Motiejaus has settled into
grand new red-brick digs in the heart of
Vilniaus gatvė. Alongside Lithuanian cookies and pastries you'll find excellent international dainties such as canelés, cupcakes,
macarons and croissants. The coffee can
also be counted on.

Rocknrolla AMERICAN €€

(☑ 8-620 81118; Vasario 16-osios gatvė 1; mains
€5-8; ⊙ noon-11pm Sun-Thu, to 3am Fri & Sat)
Stripped brick walls, craft beers and American dude food tick all the hipster boxes, attracting an appropriately young and stylish
clientele. But the kitchen can really deliver,
and there are few better places in town for
a burger, fried chicken, nachos or ribs. The
cocktails are also good, and there's a small
cinema some nights.

Casa della Pasta ITALIAN €€

(☑ 8-606 74114; www.italurestoranas.lt; Muitinės
gatvė 1-2; mains €5-9; ⊙ 11am-11pm Mon-Sat, noon-
10pm Sun) This tiny whitewashed restaurant,
tucked away on a quiet Old Town square,
does great house-made pasta. The stuffed
pastas – perhaps ravioli with braised beef,
or panzerotti with Gorgonzola, ricotta and
nuts – are particularly good.

Bernelių Užeiga LITHUANIAN €€

(☑ 37-208 802; www.berneliuuzeiga.lt; Donelaičio
gatvė 11; mains €5-8; ⊙ 11am-10pm Sun-Thu, to 1am
Fri & Sat; 🖋) The setting is rustic – aside from
the white linen tablecloths – but the traditional Lithuanian food is good. The staff will
patiently guide you through the long menu,
and at the end of the night you'll be pleasantly surprised by the reasonable tab.

Capo PIZZA €€

(☑ 8-693 99932; Palangos gatvė 9; mains €7;
⊙ noon-midnight Wed-Sat, to 10pm Sun-Tue) Capo
stands head and shoulders above most of
the other *picerijos* in Kaunas, with Italian

chefs turning out judiciously covered, hand-stretched pizzas, alongside pasta, salads, steak and fish. The venue itself is sleekly designed, with stacked logs and art against every wall, and a terrace set among Old Town brickwork.

Senieji Rūsiai
EUROPEAN €€

(Old Cellars; ☑ 37-202 806; www.seniejirusiai.lt; Vilniaus gatvė 34; mains €9-15; ⊙ 11am-midnight Mon-Fri, noon-1am Sat, to 11pm Sun; ☎) Named for its 17th-century subterranean vaults, lined with candlelit frescoes, 'Old Cellars' is one of the most atmospheric places in Kaunas to eat substantial pan-European dishes. Alongside frogs' legs, trout and other local delicacies, you can shell out extra for fillet with foie gras, or steak flame-grilled at your table.

Real Texas Grill
BARBECUE €€

(☑ 8-696 00030; www.realtexasgrill.lt; Vilniaus gatvė 48; mains €7; ⊙ noon-midnight Sun-Wed, to 6am Thu-Sat) Burgers, pulled pork, brisket, chicken wings – you'll find all the spiced, smoky meat you can handle at this modish new place in Old Town. A huge, flame-spouting barbecue, longhorn skulls and gun-slinger silhouettes in the windows complete the West meets Eastern Bloc theme.

Pilies Sodas
BARBECUE €€

(☑ 8-655 55162; www.piliessodas.lt; Pilies gatvė 12; mains €8-10; ⊙ 11am-1am Sun-Thu, to 3am Fri & Sat) Making the most of its plum location, 'Castle Gardens' mixes good cheer with craft beer and the fruits of the grill: burgers, fish, pork chops and more. It also has live music from time to time.

Avilys
LITHUANIAN €€

(☑ 8-655 02626; www.avilys.lt; Vilniaus gatvė 34; mains €8-11; ⊙ noon-midnight Sun-Thu, to 2am Fri & Sat) Avilys is an offshoot of the award-winning brewery in Vilnius. It serves unusual beers alongside Lithuanian standards and international dishes to an avid crowd, street-side or underground in the brick cellar.

Self-Catering

Maxima
SUPERMARKET €

(Kęstučio gatvė 55; ⊙ 8am-10pm Mon-Fri, from 9am Sat & Sun) A full-scale supermarket between Old Town and New.

Iki
SUPERMARKET €

(Jonavos gatvė 3; ⊙ 8am-10pm) This small supermarket is handy for Old Town self-caterers.

🍷 Drinking & Nightlife

W1640
BAR

(☑ 37-203 984; www.viskiobaras.lt; Kurpių gatvė 29; ⊙ 5pm-1am Tue-Thu, to 5am Fri & Sat; ☎) Tucked away down a shabby side street, this bar is a real find. Not only does it have a mind-boggling collection of whiskiess (150 types, to be precise) – mostly Scotch, but also some rarer Japanese ones – the bar staff are the friendliest in town. If whisky isn't your poison, then one of its ales just might be.

Skliautas
BAR

(☑ 37-206 843; www.skliautas.com; Rotušės aikštė 26; ⊙ 11am-midnight Mon-Thu, to 2am Fri & Sat, to 11pm Sun) Great for cheap Lithuanian food and a boisterous atmosphere, Skliautas bursts with energy most times of the day and night, and in summer its crowd takes over the adjoining alley. Also good for coffee and cake.

Shamrock
IRISH PUB

(☑ 8-641 54100; Vilniaus gatvė 13; ⊙ 10am-midnight) While the name might be the most Irish thing about it, the Shamrock is a decent and genuinely hospitable pub. Irish and British beers (Guinness, Murphy's, Newcastle Brown) are sold, and the outdoor tables are great for watching the Vilniaus gatvė promenade. Cheap pizzas are another plus.

Alaus Sapnas
PUB

(☑ 8-698 36724; Gedimino gatvė 30; ⊙ noon-10pm Sun-Wed, to midnight Thu-Sat) Who would have thought that 'Beer Dream' would be a dive bar, with plenty of scuzzy charm? There are plenty of draught beer options to augment the friendly vibe.

BO
BAR

(☑ 37-206 542; www.blueorange.lt; Muitinės gatvė 9; ⊙ 6pm-2am Sun-Fri, to 3am Sat) This laidback bar attracts a student/alternative set, gets rammed to overflowing on weekends, and has more than 20 beers on tap. The name is an acronym for 'Blue Orange', in case you're wondering…

Džem Pub
BAR

(☑ 8-657 45003; www.dzempub.lt; Laisvės alėja 59, 5th fl; admission €5; ⊙ 5pm-3am Tue-Thu, to 4am Fri & Sat) With excellent views from its 5th-floor balcony, a wide choice of beers and an ever-changing program of live acts and DJs, Džem is a gem for music lovers.

LITHUANIA KAUNAS

☆ Entertainment

Check daily newspaper *Kauno diena* (www. kaunodiena.lt, in Lithuanian) for listings.

Cinemas

Forum Cinemas CINEMA
(📋1567; www.forumcinemas.lt; Karaliaus Mindaugo prospektas 49; ☺box office 10am-10pm) Forum, on the 3rd floor of the Akropolis shopping centre, shows films in their original language, with Lithuanian subtitles.

Theatre & Classical Music

Kaunas is almost over-stuffed with performing arts venues and associated companies.

Kaunas State Drama Theatre THEATRE
(Naciolinis Kauno Dramos Teatras; 📋37-224 064; www.dramosteatras.lt; Laisvės alėja 71; ☺box office 10.30am-7pm) Kaunas' principal dramatic venue, and one of the oldest in Lithuania, the State Drama Theatre closes between 15 June and 15 August.

Kaunas Chamber Theatre THEATRE
(Jaunimo kamerinis teatras; 📋37-228 226; www. kamerinisteatras.lt; Kęstučio gatvė 74a; ☺2-6pm Tue-Fri, 11am-5pm Sat) Known originally as the Kaunas Youth Musical Studio, the Chamber Theatre is now an established part of the city's theatrical landscape. It still stages some productions for children, in Lithuanian.

Kaunas State Puppet Theatre THEATRE
(Kauno valstybinis lėlių teatras; 📋37-221 691; www. kaunoleles.lt; Laisvės alėja 87a; ☺box office 11am-5pm Thu & Fri, 10am-2pm Sat & Sun; 🐾) This Vilnius institution has been delighting young and old since 1958, taking its productions across Europe and even South America. At the end of August the new season is inaugurated by turning the theatre and surrounding area into a wonderful fairy town. Kids can also learn how to produce their own puppet theatre at the on-site museum.

Kaunas State Musical Theatre THEATRE
(Muzikinis teatras; 📋37-200 933; www.muzikinisteatras.lt; Laisvės alėja 91; ☺box office 11am-2pm & 3-6pm Tue-Sat) This handsome late 19th-century building hosts operas, operettas and other musical theatre from September to June.

Kaunas Philharmonic CONCERT VENUE
(Kauno filharmonija; 📋37-222 558; www.kauno-filharmonija.lt; L Sapiegos gatvė 5; ☺box office 2-6pm Tue-Sun) Housed in the former Palace of Justice, the Kaunas Philharmonic is the city's main concert hall for classical music.

🛍 Shopping

Akropolis SHOPPING CENTRE
(📋8-659 38287; www.akropolis.lt; Karaliaus Mindaugo prospektas 49; ☺8am-9pm) Handy to the bus and train stations and the New Town, this modern shopping centre has plenty of clothes shops, a supermarket, a food hall, a bowling alley and a cinema.

Centrinis Knygynas BOOKS
(📋37-229 572; www.knygynai.lt/knygynai/Centrinis-knygynas; Laisvės alėja 81; ☺10am-6pm Mon-Fri, to 5pm Sat) Maps, English-language newspapers and magazines.

Egidijaus Rudinsko Grafikos Galerija ARTS
(📋8-688 24486; L Zamenhofo gatvė 13-2; ☺noon-6pm Mon-Fri, to 4pm Sat) A great place to pick up beautiful lithographs and prints by the eponymous Egidijaus.

Humanitas BOOKS
(📋37-221 530; www.humanitas.lt; Vilniaus gatvė 11; ☺9am-6pm Mon-Fri, 11am-4pm Sat) English-language books.

Brome WINE
(📋8-615 35162; www.brome.lt; A Mickevičiaus gatvė 23; ☺10am-8pm Mon-Fri, to 4pm Sat) A stylish little wine shop with a great selection of European and New World wines. Tastings and seminars are held (€10).

Buon Giorno FOOD
(📋8-616 59005; www.buongiorno.lt; V Putvinskio gatvė 72; ☺10am-10pm) This tiny grocery is the best place in town to stock up on Italian cheeses, dried pasta, preserves, meats and more.

ℹ Information

DNB Nord (Laisvės alėja 86; ☺8am-5.30 Mon-Thu, to 5pm Fri) Foreign exchange and ATM.

Kaunas (www.kaunas.lt) Official city website.

Kaunas in Your Pocket (www.inyourpocket. com) Annual city guide sold in hotels, art galleries and news kiosks for €1 (or download the PDF from the website).

Kauno Medicinos Universiteto Klinikos (📋emergency 37-326 089; www.kaunoklinikos. lt; Eivenių gatvė 2; ☺24hr) University medical clinic for emergencies. Approximately 2.5km north of the New Town; catch trolleybus 1 from the Old or New Town.

Main Post Office (☑8-700 55400; www.post.
lt; Laisvės alėja 102; ☺8am-7pm Mon-Fri, 9am-
3pm Sat) Kaunas' principal post office.

SEB Bankas (www.seb.lt; Laisvės alėja 82;
☺8.30am-5pm Mon-Fri) Bank and ATM.

Tourist Office (☑37-323 436; www.visit.
kaunas.lt; Laisvės alėja 36; ☺9am-7pm Mon-
Fri, 10am-3pm Sat & Sun) This office books
accommodation, sells maps and guides, and
arranges bicycle rental and guided tours of
Old Town.

ⓘ Getting There & Away

AIR

Kaunas International Airport (☑8-612
44442; www.kaunas-airport.lt; Vilniaus gatvė,
Karmėlava; ☺9am-midnight; 🚌29, 29E) is
situated 10km north of the city centre. **Ryanair**
(☑37-750 195; www.ryanair.com) handles
the bulk of the airport's traffic, operating
flights to/from Birmingham, Brussels, Dublin,
Frankfurt, Liverpool, London (Gatwick, Luton,
Stansted), Oslo, Paris and Stockholm. Bus 29
or minibus 120 run to the centre of town; a taxi
should cost around €18.

BUS

The **long-distance bus station** (Autobusų
Stotis; ☑37-409 060; www.autobusubilietai.
lt; Vytauto prospektas 24; ☺ticket office
5.45am-9.30pm) handles intercity buses within
Lithuania and buses further afield. Information
is available from the timetable on the wall or
from the helpful information desk (open 7am
to 8pm).

For domestic tickets, try the Eurolines subsidiary **Kautra** (☑37-342 440; www.kautra.lt). Buy
tickets inside the main bus terminal or on the
company's website.

Several companies offer international services, including **Eurolines** (www.eurolines.
lt) and its **Lux Express** (www.luxexpress.lt)
subsidiary. You can buy tickets in the main
hall. **Ecolines** (☑37-202 022; www.ecolines.
net; Vytauto prospektas 27; ☺9am-6pm Mon-
Fri, to 3pm Sat), across the road, also sells
tickets for international destinations. **Simple
Express** (☑5-233 6666; www.simpleexpress.
eu) offers budget travel within the Baltics, but
doesn't have a local office, so you'll have to
book online.

Daily services within Lithuania and the Baltics
include the following:

Birštonas (€3, 50 minutes, hourly)
Druskininkai (€8, two to three hours, hourly)
Klaipėda (€14, 2¾ to four hours, 20 daily)
Palanga (€17, 3½ hours, nine daily)
Panevėžys (€8, 2¼ hours, 30 daily)

Rīga (€19, 4½ hours, three daily)
Šiauliai (€10, 2¾ hours, 20 daily)
Tallinn (€38, 10 hours, three daily)
Vilnius (€6, 1¾ hours, at least every 30 minutes)

CAR

Autobanga (☑5-212 7777; www.autobanga.
lt; Oro uosto gatvė 4) provides car hire at the
airport.

TRAIN

From the **train station** (Geležinkelio Stotis;
☑7005 5111; www.litrail.lt; MK Čiurlionio gatvė
16; ☺ticket office 4.10am-9.20pm) there are
14 trains daily to/from Vilnius (€5, 1¼ to 1¾
hours).

ⓘ Getting Around

Buses and trolleybuses run from 5am to 11pm
and tickets cost €0.70 from the driver. Alternatively, you can buy a Kauno Miesto Kortelė
(Kaunas City Card) from a Kauno Spauda or
Naversen kiosk for €1.74, top it up, and pay only
€0.58 each time you press it to the on-board
card reader. While the City Card is cheaper, it's
only really worth it if you'll be in Kaunas for an
extended stay.

Minibuses shadow routes and run later than
regular buses; drivers sell tickets for €0.87,
and will stop wherever you wish. For information on public transport, including routes and
timetables, see the website **Kaunas Public
Transport** (www.kvt.lt).

To get to/from the airport, take minibus 120
from the local bus station on Šv Gertrūdos gatvė
or bus 29 from the stop on Vytauto prospektas.
Buses depart at least once an hour between 7am
and 9.30pm.

Trolleybuses 1, 5 and 7 run north from the train
station along Vytauto prospektas, west along
Kęstučio gatvė and Nemuno gatvė, then north
on Birštono gatvė. Returning, they head east
along Šv Gertrūdos gatvė, Ožeškienės gatvė
and Donelaičio gatvė, then south down Vytauto
prospektas to the bus and train stations.

There's also a couple of skeletal night-bus
routes – 13N, 14N and 37N – from Thursday to
Saturday.

Several taxi companies operate in Kaunas and
you're always best advised to order one in advance by telephone. Try **Einesa** (☑37-331 533;
www.eines.lt) or **Žaibiškas** (☑37-333 111; www.
zaibiskasgreitis.lt).

Outside Old Town, driving in Kaunas is a
relatively simple affair, with plentiful parking
and few one-way streets. Old Town is a warren
of small cobbled alleys, however, and parking
is scarce.

LITHUANIA KAUNAS

Birštonas

📱 319 / POP 3100

Birštonas (bir-shto-nas), some 40km south of Kaunas, resides on a pretty loop of the Nemunas River. It's famous as a spa town and for hosting **Birštonas Jazz** – arguably Lithuania's top jazz festival – in March in even-numbered years.

◉ Sights & Activities

For Lithuanians, Birštonas is best known for its spa treatments, built around the region's mineral springs and mud. These are considered serious medical treatments and are used for treating circulatory, heart, stomach and lung ailments. If you're of a more active bent, canoeing, cycling and hiking in the Nemunas Loops Regional Park – which encompasses most of the surrounding countryside – are delightful pastimes.

The tourist office is the best source of information for all sights and activities.

Eglė Sanitorija   SPA
(📱 319-42 142; www.birstonas.sanatorija.lt; Algirdo gatvė 14; ☻8am-5pm Mon-Fri) Offering spas, mud baths, week-long treatments and bed-and-breakfast from €48 per night, Eglė is a well-established spa in central Birštonas, not far from the broad Nemunas. It's excellent value: a 60-minute massage can be had for as little as €29, or a mineral bath for €7.

Bicycles Birštonas   BICYCLE RENTAL
(Dviračiai Birštone; 📱8-677 77472; Pušyno St 75; ☻9am-10pm) Hires bikes for €2 per hour or €10 per day, between May and September.

Canoeing   CANOEING
The fast-flowing Verknė River provides excellent opportunities for canoeing, particularly in spring when the water is high. Half-day, full-day and two-day trips are possible, and can be arranged through the tourist office. Canoes (€4/15 per hour/day) can be hired from the **Birštonas Sport Centre** (📱 319-65 640; www.birstonosportas.lt; B Sruogos gatvė 18; ☻9am-6pm).

Boat Hire   BOATING
(📱8-640 26638; Birutės gatvė 17; rowboats per hour €6) Pedalos and motorboats are also to be had, from the jetty near Birutės gatvė.

Birštono Nemunas   BOAT TOUR
(📱 319-56 360; www.birstononemunas.lt; Prienų gatvė 21; ☻by appointment) This boating club arranges Nemunas cruises on one of three Viking longboats – the nine-seat royal boat, the 15-seat Finnish Viking boat or the 20-seat Viking Dragon boat. Prices depend on the boat hired and the number and age of the passengers.

Vytenis   CRUISE
(Pušyno gatvė; adult/child €10/5; ☻3pm Sun) Leaving from the pier on Pušyno gatvė, this two-tiered pleasure craft takes up to 50 for a one-hour jaunt to the Verknė River.

🛏 Sleeping

Audenis   GUESTHOUSE €
(📱 319-61 300; www.audenis.lt; Lelijų gatvė 3; s/d €35/47; 🅿@🛜) This very pleasant guesthouse has simple rooms in an array of pastel colours and friendly staff. They can organise kayaking, bikes, hot-air ballooning and other pastimes, and the terraced cafe is a fine spot for a light lunch.

Sofijos Rezidencija   HOTEL €€
(📱 319-45 200; www.sofijosrezidencija.lt; Jaunimo gatvė 6; d/ste €75/105; 🅿@🛜🏊) Rooms at Sofijos may border on kitsch (the rooms are all themed for great figures of Lithuanian history) but can win you over with pseudo-Renaissance splendour, four-poster beds, comfy couches and plenty of mod cons. There's also a small wellness centre on-site.

Nemuno Slėnis   HOTEL €€€
(📱8-699 64028; www.nemunoslenis.lt; Kampiškių gatvė 8; r €58-144; 🅿@🛜🏊) Located on the banks of the Nemunas, away from the town centre and surrounded by forest, Nemuno Slėnis offers seclusion and comfort. The interior is lavish, with rooms decorated in plush, antique furniture and draped in deep, warm colours. There's a spa, a restaurant and a fitness centre in the complex. Prices rise steeply from Thursday to Sunday.

ℹ Information

Tourist Office (📱 319-65 740; www.visit birstonas.lt; B Sruogos St 4; ☻9am-6pm Mon-Fri, 10am-6pm Sat, to 4pm Sun) While some of the printed information isn't available in English, the helpful staff can advise on spas, river activities, hiking, accommodation and more.

Nemunas Loops Regional Park Visitor Centre (Nemunas kilpų regioninio parko; 📱 319-65 610; www.nemuno kilpos.lt; Tylioji gatvė 1; ☻8am-5pm Mon-Thu, to 3.45pm Fri, 10am-4pm Sat May-Oct) Provides essential information on hiking, camping, cycling and nature-watching in the gorgeous Nemunas Loops National Park, 250 sq km of meandering waterway, forests and gentle hills. Guides can also be arranged (22 per hour).

ⓘ Getting There & Away

From Kaunas bus station there are buses every hour or so to and from Birštonas (€3, 50 minutes).

Šiauliai

🛈 41 / POP 128,400

Lithuania's fourth-largest city, Šiauliai (show-ley), is a workaday town and not worth a special trip. That said, its central location makes it a handy stopover, whether you are moving north to south or east to west. The city's main claim to fame, at least during Soviet times, was the massive military airfield on the outskirts of town. To this day, Šiauliai retains a whiff of lingering communism.

That's not to say it's not attractive. The main drag, Vilniaus gatvė, is prime strolling turf, lined with the usual mix of cafes and bars. The city's biggest drawcard is the incredible Hill of Crosses, 10km to the north. Outside of that, there are several offbeat museums that warrant a few hours of attention.

◉ Sights

Šiauliai is home to some of Lithuania's most unusual museums, all of which lie either on or near the main avenue, Vilniaus gatvė.

◉ Hill of Crosses

Atop a small hill about 10km north of Šiauliai is a strange and inspiring sight. Here stand thousands upon thousands of crosses planted by countless pilgrims and, on Saturdays, one newlywed couple after the next.

Large and tiny, expensive and cheap, wood and metal, the crosses are devotional, to accompany prayers, or finely carved folk-art masterpieces. Others are memorials tagged with flowers, a photograph or other mementoes of the deceased, and inscribed with a sweet or sacred message. Traditional Lithuanian *koplytstulpis* (wooden sculptures of a figure topped with a little roof) intersperse the crosses, as do magnificent sculptures of the Sorrowful Christ (Rūpintojėlis). If you wish to add your own, souvenir

LITHUANIA ŠIAULIAI

THE ART OF CRAFTING CROSSES

Crosses were once symbols of sacred fervour and national identity, both pagan and Catholic; cross crafting is the embodiment of Lithuanian contradiction.

Handed down from master to pupil, the crosses were carved from oak, the sacred pagan tree. They were made as offerings to gods, and were draped with food, coloured scarves (for a wedding) or aprons (for fertility). Once consecrated by priests, they became linked with Christian ceremonies, with unmistakable sacred significance. The crosses, which measure up to 5m in height, then became symbols of defiance against occupation.

When it comes to explaining the origin of the Hill of Crosses, there are almost as many myths as crosses. Some claim it was created in three days and three nights by the bereaved families of warriors killed in a great battle. Others say it was the work of a father who, in a desperate bid to cure his sick daughter, planted a cross on the hill. Pagan traditions tell stories of sacred fires being lit here and tended by celestial virgins.

Crosses first appeared here in the 14th century. They multiplied after bloody anti-tsarist uprisings to become a potent symbol of suffering and hope.

During the Soviet era planting a cross was an arrestable offence – but pilgrims kept coming to commemorate the thousands killed and deported. The hill was bulldozed at least three times. In 1961 the Red Army destroyed the 2000-odd crosses that stood on the mound, sealed off the tracks leading to the hill and dug ditches at its base, yet overnight more crosses appeared. In 1972 they were destroyed after the immolation of a Kaunas student in protest at Soviet occupation. But by 1990 the Hill of Crosses comprised a staggering 40,000 crosses, spanning 4600 sq metres. Since Independence they have multiplied at least 10 times – and are multiplying still. In 1993 Pope John Paul II celebrated mass here (his pulpit still stands) and graced the hill a year later with a papal cross, adding his own message to the mountain of scribbled-on crosses: 'Thank you, Lithuanians, for this Hill of Crosses which testifies to the nations of Europe and to the whole world the faith of the people of this land'.

Šiauliai

Šiauliai

traders in the car park sell crosses big and small.

An alternative view of the cross-swamped hill is from inside the chapel of the modern brick monastery. Now home to around a dozen Franciscan monks, it was built behind the hill from 1997 to 2000. The mon-

astery was allegedly the idea of the late Pope John Paul II, who said after visiting the hill in 1993 that he would like to see a place of prayer here. Behind the altar in the church, the striking backdrop seen through the ceiling-to-floor window of the Hill of Crosses is very moving; Italian architect Angelo Polesello designed it.

The Hill of Crosses (Kryžių kalnas) is 10km north of Šiauliai, 2km east off the road to Joniškis and Rīga, in the village of Jurgaičiai. To get here, take one of up to eight daily buses from Šiauliai bus station to Joniškis and get off at the Domantai stop, from where it is a 2km walk to the hill. Look for the sign 'Kryžių kalnas 2'. By taxi, the return taxi fare is around €18, with a 30-minute stop at the hill (€22 with a one-hour stop); ask the Šiauliai tourist office or your hotel to order one for you by telephone to avoid being ripped off.

By bicycle, the Hill of Crosses makes for a gentle three-hour trip out and back, mostly along paved bicycle paths that lie to the side of the main road. The tourist office hires out bikes (€1.50 per hour) and can show the route (mostly straight along the main road in the direction of Rīga, turning right at the sign for the last 2km).

⊙ Town Centre

Bicycle Museum
MUSEUM

(Dviračių muziejus; ☑ 41-524 395; www.ausros muziejus.lt; Vilniaus gatvė 139; adult/child €2/1; ⊙ 10am-6pm Tue, Thu & Fri, to 7pm Wed, 11am-5pm Sat) This fun museum has several rooms of glorious bone-rattlers and torturous bicycles with wooden tyres, as well as exhibits dedicated to pioneering Lithuanian cyclists and their incredible exploits, including one trip from Lithuania to far-eastern Vladivostok (completed in six months, though it claimed the life of one cyclist).

Photography Museum
MUSEUM

(☑ 41-524 396; www.ausrosmuziejus.lt; Vilniaus gatvė 140; adult/child €2/1; ⊙ 10am-6pm Tue, Thu & Fri, to 7pm Wed, 11am-5pm Sat & Sun) The permanent collection features Lithuanian photography from the mid-20th century, and there's an interesting program of special exhibitions.

Museum of Cats
MUSEUM

(Katinų muziejus; ☑ 8-683 69844; Žuvininkų gatvė 18, Jaunųjų gamtininkų centras; adult/child €1.16/0.58; ⊙ 10am-5pm Tue-Fri, 9am-4pm Sat) Cat lovers will certainly want to venture out to this museum southeast of the centre to see an unusual collection of feline memorabilia, including endless displays of porcelain cats and photogenic felines on the walls. There are even a couple of live cats on the premises that shadow you as you take in the various rooms. In the back room there's a mini-zoo that will likely appeal to kids but may give animal-rights activists pause.

Radio & Television Museum
MUSEUM

(Radijo ir televizijos muziejus; ☑ 41-524 399; www.ausrosmuziejus.lt; Vilniaus gatvė 174; adult/child €0.50/0.25; ⊙ 10am-5pm Wed-Fri, from 11am Sat) Šiauliai was home to some of Lithuania's first amateur radio operators in the 1920s, so it's a fitting locale for this eclectic collection of radios, TVs and phonographs. Particularly enjoyable are the big old radio receivers and some Soviet-era TV sets that were produced at nearby factories.

Frenkelis Villa
MUSEUM

(Ch Frenkelio vila; ☑ 41-524 389; www.ausros muziejus.lt; Vilniaus gatvė 74; adult/child €3/1.50; ⊙ 10am-6pm Tue, Thu & Fri, to 7pm Wed, 11am-5pm Sat & Sun) To the east of the town centre stands Frenkelis Villa, built in art nouveau style in 1908 for the then leather baron of Šiauliai. It survived WWII unscathed and was used as a military hospital by the Soviets from 1944 until 1993, at which time it was turned over to the city. The exterior has been spruced up, and the interior has been lovingly restored to its former glory, with dark-wood panelling and period furniture featuring heavily throughout.

SS Peter & Paul Cathedral
CHURCH

(Šv Petro ir Povilo bažnyčia; ☑ 41-528 077; www.siauliukatedra.lt; Aušros takas 3) Towering over Priskėlimo aikštė is the 75m spire of the Peter & Paul Cathedral, Lithuania's second-highest. It was constructed between 1595 and 1625 from the proceeds of the sale of four-year-old bulls donated by local farmers. Legend says that the hillock it stands on was created from sand and dust, which blew over the corpse of an ox that wandered into Šiauliai, sat down and died.

Sundial
MONUMENT

(☑ 41-528 077; cnr Salkauskjo gatvė & Ežero gatvė) A distinctive city landmark is the mammoth sundial, topped by a shining bronze statue of an archer in what has become known as 'Sundial Sq'. It was built in 1986 to commemorate the 750th anniversary of the Battle of Saulė (1236), the battle in which local Samogitians defeated the Knights of the Sword and founded the town.

St George's Church
CHURCH

(Šv Jurgio bažnyčia; Kražių gatvė 17) This attractive Catholic church has an unlikely onion dome – a reminder of its Russian origins.

🛏 Sleeping

The tourist office has information on homestay accommodation around Šiauliai.

Šiauliai College Youth Hostel
HOSTEL €

(Šiaulių Kolegijos Jaunimo Navynės Namai; ☑ 41-523 764; www.jnn.svako.lt; Tilžės gatvė 159; d/tr €18/22; ⊙ reception 7am-11pm; ℗) This former college has been renovated with EU funds to create a spanking clean and sparkling hostel with kitchen and TV room. The reception staff don't speak much English, but they do their best to help.

Šiauliai
HOTEL €€

(☑ 41-437 333; www.hotelsiauliai.lt; Draugystės prospektas 25; s/d/ste €28/48/77; ℗ @ 🛜) The town's old 14-storey Soviet hotel has enjoyed recent renovation both inside and out, leaving it with pleasant rooms dressed in pale yellow and brown. The views are still as great as ever but the breakfast buffet is underwhelming.

Šaulys
HOTEL €€

(☑41-520 812; www.saulys.lt; Vasario 16-osios gatvė 40; s/d/tr €60/80/110; P@🛜) This four-star establishment is Šiauliai's swankiest choice. Hidden behind its deep-red facade are suitably plush rooms and staff who can organise paragliding, parachuting and biplane flights.

✖ Eating

Most restaurants are clustered along central Vilniaus gatvė.

ČinČin
CAFE €

(☑8-640 27701; Aušros alėja 25; mains €4-6; ☉11am-10pm Mon-Fri, noon-midnight Sat) This charismatic little place is a cafe, grocery and deli in one, with good coffee, beer, simple plates and pillows to recline on.

Cask 215
PUB FOOD €

(☑8-686 67006; Vilniaus gatvė 215; mains €5-7; ☉11am-11pm) A rare nod to contemporary dining fashion in Šiauliai, Cask 215 is a pub that serves mainly American dude food: burgers, ribs, pulled pork and the like.

Ikiukas
SUPERMARKET €

(Trakų gatvė 43; ☉7.30am-11pm) A small supermarket handy to central Šiauliai.

Arkos
LITHUANIAN €€

(☑41-520 205; www.arkos.lt; Vilniaus gatvė 213; mains €6-8; ☉10am-midnight) Arkos is the nicest of several restaurants on the main pedestrian drag. A warm and welcoming red-brick cellar lures an office crowd for lunch (and everyone else at dinner) with good-value daily specials and a broad menu of Lithuanian and international dishes.

Kapitonas Morganas
INTERNATIONAL €€

(☑41-526 477; www.kapitonasmorganas.lt; Vilniaus gatvė 183; mains €7-9; ☉11am-11pm Sun-Wed, noon-midnight Thu-Sat) Captain Morgan's pirate ship is more than just a great place for carousing on the street-side terrace. Its international menu, featuring dishes such as prawns in cream and garlic and pork with grilled vegetables, has something for everyone.

☆ Entertainment

Drama Theatre
THEATRE

(☑41-523 209; www.sdt.lt; Tilžės gatvė 155) Stages productions in Lithuanian.

Saulė
CONCERT VENUE

(☑41-424 424; www.saule.lt; Tilžės gatvė 140) Šiauliai's principal concert hall.

ℹ Information

Post Office (☑8-700 55400; Aušros alėja 42; ☉7.30am-7pm Mon-Fri, 8am-3pm Sat) Šiauliai's main post office.

Šiauliai Bankas (☑8-700 55055; www.sb.lt; Vilniaus gatvė 167; ☉8am-6pm Mon-Fri) A major bank outlet handy to the centre of town.

Tourist Information Centre (☑41-523 110; www.siauliai.lt/tic; Vilniaus gatvė 213; ☉9am-1pm & 2-6pm Mon-Fri, 10am-4pm Sat, to 3pm Sun) Sells maps and guides, rents bicycles for €1.50 per hour and makes accommodation bookings. The website has detailed transport information for the Hill of Crosses.

ℹ Getting There & Away

BUS

Services to/from Šiauliai **bus station** (☑41-525 058; Tilzes gatvė 109):

Kaunas (€10, 2¾ hours, 20 daily)
Klaipėda (€11, three hours, eight daily)
Palanga (€11, three hours, eight daily)
Panevėžys (€6, 1½ hours, 18 daily)
Rīga (€9, 2½ hours, four daily)
Vilnius (€15, 3¾ hours, six daily)

TRAIN

Services to/from Šiauliai **train station** (☑41-203 445; Dubijos gatvė 44) include Klaipėda (€8, two to three hours, five daily), Panevėžys (€4, 1½ hours, three daily) and Vilnius (€10, 2½ to three hours, five daily).

Radviliškis & Around

Grim Radviliškis (rad-vi-lish-kis; population 19,700), 22km southeast of Šiauliai, is notable only as the central hub of the rail network, but there are a couple of interesting stops on the stretch of the A9 heading towards Panevėžys.

Šeduva (she-du-va; population 3200), 15km east of Radviliškis, is a large village with a faded yellow-and-white baroque church framed by cobbled streets. **Šeduvos Malūnas** (☑42-256 300; www.seduvosmalunas.lt; Vytauto gatvė 89a; mains €6-8) is a kitsch but fun restaurant, in a windmill on the western edge of Šeduva that was built in 1905 and retains the original central-core cog mechanism. Serving traditional Lithuanian cuisine over four levels, the owners also run the pleasant hotel next door, housed in a modern building (double rooms €41).

In **Kleboniškiai**, signposted on the A9 between Radviliškis and Panevėžys, is a windmill (1884) and – 1km down a dusty road – the **Kleboniškiai Rural Life Exhibition**

(Kleboniškių kaimo buites ekspozicija; ☑42-242 005; adult/student €1.74/0.87; ☺9am-5pm Tue-Sun Apr-Oct). This beautiful farmstead, with 19th- and early 20th-century farm buildings, offers a picture-postcard peek at rural Lithuania. It is brimful with collectors' items, including wooden sleds, farming tools and a tractor dating from 1926. The exhibition is part of the **Daugyvenė Cultural History Museum Reserve** (Daugyvenės kultūros istorijos muziejus-draustinis), which encompasses burial grounds, mounds and other local sights.

Panevėžys

☑45 / POP 114,600

Panevėžys (pa-ne-vey-zhees) is far from a tourist hot spot, and most people who venture to the town will do so en route from Vilnius to Rīga by bus. If you've got time to kill, there are a couple of sights to explore in this, Lithuania's fifth-largest city.

At the centre of town is Laisvės aikštė, bordered at its northern end by east–west Elektros gatvė and at its southern end by Vilniaus gatvė. Basanavičiaus gatvė runs north to the Rīga road and south to Kaunas and Vilnius. The train station is 2km northwest of the centre; the bus station is on Savanorių aikštė.

◉ Sights & Activities

Triangular-shaped **Laisvės aikštė** is a central tree-lined pedestrianised spot, pleasant for two months in summer and quiet the rest of the year. It is surrounded by a few simple cafes and shops and the Juozas Miltinio Drama Theatre, in action since 1940. By the river, a **small bridge** and **statues** make for a pleasant stroll.

Regional Museum   MUSEUM
(Kraštotyros muziejus; ☑45-462 331; www.panevezi omuziejus.lt; Vasario 16-osios gatvė 23; adult/child €1.16/0.58; ☺9am-5pm Tue-Fri, 11am-4pm Sat) This tiny museum focuses on ethnography and also hosts temporary exhibitions.

⌂ Sleeping & Eating

Hotel Panevėžys   HOTEL €€
(☑8-678 24640; www.panevezyshotel.lt; Laisvės aikštė 26; s/d €30/60; ꟼ☎) Perched on the 5th floor of a Soviet-style high-rise (the rest is now office space), this modern hotel is a decent option should you need to stay in central Panevėžys. The entrance to the reception area is located behind the building, beside the car park.

Panevėžys

Panevėžys

Hotel Romantic   HOTEL €€€
(☑45-848 60; www.romantic.lt; Kranto gatvė 24; s/d/ste €105/175/200; ꟼ@☎☒) Housed in a converted old mill, rooms here are suitably plush (and priced accordingly). The restaurant terrace overlooking the park – definitely the best place in town to dine – is a delight (mains €11 to €16).

Taverna   ITALIAN €
(☑8-683 72255; Laisvės aikštė 6; mains €4-6; ☺6pm-1am Thu-Sun, to midnight Mon-Wed) With an ideal location on Laisvės aikštė, this casual Italian is good for a glass of wine,

SAMPLING THE NORTHERN ALES

Northern Lithuania is the land of barley-malt beer, with ale-makers keeping to recipes and rituals practised by their ancestors 1000 years ago. People here drink 160L of beer a year, say proud locals. The biggest drinkers in the world, the Czechs, consume around the same amount. The Australians down around 110L per year, the Brits a meagre 100L.

Big-name brews to glug include **Horn**, brewed in Kaunas since 1853; Šiauliai-made **Gubernija** (www.gubernija.lt); and **Kalnapilis** from Panevėžys.

Lakeside Biržai, 65km north of Panevėžys and the true heart of Lithuanian beer country, hosts the annual two-day **Biržai Town Festival** in August, a madcap fiesta where the town's breweries sell their wares on the street; expect plenty of beer swilling and general drunken behaviour. Its **Rinkuškiai Brewery** (☑ 45-035 293; www.rinkuskiai.lt; Alyvų gatvė 8) can be visited, and its beer – everything from light lager to lead-heavy stout – can be bought in bulk in its factory shop. A lesser-known label to look out for is the sweet **Butautų alaus bravoras**, an ale bottled in brown glass with a ceramic, metal-snap cap. It has been brewed in the village of Butautų since 1750.

a panino, pasta with pesto, or something meaty from the grill.

Galerija XX　　　　　　　LITHUANIAN €
(☑ 45-438 701; www.galerijaxx.lt; Laisvės aikštė 7; mains €4-6; ⊙ 10am-11pm) With a terrace on the main square, this gallery-cafe does good-value Lithuanian cuisine.

Iki　　　　　　　　　　SUPERMARKET €
(Ukmerges gatvė 18; ⊙ 8am-10pm) Get snacks for the trip here, near the bus station.

☆ Entertainment

Puppet Wagon Theatre　　　　THEATRE
(Pasakų traukinukas; ☑ 45-511 236; www.leliu vezimoteatras.lt; Respublikos gatvė 30; ⊙ 8am-5pm Mon-Fri) Lithuania's only travelling-cart theatre is rarely at home (it travels most of the summer), but the characters displayed in this old narrow-gauge train carriage are enchanting.

ℹ Information

E-kopija (☑ 8-652 89145; Laisvės aikštė 16; internet access per hour €0.70; ⊙ 8.30am-6.30pm Mon-Fri, 10am-3pm Sat)
SEB Bankas (☑ 1528; www.seb.lt; Ukmergės gatvė 20; ⊙ 8.30am-5pm Mon-Thu, to 4pm Fri) Handy to the bus station.
Tourist Information Centre (☑ 45-508 080; www.panevezysinfo.lt; Laisvės aikštė 11; ⊙ 9am-6pm Mon-Fri, 9am-2pm Sat Apr-Sep, reduced hours rest of year)

ℹ Getting There & Away

BUS

Services to and from the **bus station** (☑ 463 333; Savanorių aikštė 5) include the following:

Kaunas (€8, 2¼ hours, 30 buses daily)
Rīga (€11, 2½ to three hours, six daily)
Šiauliai (€6, 1½ hours, 18 daily)
Vilnius (€10, 1¾ to three hours, regularly from 6am to 10pm)

TRAIN

Service to/from the **train station** (☑ 45-463 615; Kerbedžio gatvė 9) is limited but includes Šiauliai (€4, 1½ hours, two daily), from where you can connect to onward rail destinations.

Biržai

☑ 450 / POP 15,000

The quiet town of Biržai (ber-zhay) – Lithuania's northernmost, and one of its oldest – has a beautiful lakeside situation, and several worthwhile sights. To get here, follow the A10 north from Panevėžys, then take highway 125 east at Raubonys. Buses also run to/from Panevėžys (€5, 1¼ hours, 14 daily), Vilnius (€10, two hours, hourly) and other centres.

⊙ Sights

Biržai Castle　　　　　　CASTLE
(☑ 450-33 390; www.birzumuziejus.lt; adult/child €2/1; ⊙ 10am-6.30pm Wed-Sat, to 5.30pm Tue & Sun) As permanent as it looks, its huge, white-washed bastions striking skywards from artificial Lake Širvėna, Biržai Castle was largely restored in the 1980s, having been twice destroyed. First built by Duke Kristupas Radvila in the late 16th century, it was the seat of the Dukes of Biržai, and found itself in the front line in two wars with Sweden. The main castle and arsenal house exhibitions of local ethnography, military history, and the story of the Duchy and Radvilas family.

Astravas Manor
HISTORIC BUILDING

This once-grand Romantic estate, built by Count Mykolas Tiškevičius in 1862, is beautifully sited on the northern shore of Lake Širvėna. It's subsequently been used as a dairy, a sacking factory and a linen warehouse, but restoration of the buildings and classical park in the '50s and '60s returned some of its original grandeur. It's not officially open to the public, but you can walk over the 525m footbridge (Lithuania's longest), admire the views, and possibly have a peek inside.

Biržai Regional Park
NATIONAL PARK

(☑ 450-35 805; www.birzuparkas.lt; Rotušės gatvė 10) The region around Biržai is famous for its karst sink-holes, formed when underground water sources wash away the gypsum supporting the soil. More than 9000 of these holes, including the 12.6m-deep 'Cow's Cave' (so-called because an unhappy bovine was swallowed up when it opened, 200 years ago) can be found in the area, many within the 146-sq-km regional park. The park office has more information on the topography, plus walks, tours and other activities.

St John the Baptist Church
CHURCH

(www.birzuparapija.lt; Radvilos gatvė 5) The white-walled St John's, built in neoclassical and baroque styles in the 19th century, is the second-most imposing building in Biržai, after the castle.

🍴 Sleeping & Eating

Helveda
GUESTHOUSE €

(☑ 450-31 150; J Janonio gatvė 7; d €29) Handy for the bus station and Biržai's main sights, this functional guesthouse lacks charm, but does the job.

Pilies Skliautai
LITHUANIAN €

(☑ 450-33 032; J Radvilos gatvė 3; mains €6; ⊙noon-9pm Tue-Sun) Pilies Skliautai has probably the best food in Biržai, and certainly wins the rosette for atmosphere. It's housed in the vaulted cellars of the Duke's castle, serving a typical Lithuanian mix of soups, grilled meats, dumplings and fish.

ℹ Information

Tourist Information Centre (☑ 450-33 496; www.visitbirzai.lt; J Janonio gatvė 2; ⊙8am-5pm Mon-Fri year-round, plus 10am-3pm Sat & Sun mid-Jun–Aug) Bursting with pamphlets and good advice, this friendly little centre can help arrange accommodation, local tours, cycling, walks and more.

Anykščiai
☑ 381 / POP 12,000

Lovely Anykščiai (a-neeksh-chey), 60km southeast of Panevėžys, sits on the confluence of the Šentoji and Anykšta Rivers. Fanning eastward are 76 lakes, the largest of which – Lake Rubikiai (9.68 sq km and 16m deep) – is freckled with 16 islands. There are a handful of sights here, and in winter the city transforms itself into that rarity of rarities, a Lithuanian ski resort. In summer, the Devilstone Music Festival (www.devilstone.net) brings hard rock to Anykščiai's Dainuva Valley.

⊙ Sights & Activities

The chance to clamber over train cars and even to take a ride on an old narrow-gauge locomotive is arguably the town's biggest attraction, and a big draw for kids.

Narrow-Gauge Railway Museum
MUSEUM

(Siaurojo geležinkelis istorijos ekspozicija; ☑ 381-54 597; www.baranauskas.lt; Viltis gatvė 2; adult/child €2/1.60; ⊙10am-5pm May-Oct) Housed in Anykščiai's old station, this museum gives visitors the chance to ride on manual rail cars and, on weekends from May to October, take a trip along the line to either Troškūnai or Rubikiai. Trains leave at 11am and return around 3pm; tickets cost €5.80. More information can be found at www.siaurukas.eu or at the Anykščiai tourist information office.

Horse Museum
MUSEUM

(Arklio muziejus; ☑ 381-6237 0629; www.arkliomuziejus.lt; adult/child €3/2; ⊙9am-6pm May-Aug, 8am-4pm Sep-Apr) Horse lovers – and kids – will want to make the journey 6km north to Lithuania's only horse museum, in the tiny village of Niūronys. Set out as a traditional farmstead, the museum displays black-and-white photos of horse-drawn transport in Vilnius alongside a fine collection of horse-drawn fire engines, carriages and taxis. Horse and carriage rides are available (adult/child €1.50/1) and there's a playground for bipedal fun. Two buses daily (€0.70, 20 minutes) connect Niūronys with Anykščiai.

Puntukas Stone
LANDMARK

A pine forest 10km south of Anykščiai contains the Puntakas Stone (Puntuko akmuo), a boulder 5.7m tall, 6.7m wide and 6.9m long, which legend says was put there by the devil. While he was trying to destroy Anykščiai's twin-steeple church, St Mathew's (1899–1909), a rooster crowed and the devil thundered to hell – prompting the boulder to hurtle down from the sky.

Kalitos Kalnas
SNOW SPORTS

(☑381-78 144; www.kalitoskalnas.lt; Kalno gatvė 25; ☉11am-6pm Mon-Fri, 10am-7pm Sat & Sun) In winter, Anykščiai transforms itself into one of the country's few 'ski resorts'. This ski centre operates two ski lifts in season (December to March), has equipment for hire and offers skiing lessons. Throughout the rest of the year, the 'Alpine Coaster' (a sled on tracks) can still satisfy your desire to speed down a hill.

🛏 Sleeping

The Anykščiai tourist information office can suggest homestays and farmstays, which are the most common accommodation options in town.

Nykščio Namai
HOTEL €

(☑8-655 43379; www.nykscionamai.lt; Liudiškių gatvė 18; s/d €29/52; 🏊) Keturi Kalnai is a reasonably slick modern hotel that offers excellent value in understated but comfortable rooms. Plus, there's a gym, a tennis court and a pool on-site.

ⓘ Information

Tourist Information Office (☑381-59 177; www.antour.lt; Gegužės gatvė 1; ☉8am-5pm Mon-Sat year-round, plus 9am-4pm Sun May-Sep) Anykščiai's extremely helpful tourist information office should be your first port of call. The enthusiastic staff can help book homestays as well as advise on sights and travel info.

ⓘ Getting There & Away

With Anykščiai's rail line effectively transformed into a tourist attraction, that leaves just the bus. From the **bus station** (☑381-51 333; A Vienuolio gatvė 1; ☉6am-7pm), opposite the tourist office, there are buses to/from Panevėžys (€5, 1¼ hours, two daily), Vilnius (€8, 2½ hours, 14 daily), Kaunas (€7, 2¼ hours, 15 daily) and Utena (€7, one hour, six daily).

WESTERN LITHUANIA

Lithuania's Baltic coastline is one of the country's leading tourist draws. While the season is mercilessly short (running from just mid-May to mid-September, with only July and August suitable for swimming), locals and visitors alike come here in droves to enjoy the nearly 100km stretch of glistening sea, white-sand beaches and vibrant summertime energy.

Topping the bill is a unique gem: Curonian Spit (Kuršių Nerija), a skinny leg of sand that stalks into Russia. So precious and extraordinary is this slice between the relentless Baltic Sea and the lapping Curonian Lagoon that Unesco added it to its World Heritage list in 2000. Its historical fishing villages and East Prussian past are fascinating backdrops to the real attraction: giant sand dunes and dense pine forests.

The gateway to the spit is Klaipėda, the country's third-largest city and only major port. This busy city with its tiny Old Town and constant flow of ferries has its own rhythms. To the north is Palanga, a party town if ever there was one; finding a room here in summer can be a challenge.

South of Klaipėda, the Nemunas Delta Regional Park is an oasis for birds and bird lovers. Inland, the Žemaitija National Park was once home to a secret Soviet nuclear base. The base has been converted to the Cold War Museum and is a must for history buffs.

Klaipėda

☑46 / POP 161,300

Lithuania's third-largest city is a mix of old and new. This former Prussian capital (when it was named Memel) has retained a distinct German flavour in the architecture of its heavily cobbled Old Town and one remaining tower of its red-brick castle. It's also Lithuania's only port of call for *Titanic*-sized cruise ships, and a vital sea link for cargo and passenger ferries between Lithuania, Scandinavia and beyond.

Most people will only catch a glimpse of Klaipėda (klai-pey-da) as they rush headlong for the ferry to Curonian Spit, but spend a few hours – or even better, a day – and you'll be justly rewarded.

The Danė River flows westward across the city centre and enters the Curonian Lagoon 4km from the Baltic Sea. The river cuts the city into two distinct parts. North of the river is the more modern New Town, where you'll find some hotels, the train and bus stations, and Klaipėda University. The main axis here is Manto gatvė, which runs north–south. South of the river is the gentrifying Old Town, which has the tourist information office as well as shops, bars, restaurants and

Western Lithuania

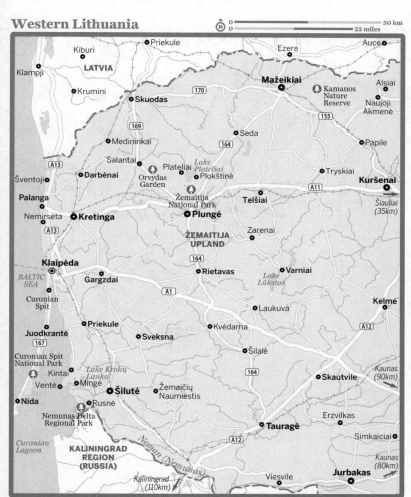

a smattering of hotels. The main drag here is Tiltų gatvė and Taikos prospektas.

A third district, Smiltynė, lies across the Curonian Lagoon from the rest of the city on the northern tip of Curonian Spit. It has a handful of interesting sights and is reachable only by ferry.

History

Klaipėda was Memel until 1925. Founded in 1252 by the Teutonic Order, who built the city's first castle, it was a key trading port from the 15th century until 1629, when Swedish forces destroyed it. After the Napoleonic Wars of the early 19th century, it became part of Prussia and stayed in Prussian hands until WWI. The population at this time was an even split of Germans and Lithuanians.

Under the Treaty of Versailles that ended WWI, Memel town, the northern half of Curonian Spit and a strip of land (about 150km long and 20km wide) along the eastern side of the Curonian Lagoon and the northern side of the Nemunas River were separated from Germany as an 'international territory'. It remained stateless until 1923, when Lithuanian troops marched in, annexed it, and changed the name of Memel to Klaipėda.

Klaipėda

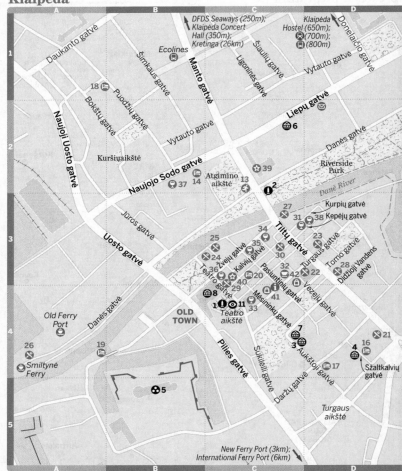

Germany eventually reclaimed Klaipėda during WWII and the city served as a Nazi submarine base. The city's strategic value ensured that it was all but destroyed during the war. After much rebuilding and repopulating, it has developed into an important city on the back of shipbuilding and fishing. In 1991 its university opened, followed in 2003 by a new cruise ship terminal. In recent years the town has begun to focus its attention on the tourist trade, building smart new hotels and restaurants.

⊙ Sights

◎ Old Town

Little of German Klaipėda remains but there are some restored streets in the oldest part of town wedged between the river and Turgaus aikštė. Pretty **Teatro aikštė** (Theatre Sq) is the Old Town focus.

In front tinkles a **fountain** dedicated to Simon Dach, a Klaipėda-born German poet (1605–59) who was the focus of a circle of

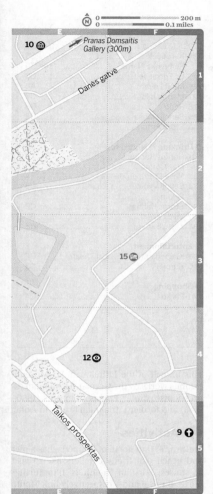

(incorporation) of Memel into Germany from its balcony.

Castle
RUIN

Originally built by the Teutonic Order in the 13th century, and nearly completely razed in the late 19th (after centuries of neglect), Klaipėda Castle is rising again. Above the surviving moat and earth ramparts a huge reconstruction project is underway, promising to restore the seaward focal point to the city. While it remains to be seen how convincing the reconstruction is, the first phase was expected to be complete by 2016.

Švyturys
BREWERY

(📞 46-484 000; www.svyturys.lt; Kūlių Vartų gatvė 7) Klaipėda is home to the country's oldest operating brewery, where its biggest beer, Švyturys, has been brewed since 1784. Organised by the tourist office, tours of the brewery are 1½ to two hours, cost €10 per person (including tastings), and leave any time between 10am and 4pm Monday to Friday.

History Museum of Lithuania Minor
MUSEUM

(Mažosios Lietuvos Istorijos Muziejus; 📞 46-410 524; www.mlimuziejus.lt; Didžioji Vandens gatvė 6; adult/child €1.45/0.72; ⊙10am-6pm Tue-Sat) This small museum traces the origins of 'Lithuania Minor' (Kleinlitauen) – as this coastal region was known during several centuries as part of East Prussia. It exhibits Prussian maps, coins, artefacts of the Teutonic Order, traditional weaving machines and traditional folk art.

Blacksmith's Museum
MUSEUM

(Kalvystės muziejus; 📞 46-410 526; www.mlimuz iejus.lt; Šaltkalvių gatvė 2; adult/child €1.45/0.72; ⊙10am-6pm Tue-Sat) One branch of the quadripartite Lithuania Minor History Museum, the cute Blacksmith's Museum displays ornate forged-iron works such as elaborate crosses transferred from the town's former cemetery (Martynas Mažvydas Sculpture Park).

Mary Queen of Peace Church
CHURCH

(Švč Mergelės Marijos Taikos Karalienės bažnyčia; 📞 46-410 120; Rumpiškės gatvė 6a; ⊙8am-6pm) This is that rarest of beasts: a Catholic church built during the Soviet era (it is, in fact, unique in the Baltics). Its 46.5m tower is one of the highest points in the city, and visits can be booked through the tourist office.

Königsberg writers and musicians. On a pedestal in the middle of the water stands **Ännchen von Tharau** (1912), a statue of Ann from Tharau sculpted by Berlin artist Alfred Kune (a replica; the original was destroyed in WWII) and inspired by a famous German wedding and love song originally written in the East Prussian dialect.

Klaipėda Drama Theatre
HISTORIC BUILDING

(📞 46-314 453; www.kldteatras.lt; Teatro aikštė 2; ⊙noon-6pm Tue-Sat) This fine neoclassical theatre, built in 1857, stages productions in Lithuanian. Hitler proclaimed the *Anschluss*

Klaipėda

Baroti Gallery　　　　　　　　　　GALLERY
(Baroti galerija; ☎46-313 580; www.barotigalerija.
lt; Aukštoji gatvė 1; ☉11am-6pm Tue-Fri, to 4pm Sat)
FREE This gallery, with its lively program of
visiting exhibitions, is partly housed in a
converted fish warehouse dating to 1819.

◉ New Town

A **riverside park** skirts the northern bank
of the Danė. A little further north, Liepų
gatvė – called Adolf-Hitler-Strasse for a
brief spell – has a few attractions of its own.

Clock Museum　　　　　　　　　　MUSEUM
(Laikrodžių muziejus; ☎46-410 414; Liepų gatvė
12; adult/child €1.74/0.86; ☉noon-6pm Tue-Sat, to
5pm Sun) This niche museum is divided into
two sections: the first explores the principles
of chronology from its earliest times; the
second looks at the evolution of design and
form in clocks over the past four centuries.
The sundial garden can be worth the price
of admission, on sunny days.

Pranas Domšaitis Gallery　　　　MUSEUM
(☎46-410 416; www.ldm.lt; Liepų gatvė 33; adult/
child €1.73/0.87; ☉noon-6pm Tue-Sat, to 5pm Sun)

This branch of the Lithuanian Art Museum
exhibits works by the German-Lithuanian expressionist painter Pranas Domšaitis (1880–
1965) and former Lithuanian artists-in-exile.

Activities

Melnragė, 1km north of Klaipėda, has a pier
and beach which city dwellers like to visit
at sunset; **Giruliai Beach** is 1km further
north. Buses 6 and 4 respectively link Manto
gatvė with both. **Karklė**, another 1km north,
is known for having amber specks wash up
on its unusually stony beach after autumn
storms and for the protected **Dutch Cap**, a
24m sea cliff.

Klaipėda's tourist office can arrange boat
trips, sailing (during July's Sea Festival), and
ice-fishing in winter.

✵ Festivals & Events

Sea Festival　　　　　　　　　　CULTURAL
(Juros Svente; ☎46-400 300; www.jurossvente.lt)
Klaipėda celebrates its rich nautical heritage
in late July with the flamboyant Sea Festival.
The three-day event brings music, workshops,
fairs and (naturally) watercraft to town.

🛏 Sleeping

Try to book in advance during the summer season, especially during the Sea Festival. The tourist office can help with private rooms and country stays.

Litinterp Guesthouse　　GUESTHOUSE €
(📞 46-410 644; www.litinterp.lt; Puodžių gatvė 17; s/d/tr from €25/34/51; 🅿🛜) A commercial building since the 18th century, this guesthouse retains timber stairs, brick arches and other lovely old touches. Its 19 rooms are spotless, with light pine furnishings. The breakfast (€2.90) is spartan, but with overall value this good we're not complaining.

Klaipėda Hostel　　HOSTEL €
(📞 46-211 879; www.klaipedahostel.com; Butkų Juzės gatvė 7/4; dm/d €12/32; 🅿@🛜) This friendly hostel close to the bus station looks terrible from the outside but is very homey and pleasant inside. Two small dorms sleep 12 people and there's one double, as well as a kitchen and free tea and coffee. Book in advance; no credit cards accepted.

Pajūrio Kempingas　　CAMPGROUND €
(📞 8-677 73227; www.campingklaipeda.lt; Šlaito gatvė 3, Giriuliai; sites per person/tent €4.34/4.34; 🅿) This quiet camping ground is around 8km north of Klaipėda's Old Town near the village of Giriuliai. It's conveniently situated close to both the sea and the local train station, with regular services to and from Klaipėda.

★Hotel Euterpė　　HOTEL €€
(📞 46-474 703; www.euterpe.lt; Daržų gatvė 9; s/d €73/93; 🅿➔@🛜) Our bet for the best small hotel in Klaipėda is this upscale number, tucked among former German merchant houses in Old Town. Expect a warm welcome at reception and snug rooms in earthy colours and a neat, minimalist look. The downstairs restaurant is excellent and there's a small terrace to enjoy your morning coffee.

Preliudija Guesthouse　　GUESTHOUSE €€
(📞 46-310 077; www.preliudija.com; Kepėjų gatvė 7; s/d €58/70; @🛜) This handsome mid-19th-century guesthouse is right in the heart of Old Town Klaipėda. Despite its history, the rooms are minimalist and modern; each has a single fresh flower in a vase and a sparkling bathroom.

Old Mill Hotel　　HOTEL €€
(📞 46-219 215; www.oldmillhotel.lt; Žvejų gatvė 22; d €70; 🛜) Occupying two old merchants' buildings in a commanding position either side of the Klaipėda dock swing-bridge, this well-established hotel is close to the castle, Old Town and ferries to Curonian Spit. The claret-carpeted rooms are bright and generous, with quality beds and sparkling bathrooms. The Old Port and Ferryman House restaurants are part of the complex.

Friedricho　　GUESTHOUSE €€
(📞 46-391 020; www.pasazas.lt; Šaltkalvių gatvė 3; s/d €60/70; 🅿🛜) This pretty six-room guesthouse is run by the same people who operate the restaurants along Friedricho Pasažas. The rooms themselves are more like small apartments, with kitchenettes and sitting rooms, and are perfect for families. The Old Town setting is ideal.

Aribė　　HOTEL €€
(📞 46-490 940; www.aribe.lt; Bangų gatvė 17a; s/d €41/58; 🅿@🛜) This three-star establishment lies behind an unassuming facade, and is a 10-minute walk from Old Town. Rooms are quiet, pleasant and dressed in light, bright colours, and the staff couldn't be more helpful.

Amberton Klaipėda　　HOTEL €€€
(📞 46-404 372; www.ambertonhotel.com; Naujoji Sodo gatvė 1; r/ste from €94/350, older r from €54; 🅿✳@🛜♨) This four-star hotel is one of the top addresses in town and occupies the unusual red-brick tower and 'K' buildings just to the north of the river. There's a good range of accommodation on offer from relatively simple singles and doubles in the older wing, at reasonable prices, all the way up to multiroom, luxury suites in the newer K building that include Jacuzzis and sea views. All guests have access to amenities like the spa, tennis courts and casino.

🍴 Eating

Katpėdėlė　　LITHUANIAN €
(📞 8-618 28343; www.katpedele.lt; Žvejų gatvė 12; mains €4-6; ⏰10am-1am Sun-Wed, to 2am Thu, to 3am Fri & Sat; 🛜) While it may be a franchise, Katpėdėlė does the Lithuanian standards really well, and makes the most of a brick merchant's building in a prime spot by the Danė. Try the grilled pork neck with thyme and whisky sauce, or the salmon with peanuts.

Ikiukas　　SUPERMARKET €
(Turgaus gatvė 16; ⏰7.30am-11.30pm) Only a mini-supermarket, but handy for Old Town.

KLAIPĖDA'S SCULPTURE SCAPE

In true Lithuanian style, Klaipėda is studded with great sculptures, including 120-odd pieces from the late 1970s in the **Martynas Mažvydas Sculpture Park** (Liepų gatvė), the city's main cemetery until 1977. Not far from the park on Lietuvninkų aikštė is a monumental 3.5m sculpture in granite of the eponymous Martynas Mažvydas, author of the first book published in Lithuanian, in 1547.

The red granite pillar propping up a broken grey arch of almighty proportions at the southern end of Manto gatvė is Lithuania's biggest granite sculpture. Engraved with the quote 'We are one nation, one land, one Lithuania' by local poet Ieva Simonaitytė (1897–1978), the *Arka* (Arch) celebrates Klaipėda joining Lithuania in 1923.

Outside the train station stands *Farewell* (2002), a moving statue of a mother with a headscarf, a suitcase in one hand, and the hand of a small boy clutching a teddy bear in the other. It was given by Germany to Klaipėda to remember Germans who said goodbye to their homeland after the city became part of Lithuania in 1923.

Smaller works seem to pop up overnight in Klaipėda. Inside Old Town are sculptures of a dog, a cat, a mouse, a spider and a disturbing red dragon, while on its outskirts reside an apple, a row of oversized yellow chairs, and a boy with a dog waving off the ferries. Discover them on your wanders.

Friedricho Pasazas
INTERNATIONAL €€

(☑46-391 020; www.pasazas.lt; Tiltų gatvė 26a; mains €5-10; ☺11am-1am Mon-Sat, noon-midnight Sun; ☎) Lining this snug carriageway on the southern side of Old Town is Friedricho Pasazas – not just one restaurant, but a whole complex of them. Friedricho Restoranas, the main show, is top of the pile, with creative Mediterranean dishes and wine to match. Following closely behind, there's a pizzeria, a steakhouse and a Lithuanian tavern.

Meat Lovers
PUB FOOD €€

(☑8-652 21998; Danės gatvė 1; mains €5-11; ☺9am-10pm Mon-Fri, from 10am Sat & Sun) Should you find yourself peckish while waiting for the ferry to Smiltynė (and provided you're not vegetarian), Meat Lovers has you covered. Perched above the terminal building, it can whip up a burger and beer in no time, served with a view of the upper Curonian Lagoon.

Keltininko Namas
LITHUANIAN €€

(☑8-616 23551; www.oldporthotel.lt; Žvejų gatvė 20; mains €7-10; ☺11am-10pm; ☎) The house restaurant of the Old Port Hotel has a lovely port setting overlooking the Danė. The chefs here really try to incorporate fresh local ingredients, including ample fish dishes. Linen and silverware lend a fancy touch, but the prices are surprisingly reasonable.

Rene
BELGIAN €€

(☑46-215 068; www.restoranasrene.lt; Tiltų gatvė 13; mains €7; ☺11am-11pm Mon-Sat, to 9pm Sun; ☎) A smart, kooky place serving *cuisine à la bière:* mussels, beef and other dishes cooked in (primarily Belgian) beer.

La Terrasse
ITALIAN €€

(☑8-620 46685; Žvejų gatvė 10; mains €5-8; ☺11am-midnight Sun-Thu, to 2am Fri & Sat; ☎) This popular place on the Danė River focuses on well-made Italian dishes, including pizzas, pastas, salads and fish. The decor is a stripped-down contemporary, and, in nice weather, you can dine on the river.

Jing Bin Lou
CHINESE €€

(☑46-257 937; Turgaus gatvė 23; mains €5-9; ☺11am-10pm Mon-Sat, from noon Sun) There aren't too many alternatives to Lithuanian and Italian in Old Town Klaipėda, but Jing Bin Lou does decent Westernised Chinese. It even takes a stab at a few dishes from Sichuan and Xinjiang.

Senoji Hansa
LITHUANIAN €€

(☑46-300 171; www.senojihansa.lt; Kurpių gatvė 1; mains €6-10; ☺10am-10pm Mon-Sat, to 6pm Sun; ☎) This combination bar, restaurant and cafe overlooking Teatro aikštė is popular for its meat dishes, pancakes and *cepelinai*. The covered terrace is open year-round and draws a fun crowd on weekend evenings.

★Stora Antis
LITHUANIAN €€€

(☑46-493 910; www.storaantis.lt; Tiltų gatvė 6; mains €15-18; ☺5pm-midnight Tue-Fri, from noon Sat) Taking full advantage of a stunning 19th-century cellar (a restaurant was first established here in 1856), Stora Antis is charming, full of bric-a-brac and one of the best places to eat in Klaipėda's Old Town.

Meridianas EUROPEAN €€€
(☑46-411 660; www.pasazas.lt/restoranas-meridianas; Danė embankment, near Tiltų gatvė; mains €19-20, 7-course degustation with wine €84; ☉noon-1am Mon-Sat, to 10pm Sun) The *Meridianas* – a barquentine built by Finland for the USSR as part of imposed war reparations – has been restored to the glory befitting this icon of Klaipėda, and is now a floating restaurant moored in a prominent position on the Danė. Aboard, it's all gleaming fittings, starched tablecloths, wagyu, foie gras, scallops and fine wine.

🍷 Drinking & Nightlife

Klaipėda is bursting with places to drink, with plenty of new additions over the past several years.

Žvejų Baras BAR
(☑46-412 060; www.zvejubaras.lt; Kurpių gatvė 8; ☉5pm-midnight Sun-Wed, to 2am Thu-Sat) The beautiful, lead-lit, timbered interior of this portside pub (the name means 'Fisherman's Bar') is one of Klaipėda's nicest places to catch live music, or grab a few interesting beers.

Herkus Kantas PUB
(☑8-685 87338; www.herkuskantas.lt; Kepėjų gatvė17; ☉5pm-1am Tue-Sat) One of Klaipėda's riverside pubs, Herkus has perhaps the best location of all, opposite the iconic barquentine *Meridianis,* which is permanently moored here on the Danė. There's plenty of outdoor seating for good weather, and a cosy cellar interior with great beers (including a weekly guest ale) on tap.

Seven PUB
(☑8-653 27777; Žvejų gatvė 7; ☉noon-11pm) Brand new, this riverside pub has all the clean lines, burgers and craft beers you'd expect from a place angling for a youthful crowd.

Senoji Vyninė WINE BAR
(☑8-610 41204; Žvejų gatvė 5; ☉noon-11pm Mon-Fri, from 1pm Sat) This perfectly situated riverside wine bar, with its white napery, timber bar and subdued atmosphere, is ideal for a quiet drink for two.

Storas Katinas BAR
(☑46-416 173; www.nationalhotel.lt/new/en/bar; Žvejų gatvė 21; ☉8am-midnight Mon-Thu, to 2am Fri & Sat, to 11pm Sun) The 'Fat Cat' has unusual charm for a hotel bar – it's more in line with other vaulted-brick beer cellars in Germanic Klaipėda. There's a daily menu of Lithuanian food, dark timber, leather seats and subtle yellow lamps throughout, and a good wine and beer selection.

Viva Lavita COCKTAIL BAR
(☑46-228 800; www.ambertonhotels.com; Naujojo Sodo gatvė 1; ☉noon-1am Sun-Thu, to 3am Fri & Sat) On the 20th floor of the K building of the Amberton hotel, and attached to the restaurant that shares its name, Viva Lavita offers spectacular views of Klaipėda's waterfront, the spit's northern point, and the Baltic Sea beyond. To the east stretches Lithuania as far as the eye can see.

Nesė Pramogų Bankas CLUB
(☑8-870 055555; www.nesepb.lt; Turgaus gatvė 1; ☉24hr; ☎) The 'Nesė Entertainment Bank' has many faces: the complex entails an Irish pub, a whisky bar, a casino and a lounge bar. It's not the most interesting place to drink in Klaipėda, but there are four floors of options, some open around the clock.

Max Coffee CAFE
(☑8-657 30557; www.maxcoffee.lt; Turgaus gatvė 11; ☉7.30am-10pm Mon-Fri, from 9am Sat, 10am-9pm Sun; ☎) Coffee culture isn't that rich in Klaipėda, and you can do worse than this decent cafe, with cakes, muffins and wi-fi.

☆ Entertainment

Klaipėda Concert Hall CONCERT VENUE
(☑46-410 561; www.koncertusale.lt; Šaulių gatvė 36) Orchestral, choral and chamber performances are held in this handsome 19th-century building.

Kurpiai JAZZ
(☑46-410 555; Kurpių gatvė 1; entry on weekends €5; ☉7pm-1am Wed, to 2am Thu, to 4.30am Fri & Sat) This Old Town club has been a Klaipėda legend for years, opening way before the post-Independence bar scene mushroomed. Its cobbled terrace and dark old-world interior are the best place in town to catch live jazz.

Klaipėda State Musical Theatre THEATRE
(Muzikinis teatras; ☑46-397 404; www.muzikinis-teatras.lt; Danės gatvė 19; ☉11am-2pm & 3.30-6.30pm Tue-Sat, noon-5pm Sun) Founded in 1987, this Klaipėda institution stages all kinds of musical theatre, taking some productions on the road. It's also home to the Klaipėda Philharmonic.

🛍 Shopping

Klaipėda is known for its amber (stalls selling souvenirs dot Teatro aikštė), and it's possible to pick up fine linen and artwork in town.

Parko
ARTS
(☎8-652 11112; Turgaus gatvė 9; ⊗11am-5.30pm Mon-Fri, to 3pm Sat) Great if you're in the market for contemporary etchings, paintings or sculpture.

Pėda
ARTS
(☎46-410 710; www.karciauskas.com; Turgaus gatvė 10; ⊗11am-6pm Mon-Fri) Stunning sculpture and designs by contemporary artist Karčiauskas Vytautas.

Pegasas
BOOKS
(☎46-469 196; www.pegasas.lt; Taikos prospektas 61; ⊗10am-10pm) Arguably the best bookshop in Klaipėda, Pegasas is south of Old Town, in the Akropolis shopping centre.

ℹ Information

Jāņa sēta's Klaipėda Neringa map covers Klaipėda's northern beach suburbs, Smiltynė and Curonian Spit as well as central Klaipėda (1:10,000). Bookshops sell it for around €2.50.

Balt Tours (☎46-212 929; www.balttours. lt; Kepėjų gatvė 11a; ⊗10am-6pm Mon-Fri) If you're happier working with an all-in-one shop, Balt Tours can organise trips to the Curonian Lagoon, Nemunas Delta and other Baltic states, plus accommodation, cultural tours and more.

Klaipėda in Your Pocket (www.inyourpocket. com) Annual city guide published locally and sold in hotels and news kiosks for €1. Also available as a PDF download.

Krantas Travel (☎46-395 215; www.krantas.lt; Teatro gatvė 5; ⊗8am-6pm Mon-Fri, 9am-3pm Sat) Sells Sassnitz, Kiel and Karlshamn ferry tickets.

Post office (☎8-700 55400; www.post.lt; Liepų gatvė 16; ⊗8am-7pm Mon-Fri, 9am-4pm Sat) Klaipėda's principal post office occupies a delightful neo-Gothic red-brick building from the late 19th century.

Tourist office (☎46-412 186; www.klaipedainfo. lt; Turgaus gatvė 7; ⊗9am-7pm Mon-Fri, 10am-4pm Sat & Sun) Exceptionally efficient tourist office selling maps and locally published guidebooks, and arranging accommodation, tours and more. Operates reduced hours outside high season, closing on Sundays.

ℹ Getting There & Away

BOAT
From Klaipėda's **International Ferry Port** (☎46-395 051; www.dfdsseaways.lt; Perkėlos gatvė 10), **DFDS Seaways** (☎46-395 000; www.dfds seaways.lt; Šaulių gatvė 19) runs big passenger and car ferries regularly to Kiel and Sassnitz (in Germany) and to Karlshamn (in Sweden).

Smiltynės Perkėla (☎46-311 117; www.keltas. lt; Nemuno gatvė 8; adult/child over 7 yr €12/8.40) runs a quick ferry from Klaipėda's Old Ferry Port to and from Nida, stopping at Juodkrantė for 10 minutes. The trip takes about two hours, and kids under seven travel free. There are two daily services between late May and August, and only one, on Saturdays and Sundays, the rest of the year.

BUS
Ecolines (☎46-310 103; www.ecolines.net; Mažvydo alėja 1; ⊗9am-6pm Mon-Fri, 9am-3pm Sat) sells tickets for international destinations.

At the **bus station** (Autobusų Stotis; ☎46-411 547; www.klap.lt; Butkų Juzės 9; ⊗ticket office 3.30am-7.30pm) the information window has timetable information. Most buses to/from Juodkrantė and Nida depart from the ferry landing at Smiltynė on Curonian Spit.

Services to/from Klaipėda bus station include the following:

Kaliningrad (€11, 3½ hours, one daily)
Kaunas (€14, 2¾ to four hours, 20 daily)
Kretinga (€1.70, 30 to 50 minutes, half-hourly between 6.25am and 9.30pm)
Liepāja (€5.40, 1¾ hours, one daily)
Nida (€3.40, 1½ hours, seven daily from Smiltynė)
Palanga (€1.80, 30 minutes, 22 daily)
Pärnu (€35, 8¾ hours, three daily via Rīga)
Rīga (€19, five hours, eight buses daily)
Šiauliai (€11, three hours, eight daily)
Tallinn (€41, 10 hours, three buses daily via Rīga)
Vilnius (€18, four to 5½ hours, 17 daily)

TRAIN
The **train station** (☎8-700 55111; www.litrail.lt; Priestočio gatvė 1; ⊗ticket office 6.10am-7pm), 150m from the bus station, has an unusual helmeted clock tower and a moving sculpture in front.

Daily services include three trains to/from Vilnius (€18, four hours) and five trains to/from Šiauliai (€7, two to three hours) and Kretinga (€1.70, 30 minutes).

ℹ Getting Around

BICYCLE
Baltic Cycle (☎8-615 91773; www.bicycle. lt; Naujoji Uosto gatvė 3; per day €12; ⊗9am-7pm May-Sep, by reservation Oct-Apr) Handy to pick up two wheels to see Klaipėda or Curonian Spit.

BOAT

Everything about **Smiltynė Perkėla** (www.keltas.lt) – timetables, fares, newsflashes – is online.

The passenger ferry for Smiltynė (principal point of access for Curonian Spit) leaves from the **Old Ferry Port** (Senoji perkėla; ☑ 46-311 117; www.keltas.lt; Danės gatvė 1; per passenger/bicycle €0.90/free): look for signs to 'Neringa'. It docks on the eastern side of Smiltynė, at the start of the Nida road. Ferries sail at least every half-hour between 6.30am and midnight June to August (at least hourly until 11pm the rest of the year). The crossing takes five minutes and a return passenger fare is €0.80 per person; bicycles and children under the age of seven sail for free.

Year-round, vehicles can use the **New Ferry Port** (Naujoji perkėla; ☑ 46-311 117; www.keltas.lt; Nemuno gatvė 8; per passenger/car €0.80/11.50, bicycle free), around 2km south of the mouth of the Danė River. Look for road signs to 'Neringa'. Ferries sail half-hourly between 5.40am and 1.10am and dock on Curonian Spit 2.5km south of the Smiltynė ferry landing. Bus 1 links Klaipėda city centre with the New Ferry Port.

BUS

Local bus tickets cost €0.64 from news kiosks or €0.70 from the driver. Bus 8 (known for pickpockets) links the train station with Manto gatvė, the city centre and the Turgaus stop, on Taikos prospektas. Bus 11 links the bus station with Manto gatvė. Minibuses, which follow the same routes, can be flagged down on the street and cost €0.70 (or €1 before 6am and after 11pm).

Curonian Spit National Park

☑ 469 / POP 3100

Curonian Spit National Park (Kuršių Nerijos Nacionalinis Parkas) was established in 1991 to protect the rare ecosystems found on Curonian Spit, including the sand dunes, the Curonian Lagoon and the surrounding sea. It covers most of the Lithuanian section of the spit, running from the village of Smiltynė in the north down to Nida, 50km to the south.

The park is refreshingly wild and undeveloped. Pine forests populated by deer, elk and wild boar cover about 70% of the park. Sand dunes make up 25% of it. Just a small fraction is urban, namely four main villages – Nida, Juodkrantė, Pervalka and Preila – known collectively on maps and signs as 'Neringa'. The main industry is tourism, centred on the villages of Nida and Juodkrantė, a double-edged sword that yields both its main source of income and its biggest environmental threat.

Up until the first decades of the 20th century, most of the spit was German territory. The area used to have a hugely magnetic attraction for German exiles, and continues to attract a large number of German tourists to this day.

These days, Lithuania shares the spit with the Russian-controlled Kaliningrad Region. A road runs the whole length of the spit all

LITHUANIA CURONIAN SPIT NATIONAL PARK

SHIFTING SANDS & DELICATE DUNES

Legend has it that motherly sea giantess Neringa created the spit, lovingly carrying armfuls of sand in her apron to form a protected harbour for the local fishing folk. The truth is just as enchanting. The waves and winds of the Baltic Sea let sand accumulate in its shallow waters near the coast 5000 or 6000 years ago to create an original beauty found nowhere else.

Massive deforestation in the 16th century started the sands shifting. Trees were felled for timber, leaving the sands free to roam unhindered at the whim of the strong coastal winds. At a pace of 20m a year, the sands swallowed 14 villages in the space of three centuries.

It was soon dubbed the 'Sahara of Lithuania' due to its desert state; drastic action was needed. In 1768 an international commission set about replanting. Today this remains a priority of the national park authorities. Deciduous forest (mainly birch groves) covers 20% of the national park; coniferous forest, primarily pine and mountain pine trees, constitutes a further 53%. Alder trees can be found on 2.6 sq km (3% of the park's area). Lattices of branches and wooden stakes have pinned down the sand.

But the sands are still moving – at least 1m a year. Slowly the spit is drifting into the Baltic Sea. Each tourist who scrambles and romps on Parnidis Dune – the only remaining free-drifting dune – meanwhile pushes down several tonnes of sand. With 1.5 million people visiting the dunes each year, the threat posed by them wandering off designated paths – not to mention the risk of forest fire – is high.

The dunes are also shrinking. Winds, waves and humans have reduced them by 20m in 40 years. Its precious beauty may yet be lost forever.

Curonian Spit National Park

0 ——— 5 km
0 ——— 2.5 miles

LITHUANIA CURONIAN SPIT NATIONAL PARK

Nida Jazz Marathon   JAZZ
(www.nidajazz.lt) Held over three days in late
July or early August, this festival culminates
in a jam session each night.

❶ Information

Kopos (www.kopos.lt) Searchable listings of
accommodation in Nida, Juodkrantė and Preila.

Visit Neringa (www.visitneringa.com)
Well-maintained site covering most of Neringa's
attractions and facilities.

❶ Getting There & Around

Curonian Spit is accessible only via boat or
ferry (there are no bridges linking the spit to
the mainland). From Klaipėda, two ferries run
regularly: a passenger ferry, known as the 'Old
Ferry', goes to Smiltynė; and a vehicle ferry,
the 'New Ferry', connects to a point on the spit
around 2km south of Smiltynė. The New Ferry
departs from a port 2km south of Klaipėda's
Old Town.

Regular buses run to villages on the spit,
including Nida (€3.40) and Juodkrantė (€1.40),
but these depart from **Smiltynė** (Smiltynės
gatvė), meaning you'll first have to use the passenger ferry to get to the bus.

If you've got the weather for it, cycling is a
great way to explore the spit. There is a well-
marked trail that runs the entire length of the
spit from Smiltynė to Nida via Juodkrantė
(about 50km). Hire bikes in Klaipėda and take
them across the lagoon via the passenger ferry
for free.

You can also reach Kaliningrad (south) in Russia from here. The Russian border post is 3km
south of Nida on the main road. Don't contem-
plate this without the necessary Russian visa
and paperwork.

the way to Kaliningrad and indeed, with the
proper paperwork, it's possible to combine
a visit to the spit with a mini-trip to Russia.

✹ Festivals & Events

The summer season – mid-June to the end
of August – is lined end to end with festivals.

International Folk Festival   MUSIC
Showcasing Lithuanian and European folk
music, and held on a weekend in late June,
this folk fiesta swamps Nida with visitors.
Book accommodation ahead.

Smiltynė

📍 46 / POP 50

The small village of Smiltynė is a hop, skip and five-minute ferry ride away across the thin strait that divides Klaipėda from Curonian Spit. This strait-side patch of paradise – packed on summer weekends with Klaipėda residents – has beautiful beaches, sandy dunes and sweet-smelling pine forests.

◎ Sights & Activities

Grab your Speedos and take a footpath through pine forests across the spit's 1km-wide tip to a bleached-white sandy beach. From the ferry landing, walk straight ahead across the car park, then bear left towards Nida; on your right a large sign marks a smooth footpath that leads through pine forest to a women's beach (Moterų pliažas; 1km), mixed beach (Bendras pliažas; 700m) and men's beach (Vyrų pliažas; 900m). Nude or topless bathing is the norm on single-sex beaches.

Lithuania Sea Museum   AQUARIUM
(Lietuvos Jūrų Muziejus; 📍 46-490 740; www.juru. muziejus.lt; Smiltynės gatvė 3; adult/student €9/6; ⊙10.30am-6.30pm Tue-Sun Jun-Aug; 🚻) This popular museum, set in a 19th-century fort, has some fascinating stuffed sea animals, aquariums and live shows featuring seals, sea lions and dolphins. Admission drops to €7/4 between September and April, but opening hours also contract.

Exposition of the National Park
of the Curonian Spit   MUSEUM
(Kuršių nerijos nacionalinis parkas gamtos muziejus ekspozicija; 📍 46-402 256; www.nerija.lt; Smiltynės gatvė 11; adult/child €1.16/0.58; ⊙11am-6pm Wed-Sun May-Sep) Dedicated to the flora and fauna of the park, this museum is spread across three wooden houses. Alongside stuffed examples of wild pigs, badgers, beavers and elk there's a large collection of insects, and information on measures being taken to protect the dunes.

Ethnographic Sea
Fishermen's Farmstead   MUSEUM
(Smiltynės gatvė; ⊙dusk-dawn) `FREE` This farmstead, with its collection of traditional 19th-century buildings (granary, dwelling house, cellar, cattle shed and so on), offers a glimpse of traditional Curonian fishing life. Outside are old fishing vessels to explore, including three Baltic Sea fishing trawlers built in the late 1940s and a 1935 *kurėnas* (a traditional flat-bottomed Curonian fishing boat).

ℹ Information

Curonian Spit National Park Visitors Centre
(Smiltynė) (📍 46-402 256; www.nerija.lt; Smiltynės gatvė 11, Smiltynė; ⊙9am-5pm Sun-Thu, to 6pm Fri & Sat) The visitors centre is packed with information about the park's ecology and attractions, and can arrange guided nature tours (€20 to €34, two to eight people). It closes for lunch between noon and 1pm, and on weekends between September and April.

Juodkrantė

📍 469 / POP 720

The long, thin village of Juodkrantė (ywad-kran-tey) – 'Black Shore', or Schwarzort to Germans – is 20km south of Smiltynė and is spread out along the lagoon. The pace of life here is slow even in the height of summer, and the sweet smell of smoked fish follows you wherever you go.

◎ Sights

Contemporary stone sculptures and a silky-smooth promenade sidle up to the water's edge, while the main road – Liudviko Rėzos gatvė – is lined with holiday homes and quaint *žuvis* (fish) outlets.

At Juodkrantė's northern end is an area around a fishing harbour known as **Amber Bay** (Gintaro įlanka), recalling the amber excavated in the village in three separate clusters – 2250 tonnes in all – in 1854 to 1855 and 1860. The spit is about 1.5km wide at this point and the fine stretch of forest – good for spotting elk in the early morning and evening – is among the loveliest you will find on the peninsula.

★ Cormorant &
Heron Colony   BIRD SANCTUARY
Just south of Juodkrantė is Lithuania's largest colony of grey herons and cormorants, observed here since the 19th century. Wooden steps lead from the road to a viewing platform where the panorama of thousands of nests amid pine trees – not to mention the noise of the 6500-strong colony – is astonishing. Fisherman blame the cormorants in particular for reduced catches, but both species are protected.

Cormorants arrive in early February (herons a little later) to rebuild their nests. By May chicks are screaming for food. Starlings,

SPIT RULES

→ Neringa municipality entrance fee: motorbike/car July to August €5/10, September to June €5/5.

→ Speed limit: 50km/h in villages, 70km/h on open roads.

→ Don't romp in the dunes, pick flowers or stray off designated footpaths.

→ Don't damage flora or fauna, mess with bird nests or light campfires.

→ Don't pitch a tent or park a camper overnight anywhere in the park.

→ Don't fish without a permit; purchase them at tourist offices.

→ Beware of elk and wild boar crossing the road, and don't feed them!

→ Break a rule and risk an on-the-spot fine of up to €150.

→ In case of forest fire, call ☑ 01, ☑ 112, Smiltyne ☑ 8-656 35025, Juodkrantė ☑ 8-656 34998, Préila and Pervalka ☑ 8-687 27758, Nida ☑ 8-656 34992.

thrushes, warblers, and grey, spotted and black woodpeckers can also be seen here.

Witches' Hill
SCULPTURE TRAIL

(Ragany Kalnas; ⛢) Carved by local artists and growing in number since 1979, the Witches' Hill is a collection of devils, witches and other fantastical and grotesque wooden carvings from Lithuanian folklore that skulk along a wooded sculpture trail ranging from fairy tale to playful (slide down a giant devil's tongue) to nightmare. It's signposted immediately south of Liudviko Rēzos gatvē 46.

Weathervane Gallery
MUSEUM

(Vetrungiy Galerija; ☑ 8-698 27283; www.autentic.lt; L Rēzos gatvē 13; ☻ 9am-7pm May-Sep, 10am-5pm Apr & Oct) The Weathervane Gallery, a museum selling authentic Curonian weathervanes and amber jewellery, is worth a visit.

Evangelical-Lutheran church
CHURCH

(Liudviko Rēzos gatvē 56) This red-brick German church at the southern end of Juodkrantē was built in 1885.

🛌 Sleeping & Eating

Many places close down during the 'cold' season (October to April) so be sure to book in advance to avoid disappointment. Smoked fish is sold all along Liudviko Rēzos gatvē and self-caterers are limited to an expensive store (open 8am to 10pm) near the start of the Witches' Hill trail.

Vila Flora
GUESTHOUSE €€

(☑ 469-53 024; www.vilaflora.lt; Kalno gatvē 7a; d/tr €80/115; ℗) This delightful 19th-century

timber villa in the heart of Juodkrantē is open all year. It has 15 bright, stylish rooms, some with balconies and conservatories. The restaurant on the ground floor is the best in town, offering traditional Lithuanian with a twist. Prices are cheaper in winter, but the restaurant, sadly, closes.

Kurēnas
HOTEL €€

(☑ 8-698 02711; kurenas@gmail.com; Liudviko Rēzos gatvē 10; r from €75; ℗⏱) Named after the traditional flat-bottomed Curonian fishing boat, this busy and bright cafe-bar with street-side terrace sports large, individually decorated rooms with wooden floors and clean white walls. Reserve one with a balcony overlooking the lagoon (and pay half the price between September and May).

Hotel Ažuolynas
HOTEL €€

(☑ 469-53 310; www.hotelazuolynas.lt; Liudviko Rēzos gatvē 54; s/d €76/114; ℗⏱) This modern hotel lacks character, but has decent rooms and all the facilities – tennis courts, pool table, sauna, swimming pool – that smaller places lack. It's open all year, and prices in the low season (between September and May) fall appreciably.

Pamario Takas
LITHUANIAN €€

(☑ 8-650 97491; L Rēzos gatvē 42; mains €8; ☻ 10am-midnight) This fun, family-run restaurant is set in a quaint wooden cottage with accompanying flower-filled garden. They make their own bread, and the food is really good.

ℹ Information

Post Office (L Rēzos gatvē 54; ☻ 8.30am-4.30pm Mon-Fri) Closes for lunch for an hour from noon.

Tourist Information Centre (☑ 469-53 490; juodkrante@visit neringa.lt; Liudviko Rėzos gatvė 8; ☺10am-8pm Mon-Sat, to 3pm Sun) Located opposite the bus stop; has accommodation and activity information. Closes for lunch between 1pm and 2pm; has reduced hours (including closing on Sundays) from September to May.

❶ Getting There & Away

Buses to/from Nida (€2.30, 45 minutes) and Smiltynė (€1.40, 15 to 20 minutes) stop in Juodkrantė. Bicycle hire (€3/12 per hour/day) can be found near the tourist office.

Juodkrantė to Nida

Heading south from Juodkrantė the road switches to the western side of the Spit. The 16.8-sq-km **Naglių Strict Nature Reserve** (Naglių rezervatas) here protects the Dead or Grey Dunes (named after the greyish flora that covers them) that stretch 8km south and are 2km wide; a marked footpath leads into the reserve from the main road.

Shifting sands in the mid-19th century forced villagers here to flee to **Pervalka** and **Preila** on the east coast, accessible by side roads from the main road. Pine-forested **Vecekrugas Dune** (67.2m), the peninsula's highest dune, south of Preila, stands on a ridge called Old Inn Hill – named after an inn that stood at the foot of the dune before being buried by sand; view it from the Juodkrantė–Nida cycling path.

🛏 Sleeping & Eating

Accommodation and eating options are limited here; don't count on cash machines.

Kuršmarių Vila   HOTEL **€€**
(☑8-685 56317; kursmariuvila@gmail.com; Preilos gatvė 93; d €70; ℗) At the southern end of Preila is thatch-roofed Kuršmarių Vila, which offers bed and board all year. The fishing family that runs it produces great fish from its old smokehouse, and can introduce you to ice-fishing in winter (if you can handle the cold). The price for a double plummets to €30 in the low season.

Karalienė Luizė   LITHUANIAN **€€**
(☑8-6121 2111; Pervalkos gatvė 29e; mains €8-11) Right on the lagoon at Pervalka, this welcome respite for cyclists on the Nida–Juodkrantė trail combines a decent restaurant (in summer) with well-appointed rooms.

Nida

☑469 / POP 1650
Lovely Nida (Nidden in German) is the largest settlement on the Lithuanian half of Curonian Spit; it's also the spit's tourist hot spot. Remnants of a former life as an old-fashioned fishing village are plain to see in its pretty wooden cottages and harbour jammed with seafaring vessels, but these days Nida makes its money from holidaymakers and busloads of Germans exploring historical East Prussia.

Natural beauty abounds here, and whitesand beaches are only a 2km walk away through hazy pine forests. To the south is the most impressive dune on the peninsula, Parnidis Dune (Parnidžio kopa), which has steps up to its 52m summit from where there are stunning views of rippling, untouched dunes stretching into Russia.

From the late 19th century a colony of artists drew inspiration from the area. Nida developed as a tourist resort and there were five hotels by the 1930s, when the German writer Thomas Mann (1875–1955) had a summer home built here. In 1965 French philosopher Jean-Paul Sartre and companion Simone de Beauvoir were granted special permission by Khrushchev to spend five days on the dunes, and Lithuanian photographer Antanas Sutkus was allowed to shoot the pair in the sand.

Nida is 48km from Klaipėda and 3km from the Russian border; the town stretches for 2km, but its centre is at the southern end, behind the harbour.

◉ Sights & Activities

There's plenty to keep you occupied on land and water, or you could avoid it all and simply chill out. Outside the high season, scour the beaches for speckles of amber washed up on the shores during the spring and autumn storms, and in the depths of winter brave the lagoon and ice-fish for smelt and burbot.

NORTH OF THE HARBOUR

Find breathtaking views of Parnidis Dune at the harbour; from there a pleasant waterfront lagoon promenade stretches for over 1km.

Neringa History Museum   MUSEUM
(Neringos Istorijos Muziejus; ☑469-52 372; www.neringosmuziejus.lt; Pamario gatvė 53; adult/child €0.58/0.29; ☺10am-6pm) Black-and-white photographs of more rough-and-ready days fill the thoughtfully laid-out displays here, where Nida's tale from the Stone Age to 1939 is told. Particularly brilliant are the images of local

Nida

hunters biting a crow's neck to kill the bird, followed by them a taking a shot of vodka to dull the taste. Eating crows and seagulls' eggs was common on the spit in the 17th to 19th centuries, when continually drifting sands rendered previously arable land useless.

Thomas Mann Memorial Museum   MUSEUM
(Tomo Mano memorialinis muziejus; ☑ 469-52 260; www.mann.lt; Skruzdynės gatvė 17; adult/child €1.74/0.87; ☺ 10am-6pm daily Jun-Aug, 10am-5pm Tue-Sat Sep-May) The German writer and Nobel laureate Thomas Mann used to own this beautifully situated villa, which is now a museum. Mann spent each summer between 1930 and 1932 here, with his wife and children, before fleeing Germany in 1933.

Hermann Blode Museum   MUSEUM
(☑ 469-52 219; Skruzdynės gatvė 2; adult/child €0.58/0.29; ☺ 9am-7pm Sep-Mar) This small museum, occupying a hotel dating to 1867, commemorates the famous artists that have stayed here: Thomas Mann, Ludwig Passarge and (not least) Engelbert Humperdinck.

Evangelical-Lutheran Church   CHURCH
(Pamario gatvė 43; ☺ 10am-6pm) This graceful red-brick church dates to 1888. Its peaceful woodland cemetery is pinpricked with *krikstai* – crosses carved from wood to help the deceased ascend to heaven more easily.

Amber Gallery   GALLERY
(Gintaro Galerija; ☑ 469-52 573; www.ambergallery. lt; Pamario gatvė 20; adult/child €1.20/0.60;

☺ 10am-7pm Apr-Oct) In an old fisherman's hut on the north side of town is this museum, with a small amber garden and exceptional pieces of amber jewellery. It runs a second gallery, Kurėnas, in a striking glass box encased in an old wooden boat near the harbour.

Nemunas Delta Tours   BOAT TOUR
(www.visitneringa.com; Nida harbour; tours €35) If you have the time, and particularly if the weather is fine, a visit to the stunning Nemunas Delta, with its waterbirds, whispering rushes and gleaming carpets of lilies, is not to be missed. Numerous operators lining the pier at Nida harbour sail across the lagoon, throwing in lunch at Mingė and an excursion to the Ventės Ragas Ornithological Station. Tours leave around 10am, and take six hours.

Velo Nida   BICYCLE RENTAL
(☑ 8-682 14798; Naglių gatvė 18e; per day €12; ☺ 9am-9pm May-Oct) Behind the bus station you'll find this well-run bike-hire place. It has a branch in Juodkrantė, where bikes can be left, exchanged or repaired, and luggage transport can be arranged.

Kuršis   SAILING
(☑ 8-686 65242; Nida harbour; adult/child per hour €8/5) This handsome replica of a *kurėnas*, a traditional 19th-century fishing boat, takes passengers on lagoon tours between June and September.

Nida

Juodkrantė (28km);
Smiltynė (47km);
Klaipėda (48km)

Audrone (200m);
Thomas Mann
Memorial Museum (200m)

Kuverto gatvė

Pamario gatvė

Curonian
Lagoon
(Kuršių marios)

Urbas Hill
Lighthouse

Beach
(1.3km)

Bus
Station

Harbour

Taikos gatvė

Nidos Kempingas
(800m); Beach (1.3km);
Felikso (1.3km)

Lotmiškio gatvė

Naglių gatvė

Curonian Spit
National Park
Visitors Centre (Nida)

Harbour

PARNIDIS
DUNE

Parnidis Dune (800m)

WEST OF THE HARBOUR

All westward routes lead to the beach. Or you can turn north off Taikos gatvė opposite the post office, folllow the street as it turns left after 150m, and climb the path up the hill to the 29.3m **Urbas Hill Lighthouse** (closed to visitors). Continue 700m along the path behind the lighthouse to come out on a straight path that leads back down to the main road and, 400m beyond that, to the beach.

A less adventurous option is to follow Taikos gatvė westward until it meets the main Smiltynė–Nida road, then continue in the same direction along a paved footpath (signposted) through pine forest until you hit sand.

SOUTH OF THE HARBOUR

To the south of town are two or three streets of fishing cottages with pretty flower-filled gardens.

Beyond Lotmiškio gatvė a path leads along the coastline and through a wooded area to a meadow, dubbed 'Silence Valley'. Here walkers can pick up the **Parnidis Cognitive Path** (Parnidžio pažintinis takas), a 1.8km nature trail leading to the mighty Parnidis Dune itself.

From here, the Kaliningrad border is 3km south. If you stick to the designated wooden footpaths, you have no chance of wandering into Russia by mistake. From the dune, the Parnidis Cognitive Path continues past the lighthouse and pine forest to Taikos gatvė.

★ **Parnidis Dune**   LANDMARK
(Parnidžio kopos) The panorama of coastline, forests and this unforested, 7km thread of golden sand snaking south into Russia is unforgettable. Make sure you don't stray from the wooden boardwalk as the dune is very fragile. At the bottom of the flight of 180 steps, two photographs are displayed – one taken in 1960, the other in 2002. The difference in dune height – 20m in 40 years – is a warning to those keen to romp in the sand.

Park authorities have left the smashed remains of the granite sundial that stood 12m tall on the 52m dune peak until 1999, when a hurricane sent it crashing to the ground as a symbol of 'nature's uncontrollable forces' – another warning to wannabe sand rompers.

Ethnographic Fisherman's Museum   MUSEUM
(Žvejo Etnografinė Sodyba; ☑ 469-52 372; Naglių gatvė 4; adult/child €0.58/0.29; ☺10am-6pm) The Ethnographic Museum is a peek at Nida in the 19th century, with original weathervanes decorating the garden, and rooms inside arranged as they were a couple of centuries ago. Closes on Sundays and Mondays between September and May.

🛏 Sleeping

Prices in Nida fluctuate wildly between high season (June to August) and the rest of the year. Rates can fall by half in the 'cold season', and some places close down altogether (be sure to call ahead).

Nidos Kempingas   CAMPGROUND €
(☑469-52 045; www.kempingas.lt; Taikos gatvė 45a; tent/adult/child €5/6.50/3.50, d/apt €64/96; P 🔐 🚲 🏀) Set in pine forest at the foot of a path that leads to Parnidis Dune, this spruced-up camping ground has accommodation to suit all budgets. Double rooms have satellite TV and fridge, and apartments are equipped for self-caterers. There are also bikes for hire, and basketball and tennis courts to use.

Miško Namas   GUESTHOUSE €€
(☑ 469-52 290; www.miskonamas.com; Pamario gatvė 11; d €75, 2-/4-person apt €95/100; P @ 🚲) This immaculately maintained guesthouse is picked out in Curonian blue-and-white and strewn with flowers. Every room has a fridge, a sink and a kettle, and some have fully fledged kitchens and balconies. Guests can cook meals in a communal kitchen, hire bicycles, choose books from the small library or laze in the garden.

Vila Banga   GUESTHOUSE €€
(☑8-686 08073; www.nidosbanga.lt; Pamario gatvė 2; d/apt €95/115; 🚲) This pristine wooden establishment with bright-blue shutters and perfect thatched roof is a gem of a guesthouse. It has seven comfortable rooms in its pinewood interior, a sauna, and bikes for rent (€9 per day).

Naglis   GUESTHOUSE €€
(☑8-699 33682; www.naglis.lt; Naglių gatvė 12; d/apt €75/100; P) This charming guesthouse in a wooden house near the main port is full of smiles. Doubles comprise two rooms, and some have a door opening out to the table-dotted, tree-shaded garden. There's a dining room and kitchen for guests to share; one room has a fireplace. The guesthouse hires out bikes (€2.40/9 per hour/day).

Inkaro Kaimas   GUESTHOUSE €€
(☑469-52 123; www.inkarokaimas.lt; Naglių gatvė 26-1; d/apt €64/87; P) Blue pillars prop up this beautifully maintained red wooden house on the water's edge. Accommodation is in individual apartments, each with its own entrance. The place dates from 1901

SEAFARING WEATHERVANES

Nowhere are Juodkrantė's and Nida's seafaring roots better reflected than on top of the 19th-century wooden cottages that speckle the spit villages. A ruling in 1844 saw weathervanes or cocks used to identify fishing vessels. They quickly became ornamentation for rooftops. Originally made from tin and later from wood, these 60cm x 30cm plaques were fastened to the boat mast so other fishermen could see where a *kurėnas* (Neringa boat) had sailed. Each village had its own unique symbol – a black-and-white geometrical design – incorporated in the weathercock and then embellished with an eclectic assortment of mythical cut-outs; see the different designs first-hand in the Neringa History Museum.

and a couple of pine-furnished rooms boast a balcony overlooking the lagoon.

Poilsis Nidojė
GUESTHOUSE €€

(📞 8-686 31698; www.neringahotels.lt; Naglių gatvė 11; d/apt €80/108; 🅿🛜) A wooden-house favourite, Poilsis Nidojė sports spacious yet cosy doubles and apartments with kitchenettes. Interior design is rustic, an optional breakfast (€8) is served in the shared kitchen, and guests can cook up dinner on a barbecue in the pretty garden.

Audrone
APARTMENT €€

(📞 8-619 61943; Skruzdynės gatvė 14-4; apt €100; 🅿) Located next to the Thomas Mann Memorial Museum, this apartment is attached to a private house and has enormous rooms and really stunning views of the lagoon. Prices are lower outside July and August.

Hotel Jūratė
HOTEL €€

(📞 469-52 300; www.hotel-jurate.lt; Pamario gatvė 3; s/d from €47/67; 🅿🛜) This hotel looks and feels like a sanatorium but its supremely central position and relatively cheap rooms help to balance things out. Soviet kitsch-spotters will be thrilled to know that the hotel's most recent facelift didn't get rid of the glitter cement on the corridor walls.

✕ Eating

Opening hours generally follow the Nida standard: 10am to 10pm daily mid-May to mid-September. Out of season, little is open.

★ Tik Pas Jona
SEAFOOD €

(📞 8-620 82084; Naglių gatvė 6-1; mains €3; ◷10am-10pm daily Apr-Nov, Sat & Sun only Dec-Mar) This unfussy place has to be the best in Neringa to eat the Lagoon's famous smoked fish. Grab a bream straight from the smoker, sit on the terrace with a beer, rye bread, lemon and fresh tomato, watch the boats come into harbour, and make a mess of yourself.

Laumė
EUROPEAN €

(📞 469-52 335; www.nidospastoge.com; Pamario gatvė 24-3a; mains €5-7; ◷10am-midnight Jun-Aug) Laumė is an unpretentious little place with great views of the lagoon from its flower-girt terrace. Alongside basic Lithuanian staples you'll find pizzas, pastas, salads and the like. Closed outside the summer season.

Nidos Seklyčia
EUROPEAN €€

(📞 469-50 000; www.neringaonline.lt; Lotmiškio gatvė 1; mains €12-17; ◷10am-11pm; 🛜) Open all year, this beautifully situated restaurant,

almost in the lee of the Parnidis Dune, is one of Nida's best. Prices can seem a little steep by Lithuanian standards, but the food, especially the fish, is really good.

Užeiga Sena Sodyba
LITHUANIAN €€

(📞 8-652 12345; www.senasodyba.lt; Naglių gatvė 6; mains €5-8; ◷11am-10pm Mon-Fri) The selection of fish dishes at this delightful wooden cottage restaurant is impressive – and inviting – but it's the pancakes that win the day. If you're here during berry season you'll be in gastronomic heaven.

Grill House'as
EUROPEAN €€

(📞 8-614 15470; Naglių gatvė 14a; mains €6-10; ◷10am-midnight) A good option for a burger, steak or salad (or just a beer), the Grill House also has a terrace with harbour views, for the sunny season.

Kuršis
LITHUANIAN €€

(📞 8-612 18868; Naglių gatvė 29; mains €6-8; ◷8am-midnight; 🛜) A dependable allrounder, Kuršis pumps out omelettes and scrambled eggs at breakfast time, salads and seafood and lunch, and *cepelinai*, pork, pasta and other heavier fare in the evening. It runs shortened hours outside summer.

Ešerinė
LITHUANIAN €€

(📞 469-52 757; www.eserine.lt; Naglių gatvė 2; mains €8-13; ◷10am-midnight) Vaguely Polynesian in look, with its thatched pavilion and carved wood, Ešerinė offers a vast waterfront terrace (with views of the Parnidis Dune) and excellent fish and Lithuanian food. It's one of the most popular places in town.

Pastoge
LITHUANIAN €€

(📞 469-51 149; www.nidospastoge.com; GD Kuverto gatvė 2; mains €8-11; ◷10am-midnight) This weather-darkened timber A-frame by the lagoon is an ideal setting for a restaurant. Lithuanian dishes such as halibut with potatoes share menu-space with delights from further afield, such as Georgian chicken *tabaka* (a whole chicken, pressed and pan-fried). Closes outside the summer season.

🍸 Drinking & Nightlife

People generally don't come to Nida to party, but there are a few options.

Faksas
BAR

(📞 8-648 53665; Taikos gatvė 32a; ◷3pm-4am summer) This party cabin in the pinewoods is one of the few real nightspots in Nida. Proclaiming itself 'Friendly to rockers, bikers, and freaky people', Faksas puts on live acts in summer, and the beer and shots are usually flowing.

In Vino BAR
(☑8-655 77997; www.invino.lt; Taikos gatvė 32; ☺10am-midnight May-Sep) Perched in an unlikely position above a block of flats set back from the main road is this wine bar, one of Nida's few dedicated drinking establishments. Inside is cosy, lit during daylight hours by picture windows, while outside the rooftop terrace overlooks the Parnidis Dune.

Kolibris BAR
(☑469-52 557; Naglių gatvė 14a; ☺9am-11pm) Kolibris is a dependable *kavinė-baras* (cafe-bar) near the harbour, good for a beer in the tented terrace after a day on the water, or for grilled pork, *šaltibarščiai* (cold beetroot soup), dumplings and other Lithuanian classics.

☆ Entertainment

Agila Cultural Centre LIVE PERFORMANCE
(☑469-52 538; www.visitneringa.com; Taikos gatvė 4) The centre organises festivals, events, folk performances, discos and more.

🛍 Shopping

Smoked Fish Outlet FOOD
(Rūkyta žuvis; Naglių gatvė 18; ☺10am-10pm May-Sep) Sells *ungurys* (long slippery eel), *stark-is* (pikeperch), *stinta* (smelt), *ešerys* (perch) and *karšis* (bream).

Market MARKET
(opposite Naglių gatvė 17; ☺variable, usually 10am-10pm) In season the one-stall market sells plastic cups of wild strawberries, blueberries and other berries picked fresh from the forest.

ℹ Information

Curonian Spit National Park Visitors Centre (Nida) (Lankytojų centras; ☑469-51 256; www.nerija.lt; Naglių gatvė 8; ☺9am-5pm Mon-Wed, to 6pm Thu-Sun) A wealth of information about the park, the centre can also arrange guided nature tours (€20 to €34, two to eight people). It closes for lunch between noon and 1pm, and on weekends between September and April.

Eurovaistinė (☑8-005 0005; www.eurovaistine.lt; Naglių gatvė 29a; ☺9am-7pm Mon-Fri, 10am-4pm Sat, to 3pm Sun) Pharmacy in the middle of Nida.

Police (☑469-52 202; Taikos gatvė 5)

Post Office (www.post.lt; Taikos gatvė 13; ☺8.30am-4.30pm Mon-Fri) Neringa's main post office. Closed for lunch from 1pm to 2pm.

Šiaulių Bankas (www.sb.lt; Naglių gatvė 18e; ☺8am-4pm Mon-Fri) Closed for lunch between 12.30pm and 1.30pm.

Tourist Information Centre (☑469-52 345; www.visitneringa.com; Taikos gatvė 4; ☺9am-7pm Mon-Sat, 10am-5pm Sun; 🛜) Sells maps, books accommodation and stocks loads of

---

BY BIKE FROM NIDA TO JUODKRANTĖ

One of Lithuania's best cycling trips follows Curonian Spit end to end, connecting in the south with a path that leads into the Kaliningrad Region and to the north with another trail that heads off eventually to Palanga and onward towards Latvia. The trail forms part of Eurovelo cycling route No 10, the 'Baltic Sea Circuit'. For our money, arguably the best section of the entire trail runs the 30km from Nida to Juodkrantė.

This part of the trail passes some of the spit's greatest natural treasures, including the Vecekrugas Dune and an authentic fish smoker in Preila. Footpaths lead from the cycling path to Karvaičiai Reservation, where entire villages were buried by sand. Cycling the path also provides the perfect opportunity to spot wild boar and elk, something not so easily accomplished while seated in a car or bus.

To pick up the path in Nida, follow the red-paved cycling track north along the lagoon promenade and, after passing the Thomas Mann Memorial Museum, follow the track left around the corner onto Puvynės gatvė. On the road, turn immediately right and follow it for 3.5km until you see a dirt track forking left into pine forest: this is the start of the cycling path, complete with 0.0km marker.

Heading north, at Pervalka you can cycle through or around the village (the quicker route), arriving 4km later at the entrance to the Naglių Strict Nature Reserve. Shortly afterward, the cycling path crosses the main road to take cyclists along the opposite (western) side of the spit for the remaining 9km to Juodkrantė.

The first 5km snake beneath pine trees alongside the main road and the final 4km skirt sand dunes. Once you're out of the reserve, leap into the sea for a quick cool-down before the last leg – an uphill slog through forested dunes to arrive in Juodkrantė.

information (including photographs) of private rooms and flats to rent. Can also advise on ferries to and from the Nemunas Delta. Operates reduced hours September to May.

ⓘ Getting There & Away

The Nida **bus station** (☏ 469-54 859; www.mare travel.lt; Naglių gatvė 18e; ☉ 7.45am-7.45pm, to 4.45pm 1 Sep-14 Jun) has services every one or two hours to and from Smiltynė (€3.40, one hour) between 6am and 8pm, stopping en route in Juodkrantė (€2.30, 35 minutes). From Smiltynė take the passenger ferry to Klaipėda. For longer trips, there are two buses daily to Vilnius (€24, 5½ hours) and Kaunas (€19 4½ hours), and at 8.09am to Kaliningrad (€7, two hours).

Nemunas Delta

☏ 441

The low-lying, marsh-dotted eastern side of the Curonian Lagoon (Kuršių marios) could be the end of the world. Tourism has scarcely touched this remote, rural and isolated landscape where summer skies offer magnificent views of the spit's white dunes across the lagoon. In winter ice-fishers sit on the frozen lagoon – up to 12km wide in places – waiting for a smelt to bite.

The gateway into the extraordinary Nemunas Delta (Nemuno Delta), where the Nemunas River ends its 937km journey from its source in neighbouring Belarus, is Šilutė (population 21,000), a sleepy town an hours' drive south of Klaipėda. Rusnė Island, the largest island, covers 48 sq km and increases in size by 15cm to 20cm a year.

Boat is the main form of transport; villagers travel in and out of the park by an amphibious tractor from March to mid-May, when merciless spring floods plunge about 5% of the park under water. In 1994 floodwaters rose to 1.5m in places, although 40cm to 70cm is the norm.

From Nida there are seasonal boats across the lagoon to the delta settlement of Mingė (also called Minija after the river that forms the main 'street' through the village). No more than 100 people live in Mingė – dubbed the 'Venice of Lithuania' – and only a handful of people still speak Lietuvinkai, an ethnic dialect of Lithuanian distinct to the delta. The 19th-century riverside houses are made of wood with reed roofs and are protected architectural monuments.

A good way to explore this area is by bicycle; from Mingė a cycling track runs

around Lake Krokų Lanka, the largest lake in the park at 4km long and 3.3km wide.

◉ Sights & Activities

In the heart of the Nemunas Delta is Rusnė, on the island of the same name, 8km southwest of Šilutė, where the main stream divides. There's not much to do here but picnic on the pretty riverbanks and visit two small museums.

Dike-protected polders (land reclaimed from the sea) cover the park, the first polder being built in 1840 to protect Rusnė. Many lower polders still flood seasonally and serve as valuable spawning grounds for various fish species (there are some 60 in the park). Close by, on the shores of Lake Dumblė, is Lithuania's lowest point, 1.3m below sea level.

Ventės Ragas (Ventė Horn) is a sparsely inhabited area on the south-pointing promontory of the delta, which, with its dramatic nature and uplifting isolation, is beautifully wild. A Teutonic Order castle was built here in the 1360s to protect shipping, only for it to collapse within a couple of hundred years due to severe storms on this isolated point. The church was rebuilt, only to be storm-wrecked again in 1702. Its stones were used to build a new church at Kintai, 10km north on the regional park's northeastern boundary.

Bar a few fishers' houses and the lighthouse (1862), the main attraction here is the Ventės Ragas Ornithological Station, 66km south of Klaipėda at the end of the Kintai–Ventė road.

★ **Nemunas Delta**
Regional Park   NATIONAL PARK
(Nemuno Deltos Regioninis Parkas; www.nemuno delta.lt) Where the Nemunas, Lithuanian's largest river, spills into the Curonian Lagoon, it splits into four distributaries: the Skirvytė, the Atmata, the Pakalnė and the Gilija. The result is a wetland delta of surpassing beauty, teeming with birds and bristling with rushes, lilies and small patches of forest. If you're in Nida, or Šilutė, or really anywhere nearby, and have the chance to visit this incredible place, take it. The park administration is on Rusnė, the delta's largest island.

The delta should have twitchers in spasms. Its 240 sq km are dotted with islands, marshes and flooded meadows, creating the perfect environment for the 294 different species of bird noted here. It's located on a migration route running from the

BIRDING IN THE NEMUNAS DELTA

This wetland is a birder's heaven. Almost 300 of the 330 bird species found in Lithuania frequent the Nemunas Delta Regional Park and many rare birds breed in the lush marshes around Rusnė, including black storks, white-tailed eagles, black-tailed godwits, pintails, dunlin, ruff and great snipe. The common white stork breeds like there's no tomorrow in Ventė.

The Arctic–European–East African bird-migration flight path cuts through the park, making it a key spot for migratory waterfowl. But it's not just a stopover or feeding site – the park is a breeding ground for around 170 species of bird, and some, such as the pintail, don't breed anywhere else in Lithuania.

Rare aquatic warblers, corncrakes, black-headed gulls, white-winged black terns and great crested grebes have their biggest colonies in the delta. In autumn up to 200,000 birds – 80% of which are tits and finches – fly overhead at any one time in the sky above Ventės Ragas Ornithological Station, and up to 5000 are ringed each day for research into world migration.

Arctic, through Europe to Eastern Africa, so many birds stop here to breed.

Ventės Ragas Ornithological Station
BIRD SANCTUARY

(☑ 8-638 90619; www.vros.lt; adult/child €3/2; ⊘ 10am-6pm Mon-Fri, to 7pm Sat & Sun) The first bird-ringing station was established here in 1929, but it was not until 1959 to 1960 that large bird traps were installed. Today, around 100,000 birds pass through the station each migratory period; zigzag, snipe, cobweb and duck traps ensnare birds to be ringed. Two exhibition rooms inside the station explain the birdlife, and an observation deck encourages visitors to spot species firsthand. The station or tourist office can put you in contact with local English-speaking ornithological guides.

Ethnographic Farmstead Museum
MUSEUM

(Etnografinė Sodyba Muziejus; ☑ 441-58 169; Skirvytėlės gatvė; admission by donation; ⊘ 10am-6pm mid-May–mid-Sep) This museum (signposted 1.8km from Rusnė) exhibits tools, furnishings and three venerable farm buildings, giving a sense of the harsh basics of traditional delta life.

Polder Museum
MUSEUM

(☑ 441-62 230; admission by donation; ⊘ variable) Housed in an old water-pumping station on the Vilkinė, this museum shows the basic technology with which Nemunas farmers have tried to keep the waters at bay. In Uostadvaris village, on Rusnė.

🛏 Sleeping & Eating

Campers can pitch tents at designated spots in the park – the regional park headquarters can tell you where – but bring food provi-

sions with you. Wonderful farm accommodation is spread throughout the delta and can be organised through the regional park headquarters or the tourist office in Šilutė; many also advertise their services. Beds cost on average €20 a night and meals can often be arranged for a little extra; a taste of delta life, though, is priceless.

Laimutės
HOTEL €€

(☑ 8-698 18402; Žemaičių Naumiestis; r €44; P ⛱) Laimutės is an all-in-one package, offering eye-catching rooms, a wellness- and sauna-centre, bicycle hire, boat and farm trips, winter lake fishing, and, despite all the activities, peace and relaxation. Its restaurant only uses organic produce from local farms and waterways, and breakfast and dinner are included. Find Laimutės in Žemaičių Naumiestis, about 15km east of Šilutė.

Kintai
GUESTHOUSE €€

(☑ 441-69 501; www.kintai.lt; d €50, camping per person/tent €1.45/2.90; P) This hotel, restaurant and boating complex offers comfort, seclusion and a plethora of water-bound activities. All rooms come with balcony, and some literally sit on the water (located in a house boat). Fishing trips can be organised, as can tours of the delta by boat. Find Kintai 6km east of Kintai village on the Minija River.

Ventainė
HOTEL, CAMPGROUND €€

(☑ 441-68 525; www.ventaine.lt; Marių gatvė 7; d/apt €60/100, camping per adult/car/tent €2.90/2.90/2.90; P @ ⛱) This complex, a 20-minute walk from the ringing station, sits on the lagoon shore with views of the spit's dunes. Comfy villa rooms have fridges and heated bathroom floors, and campers are well catered for with wooden huts, campsites and a clean, modern shower-and-toilet block. Its restaurant serves Lithuanian cuisine (mains €8 to €10), including very good fish soup.

ℹ Information

An influx of government and EU money to increase tourism is steadily making the region more accessible.

Regional Park Headquarters (☑441-75 050; www.nemunodelta.lt; Kuršmarių gatvė 13; ⊙8am-5pm Mon-Thu, to 3.45pm Fri) In the tiny village of Rusnė, this office has information about the delta, can help with organising itineraries, and even has rooms and bicycles for hire. Closes between noon and 12.45pm for lunch.

Šilutė Tourist Office (☑441-77 785; www. silute.info.lt; Lietuvininkų gatvė 4; ⊙8am-5pm Mon-Thu, to 3.45pm Fri) This immensely helpful office on Šilutė's main road should be the first port of call for those seeking information on accommodation, activities and transport. It produces a handy cycling guide to the region and the annual newspaper *Šilutės kraštas*, which covers accommodation and cultural events in the delta.

ℹ Getting There & Around

Getting to the area without your own wheels is tough. In summer Šilutė is served by 10 buses a day to/from Klaipėda (€3.90, one hour), and the same number to/from Kaunas (€12, 3½ hours) and Vilnius (€22, 5¼ hours).

Boats are the best means of exploring the delta (it's 8km from Pakalnė to Kintai by boat but 45km by road). The main routes follow the three main delta tributaries – the Atmata (13km), Skirvytė (9km) and Pakalnė (9km) Rivers – which fan out westwards from Rusnė.

At Kintai, Ventainė and Laimutės you can hire out boats with a boatman-guide. The office in Šilutė can also help.

Palanga

☑460 / POP 17,600

Palanga is a seaside resort with a split personality – peaceful pensioner paradise in winter, pounding party spot in summer. Tourists from all over Lithuania and abroad come for its idyllic 10km sandy beach backed by sand dunes and scented pines.

Despite the crowds and encroaching neon, Palanga is not without charm, with wooden houses and the ting-a-ling of bicycle bells and pedal-powered taxis in the air.

History

Palanga has often been Lithuania's only port over the centuries; however, it was destroyed by the Swedes in 1710. It was a resort in the 19th century, and a Soviet hot spot. After 1991, villas and holiday homes nationalised under the Soviets were slowly returned to their original owners, and family-run hotels and restaurants opened. In 2005 the city's main pedestrian street enjoyed a facelift befitting the sparkling reputation Palanga now enjoys.

◎ Sights & Activities

Nearly all of the action happens on Basanavičiaus gatvė, a long pedestrian-only concourse that runs perpendicular to the coast and is lined end to end with restaurants, cafes, bars and shops. South of here are the city's two leading non-beach attractions: the Botanical Park and the Amber Museum.

A stroll along Basanavičiaus gatvė is a sight in itself – and it's the way most holidaymakers pass dusky evenings. Stalls selling amber straddle the eastern end and amusements dot its entire length – inflatable slides, bungee-jump simulators, merry-go-rounds, electric cars, portrait artists, buskers and street performers with monkeys.

From the end of Basanavičiaus gatvė, a boardwalk leads across the dunes to the pier. By day, street vendors sell popcorn, *ledai* (ice cream), *dešrainiai* (hot dogs), *alus* (beer) and *gira* (a cloudy, nonalcoholic drink made from bread) here. At sunset (around 10pm in July), families and lovers gather here on the sea-facing benches to watch the sunset.

From the pier end of Basanavičiaus, a walking and cycling path wends north and south through pine forest. Skinny paths cut west onto the sandy beach at several points. Follow the main path (Meilės alėja) about 500m south onto Darius ir Girėno gatvė, to reach the Botanical Park, where cycling and walking tracks are plentiful.

★ **Amber Museum** MUSEUM
(Gintaro Muziejus; ☑460-51 319; www.pgm. lt; Vytauto gatvė 17; adult/student €2.32/1.16; ⊙10am-8pm Tue-Sat, to 7pm Sun) This highly popular museum showcases what is reputedly the world's sixth-largest collection of Baltic gold – 20,000-odd examples in all. It's housed in a sweeping neoclassical palace built by Count Feliksas Tiskevicius in 1897. Visitors are welcome until one hour before closing.

Palanga

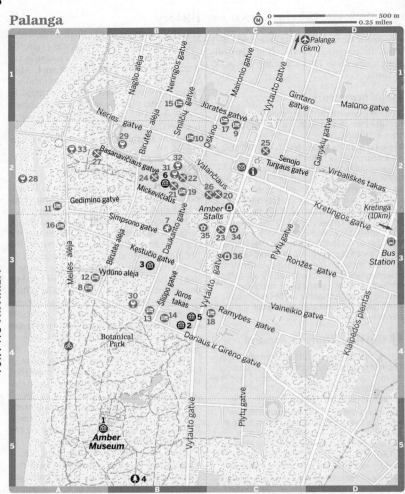

Botanical Park

PARK

(☑ 460-49 270; www.pgm.lt; 15 Vytauto gatvė) The 1-sq-km park includes a rose garden, 18km of footpaths and Birutė Hill (Birutės kalnas), once a pagan shrine. According to legend, it was tended by vestal virgins, one of whom, Birutė, was kidnapped and married by Grand Duke Kęstutis. A 19th-century chapel tops the hill. The wonderful Amber Museum is inside the park.

Amber Processing Gallery

GALLERY

(Gintaro Dirbtuvės Galerija; ☑ 8-682 69139; Darius ir Girėno gatvė 27; ⊙ 10am-6pm Tue-Sat) FREE This is the last of the dozen or so amber shops Palanga boasted in the late 19th century, when it was one of the largest processing centres in the Baltic. Run by the Palanga Guild of Amber Masters, the gallery sells beautiful amber pieces, and lets you try your hand at fashioning your own jewellery.

Antanas Mončys House Museum

MUSEUM

(Antano Mončio Namai-Muziejus; ☑ 460-49 366; www.antanasmoncys.com; Daukanto gatvė 16; adult/student €1.16/0.58; ⊙ 11am-5pm Wed-Sun) This museum displays large wooden sculptures, collages and masks by Lithuanian émigré artist Antanas Mončys (1921–93).

Palanga

Dr Jono Šliūpas Memorial House MUSEUM
(Jono Šliūpo Memorialinė Sodyba; ☑460-54 559; Vytauto gatvė 23a; adult/child €1.16/0.58; ⊙11am-6pm Tue-Sun) Fascinating black-and-white photos of old Palanga fill this house, the former home of the town's first mayor. Closed on Sunday between September and May.

Exile & Resistance Museum MUSEUM
(☑460-484 72; J Basanavičiaus gatvė 21; ⊙4-6pm Wed, Sat & Sun) FREE A modest permanent exhibition detailing resistance to foreign (particularly Soviet) occupation in Lithuania's troubled 20th century.

Bike House BICYCLE RENTAL
(☑8-696 10010; www.bikehouse.lt; Vytauto gatvė 10a; per day €12; ⊙9am-8pm) Bike House lets you order online, and can deliver the bike to your accommodation.

✸ Festivals & Events

Palanga Seals FOOD
(Palangos ruoniai) The 'seals' in question are actually smelts, the tiny fish delicacy that arrive on Palanga's shores for a short period in February. During this three-day festival in mid-February the smelts are prepared around town in all their glory. As an added attraction, hundreds of hardy souls brave the cold waters of the Baltic for a polar bear swim.

Palanga Summer Festival CULTURAL
The highlight of the summer season, the festival takes place on a different week each summer, closing with a massive street carnival, song festival and pop concert on the last day.

⌂ Sleeping

Summer season is when everything gets booked up fast; winter sees rates slashed by up to 50%. In season (June to August), try haggling with one of the many locals who stand at the eastern end of Kretingos gatvė touting 'Nuomojami kambariai' (rooms for rent) signs. Many houses on Nėries gatvė and Birutės alėja carry the same sign. Count on paying €15 to €30 a night, depending on room quality and facilities. Alternatively, check with the tourist office or contact the apartment-rental agency **Palbiuras** (☑460-51 500; www.palbiuras.lt; Kretingos gatvė 12; ⊙9am-6pm Mon-Fri).

Laguna GUESTHOUSE €
(☑460-49 191; www.laguna-hotel.lt; Meiles alėja 12; d from €40) It's hard to better Laguna's location, nestled under pines where Palanga meets the sea. It's a lovely three-storied timber guesthouse divided into six 'apartments' equipped with fridges, orthopedic mattresses, safes and other conveniences. Great value.

Seklytėlė
APARTMENT €€

(☎460-57 415; seklytele@gmail.com; Jūratės gatvė 18; per week from €280) Above the restaurant of the same name is a well-appointed, one-bedroom apartment. It's ideal for a couple spending more than a day or two in Palanga.

Vila Mama Rosa
GUESTHOUSE €

(☎460-48 581; Jūratės gatvė 28a; s/d from €42; P@☎) Vila Mama Rosa has eight sweet rooms, each cosily furnished English-style with fireplace, heated bathroom floor and wrought-iron bedheads. There is a stylish lounge and restaurant as well as a sauna complex and Jacuzzi.

Ema
GUESTHOUSE €

(☎460-48 608; www.ema.lt; Jūratės gatvė 32; s/d €23/40; P) This basic guesthouse is distinguished by friendliness and decor that wouldn't be out of place in a nursery. There's a decent cafe and tackle shop on premises.

Vasaros Ambasada
HOTEL €

(☎8-698 08333; www.palangosambasada.lt; Meilės alėja 16; r from €35; P☎) This attractive smaller hotel enjoys one of the most enviable locations in town: right on the coast, but only metres from the throngs on Basanavičiaus gatvė. The rooms are plainly furnished and there's not much English spoken here, but everything is clean and well tended. Prices jump extravagantly in high season (June to September).

Vila Ramybė
BOUTIQUE HOTEL €€

(☎460-54 124; www.vilaramybe.lt; Vytauto gatvė 54; s/d €55/70; @☎) It is tricky to snag a room at this stylish, unpretentious standout. Pine-clad rooms come in soothing pastel hues of blues and greens, seven of the 12 have a terrace and most have a little lounge. Apartments are also available.

Hotel Alanga
HOTEL €€

(☎460-49 215; www.alanga.lt; S Nėries gatvė 14; d/ste/apt from €41/47/73; P@☎☰) Families will love this hotel. It has a children's playroom, nanny care, billiard room and fitness centre alongside spotlessly clean and comfortable rooms. The decor is a bit bleak but balconies are livened up with bright-red dahlias. Prices vary hugely across the year, with high-season prices more than double the rate listed here.

Palangos Vėtra
HOTEL €€

(☎460-53 032; www.palangosvetra.lt; S Daukanto gatvė 35; s/d from €86/98; P@☎☰) Situated on a prominent corner in a quiet area of town, Vėtra's glass and clean lines give it a Scandinavian feel. There's a spa and wellness centre on-site, together with a cafe and a very good restaurant.

Vila Žvaigždė
GUESTHOUSE €€

(☎460-49 012; www.vilazvaigzde.lt; S Daukanto gatvė 6; r from €60; P) Žvaigždė has been running since 1932, and seems a world away from the modern bustle of Palanga. The large, welcoming rooms have a touch of romance about them, and the ground floor is given over to a popular Ukrainian restaurant.

★ Palanga Hotel
HOTEL €€€

(☎460-41 414; www.palangahotel.lt; Birutės gatvė 60; d/ste from €130/295, 1-room apt from €225; P✷@☎☰) Wrapped in a grove of pine trees, the Palanga is a stunner. Rooms peer out on blue sky and tree trunks, treetops or sea, while furnishings are subtle and luxurious, with natural hues of amber, cream and sand predominating. Some even sport their own sauna or Jacuzzi.

Pusų Paunksnėje
GUESTHOUSE €€€

(☎460-49 080; www.pusupaunksneje.lt; Dariaus ir Girėno gatvė 2; apt from €160; P@☰) We love this upscale, rustic guesthouse owned by Lithuanian basketball star Arvydas Sabonis. The guesthouse has a pool, a restful courtyard and 14 luxury apartments, each with fireplace.

Corona Maris
APARTMENT €€€

(☎8-620 31535; www.coronamaris.lt; Dariaus ir Girėno gatvė 5; d/q €130/215; P@☎) Wedged between the pines and the sea, this smart guesthouse offers accommodation in luxury apartments in two sizes, for two or four persons. All come with kitchens, sitting rooms, living rooms with under-floor heating; the larger also have fireplaces.

✗ Eating

Basanavičiaus gatvė plays host to the majority of restaurants in town.

City Chef
FAST FOOD €

(☎8-656 88926; Vytauto gatvė 39a; mains €4; ⊙4pm-2am) When the weather's good it's hard to beat a chorizo hot dog, fries and beer from this semi-permanent food van. There are plenty of benches and trestles on the terrace and, in summer, movies, live music, free dance lessons and more.

Mini Maxima
SUPERMARKET €

(Senojo Turgaus gatvė 1; ⊙8am-11.30pm) Self-caterers can stock up here.

1925 Baras
LITHUANIAN €€

(✆460-52 256; www.baras1925.lt; Basanavičiaus gatvė 4; mains €8-12; ⊙10am-midnight) This handsome timbered tavern has provided relief from the main-street madness since 1925. The Lithuanian cuisine is good and simple, and the restaurant's back garden as charming as you'll find in Palanga.

Molinis ąsotis
EUROPEAN €€

(✆460-40 208; www.molinisasotis.lt; Basanavičiaus gatvė 8; mains €8-12; ⊙11am-midnight; 🛜) This handsomely timbered restaurant distinguishes itself from the plentiful competition on Palanga's main strip by selling art and jewellery, and serving excellent food. Its broadly European menu also includes Lithuanian dishes such as meat-stuffed potato pancakes and pork shank with peas and crackling.

Čagino
RUSSIAN €€

(✆460-53 555; www.cagin.lt; Basanavičiaus gatvė 14a; mains €8-12; ⊙noon-midnight) Čagino is something a little different in Palanga, offering *pirozhki* (pies) and *pelmeni* (dumplings), stewed venison, veal with cherries and other substantial Russian dishes. On Thursday nights diners are immersed in total darkness, while Fridays and Saturdays the lights come back on, and live music kicks off at 8pm.

Armėniška Virtuvė
ARMENIAN €€

(✆8-652 87579; www.armeniskavirtuve.lt; Basanavičiaus gatvė 17; mains €5-9; ⊙11am-10pm) For a diversion from Lithuanian, pizza and fun-fair-fare, this authentic Armenian restaurant is definitely worth a visit. Spiced lamb and beef soups, pigeon in sour-milk sauce, charcoal-grilled shashliks, pickled vegetables to be eaten with vodka: all can be enjoyed on the summer terrace, or indoors by the light of flat-screen TVs.

Lašas Steak House
STEAK €€€

(✆460-44 880; www.steakhousehotel.lt; Basanavičiaus gatvė 29; mains €8-14; ⊙10am-midnight) Attached to a hotel of the same name, this place does what it says on the tin, and does it well. Steaks, pork, duck and venison are cooked to order, and the terrace beckons in nice weather.

Žuvinė
FISH €€€

(✆460-48 070; www.zuvine.lt; Basanavičiaus gatvė 37a; mains €12-16; ⊙11am-midnight; 🛜) It would be a crime to come to the Baltic coast, and not sample some of the local fish, and Žuvinė, while more expensive than most

other options in Palanga, has you covered. Try the *zander* with spinach and beetroot cream, or the monkfish with *porcini*.

🍷 Drinking & Nightlife

Kablys: Jūra. Kultūra
BAR

(✆8-610 34231; Dariaus ir Girėno gatvė 13; ⊙10am-midnight; 🛜) The most offbeat and diverse venue in Palanga, Kablys ('hook') faces the Botanical Park, away from the noise and action of central Palanga. It's a bar, cafe, gallery, cinema and event space rolled into one.

Beach Bars
BAR

(Palanga seafront; ⊙24hr) Between June and September tents housing round-the-clock bars sprout on the beach, and can be lovely places to see the sun set over the Baltic (or feel it rise behind you). DJs play at the busiest times.

Piano
CLUB

(✆460-64 188; Basanavičiaus gatvė 24a; ⊙11am-5am; 🛜) Outdoor barbecue restaurant and terrace by day, cocktail bar and club by night, Piano tries to keep the throngs happy throughout the day. A crowded summer event schedule sees themed parties alternate with live acts and DJs. The eponymous piano is a white grand, kept out front.

Laukinių Vakarų Salūnas
BAR

(✆460-52 831; www.salunas.lt; Basanavičiaus gatvė 16; ⊙10am-5am) Improbably Western-themed, this 'saloon' doubles as a lunch-spot by day and club by night, making use in both cases of a wide frontage on Palanga's main strip. It can be raucous, and a bit tacky, but that's really not so unusual in Palanga.

Šachmatinė
CLUB

(✆8-604 58617; www.sachmatine.lt; Basanavičiaus gatvė 45; ⊙11pm-5am Wed-Sun) One of the biggest, most raucous clubs in Palanga, playing mainly house and mainstream dance music.

Exit
CLUB

(✆8-698 59116; Neries gatvė 39; ⊙11pm-5am Wed-Sun) One of Palanga's best clubs, Exit attracts international DJs.

☆ Entertainment

The tourist office knows what's on where.

Kino Teatras Naglis
CINEMA

(✆460-57 575; www.kinoteatrasnaglis.lt; Vytauto gatvė 82; ⊙2-10pm) Shows films in their original languages, with Lithuanian subtitles.

Open-air Concert Hall CONCERT VENUE
(Vasaros Estrada; ☎ 460-52 210; Vytauto gatvė 43)
The old bandstand has been replaced by a
swanky new 2200-seat auditorium, which
opened in late 2015.

Shopping

Baltijos Auskas JEWELLERY
(☎ 460-51 386; Vytauto gatvė 66; ⏰ 10am-2pm
& 3-6pm Mon-Fri, 10am-5pm Sat) 'Baltic Gold'
is among the best of the many galleries for
amber jewellery and handicrafts in Palanga.

ℹ Information

Jāņa sēta's *Palanga* town plan (1:15,000), featuring Palanga and Šventoji, costs €1.60 and is
available from the tourist office.

Palangos vaistinė (Vytauto gatvė 33; ⏰ 9am-
8pm Mon-Fri, to 6pm Sat, to 4pm Sun) Pharmacy
in the former KGB headquarters (1944–51).

Police Station (☎ 460-53 837; Vytauto gatvė 4)

Post Office (Vytauto gatvė 53; ⏰ 9am-5.30pm
Mon-Fri, to 1pm Sat) Palanga's most centrally
convenient post office.

Tourist Information Centre (☎ 460-48 811;
www.palangatic.lt; Vytauto gatvė 94; ⏰ 9am-
7pm Mon-Fri, 10am-4pm Sat & Sun) Books
accommodation and sells maps and guides.
Reduced hours outside July and August.

ℹ Getting There & Away

Reach Palanga by road or air; services are substantially more frequent in summer.

AIR

Palanga Airport (Palangos Oro Uostas; ☎ 6124
4442; www.palanga-airport.lt; Liepaja plentas 1),
6km north of the centre, has passenger services
to Copenhagen and Oslo via SAS (www.flysas.
com), as well as intermittent services to Oslo
with Norwegian Air Shuttle (www.norwegian.
com) and Rīga via airBaltic (www.airbaltic.com).

BUS

Services from the new **bus station** (☎ 460-
53 333; www.naujapalangosautobusustotis.
lt; Klaipėdos plentas 42; ⏰ ticket office 7am-
7.30pm) include Kaunas (€17, 3½ hours, nine
daily), Klaipėda (€1.80, 30 minutes, 22 daily),
Šiauliai (€11, three hours, eight daily) and Vilnius
(€18, 4¼ to six hours, 14 daily).

ℹ Getting Around

Bus 3 runs to and from the airport roughly every
hour from 7am to midnight. Timetables are posted
at its stop on Vytauto gatvė near the bus station.

The main taxi stand is on Kretingos gatvė in
front of the bus station; a taxi from the airport
into town costs between €9 and €11.

Pedal-powered taxis are at the eastern end of
Basanavičius gatvė. From May to September,
bicycle-hire stalls pepper the town. Hourly/daily
rates are €9/12 for a bicycle, €12 per day for
a four-wheel buggy for two and €12 for a kid's
buggy.

Around Palanga

Brash Šventoji, 12km north, lacks the pa-
nache of Palanga but – with its inflatable
fish that spit out kids, its dodgem cars and
its merry-go-round of restaurant entertainers
and funfair rides – it entertains. Nemirseta,
a couple of kilometres south of Palanga, is
known for its incredible sand dunes and for
being the furthest east the Prussians ever got.
Five buses daily run to Šventoji from Palanga,
but to reach Nemirseta you'll need your own
transport.

About 10km east of Palanga, the town of
Kretinga is connected to Palanga by frequent buses (€1.16, 15 minutes).

⊙ Sights

Kretinga Museum MUSEUM
(Kretingos muziejus; ☎ 445-77 323; www.
kretingosmuziejus.lt; Vilniaus gatvė 20; adult/stu-
dent €2.90/1.16; ⏰ museum 10am-6pm Wed-Sun,
winter garden 10am-6pm Tue-Sun) A crumbling
winter garden attached to the Kretinga
Museum houses a tropical mirage of 850
species of exotic plants. The museum itself is located in one of the many homes
of the Tyszkiewicz family of Polish nobles.
Find the museum west of the centre in the
Kretinga city park.

★ **Orvydas Garden** GARDENS
(☎ 613-28 624; Gargždelė; adult/child €2.32/1.16;
⏰ 10am-7pm Tue-Sun) The Orvydas Garden
was the work of stonemason Kazys Orvydas
(1905–89) and his oldest son turned Franciscan monk, Vilius (1952–92). The carvings
were originally created for the village cemetery in nearby Salantai but were brought
here to the Orvydas homestead after then
Soviet leader Nikita Khrushchev turned his
wrath on religious objects in the 1960s. The
Soviets later blocked access to the house to
prevent visitors getting to the persecuted
Orvydas family.

Today, visitors can walk through the
lovely farmstead gardens admiring literally hundreds of statues, carvings, busts and
just plain oddities. Three daily buses between Kretinga and Skuodas stop in Salan-

tai and Mosėdis. For the Orvydas Garden get off at the last stop before Salantai and walk about 1km.

Žemaitija National Park

☑ 448 / POP 3500

The 200-sq-km Žemaitija National Park, a magical landscape of lake and forest, is as mysterious as it is beautiful. It's easy to see why it spawns fables of devils, ghosts and buried treasure.

The draw here is two-fold. You can swim, boat and bike around at your leisure, as well as pay a visit to one of the country's newest and most bizarre attractions: a museum to the Cold War, housed in what was once a Soviet nuclear missile base.

The best access point is the small town of Plateliai, on the western shore of the lake of the same name and home to the helpful Žemaitija National Park Visitor Centre.

About 20km northeast of the park is Samogitian Calvary (Žemaičių Kalvarija), built on the site of 9th- to 13th-century burial grounds. Pilgrims come here during the first two weeks of July to climb the seven hills where 20 chapels form a 7km 'Stations of the Cross' route in commemoration of Christ's life, death and resurrection.

◉ Sights

★ Cold War Museum   MUSEUM

(Šaltojo Karo Muziejus; ☑ 8-677 86574; www. zemaitijosnp.lt; Plokštinė; adult/child €5/2.50; ⊙9am-6pm Tue-Fri, 10am-5pm Sat & Sun) This museum on the site of a former Soviet nuclear missile base is situated deep in the heart of the Žemaitija National Park. There's a small exhibition on the history of the Cold War, particularly on how it played out in the Baltic countries, and on the construction and role of the base. The highlight, however, is the chance to poke around inside one of the former missile bunkers.

Built in the 1960s in secret from the Lithuanian people, the base had enough firepower to flatten most of Europe, and may have played a role in the Cuban missile crisis. It's about 8km from Plateliai: follow the main road to Plokštinė, then 5km along a sign-posted gravel road through the pines.

Plateliai Manor Museum Complex MUSEUM

(☑ 8-659 07918; www.zemaitijosnp.lt; Didžioji gatvė 22; adult/child €2.50/1.50; ⊙10am-5pm Tue-Sun) The old granary and stable of the former Plateliai Manor now houses a highly worthwhile museum complex. The granary holds a multistorey exhibition dedicated to the nature, history and ethnography of the area, as well as archaeological findings from Sventrokalnis and Pilies islands on the lake. The stable houses a fascinating exhibition of local Shrove Tuesday Carnival customs, complete with around 250 (scary) masks. Hours and entrance fees contract in winter.

Žemaitija Art Museum   MUSEUM

(Žemaičių dailės muziejus; ☑ 448-52 492; www. oginski.lt; Parko gatvė 1; adult/child €1.16/0.58; ⊙10am-9pm Tue-Sun) The 19th-century Oginski Palace, in the nearby city of Plungė, holds an interesting collection of modern Samogitian art (carvings and metal works). The landscaped grounds surrounding the palace, criss-crossed with terraced ponds, are a sight in themselves. The museum closes at 5pm, and all day Sunday, in winter.

🏃 Activities

Most activities centre on Lake Plateliai (Platelių ežeras), renowned for its seven islets and seven ancient shore terraces. It's the park's most stunning natural feature, and the site of Midsummer celebrations on 23 and 24 June, when bonfires are lit and traditional songs sung. Legend says the lake was swept into the sky by a storm before being dropped where it lies now after the magic words 'Ale plate lej' (the rain goes wide) were uttered.

If it gets warm enough, swim in the lake. Otherwise, boats for excursions on the lake can be hired from the Yacht Club (☑ 8-682 42062; Ežero gatvė 40).

Many of the traditional Samogitian festivals are celebrated in the small town of Plateliai on the lake's western shore, including the amazingly colourful Shrove Tuesday Carnival (Mardi Gras; the Tuesday before Ash Wednesday in the Christian calendar).

The national park visitor centre can assist in bike rentals and hands out cycling maps. One of the easiest and most enjoyable rides is to remote Plokštinė (8km), the site of the former missile base and now home to the Cold War Museum.

LITHUANIA ŽEMAITIJA NATIONAL PARK

🛏 Sleeping & Eating

Plateliai's visitor centre has a list of B&Bs (around €20 to €25 per person) in some fabulous farms and private homes in the park.

Eating options in Plateliai are limited, but you could do worse than dine in its **Yacht Club** (Platelių jachtklubas; ☑8-6152 7350; www.plateliuose.lt; Ežero gatvė 40; mains €5-8) right on the lake, which has a limited menu but breathtaking lake views.

Audronės GUESTHOUSE €
(☑8-672 46572; www.poilsisplateliuose.lt; Ežero gatvė 37; d €40; 🖥) This delightful farmstead guesthouse is spread over several buildings, centred on a Swedish-style house. You'll find comfortable rooms, bikes for hire, swings and a grass-fringed pond for family leisure, and a welcome of real generosity from the owners. To find it, walk uphill from the centre of town (not down towards the lake).

Mortos GUESTHOUSE €
(☑448-49 117; Ezero gatvė 33; per person €15) A cluster of neat little timber cabins near the lake in Plateliai, Mortos is delightfully restful.

Julija and Bronius Staponkai GUESTHOUSE €
(☑8-617 03418; jb@zebra.lt; Ežero gatvė 38; r €25-40; 🅿) Cosy apartments for rent, a short walk from the lake.

Hotel Linelis HOTEL €
(☑8-655 77666; www.linelis.lt; Paplatelės; s/d/tr €40/45/55; 🅿🖥) Linelis has a fine restaurant and spa centre on the lake's eastern edge. Breakfast costs an additional €5.

ℹ Information

National Park Visitor Centre (☑448-49 231; www.zemaitijosnp.lt; Didžioji gatvė 8; ⊙8am-5pm Mon-Thu, to 3.45pm Fri, 10am-5pm Sat Jun-Aug) In Plateliai. Issues fishing permits (€1.40 for two days), arranges guides (around €40, must be booked in advance), has information on yacht, windsurfer and boat hire, and can direct you to the workshops of local folk artists. It also hosts a small exhibition on park flora and fauna.

ℹ Getting There & Away

Plungė, the nearest city, is best reached by train from Klaipėda (€4, one hour, four daily) and from Vilnius (€13, four hours, two daily). There are several buses daily from Kaunas (€13, four hours) and from Palanga (€6.50, 1¼ hours). From Plungė, there are limited buses onward to Plateliai.

UNDERSTAND LITHUANIA

Lithuania Today

Lithuania today is in the best place it's been since Independence. Economically and culturally it's making strides: it's becoming an ever-more confident member of the EU; and emigrants are returning (and tourists are visiting) in unprecedented numbers. It's palpably modernising, but not at the expense of its own deep-rooted, idiosyncratic culture, still widely celebrated in song, craft and cuisine.

The Lithuanian economy has grown significantly since Independence, moving swiftly from full central control under Soviet rule to the market economy of today. Boosted by admission to the World Trade Organization in 2001 and the EU in 2004, its GDP grew by 77% between 2000 and 2008, leading to widespread admiration for the 'Baltic Tiger'. However, things stalled dramatically with the 2008–09 economic crisis, and GDP only recovered to its 2009 level in 2015. Now, it's once more one of the fastest growing economies in the EU.

What the dry statistics translate to in everyday life, especially on the streets of Vilnius, is a greater sense of prosperity and optimism, flashier cars and clothes, and flourishing restaurant and bar scenes. Of course, there are plenty left behind by the new prosperity: unemployment is still at 9% and homelessness is a visible problem on city streets.

History

A powerful state in its own right at its peak in the 14th to 16th centuries, Lithuania subsequently disappeared from the map in the 18th century, only to reappear briefly between the wars, and ultimately regain Independence (from the Soviets) in 1991. Kaunas' Vytautas the Great War Museum and Vilnius' National Museum of Lithuania cover the whole span of Lithuania's history.

Tribal Testosterone

Human habitation in the wedge of land that makes up present-day Lithuania goes back to at least 9000 BC. Trade in amber started during the Neolithic period (6000 to 4500 years ago), providing the Balts – the ancestors of modern Lithuanians – with a ready-made source of wealth when they arrived on the scene from the southeast some time around 2000 BC.

Two millennia on, it was this fossilised pine resin and the far-flung routes across the globe its trade had forged – all brilliantly explained in Palanga's Amber Museum – that prompted a mention of the amber-gathering *aesti* on the shores of the Baltic Sea in *Germania,* a Roman book about the Germanic tribes written in AD 98. It wasn't until AD 1009 that Litae (Latin for Lithuania) first appears in written sources (the *Kvedlinburgh Chronicle*) as the place where an archbishop called Brunonus was struck on the head by pagans.

By the 12th century Lithuania's peoples had split into two tribal groups: the Samogitians (lowlanders) in the west and the Aukštaitija (highlanders) in the east and southeast. Around this time, some sources say, a wooden castle was built on the top of Gediminas Hill in Vilnius.

Medieval Mayhem

In the mid-13th century Aukštaitija leader Mindaugas unified Lithuanian tribes to create the Grand Duchy of Lithuania, of which he was crowned king in 1253 at Kernavė. Mindaugas accepted Catholicism in a bid to defuse the threat from the Teutonic Order – Germanic crusaders who conquered various Prussian territories, including Memel (present-day Klaipėda). Unfortunately, neither conversion nor unity lasted very long: Mindaugas was assassinated in 1263 by nobles keen to keep Lithuania pagan and reject Christianity.

Under Grand Duke Gediminas (1316–41), Lithuania's borders extended south and east into modern-day Belarus and Ukraine, and even included Kyiv for a time. After Gediminas' death, two of his sons shared the realm: in Vilnius, Algirdas pushed the southern borders of Lithuania past Kyiv, while Kęstutis – who plumped for a pretty lake island in Trakai as a site for his castle – fought off the Teutonic Order.

Algirdas' son Jogaila took control of the country in 1382, but the rising Teutonic threat forced him to make a watershed decision in the history of Europe. In 1386 he wed Jadwiga, crown princess of Poland, to become Władysław II Jagiełło of Poland and forge a Lithuanian-Polish alliance that would last 400 years. The Aukštaitija were baptised in 1387 and the Samogitians in 1413, making Lithuania the last European country to accept Christianity.

Glory Days

Jogaila spent most of his time in Kraków, but trouble was brewing at home. In 1390 his cousin Vytautas revolted, forcing Jogaila's hand. In 1392 he named Vytautas Grand Duke of Lithuania on condition that he and Jogaila share a common policy. The decisive defeat of the Teutonic Order by their combined armies at Grünwald (in modern-day Poland) in 1410 ushered in a golden period of prosperity, particularly for the Lithuanian capital Vilnius, which saw its legendary Old Town born.

LITHUANIA HISTORY

TOP FIVE HISTORICAL READS

The Last Girl (Stephan Collishaw) Absolutely spellbinding, this superb historical novel set in Vilnius flits between WWII and the 1990s.

Lithuania Awakening (Alfred Senn) From 'new winds' (the birth of the Independence movement in the 1980s) to a 'new era' (Independence), Senn's look at how the Lithuanians achieved Independence remains the best in its field; read the entire thing free online at http://ark.cdlib.org/ark:/13030/ft3x0nb2m8.

And Kovno Wept (Waldemar Ginsburg) Life in the Kovno ghetto is powerfully retold by one of its survivors.

Lithuania – Independent Again: The Autobiography of Vytautas Landsbergis The scene outside parliament on 13 January 1991 is among the dramatic moments Landsbergis brings vividly to life in his autobiography.

Forest of the Gods (Balys Sruoga) The author's powerful account of his time spent in the Stutthof Nazi concentration camp in the early 1940s was censored, and hence not published until 1957. It was transferred onto celluloid by Algimantas Puipa in 2005.

Vytautas ('the Great') extended Lithuanian control further south and east. By 1430, when he died, Lithuania stretched beyond Kursk in the east and almost to the Black Sea in the south, creating one of Europe's largest empires. Nowhere was its grandeur and clout better reflected than in 16th-century Vilnius, which, with a population of 25,000-odd, was one of Eastern Europe's biggest cities. Fine late-Gothic and Renaissance buildings sprang up, and Lithuanians such as Žygimantas I and II occupied the Polish-Lithuanian throne inside the sumptuous Royal Palace.

In 1579 Polish Jesuits founded Vilnius University and made the city a bastion of the Catholic Counter-Reformation. Under Jesuit influence, baroque architecture also arrived.

Polonisation & Partitions

Lithuania gradually sank into a junior role in its partnership with Poland, climaxing with the formal union of the two states (instead of just their crowns) at the Union of Lublin in 1569, during the Livonian War with Muscovy.

Under the so-called Rzeczpospolita (Commonwealth), Lithuania played second fiddle to Poland. Its gentry adopted Polish culture and language, its peasants became serfs and Warsaw usurped Vilnius as political and social hub.

A century on it was Russia's turn to play tough. In 1654 Russia invaded the Rzeczpospolita and temporarily snatched significant territory from it. By 1772 the Rzeczpospolita was so weakened that the states of Russia, Austria and Prussia simply carved it up in the Partitions of Poland (1772, 1793 and 1795). Most of Lithuania went to Russia, while a small chunk in the southwest was annexed by Prussia, but passed into Russian hands after the Napoleonic Wars.

Russification & Nationalism

While neighbouring Estonia and Latvia were governed as separate provinces, Russian rule took a different stance with rebellious Lithuania.

Vilnius had quickly become a refuge for Polish and Lithuanian gentry dispossessed by the region's new Russian rulers and a focus of the Polish national revival, in which Vilnius-bred poet Adam Mickiewicz was a leading inspiration. When Lithuanians joined a failed Polish rebellion against

Russian rule in 1830, Tsarist authorities clamped down extra hard. They shut Vilnius University, closed Catholic churches and monasteries and imposed Russian Orthodoxy. Russian law was introduced in 1840 and the Russian language was used for teaching. A year after a second rebellion in 1863, books could only be published in Lithuanian if they used the Cyrillic alphabet, while publications in Polish (spoken by the Lithuanian gentry) were banned altogether.

National revival gained some momentum in the 19th and early 20th centuries. While most Lithuanians continued to live in rural areas and villages, the rapid industrialisation of Vilnius and other towns gave nationalist drives more clout. Vilnius became an important Jewish centre during this period, with Jews making up around 75,000 of its 160,000-strong population in the early 20th century to earn it the nickname 'Jerusalem of the North' (p386).

Independence

Ideas of Baltic national autonomy and independence had been voiced during the 1905 Russian revolution, but it was not until 1918 that the restoration of the Independent State of Lithuania was declared. During WWI Lithuania was occupied by Germany and it was still under German occupation on 16 February 1918 when a Lithuanian national council, the Taryba, declared independence in Vilnius in the House of Signatories. In November Germany signed an armistice with the Western Allies, and the same day a Lithuanian republican government was set up.

With the re-emergence of an independent Poland eager to see Lithuania reunited with it or to cede the Vilnius area, which had a heavily Polish and/or Polonised population, things turned nasty. On 31 December 1918 the Lithuanian government fled to Kaunas, and days later the Red Army installed a communist government in Vilnius. Over the next two years the Poles and Bolsheviks played a game of tug-of-war with the city, until the Poles annexed Vilnius once and for all on 10 October 1920. Thus from 1920 until 1939 Vilnius and its surrounds formed a corner of Poland, while the rest of Lithuania was ruled from Kaunas under the authoritarian rule (1926–40) of Lithuania's first president, Antanas Smetona (1874–1944).

In 1923 Lithuania annexed Memel (Klaipėda), much to the displeasure of its former ruler, a much-weakened Germany.

LATE TO THE CHURCH

While today Lithuanians are staunchly Roman Catholic (a short stroll through steeple-rich Vilnius is enough to convince any doubters), it wasn't always this way. In fact, Lithuania is considered to be the last pagan country in Europe. It wasn't fully baptised into Roman Catholicism until 1413.

There are lots of reasons for this: foremost among them was the Lithuanians' fierce independence, militating against attempts to convert them. The country's relatively recent experience (if you can call the 15th century 'recent') with paganism explains why so much of its religious art, national culture and traditions have pagan roots.

During the Soviet years, Catholicism was persecuted and hence became a symbol of nationalistic fervour. Churches were seized, closed and turned into 'museums of atheism' or used for other secular purposes (such as a radio station in the case of Christ's Resurrection Basilica in Kaunas, open for business as usual today) by the state.

After Independence in 1991, the Catholic Church quickly began the ongoing process of reacquiring church property and reconsecrating places of worship.

These days, around 80% of Lithuanians consider themselves to be Catholics. There are small minorities of other sects and faiths, including Russian Orthodox (4%) and Protestant Christians (2%).

WWII & Soviet Rule

With the signing of the Nazi-Soviet non-aggression pact in 1939 and the German invasion of Poland in September of that year, Lithuania fell into Soviet hands. The USSR insisted on signing a 'mutual-assistance pact' with Lithuania in October and returned Vilnius to the Lithuanian motherland as part of the inducement. But this was little consolation as the terror Lithuania experienced as a USSR republic – Soviet purges saw thousands upon thousands of people killed or deported.

Following Hitler's invasion of the USSR and the German occupation of the region in 1941, nearly all of Lithuania's Jewish population – more than 90% of the country's 200,000 Jews – was killed; most Vilnius Jews died in its ghetto or in the nearby Paneriai Forest. Ethnic Lithuanians suffered proportionately much less, but thousands were killed, and between 1944 and 1945 some 80,000 fled West to avoid the Red Army's reconquest of the Baltic countries.

Immediate resistance to the reoccupation of Lithuania by the USSR, in the form of the partisan movement 'Forest Brothers', began in 1944. Discover their story in museums across the country, including the Museum of Deportation & Resistance in Kaunas.

Between 1944 and 1952 under Soviet rule, a further 250,000 Lithuanians were killed, arrested or deported, as patriotic spirit and thought were savagely suppressed. Nowhere is this dark period explained more powerfully than at the Museum of Genocide Victims in the old KGB headquarters in Vilnius.

Finally Free

A yearning for independence had simmered during the *glasnost* years of the mid-1980s, but it was with the storming success of Lithuania's popular front, Sajūdis, in the March 1989 elections for the USSR Congress of People's Deputies (Sajūdis won 36 of the 42 directly elected Lithuanian seats) that Lithuania surged ahead in the Baltic push for independence. The pan-Baltic human chain, which was formed to mark the 50th anniversary of the Nazi-Soviet nonaggression pact a few months later, confirmed public opinion and, in December that year, the Lithuanian Communist Party left the Communist Party of the Soviet Union.

Vast pro-independence crowds met then Soviet leader Mikhail Gorbachev when he visited Vilnius in January 1990. Sajūdis won a majority in the elections to Lithuania's supreme Soviet in February, and on 11 March the assembly declared Lithuania an independent republic. In response, Moscow carried out weeks of troop manoeuvres around Vilnius and clamped an economic blockade on Lithuania, cutting off fuel supplies.

Soviet hardliners gained the ascendancy in Moscow in the winter of 1990–91, and in January 1991 Soviet troops and paramilitary police stormed and occupied Vilnius' TV Tower and Parliament, killing 14 people. Some of the barricades put up around the

Parliament remain. On 6 September 1991 the USSR recognised the independence of Lithuania.

Towards Europe

Lithuanians have a sense of irony: they led the Baltic push for independence then, at their first democratic parliamentary elections in 1992, raised eyebrows by voting in the ex-communist Lithuanian Democratic Labour Party (LDDP). Presidential elections followed in 1993, the year the last Soviet soldier left the country, with former Communist Party first secretary Algirdas Brazauskas winning 60% of the vote.

It was a painful time for the country. Corruption scandals dogged Brazauskas' term in office and inflation ran wild, peaking around 1000%. Thousands of jobs were lost and the country's banking system collapsed in 1995–96.

But change was under way that would eventually fuel economic growth. The litas replaced the *talonas* (coupon), the transitional currency used during the phasing out of the Soviet rouble in Lithuania, and a stock exchange opened.

Presidential elections in 1998 ushered in wild card Valdas Adamkus (b 1926), a Lithuanian émigré and US citizen who had come to the US after WWII when his parents fled the Soviet advance.

Adamkus appointed a member of the ruling Conservative Party, 43-year-old Rolandas Paksas, prime minister in 1999. The popular Vilnius mayor and champion stunt pilot won instant approval as 'the people's choice' – so much so that he challenged Adamkus for the presidency in 2003 and won.

Large-scale privatisation took place in 1997–98, but a deep recession struck following the 1998 economic crisis in Russia. Nevertheless, Lithuania managed to claw its way back and by 2001 its economy was being praised by the International Monetary Fund as one of the world's fastest growing.

Lithuania joined the World Trade Organization in 2001, and in 2002 – in a bid to make exports competitive and show a determination to join the EU – pegged its currency to the euro instead of the US dollar. It joined the Eurozone in 2015.

True to his Lithuanian heritage, Adamkus battled hard in the political ring and regained the presidency in 2004 following the impeachment of Paksas for granting Lithuanian citizenship to a shady Russian businessman who was a major financial supporter. Adamkus finished his five-year term in office in 2009 and was replaced by Dalia Grybauskaitė, who became the country's first female head of state, and was re-elected in 2014.

In 2004 Lithuania joined the EU and NATO and has been a staunch supporter of both ever since. In November 2004 it became the first EU member to ratify the EU constitution. The former USSR military base outside Šiauliai is now home to NATO F-16 fighter jets that protect the air space of all three Baltic countries.

VILNIUS: THE 'JERUSALEM OF THE NORTH'

One of Europe's most prominent Jewish communities flourished in pre-WWII Vilnius (Vilne in Yiddish), but Nazi (and later Soviet) brutality virtually wiped it out.

The city's Jewish roots go back some eight centuries when 3000 Jews settled in Vilnius at the invitation of Grand Duke Gediminas (1316–41). In the 19th century Vilnius became a centre for the European Jewish language, Yiddish. Famous Jews from the city's community include rabbi and scholar Gaon Elijahu ben Shlomo Zalman (1720–97), who led opposition to the widespread Jewish mystical movement Hassidism, and landscape artist Isaak Levitan (1860–1900).

The city's Jewish population peaked on the eve of WWI at almost 100,000 (out of 240,000 in Lithuania). However, plagued by discrimination and poverty, the Jewish community diminished in the interwar years when Vilnius was an outpost of Poland.

Despite this, Vilnius blossomed into the Jewish cultural hub of Eastern Europe, and was chosen ahead of the other Yiddish centres, Warsaw and New York, as the headquarters of the Yiddish-language scientific research institute YIVO in 1925 (the institute stood on Vivulskio gatvė). Jewish schools, libraries, literature and theatre flourished. There were 100 synagogues and prayer houses, and six daily Jewish newspapers.

By the end of WWII Lithuania's Jewish community was all but destroyed and during the mid-1980s *perestroika* (restructuring) years an estimated 6000 Jews left for Israel.

The People

The Lithuanian population is predominantly urban: two-thirds of people live in urban areas, with the five largest cities – Vilnius, Kaunas, Klaipėda, Šiauliai and Panevėžys – accounting for nearly half the population.

Lithuania is also the most ethnically homogeneous population of the three Baltic countries; indigenous Lithuanians count for almost 85% of the total population, making multiculturalism less of a hot potato than in Latvia or Estonia. Poles form the second-biggest grouping, making up around 6% of the population, approaching 250,000 people. Russians form around 5% of the population, while Jews make up just 0.1%.

The country's smallest ethnic community, numbering just 280, are the Karaites. An early 19th-century prayer house and ethnographic museum in Trakai provide insight into the culture and beliefs of this tiny Turkic minority.

Lithuanian Roma officially number around 2800. Vilnius' Human Rights Monitoring Institute (www.hrmi.lt) reckons some 46% are aged under 20 and many, unlike the Roma elders they live with, don't speak Lithuanian.

Net migration has been negative for the past several years, with literally hundreds of thousands of Lithuanians emigrating to countries where, even cleaning homes and tending bars, they can earn salaries two to three times higher than those available locally. Initially, Ireland and the UK were popular destinations, but Scandinavia is also now in favour.

More than three million Lithuanians live abroad, including an estimated 800,000 in the USA. Other large communities exist in Canada, South America and Australia.

Life expectancy for males is relatively low compared with other European countries – around 70 years (2013 estimate). The life expectancy for women is around 80 years.

Until 1998 there were only a handful of places in Lithuania to offer a university degree. Since then, several dozen colleges and universities have sprung up. Almost 90% of Lithuanians complete secondary school, and the majority of pupils go on to some form of further education. Many students work full time alongside studying and live in university dorms or with friends rather than remaining in the parental nest.

Family ties remain strong, however, and married couples often choose to live with elderly parents who can no longer live alone. Despite increased career prospects, especially for women, Lithuanians tend to marry relatively young – the majority of women who marry do so between the ages of 20 and 24. A high number of marriages – almost half – end in divorce, but this figure is falling. This is partly due to the fact that many couples choose cohabitation over marriage and thus don't figure in the official divorce statistics.

LITHUANIA THE PEOPLE

Rural vs Urban

The contrast between life in Vilnius and elsewhere is stark. Citizens of the capital enjoy a lifestyle similar to those in Western Europe, living in nice apartments, working in professional jobs and often owning a car. Many have gained a cosmopolitan view of the world and consumerism has become a way of life.

In provincial towns and rural areas poverty is still prevalent – urban dwellers have around a third more income at their disposal than their rural counterparts, and about a third of homes in farming communities are below the poverty line, compared to about 20% in built-up areas.

Lithuania's Hoop Dreams

Though Lithuanians traditionally excel at many sports – including recent Olympic medals in events as disparate as the discus throw, the modern pentathlon and the decathlon – there's really only one sport that gets their blood pumping: basketball.

For Lithuanians, b-ball is more than a sport: it's a religion. During Soviet times success at basketball within the Soviet National League was one of the few acceptable ways for Lithuanians to express their national identity. Since Independence, Lithuanians have looked to basketball to help put them on the world map. The worshipped national team scooped bronze in three successive Olympic Games (1992, 1996 and 2000), only to be nosed out for bronze in both 2004 and 2008. The team also took the bronze in the FIBA World Basketball Championship in Istanbul in 2010, and came fourth in Spain in 2014.

Lithuanians have been a global basketball power since the 1930s, but the glory years came in the mid-1980s with the unparalleled success of the leading Lithuanian team at the time, Žalgiris Kaunas. Led by phenom centre Arvydas Sabonis, Žalgiris won the Soviet national championship three years running in 1985, '86 and '87 – each time defeating the dreaded Red Army superpower CSKA Moscow. Lithuanians made up the core of the Soviet team that won Olympic gold in Seoul in 1988.

Lithuanians' success at the time did more than prove their dominance on the basketball court; it was part of the national revival that ultimately led to Independence in 1991.

In 2011 Lithuania hosted the FIBA Eurobasket 2011 championship, the most prestigious basketball tournament in Europe, for the first time since 1939. Though the home team didn't win, the event was deemed a big success in the main host cities of Vilnius and Kaunas.

The Arts

Lithuania is Baltic queen of contemporary jazz, theatre and the avant-garde, while its arts scene is young, fresh and dynamic.

Contemporary Crafts

Lithuania may be striding expectantly into its new European destiny, but the old ways haven't died. Traditional crafts are enjoying a huge renaissance, with many of the younger generation becoming intrigued with skills going back centuries.

One of the most visible of these is wood-carving, with many a front garden or forest trail graced by elaborately decorated totems that seem living relics of the country's pagan past. In fact, they're as likely to show Christian as pagan motifs, both common subject matter for traditional Lithuanian folk artists called *dievdirbiai*. Once blanketed in dense forests that now survive in the country's many national parks, Lithuania has long entertained a special reverence for wood. Traditionally, trees could only be cut down when 'asleep', in winter, and in pagan times some groves were designated sacred, and could never be felled.

The abundance of raw material on the Baltic coast also gave rise to a long tradition of amber craftsmanship, and many noted Lithuanian jewellers still prize the medium. Black pottery, a Neolithic craft in which pine resin (and sometimes dung) gives the finished wares their characteristic dark tint, is another age-old Lithuanian skill that has been revived in recent years. Add to that weaving, papermaking, the decoration of *margučiai* (Easter eggs) and many other traditional crafts, and today's Lithuania has a plethora of means to keep its past alive.

TOP FIVE CONTEMPORARY READS

Online, visit Books from Lithuania (www.booksfromlithuania.lt), a comprehensive literary information centre reviewing the latest in Lithuanian poetry and prose, including English-language translations.

Lithuanian Literature (ed Vytautas Kubilius) Read this to get the big picture.

The Issa Valley (Czesław Miłosz) Semiautobiographical account of boyhood life in a valley north of Kaunas.

Tūla (Jurgis Kunčinas) Spellbinding story of two lovers caught in the Soviet system, and battling it with every step.

Bohin Manor (Tadeusz Konwicki) Set in the aftermath of the 1863 uprising, this novel by a leading modern Polish writer born in the Vilnius area uses the past to comment on current events and evokes tensions between locals, their Russian rulers and a Jewish outsider, as well as the foreboding and mysterious nature of the Lithuanian backwoods.

Raw Amber (ed Laima Sruoginis) Anthology of contemporary Lithuanian poetry.

Literature

The Renaissance ushered in the first book to be published in Lithuanian – a catechism by Martynas Mažvydas, whose statue stands in Klaipėda – in 1547 and the creation of Vilnius University in 1579. But it wasn't until a couple of centuries later that a true Lithuanian literature emerged.

The land was the focus of the earliest fiction: *The Seasons (Metai)*, by Kristijonas Donelaitis, described serf life in the 18th century in poetic form, and a century later Antanas Baranauskas' poem *Anykščiai Pine Forest (Anykščiū šilelis;* 1860–61) used the deep, dark forest around Anykščiai as a symbol of Lithuania, bemoaning its destruction by foreign landlords. The poem is mostly known for its expressive language, and Baranauskas wrote the poem, at least in part, to show that the language need not be limited to kitchen talk.

Russia's insistence on the Cyrillic alphabet for publishing from 1864 (until 1904) hindered literature's development – and inspired poet Jonas Mačiulis (1862–1932) to push for its national revival. A statue of the Kaunas priest, whose pen name was Maironis, stands in Kaunas' Old Town. The city's Maironis Lithuanian Literary Museum, in Maironis' former home, tells his life story. Maironis' romantic *Voices of Spring (Pavasario balsai;* 1895) is deemed the start of modern Lithuanian poetry.

Several major Polish writers grew up in Lithuania and regarded themselves as partly Lithuanian, notably Adam Mickiewicz (1798–1855), the inspiration of 19th-century nationalists, whose great poem *Pan Tadeusz* begins 'Lithuania, my fatherland...' The rooms in Vilnius' Old Town, where he stayed while studying at Vilnius University, form a museum.

Winner of the 1980 Nobel Prize, Czesław Miłosz (1911–2004) was born in the central Lithuanian town of Šeteniai. While he's best known abroad for his nonfiction book *The Captive Mind* (1953), concerning the effects of Stalinism on the minds of Polish intellectuals, he was passionate about his Lithuanian roots and wrote movingly of his childhood there in books such as *The Issa Valley* (1955), and in his memoir *Native Realm* (1959).

Novelists at the fore of contemporary Lithuanian literature include Antanas Škėma (1910–61), whose semiautobiographical

novel *The White Shroud (Balta drobulė;* 1954) recounts a childhood in Kaunas, then emigration to Germany and New York. It pioneered stream of consciousness in Lithuanian literature. Realist novelist and short-story writer Ričardas Gavelis (1950–2002) shocked the literary world with *Vilnius Poker* (1989) and *Vilnius Jazz* (1993), which openly criticised the defunct Soviet system and mentality. Equally controversial was the story of a priest's love affair with a woman, *The Witch and the Rain (Ragana ir lietus)* by Jurga Ivanauskaitė (1961–2007). It was condemned by the Vilnius City Council on publication in 1992, which limited initial distribution of the book. Her subsequent novel *Gone with Dreams* (2000) highlighted new issues and subjects, such as religion, travel and perceptions of others' religion and cultures, that couldn't be addressed in Lithuanian literature until after 1989 and the collapse of communism throughout Eastern Europe.

Herkus Kunčius (b 1965) has gained a reputation for scandalous novels that tear at the fabric of cultural norms; his *The Tumulus of Cocks* (2004) introduced gay and lesbian scenes to Lithuanian literature. Marius Ivaškevičius (b 1973), on the other hand, has distinguished himself by looking at historical themes through a modern lens. *The Greens* (2002), detailing the partisan movement after WWII, has proven to be Ivaškevičius' best seller to date.

Cinema & TV

Lithuania has a long cinematic history – the first short films were shot way back in 1909 – but it wasn't until the late 1980s that independent film truly began to flourish, and now Lithuanian films capture nearly 25% of the local box office.

The grim reality of the post-Soviet experience is the focus for talented film director

Šarūnas Bartas (b 1964), whose silent black-and-white movie *Koridorius* (*The Corridor;* 1994) – set in a dilapidated apartment block in a Vilnius suburb – received international recognition. Bartas opened Lithuania's first independent film studio in 1987.

The 11 documentaries and one short film made by Audrius Stonys are acclaimed Europe-wide: *510 Seconds of Silence* (2000) – an angel's flight over Vilnius' Old Town, the lake-studded Aukštaitija National Park and Neringa – is awesome; watch it at www.stonys.lt.

Stonys codirected *Baltic Way* (1990) – which landed best European documentary in 1992 – with director-producer and European Film Academy member Arūnas Matelis (b 1961). Matelis won critical acclaim and a heap of awards for *Before Flying Back to the Earth* (2005), a documentary on children with leukaemia. Find him and his film crew at www.nominum.lt.

Algimantas Puipa became prominent with *Vilko dantu karoliai* (*The Necklace of Wolf's Teeth;* 1998) and *Elze is Gilijos* (*Elsie from Gilija;* 1999), and hit the headlines again with both *Forest of the Gods* (2005) and *Whisper of Sin* (2007).

Flying the flag for young female directors in Lithuania is Kristina Buožytė, whose *Vanishing Waves* (2012) imagines a relationship between a comatose young woman and the scientist that manages to connect with her subconscious.

Lithuania has been the location for a number of big-budget TV series, due to its reputation as a low-cost film location. They include *The New Adventures of Robin Hood* (1995–96) and *Elizabeth I* (filmed 2005), starring Jeremy Irons and Helen Mirren.

The Lithuanian Film Studios (www.lfs.lt), founded in Kaunas in 1948 and now located in Vilnius, has had a hand in all major foreign productions in the country.

More information on Lithuania's cinema and TV heritage can be gleaned at the Theatre, Music & Cinema Museum in Vilnius.

Music

Dainos – the Lithuanian name for songs – form the basis of the country's folk music. Their lyrics deal with every aspect of life, from birth to death, and more often than not they are sung by women, alone or in a group. Instruments include the *kanklė,* a Baltic version of the zither, a variety of flutes, and reed instruments. Kaunas' Folk Music Instruments Museum has a fine collection to peer at.

Romantic folk-influenced Mikalojus Konstantinas Čiurlionis (1875–1911) is Lithuania's leading composer from earlier periods. Two of his major works are the symphonic poems *Miske* (*In the Forest*) and *Jūra* (*The Sea;* 1900–07), but Čiurlionis also wrote many piano pieces.

Bronius Kutavičius (b 1932) is heralded as the harbinger of minimalism in Lithuanian music, while Rytis Mažulis (b 1961) represents a new generation of composers with his neo-avant-garde stance expressed in minimalist compositions for voice. Country-and-western icon Virgis Stakėnas is the larger-than-life force behind the country's cult country music festival, the Visagano Country, in the eastern city of Visaginas.

Lithuania is the Baltic jazz giant. Two noteworthy musicians are sparkling pianist Gintautas Abarius and cerebral saxophonist Petras Vysniauskas. As famed is the Ganelin Trio, whose avant-garde jazz stunned the West when discovered in the 1980s. The club Kurpiai in Klaipėda and the Birštonas and the Kaunas jazz festivals are *the* spots to catch Lithuanian jazz.

Lithuania has yet to break into the international rock and pop scene, but that doesn't mean there aren't any local heroes. Andrius Mamontovas has been a household name for almost two decades; Amberlife, Mango and Auguestė dominate the boy- and girl-band genre; and Skamp is an interesting mix of hip-hop, R'n'B, and funk. The biggest bands to explode onto the scene in recent years are Inculto, an eclectic group whose creative output reflects diverse world influences, and Gravel, a Brit-pop-esque four-piece with talent and attitude.

Music Export Lithuania (www.mxl.lt) is a helpful online information source on Lithuania's various music genres.

Visual Arts

Lithuania's finest painter and musician is Varėna-born Mikalojus Konstantinas Čiurlionis, who spent his childhood in Druskininkai, where his home is now a museum. He produced romantic masterpieces in gentle, lyrical tones, theatre backdrops and some exquisite stained glass. The best collection of these works is in the National Čiurlionis Art Museum in Kaunas. Depression dogged Čiurlionis, although when he died aged 35 it was of pneumonia.

Lithuania has a thriving contemporary art scene. Vilnius artists created the tongue-in-cheek Republic of Užupis (p302), which hosts alternative art festivals, fashion shows and exhibitions in its 'breakaway' state. Some 19km north, Lithuanian sculptor Gintaras Karosas heads up a sculpture park, Europos Parkas.

From Lenin to rock legend, Konstantinas Bogdanas was famed for his bronzes of communist heroes (see some in Druskininkai's Grūtas Park) and for his bust of American musician and composer Frank Zappa.

Lithuanian photography has achieved international recognition. Vytautas Stanionis (1917–66) was the leading postwar figure, while artist Antanas Sutkus (b 1939) stunned the photographic world with his legendary shots of French philosopher Jean-Paul Sartre and novelist Simone de Beauvoir cavorting in the sand on Curonian Spit. Vitalijus Butyrinas's (b 1947) famous series *Tales of the Sea* uses abstract expressionism to make powerful images. For more on these and others, visit the Union of Lithuanian Art Photographers (www.photography.lt).

Theatre

Lithuanian theatre has become an international force, with several young experimental directors turning European heads left, right and centre.

The superstar of Lithuanian theatre directors is arguably Eimuntas Nekrošius, who has won many international awards. Another well-known name, Vilnius-based Oskaras Koršunovas (b 1969), has done Europe's theatre-festival circuit with *Old Woman, Shopping and Fucking, PS Files OK* and his 2003 adaptation of *Romeo and Juliet*. In 1998 he established his own theatre company in Vilnius, the Oskaras Koršunovas Theatre (OKT), albeit one with no fixed stage.

Other big names include Gintaras Varnas (b 1961), artistic director at the Kaunas Academic Drama Theatre, voted Lithuania's best director of the year five times, and Rimas Tuminas (b 1952), who heads the Small Theatre of Vilnius.

For more on Lithuanian theatre, visit www.theatre.lt.

Food & Drink

Long, miserable winters are to blame for Lithuania's hearty, waist-widening diet based on potatoes, meat and dairy products. Cuisine between regions does not vary enormously, although certain traits become noticeable as you eat your way around: mushrooms, berries and game dishes dominate in heavily forested eastern and southern Lithuania; beer sneaks its way into northern cooking pots; while fish reigns on the coast and in lake districts like Trakai. Bread (usually rye, sometimes quite sweet) is excellent.

Staples, Specialities & 'Zeppelins'

Lithuanian food is epitomised in the formidable *cepelinai* (tsep-e-lin-ay), sometimes jokingly called zeppelins. These are parcels of thick potato dough stuffed with cheese, *mesa* (meat) or *grybai* (gree-bai; mushrooms). They come topped with a rich sauce made from onions, butter, sour cream and bacon bits.

Another favourite is sour-cream-topped *kugelis* – a 'cannon ball' dish borrowed from German cuisine that bakes grated potatoes and carrots in the oven. *Koldūnai* (koldoon-ay) are hearty ravioli stuffed with meat

LITHUANIA FOOD & DRINK

THE TWELVE DISHES OF CHRISTMAS

Christmas is the major culinary feast of the year. On 24 December families sit down to dinner in the evening around a candlelit hay-covered table topped with a white linen cloth; the hay anticipates Jesus' birth and serves as a place for the souls of dead family members to rest. (Indeed, one place around the table is always laid for someone who died that year.)

The Christmas Eve feast that unfolds comprises 12 dishes – one for each month of the coming year to ensure year-long happiness and plenty. Dishes are fish and vegetable based, and often include festive *kūčiukai* (koo-chiu-kai) – small cubed poppy-seed biscuits served in a bowl of poppy-seed milk; others like herrings, pike, mushrooms and various soups are not necessarily seasonal.

Šakotis (sha-ko-tis) – 'egg cake' – is a large tree-shaped cake covered with long spikes (made from a rather dry, spongecake mixture of flour, margarine, sugar, sour cream and dozens and dozens of eggs), which is served at weddings and other special occasions.

or mushrooms, and *virtiniai* are stodgy dumplings.

Lithuanians tend to like the less popular bits of animals: *liežuvis* (lea-zhu-vis; cow's tongue) and *alionių skilandis* (a-lyo-nyoo ski-lan-dis; minced meat smoked in pork bladders) are delicacies, and Lithuanians pork out on *vėdarai* (fried pork innards).

Hodgepodge or *šiupinys* (shyu-pi-nees) – often mistakenly assumed to be hedgehog – is pork snout stewed with pork tail, trotter, peas and beans. Smoked pigs' ears, trotters and tails are popular beer snacks alongside *kepta duona* (kep-ta dwa-na) – sticks of black rye bread heaped with garlic

and deep-fried. Order them with or without a gooey cheese topping.

Wild boar, rabbit and venison are popular in the Aukštaitija National Park, where hunted birds and animals were traditionally fried in a clay coating or on a spit over an open fire in the 18th century. When perpetually drifting sands on Curonian Spit on the Baltic Sea in the 17th to 19th centuries made growing crops impossible, locals took to hunting and eating migrating crows in winter: one bite (followed by a generous slug of vodka) at the crow's neck killed the bird, after which its meat was eaten fresh, smoked or salted.

EAT YOUR WORDS

Caught in a restaurant without a phrasebook? Here are a few useful sentences to get by.

Useful Phrases

A table for ..., please.	*Stalą ..., prašau.*	*stah*-lah ... prah-*show*
May I see the menu, please?	*Ar galėčiau gauti meniu, prašau?*	ahr gah-*leh*-chow gow-ti man-*yew* prah-*show*
Do you have the menu in English?	*Ar jūs turite meniu anglieškai?*	ahr yoos *tu*-ri-ta man-*yew* *ahn*-glish-kai
I'd like to try that.	*Aš norėčau išbandyti to.*	ahsh naw-*reh*-chow ish bahn-*dee*-ti taw
I don't eat ...	*Aš nevalgau ...*	ahsh na-*vahl*-gow
meat	*mėsiško*	*meh*-sish-kaw

Food Glossary

beef	*jautiena*	*yoh*-tien-a
beer	*alus*	*ah*-lus
boiled potato dumplings stuffed with meat	*cepelinai*	tsep-e-*lin*-ay
breaded pork chop	*karbonadas*	kar-bo-*na*-das
butter	*sviestas*	*svie*-stas
cheese	*sūris*	*soo*-ris
chicken	*vištiena*	vi-*shtie*-na
coffee	*kava*	ka-*va*
cold beetroot soup	*šaltibarščiai*	shal-*ti*-barshi-ay
eggs	*kiaušiniai*	(ki-o)-*shin*-i-ay
Lithuanian dumplings	*koldūnai*	kol-*doon*-ay
milk	*pienas*	*pien*-as
mushrooms	*grybai*	*gree*-bay
pancakes	*blyneliai*	blee-*nyal*-i-ay
pork	*kiauliena*	ki-ow-*lie*-na
tea	*arbata*	ar-ba-*ta*

Blyneliai (blee-nyal-i-ay; pancakes) – a real favourite – are sweet or savoury and eaten any time of the day. *Varskečiai* (vars-ko-chyai) are stuffed with sweet curd, and *bulviniai blyneliai* are made with grated potato and stuffed with meat, *varske* (cheese curd) or fruit and chocolate.

Cold Pink Soup & Other Starters

Lithuanians love soup and no self-respecting chef would plan a meal without one, but one soup rises above all others (maybe for its shocking pink colour, or maybe simply because it's delicious). *Šaltibarščiai* (shal-ti-barshi-ay) is a cold beetroot soup popular in summer and served with dill-sprinkled boiled potatoes and sour cream.

Other soups to look out for include nettle, sorrel, cabbage and bread soup (not to mention blood soup, which does indeed have goose, duck or chicken blood in it). Eel soup is specific to Curonian Spit, where eel also comes as a main course. In Aukštaitija, fish soup is served in a loaf of brown bread.

Popular starters include *silkė* (herring), *sprotai* (sprats) and salads. *Lietuviškos salotos* (lea-tu-vish-kos sa-lo-tos; Lithuanian salad) is a mayonnaise-coated mix of diced gherkins, boiled carrots, meat and anything else that happens to be in the fridge.

Mushrooms are popular, especially in August and September when forests are studded with dozens of different varieties – some edible, some deadly. Mushrooms are particularly abundant in the Aukštaitija and Dzūkija National Parks. In spring and early summer the same forests buzz with berry pickers; locals stand at roadsides in the region selling glass jam jars of wild strawberries, blueberries, blackberries and so on.

Beer & Other Beverages

Alus (beer) is the most widespread drink, local brands being Švyturys, Utenos and Kalnapilis. Brewing traditions are oldest in the northern part of Lithuania, where small family-run breweries treat lucky palates to natural beer free of preservatives.

Midus (mead) – honey boiled with water, berries and spices, then fermented with hops to produce an alcoholic drink of 10% to 15% proof – is Lithuania's oldest and most noble drink. It was popular until the decline of beekeeping in the 18th century, but made a comeback in 1959 when Lietuviškas midus (www.midus.lt) in Stakliškės in central Lith-

uania started making authentic mead; it produces several varieties today.

Vynas (wine) has made inroads into the drinking habits of Vilnius locals, but provincial Lithuania is still in two minds about it. *Degtinė* (vodka) is widely consumed and best enjoyed neat, chilled and with company.

The more sober-minded might enjoy the honey liqueur *stakliskes* or *starka,* made from apple-tree and pear-tree leaves. Herbal and fruit teas and brews made from linden, thyme, caraway, ginger, mint, rhubarb and a bounty of other sweet ingredients are age-old; Skonis ir Kvapas (p312) in Vilnius provides a unique opportunity to taste some.

Gira, another nonalcoholic drink, is a cloudy liquid made from bread. It's available across the country.

Where to Eat & Drink

Dining Lithuanian-style can mean spending anything from €7 for a three-course meal in a self-service cafe in a provincial town well off the tourist trail to €35 or more in a swish upmarket restaurant in the capital.

In Vilnius, the choice of cuisine and price range covers the whole gamut, and an English-language menu is usually available (likewise along the coast); elsewhere the choice is limited and menus are not always translated. Service is at its best in the capital – and generally average to poor everywhere else.

Eating Habits & Customs

A traditional dose of hospitality means loosening your belt several notches and skipping breakfast. Feasting is lengthy and plentiful, punctuated by many choruses of *Išgeriam!* (ish-ge-ryam; Let's drink!) and *Iki dugno!* (Bottoms up!). Starter dishes can be deceptively generous, leading unsuspecting guests to think they're the main meal. To decline further helpings may offend and be taken to mean that you don't like the food or the hospitality.

The family meal is a ceremonious affair and one that is taken very seriously, albeit one increasingly reserved for feast days, birthdays and other occasions in urban Lithuania's quicker-paced society. Each member of the family has a set place at the table – father at the head, mother opposite. If you arrive at someone's home while the family is seated, be sure to say *'skanaus'* (enjoy your meal!).

SURVIVAL GUIDE

 Directory A–Z

ACCOMMODATION

Lithuania has a wide choice of accommodation options to suit most budgets, including hotels, guesthouses, farmstays, hostels and campgrounds. Prices across these categories have risen in recent years but are generally lower than comparable facilities in Western Europe.

Budget properties can include hostels, cheaper guesthouses, farmsteads and campgrounds. Midrange accommodation includes most hotels and better guesthouses. Top end usually means corporate chains, luxury hotels and high-end boutiques.

➡ The resort areas on the Baltic coast during the summer season are the most expensive places to stay, followed by Vilnius then Kaunas.

➡ Watch for seasonal fluctuations on rates. Summer resorts, particularly on the Baltic coast, have much higher prices in season (June to August). Rates fall by as much as half during the 'cold season' (October to May). Many resort properties close for the winter.

➡ Prices do not always include breakfast. This is particularly true for guesthouses, which sometimes reckon a fee of €4 to €7 for breakfast.

➡ Parking may or may not be included in the room rate. Paid parking usually adds another €4 to €7 per night to the tab.

Hotels

A stay in a *viešbutis* (hotel) is the most common type of accommodation offering. The term encompasses a variety of old and new places, ranging from very basic to ultra-plush.

SLEEPING PRICE RANGES

The following price ranges refer to the cost of a double room with private bathroom.

€ less than €50

€€ €50 to €100

€€€ more than €100

At the top end are the international hotel chains that offer high-standard accommodation to a mostly business-oriented clientele, usually at prices aimed at expense accounts. Going down the line, there are many smaller, privately owned hotels that cater to the midrange market. While rates at these places vary, expect to pay around €45 for a single and from €60 for a double room.

Guesthouses

Svečių namai (guesthouses) can be found all around Lithuania, particularly in the larger cities. They can run the gamut from simple rooms in private houses to near-luxury-level boutiques, but usually represent better value than hotels, and are often much more atmospheric. While prices vary depending on the location and comfort level, expect to pay around €35/50 for a single/double, usually not including breakfast.

Homestays & Farmstays

Staying on a farm or rural homestead (*sodyba*) is a popular and highly recommended way of seeing the country. Homestays and farmstays are far more common in rural areas and small towns, and in the central and eastern parts of Lithuania, particularly in small cities like Utena or Anykščiai or around national parks, may be the only game in town.

The local tourist offices will generally keep a list of homestays on hand and can make recommendations based on your needs. Otherwise, check the helpful website of the Lithuanian Countryside Tourism Association (www.countryside.lt), which maintains a list of properties by region and has lots of good info on what to expect.

Rates vary greatly depending on the facilities and the season, but expect to pay around €40 per room in season (June to August), and half that out of season. Rates do not normally include breakfast.

Hostels

Lithuania does not have a particularly well-developed infrastructure of youth hostels, and what does exist is usually of the old-school variety, often in a school dormitory or very basic sport hotel. Most hostels are located in large cities; and outside of these you're better off choosing guesthouses or farmstays.

The Lithuanian Hostel Association (www.lha.lt) provides a directory of youth hostels, with links to individual properties.

Expect to pay around €9 to €11 per bed in dorm accommodation, depending on the property, location and time of year.

Campgrounds

Lithuania is dotted with campgrounds; some are in highly scenic areas such as along the Baltic coast or occupying desirable spots in national parks. Most campgrounds are equipped to handle both tent camping and caravans. Some also offer basic accommodation in bungalows or similar.

The Lithuanian Camp Site Association (www. camping.lt) maintains a helpful website that lists campgrounds and provides contact info and photos. The association also publishes the very helpful brochure *Kempingai Lietuvoje (Campsites in Lithuania)*, usually available at tourist offices or as a download from the association website.

Rates vary but expect to pay around €5 per person to camp and another €5 or so for a tent site. You will likely have to pay extra for parking a car or access to electricity. Some campgrounds operate only in season (May to September), so be sure to contact the campground in advance to ensure that it will be open during your visit.

ACTIVITIES

Lithuanians love nature. People were still worshipping ancient oak trees a mere six centuries ago, and these days in their free time they make regular pilgrimages to their country's many luscious lakes and forests and its long, sandy coastline. Boating, berrying, mushrooming, birdwatching and ballooning are uplifting pursuits. Travellers can walk and cycle into the wilderness, sweat in traditional lakeside saunas and enjoy ice-fishing in winter.

CUSTOMS REGULATIONS

The Lithuanian Customs Department (www. cust.lt) in Vilnius has online updates.

From outside the EU you can import duty-free into Lithuania: 1L of spirits, 2L of wine or champagne, and 200 cigarettes or 250g of tobacco. Meat and dairy products cannot be brought in as hand luggage from outside the EU. Upon entering, you must declare foreign currency in cash above €10,000, and the same amount when exiting.

When travelling within the EU, there are no restrictions on what you can take in and out of Lithuania providing it's for personal use.

Lithuania limits amber exports, but a few souvenirs should be OK providing the value doesn't exceed €1000. You need a Culture Ministry permit, and to pay 10% to 20% duty, to export artworks over 50 years old. Contact the Committee of Cultural Heritage (www.kpd. lt) for info.

EMBASSIES & CONSULATES

The website www.embassy-finder.com maintains an up-to-date list of consulates and embassies around the world. Embassies are located in Vilnius. For Lithuanian embassies abroad, see the website of the Lithuanian Foreign Affairs Ministry (www.urm.lt).

Australian Embassy (☑ 5-212 3369; Vilniaus gatvė 23; ☺10am-1pm Tue, 2-5pm Thu)

Belarusian Embassy (☑ 5-266 2200; www. lithuania.mfa.gov.by; Mindaugo gatvė 13; ☺8.30am-noon & 1-5.30pm Mon-Fri)

Canadian Embassy (☑ 5-249 0950; www. canada.lt; Jogailos gatvė 4; ☺8.30am-5pm Mon-Fri)

Danish Embassy (☑ 5-264 8760; www.amb vilnius.um.dk; T Kosciuškos gatvė 36; ☺8.30am-4.30pm Mon-Thu, to 4pm Fri)

Estonian Embassy (☑ 5-278 0200; www. estemb.lt; Mickevičiaus gatvė 4a; ☺8.30am-5pm Mon-Fri)

Finnish Embassy (☑ 5-266 8010; www.finland. lt; Kalinausko gatvė 24, 2nd fl)

French Embassy (☑ 5-219 9600; www.amba france-lt.org; Švarco gatvė 1; ☺9am-1pm & 2-5.30pm Mon-Fri)

German Embassy (☑ 5-210 6400; www.wilna. diplo.de; Z Sierakausko gatvė 24; ☺8.30am-noon & 1.30-4.30pm Mon-Thu, to 4pm Fri)

Latvian Embassy (☑ 5-213 1260; www.latvia.lt; Čiurlionio iela 76; ☺8.30am-5pm Mon-Fri)

Netherlands Embassy (☑ 5-211 3600; www. lithuania.nlembassy.org; Kosciuskos gatvė 36; ☺8.30am-12.30pm & 1.30-4.30pm Mon-Thu, to 4pm Fri)

Polish Embassy (☑ 5-219 7400; www.wilno. msz.gov.pl/en; Smėlio gatvė 20a)

Russian Embassy (☑ 5-272 3893; www. lithuania.mid.ru; Latvių gatvė 53; ☺8am-noon & 1.30-4pm Mon-Fri)

UK Embassy (☑ 5-246 2900; www. ukinlithuania.fco.gov.uk; Antakalnio gatvė 2; ☺8.30am-4.45pm Mon-Thu, to 1pm Fri)

US Embassy (☑ 5-214 0560; www.vilnius. usembassy.gov; Akmenų gatvė 6; ☺9am-9pm Mon-Fri)

INTERNET ACCESS

Internet use has developed at a staggering pace in Lithuania (at least in the country's larger urban centres), outstripping much of Western Europe. With the introduction of wireless technology, and more affordable PCs and laptops, an ever-increasing number of Lithuanians are becoming internet savvy. What this means for travellers is a decrease in the number of internet cafes and an increase in wi-fi hotspots. Most major cities still sport a cafe dedicated to internet access (on average €1.50 per hour), but in rural areas you'll be hard-pressed to find one.

Almost all hotels, including even most budget options, advertise internet access in rooms. This usually means wi-fi (often free but occasionally charged for), but there are a few hotels that still use LAN connections (and have Ethernet cables to borrow at the reception desk). Of course, you'll need your laptop or wi-fi enabled smartphone to use such services. The quality of the wi-fi connection can vary considerably

TIPPING TIPS

➡ In restaurants, tip 10% of the bill to reward good service. Leave the tip in the pouch that the bill is delivered in or hand the money directly to the waiter.

➡ Tip hairdressers and other personal services around 10% of the total.

➡ Taxi drivers won't expect a tip, but it's fine to add €2 to €4 to reward special service.

➡ Tipping in hotels is essentially restricted to the top-end establishments, which usually have decent room service and porters, who all expect to be tipped.

depending on how far your room is from the wi-fi router. If an internet connection is important, be sure to make this clear at the reception desk and request a room with a strong signal.

A couple of top-end hotels in Vilnius and Kaunas have computer-equipped business centres for guests to use at a fairly substantial fee. Many budget and midrange places, meanwhile, have a computer terminal in the lobby, on which guests can surf for free. Another option is to ask to use the hotel's computer to check email (sometimes possible, sometimes not).

MAPS

For Lithuania nothing can beat the interactive and searchable maps covering the entire country at www.maps.lt.

In print, Lithuania is best covered by the *Lietuva* (1:300,000) road map, published by Vilnius-based map publisher Briedis (p315) and sold by the publisher online. Bookshops, tourist offices and supermarkets in Lithuania sell it for €4.50. Jāņa sēta's *Lietuva* (1:500,000) is also good, and is available for around the same price.

For stress-free navigation buy Jāņa sēta's *miesto planas* (city maps) covering Vilnius, Kaunas and Klaipėda at a scale of 1:25,000, with a 1:10,000 inset of the centre, and Palanga (1:15,000), Šiauliai and Panevėžys (1:20,000). They cost €1.70 to €3.50 apiece in bookshops and some tourist offices.

Note too that most international SatNav and GPS systems (including TomTom and Garmin) offer Lithuanian maps as part of their European downloads. If you're planning on renting a car, pack your home GPS and use it on the road here just like you do at home.

MONEY

Lithuania joined the Eurozone in January 2015, trading in its litas for the euro.

ATMs are ubiquitous in cities and towns, and even the smallest hamlet is likely to have at least one. The majority accept Visa and MasterCard. Change money at banks, though the easiest way to carry money is in the form of a debit card, and withdraw cash as needed from an ATM.

Visa and MasterCard are widely accepted for goods and services. The only place you may experience a problem is at a very small establishment or for a very small transaction. American Express cards are typically accepted at larger hotels and restaurants, though they are not as widely recognised as other cards.

POST

Lithuania's postal system (www.post.lt) is quick and cheap. Posting letters or postcards costs €0.75 to other EU countries, €0.84 outside the EU and €0.39 domestically. Mail to the USA takes about 10 days, to Europe about a week. State-run EMS is the cheapest express mail service; find it in Vilnius at the central post office.

PUBLIC HOLIDAYS

New Year's Day 1 January

Independence Day (Nepriklausomybės diena) 16 February; anniversary of 1918 independence declaration

Lithuanian Independence Restoration Day 11 March

Easter Sunday March/April

Easter Monday March/April

International Labour Day 1 May

Mothers' Day First Sunday in May

Fathers' Day First Sunday in June

Feast of St John (Midsummer) 24 June

Statehood Day 6 July; commemoration of coronation of Grand Duke Mindaugas in the 13th century

Assumption of Blessed Virgin 15 August

All Saints' Day 1 November

Christmas (Kalėdos) 25 and 26 December

Lithuania also celebrates such days as the Day of the Lithuanian Flag (1 January), St Casimir's Day (4 March), Earth Day (20 March), Partisans' Day (fourth Sunday in May), Black Ribbon Day (23 August) and the Genocide Day of Lithuanian Jews (23 September). People still work on these days, but the national flag flutters outside most public buildings and private homes.

TELEPHONE SERVICES

Lithuania's digitised telephone network, run by TEO (www.teo.lt), is quick and efficient, although knowing what code to dial can be confusing.

To call other cities from a landline within Lithuania, dial ☎ 8, wait for the tone, then dial the area code and telephone number.

To make an international call from Lithuania, dial ☎ 00 followed by the country code.

To call Lithuania from abroad, dial Lithuania's country code (☎ 370), the area code and telephone number.

Then of course there are mobile telephones. No self-respecting Lithuanian would be seen without a mobile surgically attached to their ear, and indeed, many a hotel and restaurant – especially in more rural parts – lists a mobile telephone as its main number. Mobile numbers comprise a three-digit code and a five-digit number.

To call a mobile within Lithuania, dial ☎ 8 followed by the eight-digit mobile number. To call a mobile from abroad, dial ☎ 370 followed by the eight-digit mobile number.

Mobile companies Bitė (www.bite.lt), Omnitel (www.omnitel.lt) and Tele 2 (www.tele2.lt) sell prepaid SIM cards; Tele2 offers free roaming with its prepaid cards, making it the best choice for those travelling in Estonia, Latvia and Poland too. It also offers the cheapest rates.

Public telephones – increasingly rare given the widespread use of mobiles – are blue and only accept phone cards, sold at newspaper kiosks.

TOURIST INFORMATION

Most towns have a tourist office with staff who usually speak at least some English. Tourist offices range from the superbly helpful, useful and obliging to the downright useless, and are coordinated by the Vilnius-based State Department of Tourism (www.tourism.lt). Tourist offices will often help in finding a room. Among the best tourist offices in the country are those in Vilnius, Kaunas, Klaipėda and Trakai, all of which stock a wealth of highly useful brochures.

For more info on Lithuania's four Unesco World Heritage Sites – Neringa, Vilnius' Old Town, Kernavė and Struve Geodetic Arcs – visit the Vilnius-based **Lithuanian National Commission for Unesco** (Map p294; ☎ 5-210 7340; www.unesco.lt; Šv Jono gatvė 11).

ⓘ Getting There & Away

AIR

AirBaltic (☎ +371 6700 6006; www.airbaltic.com) Flies to Vilnius from Rīga several times daily and from Tallinn on most days. Also offers scheduled if sporadic service from Rīga to Palanga. These flights are more common in summer (May to September).

Estonian Air (☎ 5-232 9300; www.estonian-air.com) Flies between Tallinn and Vilnius twice each weekday.

BUS

Simple Express (☎ 5-233 6666; www.simpleexpress.eu) Budget bus carrier offering arguably the lowest prices to Lithuania from destinations in the Baltics, including daily buses to Vilnius from Rīga and Tallinn and to Kaunas from Rīga.

CAR & MOTORCYCLE

The three Baltic countries are all part of the EU's common-border Schengen Agreement, so there are no border checks when driving between Lithuania and Latvia. There's usually no problem taking hire cars across the border but it pays to let the rental company know at the time of hire if you intend to do so.

TRAIN

There is no longer a direct train from Vilnius to Rīga. There is one daily departure for Rīga, but it requires a change of train and six-hour layover at the Rēzekne 2 station in Latvia. The bus is a much better option.

Train service from Vilnius to Tallinn is simply impractical. The comically circuitous route requires two changes and some 36 hours of travel time. Here again, the bus is a better option.

ⓘ Getting Around

BICYCLE, CAR & MOTORCYCLE

Lithuanian roads are generally very good and driving is easy. Four-lane highways link the main cities of Vilnius, Kaunas and Klaipėda and the drive from Vilnius all the way to the Baltic coast (330km) generally takes three to four hours.

Touring cyclists will find Lithuania mercifully flat. In rural areas, some roads are unsealed but they're usually kept in good condition. Winter poses particular problems for those not used to driving in ice and snow. Car and bike hire is offered in all the major cities.

BUS

The national bus network is extensive, linking all the major cities to each other and the smaller towns to their regional hubs. Most services are summarised on the extremely handy website Bus Tickets (www.autobusubilietai.lt).

TRAIN

Local services are operated by Lithuanian Rail (www.litrail.lt), with regional hubs in Vilnius, Kaunas and Klaipėda. The Lithuanian Rail website is a model of user-friendliness and has routes, times and prices in English. Whether you take the bus or the train depends very much on the route. For common train journeys like Vilnius to Kaunas or to Klaipėda, the train is often more comfortable and better value than the bus. For other routes, the opposite might be true.

Kaliningrad Excursion

☑4012 / POP 423,000

Best Places to Eat

➡ Dolce Vita (p404)

➡ Borsch and Salo (p403)

➡ Zarya (p403)

Best Places to Stay

➡ Chaika (p403)

➡ Skipper Hotel (p402)

➡ Amigos Hostel (p401)

Why Go?

An intriguing and obscure destination, Kaliningrad is one of the grandest could-have-beens on the map of Europe. Having emerged, matured and indeed grown old as the grandiose German city of Königsberg, it is now the capital of a Russian exclave, surrounded on all sides by EU countries, and bearing the name of a Stalin-era Communist bigwig.

But the legacy left by the Germans, deported from East Prussia (as the region was known for centuries) at the end of WWII, shines through the Soviet architectural brutality and curiously affects local Russians, who have developed a peculiar Westernised identity, living in isolation from their mainland.

The three-day on-demand visa arrangement, still valid at the time of writing, gives a chance to explore this fascinating region of medieval German ruins, wide sandy beaches and amber-filled dunes, as well as to get a glimpse of Russia at yet another poignant moment in its history.

When to Go

➡ On 9 May troops and tanks parade through central streets to celebrate the Soviet victory in WWII. In mid-May museums welcome visitors for the museum night.

➡ Russian Navy Day at the start of the fourth week of July offers a rare chance to visit the nearby naval port of Baltiysk, which is usually off-limits to tourists unless they are on pre-organised tours.

➡ The Kaliningrad Jazz Festival is held in Kaliningrad every August, with the main shows taking place in the city's Central Park.

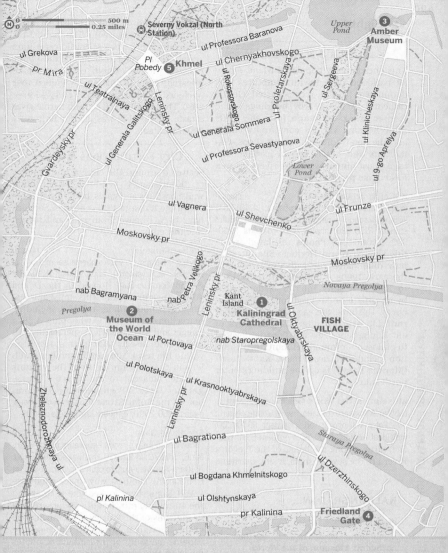

Kaliningrad Highlights

1 Visit the grave of philosopher Immanuel Kant and listen to an organ concert in **Kaliningrad Cathedral** (p400).

2 Learn about Russian maritime history at Kaliningrad's fascinating **Museum of the World Ocean** (p400).

3 Admire beautiful pieces of jewellery and art made from petrified pine resin at the **Amber Museum** (p400).

4 Be transported back to old Königsberg at the **Friedland Gate** (p400).

5 Spend a night out at **Khmel** (p404), where Central European beer culture meets Siberian culinary exoticism.

⊙ Sights

⊙ Kant Island & Around

This once densely populated island – now all parkland dotted with sculptures – is dominated by the reconstructed Gothic cathedral. A few nearby buildings – the **former stock exchange** from the 1870s (now housing various community clubs) and the neo-traditional row of shops, restaurants and hotels known as **Fish Village** – just hint at what this riverside area looked like pre-WWII.

Kaliningrad Cathedral   CHURCH
(Кафедральный собор Кёнигсберга; ☎ 4012-631 705; www.sobor-kaliningrad.ru; Kant Island; adult/student R150/130, photos R50, concerts R250-300; ☺10am-5pm) Photos displayed inside this Unesco World Heritage Site attest to how dilapidated the cathedral was until the early 1990s – the original dates back to 1333. The lofty interior is dominated by an ornate organ used for regular **concerts**. Upstairs, the carved-wood **Wallenrodt Library** has interesting displays of old Königsberg. The top floor is devoted to philosopher Immanuel Kant; the exhibition includes his death mask. Kant's **tomb** (Могила Канта) is on the building's outer north side.

Museum of the World Ocean   MUSEUM
(Музей Мирового океана; www.world-ocean.ru; nab Petra Velikogo 1; adult/student R300/200, individual vessels R100/80; ☺10am-6pm Wed-Sun) Strung along the banks of the Pregolya River are the several ships, a sub, maritime machinery and exhibition halls that make up this excellent museum. The highlight is the handsome former scientific expedition vessel *Vityaz*, moored alongside the *Viktor Patsaev*, with its exhibits relating to space research; visits to this are by guided tour (included in admission price, every 45 minutes). The pre-atomic B-413 submarine gives a taste of what life was like for its former 300 inhabitants.

⊙ City Fortifications & Gates

Scattered around the city are the remains of Königsberg's red-brick fortification walls, bastions and gates, built in stages between the 17th and 19th centuries. Sections have been rescued from ruin and turned into museums.

Amber Museum   MUSEUM
(Музей янтаря; www.ambermuseum.ru; pl Marshala Vasilevskogo 1; adult/student R190/130; ☺10am-6pm Tue-Sun) Housed in the Dohna Tower (Башня Дона), this museum features over 6000 amber exhibits, including marvellous artworks, a whopping 4.28kg nugget and several ancient specimens with prehistoric insects and plants fossilised within the resin. You can buy amber jewellery in the museum or from the vendors outside. Adjacent to the museum, **Rossgarten Gate** (Росгартенские Ворота) houses the **Solar Stone** (Солнечный камень; mains R280-2000; ☺noon-2am) restaurant.

Friedland Gate   MUSEUM
(Ворота Фридланд; www.fvmuseum.ru; pr Kalinina 6; adult/child R20/10, multimedia show R30; ☺10am-7pm May-Aug, to 6pm Sep-Apr, closed 1st Fri of month) The best way to see what pre-WWII Königsberg looked like is to attend the 40-minute **multimedia show** screened in the halls of this museum occupying one of the 13 original city gates. The evocative show is made up of projections of photos taken in the city between 1908 and 1913, and grainy footage shot around the castle in 1937.

King's Gate   MUSEUM
(Королевские ворота; ul Frunze 112; adult/student R60/30; ☺11am-7pm Wed-Sun) Focusing on Peter the Great's Grand Embassy to the city in 1697, this revamped gate also has good models of old Königsberg and exhibits on the personalities who shaped the region's history. If you venture a little south

---

KALININGRAD IN...

One Day
If your time is limited to a day, see the **cathedral**, **Museum of the World Ocean** and **Amber Museum** and stroll around Kaliningrad's leafy **parks**. End the day with a meal at **Fish Club**.

Two Days
With more time, check out Soviet art at the **Kaliningrad Art Gallery** and stroll through the leafy old German suburbs of **Amalienau** and **Maraunenhof**. Get a feel for the local bar scene at **Stoned Pony** in Kaliningrad city.

KALININGRAD AT A GLANCE

Area 15,100 sq km (region)

Departure tax none

Money rouble; €1 = R41.40; US$1 = R29.1; UK£1 = R47.2

Official language Russian

Visa You need a Russian visa to enter Kaliningrad. Citizens of Schengen countries, the UK, Switzerland and Japan can enter with an on-demand 72-hour tourist visa. These need to be arranged via local private travel agencies.

of here, where Moskovsky pr meets Litovsky val, you can find the twin-towered **Sackheim Gate** (Закхаймские ворота).

👁 Other Sights

Amalienau & Maraunenhof   NEIGHBOURHOOD

(Амалиенау и Марауненхоф) Casual strolls through the linden-scented, tree-lined neighbourhoods of Amalienau (to the city's west along pr Mira) and Maraunenhof (at the north end of the Upper Pond) provide a glimpse of cultured pre-WWII Königsberg. Amalienau is particularly lovely, with an eclectic range of villas along ul Kutuzova, the street connecting prs Pobedy and Mira. Maraunenhof has several appealing small hotels as well as the **German consulate** (ul Telmana 14) where visas can be issued.

History & Arts Museum   MUSEUM

(Калининградский областной историко-художественный музей; ☎ 4012-453 844; www.westrussia.org; ul Klinicheskaya 21; adult/student R80/70; ⏰10am-6pm Tue-Sun) Housed in a reconstructed 1912 concert hall on the banks of the pretty Lower Pond (Нижний пруд), this museum mainly focuses on events since Russia's takeover of the region, though Kaliningrad's German past does get a look-in.

Bunker Museum   MUSEUM

(Музей "Бункер"; ul Universitetskaya 3; adult/student R100/70; ⏰10am-6pm Tue-Sun) The city's last German commander, Otto van Lasch, capitulated to the Soviets from this buried command post in 1945. It now houses informative presentations about East Prussia during WWII.

Kaliningrad Art Gallery   GALLERY

(Калининградская художественная галерея; www.kaliningradartmuseum.ru; Moskovsky pr 60-62; adult/student R100/80; ⏰10am-6pm Tue & Wed, Fri-Sun, to 9pm Thu) View modern and contemporary works by local artists, including some striking pieces from the Soviet decades. The gallery shop sells art books and local creations.

Ploshchad Pobedy   SQUARE

(Площадь победы) The city's centre has come a long way since 1934, when it was known as Adolf-Hitler Platz. Today it's surrounded by shopping malls and features the gold-domed Cathedral of Christ the Saviour (Кафедральный Собор Христа Спасителя), built in 2006 in the Russo-Byzantine style.

Kaliningradsky Zoopark   ZOO

(Калининградский Зоопарк; www.kldzoo.ru; pr Mira 26; weekend/weekday R150/100; ⏰9am-8pm May-Sep, until 5pm Oct-Apr) Bears, hippos, seals and flamingos are among the creatures that call this zoo home.

Central Park   PARK

(Центральный парк; main entrance pr Pobedy 1) This forest-like park, on the grounds of an old German cemetery, has statues, funfair rides and an amphitheatre hosting summer concerts.

🛏 Sleeping

Kaliningrad is well served with midrange and top-end hotels, but budget accommodation is thin on the ground. Unless noted, rates include breakfast.

Amigos Hostel   HOSTEL €

(Амигос Хостел; ☎8-911-485 2157; www.amigoshostel.ru; ul Yablonevaya Alleya 34; dm R500-550, d R1200; 🛜) One of Kaliningrad's first hostels, Amigos has a new home in a charming house in a lovely part of town. The rooms are airy and bright, the kitchen and common areas are super clean and there are loads of public transport options

SLEEPING PRICE RANGES

€ less than R1500 per night for the cheapest double room

€€ cheapest double R1500 to R4000

€€€ cheapest double more than R4000

Kaliningrad

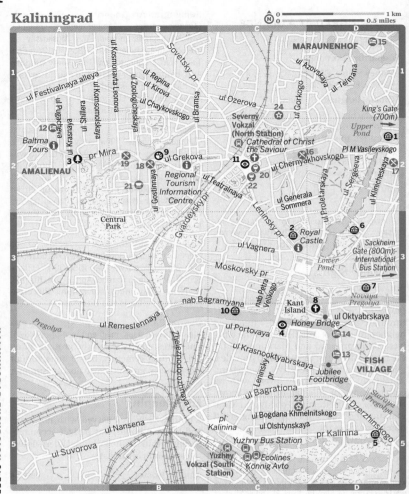

on the doorstep. It also rents bicycles (R250 per hour) and roller skates (R70 per hour).

Akteon Lindros Hostel   HOSTEL €
(Хостел Актеон Линдрос; ☎8-900-568 3333; ul Engelsa 14; dm/d from R500/1190; ☎) Quiet and clean, this new hostel offers standard-issue bunks, a good kitchen and happy-to-help staff. It's well serviced by public transport: buses 5, 9, 12, 14 and 35 will get you there from the city centre.

★**Skipper Hotel**   HOTEL €€
(Гостиница Шкипер; ☎4012-307 237; www.skipperhotel.ru; ul Oktyabrskaya 4a; r from R2800; ❄☎⑦) Location, ahoy! In a quaint period building with a superb riverside position in Fish Village, the Skipper Hotel is within stumbling distance of many of Kaliningrad's main attractions, cafes and bars. Rooms are clean with a vague nautical theme and have great views of the bustling surrounds.

Kaliningrad

Villa Severin GUESTHOUSE €€

(Вилла Северин; ☎4012-365 373; www. villa-severin.ru; ul Leningradskaya 9a; s/d from R1600/2200; ❄@🗑) This villa looks like a doll's house, with an adorable garden and lovely setting by Upper Pond (Prud Verkhny) to match. There are 10 comfortably furnished rooms, including one simple student room (R1000 without breakfast). It also has a small sauna and cafe.

Chaika HOTEL €€€

(Чайка; ☎4012-352 211; www.hotelchaika.ru; ul Pugacheva 13; s/d from R3500/4450; ❄@🗑) On a leafy street near the picturesque Amalienau area, 'Seagull' is a delightful 28-room property decorated with classy heritage touches. It also has a restaurant, comfy lounge and fitness room.

Heliopark Kaiserhof HOTEL €€€

(☎4012-592 222; www.heliopark.ru; ul Oktyabrskaya 6a; s/d from R4500/4950; ❄@🗑🏊) Part of the Fish Village development, this nicely designed and furnished hotel has light-filled rooms and a full-service spa and sauna. Rates are almost halved Friday to Sunday.

EATING PRICE RANGES

The following price ranges refer to the price of a main meal.

€ less than R500

€€ R500 to R1000

€€€ more than R1000

✖ Eating

Self-caterers should visit the lively **central market** (Центральный рынок; ul Chernyakhovskogo; ⊙8am-6pm).

Tabasko INTERNATIONAL €

(Табаско; pr Mira 19; pizzas R140-630, sushi R35-100; ⊙11am-11.30pm Sun-Thu, to 1.30am Fri & Sat) That time-honoured Russian classic – pizza and sushi – gets a good workout at this popular joint, with a massive range of both on offer.

Borsch and Salo UKRAINIAN €€

(Борщ и Сало; pl Pobedy 10; meals R300-500; ⊙noon-midnight Sun-Thu, to 2am Fri & Sat; 🗑) Decked out like a Ukrainian village hut, this cosy cafe has all the flavoursome, fattening treats you'd expect from its name. It also has a huge variety of flavoured brandies; if you're nice, they might even give you one on the house.

Zarya RUSSIAN, EUROPEAN €€

(Заря; ☎4012-300 388; pr Mira 43; meals R200-540; ⊙10am-3am; 🗑) This fashionable brasserie in the Scala cinema lobby is beautifully decorated and has an attractive outdoor area. A popular hang-out for pre- and post-movie nibbles, it whips up everything from steak and seafood to the inutterably sinful deep-fried Camembert.

★ Fish Club SEAFOOD €€€

(Рыбный клуб; ul Oktyabrskaya 4a; meals R500-1500; ⊙noon-midnight) For a seafood splurge with a view, this classy waterfront restaurant cannot be beaten. Everything on the menu is fresh and elegantly prepared and the service is the best in the city. If you're not supping in the sunshine, ask for a table near the aquarium.

Dolce Vita EUROPEAN, RUSSIAN €€€
(✆4012-351 612; www.dolcevita-kaliningrad.ru; pl Marshala Vasilevskogo 2; mains R420-1450; ☺noon-midnight; 🖥🍴) Many of Dolce Vita's inventive dishes appear overly fussy on the menu, but the competent chef makes them work. There's an excellent selection for vegetarians, superb seafood and divine pastas.

🍷 Drinking & Nightlife

Major DJs from Russia and Western Europe jet in for gigs at Kaliningrad's clubs, which open around 9pm but typically don't get going until well after midnight.

Teahouses and pubs also serve food and are often good alternatives to restaurants and cafes.

Khmel MICROBREWERY
(Clover City Centre, pl Pobedy 10; ☺noon-2am) Four types of beer are brewed at this appealing multilevel gastropub. An interesting menu (R350 to R600) includes unusual dishes such as reindeer and wild boar.

DON'T MISS

KVARTIRA

Hiding on the ground floor of an apartment block, **Kvartira** (Apartment; ✆4012-216 736; ul Serzhanta Koloskova 13; 🖥) is unquestionably one of Kaliningrad's coolest hang-outs. Lined with a fascinating range of pop-culture books, CDs, records and DVDs, all for sale or rent (as is everything else, including the stylish furniture), Kvartira – which means 'apartment' – also serves drinks and snacks, but there's no menu.

Movies are screened for free on several nights, while on others there may be a party or an art event. Whatever's happening, you're sure to make friends with locals. It's best to visit in the early evening, but opening hours are erratic, so call before setting off.

Stoned Pony NIGHTCLUB
(ul Chernyakhovskogo 2a; ☺11am-2am Mon-Thu, to 6am Fri & Sat, to midnight Sun) This fun indie club attracts a young and open-minded crowd; talented mixologists add fuel to the frivolities.

Bar Verf WINE BAR
(ul Oktyabrskaya 4a, Fish Village; ☺11am-midnight; 🖥) This relaxed wine bar has outdoor tables overlooking the cathedral. It screens movies and provides coloured pencils and paper for doodling.

Universal NIGHTCLUB
(✆4012-921 005; pr Mira 43; admission from R500) Kaliningrad's classiest club hosts DJs and fashion shows. It shares a location with Scala cinema.

Amsterdam NIGHTCLUB
(www.amsterdam-club.ru; 38/11 Litovsky val; admission R1000; ☺9am-6am Fri & Sat) This large alternative and gay-friendly club is in an old brick building 200m down an unnamed side street off Litovsky val.

☆ Entertainment

Classical concerts are occasionally held at the cathedral.

Reporter LIVE MUSIC
(Клуб Репортёр; ✆4012-571 601; www.reporter-club.ru; ul Ozerova 18; ☺11am-1am) Eclectic live gigs and jams kick off at this industrial-cool club most nights at 9pm. It also does set lunches for R150.

Philharmonic Hall CLASSICAL MUSIC
(Филармония; ✆4012-643 451; www.kenigfil.ru; ul Bogdana Khmelnitskogo 61a; tickets from R200) This beautifully restored neo-Gothic church has excellent acoustics, perfect for organ concerts, chamber-music recitals and the occasional symphony orchestra.

ℹ Information

Baltma Tours (✆4012-931 931; www.baltma.ru; 4th fl, pr Mira 94) The multilingual staff can arrange visas, accommodation, city tours and local excursions.

Emergency Hospital (Городская больница скорой медицинской помощи; ✆4012-466 989; ul A Nevskogo 90; ☺24hr)

Konigsberg.ru (www.konigsberg.ru) Loads of info on visas, hotels and what's happening in Kaliningrad.

Regional Tourism Information Centre
(☑4012-555 200; www.visit-kaliningrad.ru; pr
Mira 4; ⊙9am-8pm Mon-Fri, 11am-6pm Sat
May-Sep, 9am-7pm Mon-Fri, 11am-4pm Sat Oct-
Apr) Helpful, English-speaking staff and lots of
information on the region.

Royal Castle (☑4012-350 782; www.
kaliningradinfo.ru; Hotel Kaliningrad, Leninsky
pr 81; ⊙8am-8pm Mon-Fri, 9am-4pm Sat)
Access the internet and book tours to Kurshskaya Kosa (Curonian Spit) and elsewhere.

UNDERSTAND KALININGRAD

Kaliningrad Today

Russia's latest fallout with the West has
resulted in a bit of a siege complex in Kaliningrad, surrounded on all sides by NATO
countries. This is especially visible during
the pompous Victory Day parades on 9
May. But for most people, the annoyance
of poor relations with the neighbours is
gradually turning into a headache. Much of
the region's economy, after all, is dependent on cross-border trade with Poland and
Lithuania. With a huge devaluation of the
rouble, caused by the oil price slump and
Western sanctions against Russia, people's
ability to buy goods in the EU has diminished. That, on the other hand, means the
region has become much cheaper for foreign visitors.

The ongoing economic crisis does bite,
but the cushion of the wealth accumulat-
ed in the 'golden' 2000s is still protecting
people from outright poverty or unemployment. A new football stadium is being built, as Kaliningrad prepares to host
group matches of the World Cup in 2018.

History

Founded in 1255, Königsberg joined the
Hanseatic League in 1340, and from 1457
to 1618 was the residence of the grand
masters of the Teutonic order and their
successors, the dukes of Prussia. Prussia's
first king, Frederick I, was crowned in 1701
in the city's castle. For the next couple of

WORTH A TRIP

KURSHSKAYA KOSA NATIONAL PARK

Over half of the 98km-long Curonian
Spit lies in Russian territory and is
protected within the **Kurshskaya
Kosa National Park** (Национальный
парк Куршская коса; www.park-kosa.ru;
admission per person/car R40/300). Easily accessible in a day from Kaliningrad
city, it's a fascinating place to explore,
go wildlife- and bird-spotting or simply relax on pristine beaches. Highlights include the spectacular views
of the dunes from raised platforms
at **Vistota Efa**, and the **Dancing
Forest** (Танцующий лес; km37) where
wind-sculpted pines do indeed appear
to be frozen mid-boogie.

Buses from Kaliningrad head up
the spit (R101, two hours, four daily);
all stop in the coastal resort of Zelenogradsk on the way there and back.
Kaliningrad's Regional Tourism Centre
has the current timetable. Alternatively, hire a car (from around R1500) or
arrange a tour (around R700) in either
Kaliningrad or Zelenogradsk.

centuries Königsberg flourished, producing
citizens such as the 18th-century philosopher Immanuel Kant.

The city centre was flattened by British
air raids in August 1944 and the Red Army
assault from 6 to 9 April 1945. The Soviet
authorities deported all the remaining Germans and re-populated the area, mostly
with Russians. Renamed Kaliningrad on
4 July 1946, the city was rebuilt in grand
Soviet concrete style, albeit tempered by
parks, a network of ponds and waterways
and Kaliningrad Lagoon.

The remains of the castle were destroyed
and replaced by the outstandingly ugly
Dom Sovetov (House of Soviets) in the
1960s. During the eyesore's construction it
was discovered that the land below it was
hollow, with a (now flooded) four-level underground passage connecting to the cathedral. The decaying half-finished building
has never been used.

ⓘ VISAS

Visa barrier is what largely prevents mass tourism in Russia, but Kaliningrad is (or was) a lucky exception. It was unclear at the time of writing whether Russia was going to continue the experiment, which allowed citizens of Schengen-zone countries (most of the EU, that is), as well as Britain and Japan, to enter Kaliningrad region by obtaining 72-hour visas at the border. The experiment was originally expected to be discontinued at the end of 2014, but the authorities decided to prolong it for another year. With Kaliningrad hosting group matches of the 2018 World Cup, it is likely that the option will still be on the table for the next few years.

Here is how it works. No later than 10 days before the visit, you need to send a passport scan, your address and the date of arrival to one of the accredited tour agencies listed on www.visit-kaliningrad.ru. Check this website for exact requirements, which may change. After sending the scan and the info, you can get your visa when crossing the border at Khrabrovo airport and also at Bagrationovsk and Khrabrovo crossings on the Polish border. The latter two are convenient if you are travelling via Gdansk, which has an international airport. Note that on the Lithuanian border the 72-hour visa is not an option.

SURVIVAL GUIDE

ⓘ Getting There & Away

AIR

Khrabrovo airport (☏ 4012-610 620; www.kgd.aero) is 24km north of the city. There are daily flights to Moscow, St Petersburg and Berlin; see the website for other connections.

BUS

Mainly local buses depart from the **Yuzhny bus station** (ul Zheleznodorozhnaya 7) as well as international bus services run by **Ecolines** (☏4012-758 733; www.ecolines.net) to Warsaw and several German cities. **König Avto** (☏4012-999 199; www.kenigavto.ru) international services to the Baltic countries leave from its own bus station. Services to Vilnius, Klaipeda and Rīga are available.

TRAIN

All long-distance and most local trains go from **Yuzhny Vokzal** (Южный вокзал, South Station; pl Kalinina), some passing through, but not always stopping at, **Severny Vokzal** (Северный вокзал, North Station; pl Pobedy).

Long-distance destinations include Moscow, St Petersburg and Minsk; local services are to Svetlogorsk and Zelenogradsk.

ⓘ Getting Around

Trams (R10), trolleybuses (R10), buses (R12) and minibuses (R12 to R17) will get you most places. For the airport, take bus 144 from the bus station (R30, 30 minutes). A taxi to/from the airport is R600 with **Taxi Kaliningrad** (☏4012-585 858; www.taxi-kaliningrad.ru).

Car hire is available from **City-Rent** (☏4012-509 191; www.city-rent39.com; Moskovsky pr 182a), which also has a branch at the airport.

KALININGRAD EXCURSION GETTING THERE & AWAY

Survival Guide

Directory A–Z

Accommodation

In the Baltic, the Eastern Bloc bedtime blues are a thing of the past. Many hotels have been renovated and though there are still a few grey Soviet monsters lurking about, nowadays plenty of other options are available. The capitals tend to have the best range – from hostels to international hotel chains – but things can get tight on summer weekends.

Generally speaking, hostels, camp sites and cheaper guesthouses fall into the budget category; most of the guesthouses and the less expensive hotels are rated midrange; and top-end places include the ritzier hotels and boutique properties. In the capitals, especially Tallinn, it's hard to come by a decent double in the budget category, but competition is fierce, so in most cases you should be able to find something after a bit of online research.

The peak tourist season is from June to August (the ski resorts have a second peak in winter); if you're travelling then, you should book well in advance. This is essential in Tallinn, Vilnius and Rīga, as well as in popular summer-lovin' destinations, including the Estonian islands and all the coastal resorts.

From October to April (and to a lesser extent September and May), room prices typically drop by about 30% – sometimes substantially more, depending on your powers of persuasion. Also keep in mind that popular seaside spots and other weekend getaway destinations (including Tallinn) are pricier on Friday and Saturday than during the week.

Camping

Many Baltic camping grounds are beautifully located by lakes or within forests, but most are difficult to reach unless you have a private vehicle. Some have permanent wooden cottages or, occasionally, brick bungalows. Cabins vary in shape and size but are usually small, one-room affairs with three or four beds. Showers and toilets are nearly always communal and vary dramatically in cleanliness.

Camping grounds usually open in May or June and close in mid-to-late September. A night in a wooden cottage typically costs €10 to €30 per person, while tent sites range from €4 to €10 per person.

Estonia, in particular, has an extremely well-organised outfit overseeing camping. **RMK** (☑676 7500; www.rmk. ee) maintains dozens of free basic camp sites in forests all over the country: check its dedicated website www. loodusegakoos.ee for details.

Farmstays

The term 'farmstay' can vary widely – and isn't always the farm-based homestay experience you might be expecting. Many 'tourist farms' are set up as small guesthouses, while others offer self-contained apartments or whole cottages. Regardless, farmstays can prove to be a memorable choice. For a fee, host families will often

---

COTTAGE RENTALS

Baltcott (www.baltcott.com) An Estonian company with dozens of cottages and apartments on its books, throughout Estonia (☑648 5788) and Latvia (☑6756 9435). Scour its website for a log cabin in Lahemaa National Park, a farmstead on Saaremaa, a beachside apartment in Pärnu or Jūrmala, or a city base in Tallinn or Rīga.

Lauku Celotajs (www.celotajs.lv) This Latvian tourism company catalogues dozens of rural hotels and farmsteads in Latvia and beyond on its excellent website.

BOOK YOUR STAY ONLINE

For more accommodation reviews by Lonely Planet authors, check out http://lonelyplanet.com/hotels/. You'll find independent reviews, as well as recommendations on the best places to stay. Best of all, you can book online.

provide home-cooked meals and arrange fishing, boating, horse riding, mushrooming, berry-gathering and other activities.

Baltic Country Holidays
(Lauku Ceļotājs; ☑6761 7600; www.traveller.lv) Latvia-based but books accommodation in rural settings all over the Baltic. Options include B&B and guesthouse rooms, whole cottages and camp sites.

Countryside Tourism Association of Lithuania
(☑37-400 354; www.country side.lt) Arranges accommodation in farmhouses and rural cottages throughout Lithuania.

Estonian Rural Tourism
(☑600 9999; www.maaturism. ee) The full range of accommodation – from camping and farm-based B&Bs to palaces and castle hotels – can be booked through this umbrella organisation.

Guesthouses

Somewhat bigger than B&Bs but smaller than hotels, private guesthouses are a good bet for affordable travel in the Baltic and often offer a cosy, informal setting. Typically they have fewer than a dozen rooms but beyond that there are no hard and fast rules. Some have en suite bathrooms while others' are communal, some offer breakfast and others don't; these days, free wi-fi is more common than not. Standards of cleanliness can also vary but generally the quality is high. Prices range from around €20 to €90 per room.

Hostels

There are a growing number of hostels scattered throughout the Baltic, mostly con-

centrated in the capitals and larger cities. Dorm beds in the capital cities in high season range from about €10 to €15. Book your bed well in advance if you come in the summer.

You'll find **Hostelling International** (www.hihostels. com) hostels in all of the Baltic countries. For backpacker recommendations, check out **Hostelworld** (www. hostelworld.com). Some websites with a (not comprehensive) list of hostels in each country:

➡ **Estonia** www.hostels.ee

➡ **Latvia** www. hostellinglatvia.com

➡ **Lithuania** www.lha.lt

Hotels

The Baltics have hotels to suit every price range, although budget doubles and singles in the increasingly glam capitals have become dishearteningly scarce. (The hostel scene, on the other hand, is thriving.) As more cheap hotels make the effort to brighten up their image, nightly rates are being yanked up, too. Delightfully horrible relics from the Soviet era still exist – but though they may retain their blocky exteriors, the interiors will have generally been modernised.

The midrange option, both in and outside the capitals,

Climate

Rīga

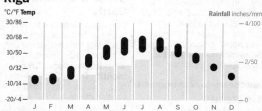

Tallinn

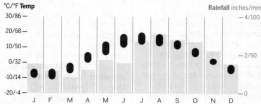

Vilnius

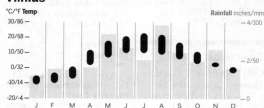

includes small, family-run hotels – whose only downside is that they have few rooms and get booked up quickly.

Top hotels are a dime a dozen. Many are under Western management or are part of a recognised international hotel chain, while others – such as Dome Hotel (p215) in Rīga, the Radisson Blu Royal Astorija (p307) in Vilnius and the Three Sisters (p72) in Tallinn – are housed in exquisitely renovated, historic buildings dating from the 13th to 19th centuries.

Spa Hotels

Spa hotels are both an excellent place to be pampered and – for those with water parks attached – to take the kids. Even if you don't stay overnight, you can pop in for treatments: mud baths, massages, herbal baths and dozens of other options.

Estonia and Latvia have the most selections, with Jūrmala in Latvia known as the spa centre of the Baltic. Druskininkai is Lithuania's premier spa connection; Birštonas is also popular. Kuressaare on Saaremaa is known as the spa capital of Estonia.

Customs Regulations

If you think that a painting or other cultural object you'd like to buy in one of the Baltic countries might attract customs duty or require special permission to export, check with the seller before purchasing – you may have to get permission from a government office before it can be exported. For country-specific customs information, see Estonia (p177), Latvia (p282) and Lithuania (p395).

Discount Cards

City Discount Cards

All three capitals offer discount cards. Ventspils has its own virtual currency that can be earned by and spent on visiting its sights.

Hostel Cards

A Hostelling International (HI) card yields discounts of up to 20% at affiliated hostels (though there are many non-HI hostels throughout the Baltic). You can buy one at participating hostels en route, or purchase it before you go via your national **Youth Hostel Association** (YHA; www.hihostels.com).

Seniors Cards

There are some discounts available to older people – museums often reduce the entrance fee, and concert and performance tickets may also be reduced, so it's always worth asking. Ferries and long-distance buses will often have seniors' fares (discounts of around 10%). To take advantage of discounts, be sure to carry ID providing proof of your age.

Student & Youth Cards

Carrying a student card entitles you to a wide variety of discounts throughout the Baltics. The most common card is the **International Student Identity Card** (ISIC; www.isic.org), which is issued to full-time students aged 12 years and over, and gives the bearer discounts on accommodation, transport and admission to some attractions. It's available from student unions, hostelling organisations and some travel agencies; for more information, see the website of the **International Student Travel Confederation** (ISTC; www.istc.org).

The ISTC is also the body behind the **International Youth Travel Card** (IYTC or Go25), which is issued to people who are between 12 and 26 years of age and not full-time students, and gives equivalent benefits to the ISIC.

A similar ISTC brainchild is the **International Teacher Identity Card** (ITIC), available to teaching professionals.

Electricity

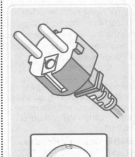

220V/50Hz

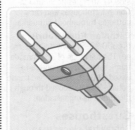

220V/50Hz

Embassies & Consulates

Estonia, Latvia and Lithuania each have numerous diplomatic missions overseas. Likewise, many countries have their own embassies or missions in the Baltic capitals. See Estonia (p177),

Latvia (p282) and Lithuania (395) for details.

It's important to realise what your own embassy can and can't do for you if you get into trouble. Remember that you are bound by the laws of the country you are in. Your embassy will not be sympathetic if you end up in jail after committing a crime locally, even if such actions are legal in your own country.

Some countries opt to have only one diplomatic mission for the entire Baltic region (usually in Rīga), while others may be served out of embassies in Stockholm or Berlin.

Gay & Lesbian Travellers

Following independence, all three Baltic States decriminalised homosexual acts and today there is an equal age of consent for sexual acts for all citizens. Yet not all is as rosy as it seems. Of the three, secular Estonia is the most tolerant, while life is considerably harder for gays and lesbians in Catholic Lithuania, and arguably worse still in Latvia. On the 2015 Rainbow Europe Map website, which ranks each nation according to the legal protection offered to its lesbian, gay, bisexual and transgender (LGBT) citizens, Estonia scored 34%, Lithuania 19%, and Latvia 18%. (By comparison, Britain is at 86%, while nearby Sweden scores 72%.)

In all three countries, being 'out' creates multiple risks, as small displays of public affection can provoke some nasty responses. While there is a small gay scene in Tallinn (p79), Rīga and Vilnius (p312), there's almost nothing elsewhere.

That said, Baltic Pride has become an annual festival, with successful, problem-free celebrations hosted by one of the three capitals each year. In 2015, Rīga was the first Baltic capital to host Euro-

pride; the march proceeded without any incidents.

Resources

Estonian LGBT portal (www.gay.ee)

ILGA Europe (www.ilga-europe.org) Excellent, country-by-country information on gay life and acceptance in all of Europe, including the Baltic countries.

Latvian LGBT portal (www.gay.lv)

Lithuanian LGBT portal (www.gay.lt)

Health

The Baltic region is, on the whole, a pretty healthy place to travel in, though medical facilities outside of the capital cities may not be entirely up to Western standards. Practically all pharmacies in the capitals and larger towns stock imported Western medicines. In the capitals, private clinics offer Western-standard, English-speaking medical care, but they are often expensive. In an emergency, seek your hotel's help first (if you're in one); the bigger hotels may have doctors on call. Emergency care is free in all three countries.

If you're an EU citizen, a European Health Insurance Card (EHIC) covers you for most medical care, but not for nonemergencies or the cost of repatriation. You can apply for one online in many EU countries via your government health department's website.

Insect Bites & Stings

Spread by tick bites, tick-borne encephalitis is a serious infection of the brain. If you intend to spend a lot of time in forested areas, including by the coast where pine forest prevails, vaccination is advised. Two doses of vaccine will give a year's protection; three doses are good for up to three years. You should always check

all over your body if you have been walking through a potentially tick-infested area; signs along the Lithuanian coast alert walkers and beachgoers to areas where ticks are particularly rampant. If you find an attached tick, press down around its head with tweezers, grab the head and gently pull upwards. Avoid pulling the rear of the body as this may squeeze the tick's gut contents through the attached mouth parts into the skin, increasing the risk of infection and disease.

Mosquitoes are a voracious pest in the region, and can cause irritation and infected bites. Use a DEET-based insect repellent.

Water

Some official travel advisories detail the need to avoid tap water and drink only boiled or bottled water, but locals insist the tap water is perfectly safe to drink (if not altogether pleasant-tasting). Do not drink water from rivers or lakes – it may contain bacteria or viruses that can cause diarrhoea or vomiting.

Insurance

A travel insurance policy to cover theft, loss of property and medical problems is a good idea. Worldwide travel insurance is available at www.lonelyplanet.com/travel-insurance. You can buy, extend and claim online anytime – even if you're already on the road.

Some policies offer lower and higher medical expense options. Policies can vary widely, so be sure to check the fine print. Some insurance policies will specifically exclude 'dangerous activities', which can include hiking.

You may prefer a policy that pays doctors or hospitals rather than requiring you to pay on the spot and claim later. If you do have to claim later make sure you keep all documentation.

Some policies ask you to call (reverse charges) a centre in your home country, where an immediate assessment of your problem is made. Check that your policy covers ambulances and an emergency flight home.

Internet Access

Internet use has developed at a staggering pace in the Baltic, outstripping much of Western Europe. With the introduction of wireless technology and more affordable laptops and smartphones, an ever-increasing number of locals are becoming internet-savvy. What this means for travellers is a decrease in the number of internet cafes and an increase in wi-fi hot spots – Estonia in particular is virtually blanketed in wi-fi. Most major cities still sport a cafe or two with computers for internet access, but in rural areas you'll be hard-pressed to find one. In these parts tourist offices or libraries are your best bet. Public libraries are also a reliable source of free wi-fi.

Almost all top-end hotels, an ever-expanding number of midrange places and even many budget options have internet access in the rooms. However the speed varies wildly.

A cheap way to ensure you have internet access at all times is to procure a local SIM card that provides mobile internet access. You can then use your smartphone to create a personal hot spot and get your other gadgets connected.

Each of the countries maintains lists of wi-fi hot spots you can tap into. For details:

Estonia www.wifi.ee

Latvia http://wifi.inbox.lv

Lithuania www.wifi.lt

Legal Matters

If you are arrested in the Baltics you have the same basic legal rights as anywhere else in Europe, including the right to be informed of the reason for your arrest (before being taken to the police station); to inform a family member of your misfortune (once you are there); and to have your lawyer present during questioning. You cannot be detained for more than 72 hours without being charged with an offence.

Smoking is not permitted in restaurants, bars, nightclubs and cafes in all three countries, although it is permitted on outdoor terraces or in closed-off smoking rooms (with proper ventilation).

Drinking alcohol outside restaurants and bars is generally not permitted. The risk of being fined is high in larger capitals.

Maps

Decent regional and country maps are widely available outside the region, as are quality city maps in each country. A map covering the whole region can be useful for planning: *Estonia, Latvia, Lithuania* from **Cartographia** (www.cartographia.hu) has a 1:700,000-scale map of the three countries, and many publishers produce something similar. Insight Travel Maps has a useful 1:800,000 *Baltic States* map, which includes city plans of Tallinn and Rīga.

Good maps to look for in the region include *Eesti Latvija Lietuva* (1:700,000) published by Vilnius-based **Briedis** (www.briedis.eu). In Estonia, **EO Map** (www.eomap.ee) does a pretty mean *Baltimaad* (Baltic States, 1:800,000), which is widely

---

PRACTICALITIES

Print & Digital Press Major global English-language publications, such as the *Economist* and *National Geographic,* are available at centrally located press kiosks in all three capitals. The *Baltic Times* is a Rīga-based pan-Baltic newspaper covering politics and life in all three countries. The Estonian public broadcaster's English-language portal is at news.err.ee, Latvian public broadcaster's English-language portal is at lsm.lv/en and Lithuanian news in English canbe found at en.delfi.lt. For long reads on Latvian and international politics translated into English, visit rebaltica.lv/en.

Radio The BBC World Service airs on 100.5 FM in Rīga, 103.5 FM in Tallinn and 95.5 FM in Vilnius.

TV English-language channels are available in most hotels and in cable packages.

Weights & Measures All three countries use the metric system for length (metres), weight (kilograms) and temperature (Celsius).

Smoking In all three countries, smoking is banned in restaurants, bars and night clubs (except for on open-air terraces). Additional restrictions on smoking near schools apply in Latvia.

available in Estonian bookshops.

In Latvia, map publisher **Jāņa Sēta** (www.kartes.lv) is the market leader, with its pocket-sized, spiral-bound, 152-page *Baltic Countries & Kaliningrad Region* (1:500,000), which contains 72 city and town plans as well as road maps covering the entire region. It also has a *Baltic Countries* (1:700,000) road map, which is equally good.

The website www.maps.com is a decent digital map resource.

See also p177 for Estonia, p283 for Latvia and p396 for Lithuania.

Money

ATMs

ATMs accepting Cirrus, Visa and MasterCard are widespread in cities and larger towns, enabling you to get cash 24 hours a day. Most ATMs are multilingual, using the main European languages.

Credit Cards

Credit cards are widely accepted in hotels, restaurants and shops, especially at the upper end of the market. Visa and MasterCard are the most commonly accepted but Diners Club and American Express also crop up. They are essential for hiring a car. It's generally easiest to use an ATM for a Visa or MasterCard cash advance.

Moneychangers

Every town has somewhere you can change cash: usually a bank, exchange office or currency exchange kiosk. The latter crop up in all sorts of places, particularly airports, bus stations and train stations. Rates vary from one outlet to another. Exchange places are generally open during usual business hours.

Tipping & Bargaining

It's fairly common, though not compulsory, to tip waiters 5% to 10% by rounding up the bill. Some bargaining (but not a lot) goes on at flea markets; you're not likely to get more than a 10% to 20% discount off the initial asking price.

Travellers Cheques

Given the explosion of ATMs accepting international cards, travellers cheques are going the way of the dinosaurs, but you should still be able to exchange them (for a hefty commission) at banks in major cities.

Opening Hours

The following are standard opening hours throughout the region.

Banks 9am to 4pm or 5pm Monday to Friday.

Bars 11am or noon to midnight from Sunday to Thursday; until 2am or 3am Friday and Saturday.

Cafes 8am or 9am to 10pm or 11pm daily.

Clubs 10pm to 4am or 5am Thursday to Saturday. In Latvia they start filling up at 11pm and close around 6am, Wednesday to Saturday; in warmer months they often open Sunday to Tuesday as well.

Post offices 8am to 6pm or 7pm Monday to Friday; 8am or 9am to 2pm or 3pm on Saturday.

Restaurants Noon to 11pm or midnight daily.

Shops 10am to 6pm or 7pm Monday to Friday; 10am to 3pm or 4pm Saturday.

Supermarkets 8am or 9am to 10pm daily.

Post

Letters and postcards from any of the three countries take about two to four days to Western Europe, seven to 10 days to North America

WHICH FLOOR?

Before you start traipsing up the stairs, note that in the Baltic countries the ground floor is referred to as the 1st floor.

and two weeks to Australia, New Zealand and South Africa. Occasionally, as in any other country, a letter or parcel might go astray for a couple of weeks, but generally everything arrives.

You can buy your stamps at a post office (Estonian: *postkontor;* Latvian: *pasts;* Lithuanian: *paštas*) and post your mail there. In Estonia, you can bypass the post office, buy stamps in shops and slip the envelope in any post box.

For postal rates and other information, take a look at the websites of the postal companies:

Eesti Post (www.post.ee) Estonia.

Latvijas Pasts (www.pasts.lv/en/) Latvia.

Lietuvos Paštas (www.post.lt) Lithuania.

Expensive international express-mail services are available in the capital cities.

Written address format conforms to Western norms, for example:

Kazimiera Jones
Veidenbauma iela 35-17
LV-5432 Ventspils
Latvia

Veidenbauma iela 35-17 means Veidenbaum St, building No 35, flat No 17. Postcodes in Estonia are the letters 'EE' plus five digits; in Latvia 'LV-' plus four digits; and in Lithuania 'LT-' plus five digits (although the LT isn't essential).

For people wanting to receive mail on the move, there are poste-restante services in the main post offices in Tallinn and Vilnius, and at the post office next to Rīga train station. All three keep mail for a month. Address letters to poste restante as follows, preceded by the full name of the recipient:

Estonia Poste Restante, Narva maantee 1, EE10101 Tallinn, Estonia

Latvia Poste Restante, Rīga, LV-1050 Latvia

Lithuania Poste Restante, Vilnius ACP, Gedimino prospektas 7, LT-01001 Vilnius, Lithuania

Telephone

City codes are a thing of the past in little Estonia and Latvia – if you're calling from abroad, dial just the country code then the listed number. In Lithuania things are a little more complicated. Futher details can be found in the country directories (see Estonia, p178; Latvia, p283; and Lithuania, p396).

Speaking of mobile phones, Estonia, Latvia and Lithuania all use GSM 900/1800 – compatible with the rest of Europe and Australia, but not with the North American GSM 1900 or the totally different system in Japan. If your phone is GSM 900/1800-compatible you can buy a cheap SIM card package from a choice of mobile-phone providers in all three countries.

Time

Estonia, Latvia and Lithuania are on Eastern European Time (GMT/UTC +2). All three countries adhere to daylight savings, which runs from the last Sunday in March to the last Sunday in October (at this time it's GMT +3).

The 24-hour clock is used for train, bus and flight timetables, while letters (the initial letter of each day) or numerals (I or 1 = Monday; VII or 7 = Sunday) may indicate the days of the week in posted opening hours or timetables. Dates

---

WHICH DOOR IS WHICH?

We hope you're not busting for a pee, as working out which toilet door to enter may require some thinking time. Men's toilets are marked by the letter 'M' in Estonia and 'V' in Latvia or Lithuania; women's toilets are indicated by 'N' in Estonia, 'S' in Latvia and 'M' in Lithuania. Some doors sport the triangle system: a skirtlike triangle for women and a broad-shouldered, upside-down triangle for men. To add even more confusion, in Lithuania (as in neighbouring Poland), male toilets may be indicated by a triangle and female toilets by a circle.

---

are listed in European style: date, then month, then year – 01.06.1974 stands for 1 June 1974.

Toilets

Public toilets in the Baltic countries are wondrous things compared with the stinking black holes of the past: today you'll find mostly clean, modern systems (no grubby baskets in the corner; just flush the paper). That isn't to say that we recommend spending much time in the public restrooms of train or bus stations: they aren't the most inviting of places. Although there are public toilets in some places, you can also stroll into large hotels in major cities and use the toilets without upsetting the staff too much (or else just pop into the nearest McDonald's).

Tourist Information

All three capitals, plus most cities, towns and seaside resorts, sport an efficient tourist office of sorts that doles out accommodation lists and information brochures, often in English and usually delivered with a smile. These tourist offices are coordinated by each country's national tourist board, listed in the country directories (Estonia, p178; Latvia, p227; and Lithuania, p316). Pretty

much all locations covered in this book have websites for tourists.

Travellers with Disabilities

With its cobbled streets, rickety pavements and old buildings (often without elevators), the Baltic region presents challenges for travellers with disabilities. That said, many city hotels have rooms equipped for disabled travellers; your first port of call for this information should be the tourist information centres of the capitals. Some beaches on the western Lithuanian coast in Nida and Palanga have ramps to allow wheelchair access to the sand.

Useful resources:

Able Travel (www.able-travel. com) Has information on its website. (Sadly, there's no information for either Latvia or Lithuania.)

Apeirons (☑6729 9277; www. apeirons.lv) This organisation of people with disabilities and their friends is a good first contact in Latvia.

Freedom of Movement (Liikumisvabadus; http:// liikumisvabadus.invainfo.ee) This fantastic resource provides detailed information (in English) about accessibility in Estonia for wheelchair-users and those with limited movement, split into regions, towns and places of interest.

Visas

Your number-one document is your passport; make sure it's valid for at least three months after the end of your Baltic travels. Only some nationalities need visas. Citizens from the EU, Australia, Canada, Japan, New Zealand and the US do not require visas for entry into Estonia, Latvia or Lithuania.

Other nationalities should check the websites of the relevant Ministries of Foreign Affairs:

Estonia Välisministeerium; www.vm.ee

Latvia www.pmlp.gov.lv

Lithuania www.migracija.lt

Visa Extensions

Single-entry visas can sometimes be extended in the Baltics. In Latvia visit the foreigners' service centre of the **Office of Citizenship & Migration Affairs** (Pilsonības un migrācijas lietu pārvalde; ☑6721 9656; www.pmlp. gov.lv; Alunāna iela 1, Rīga). In Lithuania your first port of call should probably be the migration department inside the **Ministry of Interior** (Migracijos Departamentas; ☑52-717 112; www.migracija.lt; L. Sapiegos 1, Vilnius).

Belarusian Visas

You will need a Belarusian visa, arranged in advance, even to transit within the country. Visas are not issued at road borders. Belarusian embassies in all three Baltic capitals issue visas – see www.belembassy.org for contact details. For the low-down, see the **Ministry of Foreign Affairs of the Republic of Belarus** (www. mfa.gov.by).

Russian Visas

All foreign visitors need a visa to enter Russia. Getting the visa can be time-consuming, and our strongest advice is that you obtain one before you leave home. A tourist visa requires an invitation, which can be issued from a hotel or some hostels in Russia or from online visa specialists (eg www.visatorussia. com). You then present your invitation and application to a Russian consulate and receive your visa a few weeks later (or an agency can do that step too, for a fee – this is recommended, as they're experts in dealing with the bureaucracy).

If you didn't get the urge to enter Russia until arriving in the Baltics, you can try your luck in obtaining a Russian visa from one of the embassies in Tallinn, Rīga or Vilnius. There you'll get a heavy dose of bureaucracy and perhaps a visa – there are no guarantees, and this might come down to your nationality. You might also consider asking a local travel agency for help.

A special Kaliningrad 72-Hour Express Visa is available for Russia's Kaliningrad region for citizens of Schengen countries (ie most countries of the EU, excluding the UK and Ireland), the UK and Japan, but you'll still need to apply in advance – and it's available only for those arriving by plane or crossing from Poland. It's probably best to plan on obtaining a regular Russian visa, arranged in advance.

Volunteering

Estonia has an established WWOOF (World Wide Opportunities on Organic Farms) organisation, facilitating volunteer work on organic farms in exchange for accommodation and meals. Lithuania's branch is just starting out (www.wwoof.lt) and Latvia has only a couple of farms listed with **WWOOF Independents** (www.wwoof. org/wwind). Volunteer opportunities for English speakers are occasionally advertised locally in the *Baltic Times* (www.baltictimes.com) newspaper.

Women Travellers

The Balts have some fairly traditional ideas about gender roles, but on the other hand they're pretty reserved and rarely impose themselves upon other people in an annoying way. Women are not likely to receive aggravation from men in the Baltics, although unaccompanied women may want to avoid a few of the sleazier bars and beer cellars. Many women travel on overnight buses and trains alone, but if you're travelling on a train at night, play safe and use the hefty metal lock on the inside of the carriage door.

Work

The Baltic region has enough difficulty keeping its own people employed, meaning there's little temporary work for visitors. Most nonlocals working here have been posted by companies back home. However, these are times of change, and there is some scope for people who want to stay a while and carve themselves a new niche – though, in Western terms, you shouldn't expect to get rich doing so. The English language is certainly in demand and you might be able to earn your keep (or part of it) teaching it in one of the main cities. For teaching and other postings, try www.goabroad.com.

Transport

GETTING THERE & AWAY

There are numerous ways to enter the Baltic countries, either directly or via a close neighbour. For example, it's feasible to fly or take a bus to Warsaw and then enter Lithuania by train, or fly to Helsinki and sail from there to Estonia. Within the Baltics, distances are relatively small.

This section focuses on getting to Estonia, Latvia and Lithuania from outside the region. Flights, tours and rail tickets can be booked online at www.lonelyplanet.com/bookings.

Entering Estonia, Latvia & Lithuania

Whether you arrive by bus, boat, plane or train, entry procedures are fairly quick and painless. If you're travelling from within the Schengen zone (ie most countries of the EU, excluding the UK and Ireland), there are no longer any arrival formalities.

Passport

Travellers arriving from outside the Schengen zone need a passport, valid for three months beyond the planned stay. Citizens of EU countries, the US, Canada, Australia and New Zealand don't need a visa for entering Estonia, Latvia or Lithuania. See p408 for more information.

Air

Airports & Airlines

Estonia's national carrier is **Estonian Air** (www.estonian-air.ee), while Latvia's is **airBaltic** (☑9000 1100; www.airbaltic.com). Lithuania's former national carrier is now defunct. International airports within the region:

Kaunas Airport (KUN; ☑6124 4442; www.kaunas-airport.lt)

Palanga Airport (Palangos Oro Uostas; ☑6124 4442; www.palanga-airport.lt; Liepaja plentas 1) Nonstop flights to Copenhagen.

Rīga International Airport (Starptautiskā Lidosta Rīga; ☑1817; www.riga-airport.com; Mārupe District; ☐22)

Tallinn Airport (TLL; ☑605 8888; www.tallinn-airport.ee; Tartu mnt 101; ☐2)

Tartu Airport (TAY; ☑605 8888; www.tartu-airport.ee; Lennu tn 44, Reola küla)

Vilnius International Airport (Tarptautinis Vilniaus Oro Uostas; ☑6124 4442; www.vno.lt; Rodūnios kelias 10a; W; g1, 2) Lithuania's major international air gateway, with a handful of direct flights to major European cities.

Tickets

Automated online ticket sales work well if you're planning a simple one-way or return trip on specified dates, but for complicated routing they are no substitute for

---

CLIMATE CHANGE & TRAVEL

Every form of transport that relies on carbon-based fuel generates CO_2, the main cause of human-induced climate change. Modern travel is dependent on aeroplanes, which might use less fuel per kilometre per person than most cars but travel much greater distances. The altitude at which aircraft emit gases (including CO_2) and particles also contributes to their climate change impact. Many websites offer 'carbon calculators' that allow people to estimate the carbon emissions generated by their journey and, for those who wish to do so, to offset the impact of the greenhouse gases emitted with contributions to portfolios of climate-friendly initiatives throughout the world. Lonely Planet offsets the carbon footprint of all staff and author travel.

a travel agent with the low-down on deals, strategies for avoiding stopovers and other useful advice.

Paying by credit card offers some protection if you end up dealing with a rogue fly-by-night agency, as most card issuers provide refunds if you can prove you didn't get what you paid for. Even better, buy a ticket from a bonded agent, such as one covered by the **Air Travel Organisers' Licence** (ATOL; www.atol.org.uk) scheme in the UK. If you have doubts about the service provider, at the very least call the airline and confirm that your booking has been made.

Australia & New Zealand

If you're coming from Australasia, a trip to the Baltic will necessitate at least three separate flights; there's no one airline that services the entire route. **Star Alliance** (www.staralliance.com) has the most partner airlines serving the Baltic states – Austrian Airlines, Brussels Airlines, LOT, Lufthansa, SAS and Turkish Airlines – making an Air New Zealand or Thai Airways code-share the most flexible choice. Qantas is a member of **One World** (www.oneworld.com), but **Finnair** (AY; ☑Estonia 626 6309, Latvia 6720 7010, Lithuania 5-261 9339; www.finnair.com) is the only One World member that flies directly to the Baltic.

The cheapest fares to Europe tend to be for routes through Asia, although you can sometimes get a good deal through the USA from New Zealand. If you're considering a route via London, note that no Baltic flights leave from Heathrow, which is where most Australian and New Zealand flights land.

Caucasus & Central Asia

AirBaltic flies from Rīga to Tbilisi (Georgia) and Baku (Azerbaijan). **Uzbekistan Airways** (HY; www.uzairways.com) operates flights from Rīga to Tashkent (Uzbekistan).

Continental Europe

Budget airlines have revolutionised European air transport in the past decade, so you are spoilt for choice when it comes to getting from Baltic airports to EU countries. The Rīga-based airBaltic alone flies to a few dozen cities all over the EU. **Ryanair** (FR; www.ryanair.com), **Wizz Air** (W6; ☑Latvia 9020 0905; www.wizzair.com) and **easyJet** (U2; ☑UK 870 600 0000; www.easyjet.com) also connect Baltic capitals with a host of destinations, notably in Germany.

AirBaltic also flies to Ukraine, Belarus and Moldova, code-sharing with these countries' national carriers. In addition, **Ukrainian International Airlines** (PS; www.flyuia.com) fly from Kyiv to Vilnius, as does **Belavia** (B2; ☑Estonia 6732 0314; http://en.belavia.by) from Minsk.

Middle East

Turkish Airlines (TK; ☑Latvia 6735 9440; www.turkishairlines.com) connects Tallinn and Rīga with Istanbul. AirBaltic flies to Tel Aviv.

Nordic Countries

AirBaltic, along with **SAS** (☑Lithuania 5-230 6638; www.scandinavian.net), Finnair, **Norwegian** (DY; ☑Norway 2149 0015; www.norwegian.no), Ryanair and Wizz Air connect all Baltic airport to any Scandinavian city of note.

North America

There is a direct flight from New York (JFK) to Rīga on Uzbekistan Airways. Otherwise, book a codeshare flight through Star Alliance on **Austrian Airlines** (OS; ☑Lithuania 5-210 5030; www.aua.com), **Brussels Airlines** (SN; ☑Lithuania 5-252 5555; www.brusselsairlines.com), **LOT** (LO; ☑Estonia 668 1008, Latvia 6720 7113, Lithuania 5-273 9000; www.lot.com),

Lufthansa (LO; ☑Latvia 6728 5901, Lithuania 5-212 0220; www.lufthansa.com), SAS or Turkish Airlines; through One World on Finnair; or through **SkyTeam** (www.skyteam.com) on Aeroflot or **ČSA** (Czech Airlines, OK; ☑Estonia 630 9397, Latvia 6720 7636, Lithuania 5-215 1511; www.czechairlines.com).

Russia

Russia's **Aeroflot** (SU; ☑Estonia 605 8887, Latvia 6778 0770, Lithuania 212 4189; www.aeroflot.com) operates flights from Moscow to all three Baltic capitals. AirBaltic also flies to St Petersburg from Rīga.

UK & Ireland

Budget airlines Ryanair, easyJet and Wizz Air fly numerous routes from Ireland and the UK to the Baltics, including departures from many small regional airports. If you're considering connecting flights via London, allow several hours to travel between airports, as 'London airports' are a long way from the city and from each other.

Land

Bicycle

Bicycles can be carried cheaply (or free) on ferries from the Nordic countries and Germany to the Baltics; see p419 for ferry routes. Pedallers through Poland face the same choice of routes as drivers; see p418 for more information.

Border Crossings

Travelling from north to south, Estonia shares borders with Russia and Latvia; Latvia shares borders with Estonia, Russia, Belarus and Lithuania; and Lithuania borders Latvia, Belarus, Poland and the Kaliningrad Region (part of Russia).

Now that the Baltic countries are in the EU and part of the Schengen Agreement, border checkpoints between

Estonia, Lithuania, Latvia and Poland have disappeared.

Travel to Belarus and Russia is another matter entirely. These borders continue to be rigorously controlled, and you'll need to get a visa in advance. Expect to spend at least an hour at the border regardless.

Private cars queue for hours to get in and out of Russia and Belarus at major checkpoints. In Estonia, however, you can avoid the wait by booking a time slot for the border crossing at www.estonianborder.eu (unfortunately it doesn't work for cars coming back into Estonia). International buses bypass the queue.

The Kaliningrad Region enjoys quieter road borders with Lithuania at Panemunė–Sovietsk, between Kybartai (Lithuania) and Nesterov, and on Curonian Spit along the Klaipėda–Zelenogradsk road. But note that the three-day visa-on-demand arrangement for Kaliningrad Region only works if you cross from Poland or fly into Khrabrovo airport.

Bus

With a few exceptions, buses are the cheapest but least comfortable method of reaching the Baltic from within Europe. Direct buses arrive from as far north as St Petersburg, as far west as Paris, as far south as Sofia and as far east as Moscow. From much of the rest of Europe you can reach the Baltic with a single change of bus in Warsaw. Pan-European bus companies run services from Baltic capitals to a multitude of destinations in the EU, as well as Russia and Belarus.

See bus company websites for route maps, prices, schedules, ticketing agents and more; you can also purchase tickets online. There are 10% discounts for passengers under 26 or over 60. Return tickets cost about 20% less than two one-way tickets.

Ecolines www.ecolines.net

Eurolines www.eurolines.com

Lux Express www.luxexpress.eu

Simple Express www.simple-express.eu

Car & Motorcycle

If you take your own vehicle to the Baltic, make sure it's in good condition before you leave home.

It's worth contacting motoring clubs, as well as Estonian, Latvian and Lithuanian embassies, for information on regulations, border crossing and so on.

AA (www.aa.co.nz) New Zealand

AA (www.theaa.com) UK

AAA (www.aaa.asn.au) Australia

AAA (www.aaa.com) USA

RAC (www.rac.co.uk) UK

DOCUMENTS

Bring your vehicle's registration document, preferably in the form of an international motor vehicle certificate, which is a translation of the basic registration document. Motoring associations should be able to provide one. An International Driving Permit (IDP; also obtainable from motoring associations) is recommended but your own licence will suffice in most situations. All three Baltic countries demand compulsory accident insurance for drivers.

Insurance policies with limited compensation rates can be bought at the Estonian, Latvian and Lithuanian borders. Remember that you'll also need appropriate documentation for all the countries you pass through on the way to or from the Baltics; motoring associations can advise you.

BELARUS

There is no particular reason to venture into Belarus, unless it is your destination, or you are transiting into Ukraine, having acquired a Belarusian transit visa in advance.

Do not attempt to approach the border or set foot in the country without a Belarusian transit visa – available only at Belarusian embassies. No visas are sold at any Belarus border. Even with a visa, expect to wait several hours (at least) at the border.

Note that although Belarus and Russia are united in a customs union and there are no checks on the border between them, you still can't enter Belarus on a Russian visa.

FINLAND

The quickest and best-served car ferry connection is from Helsinki to Tallinn. Alternatively, from Finland you can drive through Russia; from the Finnish–Russian border at Vaalimaa–Torfyanovka it's 360km to Narva (Estonia). You could do it in a day but there's little point coming this way unless you want to look at St Petersburg on the way through.

GERMANY

Bringing a vehicle into the Baltics usually entails a ferry trip from the German ports of Kiel or Lübeck, to Klaipėda (Lithuania) or to Ventspils or Liepāja (Latvia). But you can also drive into Lithuania through Poland.

POLAND

It will take some minutes before you notice you've crossed the border as it's neither guarded nor really marked; now that Lithuania and Poland are both part of the Schengen Agreement, border formalities are minimal to nonexistent. Brace for a nervous and painstaking drive on the truck-ridden, single-lane roads in eastern Poland. It gets better once you get into Lithuania or once you reach Warsaw on the way back.

RUSSIA

From St Petersburg the drive to the Estonian border at Ivangorod–Narva is only 140km. Driving from all three Baltic countries into Moscow, the Rīga–Moscow highway is the most straightforward route, and both its Russian and Latvian sections are now in good shape. Coming from Estonia, you can cross the border at Lütä (book your crossing time slot at www.estonianborder.eu to avoid queues) and then drive south to the Rīga–Moscow highway. Coming from Lithuania, note that you'll need a Belarusian transit visa to use the convenient Minsk–Moscow highway. Unless you manage to get it, you'll have to drive via Zilupe checkpoint on the Moscow–Rīga highway, where the waiting time often takes a good half of the day.

SWEDEN

Vehicle ferries run from Stockholm to Tallinn or Rīga, from Nynäshamn to Venstpils and Liepāja (Latvia) and from Karlshamn to Klaipėda.

Train

Train travel is not really much of an option for Baltic countries these days, unless you are coming from Russia or Belarus. There is also a weak link connecting the region to the rest of the EU via Poland.

POLAND

Surprisingly, there is no longer a direct train route operating between Warsaw and Vilnius. You can make a daytime journey on local trains from Warsaw to Kaunas or Vilnius, changing trains in Šeštokai, in Lithuania (close to the Poland–Lithuania border). Timetables are designed to give a 15-minute window to transfer. Total journey time is about 9½ hours. Note, too, that this option doesn't pass through Belarus.

RUSSIA & BELARUS

The old Soviet rail network still functions over most of the former USSR. Trains linking Moscow with all the main Baltic cities enable you to combine the Baltics with a Trans-Siberian trip or other Russian or Central Asian travels. Check the Russian railways website http://pass.rzd.ru for details.

If you can make sense of it, the website www.poezda.net allows you to search timetables for trains within the former USSR, but we prefer the simpler http://bahn.hafas.de for European train schedules (although prices aren't given).

Overnight trains connect Rīga and Tallinn with both Moscow and St Petersburg. Note that the latter is connected by fast train services with Helsinki in Finland, which allows you to make a neat circle, coming back to Tallinn by ferry. (That's provided you have a Russian visa.)

From Vilnius, there are two daily trains to Moscow's Belarus train station. These pass through Belarus, however, so you'll need a Belarusian visa. From Vilnius, two daily trains travel west to Kaliningrad (a journey of about seven hours).

Sea

Numerous seafaring options offer a slower but more relaxed journey. You can sail directly from Finland to Estonia (a distance of only 85km); from Germany to Latvia and Lithuania; from Denmark to Lithuania; and from Sweden to all three Baltic countries. The Tallinn–Helsinki route has so many competing services that you should have no difficulty in getting a passage any day, but some of the other services – notably Stockholm to Tallinn and the cargo ferries to Denmark – can get booked up far in advance.

Schedules and fares change frequently – be sure to double-check both when you are planning your trip. Ferry and hydrofoil operators' websites have up-to-date schedules and fares.

Denmark

The shipping company **DFDS Seaways** (☑ in Denmark 7620 6700, in Lithuania 4639 5088; http://freight.dfdsseaways.com) operates a cargo service connecting Fredericia (Denmark) and Klaipėda (Lithuania) via Copenhagen, twice a week. There is limited cabin capacity for passengers – book ahead.

Finland

A fleet of ferries now carries well over two million people each year across the 85km Gulf of Finland separating Helsinki and Tallinn. There are dozens of crossings each way every day (ships take two to 3½ hours; hydrofoils take approximately 1½ hours). Note that in high winds or bad weather, hydrofoils are often cancelled; they operate only when the sea is free from ice (generally around late March/April to late December); larger ferries sail year-round.

Shop around: the best deals are often for advance tickets purchased on the internet. Fares vary widely, depending on season, day and time of travel, and other factors (check if the company has a fuel surcharge that's included – or not – in the advertised price). Fares are generally higher at high-demand times such as Friday evening, Saturday morning and Sunday afternoon. On most ferry lines, students and seniors get a 10% to 15% discount, children between ages six and 17 pay half price and those under six sail for free. Most operators offer special deals for families and serial tickets for frequent passengers.

Germany

Scandlines (☑ in Latvia 4631 0561; www.scandlines.lt) ferries sail twice weekly in each direction from Travemünde (Lübeck) to both Ventspils and Liepāja in Latvia. DFDS Seaways runs service between Klaipėda and Kiel.

Railway & Ferry Routes

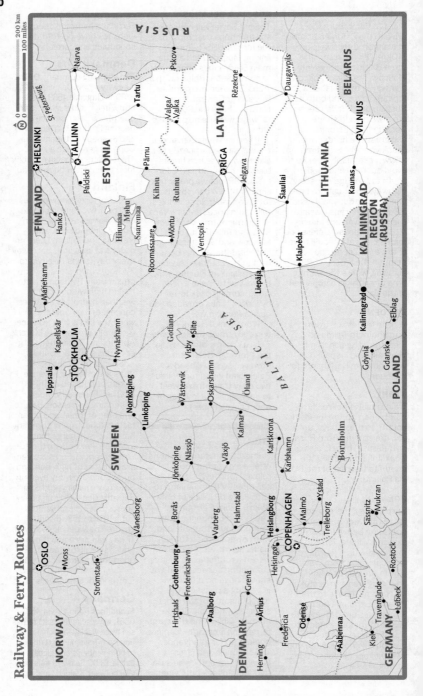

Sweden

TO/FROM ESTONIA

Tallink Silja (☑in Estonia 640 9808, in Sweden 8222 140; www.tallinksilja.com) Sails every night between Tallinn and Stockholm, stopping at Mariehamn on the Åland Islands (Finland) en route. Ferries make the 17-hour crossing year-round, leaving from Terminal D in Tallinn and the Värtahamnen Terminal in Stockholm. This service gets heavily booked, so make your reservation a month or two ahead.

TO/FROM LATVIA

Tallink Silja operates overnight services daily between Rīga and Stockholm.

Scandlines has boats connecting the ports of Liepāja and Ventspils with Nynäshamn (about 60km from Stockholm), departing five times weekly from both ports.

TO/FROM LITHUANIA

DFDS Seaways (☑in Lithuania 4632 3232, in Sweden 4543 3680; www.dfdsseaways.com) Has daily ferries from Karlshamn to Klaipėda (seat/berth €38/80; 14 hours).

Yacht

The Baltics – particularly Estonia with its islands and indented coast – attract hundreds of yachts a year, mainly from Finland and Scandinavia. Good online resources:

http://marinas.nautilus.ee Information on entry regulations, a database of all the local marinas and details for ordering the *Estonian Cruising Guide*.

www.balticyachting.com Covers southern Finland as well as western Estonia.

It's also possible to rent yachts throughout the region.

Tours

Several international travel operators specialise in the Baltic region.

Baltic Holidays (☑in the UK 0845 070 5711; www.balticholidays.com) This UK op-

erator offers spa or city breaks, beach, family or countryside holidays and tailor-made themed holidays. Can help with genealogy research.

Baltics and Beyond (in UK ☑0845 094 2125; www.balticsandbeyond.com) A UK-based company offering regular tours, self-guided options and tailor-made trips to the three Baltic countries and some of their neighbours (including Belarus, Russia and Poland).

Regent Holidays (☑in the UK 0117 921 1711; www.regent-holidays.co.uk) A UK company with an array of Baltic options, including fly/drive and city breaks.

Vytis Tours (☑in the US 718-423-6161; www.vytistours.com) A US company offering a range of tours, from an economical eight-day jaunt round the region's capitals to a more extensive 17-day 'Grand Tour'.

GETTING AROUND

Air

There are plenty of scheduled flights between the three Baltic capitals, but domestic flights within each country are minimal.

Airlines flying within Estonia, Latvia & Lithuania

airBaltic (☑17107; www.airbaltic.com) Flies from Rīga to Palanga, Tallinn and Vilnius; and from Vilnius to Tallinn.

Avies (U3; ☑680 3501; www.avies.ee) Flies to/from Tallinn and Kärdla (Hiiumaa).

Estonian Air (OV; ☑640 1160; www.estonian-air.ee) Flies from Tallinn to Vilnius.

Bicycle

The flatness and small scale of Estonia, Latvia and Lithuania, and the light traffic on most roads, make them good cycling territory. On the

Estonian islands especially you'll see cyclists galore in summer. Most bring their own bicycles but there are plenty of places where you can hire one, including each of the capitals and most major towns.

Cyclists should bring waterproof clothing, and perhaps a tent if touring: you may not find accommodation in some out-of-the-way places. Travel agencies and organisations both within and outside the region organise cycling tours.

Boat

Ferry

At the time of writing there were no ferry links between the Baltic countries. Estonia has ferry connections to many of its islands, although smaller boats don't run in winter once the seas ice up. Ferries within Latvia are few, although you can catch a slow boat between Rīga and Jūrmala. In Lithuania, people travel by boat from Klaipėda to Curonian Spit.

Yacht

Private yachting is a popular way to get around the Baltic Coast – particularly Estonia's coast, with its many islands and bays. **Sailing.ee** (☑in Estonia 5333 1117; www.sailing.ee; Regati puiestee 1, Tallinn) rents out yachts with or without a skipper.

http://marinas.nautilus.ee For information and advice on Estonia's dozens of marinas.

www.marinaslatvia.lv Details of Latvia's marinas.

Bus

The region is well served by buses, although services to off-the-beaten-track villages are infrequent. Direct bus services link the three capitals and there are other cross-border services between main towns.

Buses are generally faster than trains and often slightly cheaper. Those used for local journeys, up to about two hours long, offer few comforts. Avoid window seats in rainy, snowy or very cold weather; travel with someone you're prepared to snuggle up to for body warmth; and sit in the seat allocated to you (to avoid tangling with a merciless *babushka* – grandmother – who wants *her* seat that *you're* in).

Some shorter routes are serviced by nippier and more modern microbuses, holding about 15 passengers and officially making fewer stops than their big-bus counterparts.

By contrast, buses travelling between the Baltic countries are equal to long-distance coaches anywhere else in Europe. Most are clean and have a heating system, a toilet, hot drinks dispenser and TV on board. Many scheduled buses to/from Tallinn, Rīga and Vilnius run overnight; it's a convenient and safe way of travelling, even for solo female travellers.

Buses operating within Estonia, Latvia & Lithuania

BussiReisid (☑12550; www.bussireisid.ee) Umbrella for all Estonian services.

Ecolines (☑in Rīga 6721 4512, in Tallinn 606 2217, in Vilnius 5213 3300; www.ecolines.net) Major routes include: Rīga–Salacgrīva–Pärnu–Tallinn; Rīga–Valmiera–Valga–Tartu–Narva; Rīga–Panevėžys–Vilnius–Kaunas; Liepāja–Palanga–Klaipėda; and Rēzekne–Daugavpils–Utena–Vilnius–Kaunas.

Hansabuss (☑627 9080; www.hansabuss.ee) Four daily buses between Rīga and Tallinn, three of which stop in Pärnu.

Lux Express (☑680 0909; www.luxexpress.eu) With its associated budget line Simple Express (www.simpleexpress.eu), major routes include: Tallinn–Pärnu–Rīga–Vilnius; Narva–Tartu–Valga–Rīga; Rīga–Vilnius; Rīga–Kaunas; Rīga–Šiauliai; and Vilnius–Kaunas.

Tickets & Information

Ticket offices/windows selling national and international tickets are clearly marked in the local language and occasionally in English, too. Tickets are always printed in the local language and are easy to understand once you know the words for 'seat', 'bus stop' etc.

For long-distance buses, tickets are sold in advance from the station from which you begin the journey. For local buses to nearby towns or villages, or for long-distance buses that are midroute (in transit), you normally pay on board. This may mean a bit of a scrum for seats if there are a lot of people waiting.

Most bus and train stations in towns and cities have information windows with staff who generally speak some English.

Timetables & Fares

See timetables on bus company websites before leaving home or, upon arrival in the region, check schedules at the local tourist office. The offices in Tallinn, Rīga and Vilnius in particular maintain up-to-the-minute transport schedules. The **In Your Pocket** (www.inyourpocket.com) city guides to the capitals include fairly comprehensive domestic and pan-Baltic bus schedules, updated every two months.

Comprehensive timetables are posted in bus stations' main ticket halls. A rare few need careful decoding. Most simply list the departure time and the days (using either Roman or Arabic numerals, the number 1 being Monday) on which the service runs.

Fares vary slightly between the three countries, and between bus companies, reflecting the speed of the bus, comfort levels and time of day it arrives/departs.

Online bus timetable resources:

Estonia www.tpilet.ee

Latvia www.autoosta.lv

Lithuania www.stotis.lt

Car & Motorcycle

For flexibility and access to out-of-the-way destinations, you can't beat driving.

Fuel & Spare Parts

Petrol stations run by major companies are open 24 hours along all the major roads; many are self-service with an automated pay system accepting notes or credit cards with PINs. Western-grade fuel, including unleaded, is readily available.

Road Rules

The whole region drives on the right. The legal maximum blood alcohol limit varies in each country (Estonia 0.02%; Latvia 0.05%; Lithuania 0.04%). Seat belts are compulsory and headlights must be on at all times while driving. The speed limit in built-up areas is 50km/h; limits outside urban areas vary from 70km/h to 110km/h – look out for signs, as these limits are often strictly enforced. Fines may be collected on the spot – the amounts vary and the only way to ensure officers don't also add a little pocket money for themselves is to ask for a receipt.

It is illegal to use a mobile phone while operating a vehicle (hands-free kits are allowed). Winter tyres are a legal requirement, usually from December to March every year, but if there are severe weather conditions outside these dates (likely in most years), the dates will change accordingly, so check local conditions if driving between October and April.

Traditional coin-fed parking meters are still found in some parts of the Baltics, though both Tallinn and Vilnius have moved towards electronic systems – drivers pay for parking via SMS, dialling a number and inputting the car's licence plate and location number (posted nearby).

Driving into the old towns in Rīga, Tallinn, Vilnius and Kaunas is free, but parking is pricey, and often involves confusing regulations – ask at your hotel or the tourist office to avoid being fined. Motorists must pay a small entrance fee to drive into Latvia's prime seaside resort, Jūrmala, and to enter Curonian Spit National Park.

Take care driving near trams, trolleybuses and buses in towns: passengers may run across the road to catch a tram that's still in motion. Traffic behind a tram must stop when it opens its doors to let people in and out. Trolleybuses often swing far out into the road when leaving a stop.

ROAD DISTANCES (KM)

	Tallinn	Tartu	Pärnu	Narva	Valka/Valga	Rīga	Liepāja	Daugavpils	Ventspils	Vilnius	Kaunas	Klaipėda	Panevėžys
Tartu	190												
Pärnu	130	205											
Narva	210	194	304										
Valka/Valga	276	86	140	268									
Rīga	310	253	180	435	167								
Liepāja	530	473	400	655	387	220							
Daugavpils	540	377	410	559	291	230	450						
Ventspils	510	453	380	635	367	200	119	430					
Vilnius	600	543	470	725	457	290	465	167	584				
Kaunas	575	523	460	715	447	280	230	267	349	100			
Klaipėda	620	538	490	745	477	310	155	477	274	310	210		
Panevėžys	460	403	330	585	317	150	270	168	350	140	110	235	
Šiauliai	465	383	310	565	297	130	192	387	330	220	140	155	80

Hitching

Hitching is never entirely safe in any country in the world, and we don't recommend it. Travellers who decide to hitch should understand that they are taking a small but potentially serious risk. People who do choose to hitch will be safer if they travel in pairs and let someone know where they are planning to go.

Locally, hitching is a popular means of getting around. The **Vilnius Hitchhiking Club** (VHHC; www.autostop.lt) provides practical information and contacts for travellers hoping to hitch a ride in all three Baltic countries. Hostel notice boards in capital cities are a good place to find or offer a ride-share; the website www.digihitch.com might also be helpful.

Local Transport

Bus, Tram & Trolleybus

A mix of trams, buses and trolleybuses (buses run by electricity from overhead wires) provides thorough public transport around towns and cities in all three countries. All three types of transport get crowded, especially during the early-morning and early-evening rush hours.

Trams, trolleybuses and buses all run from about 5.30am to 12.30am, but services get pretty thin in outlying areas after about 7pm. In Tallinn and Vilnius, the same ticket is good for all types of transport except minibuses; in Rīga a bus ticket must be purchased on board, but trolleybus and tram tickets are interchangeable. In all three countries, you validate your flat-fare ticket by punching it in one of the ticket punches fixed inside the vehicle. Tickets are sold from news kiosks displaying them in the window and by some drivers (who are easier to find but charge a little more for tickets). Multitrip, weekly and monthly tickets are available. The system depends on honesty and lends itself to cheating but there are regular inspections, with on-the-spot fines if you're caught riding without a punched ticket.

Travelling on all trams, trolleybuses and buses involves a particular etiquette. If you are young, fit and capable of standing for the duration of your journey, do not sit in the seats at the front – these are only for babushkas (senior-age women) and small children. Secondly, plan getting off well ahead of time. It's good to know how to say 'excuse me' in the language of your Baltic country or in Russian, so people understand that you want to get to the door on a crowded bus.

All airports are served by regular city transport as well as by taxis.

Taxi

Taxis are plentiful and usually cheap. Night-time tariffs, which generally apply between 10pm and 6am, are higher. To avoid rip-offs, insist on the meter running. In any of the cities, it's always cheaper and safer to order a cab by phone.

Train

Suburban trains serve the outskirts of the main cities and some surrounding towns and villages. They're of limited use as city transport for visitors, as they mostly go to residential or industrial areas where there's little to see. But some are useful for day trips to destinations outside the cities.

Tours

Numerous local travel operators specialise in travel around the Baltic region and can help you organise a trip.

City Bike (☑in Estonia 511 1819; www.citybike.ee) Reputable and longstanding Tallinn-based company, which arranges multiday cycling tours through Estonia, Latvia and Lithuania.

Scanbalt Experience (☑in Estonia 5301 9139; www.scanbaltexperience.com) A backpacker-focused company offering adventure bus trips through Scandinavia and the Baltic region.

TrekBaltics (☑in Estonia 5623 3255; www.trekbaltics.com) An Estonian-based operator with a great range of camping treks, adventure and activities packages (eg cycling tours) and spa breaks, taking in the three Baltic countries. The comprehensive 19-day Grand Baltics Trek can be done as a camper, or in more comfort (overnighting in cabins, farmhouses and hostels).

Train

Estonia, Latvia and Lithuania have railways, although services have been scaled back significantly in recent years and most long-distance travel within the Baltics is done by bus or plane. A planned intra-country rail network (the Rail Baltica Project) seemed to have been shelved at the time of writing.

In the meantime, Baltic trains are slow and cheap, and not terribly comfortable. You can almost never open the windows, so it can be stuffy (and smelly, depending on your travelling companions), while you stand equal chances of freezing or baking, depending on whether the heating is turned on or not. Local trains, known as suburban or electric, are substantially slower and make more frequent stops than long-distance trains.

Routes

There are no direct train services running between the Baltic capitals, although you can travel from Tallinn to Rīga by train with a stop at Valga (on the Estonia–Latvia border).

Tickets & Information

In Latvia and Lithuania, tickets can be purchased in advance and right before departure at train stations. In larger stations, such as Rīga, you can only buy tickets for certain types of trains or destinations at certain windows.

Except for Tallinn, Estonia's train stations are deserted places, with no ticket offices or other services of any kind. You buy your tickets on the train; don't head to the train station (which is usually quite far from the city centre) unless you know the exact departure time. You can also purchase domestic tickets online at www.elron.ee.

On long-distance trains between the Baltics and other countries, tickets must be surrendered to the carriage attendant, who will safeguard it for the journey's duration and return it to you 15 minutes before arrival at your final destination (a handy 'alarm clock' if you're on an overnight train).

Timetables

The following websites provide railway timetables online.

Estonia www.elron.ee

Latvia www.pv.lv

Lithuania www.slotis.lt

At train stations, the timetables generally list the number of the train, departure and arrival times, and the platform from which it leaves. Some list return journey schedules, the number of minutes a train waits in your station or the time a train left the place it began its journey. Always study the small print on timetables, as many trains only run on certain days or between certain dates.

Language

ESTONIAN

Estonian belongs to the Baltic-Finnic branch of the Finno-Ugric languages. It's closely related to Finnish and distantly related to Hungarian. Most Estonians, especially the younger generations, understand some English and Finnish, but you'll find that people are welcoming of visitors who make an effort to speak their language.

Most Estonian consonants are the same as in English. If you read our pronunciation guides as if they were English, you'll be under-stood. Note that p is pronounced between the English 'p' and 'b', d between the English 't' and 'd', rr is trilled and zh sounds like the 's' in 'treasure'. As for vowels, aeh is pronounced as the 'ae' in 'aesthetic', err as the 'yrr' in 'myrrh' (rounding the lips) and ü as the 'oo' in 'too' (rounding the lips).

Stressed syllables are indicated with italics, and stress generally falls on the first syllable.

Basics

Hello.	Tere.	te·rre
Goodbye.	Head aega.	head ae·gah
Yes.	Jah.	yah
No.	Ei.	ay
Thank you.	Tänan.	ta·nahn
You're welcome.	Palun.	pah·lun

WANT MORE?

For in-depth language information and handy phrases, check out Lonely Planet's *Baltic Phrasebook*. You'll find it at **shop.lonelyplanet.com**, or you can buy Lonely Planet's iPhone phrasebooks at the Apple App Store.

Excuse me/ Sorry.	Vabandage.	vah·bahn·dah·ge
How are you?	Kuidas läheb?	kuy·dahs la·heb
Fine.	Hästi.	has·ti

What's your name?
Mis te nimi on? mis te ni·mi on

My name is ...
Mu nimi on ... mu ni·mi on ...

Do you speak English?
Kas te räägite inglise keelt? kahs te rraa·gi·te ing·li·se kehlt

I don't understand.
Ma ei saa aru. mah ay saah ah·rru

Accommodation

Where's a ...?	Kus asub ...?	kus ah·sub ...
campsite	kämping	kam·ping
hotel	hotell	ho·tell
pension	võõrastemaja	vyy·rrahs·te·mah·yah

I'd like a single/double room.
Ma tahaksin ühe/ kahe voodiga tuba. mah tah·hak·sin ü·he/ kah·he vaw·di·gah tu·bah

How much is it per person/night?
Kui palju maksab voodikoht/ööpäev? kui pahl·yu mahk·sab vaw·di·koht/err·paehv

Directions

Where is ...?
Kus on ...? kus on ...

How far is it?
Kui kaugel see on? kuy kau·gel seh on

Please show me on the map.
Palun näidake mulle seda kaardil. pah·lun nai·dah·ke mul·le se·dah kaahrr·dil

EATING & DRINKING

SIGNS – ESTONIAN

Sissepääs	Entrance
Väljapääs	Exit
Avatud/Lahti	Open
Suletud/Kinni	Closed
WC	Toilets
Meestele	Men
Naistele	Women

Eating & Drinking

Can I have a menu?
Kas ma saaksin menüü?
kas mah saahk·sin me·nüü

I'd like ...
Ma sooviksin ...
ma saw·vik·sin ...

I'm a vegetarian.
Ma olen taimetoitlane.
mah o·len tai·me·toyt·lah·ne

Bon appetit!
Head isu!
head i·su

To your health! (Cheers!)
Terviseks!
ter·vi·seks

The bill, please.
Palun arve.
pah·lun ahrr·ve

Emergencies

Help!	Appi!	ahp·pi
Go away!	Minge ära!	min·ge a·rrah
Call a doctor!	Kutsuge arst!	kut·su·ge ahrrst
I'm ill.	Ma olen haige.	mah o·len hai·ge
I'm lost.	Ma olen eksinud.	mah o·len ek·si·nud

Shopping & Services

What time does it open/close?
Mis kell see avatakse/suletakse?
mis kell seh ah·vah·tahk·se/su·le·tahk·se

How much does it cost?
Kui palju see maksab?
kui pahl·yu seh mahk·sahb

bank	pank	pahnk
chemist/ pharmacy	apteek	ahp·tehk
market	turg	turrg
police	politsei	po·lit·say
post office	postkontor	post·kon·torr
toilet	tualett	tua·lett
tourist office	turismibüroo	tu·rris·mi·bü·rroo

Time & Numbers

What time is it? Mis kell on? mis kell on

It's one o'clock. Kell on üks. kell on üks

in the morning hommikul hom·mi·kul

in the evening õhtul yh·tul

1	üks	üks
2	kaks	kahks
3	kolm	kolm
4	neli	ne·li
5	viis	vees
6	kuus	koos
7	seitse	sayt·se
8	kaheksa	kah·hek·sah
9	üheksa	ü·hek·sah
10	kümme	küm·me

Transport

Where's the ...?	Kus on ...?	kus on ...
airport	lennujaam	len·nu·yaahm
bus station	bussijaam	bus·si·yaahm
ferry terminal	sadam	sah·dahm
train station	rongijaam	rron·gi·yaahm

Which ... goes there?	Mis ... ma sinna saan?	mis ... mah sin·nah saahn
bus	bussiga	bus·si·gah
tram	trammiga	trrahm·mi·gah
trolleybus	trolliga	trrol·li·gah

What time is the next bus/train?
Mis kell on järgmine buss/rong?
mis kell on yarrg·mi·ne buss/rrong

Please give me a one-way/return ticket.
Palun üks/edasi-tagasi pilet.
pah·lun üks/e·dah·si·tah·gah·si pi·let

LATVIAN

Latvian belongs to the Baltic language family. Only about 55% of the population, and just over 45% of the inhabitants of Rīga speak it as their first language. Latvian and Lithuanian have a lot of vocabulary in common, but are not mutually intelligible.

In our pronunciation guides, a line above a vowel indicates that it is a long sound. Note that uh is pronounced as the 'u' in 'fund', eh as the 'ai' in 'fair', ea as in 'fear', dz as the 'ds' in 'beds', zh as the 's' in 'pleasure' and jy is similar to the 'dy' sound in British 'duty'. Word stress is indicated with italics. The markers (m) and (f) indicate the options for male and female speakers respectively.

Basics

Hello.	Sveiks. (m)	svayks
	Sveika. (f)	svay·kuh
Goodbye.	Uz redzēšanos.	uz redz·eh·shuhn·aws
Yes.	Jā.	yah
No.	Nē.	neh
Please.	Lūdzu.	loo·dzu
Thank you.	Paldies.	puhl·deas
You're welcome.	Lūdzu.	loo·dzu
Excuse me.	Atvainojiet.	uht·vai·naw·yeat
Sorry.	Piedodiet.	pea·doad·eat

How are you?
Kā jums klājas?   kah yums klah·yuhs

Fine, thank you.
Labi, paldies.   luh·bi puhl·deas

What's your name?
Kā jūs sauc?   kah yoos sowts

My name is ...
Mani sauc ...   muhn·i sowts ...

Do you speak English?
Vai jūs runājat angliski?   vai yoos run·ah·yuht uhn·gli·ski

I don't understand.
Es nesaprotu.   es ne·suh·praw·tu

Accommodation

I'm looking for a ...	Es meklēju ...	es mek·leh·yu ...
hotel	viesnīcu	veas·neets·u
youth hostel	jauniešu mītni	yow·nea·shu meet·ni

I'd like a single/double room.
Es vēlos vienvietīgu/ divvietīgu istabu.   es vaa·laws vean·vea·tee·gu/ div·vea·tee·gu is·tuh·bu

How much is it per night?
Cik maksā diennaktī?   tsik muhk·sah dean·nuhk·tee

Directions

How do I get to ...?
Kā es tieku līdz ...?   kah es tea·ku leedz ...

Is it far from here?
Vai tas atrodas tālu?   vai tuhs uht·raw·duhs tah·lu

SIGNS – LATVIAN

Ieeja	Entrance
Izeja	Exit
Atvērts	Open
Slēgts	Closed
Tualetes	Toilets
Vīriešu	Men
Sieviešu	Women

Could you show me (on the map), please?
Lūdzu parādiet man (uz kartes)?   loo·dzu puhr·ah·deat muhn (uz kuhrt·es)

Eating & Drinking

A table for ... people, please.
Lūdzu galdu ... personām.   loo·dzu gahl·du ... per·so·nahm

Do you have a menu?
Vai jums ir ēdienkarte?   vai yums ir eh·dean·kar·te

What do you recommend?
Ko jūs iesakāt?   kwo yoos eah·sah·kut

I'm a vegetarian.
Es esmu veģetārietis/te. (m/f)   es es·mu ve·gye·tah·reah·tis/te

I'd like ...
Es vēlos ...   es vaa·lwos ...

The bill, please.
Lūdzu rēķinu.   loo·dzu reh·kyi·nu

Emergencies

Help!
Palīgā!   puh·lee·gah

Go away!
Ejiet projam!   ay·eat praw·yam

Call a doctor!
Izsauciet ārstu!   iz·sowts·eat ahr·stu

I'm ill.
Es esmu slims/ slima. (m/f)   es as·mu slims/ slim·uh

I'm lost.
Es esmu apmaldījies/ apmaldījusies. (m/f)   es as·mu uhp·muhl·dee·yeas/ uhp·muhl·dee·yu·seas

Shopping & Services

What time does it open?
No cikiem ir atvērts?   naw tsik·eam ir uht·vaarts

What time does it close?
Cikos slēdz?   tsik·aws slaadz

How much is it?
Cik tas maksā?   tsik tuhs muhk·sah

Where are the toilets?
Kur ir tualetes?   kur ir *tu*·uh·le·tes

bank	*banka*	*buhn*·kuh
chemist/ pharmacy	*aptieka*	*uhp*·tea·kuh
currency exchange booth	*valūtas maiņa*	*vuh*·loo·tuhs *mai*·nyuh
market	*tirgus*	*tir*·gus
post office	*pasts*	puhsts

Time & Numbers

What time (is it)?
Cik (ir) pulkstenis?   tsik (ir) *pulk*·sten·is

It's five o'clock.
Ir pieci.   ir *peats*·i

morning	*rīts*	reets
afternoon	*pēcpus-diena*	*pehts*·pus·dea·nuh
night	*nakts*	nuhkts

1	*viens*	veans
2	*divi*	*di*·vi
3	*trīs*	trees
4	*četri*	*chet*·ri
5	*pieci*	*peats*·i
6	*seši*	*sesh*·i
7	*septiņi*	*sep*·ti·nyi
8	*astoņi*	*uhs*·taw·nyi
9	*deviņi*	*de*·vi·nyi
10	*desmit*	*des*·mit

Transport

Where's the ...?	*Kur atrodas ...?*	kur *uht*·raw·duhs ...
airport	*lidosta*	*lid*·aw·stuh
bus station	*autoosta*	*ow*·to·aws·tuh
ferry terminal	*pasažieru osta*	*puh*·suh·zhea·ru *aw*·stuh
train station	*dzelzceļa stacija*	*dzelz*·tse·lyuh *stuhts*·i·ya
tram stop	*tramvaja pietura*	*truhm*·vuh·yuh *pea*·tu·ruh
I want to buy a ... ticket.	*Es vēlos nopirkt ... biļeti.*	es *vaa*·laws *naw*·pirkt ... *bi*·lyet·i
one-way	*vien-virziena*	*vean*·virz·ean·uh
return	*turp-atpakaļ*	*turp*·uht·puh·kuhly

LITHUANIAN

Lithuanian belongs to the Baltic language family, along with Latvian. Low Lithuanian (*Žemaičiai*), spoken in the west, is a separate dialect from High Lithuanian (*Aukštaičiai*), spoken in the rest of the country and considered the standard dialect.

Note that in our pronunciation guides eah sounds as the 'ea' in 'ear', ew as in 'new', uaw as the 'wa' in 'wander', dz as the 'ds' in 'roads', zh as the 's' in 'treasure', and the r sound is trilled. Stressed syllables are in italics.

Basics

Hello.	*Sveiki.*	*svay*·ki
Goodbye.	*Sudie.*	su·*deah*
Yes./No.	*Taip./Ne.*	tayp/na
Please.	*Prašau.*	prah·*show*
Thank you.	*Dėkoju.*	deh·*kaw*·yu
You're welcome.	*Prašau.*	prah·*show*
Excuse me.	*Atsiprašau.*	aht·si·prah·*show*
Sorry.	*Atleiskite.*	aht·*lays*·ki·ta

How are you?
Kaip gyvuojate?   kaip gee·*vuaw*·yah·ta

What's your name?
Kaip jūsų vardas?   kaip yoo·soo *vahr*·dahs

My name is ...
Mano vardas yra ...   mah·naw *vahr*·dahs ee·*rah* ...

Do you speak English?
Ar kalbate angliškai?   ahr *kahl*·bah·ta *ahn*·glish·kai

I don't understand.
Aš jūsų nesuprantu.   ahsh yoo·soo na·su·prahn·*tu*

Accommodation

I'm looking for a hotel.
Aš ieškau viešbučio.   ahsh *yeash*·kow *veash*·bu·chaw

I'd like a single/double room.
Aš noriu vienviečio/ dviviečio kambario.   ahsh *nawr*·yu veahn·*veah*·chaw/ dvi·*veah*·chaw *kahm*·bahr·yaw

How much is it per night, per person?
Kiek kainuoja apsistoti naktiai asmeniui?   keahk kai·*nuaw*·yah ahp·si·*staw*·ti nahk·chay ahs·man·wi

Directions

How do I get to the ...?
Prašom pasakyti, kaip patekti į ...?   *prah*·shom pah·sah·*kee*·ti kaip pah·*tak*·ti i ...

Is it far?
Ar toli? — ahr taw·*li*

Can you show me (on the map)?
Galėtumėt man parodyti (žemėlapyje)? — gah·*leh*·tu·met mahn pah·*raw*·dee·ti (zham·*eh*·lah·pee·ya)

Eating & Drinking

A table for ..., please.
Stalą ..., prašau. — stah·lah ... prah·*show*

Can I see the menu, please?
Ar galėčiau gauti meniu prašau? — ahr gah·*leh*·chow gow·ti man·yew prah·*show*

Do you have the menu in English?
Ar jūs turite meniu angliškai? — ahr yoos tu·ri·ta man·yew ahn·glish·kai

I'd like to try that.
Aš norėčau išbandyti to. — ahsh naw·*reh*·chow ish·bahn·*dee*·ti taw

I don't eat (meat).
Aš nevalgau (mėsiško). — ahsh na·*vahl*·gow (meh·sish·kaw)

Emergencies

Help! *Gelbėkite!* — gal·beh·ki·te
Go away! *Eik šalin!* — ayk shah·*lin*
I'm ill. *Aš sergu.* — ahsh sar·gu

Call a doctor!
Iššaukite gydytoją! — ish·*show*·ki·ta gee·dee·taw·yah

I'm lost.
Aš paklydusi/ paklydęs. (m/f) — ahsh pah·*klee*·du·si/ pah·*klee*·das

Shopping & Services

What time does it open/close?
Kelintą valandą atsidaro/ užsidaro? — kal·*in*·tah vah·lahn·dah aht·si·*dah*·raw/ uzh·si·*dah*·raw

How much is it?
Kiek kainuoja? — keahk kai·*nu* aw·yah

I'm looking for the ...	*Aš ieškau ...*	ahsh yeahsh·kow ...
bank	*bankas*	ban·kas
chemist/ pharmacy	*vaistinė*	vais·ti·neh
currency exchange	*valiutos*	vah·*lyu*·taws
market	*turgus*	tur·gows
police	*policijos*	paw·*lit*·si·yaws
post office	*pašto*	pahsh·taw
public toilet	*tualeto*	tu ah·*lat*·aw

SIGNS – LITHUANIAN

Įėjimas	Entrance
Išėjimas	Exit
Atidara	Open
Uždara	Closed
Dėmesio	Caution
Patogumai	Public Toilets

Time & Numbers

What time is it?
Kiek dabar laiko? — keahk dah·bahr lai·kaw

It's two o'clock.
Dabar antra valanda. — dah·*bahr* ahn·*trah* vah·lahn·*dah*

morning	*rytas*	ree·tahs
afternoon	*popietė*	paw·peah·teh
night	*naktis*	nahk·tis

1	*vienas*	veah·nahs
2	*du*	du
3	*trys*	trees
4	*keturi*	kat·u·ri
5	*penki*	pan·ki
6	*šeši*	shash·i
7	*septyni*	sap·tee·ni
8	*aštuoni*	ahsh·tu aw·ni
9	*devyni*	dav·ee·ni
10	*dešimt*	dash·imt

Transport

Where's the ...?	*Kur yra ...?*	kur ee·*rah* ...
airport	*oro uostas*	aw·raw u aws·tahs
bus stop	*autobuso stotelė*	ow·*taw*·bu·saw staw·ta·leh
ferry terminal	*kelto stotis*	kal·taw staw·tis
train station	*geležin-kelio stotis*	gal·azh·in·kal·yaw staw·tis

I'd like (a) ... ticket.	*Aš norėčiau bilietą į ...*	ahsh naw·*reh*·chow bil·eah·tah i ...
one-way	*vieną galą*	veah·nah gah·lah
return	*abu galus*	ah·bu gah·lus

GLOSSARY

See the individual destination chapters for some useful words and phrases dealing with food and dining; see the Language chapter (p425) for other useful words and phrases. This glossary is a list of Estonian (Est), Finnish (Fin), German (Ger), Latvian (Lat), Lithuanian (Lith), and Russian (Rus) terms you might come across during your time in the Baltic.

aikštė (Lith) – square
aludė (Lith) – beer cellar
alus (Lat, Lith) – beer
apteek (Est) – pharmacy
aptieka (Lat) – pharmacy
Aukštaitija (Lith) – Upper Lithuania
autobusų stotis (Lith) – bus station
autoosta (Lat) – bus station
autostrāde (Lat) – highway

baar (Est) – pub, bar
babushka (Rus) – grandmother/pensioner in headscarf
bagāžas glabātava (Lat) – left-luggage room
bagažinė (Lith) – left-luggage room
bāka (Lat) – lighthouse
Baltic glint – raised limestone bank stretching from Sweden across the north of Estonia into Russia
baras (Lith) – pub, bar
baznīca (Lat) – church
bažnyčia (Lith) – church
brokastis (Lat) – breakfast
bulvāris (Lat) – boulevard
bussijaam (Est) – bus station

ceļš (Lat) – railway track, road
centras (Lith) – town centre
centrs (Lat) – town centre
Chudckoye Ozero (Rus) – Lake Peipsi
Courland – Kurzeme

daina (Lat) – short, poetic oral song or verse

datorsalons (Lat) – internet cafe
dzintars (Lat) – amber

ebreji (Lat) – Jews
Eesti (Est) – Estonia
ežeras (Lith) – lake
ezerpils (Lat) – lake fortress
ezers (Lat) – lake

gatvė (Lith) – street
geležinkelio stotis (Lith) – train station
gintarinė/gintarinis (Lith) – amber

hinnakiri (Est) – price list
hommikusöök (Est) – breakfast

iela (Lat) – street
iezis (Lat) – rock
informacija (Lith) – information centre
internetas kavinė (Lith) – internet cafe
interneti kohvik (Est) – internet cafe

järv (Est) – lake

kafejnīca (Lat) – cafe
kalnas (Lith) – mountain, hill
kalns (Lat) – mountain, hill
kämping (Est) – camp site
katedra (Lith) – cathedral
katedrāle (Lat) – cathedral
kauplus (Est) – shop
kavinė (Lith) – cafe
kelias (Lith) – road
kempingas (Lith) – camp site
kempings (Lat) – camp site
kesklinn (Est) – town centre
kino (Est, Lat, Lith) – cinema
kirik (Est) – church
kohvik (Est) – cafe
kõrts (Est) – inn, tavern
krogs (Lat) – pub, bar
Kurshskaya Kosa (Rus) – Curonian Spit
Kuršių marios (Lith) – Curonian Lagoon

Kuršių Nerija (Lith) – Curonian Spit

laht (Est) – bay
Latvija (Lat) – Latvia
laukums (Lat) – square
lennujaam (Est) – airport
lidosta (Lat) – airport
Lietuva (Lith) – Lithuania
looduskaitseala (Est) – nature/landscape reserve
loss (Est) – castle, palace

maantee (Est) – highway
mägi (Est) – mountain, hill
Metsavennad (Est) – Forest Brothers resistance movement
midus (Lith) – mead
mõis (Est) – manor
muuseum (Est) – museum
muzejs (Lat) – museum
muziejus (Lith) – museum

nacionālais parks (Lat) – national park

õlu (Est) – beer
oro uostas (Lith) – airport
osta (Lat) – port/harbour

pakihoid (Est) – left luggage
parkas (Lith) – park
parks (Lat) – park
paštas (Lith) – post office
pasts (Lat) – post office
Peko (Est) – pagan god of fertility in Seto traditions
perkėla (Lith) – port
piletid (Est) – tickets
pilies (Lith) – castle
pils (Lat) – castle, palace
pilsdrupas (Lat) – knights' castle
pilskalns (Lat) – castle mound
plats (Est) – square
plentas (Lith) – highway, motorway
pliažas (Lith) – beach
pludmale (Lat) – beach
pood (Est) – shop

GLOSSARY

postkontor (Est) – post office
prospektas (Lith) – boulevard
prospekts (Lat) – boulevard
pubi (Est) – pub
puhketalu (Est) – tourist farm (ie a farm offering accommodation)
puiestee (Est) – boulevard
pusryčiai (Lith) – breakfast

raekoda (Est) – town/city hall
rahvuspark (Est) – national park
rand (Est) – beach
rātsnams (Lat) – town hall
raudteejaam (Est) – train station
Reval (Ger) – old German name for Tallinn
rezervāts (Lat) – reserve
Riigikogu (Est) – Parliament
rotušė (Lith) – town/city hall

rūmai (Lith) – palace

saar (Est) – island
sadam (Est) – harbour/port
Saeima (Lat) – Parliament
Seimas (Lith) – Parliament
Seto (Est) – ethnic group of mixed Estonian and Orthodox traditions
Setomaa (Est) – territory of the Seto people in southeastern Estonia and Russia
sild (Est) – bridge
smuklė (Lith) – tavern
stacija (Lat) – station
švyturys (Lith) – lighthouse

Tallinna (Fin) – Tallinn
talu (Est) – farm
tänav (Est) – street
tee (Est) – road

tiltas (Lith) – bridge
tilts (Lat) – bridge
tirgus (Lat) – market
toomkirik (Est) – cathedral
trahter (Est) – tavern
tuletorn (Est) – lighthouse
turg (Est) – market
turgus (Lith) – market
turismitalu (Est) – tourist farm (ie a farm offering accommodation)

vanalinn (Est) – old town
vaistinė (Lith) – pharmacy
väljak (Est) – square
Vecrīga (Lat) – Old Rīga
via Baltica – international road (the E67) linking Estonia with Poland

žydų (Lith) – Jews

Behind the Scenes

SEND US YOUR FEEDBACK

We love to hear from travellers – your comments keep us on our toes and help make our books better. Our well-travelled team reads every word on what you loved or loathed about this book. Although we cannot reply individually to postal submissions, we always guarantee that your feedback goes straight to the appropriate authors, in time for the next edition. Each person who sends us information is thanked in the next edition – the most useful submissions are rewarded with a selection of digital PDF chapters.

Visit **lonelyplanet.com/contact** to submit your updates and suggestions or to ask for help. Our award-winning website also features inspirational travel stories, news and discussions.

Note: We may edit, reproduce and incorporate your comments in Lonely Planet products such as guidebooks, websites and digital products, so let us know if you don't want your comments reproduced or your name acknowledged. For a copy of our privacy policy visit lonelyplanet.com/privacy.

OUR READERS

Many thanks to the travellers who used the last edition and wrote to us with helpful hints, useful advice and interesting anecdotes:

Alan Porter, Alessio Fabrizi, Amanda Kiilerich, Ben Boodman, Benjamin Deissler, Carlos Azpeitia, Chiara Manenti, Daniëlle Wolbers, Dean Meservy, Jyoti Careswell, Kingsley Ashford-Brown, Marju Mätas, Martin Hellwagner, Rodrigo Lopez, Sigitas Zemaitis

AUTHOR THANKS

Peter Dragicevich

Special thanks are due to my long-suffering travel agent David Inglis of Travel Managers, Auckland. When an airline managed to void all of my flights home (after a flight delay turned my trip to Tallinn into a 76-hour door-to-door nightmare – but that's another story), he sprang into action and got me onto a flight out of Tallinn at extremely short notice.

Hugh McNaughtan

My sincere thanks go to Helen, Tasmin, Irmantas, Saulius, Milda and, of course, my wee ladies.

Leonid Ragozin

Let me start by thanking Latvia for becoming my home at the time of troubles in Russia. Huge thanks to my dear friends Ilze and Ģirts Jankovskis for making me fall in love with their country and to Reinis Norkārkls for explaining it to me. I would also like to thank the great Latvian journalists Sanita Jemberga and Rita Ruduša for their invaluable advice on all aspects of life and travel in Latvia. Now, special thanks goes to Vita Viļuma, who is guiding me through the universe that is Latvian language. Finally, this whole project wouldn't have happened without my wife Masha Makeeva's constant support and appetite for adventure.

ACKNOWLEDGMENTS

Climate map data adapted from Peel MC, Finlayson BL & McMahon TA (2007) 'Updated World Map of the Köppen-Geiger Climate Classification', *Hydrology and Earth System Sciences*, 11, 163344.

Cover photograph: Tallinn, Estonia, Old Town skyline of Toompea Hill, Sean Pavone/Shutterstock

Many of the images in this guide are available for licensing from Lonely Planet Images: www.lonelyplanetimages.com.

THIS BOOK

This 7th edition of Lonely Planet's *Estonia, Latvia & Lithuania* guidebook was researched and written by Peter Dragicevich, Hugh McNaughtan and Leonid Ragozin. The 6th edition was written by Brandon Presser, Peter Dragicevich, Mark Baker, Simon Richmond and Andy Symington. This guidebook was produced by the following people:

Acting Destination Editor Helen Elfer

Coordinating Editor Andrea Dobbin

Product Editors Elizabeth Jones, Vicky Smith

Regional Senior Cartographer Valentina Kremenchutskaya

Book Designer Mazzy Prinsep

Assisting Editors Sarah Billington, Bruce Evans, Kate Evans, Ali Lemer, Gabrielle Stefanos

Cover Researcher Naomi Parker

Language Content Valentina Kremenchutskaya

Thanks to Gemma Graham, Anne Mason, Kirsten Rawlings, Alison Ridgway, Angela Tinson, Lauren Wellicome

Index

LONELY PLANET IN THE WILD

Send your 'Lonely Planet in the Wild' photos to social@lonelyplanet.com
We share the best on our Facebook page every week!

Map Legend

Sights

- Beach
- Bird Sanctuary
- Buddhist
- Castle/Palace
- Christian
- Confucian
- Hindu
- Islamic
- Jain
- Jewish
- Monument
- Museum/Gallery/Historic Building
- Ruin
- Shinto
- Sikh
- Taoist
- Winery/Vineyard
- Zoo/Wildlife Sanctuary
- Other Sight

Activities, Courses & Tours

- Bodysurfing
- Diving
- Canoeing/Kayaking
- Course/Tour
- Sento Hot Baths/Onsen
- Skiing
- Snorkelling
- Surfing
- Swimming/Pool
- Walking
- Windsurfing
- Other Activity

Sleeping

- Sleeping
- Camping

Eating

- Eating

Drinking & Nightlife

- Drinking & Nightlife
- Cafe

Entertainment

- Entertainment

Shopping

- Shopping

Information

- Bank
- Embassy/Consulate
- Hospital/Medical
- Internet
- Police
- Post Office
- Telephone
- Toilet
- Tourist Information
- Other Information

Geographic

- Beach
- Gate
- Hut/Shelter
- Lighthouse
- Lookout
- Mountain/Volcano
- Oasis
- Park
- Pass
- Picnic Area
- Waterfall

Population

- Capital (National)
- Capital (State/Province)
- City/Large Town
- Town/Village

Transport

- Airport
- Border crossing
- Bus
- Cable car/Funicular
- Cycling
- Ferry
- Metro station
- Monorail
- Parking
- Petrol station
- S-Bahn/S-train/Subway station
- Taxi
- T-bane/Tunnelbana station
- Train station/Railway
- Tram
- Tube station
- U-Bahn/Underground station
- Other Transport

Note: Not all symbols displayed above appear on the maps in this book

Routes

- Tollway
- Freeway
- Primary
- Secondary
- Tertiary
- Lane
- Unsealed road
- Road under construction
- Plaza/Mall
- Steps
- Tunnel
- Pedestrian overpass
- Walking Tour
- Walking Tour detour
- Path/Walking Trail

Boundaries

- International
- State/Province
- Disputed
- Regional/Suburb
- Marine Park
- Cliff
- Wall

Hydrography

- River, Creek
- Intermittent River
- Canal
- Water
- Dry/Salt/Intermittent Lake
- Reef

Areas

- Airport/Runway
- Beach/Desert
- Cemetery (Christian)
- Cemetery (Other)
- Glacier
- Mudflat
- Park/Forest
- Sight (Building)
- Sportsground
- Swamp/Mangrove

OUR STORY

A beat-up old car, a few dollars in the pocket and a sense of adventure. In 1972 that's all Tony and Maureen Wheeler needed for the trip of a lifetime – across Europe and Asia overland to Australia. It took several months, and at the end – broke but inspired – they sat at their kitchen table writing and stapling together their first travel guide, *Across Asia on the Cheap*. Within a week they'd sold 1500 copies. Lonely Planet was born.

Today, Lonely Planet has offices in Franklin, London, Melbourne, Oakland, Beijing and Delhi, with more than 600 staff and writers. We share Tony's belief that 'a great guidebook should do three things: inform, educate and amuse'.

OUR WRITERS

Peter Dragicevich

Estonia After a dozen years working for newspapers and magazines in both his native New Zealand and Australia, Peter ditched the desk and hit the road. He's since contributed to literally dozens of Lonely Planet titles, including the previous edition of this book, *Scandinavian Europe* and five successive editions of the *Eastern Europe* guidebook. He rates Tallinn as one of his favourite European cities. Peter also contributed the Plan section to this book.

Hugh McNaughtan

Lithuania A former English lecturer, Hugh decided visa applications beat grant applications, and turned his love of travel into a full-time thing. Having also done a bit of restaurant reviewing in his home town (Melbourne), he's now eaten his way across Europe, and found the best way to work up an appetite for Lithuania's great, gut-busting food is spending all day cycling in its stunning forests. He's never happier than when on the road with his two daughters. Except perhaps on the cricket field...

Leonid Ragozin

Latvia, Helsinki Excursion, Kaliningrad Excursion, Directory A–Z, Transport Leonid studied beach dynamics at the Moscow State University, but for want of decent beaches in Russia, he switched to journalism and spent 12 years voyaging through different parts of the BBC, with a break for a four-year stint as a foreign correspondent for the Russian *Newsweek*. Leonid is currently a freelance journalist focusing largely on the conflict between Russia and Ukraine (both his Lonely Planet destinations), which prompted him to leave Moscow and find a new home in Rīga. The latter turned writing this book into a literally life-changing experience.

Published by Lonely Planet Publications Pty Ltd
ABN 36 005 607 983
7th edition – May 2016
ISBN 978 1 74220 757 5
© Lonely Planet 2016   Photographs © as indicated 2016
10 9 8 7 6 5 4 3 2 1
Printed in China